Specimens Of English Literature ... 1394-1579, With Intr., Notes And Glossarial Index, By W.w. Skeat...

Anonymous

Clarendon Press Series

SPECIMENS

OF

ENGLISH LITERATURE

SKEAT

London

HENRY FROWDE

OXFORD UNIVERSITY PRESS WAREHOUSE

AMEN CORNER, E.C.

Clarendon Press Series

SPECIMENS

OF

ENGLISH LITERATURE

FROM THE 'PLOUGHMANS CREDE'
TO THE 'SHEPHEARDES CALENDER'
A. D. 1394—A. D. 1579

WITH

Introduction, Notes, and Glossarial Index

BY THE

REV. WALTER W. SKEAT, LITT. D.

LL.D. EDIN., M.A. OXON.

Elrington and Bosworth Professor of Anglo-Saxon
in the University of Cambridge

" . . . our nation is in nothing inferiour to the French or Italian for copie of language, subtiltie of device, good method and proportion in any forme of poeme"; PUTTENHAM, *Arte of English Poesie* (1589); bk. i. c. 31.

Fourth Edition

Oxford

AT THE CLARENDON PRESS

M DCCC LXXXVII

S. Lang Eng.

CONTENTS.

CONTENTS.

INTRODUCTION.

Synopsis. § 1. Object of the volume. § 2. The period considered in it. § 3. 'Edited' texts. § 4. Difficulties. § 5. The Alphabet. § 6. Abbreviations. § 7. Spelling. § 8. Pronunciation. § 9. Vocabulary. § 10. Glossarial Index. § 11. Sources whence the Extracts are taken.

General Hints. § 12. The Anglo-Saxon Dictionary. § 13. Anglo-Saxon or English Grammar. § 14. Words from the Old French. § 15. Contracted forms in Old French. § 16. Formation of French nouns. § 17. French words not all of Latin origin. § 18. English as compared with German. § 19. The difference between 'derived' and 'cognate.' § 20. Help to be obtained from the Allied Languages. § 21. Literature of the Fifteenth Century, &c. § 22. Chronological Table.

§ 1. THE object of this volume is to supply the student and general reader with trustworthy and useful extracts from writings of the fifteenth and part of the sixteenth centuries. Most of the existing books of the same character are insufficient in one or other respect; either the extracts given are too short to represent adequately the style of the author, or they are more or less modernized in such a manner as to give no clue to the real state of the language at the time when he wrote. Besides this, many of the explanations of words given by the compilers of such works are wholly wrong; the mistakes, for example, in Ellis's 'Specimens of English Poetry' are occasionally of a serious character, and only to be accounted for by supposing that he had no exact knowledge of our language in its earliest stages. Even Warton's 'History of English Poetry,' which will probably long continue to be a standard work, is by no means free from curious errors of this kind, as indicated in the Notes to Gawin Douglas ; see pp. 416-418 of this volume.

§ 2. It is most important to observe that there is nowhere any real or considerable break in our literature.[1] The changes in the language between the reigns of Ælfred and Victoria have been gradual, not violent, and our present speech differs from the Oldest English (generally called 'Anglo-Saxon') chiefly by reason of the alterations which a long lapse of time naturally and imperceptibly introduces. Hence the particular period of our literature here illustrated is determined by arbitrary boundaries. I begin with an extract from the 'Crede,' because the volume of 'Specimens of English,' by Dr. Morris, published in 1867, terminates with an extract of a slightly anterior date ; and I leave off with the year 1579, because it was remarkable for the publication of Lily's 'Euphues' and Spenser's 'Shepheardes Calender,' and because it was about this time that a marked revival in English letters took place. A glance at Professor Morley's 'Tables of English Literature' will shew that, whilst the important works published between 1560 and 1580 are not very numerous, those published soon after 1580 are many and valuable. Before the end of the century we meet with such standard works as Marlowe's Plays, Fairfax's 'Tasso,' Daniel's Poems, Sidney's 'Arcadia,' and, still better than these, the 'Faerie Queene,' 'Venus and Adonis,' 'Lucrece,' and several of the best of Shakespeare's Plays. It seems as if the comparatively unproductive period of our literature then suddenly

---

[1] This statement has been flatly contradicted by a reviewer. But as the writer omitted to state *where the break occurs,* his opinion is of no assistance to us.

ceased, and we begin to meet with writings that are to be read at length, and of which short specimens will no longer suffice.

§ 3. A great deal of the supposed difficulty of Early English, and much of the curious awe with which many Englishmen regard it (as if it were a study much beyond them, and in which they can have little interest), has been the indirect result of the injudicious way in which editors have been accustomed to tamper with their texts. Readers are so used to having their extracts from older authors modified or modernized, that they find themselves thrown out when actually meeting with a genuine old book, and are discouraged at the outset from attempting to peruse it.[1] In the present volume, all the pieces have been printed without alteration, with the exact spelling which occurs in the MS. or old black-letter book from which each is taken; and the earliest MS. copies, or first editions of printed works, have been resorted to, as being, in general, the most correct. The student who masters the contents of it will therefore make a real advance, and will be pleased to find himself able to read with considerable ease every English printed book in existence, with the exception of those which are copied from MSS. older than the time of Chaucer. He will also find that he has acquired much that will assist him in the reading of early MSS.

§ 4. There are a few difficulties that ought to be resolutely grappled with, and vanquished, at the outset.[2] Difficulties arise

---

[1] 'But for the unfortunate readiness with which editors and publishers have yielded to the popular demand for conformity to the spelling and the vocabulary of the day, the knowledge of genuine English would now be both more general and further advanced than it is.'—Marsh, Lectures on English, ed. 1861, p. 21.

[2] 'Chaucer, whom a week's labor will make almost as intelligible as Dryden,' &c.—Marsh, Lectures on English, ed. 1861, p. 174.

from three principal sources, viz. from the alphabet employed, from the spelling, and from the diction or vocabulary of words used. The alphabet and the spelling should receive immediate attention; but a knowledge of the vocabulary comes only with time, being acquired imperceptibly, yet with ever-increasing rapidity. A few hints on these subjects will probably be of service.

§ 5. *The Alphabet.* The letters employed are the same as those employed now, with two additions, and with some variations in significance. The additional letters are þ and ʒ; the capitals of which are printed Þ and ʒ. Both of these are of frequent occurrence in early MSS. The former (þ) signifies *th*. In our modern pronunciation we make a distinction between the initial sounds of *thine* and *thin,* a distinction which in the earliest times probably did not exist, the *th* in both cases being sounded as in *thin*; but at an early period we ceased to preserve this sound in all our oldest and commonest words, such as *thou, the, that, there, then,* and the like[1]. But we often find a distinction made in the fourteenth century. Some scribes used þ at the beginning of *þe, þat* (the, that), and the letters *th* at the beginning of *thin, thikke* (thin, thick). In the fifteenth century this distinction was less regarded, and the symbol þ was gradually disused. In Section I, p. 1, we find in the first line, *þanne, þouʒt, þe, þis,* for *then, thought, the,* and *this.* In Section II, p. 14, there is but one instance in the page, viz. *þee* for *thee,* in st. 299, l. 5. Very soon after this, the scribes began habitually to form the character þ so indistinctly, that no difference was made between it and the letter *y*. I denote this by printing *th* in italics. Thus, in Sect. VII, l. 5, p. 68, the word '*th*e' signifies that 'ye' is written in the MS., but 'the' is

---

. [1] See Appendix I to 'Gregory's Pastoral Care,' edited for the Early English Text Society by H. Sweet, Esq., where a different view is taken.

meant. In the same line, the word '*tha*t' signifies that the MS. has 'y^t,' where the *y* means *th*, and the *a* is only indicated by the *t* being a little above the line. Hence it is very common to find in old printed books the words 'y^e,' 'y^t,' 'yis,' which are to be read *the, that, this,* and not *ye, yat, yis,* as many persons, with a comic ignorance, seem to suppose.

The character ȝ has various powers. At the *beginning* of a word it is to be sounded as *y*, so that ȝard is our modern *yard* ; in the middle of a word it had a guttural sound, still represented in our *spelling* by *gh*, as liȝt for *light* ; at the end of a word it either had the same sound, or stood for *z*. In fact, the character for *z* was written precisely like it, although more sparingly employed ; we find, e. g. marchauntȝ for *marchauntz*, where the *z*, by the way, must necessarily have been sounded as *s*. This use of the character is French, and appears chiefly in French words. In early French MSS. it is very common, and denotes *z* only, which was sounded as *ts*.

The characters *v* and *u* require particular attention. The latter is freely used to denote *both* the modern sounds, and the reader must be prepared at any moment to treat it as a consonant. Thus the words *haue, leue, diuerse* are to be read *have, leve, diverse* ; where it will be observed that the symbol appears between two vowels. The former is used sparingly, but sometimes denotes the modern *u*, chiefly at the beginning of a word. The following are nearly all the commoner examples of it[1], and may as well be learnt at once ; viz. *vce* or *vse* (use), *vtter* (utter), *vp* (up), *vpon* (upon), and the prefix *vn-* (un-). Many readers are impatient of learning this easy lesson, and hence it is common to find, even in well-edited editions of old authors, that the *v*'s and *u*'s are altered so as to suit the modern taste ; yet a very little attention soon over-

[1] In these and other instances, it will be understood that I speak with reference to the period 1394–1579 only.

comes this difficulty, which is, after all, but a small matter to be
discouraged at. A learner of French or German has to en-
counter greater difficulties than these, and Old English is as
well worth a little pains as either one or the other.

Occasionally even *w* is used for *u*. Hence the words *swe*,
remwe (p. 29) are for *sue*, *remue* ; and, in one instance, we find
the curious form *dywlgat*=*dyuulgat*=*dyvulgat*=divulged. In
some examples of Lowland Scotch (Sections VI, XIII), *w* is
used for both *u* and *v* ; so that *gawe* means *gave*, and *hows* is
hous (house). A little practice soon renders the eye familiar
with these variations.

The letter *J* is very rare. It is generally denoted by a
capital *I*; as in *Iape*, *Ieoperdie*, *Iourney*, for *jape*, *jeopardy*,
journey. Sometimes *ij* is written for *y*, as in *wij3t*=*wy3t*=
wyght=wight. This symbol is very common in modern Dutch,
as in the words *mijn* (mine), and *wijn* (wine), which are pronounced *mine* and *vine* respectively. The combination *quh* is
common in Scotch, and answers to the modern English *wh* and
the Anglo-Saxon *hw* ; as in *quhy* for *why*, A. S. *hwí*.

Most of the early editions from which this volume is compiled are in black letter, roman letters being used occasionally
as we should now use italics. Gascoigne's ' Steel Glas,' however,
is almost wholly printed in italic letters, and a sudden demand
for a number of capital *W*'s in one passage seems to have taxed
the resources of the printers, who resorted to the use of small
letters and double *V*'s ; see p. 322. The reader should observe
that proper names more frequently begin with a small letter
than with a capital; as, e.g. *pryant* for *Priam*, p. 89. The
letters *a*, *i*, and *r*, are frequently written as capitals in MSS.,
at the beginning of words ; see *In* in l. 4, *Away* in the same
line, and *Rue* in l. 9, on p. 68. Marks of punctuation are very
rare in MSS. ; and in old printed books we frequently find only
the mark / for a comma (see p. 89), with occasional full stops

and colons. In most of the pieces the punctuation is entirely my own, and the reader may change or disregard it at pleasure ; just as he may, if he pleases, disregard it in all other editions of Old English authors, wherein it is almost always due to the editor only, and is sometimes wrong. Wherever a word has been misspelt by mere accident, I have altered it, at the same time appending a foot-note ; and sometimes I have supplied a missing letter or word within square brackets.

§ 6. *Abbreviations.* The most usual marks of contraction employed in early books and MSS. are so few that they may soon be learnt. The commonest are these following, their expansions being denoted throughout this volume by the use of italic letters.

A stroke over a vowel signifies *m* or *n* ; as in *sũ, hĩ, hoũd,* meaning su*m*, hi*m*, hou*n*d.

An upward curl, above the line, signifies *er* ; as in *man⁹,* *s⁹ue,* for man*er*, s*er*ue (serve). But if this symbol follows the letter *p*, it means *re* ; as in *p⁹che* for p*re*che. It arose from a roughly written *e*, the letter *r* being *understood*.

A small undotted *i* above the line means *ri*, the letter *r* being *understood*, as before ; hence *pⁱnce, cⁱst,* for p*ri*nce, c*ri*st (Christ).

A roughly written *a* (ω) in like manner stands for *ra* ; as in *gωce, pωy,* for g*ra*ce, p*ra*y.

A curl, of a form which arose from a roughly written *v* (for *u*) signifies *ur* ; as in *t̃ne, õ,* for t*ur*ne, o*ur*.

The reason for the upward curl after *p* being used for *re*, arose from the fact that there was already a way of writing *per*, viz. by drawing a stroke through the tail of the *p* ; as in *pil,* for p*er*il. Sometimes this sign stood for *par* ; as in *pty* for p*ar*ty.

A similar stroke, but curling, enabled the scribe to abbreviate *pro.* Thus we have *pfite, pue,* for p*ro*fite, p*ro*ue—(prove).

At the end of a word, the mark *ꝑ* signifies *es* or *is*; and the mark *⁹* signifies *us*; as in *word-ꝑ* for word*es* or word*is*, and *þ⁹* for *þus* (thus)[1].

A not very common mark of contraction is *ɑ* for *com* or *con*; as in *ɑ-fort*, *ɑ-seil*, *com*fort, *con*seil.

Other examples of contraction are *q* or *qd* for q*uod* or q*uod*, i. e. quoth; *þᵗ* or *yᵗ* for *þat* or *tha*t; *þᵘ* or *yᵘ* for *þou* or *tho*u; and *iħc*, *iħm*, for i*esus*, i*esu*m (Jesus, Jesum), where the *h* came from the Greek H (long *e*), and the *c* from the Greek C (Σ, *s*).

§ 7. *Spelling.* It is a common error to look upon the spelling of Old English as utterly lawless, and unworthy of notice. Because it is not *uniform*, the conclusion is at once rushed to that it cannot be of much service. No mistake could well be worse. It is frequently far better than our modern spelling, and helps to shew how badly we spell now, in spite of the uniformity introduced by printers for the sake of convenience. Old English spelling was conducted on an intelligible principle, whereas our modern spelling exhibits no principle at all, but merely illustrates the inconvenience of separating symbols from sounds. The intelligible principle of Old English spelling is, that it was intended to be *phonetic*. Bound by no particular laws, each scribe did the best he could to represent the sounds which he heard, and the notion of putting in letters that were not sounded was (except in the case of final *e*) almost unknown. The very variations are of value, because they help to render more clear in each case what the sound was which the scribes were attempting to represent. But to bear in mind that the spelling was *phonetic* is to hold the clue to it. Scribes differed in their modes of spelling for several reasons. Most of them

[1] The printer of Gascoigne's 'Steel Glass,' who turned 'August⁹' into 'August 9,' can hardly have understood this symbol. See note to Sect. xxvi. 770.

were guided by the pronunciation of the dialect of their place of residence, and dialects were then numerous. Some were more ignorant than others, whence the exceptional badness of the spelling of the piece called 'Chevy Chase.' Many were influenced by what they had previously themselves read, so that changes of spelling took place more slowly than changes in pronunciation, and were often a little behind it; the most marked instance of this being in the case of *e* final, which was retained in spelling after it had ceased to be pronounced, so that the spelling *serche* (p. 77, l. 1), means that the word had at one time been pronounced *serchè*, a dissyllable. Unfortunately, one result of this was that a silent *e* was often ignorantly added, as in the word *kynge* (p. 77, l. 4), which only three lines above is rightly spelt *kyng*. To determine when the final *e* is rightly added is one of the most useful exercises which occur in Middle English grammar. Somewhat similar remarks apply to final *-es*. The word *townes* (p. 77, l. 1) was once called *townès* (dissyllable), A.S. *túnas*; but it does not follow that it was dissyllabic in the time of Malory. In the extract from Surrey, the metre shews at once that *costes* (p. 208, l. 324) was a monosyllable; and so on, for other words. It is impossible to enlarge upon this here, for want of space; but experience shews that the spelling very seldom causes any *real* difficulty, and that the words which are so disguised by it as not to be at once intelligible, are very few indeed. Those who do not care to investigate the spelling, have only to read right on, making the best they can of it, and they will not find much difficulty *after the first page of each extract has been fairly considered.* To give *the beginning* of a piece of literature, in whatever language it may be written, a fair trial, is a principle of the highest importance. The present writer well remembers spending two hours over the first dozen lines of a manuscript, which, not long afterwards, he could read as easily as a newspaper.

b

§ 8. *Pronunciation.* Owing to the conservatism introduced into spelling by the invention of printing, our spelling has not suffered any very considerable alteration since the time of Caxton; and one curious result has been, that if we give our modern pronunciation to the pieces here printed, we can make shift to understand them almost as well as if we knew how they were really pronounced. In other words, the change in pronunciation causes little difficulty at first, and the consideration of it may be neglected by the beginner. The actual investigation of the pronunciation of Early English is a subject of so great difficulty, that it has been entirely neglected till the last few years, during which Mr. A. J. Ellis has attacked the subject with much success, and his great work upon it is the chief authority[1]. The results at which he arrives are most curious and striking. If I interpret him rightly, the principal ones are these.

1. The gross confusion in modern English spelling is, in a great measure, due to the great changes in pronunciation that have taken place since early times.

2. Some of the most violent of these changes probably took place during the civil wars of the fifteenth century, and during the latter part of the seventeenth and former part of the eighteenth centuries.

3. Whereas our modern English pronunciation, of the vowels especially, differs widely from the pronunciation adopted on the continent (in Germany, for example), it is certain that in early times this difference was but slight. Our insular peculiarities have increased upon us. It follows from this that a reader who

[1] 'On Early English Pronunciation, with especial reference to Shakespeare and Chaucer; by Alex. J. Ellis, F.R.S.' Trübner & Co. A short discussion (by Mr. Ellis) of the pronunciation of Chaucer's time will be found in the Introduction to my edition of Chaucer's 'Man of Law's Tale,' &c. (Clarendon Press.)

pleases to pronounce these specimens of English according to
the continental vowel-system will probably make a rough ap-
proximation to the true sounds of many of the words. It
deserves to be particularly observed, moreover, that the fact of
there being no very wide difference, in the fourteenth century,
between the French and English vowel-systems, must have
greatly assisted in that introduction into English of numerous
French words which we know to have taken place.

§ 9. *Vocabulary.* The pieces here printed do not, after all,
present very many difficulties through the use of uncommon
words, except in a few cases which may be particularly mentioned. Section I is an extract from an alliterative poem, and
poems in such metre are invariably remarkable for more or less
obscurity; yet the obscurity is not, in this case, very great.
Sections IV, VI, XI, XIII, XXII are in Lowland Scotch, and
therefore differ from the rest somewhat in the same way in
which the diction of Burns differs from that of Byron. A North-
country man will understand them readily; a Southerner will
have more trouble to do so. This remark, perhaps, hardly
applies to Section XIII, from Gawin Douglas, a piece of quite
exceptional character. Partly from his profuse employment of
Northern-English words, and partly from the freedom with
which he introduces Latin and French terms, the worthy bishop
has succeeded in producing many lines which puzzle even the
experienced. Such a line as

‘ Moich hailsum stovys ourheldand the slak’ (l. 46)

does not carry with it its obvious meaning; but it would be a
mistake to suppose this to be an average specimen of Middle
English. We can hardly find lines as unfamiliar in appearance
as this without going back at least to the thirteenth century.
But, setting these Sections aside, the language calls for but little
explanation. The prose pieces in particular, such as those in

Sections V, VIII, IX, XV, XVI, XVII, XVIII, XXI, XXV, XXVII, are perspicuous enough, and can be understood with but a very sparing use of the glossary. About the end of the fourteenth century, French words ceased to be introduced into the language in such numbers as before, and the question as to which of them should be accepted and which rejected, was soon more or less settled. Very shortly after this, the introduction of printing did very much to *fix* the language, and the result has been that the language of the fifteenth century differs less from that of the nineteenth than the language of the fourteenth from that of the thirteenth. Hence, the perusal of the pieces here printed forms an easy introduction to the study of English of a still earlier period.

§ 10. *Glossarial Index.* As to the meanings of the words, the Glossarial Index is so copious that little more need here be added. Further information about many of them may easily be obtained from such works as Nares' Glossary, or the glossaries to Dr. Morris's edition of Chaucer's 'Prologue' and 'Knightes Tale,' my own (smaller) edition of 'Piers the Plowman,' of Chaucer's 'Prioress's Tale,' &c., and of Chaucer's 'Man of Law's Tale,' &c., Mr. Kitchin's edition of Spenser's 'Faerie Queene,' books i and ii (all in the Clarendon Press Series). See also Dyce's Shakespeare, Staunton's Shakespeare, Dyce's Skelton, Morris's or Tyrwhitt's or Bell's Chaucer, &c. for further illustrations.

The references in the Glossarial Index may be readily understood. The first figure refers to the Section, and the last to the line, or (in cases where the lines are not numbered) to the stanza. Thus, *entendement* occurs in Sect. II, st. 281 (p. 14), *harborowe* in Sect. XVIII, chap. xviii, l. 16 (p. 202), *hew* in Sect. XI, Extract A, st. 3 (p. 109), and *gaudying* in Sect. XXIII, Act iii, Sc. 4, l. 1 (p. 269).

The etymological remarks appended to the explanations of the words in the Glossarial Index are of the briefest possible character, and intended to stimulate rather than to satisfy enquiry. Whilst they are in some measure a guarantee that the words have received due attention, they direct the learner to sources of fuller information. To this end, the spellings of all the Anglo-Saxon, Icelandic, and other words cited, have been carefully verified, and conformed to the spellings actually adopted in the dictionaries, of which a list is given on p. 477[1]. This is a point of some importance, as it is not uncommon to find words cited as Anglo-Saxon, Danish, &c., which are so spelt as to render the attempt to find them in a dictionary a wearisome task, instead of an easy employment. My object is to enable the student to satisfy himself that I am in the right, not to throw difficulties in the way of his proving me to be wrong[2].

§ 11. *Sources whence the Extracts are taken.* Many of the pieces here printed are from sources not always easily attainable. I have endeavoured to use the originals wherever I could gain access to them, and have always gone back to the *first* editions, because these were commonly, in former times, the most correct. A second edition of a book now generally means (or should mean) a revised and corrected copy of it; a second edition in former days commonly meant a mere reprint of the former one, with a good many additional errors. It may be as well to state exactly where the MSS. and first editions are to be found. The Bodleian Library at Oxford supplied the pieces in

---

[1] I have chiefly used common pocket-dictionaries, with the distinct object of avoiding the citation of other than commonly-used words.

[2] To coin old forms in various languages for the purposes of ' etymology' is 'one of the safest and easiest of literary frauds.'—Marsh, Lectures on English, ed. 1861, p. 58.

Sections IV, VII, XII, XVI, XIX, XX, XXI, XXIV, and XXVIII; the University Library, Cambridge, those in Sections V, IX, X, XV, XVII, XXV, XXVI; the Library of Trinity College, Cambridge, those in Sections I and XIII; the British Museum those in Sections II and III, and a second MS. of the 'Crede' (Sect. I); and the Advocates' Library at Edinburgh those in Sections VI and XI. For a loan of a copy of the first edition of Sir Thomas Elyot's 'Gouernour' (Sect. XVIII) I was indebted to the courtesy of Mr. Arber, whose excellent reprints of many of our old authors are well known. Sections XXIII and XXVII are simply copied from Mr. Arber's reprints; Sect. VIII from the reprint by Southey; Sect. XIV from the edition by Dyce; and Sect. XXII from the edition published for the Early English Text Society. I was much indebted to the kindness of the much-lamented Mr. Halkett, late Librarian of the Advocates' Library, for comparing my proof of Dunbar's 'Thrissill and Rois' with the Bannatyne MS.; and his successor, the late Mr. Jamieson, likewise did me good service by comparing my proof of Henry's 'Wallace' with the original. For some hints contained in the Notes, my thanks are due to Mr. John W. (now Professor) Hales, one of the editors of the 'Percy Folio MS.'

In preparing the second edition of this book, I have taken a few hints from the very convenient book by Professor Morley, entitled 'Shorter English Poems.' I desire also to express my thanks to a few readers of the former edition for suggestions kindly sent to me.

GENERAL HINTS.

The following general remarks may serve to correct some misconceptions commonly entertained, and to supply some fundamental notions of considerable importance.

§ 12. No previous knowledge of Anglo-Saxon is necessary to enable the student to look out, in Bosworth's (smaller) Anglo-Saxon Dictionary, the words cited in the Glossary.

§ 13. A real insight into English grammar can more easily be obtained by a week's study of Sweet's Anglo-Saxon Primer, or some similar book[1], than by years spent in reading treatises which ignore the older forms of the language. Many students lose much solid advantage, and a sure basis on which to rest their grammatical knowledge, through an ill-judged anxiety to avoid the much-dreaded 'Anglo-Saxon,' the awe of which soon disappears, and is exchanged for interest, when once it is patiently encountered. The whole of English grammar is formed upon the Anglo-Saxon grammar as a basis. A knowledge of Latin grammar is sometimes a direct hindrance, as it is apt to make the student imagine that he has the key to idiomatic constructions, when he is all the while explaining them wrongly.

§ 14. By far the greatest quantity of words introduced into English from the French were introduced in the fourteenth century. It follows from this, that English etymology frequently depends, not upon *modern*, but upon *old* French.

---

[1] Dr. Morris's 'Historical Outlines of English Accidence' is a valuable help. See also Earle's 'Philology of the English Tongue,' Abbott's 'Shakespearian Grammar,' and, especially, Sweet's 'Anglo-Saxon Reader.'

Pick's French Dictionary is of some service, as giving the Old French forms; but not much real progress can be made without consulting the Glossaries of Old French by Burguy and Roquefort, or the great work by Littré. The former of these (constituting the third volume of Burguy's 'Grammaire de la langue d'oïl,' and sold separately) is of great service, and much the best. Cotgrave's French Dictionary, published in 1611, and often reprinted, is of more use than any modern one. The difference between old and modern French is not very great, the language having changed much less than English has done during the same period.

§ 15. French words derived from Latin are remarkable for the effort which seems to be made in them to reduce the number of syllables, and to clip the full form of the word. A consonant between two vowels is often summarily dispensed with, whence the Latin words *laudare,* 'to praise,' and *locare,* 'to let,' have both produced the French form *louer* as a result. But, for further information on this important subject, the student should consult Brachet's 'Historical Grammar of the French Tongue,' translated by Mr. Kitchin (Clarendon Press Series); also Brachet's 'Dictionnaire Étymologique de la Langue Française,' a handy volume, of which a translation by Mr. Kitchin has also appeared (in the same series).

§ 16. French nouns derived from Latin are almost invariably formed from the *accusative case* of Latin nouns. See this proved in an Essay on the Romance Languages, by Sir G. C. Lewis. The same rule holds for the Spanish, Italian, and Portuguese. Thus, from the Latin *nationem* were formed the French *nation,* the Spanish *nacion,* the Italian *nazione,* the Portuguese *naçdo* (for *naçaon*), and, through the French, the English *nation.* By thinking of the *accusatives,* rather than the *nominatives* of Latin nouns, the etymologies of many words are more clearly perceived. Examples are, *font, flower, peace, part*, from Lat. *fontem, florem, pacem, partem*. The accusative case also possesses the merit of exhibiting clearly the *stem* of a Latin noun; thus, *mortem* exhibits the stem *mort-*, whence the adjective *mortal*. The latter property it of course has in common with all the other oblique cases. It is singular that it should be the fashion always to cite the nominative case in etymological dictionaries; the practice is certainly unfortunate, as it is the only case which often fails to exhibit the true form of the stem. It would be a great improvement always to choose some oblique case, and the accusative is by far the best for the purpose.

§ 17. Many French words are, after all, not of Latin, but of Teutonic or Celtic origin. In such cases, the English often possesses an older form than the French, from which, in another shape, it was derived. Thus, the word *guise* is from the French *guise*; but *guise* itself was borrowed from the Teutonic, and the word *wise* (modern English *wise*) is good Anglo-Saxon; hence we have the double forms, *wise* and *guise*, the former being genuine English, and the latter from old High German, which runs parallel with English. Such words are conveniently called *doublets*.

§ 18. The true dignity and originality of our own language seem to be very little understood and appreciated. An Englishman learning a little German soon begins to think that a good many English words appear to be 'derived' from the German. Accustomed to despise his own language, he seems to forget that there is at least an equal chance of the German being 'derived' from the English. As a matter of fact, the languages are cognate or allied, and neither language has really borrowed much from the other. But it deserves to be remembered, that the oldest Teutonic remains are in Low German, not in High German; that the English epic poem of 'Beowulf' is older than anything extant in High German; and that English ranks above German in the tables of letter-changes indicated in 'Grimm's Law.' It follows from this, that to look upon German, so to speak, as a subordinate form of English, is, although an error, an error of less magnitude than the unphilological and unpatriotic one of looking upon English as a subordinate form of German. German scholars are aware of this. It is reserved for Englishmen to be unaware, as a rule, of the dignity and importance of their own magnificent language. The difference between the two languages is strikingly illustrated by comparing the grammatical inflexions. The slowly advancing German still retains a large number of these, which English, more progressive, has abandoned whole centuries ago.

§ 19. Few words are more frequently misused than the word *derived*. English certainly contains many words derived from the Latin directly, or through the medium of the French; a few, perhaps, derived through the French from a Celtic source; a good many that are derived from Scandinavian sources; some that are derived, or rather borrowed, from the Greek; some others, few in number, borrowed from a great many various sources, such as Arabic, Hebrew, Spanish, &c., as explained in Trench's 'English, Past and Present.' But when people speak of *deriving* English words from the Sanskrit, they are often in danger of misunderstanding the whole matter. Sanskrit is not a parent of English, but an elder sister. With regard to the great mass of words in the Sanskrit, Greek, Latin, English, High German, Slavonic, and Scandinavian languages, we must place these languages *side by side*, and not one above the other, and remember that they mutually illustrate each other, some of them preserving words, or preserving them in a purer form, where others have lost them, or retained them in a more debased form. Where, for instance, the English has the word *star*, the Sanskrit only exhibits a corrupted form, *tára*, and the Latin can only shew the contracted form, *stella*, of the diminutive *ster-ula*, and the disguised form *astrum*. Similarly, the English *work* shews to advantage beside the decapitated Greek ἔργον. In many cases, therefore, we must not use the word *derived*, but the term *cognate* or allied, intimating a community of origin. Thus the English words *bear*, *know*, *foot*, are not derived from, but cognate with, the Latin *ferre*, *noscere*, *pedem* (acc. of *pes*), and the Greek φέρειν, γιγνώσκειν, and ποδά (acc. of πούς).

§ 20. As one language often preserves words which in another have become obsolete, we may try to find out the meanings of Old English words by the help of the allied languages. If the meaning of a word be at first unknown, or not quite clear, or if (which is often the case) it seems desirable to obtain some new light upon it for the sake of bringing out its peculiar shade of meaning more clearly, the process is as follows. First, we must observe whether it seems to be of French origin or not, which is frequently apparent from the look of it. If of French origin, we can find it either in modern French or in old French, or in both, and thence trace it backwards either to classical Latin or Low Latin, i. e. Latin of a later date and more corrupt type. From Low Latin it can be traced back either to some kindred form in classical Latin, or to an Old Teutonic (Old High German or Mœso-Gothic) form. Some French words, however, are not of Latin origin at all, but solely of Teutonic or Celtic origin : in the former case, we are assisted by the Old High German or Mœso-Gothic, or by the Icelandic ; in the latter case by the Breton or Welsh. If a word be not French, we naturally turn first of all to the Anglo-Saxon ; if this fails, to the Old Friesic or the Dutch, as coming nearest to English ; and, after that, to the German. Many Northern-English words are best represented by Scandinavian, thus leading us to the Icelandic or Swedish, particularly the Old Swedish, which has been called Suio-Gothic. Danish is of less assistance, as Swedish or Icelandic generally preserves the same words in a better form. Some words are directly borrowed from the Welsh. In every case, the oldest forms of the word are almost invariably the best and clearest, and this is why it is often worth while to trace them back as far as possible. Assistance is thus attainable from many quarters, and it is seldom indeed that some further light cannot be obtained. The endeavour to trace words is good practice, and more can be learnt by some-times attempting it than by accepting the results given in modern English dictionaries. Besides which, the dictionaries may be wrong ; or, if right, there is still a satisfaction in having tested and proved their truthfulness. Nothing teaches a student so much as to investigate things for himself in his own way.

For further remarks and hints of a similar character, I beg leave to refer the reader to my edition of 'Piers the Plowman, in the Clarendon Press Series, pp. xxxvii–xlii.

§ 21. For studying the literature of the period here con-sidered, the following books may be consulted. Warton's 'History of English Poetry,' of which a new edition, edited by Mr. W. Carew Hazlitt, has just appeared ; Professor Morley's 'English Writers ;' Craik's 'English Literature ;' Spalding's 'English Literature ;' Chambers's 'Encyclopædia of English Literature ;' the editions wherein some of the Extracts here printed may be found, particularly 'Pierce the Ploughmans Crede' (Early English Text Society), Mr. Babington's edition of Pecock, Jamieson's edition of Wallace, the Globe edition of the 'Morte Darthur,' Laing's edition of Dunbar, Dyce's

Skelton, Sir David Lyndesay's Works (Early English Text Society), and Sibbald's Chronicle of Scottish Poetry; also the Globe edition of Spenser, Mr. Kitchin's edition of the first two books of Spenser's 'Faerie Queene,' and the numerous reprints by the Early English Text Society, and by Mr. Arber. Other sources of information might be pointed out, but these are some of the most obvious.

§ 22. CHRONOLOGICAL TABLE.

*** See also the list of Early English Poems in Warton's History of English Poetry, ed. 1871 ; vol. ii. p. 28.

I.

PERES THE PLOUGHMANS CREDE.

ABOUT A.D. 1394.

THIS poem, consisting of 850 lines, was written in alliterative verse by a disciple of Wycliffe, whose name has not been ascertained. The title and form of it are both imitated from William Langland's more famous poem, known as 'The Vision of William concerning Piers the Plowman.' Though these two poems, the 'Crede' and the 'Vision,' are, in fact, by different authors, and express different sentiments on some points, they are, to the disgrace of students of English literature, continually being confounded with each other. There is every reason to believe that the anonymous author of the 'Crede' was also author of 'The Plowman's Tale,' a satirical poem which has often been wrongly ascribed to Chaucer.

The present text is based upon MS. R. 3. 15, in the library of Trinity College, Cambridge, as edited by the Rev. W. W. Skeat for the Early English Text Society, 1867.

The dialect is of a Midland character, and less full of unusual words than most of the poems in the same metre. The poem may have been written in the neighbourhood of London.

The numbering of the lines agrees with that in the complete edition.

[*Description of a Dominican Convent.*]

Þanne þouȝt y to frayne þe first · of þis foure ordirs,
And presede to þe prechoures · to proven here wille.
Ich hiȝede to her house · to herken of more;   155
And whan y cam to þat court · y gaped aboute.

25

Swich a bild bold, y-buld · opon erþe heiȝte
Say i nouȝt in certeine · siþþe a longe tyme.
Y ȝemede vpon þat house · & ȝerne þeroñ loked,
Whouȝ þe pileres weren y-peynt · and pulched ful clene,   160
And queynteli i-corven · wiþ curiouse knottes,
Wiþ wyndowes well y-wrouȝt · wide vp o-lofte.
And þanne y entrid in · and even-forþ went,
And all was walled þat wone · þouȝ it wid were,
Wiþ posternes in pryuytie · to pasen when hem liste;   165
Orcheȝardes and erberes · euesed well clene,
& a curious cros · craftly entayled,
Wiþ tabernacles y-tiȝt · to toten all abouten.
Þe pris of a plouȝ-lond · of penyes so rounde
To aparaile þat pyler · were pure lytel.   170
Þanne y munte me forþ · þe mynstre to knowen,
And a-waytede a woon · wonderlie well y-beld,
Wiþ arches on eueriche half · & belliche y-corven,
Wiþ crochetes on corners · wiþ knottes of golde,
Wyde wyndowes y-wrouȝt · y-written full þikke,   175
Schynen wiþ schapen scheldes · to schewen aboute,
Wiþ merkes of marchauntes · y-medled bytwene,
Mo þan twenty and two · twyes y-noumbred.
Þer is none heraud þat haþ · half swich a rolle,
Riȝt as a rageman · haþ rekned hem newe.   180
Tombes opon tabernacles · tyld opon lofte,
Housed in hirnes · harde set a-bouten,
Of armede alabaustre · clad for þe nones,
[Made vpon marbel · in many maner wyse,
Knyghtes in her conisantes · clad for þe nones,]   185
All it semed seyntes : y-sacred opon erþe;
And louely ladies y-wrouȝt · leyen by her sydes
In many gay garmentes · þat weren gold-beten.
Þouȝ þe tax of ten ȝer · were trewly y-gadered,

Nolde it nouȝt maken þat hous · half, as y trowe.   190
Þanne kam I to þat cloister · & gaped abouten
Whouȝ it was pilered and peynt · & portred well clene,
All y-hyled wiþ leed · lowe to þe stones,
And y-paued wiþ peynt til · iche poynte after oþer;
Wiþ kundites of clene tyn · closed all aboute,   195
Wiþ lauoures of latun · louelyche y-greithed.
I trowe þe gaynage of þe ground · in a gret schire
Nolde aparaile þat place · oo poynt til other ende.
Þanne was þe chaptire-hous wrouȝt · as a greet chirche,
Coruen and couered · and queyntliche entayled;   200
Wiþ semlich selure · y-set on lofte;
As a Parlement-hous · y-peynted aboute.
Þanne ferd y into fraytour · and fond þere an oþer,
An halle for an heyȝ kinge · an housholde to holden,
Wiþ brode bordes aboute · y-benched wel clene,   205
Wiþ windowes of glas · wrouȝt as a Chirche.
Þanne walkede y ferrer · & went all abouten,
And seiȝ halles full hyȝe · & houses full noble,
Chambers wiþ chymneyes · & Chapells gaie;
And kychens for an hyȝe kinge · in castells to holden,   210
And her dortour y-diȝte · wiþ dores ful stronge;
Fermery and fraitur · with fele mo houses,
And all strong ston wall · sterne opon heiþe,
Wiþ gaie garites & grete · & iche hole y-glased;
& oþere houses y-nowe · to herberwe þe queene.   215
& ȝet þise bilderes wilne beggen · a bagg-ful of wheate
Of a pure pore man · þat maie oneþe paie
Half his rente in a ȝer · and half ben behynde !
Þanne turned y aȝen · whan y hadde all y-toted,
And fond in a freitour · a frere on a benche,   220
A greet cherl & a grym · growen as a tonne,
Wiþ a face as fat · as a full bledder,

Blowen bretfull of breþ · & as a bagge honged
On boþen his chekes, & his chyn · wiþ a chol lollede,
As greet as a gos eye · growen all of grece;   225
Þat all wagged his fleche · as a quyk myre.
His cope þat biclypped him · wel clene was it folden,
Of double worstede y-dyȝt · doun to þe hele;
His kyrtel of clene whijt · clenlyche y-sewed;
Hyt was good y-now of ground · greyn for to beren.   230
I haylsede þat herdeman · & hendliche y saide,
'Gode syre, for godes loue · canstou me graiþ tellen
To any worþely wijȝt · þat wissen me couþe
Whou y schulde conne my crede · crist for to folowe,
Þat leuede lelliche him-self · & lyuede þerafter,   235
Þat feynede non falshede · but fully crist suwede?
For sich a certeyn man · syker wold y trosten,
Þat he wolde telle me þe trewþe · and turne to none oþer.
And an Austyn þis ender daie · egged me faste;
Þat he wold techen me wel · he plyȝt me his treuþe,   240
And seyde me, "serteyne · syþen Crist died
Oure ordir was euelles · & erst y-founde." '
    ' Fyrst, felawe!' quaþ he · ' fy on his pilche!
He is but abortijf · eked wiþ cloutes!
He holdeþ his ordynaunce · wiþe hores and þeues,   245
And purchaseþ hem pryuileges · wiþ penyes so rounde;
It is a pur pardoners craft · proue & asaye!
For haue þei þi money · a moneþ þerafter,
Certes, þeiȝ þou come aȝen · he nyl þe nouȝt knowen.
But, felawe, our foundement · was first of þe oþere,   250
& we ben founded fulliche · wiþ-outen fayntise;
& we ben clerkes y-cnowen · cunnynge in scole,
Proued in procession · by processe of lawe.
Of oure ordre þer beþ · bichopes wel manye,
Seyntes on sundry stedes · þat suffreden harde;   255

& we ben proued þe prijs · of popes at Rome,
& of gretest degre · as godspelles telleþ.'
'A! syre,' quaþ y þanne · 'þou seyst a gret wonder,
Siþen crist seyd hym-self · to all his disciples,
"Which of ȝou þat is most · most schal he werche,   260
& who is goer byforne · first schal he seruen."
& seyde, "he sawe satan · sytten full heyȝe
& ful lowe ben y-leyd;" · in lyknes he tolde,
þat in pouernesse of spyrit · is spedfullest hele,
And hertes of heynesse · harmeþ þe soule.   265
And þerfore, frere, fare well · here fynde y but pride;
Y preise nouȝt þi preching · but as a pure myte.'

*   *   *   *   *   *   *   *

[*The Carmelites or White Friars.*]

þANNE totede y into a tauerne · & þer y aspyede
Two frere karmes · wiþ a full coppe.   340
þere y auntrede me in · & aisliche y seide,
'Leue syre, for þe lordes loue · þat þou on leuest,
Lere me to som man · my crede for to lerne,
þat lyueþ in lel lijf · and loueþ no synne,
And gloseþ nouȝt þe godspell · but halt Godes hestes, 345
And neþer money ne mede · ne may him nouȝt letten
But werchen after Godes worde · wiþ-outen any faile.
A prechour y-professed · haþ pliȝt me his trewþe
To techen me trewlie; · but woldest thou me tellen
For þei ben certayne men · & syker on to trosten,   350
Y wolde quyten þe þi mede · as my miȝte were.'
'A trofle,' quaþ he, 'trewlie! · his treuþ is full litell!
He dyned nouȝt wiþ Domynike · siþe Crist deide!
For wiþ þe princes of pride · þe prechours dwellen;
þei bene as digne as þe devel · þat droppeþ fro heuene. 355
Wiþ hertes of heynesse · wouȝ halwen þei chirches

& deleþ in devynitie · as dogges doþ bones!

Þei medleth wiþ messages · & mariages of grete;

Þey leeuen wiþ lordes · wiþ lesynges y-nowe;

Þey biggeþ hem bichopryches · wiþ bagges of golde;   360

Þei wilneþ worchipes— · but waite on her dedes!

Herken at Herdforþe · hou þat þey werchen,

And loke whou þat þei lyven · & leeue as þou fyndest.

Þey ben counseilours of kinges · crist wot þe soþe,

Whou þey curry kinges · & her back claweþ!   365

God leue hem leden well · in lyvinge of heven,

And glose hem nouȝt for her good · to greven her soules!

Y pray þe, where ben þei pryue · wiþ any pore wiȝtes,

Þat maie not amenden her hous · ne amenden hem-seluen?

Þei prechen in proude harte · & preiseþ her order,   370

And werdliche worchype · wilneþ in erþe.

Leeue it well, lef man · & men ryȝt-lokede,

Þer is more pryue pride · in prechours hertes

Þan þer lefte in lucyfer · er he were lowe fallen;

Þey ben digne as dich-water · þat dogges in bayteþ.   375

Loke a ribaut of hem · þat can nouȝt wel reden

His rewle ne his respondes · but be pure rote,

Als as he were a connynge Clerke · he casteþ þe lawes,

Nouȝt lowli but lordly · & leesinges lyeþ.

For ryȝt as menoures · most ypocricie vseþ,   380

Ryȝt so ben prechers proude · purlyche in herte.

But, cristen creatour · we Karmes first comen

Even in Elyes tyme · first of hem all,

& lyven by our Lady · & lelly hir seruen

In clene comun life · kepen vs out of synne;   385

Nowt proude as prechours beþ · but prayen full still

For all þe soules and þe lyves · þat we by lybbeth.

We connen on no queyntyse · (crist wot þe soþe!)

But bysieþ vs in oure bedes · as vs best holdeþ.

And þerfore, leŭe leel man · leeue þat ich sygge,   390
A masse of vs mene men · is of more mede
And passeth all praiers · of þies proude freers.
& þou wilt ȝyuen vs any good · y would þe here graunten
To taken all þy penance · in peril of my soule;
And þouȝ þou conne nouȝt þy crede · clene þe assoile,   395
So þat þou mowe amenden our hous · wiþ money oþer elles,
Wiþ som katell oþer corne · or cuppes of siluer.'
    'Trewely, frere,' quaþ y þo · 'to tellen þe þe soþe,
Þer is no peny in my pakke · to payen for my mete;
I haue no good ne no gold · but go þus abouten,   400
And travaile full trewlye · to wynnen withe my fode.
But woldest þou for godes loue · lerne me my crede,
Y schuld don for þy will · whan I wele hadde.'
'Trewlie,' quaþ þe frere · 'a fol y þe holde!
Þou woldest not weten þy fote · & woldest fich kacchen! 405
Our pardon & our preiers · so beþ þey nouȝt parted,
Oure power lasteþ nouȝt so feer · but we some peny fongen.
Fare well,' quaþ þe frere · 'for y mot heþen fonden,
And hyen to an houswife · þat haþ vs bequeþen
Ten pounde in hir testament · to tellen þe soþe.   410
Ho draweþ to þe deþe-warde · but ȝet I am in drede
Lest ho turne her testament · & þerfore I hyȝe
To hauen hir to our hous · and henten ȝif y miȝte
An Anuell for myn owen vse · to helpen to cloþe.'
'Godys forbode,' quaþ his fellawe · 'but ho forþ passe   415
Wil ho is in purpose · wiþ vs to departen;
God let her no lenger lyven · for letteres ben manye.'

[*Peres the Ploughman.*]

Þanne turned y me forþe · and talked to my-selue
Of þe falshede of þis folk · whou feiþles they weren.
And as y wente be þe waie · wepynge for sorowe,   420

I seiȝ a sely man me by · opon þe plow hongen.
His cote was of a cloute · þat cary was y-called,
His hod was full of holes · & his heer oute,
Wiþ his knopped schon · clouted full þykke;
His ton toteden out · as he þe londe treddede,   425
His hosen ouerhongen his hokschynes · on eueriche a side,
Al beslombred in fen · as he þe plow folwede;
Twey myteynes, as mete · maad all of cloutes;
Þe fyngers weren for-werd · & ful of fen honged.
Þis whit waselede in þe fen · almost to þe ancle,   430
Foure roþeren hym by-forn · þat feble were worþen;
Men myȝte reken ich a ryb · so reufull þey weren.
His wijf walked him wiþ · wiþ a longe gode,
In a cutted cote · cutted full heyȝe,
Wrapped in a wynwe schete · to weren hire fro weders, 435
Barfote on þe bare ijs · þat þe blod folwede.
& at the londes ende laye · a litell crom-bolle,
& þeron lay a litell childe · lapped in cloutes,
And tweyne of tweie ȝeres olde · opon a-noþer syde,
And alle þey songen o songe · þat sorwe was to heren; 440
Þey crieden alle o cry · a carefull note.
Þe sely man siȝede sore, & seide · 'children, beþ stille!'
Þis man loked opon me · & leet þe plow stonden,
And seyde, 'sely man, why syȝest þou so harde?
Ȝif þe lakke lijflode · lene þe ich will   445
Swich good as god haþ sent · go we, leue broþer.'
Y saide þanne, 'naye, sire · my sorwe is wel more;
For y can nouȝt my crede · y kare well harde;
For y can fynden no man · þat fully beleueþ,
To techen me þe heyȝe weie · & þerfore I wepe.   450
For y haue fonded þe freers · of þe foure orders,
For þere I wende haue wist · but now my wit lakkeþ;
And all my hope was on hem · & myn herte also;

But þei ben fully feiþles · and þe fend sueþ.'

'A! broþer,' quaþ he þo · 'beware of þo foles! 455

For crist seyde him-selfe · " of swiche y ȝou warne,"

& false profetes in þe feiþ · he fulliche hem calde,

" *In vestimentis ouium* · but onlie wiþ-inne

Þei ben wilde wer-wolues · þat wiln þe folk robben."

Þe fend founded hem first · þe feiþ to destroie, 460

And by his craft þei comen in · to combren þe chirche,

By þe coueiteise of his craft · þe curates to helpen ;

But now þey hauen an hold · þey harmen full many.

Þei don nouȝt after domynick · but dreccheþ þe puple,

Ne folwen nouȝt fraunces · but falslyche lybben, 465

And Austynes rewle · þei rekneþ but a fable,

But purchaseþ hem pryuylege · of popes at Rome.

Þei coueten confessions · to kachen some hire,

And sepultures also · some wayten to cacchen ;

But oþer cures of cristen · þei coueten nouȝt to haue, 470

But þere as wynnynge lijþ · he lokeþ none oþer.'

'Whouȝ schal y nemne þy name · þat neiȝboures þe kalleþ ?'

'Peres,' quaþ he, 'þe pore man · þe plowe-man y hatte.'

'A! Peres,' quaþ y þo · 'y pray þe, þou me telle

More of þise tryflers · hou trechurly þei libbeþ ? 475

For ichon of hem haþ told me · a tale of þat oþer,

Of her wicked lijf · in werlde þat hy lybbeþ.

I trowe þat some wikked wyȝt · wrouȝte þis orders

Þoruȝ þat gleym of þat gest · þat Golias is y-calde,

Oþer ell[e]s satan him-self · sente hem fro hell 480

To cumbren men wiþ her craft · cristendome to schenden !'

'Dere broþer,' quaþ peres · 'þe devell is ful queynte ;

To encombren holy Chirche · he casteþ ful harde,

& flaricheþ his falsnes · opon fele wise,

And fer he casteþ to-forn · þe folke to destroye. 485

Of þe kynrede of Caym · he caste þe freres,

And founded hem on farysens · feyned for gode;
But þei wiþ her fals faiþ · michel folk schendeþ,
Crist calde hem him-self · kynde ypocrites;
How often he cursed hem · well can y tellen   490
He seide ones him-self · to þat sory puple,
" Wo worþe ȝou, wyȝtes · wel lerned of þe lawe!"
Eft he seyde to hem-selfe · " wo mote ȝou worþen,
Þat þe toumbes of profetes · tildeþ vp heiȝe !
ȝoure faderes fordeden hem · & to þe deþ hem brouȝte."   495
Here y touche þis two · twynnen hem I þenke;
Who wilneþ ben wisere of lawe · þan lewde freres,
And in multitude of men · ben maysters y-called,
And wilneþ worchips of þe werlde · & sitten wiþ heye,
And leueþ louynge of god · and lownesse behinde?   500
And in beldinge of tombes · þei trauaileþ grete
To chargen her chirche-flore · and chaungen it ofte.

·   ·   ·   ·   ·   ·   ·

Al her brod beldyng · ben belded withe synne,
And in worchipe of þe werlde · her wynnynge þei holden;
Þei schapen her chapolories · & streccheþ hem brode,   550
And launceþ heiȝe her hemmes · wiþ babelyng in stretes;
Þei ben y-sewed wiþ whiȝt silk · & semes full queynte,
Y-stongen wiþ stiches · þat stareþ as siluer.
And but freres ben first y-set · at sopers & at festes,
Þei wiln ben wonderly wroþ · ywis, as y trowe;   555
But þey ben at þe lordes borde · louren þey willeþ;
He mot bygynne þat borde · a beggere, (wiþ sorwe !)
And first sitten in se · in her synagoges,
Þat beþ here heyȝe helle-hous · of Kaymes kynde !
For þouȝ a man in her mynster · a masse wolde heren,   560
His siȝt schal so be set · on sundrye werkes,
Þe penounes & þe pomels · & poyntes of scheldes
Wiþ-drawen his deuocion · & dusken his herte;

I likne it tó a lym-ȝerde · to drawen men to hell,
And to worchipe of þe fend · to wraþþen þe soules. 565

   ·   ·   ·   ·   ·   ·   ·

Now mot ich soutere his sone · setten to schole,
& ich a beggers brol · on þe booke lerne, 745
& worþ to a writere · & wiþ a lorde dwell,
Oþer falsly to a frere · þe fend for to seruen!
So of þat beggers brol · a bychop schal worþen,
Among þe peres of þe lond · prese to sitten,
& lordes sones lowly · to þo losells aloute, 750
Knyȝtes croukeþ hem to · & crucheþ full lowe;
And his syre a soutere · y-suled in grees,
His teeþ wiþ toylinge of leþer · tatered as a sawe!
Alaas! þat lordes of þe londe · leueþ swiche wrechen,
And leneþ swiche lorels · for her lowe wordes! 755
Þey schulden maken bichopes · her owen breþren childre,
Oþer of some gentil blod · & so it best semed,
And foster none faytoures · ne swiche false freres
To maken fatt & full · & her fleche combren!
For her kynde were more · to y-clense diches 760
Þan ben to sopers y-set first · and serued wiþ siluer!
A great bolle-full of benen · were betere in his wombe,
And wiþ þe randes of bakun · his baly for to fillen,
Þan pertriches or plouers · or pekokes y-rosted,
And comeren her stomakes · wiþ curious drynkes. 765

   ·   ·   ·   ·   ·   ·   ·

Þei schulden deluen & diggen · & dongen þe erþe, 785
& mene mong-corn bred · to her mete fongen,
& wortes flechles wroughte · & water to drinken,
And werchen & wolward gon · as we wrecches vsen;
An aunter ȝif þer wolde on · amonge an hol hundred
Lyuen so for godes loue · in tyme of a wynter!' 790
'Leue peres,' quaþ y þo · 'y praie þat þou me tell

Whou y maie conne my crede · in cristen beleue?'
'Leue broþer,' quaþ he · · 'hold þat y segge,
I will techen þe þe trewþe · & tellen þe þe soþe.

CREDO.

Leue þou on oure Louerd God · þat all þe werld wrouȝte,   795
Holy heuen opon hey · hollyche he fourmede,
& is almiȝti him-self · ouer all his werkes,
& wrouȝt as his will was · þe werlde and þe heuen;
And on gentyl Jesu Crist · engendred of him-seluen,
His own onlyche sonne · Lord ouer all y-knowen,   800
Þat was clenly conseued · clerlye, in trewþe,
Of þe hey holy gost · þis is þe holy beleue;
And of the mayden Marye · man was he born,
Wiþ-outen synnfull sede · þis is fully þe beleue;
Wiþ þorn y-crouned, crucified · & on þe crois dyede,   805
& syþen his blissed body · was in a ston byried,
& descended a-doune · to þe derk helle,
And fet oute our formfaderes · & hy full feyn weren;
Þe þridde daye rediliche · him-self ros fram deeþ,
And on a ston þere he stod · he steiȝ vp to heuene.   810
And on his fader riȝt hand · redeliche he sitteþ,
Þat al-miȝti god · ouer all oþer whyȝtes;
And is hereafter to komen · crist, all him-seluen,
To demen þe quyke and þe dede · wiþ-outen any doute;
And in þe heiȝe holly gost · holly y beleue,   815
And generall holy Chirche also · hold þis in þy mynde;
·   ·   ·   ·   ·   ·   ·   ·   ·
And in þe sacrement also · þat soþfast god on is,
Fullich his fleche & his blod · þat for vs deþe þolede.'   823

II.

THOMAS OCCLEVE, *or* HOCCLEVE.

ABOUT A.D. 1420.

THOMAS OCCLEVE, or Hoccleve, was born about A.D. 1370, and died about A.D. 1454. He knew Chaucer personally, and calls himself Chaucer's disciple. His lament upon Chaucer's death is printed below. An edition of his minor poems was printed by G. Mason in 1796, in one of which, entitled 'La male regle de T. Hoccleve,' he recounts, in a half-penitent manner, some of his youthful excesses:—

> 'Wher was a gretter maister eek than y,
> Or bet acqweynctid at Westmynster yate,
> Among the taverneres namely
> And cookes?'

His principal poem is 'The Governail of Princes,' the greater part of which is a version of a Latin treatise called 'De Regimine Principum,' written by Ægidius, a native of Rome, who flourished about 1280, for the use of Philip le Hardi, son of Louis IX, king of France. The whole of this long poem was printed by Mr. T. Wright for the Roxburghe Club in 1860, from the Royal MS. 17 D vi. in the British Museum. The extracts here printed are from the same MS., with a *few* corrections from MS. Arundel 38. The first is of course original, and begins with stanza 281 of the poem. The remarks at the end of the second extract refer to his position in a Government office as Clerk of the Privy Seal. He requests that the salary due to him may be paid. For further information, see Morley's 'English Writers,' and Warton's 'History of English Poetry.'

[Lament for Chaucer.]

281 O maister dere and fader reuerent,
My maister Chaucers, floure of eloquence,
Mirrour of fructuous entendement,
O vniversal fader in science,
Allas! that thou thyne excellent prudence ·
In thy bedde mortalle myghtest not bequeth[e];
What eyled dethe, allas! why wold he sle the?

282 O dethe, thou didest not harme singuler
In slaughtre of hym, but alle this londe it smerteth.
But natheles yit hast thow no power
His name to slee, his hye vertu asterteth
Vnslayn fro the, which ay vs lyfly herteth
With bookes of his ornat endityng,
That is to alle this land enlumynyng.

· · · · · · ·

298 Allas! my worthy maister honorable,
This londes verray tresour and richesse,
Dethe by thy dethe hath harme irreperable
Vnto vs done; hir vengeable duresse
Dispoiled hath this londe of the swetnesse
Of Rethoryk fro vs; to Tullius
Was neuer man so like amonges vs.

299 Also who was hyer in philosofye
To Aristotle in our tunge but thow?
The steppes of Virgile in poysye
Thou folwedest eke, men wote wele ynow.
That combreworld that þee my maister slow—
Wolde I slayne were!—dethe was to hastyfe,
To renne on the and reve the thy lyfe.

· · · · · · ·
·

301 She myght han taryed hir vengeaunce a while,
   Til that som man hade egalle to the be.
   Nay, lete be that! she knewe wele that this yle
   May neuer man forth brynge like to the,
   And hir office nedes do mote she;
   God bade hir so, I truste as for the beste,
   O maister, maister, god thy soule reste!

[*Story of John of Canace.*]

598 Of foole largesse wole I talke a space,
   How it befille, I note in what contree,
   But ther was one named Iohan of Canace,
   A riche man, and two doughters hade he,
   That vnto twey worthy men of a Citee
   He wedden lete; and ther was gladnesse
   And reuelle more than I kan expresse.

599 The fader his doughters and her husbondes
   Loued fulle wele, and hade hem leef and dere;
   Tyme and tyme he yafe hem withe his hondes
   Of his goode passyngly, and they suche chere
   Hym made, and were of so plesaunt manere,
   That he ne wist how to be better at ese,
   They coude hym so wele cherisshe and plese.

600 For he as muche haunted in partie
   Her hous as he did his owen hous.
   They held[en] hym up with her flatrye,
   That of dispence he was outrageous;
   And of goode they were ay desirous;
   Alle that they axed haden they redy,
   And they euer were on hym gredy.

601 This sely man contynued his outrage,
     Til alle his goode was wasted and gone;
     And they felt his expenses swage,
     And were to hym vnkynde right anone.
     For after hade he cherisshyng none;
     They wery were of his companye,
     And he was wise and shope a remedye.

602 He to a marchaunt gothe of his notice,
     Which that his trusty frende hade be fulle yore,
     Besechyng hym that he wold hym cheuyce
     Of ten thousand pounde, no longer ne more
     Than dayes thre, and he wold it restore
     At his day; this was done, the somme he hent,
     And to his owen hous therwith he went.

603 And on the morwe praide he to sopere
     His sones bothe, and his doughters also.
     They to hym came, withouten eny daungere;
     How that they ferd[en], lete it passe and go.
     They ferden wele, without wordes mo.
     To his kunnyng grete disport he hem made,
     He did his myght to chere hem and glade.

604 After soper, whan they her tyme sye,
     They toke her leve, and home they wold algate;
     And he answerd and seide hem sikerly,
     'This nyght shulle ye not passe out at this yate,
     Your hous is ferre, and it is derk and late;
     Speke it not, for it shalle not betide.'
     And so alle nyght he made hem to abide.

605 The fader logged him, of sly purpos,
     In a chambre next to his ioynyng.

But betwixt hem nas ther but a parclos
Of bord*e*, not but of homely makyng;
Thurghout the which, at many a chynnyng, .
In eche chambre they myghten behold
And see what other did, yf that they wold.

606 I kan not sey how they slept that nyght,
Also it longeth not to my matere;
But on the morwe, at brode day-light,
The fader roos, and for they shuld here
What that he did, in a boistous manere
Vnto his chest, which thre lokkes hadde,
He went, and therat wrestede he full*e* sadde.

607 And whan it was y-opened and vnshette,
The bagged gold that the marchaunt hym lent
He hath vncofred, and streight forth with it
Vnto his beddes fete gone is and went.
What doth than this felle man and prudent,
But out this gold on a tapite hath shotte,
That in the bagges left[e] ther no grotte?

608 And all*e* this did he not but for a wile,
As that ye shull wele knowe[n] afterward;
He shope his sones and doughtres to begile.
His noise made hem dresse hem vpward;
They caste her eres to his chamberward,
And herd of gold the russhyng and the soun,
As that he rudely threwe hem adoun.

609 And to the parclos they hem haste and hye,
To wite and knowe what her fader wrought.
In at the chynnes of the bordes they prye,
And sye how he amonge the nobles sought

c

Yf defectyfe were eny, as hym thought;
And on his naile he threwe hem ofte and caste,
And bagged hem and cofred hem at the laste;

610 And opened his dore, and doun goth his wey.
And after blive out of her bedde they rise,
And came doun blive, her fader thanken they
Of his goode chere in her best wise,
And alle was for the goldes couetise.
And to gone home they axed of hym leve;
They ben departed, and there they hym leve.

611 Walkyng homward they iangled fast, and speke
Of the gold which they sawe her fader haue.
One seide, ' I wonder ther-on;' 'and I eke,'
Koth a-nother, ' for, also god me saue,
Yisterday, though I shuld in-to my graue
Haue crept, I durst on it haue leide my lyfe,
That gold with hym not hade be so ryfe.'

612 Now lete hem muse on that, what so hem leste;
And to her fader now wole I me dresse.
He alle this gold now taketh out of his cheste,
And to the marchaunt paide it more and lesse,
Thankyng hym ofte of his kyndenesse;
And thens goth he home vn-to his mete,
And to his sones hous, whan he hade ete.

613 Whan he came thider, they made of hym more
Than that they were wont, by many folde;
So grete disport they made hym not fulle yore.
'Fader,' koth they, 'this is your owen housholde;
In feith, ther is no thyng within our holde,
But it shalle be at your comaundement.
Wold god that ye were of our assent;

614 Than we shuld[en] ay to-gider dwelle.'
    Alle what they menten wist he wel ynough.
    'Sones and doughters,' koth he, 'sothe to telle,
    My wille is goode also to be with yow.
    How shuld I merier be? not wote I how,
    Than with you forto be contynuelle;
    Your companye liketh me fulle welle.'

615 Now shope it so, they held[en] hous in-fere,
    Save the fader, and as they lough and pleide,
    His doughtres bothe with laughyng chere
    Vn-to her fader spake, and thus they seide,
    And to assoile her questioun hym preide.
    'What so euer it be,' koth the fader, 'now,
    And I kan or may, I shalle it telle yow.'   .

616 'Now, goode fader, how muche money
    In your stronge bounde cheste is, I you prey?'
    'Ten thousand pound,' koth he, and lyed lowde.
    'I tolde hem,' koth he, 'not fulle longe ago,
    And þat as redily as that I coude.
    Yf ye wille after þis do to me so
    As ye haue done, ye shulle haue alle tho.'

617 After this day they alle in one hous were,
    Til the day come of her faders dying;
    Goode mete and drynke and clothes forto were
    He hade, and paide nought to his endyng.
    Whan he sawe the tyme of his departyng,
    His sones and his doughters did he calle,
    And in this wise he spake to hem alle.

618 'Not purpose I to make other testament,
    But of that is in my stronge chest ybounde;

And right anone, or I be hens hent,
An hundred pounde of nobles gode and rounde
Taketh to þe prechours, tarieth it no stounde;
An hundred pounde eke to the freres grey;
And to karmes fifty; tarye not, I you prey.

619 And whan I buryed am, of hem the keyes
Of my cheste taketh, for they hem kepe.
By every key writen ben the weyes
Of my wille;' this gold was not suffred slepe,
It was anone delt, for her hertes depe
Stak in his bounden cofre, and alle her hope
Was goode bagges, therynne forto grope.

620 To euery chirche and recluse of the toun
Bade he yeve eke of golde a quantitee;
Alle as he bade, thei were prest and boun,
And did it blive; but, so mote I thee,
Fully slily deceyued he this meyne,
His sones and his doughtres bothe I mene;
Her berdes shaued he both smothe and clene.

621 Whan he was dede, and his obsequies do
Solempnely, they to the freres yede,
And bade tho keyes deliuer hem vnto;
And, as they hem beden, so they dede.
Tho ioyfulle sones dressen hem to the stede
Where as the strong bounden chest stoode,
But or they twynned thens they pekked moode.

622 They opened the cheste, and fonde right nought
But a passyng grete sergeantes mace,
In which there gaily made was and wrought
This same scripture, ' I, Iohan of Canace,

Make suche testament here in this place;
Who bereth charge of other men, and is
Of hem dispised, slayne be he with this.'

623 Amonge folies all*e*, is none, I leeue,
More than a man his goode foole-largely
Dispende, in hope men wole hym releeue.
Whan his goode is dispent vttirly,
The indigent man sette no thyng therby.
I, Occleue, in suche caas am gilty, this me toucheth,
So seith pouert, that on foole-large hym voucheth.

624 For though I neuere were of hye degree,
Ne hade moche goode, ne grete richesse,
Yit hath the vice of prodegalitee
Smerted me, and do me hevynesse.
He that but litelle hath may done excesse
In his degree, as wele as may the riche,
Though her dispenses be not eliche.

625 So haue I plukked at my purses strenges,
And made hem oft for to gape and gane,
That his small*e* stuffe hath take hym to his wenges,
And hath sworne to be my welthes bane,
But yf releef my sorwe awey plane;
And whens it come shall*e*, kan I not gesse,
My lord, but it procede of your hyenesse.

626 I me repente of my mysreuled lyfe;
Wherfore in the wey of sauacio*u*n
I hope I be, my dotage excessife
Hath putte me to suche castigacio*u*n
Of me; O hade I helpe, now wold I thrive,
And so did I neuer yit in my live.

627   My yerely guerdoun, myne annuitee,
      That was me graunted for my longe labour,
      Is alle behynde, I may not paide be;
      Which causeth me to live[n] in langour.
      O liberalle prynce, ensaumple of honour,
      Vnto your grace like it to promote
      My poore estate, and to my woo beth boote.

628   And, worthy prynce, at cristes reuerence,
      Herkeneth what I shalle sey, and beth not greued;
      But lete me stonde in your beneuolence.
      For, yf myn hertes wille wist were and preued
      How, yow to love, it stered is and meued,
      Ye shulde knowe I your honour and welthe
      Thurste and desire, and eke your soules helthe.

III.

JOHN LYDGATE,

ABOUT A.D. 1420.

JOHN LYDGATE, a monk of Bury, was born at the village of Lydgate, near Newmarket, about A.D. 1373, and died about A.D. 1460; but these dates are uncertain. He was ordained subdeacon in the Benedictine Monastery of Bury St. Edmunds in 1389, deacon in 1393, and priest in 1397. He is remarkable for the great ease, fluency, and extent of his writings, a catalogue of which would take up a considerable space. He composed verses with such facility that we cannot expect to find his poetry of a very lofty character; still, he is generally pleasing, though too much addicted to prolixity. Some of his best poems are his minor ones, of which the best known is 'London Lickpeny,' here printed. Unfortunately there is no good copy of it; the best, occurring in the Harleian MS. 367 in the British Museum, is here accurately reproduced. Amongst his more ambitious works may be mentioned ' The Storie of Thebes,' 'The Falls of Princes' (from Boccaccio), and 'The Troy Booke.' The Storie of Thebes is intended as an additional 'Canterbury Tale,' to be added to Chaucer's Tales. It was printed, from a good MS., by Stow, in his edition of Chaucer, in 1561. An extract from it, written in the very spirit of chivalry, and detailing the adventures of Tydeus, is here printed from the Arundel MS. No. 119, in the British Museum, with a *few* corrections from MSS. R. 4. 20 and O. 5. 2, in Trinity College, Cambridge. The poet tells us that, at the time of writing it, he was nearly fifty years of age.

(A) *London Lyckpeny.*

A Ballade compyled by Dan Iohn Lydgate monke of Bery about ..
yeres agoe, and newly ouersene and amended.

1 To london once my stepp[e]s I bent,
  Where trouth in no wyse should be faynt,
To-westmynster-ward I forthwith went,
  To a man of law to make complaynt;
  I sayd, ' for marys love, that holy saynt!
Pyty the poore that wold proceede;'
But for lack of mony I cold not spede.

2 And as I thrust the prese amonge,
  By froward chaunce my hood was gone,
Yet for all that I stayd not longe,
  Tyll to the kynges bench I was come.
  Before the Iudge I kneled anon,
And prayd hym for gods sake to take heede;
But for lack of mony I myght not speede.

3 Beneth them sat clarkes a great Rout,
  Which fast dyd wryte by one assent,
There stoode vp one and cryed about,
  ' Rychard, Robert, and John of Kent.'
  I wyst not well what this man ment,
He cryed so thycke there in dede;
But he that lackt mony myght not spede.

4 Vnto the common place I yode thoo,
  Where sat one with a sylken hoode;
I dyd hym reverence, for I ought to do so,
  And told my case as well as I coode,
  How my goodes were defrauded me by falshood.
I gat not a mum of his mouth for my meed,
And for lack of mony I myght not spede.

5 Vnto the Roll[e]s I gat me from thence,
   Before the Clarkes of the Chauncerye,
Where many I found earnyng of pence,
   But none at all once regarded mee.
   I gave them my playnt vppon my knee;
They lyked it well, when they had it reade:
But, lackyng mony, I could not be sped.

6 In westmynster-hall I found out one,
   Which went in a long gown of Raye;
I crowched and kneled before hym anon,
   For maryes love, of help[1] I hym praye.
   'I wot not what thou meanest,' gan he say:
To get me thence he dyd me bede,
For lack of mony, I cold not speed.

7 Within this hall, nether rich nor yett poore
   Wold do for me ought, although I shold dye.
Which seing, I gat me out of the doore,
   Where flemynges began on me for to cry,
   'Master, what will you copen or by?
Fyne felt hattes, or spectacles to reede?
Lay down your sylver, and here you may speede.'

8 Then to westmynster-gate I presently went,
   When the sonn[e] was at hyghe pryme;
Cookes to me they tooke good entente,
   And proferred me bread, with ale and wyne,
   Rybb[e]s of befe, both fat and ful fyne.
A fayre cloth they gan for to sprede;
But, wantyng mony, I myght not then speede.

[1] MS. 'of I help.'

9 Then vnto London I dyd me hye,
     Of all the land it beareth the pryse :
' Hot pescod*es*,' one began to crye,
      ' Strabery rype,' and ' cherryes in the ryse ;'
      One bad me come nere and by some spyce,
Peper and safforne they gan me bede,
But for lack of mony I myght not spede.

10 Then to the Chepe I gan me drawne,
     Where mutch people I saw for to stand ;
One ofred me velvet, sylke, and lawne,
      An other he taketh me by the hande,
      ' Here is Parys thred, the fynest in the land ;'
I neuer was vsed to such thyng*es* in dede,
And, wantyng mony, I myght not spede.

11 Then went I forth by London stone,
     Th[o]roughout all Canwyke streete ;
Drapers mutch cloth me offred anone ;
      Then met I one, cryed ' hot shepes feete ;'
      One cryde ' makerell ;' ' Ryshes grene ' an other gan
         greete ;
On bad me by a hood to couer my head ;
But for want of mony I myght not be sped.

12 Then I hyed me into Est-Chepe ;
     One cryes ' rybb[e]s of befe,' & many a pye ;
Pewter pott*es* they clattered on a heape ;
      There was harpe, pype, and mynstralsye;
      ' Yea, by cock !' ' nay, by cock !' some began crye ;
Some songe of Jenken and Julyan for there mede ;
But for lack of mony I myght not spede.

13 Then into Cornhyll anon I yode,
　　Where was mutch stolen gere amonge;
　I saw where honge myne owne hoode,
　　That I had lost amonge the thronge;
　　To by my own hood I thought it wronge,
　I knew it well as I dyd my crede,
　But for lack of mony I could not spede.

14 The Taverner tooke me by the sleve,
　　'Sir,' sayth he, 'wyll you *our* wyne assay?'
　I answered, 'that can not mutch me greve:
　　A peny can do no more then it may;'
　　I drank a pynt & for it dyd paye;
　Yet sore a-hungerd fro*m* thence I yede,
　And, wantyng mony, I cold not spede.

15 Then hyed I me to Belyngsgate,
　　And one cryed, 'hoo! go we hence!'
　I prayd a barge-man, for gods sake,
　　That he wold spare me my expence.
　　'Thou scapst not here,' q*uo*d he, 'vnder ij pence;
　I lyst not yet bestow my Almes dede.'
　Thus, lackyng mony, I could not speede.

16 Then I convayd me into Kent,
　　For of the law wold I meddle no more;
　Because no man to me tooke entent,
　　I dyght me to do as I dyd before.
　　Now Jesus, that in Bethle*m* was bore,
　Save london, and send trew lawyers there mede!
　For who so want*es* mony w*i*th the*m* shall not spede!

Explicit London Lyckpeny.

(B) *The Storie of Thebes ; Pars Secunda.*

How manly Tydeus departed from þe king.

Whan Tydeus hadde his massage saide,   1065
Lik to the charge that was on hy*m* laide,
As he that list no lenger ther soio*u*rne,
Fro the kyng he gan his face tourne,
Nat astonned, nor in his hert afferde,
But ful proudly leyde hond on his swerde,   1070
And in despit, who that was lief or loth,
A sterne pas thorgh the halle he goth,
Thorgh-out the courte, and manly took his stede,
And oute of Thebes fast gan hy*m* spede,
Enhastyng hy*m* til he was at large,   1075
And sped hym forth touard the londe of arge.
   Thus leue I hy*m* ride forth awhile,
Whilys that I retourne ageyn my style
Vnto the kyng, which in the halle stood,
Among his lordes furious and wood,   1080
In his herte wroth and euel apayd
Of the wordes that Tydeus had[1] said,
Specialy hauyng remembrance
On the proude dispitous[2] diffiance,
Whilys that he sat in his Royal See,   1085
Vpon which he wil auenged be
Ful cruelly, what eu*e*re that befalle,
And in his Ire he gan to hy*m* calle
Chief constable of his Chyualrye,
Charchyng hym fast for to hye.   1090

[1] So in Trin. O. 5. 2; Ar. 'hath.'   [2] MS. 'dispititous.'

With al the worthy Chooce of his housholde,
Which as he knewe most manful and most bolde,
In al hast, Tydeus to swe
To-forn ar he out of his lond remwe,
Vp peyn of lyf and lesyng of her hede,   1095
With-oute mercy anon that he be dede.
And of knyghtes fyfty weren in nombre,
Myn auto*ur* seith, vnwarly hy*m* tencombre,
Armed echon in mayle and thik stiel,
And ther-with-al yhorsed wonder wiel.   1100

**How falsly Ethyocles leyde a busshement in the way
to haue slayn Tydeus.**

At a posterne forth they gan to ryde
By a geyn path, that ley oute a side,
Secrely, that no man hem espie,
Only of tresou*n* and of felonye.
They haste hem forth al the longe day,   1105
Of cruel malys, forto stoppe his way,
Thorgh a forest, all*e* of o*o*n assent,
Ful couartly to leyn a busshement
Vnder an hill*e*, at a streite passage,
To falle on hy*m* at mor au*a*ntage,   1110
 The same way that Tydeus gan drawe
At thylk[e] mount wher that Spynx was slawe.
He, nothing war in his opynyo*u*n
Of this conpassed conspiracio*u*n,
But Innocent & lich a gentyl knyght,   1115
Rood ay forth to that it drowe to nyght,
Sool by hy*m*-silf with-oute companye,
Havyng no man to wisse hy*m* or to gye.
  But at the last, liftyng vp his hede,
Toward Eue, he gan taken hede;   1120

Mid of his waye[1], riȝt as eny lyne,
Þoght he saugh, ageyn þe mone shyne,
Sheldes fresshe & plates borned bright,
The which environ casten a gret lyght;
Ymagynyng in his fantasye   1125
Ther was treson and conspiracye
Wrought by the kyng, his iourne forto lette.

How Tydeus outrayed fifty knyghtes þat lay in awayt for hym.

And of al that he no-thyng ne sette,
But wel assured in his manly herte,
List nat onys a-syde to dyuerte,   1130
But kepte his way, his sheld vpon his brest,
And cast his spere manly in the rest,
And the first platly that he mette
Thorgh the body proudely he hym smette,
That he fille ded, chief mayster of hem alle;   1135
And than at onys they vpon hym falle
On euery part, be compas envyroun.
But Tydeus, thorgh his hegh renoun,
His blody swerde lete about hym glyde,
Sleth & kylleth vpon euery side   1140
In his Ire & his mortal tene;
That mervaile was he myght so sustene
Ageyn hem alle in euery half besette;
But his swerde was so sharpe whette,
That his foomen founde[2] ful vnsoote.   1145
But he, allas! was mad light a foote,
Be force grounded, in ful gret distresse;

[1] So in Trin. O. 5. 2; Ar. 'way.'
[2] So in Trin. MSS.; Ar. 'fond.'

But of knyghthod & of gret prouesse
Vp he roos, maugre all*e* his foon,
And as they cam, he slogh he*m* oon be o*o*n,   1150
Lik a lyo*u*n rampa*u*nt in his rage,
And on this hille he fond a narow passage,
Which that he took of ful high prudence;
And liche a boor, stondyng at his[1] diffence,
As his foomen proudly hy*m* assaylle,   1155
Vpon the pleyn he made her blode to raylle
Al enviro*u*n, that the soyl wex rede,
Now her, now ther, as they fille dede,
That her lay on, & ther lay two or thre,
So mercyles, in his cruelte,   1160
Thilk[e] day he was vpon hem founde;
And, attonys his enemyes to confounde,
Wher-as he stood, this myghty champio*u*n,
Be side he saugh, with water tu*r*ned do*u*n,
An[2] huge sto*o*n, large, rounde, & squar;   1165
And sodeynly, er that thei wer war,
As it hadde leyn ther for the nonys,
Vpon his foon he rolled it at onys,
That ten of hem wenten vnto wrak,
And the remna*u*nt amased drogh a-bak;   1170
For on by on they wente[3] to mescha*u*nce.
And fynaly he broght to outra*u*nce
Hem eu*er*ycho*o*n, Tydeus, as blyve,
That non but on left of ha*m* alyue;
Hym-silf yhurt, & ywounded kene,   1175
Thurgh his harneys bledyng on the grene;
The theban knyghtes in compas rou*n*de aboute
In the vale lay[1] slayne, all*e* the hoole[4] route,

---

[1] Supplied from Trin. R. 4. 20.   [2] MS. 'And.'
[3] So in Trin. R. 4. 20; Ar. 'went.'   [4] Supplied from Trin. O. 5. 2.

Which pitously ageyn the mone gape.
For non of hem shortly myght eskape,   1180
But dede echon as thei han deserued,
Saue oon excepte, the which was reserued,
By Tydeus, of intencioun,
To the kyng to make relacioun,
How his knyghtes han on her iourne spedde,   1185
Euerich of hem his lyf left for a wed,
And at the metyng how they han hem born;
To tellen al he sured was & sworn
To Tydeus, ful lowly on his kne.

How trouth with lityl multitude hath euere in the fyn victory of falshede.

By which ensample ȝe opynly may se   1190
Ageyn trouth falshed hath no myght,
Fy on querilis nat grounded vpon riȝt!
With-oute which[1] may be no victoyre,
Therfor ech man ha this in memoyre,
That gret pouer, shortly to conclude,   1195
Plente of good, nor moch multitude,
Scleight or engyne, fors or felonye,
Arn to feble to holden Chanpartye
Ageyns trouth, who that list take hede;
For at the ende falshede may not spede   1200
Tendure long; ȝe shul fynde it thus.
Record I take of worthy Tydeus,
Which with his hand, thorgh trouthes excellence,
Fyfty knyghtes slogh in his dyffence;
But on except, as I late[2] tolde,   1205
Sworn, and assured with his honde vpholde,

---

[1] MS. 'woch.'   [2] So in Trin. MSS.; Ar. 'layt.'

The kyng tenforme how they wern atteynt.
And Tydeus, of bledyng wonder feynt,
Maat and wery, and in gret distresse,
And ouerleyd of verray feblenesse,   1210
But as he myght hym-silue tho sustene,
He took his hors stondyng on the grene,
Worthed vp, and forth he gan to ryde
An esy pas, with his woundes wyde,
And sothly ʒit, in his opynyoun,   1215
He was alway affered of tresoun.

How Tydeus, al forwounded, cam into Ligurgus lond.

But anguysshous, & ful of bysy peyne,
He rode hym forth til he did atteyne
Into the boundes of lygurgus lond,
A worthy kyng, & manly of his hond.   1220
And he, ful paal only for lak of blood,
Tydeus, saugh wher a castel stood,
Strong and myghty, belt vpon a roche,
Touard which he fast[e] gan approche,
Conveyed thider be clernesse of the ston   1225
That, be nyght, ageyn the moone[1] shoon,
On hegh toures, with crestes marcyal;
And joyneaunt almost to the wal
Was a gardyn, lityl out be-syde,
Into which Tydeus gan ride,   1230
Of aventure, be a gate smal;
And ther he fonde[2], forto rekne al,
A lusty herbere vnto his devis,
Soote and fresshe, liche a paradys,

---

[1] The Trin. MSS. have 'mone'; Ar. 'moon.'
[2] Trin. 'fonde,' 'founde'; Ar. 'fond.' So in ll. 1242, 1244, MS. Ar. has 'gren,' 'whit.'

D

Verray heuenly of inspeccioun.   1235
And first of al he alyght down,
The goodly place whan that he byheld;
And fro his nek he voyded hath his sheld,
Drogh the brydyl from his horses hede,
Let hym goon, and took no maner hede,   1240
Thorgh the gardyn that enclosed was
Hym to pasture on the grene gras;
And Tydeus, mor hevie than is led,
Vpon the herbes grene, white, & red,
As hym thought that tyme for the best,   1245
He leid hym doune forto tak his rest,
Of werynesse desirous to slepe,
And non awayt his body forto kepe,
And with dremes grocched eueramong.
Ther he lay to the larke song   1250
With notes newe, hegh vp in the ayr[1].
The glade morowe, rody & right fayr,
Phebus also casting vp his bemes,
The heghe[2] hylles gilt with his stremes,
The syluer dewe vpon the herbes rounde,   .   1255
Ther Tydeus lay vpon the grounde,
At the vprist of the shene svnne,
And stoundmele his grene[3] woundes rvnne
Round about, that the soyl depeynt
Of the grene with the rede meynt.   1260

**Hou Ligurgus[4] doghter fond Tydeus sleping in the
herber al forwounded.**

And euery morowe, for hoolsomnesse of eyre,
Lygurgus doghter maked her repeyr,

---

[1] MS. 'hayr.'   [2] Trin. MSS. 'hie,' 'hye'; Ar. 'hegh.
[3] Trin. MSS. 'grene'; Ar. 'gren.'   [4] MS. 'Barurgus.'

Of custom, ay among the flo*u*res newe
In this gardyn of many dyu*e*rse hwe;
Swich joye hadde forto taken hede   1265
On her stalkes forto sen hem sprede,
In the Allures walking to & fro.
And whan she hadde a litil while [1] goo,
Her self allo*o*n, casting vp her sight,
She byheld wher an armed knyght   1270
Lay to rest hym on the herbes colde,
And, hym besyde, she gan ek byholde
His myghty stede walkyng her & ther;
And she anon fille in a maner fer,
Speceally whan she saugh the blood   1275
Sprad al the grene aboute [2] ther she stood.
　　But at the last she kaught[e] hardynesse,
And wommanly gan her forto dresse
Toward this knyght, havyng a man*e*re drede
And gret dout, lest that he were dede,   1280
And of her will*e* sothly this was chief,
That she thought[e] forto mak a prief,
How that it stood of this man ful ofte;
And forth she gooth and touched hy*m* ful softe,
Ther as he lay, with her hondes smale;   1285
And with a face dedly, bleyk, & pale,
Lich as a man adawed in a swogh,
Vp he stert and his suerd*e* he drogh,
Nat fully out, but put it vp ageyn
Ano*o*n as he hath the lady seyn,   1290
Beseching hir*e*, only of her grace,
To han pite vpon his trespace,

---

[1] Trin. MSS. 'while'; Ar. 'whil.'
[2] So in MS. Trin. R. 4. 20; Ar. 'about.'

And rewe on hym of her wommanhede;
For, of affray, he was falle in drede,
Lest he hadde assayled ben of-newe   1295
Of the thebans, preued ful vntrewe;
For dred of which he was so rekkeles,
Ful humblely hym ȝelding to the pes,
Tryst in hym-silf he passed hadde his boundes.
And whan that she saugh his mortal woundes,   1300
She hadde routh of verrey gentyllesse
Of his desese, & of his distresse,
And bad he shulde no thing be dismayd,
Nor in hert sorouful nor affrayd,
Disconfort hym in no maner thing—   1305
'For I,' quod she, 'am doghter to the kyng,
Callyd lygurge, which gretly me delyte
Euery morowe this gardyn to visyte;
It is to me so passingly disport.

**How wommanly the lady acquyt hire to Tydeus in
his desese.**

Wherfor,' quod she, 'beth of good comfort.   1310
For no wight her, touchyng ȝoure viage,
Shal hynder ȝou, nor do ȝow no damage;
And ȝif ȝe list of al ȝour auenture
The pleyn trouth vnto me discure,
I wil in sothe do my bysynesse   1315
To reforme ȝoure greuous hevynesse
With al my myght and hool my dylygence;
That I hope of ȝoure gret offence
ȝe shal han helpe in ȝoure aduersite;
And, as ferforth as it lith in me,   1320
Trusteth right wel ȝe shul no faute fyhde.'
And whan he saugh that she was kynde,

So wommanly, so goodly & benygne
In al her poort, be many dyuers signe,
He vnto hire be ordre wold not spare   1325
His auenturis fully to declare;
In Thebes first, touching his massage,
And al the hil of the woode[1] rage,
Of his woundes and his hurtes sore;
It were but veyn to reherce it mor.   1330

Hou Tydeus was refresshed in the castel of the lady.

By and by he told her euery del,
The which in soth she liked neuere a del,
But hadde routh and compassioun
Of his meschief, wroght be fals tresoun,
Byddyng in hast that he shuld hire swe.   1335
And wommanly, as her thoght[e] dwe,
To a chambre she ladde hym vp alofte.
Ful wel beseyn; ther-in a bed right softe,
Richely abouten apparayled
With cloth of gold; al the floor yrayled   1340
Of the same, both in lengthe & brede.
And first this lady, of her wommanhede,
Hire wymmen badde, as goodly as they kan,
To be attendaunt on this wounded man.
And whan he was vnarmed to his sherte,   1345
She made first wassh his woundes smerte,
And serche hem wel with dyuers instrumentis,
And made[2] fett[en] sondry oynementis,
And leches ek, the best[e] she koude fynde,
Ful craftely to staunche hem & to bynde.   1350

[1] Trin. MSS. 'wode,' 'woode'; Ar. 'wood.'
[2] So in Trin. MSS.; Ar. 'mad.'

And eu*e*ry thing that may do hy*m* ease
Taswage his peyn, or his woo tapese,
Was in the courte and in[1] the Castel sought,
And by her byddyng to his chambre brought;
And, for his sake, she hath after sent   1355
For swich deyntees as wern co*n*uenyent,
Moost nut*r*ityf be phisikes lore,
Hem that wern syk or wounded to restore,
Makyng her wymmen ek to taken kep,
And wayt on hym anyghtes whan he slep;   1360
And be wel war that no thing asterte,
That was or myght be lusty to his herte.
    And, with al this, she preied hy*m* abyde
Til he were strong & myghty forto ride;
In the castel to pley hym & disporte,   1365
And at leysere hom ageyn resorte,
Whan he myght bywelde hym at his large.
But al for nought; he wil hom to Arge,
Toke his lyeve on the next[e] day,
With-out abood, to hast hym on his way;   1370
Lowly thonkyng vnto her goodnesse
Of her fredam and bountevous largesse,
So wo*m*manly that hir*e* list tak hede
Hym to refressh[en] in his grete[2] nede;
Beheestyng[3] hir*e* with al his ful myght   1375
He wold be her s*er*uant & her knyght,
Whyl he leueth, of what she wold hym charge,
And forth he rood til he cam to Arge
In ful gret hast, and wolde nowher dwelle.

[1] From Trin. MSS.; Ar. omits 'in.'
[2] So in Trin. MS. O. 5. 2; Ar. ' gret.'
[3] Trin. MSS. ' Bihotyng,' ' Behoting.'

Hou Tydeus repeyred hym to Arge al forwoundyd.

But what shuld I rehercen owther telle   1380
Of his repeir, the coostes or the pleyns,
The craggy Roches or the hegh mounteyns,
Or al the maner of his hoom-commynge,
Of the metyng nor the welcommynge?
Nor the Ioye that Adrastus made,   1385
Nor how his sustre & his wif were glade,
Nor how that they (wherto shuld I write?)
Enbraced hym in her Armes white,
Nor the gadryng about hym & the pres,
Nor of the sorowe that Polymytes   1390
Mad in hym-silf, to sen hym so soor wounded,
His greuous hurtes, his soorys ek vnsounded,
His dedly look, and his face pale;
Of alle this to gynne a newe tale
It were in sothe a maner ydylnesse;   1395
Nor how hym-silf in ordre did expresse,
First how that he in Thebes hath hym born,
Nor how the kyng falsly was forsworn,
Nor of the awayt nor tresoun that he sette,
Whan fyfty knyghtes on the way hym mette,   1400
As ȝe han herd al the maner howe,
With-oute [1] which my tale is long ynowe.
    But Adrastus maad men to seche
In euery Coost, for many diuerse leche,
To come in hast and make no taryinge,   1405
Vpon a peyne, be biddyng of the kynge,
To don her craft that he wer recured,
And of his force in euery part assured.

---

[1] So in Trin. MS. O. 5. 2; Ar. 'With-out.'

And they echon so her konnyng*e* shewe,
That, in space of a daies fewe,   1410
He was alhool maad of his siknesse;
Tho was ther Joye, & tho was ther gladnesse
Thorgh-out the courte, & thorgh-out al the to*w*n.
For eu*e*ry man hath swich opynyo*u*n
In Tydeus, for his gentyllesse,   1415
For his manhood and his lowlynesse,
That he was holde the most famous knyght,
And best byloued in eu*e*ry ma*n*nys sight
Thorgh-out grece, in eu*e*ry Regio*u*n.

IV.

JAMES I (OF SCOTLAND).

ABOUT A.D. 1423.

JAMES I., the second son of Robert III., was born in 1394, and was murdered on the 20th of February, 1437. In 1405 he was captured by an English vessel whilst on his way to France, and imprisoned in the Tower of London. Two years afterwards he was taken to Nottingham, but in 1414 was again sent back to the Tower, where however he remained but a few months, and was then removed to Windsor. Whilst a prisoner at Windsor, and probably not long before his release, which took place in 1424, he wrote his principal poem, known as 'The Kingis Quair,' i.e. 'The King's Quire or Book,' which extends to nearly 1400 lines. The subject of it is the poet's love for the Lady Jane Beaufort, whom he first beheld walking in the garden beneath his prison window, much as Palamon and Arcite first beheld Emelye. He married the lady in February, 1424, and in May of the same year was crowned king of Scotland at Scone. The rest of his life belongs to Scottish history. 'The Kingis Quair' is written in seven-lined stanzas, a favourite measure of Chaucer and his successors, which received the name of the 'rime roial,' from being thus employed by a king. Only one MS. of the poem is extant, with the mark Arch. Seld. B. 24, in the Bodleian Library; and from this the following extract is printed. The poem was printed by Tytler in 1783, and by Chalmers in 1824; a large portion of it occurs in Sibbald's Chronicle of Scottish Poetry. Instead of the extract usually given (which describes how the poet first saw Lady Jane) I give his curious description of Fortune and her wheel, preceded by a description of a landscape filled with animals, as seen in a vision.

From 'The Kingis Quair.'

152 Quhare, In a lusty plane, tuke I my way
Endlang a ryuer, plesant to beholde,
Enbroudin all with fresche flouris gay,
Quhare, throu the grauel, bryght as ony golde,
The cristall water ran so clere and colde,
That In myn ere maid contynualy
A maner soun, mellit with armony;

153 That full of lytill fischis by the brym,
Now here, now there, with bakkis blewe as lede,
Lap and playit, and In a rout can swym
So prattily, and dressit thame to sprede
Thair curall fynnis, as the ruby rede,
That In the sonne on thair scalis bryght
As gesserant ay glitterit In my sight.

154 And by this Ilke ryuer-syde alawe
Ane hye way [there] fand I like to bene,
On quhich, on euery syde, a long rawe
Of treis saw I full of leuis grene,
That full of fruyte delitable were to sene,
And also, as It come vnto my mynde,
Off bestis sawe I mony diuerss kynde.

155 The lyoun king, and his fere lyonesse,
The pantere, like vnto the smaragdyne,
The lytill squerell, full of besynesse,
The slawe ass, the druggar-beste of pyne,
The nyce ape, the werely porpapyne,
The percyng lynx, the lufar vnicorne,
That voidis venym with his euour horne.

156 There sawe I dress*e* him new out of [his] hau*n*t
    The fery tiger*e*, full of felonye,
    The dromydar*e*, the standar oliphant,
    The wyly fox, the wedowis Inemye,
    The clymbar*e* gayte, the elk for alblastrye,
    The herkner*e* bore, the holsum grey for hort*is*,
    The haire also, *that* oft gooth to the wortis;

157 The bugill, drawar by his hornis grete,
    The martrik, sable, the foyn3ee, and mony mo,
    The chalk-quhite ermyn tippit as the Iete,
    The riall hert, the conyng, and the ro;
    The wolf *that* of thé murthir no*ch*t say ' ho !'
    The lesty beu*er* and the ravin bare,
    For chamelot, the camel full of hare;

158 With mony an*e* othir beste diu*er*ss and strange,
    That cu*m*myth no*ch*t as now vn-to my mynd*e*.
    Bot now to p*ur*poss; straucht furth the range
    I held*e* away, our-hailing In my mynd*e*
    From quhens I come, and quhare *that* I suld*e* fynd*e*
    Fortune the goddess*e*, vnto quham In hye
    Gude hope, my gyde, has led me sodeynly.

159 And at the last behalding thus asyde,
    A round place wallit haue I found*e*,
    In myddis quhare eftsone I haue [e]spide
    Fortune the goddess*e* hufing on the grou*n*d*e*,
    And ry*ch*t befor*e* hir fete, of compas round*e*,
    A quhele, on quhich cleu*er*ing I sye
    A multitude of folk befor*e* my*n* eye.

160 And ane surcote sche werit long that tyde,
    That semyt to me of diu*er*ss hewis;
    Quhilum thus, quhen sche wald*e* turn*e* asyde,

Stude this goddesse of fortune & [of glewis].
A chapellet, with mony fresche anewis,
·Sche had vpon hir hede, and with this hong
A mantill on hir schuldris large and long,

161 That furrit was with ermyn full quhite,
Degoutit with the self In spottis blake;
And quhilum In hir chiere thus alyte
Louring sche was, and thus sone It wolde slake,
And sodeynly a maner smylyng make,
And sche were glad; [for] at ane contenance
Sche helde nocht, bot ay In variance.

162 And vnderneth the quhele sawe I there
Ane vgly pit, [as] depe as ony helle,
That to behalde thereon I quoke for fere;
Bot o thing herde I, that quho there-In fell
Came no more vp agane, tidingis to telle;
Off quhich, astonait of that ferefull sycht,
I ne wist quhat to done, so was I fricht.

163 Bot forto se the sudayn weltering
Off that Ilk quhele, that sloppar was to holde,
It semyt vnto my wit a strong thing,
So mony I sawe that than clymben wolde,
And failit foting, and to ground were rolde;
And othir eke that sat aboue on hye
Were ouerthrawe In twinklyng of ane eye.

164 And on the quhele was lytill void space,
Wele nere our-straught fro lawe [vn]to hye,
And they were ware þat long[e] sat In place,
So tolter quhilum did sche It to wrye;
There was bot clymbe[n] and rycht dounwarde hye;

And sum were eke þat fallyng had [so] sore,
There for to clymbe, thair corage was no more.

165 I sawe also *that*, quhere sum were slungin
Be quhirlyng of the quhele vnto the ground*e*,
Full sudaynly sche hath [thame] vp ythrungin,
And set thame on agane full sauf & sound*e*.
And eu*er* I sawe a new swarme abound*e*,
That [thought] to clymbe vpward vpon the quhele,
In stede of thame *that* my*ch*t no lang*er* rele.

166 And at the last, In p*r*esens[1] of thame all
That stude about, sche clepit me be name;
And ther-w*ith* apon kneis gan I fall,
Full sodaynly hailsing, abaist for schame;
And smylyng, thus sche said to me In game,
'Quhat dois thou here? quho has the hid*er* sent?
Say on anon, and tell me thyn*e* entent.

167 I se wele, by thy chere and contenance,
There is sum thing *that* lyis the on hert;
It stant no*ch*t w*ith* the as thou wald*e*, p*er* chance?'
'Madame,' q*uo*d I, 'for lufe Is all the smert
That eu*er* I fele, endlang and ou*er*-thwert;
Help, of ȝo*ur* grace, me wofull wrechit wight,
Sen me to cure ȝe powere haue and my*gh*t.'

168 'Quhat help,' q*uo*d sche, 'wold*e* thou *that* I ordeyne
To bring[en] the vnto thy hertis desire?'
'Madame,' q*uo*d I, 'bot *that* ȝo*ur* grace dedeyne
Off ȝo*ur* grete my*ch*t my wittis to enspire,
To win the well *that* slokin may the fyre,

[1] MS. 'presene.'

In quhich*e* I birn; a! goddess*e* fortunate,
Help now my game, *tha*t is In poynt to mate.'

169 'Off mate!' q*uo*d sche, 'o verray sely wrech*e*,
I se wele by thy dedely colour pale,
Thou art to feble of thy-self to streche,
Vpon my quhele to clymbe[n] or to hale
Withoutin help, for thou has fundin stale
This mony day, w*i/h*outin werdis wele,
And wantis now thy veray hertis hele.

170 Wele maistow be a wrechit man [y]callit,
That wantis the confort suld*e*[1] thy hert glade,
And has all thing within thy hert stallit,
That may thy ȝouth oppressen or defade;
Though thy begy*n*nyng hath bene retrograde,
Be froward opposyt quhare till aspert,
Now sall thai turn*e*, and luke on the dert.'

171 And therw*i/h*-all vnto the quhele In hye
Sche hath me led, and bad me lere to clymbe,
Vpon the quhich I steppit sudaynly;
'Now hald*e* thy grippis,' q*uo*d sche, 'for thy tyme,
An*e* hour*e* and more It ry*n*nis ou*er* p*r*ime;
To count the hole, the half is ner*e* away,
Spend wele ther*e*for*e* the remanant of the day.

172 Ensample,' q*uo*d sche, 'tak of this tofore
That fro my quhele be rollit as a ball;
For the nature of It is eu*er*more,
After ane hicht, to vale and geue a fall,
Thus, quhen me likith, vp or doun*e* to fall.
Fare wele,' q*uo*d sche, and by the ere me toke
So ernestly, *tha*t therw*i/h*all I woke.

---

[1] MS. '*t*bat suld*e*'; but *t*bat is better omitted.

173 O besy goste, ay flikering to & fro,
    That neuer art In quiet nor In rest
    Till thou cum to that place *that* thou cam fro,
    Quhich is thy first and verray proper nest;
    From day to day so sore here artow drest,
    That *with* thy flesche ay walking art In trouble,
    And sleping eke; of pyne so has thou double.

V.

REGINALD PECOCK.

ABOUT A.D. 1449.

THE times of Pecock's birth and death are uncertain. He was probably born about A.D. 1395, and died about A.D. 1460. He studied at Oriel College, Oxford, where he was elected to a fellowship, Oct. 30th, 1417. In 1444 he was made bishop of St. Asaph, and in 1449 bishop of Chichester. At this very time he was busy upon his principal work, named 'The Repressor of over much blaming of the clergy.' In it he undertook to combat the opinions of the 'Bible Men,' or Wycliffites, who had, as he contended, blamed the clergy overmuch for various practices which he undertook to justify. The principal things which he defended were the use of images, pilgrimages, possession of land by the clergy, the various ranks of the hierarchy, the laws framed by popes and bishops, and the religious orders of friars and monks. But his book was too bold in its expressions, and appealed too much to the reason, to be at all acceptable to his own party. He offended the bishops as much as the Lollards, perhaps more so, and may be esteemed a writer as much in favour of reformation in religion as against it. In consequence, he was deprived of his see, many of his books were publicly burnt at Oxford, and he was banished to Thorney Abbey, in Cambridgeshire, A.D. 1459, where he probably died soon after, as we hear no more of him. His works are numerous, and he was very fond of referring to and quoting from them. The 'Repressor' was edited by Churchill Babington, B.D. in 1860, in two volumes, from MS. Kk. 4. 26, in

the Cambridge University Library. For further information, see
Mr. Babington's edition, and Morley's 'English Writers,' vol. ii.
p. 401. The following extracts are taken from Mr. Babington's
edition, but the thorn-letters (þ) of the MS. have been preserved,
and the proof-sheets twice compared with the MS.

[A. *Many things are allowable that are not prescribed by the
Scriptures. From ' The Repressor,'* pt. i. c. xix.]

Þat þou maist not seie & holde ech gouernançe & deede
of goddis lawe & seruice to be expressid in holi scripture,
& þat ellis it is not goddis seruice & a deede of goddis
lawe, lo! þou maist se herbi. In al holi scripture it is not
expressid bi bidding, counseiling, or witnessing, or bi eni 5
ensaumpling of persoon, þat a lay man not preest schulde
were a breche, or þat he schulde were a cloke, or þat he
schulde were a gowne, or þat he schulde die wollen clooþ
into oþer colour þan is þe colour of scheep, or þat men
schulde bake eny fleisch or fisch in an ovyn, or þat men 10
schulde make & vse clockis forto knowe þe houris of þe dai
& nyȝt; for þouȝ in eeldist daies, & þouȝ in scripture mensioun is maad of orologis, schewing þe houris of þe dai bi
[þe] schadew maad bi þe sunne in a cercle, certis neuere
saue in late daies was eny clok telling þe houris of þe dai & 15
nyȝt bi peise & bi stroke; and open it is þat nouȝwhere in
holi scripture is expresse mensioun mad of eny suche. Also,
nouȝwhere in holi scripture is mensioun mad or eny ensaumpling doon, þat a womman schulde were upon her heer &
heed eny couercheef of lynnen þrede or of silk. Forwhi þe 20
coueryng wiþ which a wommannys heed ouȝte be couered,
wherof holi scripture spekiþ in þe pistlis of poul, was oonli þe
heer of wommennys heed vnschorn, & of noon oþer coueryng
to wommennys heedis spekiþ holi scripture. And here-aȝens
holi scripture wole þat men schulden lacke þe coueryng 25

E

which wommen schulden haue, & þei schulden so lacke bi
þat þe heeris of her heedis schulden be schorne, & schulde
not growe in lengþe doun as wommannys heer schulde growe.
Perauenture, as wijs as þou makist þee in þe bible forto re-
30 proue pilgrimage & setting up of ymagis and worschiping
doon bifore ymagis, þou couþist not aspie þis laste seid point
of wommannis coueryng; þerfore, how þou canst fynde it bi
holi scripture, lete se; & if þou canst not it fynde, it may
be founde & proued so bi holi scripture þat þou schalt not
35 kunne seie nay; & ʒit it is holde for a dede alloweable &
vertuose þat wommen were couerchefis, & þat men & wommen
were gownys & clokis, not-wiþstonding þat more synne comeþ
bi wering of wommennys couercheefis & bi wommennys
gownis þan by vce of ymagis & bi pilgrimagis; as al þe
40 world may wite, if þe mater be well & þriftili examyned, bi
what schal be seid and proued of ymagis & of pilgrimagis in
þe ijᵉ partie of þis present book, & bi what is al-redi þerof
clereli seid & proued in ' þe book of worschiping.'

Also, þou schalt not fynde expresseli in holi scripture þat
45 þe newe testament schulde be write in englisch tunge to
lay-men, or in latyn tunge to clerkis; neiþer þat þe oold
testament schulde be write in englisch tunge to lay-men,
or in latyn tunge to clerkis; & ʒit ech of þese gouernauncis þou wolte holde to be leeful, & to be a meritorie ver-
50 tuose moral deede forto þerbi deserue grace & glorie, & to
be þe seruice of god, & þerfore to be þe lawe of god; siþen
bi no deede a man haþ merit, saue bi a deede which is þe
seruice & þe lawe of god; & ech moral vertu is þe lawe of
god, as it is proued weel in oþere place of my writingis.
55   Also þus. Where is it[1] groundid expresseli in scripture,
þat men mowe lete schaue her berdis? & how dare þei so
lete, siþen it can not be founde expresseli in holi scripture þat

---

[1] MS. ' it is.'

þei ouȝten so lete, & namelich siþen it is founde in holi scripture þat men leten her berdis growe wiþoute schering or
schauyng, & also siþen it was þe oolde vsage þoruȝ al þe 60
world in cristendom? where is it in holi scripture groundid
bi wey of comendyng or of allowaunce þat men schulden or
miȝten lauȝwe? For to þe contrarie is euydence in holi
scripture, Mat. vᵉ. c., where it is seid þus: *Blessid ben þei þat*
moornen or weilen, for þei schulen be counfortid; & also, 65
gen. [xviijᵉ.] c., sara þe wijf of abraham was punyschid, for
þat sche lauȝed bihinde þe dore of þe tabernacle. where is it
also groundid in holi scripture þat men myȝten alloweabli or
schulden pleie in word bi bourding, or in deede by rennyng
or leping or schuting, or bi sitting at þe merels, or bi casting 70
of coitis? & ȝit ech of þese deedis mowe be doon & ben
doon ful vertuoseli & merytorili.

Also where in holi scripture is it grondid þat men myȝten
or schulden singe, saue oonli where-yn þei preisiden god, as
aungelis diden in erþe whanne crist was born? & so for 75
esement of a man him-silf, & for esement of his neiȝbour, it
is not expressid in holi scripture þat a man schulde singe.
& ȝit goddis forbode, but þat, into esement of him-silf &
also of his neiȝbour, a man mai singe, pleie, & lauȝe vertuoseli, & þerfore merytorili; & if he mai do it merytorili, 80
certis þanne þilk deede is goddis seruice; & if it be goddis
seruice, it is needis a deede of goddis lawe. where is it
expressid bi word or bi eny persoonys ensaumpling in holi
scripture þat men schulden make ale or beer, of whiche so
myche horrible synne comeþ, myche more þan of setting up 85
of ymagis, or of pilgrymagis? and þe defautis doon aboute
ymagis & pilgrimagis ben myche liȝter & esier to be
amendid, þan þe defautis comyng bi making of ale & of beer.
And also here-wiþ it is trewe þat wiþout ale & bere, &
wiþ-out sidir & wijn & meeþ, men & wommen myȝte lyue ful 90

long, & lenger þan þei doon now, & in lasse iolite & cherte
of herte forto bringe hem into horrible grete synnes. &
ȝit þou wolte seie þat forto make ale & beer & forto drinke
hem is þe seruice of god, & is merytorie, & þerfore is þe lawe
95 of god; for bi no deede a man schal plese god, & haue
merit & meede, saue bi deede of his seruice; & ech deede
which is his seruice is a deede of his lawe.

Þat in holi scripture is noon of þese now rehercid gouernauncis groundid or witnessid or ensaumplid bi eny persoon
100 expresseli, lo, y proue þus: no þing is expresseli spoken of
in scripture, which is not þere in special openli named; but
so it is, þat neiþer breche of lay-man, neiþer gown, neiþer
cloke, neiþer wommannis lynnen or silken couercheef, neiþer
clock, neiþer englisch tunge or langage [1], neiþer ale, neiþer
105 bere is spokun of þere in special & bi name; wherfore þe
vce of þese þingis, as to be doon bi þo þingis, is not þere
expressid.

[B. *A defence of images and pictures.   From 'The Repressor,'*
pt. ii. c. xi.]

Þat riȝt synguler avauntagis of remembring comen bi
ymagis & pilgrimagis which not comen or not so weel &
so soone comen bi writingis, I proue þus: If a man wolde be
remembrid on þe passioun of seint petir or of seint poul or
5 of the holi lijf of seint nicolas, certis þouȝ he couþe rede in
a book þe storie þerof, ȝit he schulde rede .vj. or .vij. or mo
leevis in þe book, ere he schulde bringe into knowing or into
remembraunce so myche as he may knowe & remembre
þerof in a litil & myche lasse while bi siȝt of þe iȝe in
10 biholding an ymage coruen wiþ purtenancis sett aboute him,
or in beholding a storie openli þerof purtreied or peinted in

---

[1] Here follow the words, 'neiþer latyn tunge or langage,' with a stroke
drawn through them.

þe wal or in a clooþ. as þat þis is trewe, y comytte me to þe
doom of experience & of assay, & to þe experience of þis
point,—þat þe iȝe-siȝt schewiþ & bringiþ into þe ymagina-
cioun & into þe mynde wiþ-ynne in þe heed of a man myche 15
mater & long mater sooner, & wiþ lasse labour & traueil &
peine, þan þe heering of þe eere dooþ. And if þis now seid
is trewe of a man which can rede in bokis stories writun, þat
myche sooner & in schortir tyme & wiþ lasse labour & pein
in his brayn he schal come into remembraunce of a long 20
storie bi siȝt, þan bi þe heering of oþere mennys reding or bi
heering of his owne reding; miche raþer þis is trewe of alle
þo persoones whiche kunnen not rede in bokis, namelich siþen
þei schulen not fynde men so redi for to rede a dosen leeuys
of a book to hem, as þei schulen fynde redy þe wallis of a 25
chirche peinted or a clooþ steyned or ymagis sprad abrood
in dyuerse placis of þe chirche.

Also, in beholding bi siȝt of iȝe upon manye dyuerse
stories or ymagis in þe chirche a man schal in a litil while
be remembrid, now upon þe passioun of seint laurence, & 30
now anoon aftir upon þe passioun of seint steuen, now
anoon aftir vpon þe passioun of petir, & so forþ of manye
chaungis. And if in þilk while in þe chirche were not
ymagis & picturis, he schulde not bi reding in a book in
xxti. siþis lenger tyme come into so miche remembraunce, & 35
namelich of so manye dyuerse passiouns to be rad; namelich
siþen þe reder schal not fynde writingis of alle þo passiouns
saue in dyuerse bokis, or at þe leste in dyuerse placis of oon
book; & eer oon of þo writingis schulde be ouer-rad per-
fitli, a gretter tyme schulde be spend þan in þe perfit ouer- 40
seing of alle þo seid passiouns.

Also ful ofte, whanne a man comeþ to chirche & wole
be remembrid vpon suche now seid þingis, his heed is feble
for labour or studie bifore had or for sikenes or for age; &

45 certis if he schulde be aboute forto remembre him vpon suche
seid þingis, & þat bi calling in-to mynde what he haþ bifore
þilk day red or herd red in þe book, or herd prechid, or seen
peinted, it schal be to him miche gretter labour for to laboure
so in his brayn bi taking mynde, & forto wiþinneforþ calle
50 into mynde, without siȝt of þe iȝe wiþouteforþ vpon ymagis,
what he bifore knewe & þouȝte vpon, þan it schulde be to
him if he biholde bi iȝe-siȝt upon ymagis or oþer peinting
according to his labour. & aȝenward, bi biholding upon
ymagis or upon such peinting, his witt schal be dressid &
55 lad forþ euener & more stabili & wiþ myche lasse peyne &
labour, þan forto wrastle wiþinneforþ in his owne ymagina-
ciouns, wiþoute leding wiþouteforþ had, bi biholding upon
ymagis; as experience vndoutabili wole schewe, & as men
woned forto haunte daili contemplacioun wolen bere witnes
60 herto upon perel of her soule: wherfore, þouȝ for noon
oþer commodite þan for þis now seid, þe vce of ymages
were so profitable, certis þe vce of hem were weel worþi to
be meyntened.

Also here-wiþ-al into þe open siȝt of ymagis in open
65 chirchis alle peple, men & wommen & children, mowe
come whanne euere þei wolen in ech tyme of þe day, but
so mowe þei not come in-to þe vce of bokis to be delyuered
to hem neiþer to be red bifore hem; & þerfore as forto soone
& ofte come into remembraunce of a long mater bi ech oon
70 persoon, and also as forto make þat þe mo persoones come
into remembraunce of a mater, ymagis & picturis seruen in
a specialer maner þan bokis doon, þouȝ in an oþer maner ful
substanciali bokis seruen bettir into remembrauncing of þo
same materis þan ymagis & picturis doon; & þer-fore, þouȝ
75 writingis seruen weel into remembrauncing upon þe bifore
seid þingis, ȝit not at þe ful: Forwhi þe bokis han not þe avail
of remembrauncing now seid whiche ymagis han.

Confirmacioun into þis purpos mai be þis : whanne þe dai of seint kateryn schal be come, marke who so wole in his mynde alle þe bokis whiche ben in londoun writun upon seint kate- 80 ryns lijf & passiouns, & y dare weel seie þat þouȝ þer were .x. þousind mo bokis writun in londoun in þilk day of þe same seintis lijf & passioun, þei schulden not so moche turne þe citee into mynde of þe holi famose lijf of seint kateryn & of her dignitee in which sche now is, as dooþ in 85 ech ȝeer þe going of peple in pilgrimage to þe college of seint kateryn bisidis london, as y dare putte þis into iuge- ment of whom euer haþ seen þe pilgrimage doon in þe vigil of seint kateryn bi persoones of london to þe seid college : wherfore riȝt greet special commoditees & profitis into re- 90 membraunce-making ymagis & pilgrimagis han & doon, whiche writingis not so han & doon.

Anoþer confirmacioun into þis same purpos is þis. In londoun sumtyme was a bischop whos name was Gravys- eende, & which lijþ now buried in þe chirche of seint poul at 95 londoun in þe plein pament of þe chirche weel bineþe þe myddis of þe chirche : þis bischop whanne he was chaun- celer of ynglond dide grete benefetis to þe citee of londoun, & ordeyned þerfore þat þe meir & þe aldir-men of londoun wiþ manye mo notable persoones of craftis in londoun schulde 100 at dyuerse tymes in þe ȝeer come openli to þe chirche of poulis, & stonde in euer-eiþer side of his sepulcre bi ij. longe rewis, & seie *de profundis* for his soul. Now, þouȝ it so had be þat þis bischop hadde not intendid þis to be doon for him into þis eende, þat his greet benefeting whiche 105 he dide to london schulde be had & contynued in mynde of þe citezeins, but þat he entendid oonli þis, þat preiers þer-bi schulden ȝeerli be mad þe sikirer for his soul—as dout is to me, wheþer he entendid þese boþe effectes or þe oon of hem oonli—ȝit treuþe is, þat if þe seid bischop wolde haue or- 110

deyned xx. þousand bokis to be writun of his seid benefeting, & wolde haue ordeyned hem be spred abrode in
dyuerse placis of þe cite, & forto haue be cheyned in þo
dyuerse placis of þe cite, þat of þe peple who so wolde myȝte
115 rede þer-in þe seid benefeting, þilk multitude of bokis schulden
not haue contynued so myche & so weel into þis day þe mynde
of þilk bischopis benefeting, as þe seid solempne ȝeerli goyng
bi ij. tymes in ech ȝeer, doon bi þe meir & aldir-men of londoun, haþ do & schal do in ech ȝeer to come: wherfore
120 needis it is trewe, þat writing mai not conteyne & compre-
hende in him al þe avail which þe siȝt and þe biholding of þe
iȝen mai ȝeue & is redi forto ȝeue.

VI.

HENRY THE MINSTREL.

ABOUT A.D. 1461.

OF Henry the Minstrel, commonly known as 'Blind Harry,'
nearly all that is known is contained in a single sentence written
by John Mair [or Major], the Scotch historian, who was born
about the year 1470. In Book IV, ch. xv, he has a sentence which
Jamieson thus translates :—'Henry, who was blind from his birth,
in the time of my infancy composed the whole book of William
Wallace; and committed to writing in vulgar poetry, in which
he was 'well skilled, the things that were commonly related of
him. For my own part, I give only partial credit to writings of
this description. By the recitation of these, however, in the
presence of men of the highest rank, he procured, as he indeed
deserved, food and raiment.' His poem was first printed in 1570,
and has since then been frequently reprinted, the best edition
being that by Dr. Jamieson, printed in 1820 from the unique
MS. in the Advocate's Library at Edinburgh, transcribed by
John de Ramsay in the year 1488. The date commonly assigned
to the poem is *about* 1460, but Dempster and others give it as
1361. The latter is clearly wrong (probably by an oversight) as
to the century, but may easily be right otherwise, and I have
therefore adopted 1461 as the true year. For further remarks,
see Jamieson's edition, Morley's 'English Writers,' Irving's 'Lives
of the Scottish Poets,' Warton, Craik, &c. The text is given
(with very slight alterations) as it stands in Jamieson's edition,
but has been recompared with the MS.

Wallace.   Book I.

Willȝham wallace, or he was man of armys,
Gret pitte thocht that scotland tuk sic harmys.
Mekill dolour it did hym in his mynd,
For he was wyss, rycht worthy, wicht, and kynd:
In gowry duelt still with this worthy man.   185
As he encressyt, and witt haboundyt than,
In-till hys hart he had full mekill cayr,
He saw the sothroun multipliand mayr;
And to hym-self offt wald he mak his mayne.
Off his gud kyne thai had slane mony ane.   190
Ȝhit he was than semly, stark, and bauld;
And he of age was bot auchtene ȝer auld.
Wapynnys he bur, outhir gud suerd or knyff;
For he with thaim hapnyt richt offt in stryff,
Quhar he fand ane, withoutyn othir presance,   195
Eftir to scottis that did no mor grewance;
To cut his throit, or steik hym sodanlye
He wayndyt nocht, fand he thaim fawely.
Syndry wayntyt, bot nane wyst be quhat way;
For all to him thar couth na man thaim say.   200
Sad of contenance he was, bathe auld and ȝing,
Litill of spech, wyss, curtass, and benyng.

How Wallace slew young Selbie, the Constable's Son, of Dundee.

Wpon a day to dunde he was send;
Off cruelness full litill thai him kend.
The constable, a felloun man of wer,   205
That to the Scottis did full mekill der,
Selbye he hecht, dispitfull and owtrage.

A sone he had, ner twenty ʒer of age:
Into the toun he vsyt euerilk day;
Thre men or four thar went with him to play;   210
A hely schrew, wanton in his entent.
Wallace he saw, and towart him he went;
Likle he was, richt byge, and weyle beseyne
In-till a gyde of gudly ganand greyne.
He callyt on hym, and said; 'thou scot, abyde;   215
Quha dewill the grathis in so gay a gyde?
Ane ersche mantill it war thi kynd to wer;
A scottis thewtill wndyr thi belt to ber;
Rouch rewlyngis apon thi harlot fete.
Gyff me thi knyff; quhat dois thi ger so mete?'   220
Till him he ʒeid, his knyff to tak him fra.
Fast by the collar wallace couth him ta;
Wndyr his hand the knyff he bradit owt,
For all his men that semblyt him about:
Bot help him-selff, he wyst of no remede;   225
With-out reskew he stekyt him to dede.
The squier fell: of him thar was na mar.
His men folowid on wallace wondyr sar:
The press was thik, and cummerit thaim full fast.
Wallace was spedy, and gretlye als agast;   230
The bludy knyff bar drawin in his hand,
He sparyt nane that he befor him fand.
He knew the hous his eyme had lugit in;
Thedir he fled, for owt he mycht nocht wyn.
The gude wyff than within the closs saw he;   235
And, 'help,' he cryit, 'for him that deit on tre;
The ʒong captane has fallyn with me at stryff.'
In at the dur he went with this gud wiff.
A roussat goun of hir awn scho him gaif
Apon his weyd, at coueryt all the layff;   240

A soudly courche our hed and nek leit fall;
A wowyn quhyt hatt scho brassit on with-all;
For thai suld nocht lang tary at that in;
Gaiff him a rok, syn set him doun to spyn.
The sothroun socht quhar wallace was in drede;   245
Thai wyst nocht weylle at quhat ʒett he in ʒeide.
In that same hous thai socht him beselye;
Bot he sat still, and span full conandly,
As of his tym, for he nocht leryt lang.
Thai left him swa, and furth thar gait can gang,   250
With hewy cheyr and sorowfull in thocht:
Mar witt of him as than get couth thai nocht.
The inglis men, all thus in barrat boune,
Bade byrne all scottis that war in-to that toun.
ʒhit this gud wiff held wallace till the nycht,   255
Maid him gud cher, syne put hym out with slycht.
Throw a dyrk garth scho gydyt him furth fast;
In cowart went, and vp the wattyr past;
Forbure the gate for wachis that war thar.
His modyr bade in-till a gret dispar.   260
Quhen scho him saw, scho thankit hewynnis queyn,
And said; 'der sone, this lang quhar has thow beyne?'
He tald his modyr of his sodane cass.
Than wepyt scho, and said full oft, 'allas!
Or that thow cessis, thow will be slayne with-all.'   265
'Modyr,' he said, 'god reuller is of all.
Vnsouerable ar thir pepille of ingland;
Part of thar Ire me think we suld gaynstand.'
His eme wist weyle that he the squier slew;
For dreid thar-of in gret languor he grew.   270
This passit our, quhill diuerss dayis war gane:
That gud man dred or wallace suld be tane:
For suthroun ar full sutaille, euirilk man.

A gret dyttay for scottis thai ordand than
Be the lawdayis in dunde set ane ayr : 275
Than wallace wald na langar soiorne thar.

His modyr graithit hir in pilgrame weid ;
Hym[-selff] disgysyt syne glaidlye with hir ȝeid ;
A schort swerd wndyr his weid priuale.
In all that land full mony fays had he. 280
Baith on thar fute, with thaim may tuk thai nocht.
Quha sperd, scho said, ' to sanct margret thai socht ; '
Quha serwit hir, full gret frendschipe thai fand
With sothroun folk : for scho was of Ingland.
Besyd landoris the ferrye our thai past, 285
Syn throw the ochell sped thaim wondyr fast.
In Dunfermlyn thai lugyt all that nycht.
Apon the morn, quhen that the day was brycht,
With gentill wemen hapnyt thaim to pass,
Off Ingland born, in lithquhow wounnand was. 290
The captans wiff, in pilgramage had beyne,
Fra scho thaim mett, and had ȝong wallace sene,
Gud cher thaim maid ; for he was wondyr fayr,
Nocht large of tong, weille taucht and debonayr.
Furth tawkand thus of materis that was wrocht, 295
Quhill south our forth with hyr son scho thaim brocht.
In-to lithkow thai wald nocht tary lang ;
Thar leyff thai tuk, to dunypace couth gang.
Thar duelt his Eyme, a man of gret richess.
This mychty persone, hecht to name wallas, 300
Maid thaim gud cher, and was a full kynd man,
Welcummyt thaim fair, and to thaim tald he than,
Dide him to witt, the land was all on ster ;
Trettyt thaim weyle, and said ; ' my sone so der,
Thi modyr and thow rycht heir with me sall bide, 305

Quhill better be, for chance at may betyde.'
Wallace ansuerd, said; ' westermar we will:
Our kyne ar slayne, and that me likis ill ;.
And othir worthi mony in that art:
Will god I leiffe, we sall ws wreke on part.'   310
The persone sicht, and said ; ' my sone so fre,
I cannot witt how that radress may be.'
Quhat suld I spek of frustir as this tid?
For gyft of gud with him he wald nocht bide.
His modyr and he till Elrisle thai went.   315
Vpon the morn scho for hir brothyr sent,
In corsby duelt, and schirreff was of ayr.
Hyr fadyr was dede, a lang tyme leyffyt had thar ;
Hyr husband als at lowdoun-hill was slayn.
Hyr eldest sone, that mekill was of mayn,   320
Schir malcom wallas was his nayme, but less,
His houch-senous[1] thai cuttyt in that press ;
On kneis he faucht, felle Inglismen he slew ;
Till hym thar socht may fechtaris than anew ;
On athyr side with speris bar him doun ;   325
Thar stekit thai that gud knycht of renoun.
On-to my taile I left.   At Elrisle
Schir Ranald come son till his sistyr fre,
Welcummyt thaim hayme, and sperd of hir entent.
Scho prayde he wald to the lord persye went,   330
So yrk of wer scho couth no forthir fle,
To purchess pes, in rest at scho mycht be.
Schyr Ranald had the perseys protectioune,
As for all part to tak the remissioune.
He gert wrytt ane till his systir that tyde.   335
In that respyt wallas wald nocht abyde:

[1] Jamieson prints ' houch senons.'

Hys modyr kyst, scho wepyt with hart sar,
His leyff he tuk, syne with his Eyme couth far.
Ʒonge he was, and to sothroun rycht sauage ;
Gret rowme thai had, dispitfull and wtrage.   340
Schir Ranald weylle durst nocht hald wallas thar ;
For gret perell he wyst apperand war ;
For thai had haile the strenthis of Scotland ;
Quhat thai wald do, durst few agayne thaim stand.
Schyrreff he was, and wsyt thaim amang ;   345
Full sar he dred or wallas suld tak wrang :
For he and thai couth neuir weyle accord.
He gat a blaw, thocht he war lad or lord,
That proferyt him ony lychtlynes ;
Bot thai raparyt our mekill to that place.   350
Als Ingliss clerkis in prophecyss thai fand,
How a wallace suld putt thaim of Scotland.
Schir ranald knew weill a mar quiet sted,
Quhar wilʒham mycht be bettir fra thair fede,
With his wncle wallas of Ricardtoun,   355
Schir Richart hecht that gud knycht off renoun.
Thai landis hayle than was his heretage,
Bot blynd he was, (so hapnyt throw curage,
Be ingliss-men that dois ws mekill der ;
In his rysyng he worthi was in wer ;)   360
Throuch-hurt of waynys, and mystyrit of blud.
Ʒeit he was wiss, and of his conseill gud.
In feuirʒer wallas was to him send ;
In Aperill fra him he bownd to wend.
Bot gud serwice he dide him with plesance,   365
As in that place was worthi to awance.

How Wallace past to the water of Irvine to take Fish.

So on a tym he desyrit to play,
In Aperill the thre and twenty day,
Till erewyn wattir, fysche to tak, he went;
Sic fantasye fell in[to] his entent.   370
To leide his net, a child furth with him ʒeid;
But he, or nowne, was in a felloune dreid.
His suerd he left, so did he neuir agayne;
It dide him gud, supposs he sufferyt payne.
Off that labour as than he was nocht sle: 375
Happy he was, tuk fysche haboundanle.
Or of the day ten houris our couth pass,
Ridand thar come, ner by quhar wallace wass,
The lorde persye, was captane than off ayr;
Fra-thine he turnde and couth to glaskow fair.   380
Part of the court had wallace labour seyne,
Till him raid fyve, cled in-to ganand greyne,
Ane said, sone; 'scot, martyns fysche we wald hawe.'
Wallace meklye agayne ansuer him gawe;
'It war resone, me think, ʒhe suld haif part: 385
Waith suld be delt, in all place, with fre hart.'
He bade his child, 'gyff thaim of our waithyng.'
The sothroun said; 'as now of thi delyng
We will nocht tak, thow wald giff ws our-small.'
He lychtyt doun, and fra the child tuk all.   390
Wallas said than; 'gentill men gif ʒe be,
Leiff ws sum part, we pray for cheryte.
Ane agyt knycht serwis our lady to-day;
Gud frend, leiff part and tak nocht all away.'
'Thow sall haiff leiff to fysche, and tak the ma;   395
All this forsuth sall in our flyttyng ga.
We serff a lord; thir fysche sall till him gang.'

Wallace ansuerd, said ; ' thow art in the wrang.'
' Quham thow is thow, scot ? in faith thow serwis a blaw.'
Till him he ran, and out a suerd can draw.　　　　400
Willȝham was wa he had na wappynis thar,
Bot the poutstaff, the quhilk in hand he bar.
Wallas with it fast on the cheik him tuk
Wyth so gud will, quhill of his feit he schuk.
The suerd flaw fra him a fur-breid on the land.　　405
Wallas was glaid, and hynt it sone in hand ;
And with the swerd awkwart he him gawe
Wndyr the hat, his crage in sondre drawe.
Be that the layff lychtyt about wallas ;
He had no helpe, only bot goddis grace.　　　　410
On athir side full fast on him thai dange ;
Gret perell was giff thai had lestyt lang.
Apone the hede in gret Ire he strak ane ;
The scherand suerd glaid to the colar-bane.
Ane othir on the arme he hitt so hardely,　　　　415
Quhill hand and suerd bathe on the feld can ly.
The tothir twa fled to thar hors agayne ;
He stekit him was last apon the playne.
Thre slew he thar, twa fled with all thair mycht
Eftir thar lord ; bot he was out off sicht,　　　　420
Takand the mure, or he and thai couth twyne :
Till him thai raid onon, or thai wald blyne,
And cryit ; ' lord, abide ; ȝour men ar martyrit doun
Rycht cruelly, her in this fals regioun.
Fyve of our court her at the wattir baid,　　　　425
Fysche for to bryng, thocht it na profyt maid.
We ar chapyt, bot in feyld slayne ar thre.'
The lord speryt ; ' how mony mycht thai be ?'
' We saw bot ane that has discumfyst ws all.'
Than lewch he lowde, and said, ' foule mot ȝow fall, 430

F

Sen ane ȝow all has putt to confusioun.
Quha menys it maist, the dewyll of hell him droun ;
This day for me, in faith, he beis nocht socht.'
Quhen wallas thus this worthi werk had wrocht,
Thar horss he tuk, and ger that lewyt was thar ;   435
Gaif our that crafft, he ȝeid to fysche no mar ;
Went till his Eyme, and tauld him of this dede[1].
And he for wo weyle ner worthit to weide ;
And said, 'sone, thir tithingis syttis me sor ;
And be it knawin, thow may tak scaith tharfor.'   440
'Wncle,' he said, ' I will no langar bide ;
Thir southland horss latt se gif I can ride.'
Than bot a child, him serwice for to mak,
Hys emys sonnys he wald nocht with him tak.
This gud knycht said ; ' deyr Cusyng, pray I the,   445
Quhen thow wanttis gud, cum fech ynewch fra me.'
Syluir and gold he gert on-to him geyff.
Wallace inclynys, and gudely tuk his leyff.

Explicit Liber Primus.

[1] MS. ' drede'; but see note.

VII.

CHEVY CHASE.

IT is not easy to assign the right date to this composition, but it almost certainly belonged originally to the fifteenth century, and is therefore inserted here. The oldest form in which it exists is here given, carefully reproduced from MS. Ashmole 48, in the Bodleian Library at Oxford. From the name at the end, it appears that this particular copy was dictated, or possibly written out, by Richard Sheale, a ballad-singer of the reigns of Mary and Elizabeth. He certainly was not the author, but had probably recited it very frequently, and has preserved it to us in writing. The more modern version of the poem is in 'Percy's Reliques of Ancient Poetry,' since reprinted in 'Bishop Percy's Folio MS.,' edited by Hales and Furnivall, 1868. The reader is referred to Mr. Hales' Introduction to Chevy Chase, in the second volume of that work, for further information. *Chevy Chase* means the Chase or Hunting-ground upon the Cheviot Hills, invaded by Percy, Earl of Northumberland, the consequence of the invasion being a combat between him and Earl Douglas. ' The general spirit of the ballad,' says Mr. Hales, ' is historical ; but the details are not authentic.'

[*Fytte the first.*]

the p*er*se owt off northombarlonde an avowe[1] to god mayd he,

that he wold hunte In the mowntayns off chyviat wit*h*In days iij,

---

[1] MS. ' and A vowe'; see note.

In the mag*er* of doughté dogles & all that eu*er* with him
    be ;

the fattiste hart*es* In all cheviat, he sayd he wold kyll & cary
    them Away.

' be my feth,' sayd *th*e dougheti doglas agayn, ' I wyll let
    *tha*t hontyng yf *tha*t I may.'   5

the[n] *th*e p*er*se owt off banborowe cam, w*it*h him A myghtee
    meany,

w*it*h xv.C archar*es*[1] bold off blood & bone, *th*e wear chosen
    owt of shyars iij.

this begane on a monday at morn, In cheviat the hillys
    so he ;

the chylde may Rue that ys vn-born, it wos the mor pitte.

the dryvars thorowe[2] the wood*es* went for to Reas the
    dear ;   10

bomen byckarte vppone the bent w*it*h ther browd Aros
    cleare ;

then the wyld thorowe the wood*es* went on eu*er*y syde shear ;

greahond*es* thorowe the grevis glent for to kyll thear dear.

*th*er begane In chyviat *th*e hyls Abone yerly on A monnyn-day ;

be *tha*t it drewe to the oware off none, A hondrith fat hart*es*
    ded *th*er lay.   15

the blewe A mort[3] vppone *th*e bent, *th*e semblyde on sydis
    shear,

to *th*e quyrry then the p*er*se went to se the bryttlynge off the
    deare ;

he sayd, ' it was *th*e duglas promys this day to met me hear,

but I wyste he wolde faylle verament ;' A great oth *th*e p*er*se
    swear.

at the laste A squyar off northo*mb*er*l*onde lokyde at his hand
    full ny,   20

---

[1] MS. ' archard*es*.'   [2] MS. ' throrowe.'   [3] MS. ' mot.'

he was war of[1] the doughetie doglas co*m*mynge, with him a
     myghtte meany,

both with spear, bylle[2], and brande, yt was a myghtti sight
     to se ;

hardyar men both off hart nor hande wear not In cristiante.

the wear xx.C spear-men good, withoute any feale ;

the wear borne A-long be the watt*er* A twyde yth bownd*es* of
     tividale. 25

‘ leave of the brytlyng of the dear,’ he sayd, ‘ & to your boys
     lock ye tayk good hed*e* ;

for[3] sithe ye wear on your mothars borne, had ye neu*er* so
     mickle ned*e*.’

the dougheti dogglas on A stede he Rode all*e* his men be-
     forne ;

his armor glytteryde as dyd A glede, A boldar barne was
     neu*er* born.

‘ tell me whos men ye ar ?’ he says, ‘ or whos men that
     ye be ? 30

who gave you*e* leave to hunte In this chyviat chays In *th*e
     spyt of myn & of me ?’

the first mane that eu*er* him An answear mayd yt was *th*e
     good lord p*er*se,

‘ we wyll not tell the whoys men we ar,’ he says, ‘ nor whos
     men *tha*t we be,

but we wyll hounte hear In this chays in the spyt of thyne &
     of the ;

*th*e fattiste hart*es* In all chyviat we haue kyld, & cast to carry
     them A-way.’ 35

‘ be my troth,’ sayd *th*e doughete dogglas agay[n], ‘ *th*erfor
     the ton of vs shall de this day.’

then sayd the doughté doglas vnto the lord p*er*se,

<hr>

MS. ‘ ath.’   [2] MS. ‘ brylly.’   [3] MS. ‘ for neu*er*.’

' to kyll all*e* thes giltles men, Alas! it wear great pitte ;

but, p*er*se,.thowe art A lord of lande, I am a yerle callyd
     w*ith*In my contre,

let all our men vppone a p*ar*ti stande, & do the battell off the
     & of me.'   40

' nowe crist*es* cors on his crowne !' sayd the lorde p*er*se,
     ' who-so-eu*er* *the*r-to says nay,

be my troth, doughtté doglas,' he says, ' thow shalt neu*er* se
     that day,

nethar In ynglonde, skottlonde, **nar** france, nor for no man
     of a woman born,

but, & fortune be my chance, I dar met him on man for on.'

then bespayke A squyar off northombarlonde, R*ichard* wythar-
     ryngton was his nam,   45

' it shall neu*er* be told´In sothe ynglonde,' he says, ' to kyng
     Herry *the* iiij. for sham ;

I wat youe byn great lord*es* twaw, I am A poor squyar of
     lande,

I wyll*e* neu*er* se my captayne fyght on A fylde, & stande my
     selffe & loocke on ;

but whyll*e* I may my weppone welde, I wyll*e* not [fayl*e*] both
     hart and hande.'

that day, *tha*t day, *tha*t dredfull day! *th*e first fit here I
     fynde ;   50

& youe wyll here any mor athe hountynge athe chyviat, yet
     ys *the*r mor be-hynd*e*.

[*Fytte the Second.*]

the yngglyshe men hade ther bowys ye-bent, *the*r hart*es* wer
     good ye-noughe,

the first off arros that the shote off seven skore spear-men
     the sloughe ;

yet byddys the yerle doglas vppon *the* bent, a captayne good
    ye-noughe,

& that was sene verament, for he wrought ho*m* both woo &
    wouche. 55

the dogglas p*ar*tyd his ost In iii. lyk a cheffe cheften off
    pryde,

with suar spears off myghtte tre the cu*m* In on eu*er*y syde,

thrughe our yngglyshe archery gave many A wounde full*e*
    wyde,

many a doughet*é* the garde to dy, which ganyde them no
    pryde.

the ynglyshe men let thear boys be, & pulde owt brand*es* *that*
    wer brighte ; 60

it was A hevy syght to se bryght sword*es* on basnit*es* lyghte.

throrowe ryche male and myne-ye-ple many sterne *the* strocke
    done streght ;

many A freyke that was full*e* fre ther vndar foot dyd lyght.

at last the duglas & the P*er*sé met lyk to captayns of myght
    & of mayne ;

the swapte togethar tyll*e* the both swat, w*ith* sword*es* *that*
    wear of fyn myllan. 65

thes worthe freckys for to fyght, *ther*-to *the* wear full*e* fayne,

tyll*e* the bloode owte off thear basnet*es* sprente as eu*er* dyd
    heal or Ran.

' yelde the, p*er*se,' sayde the doglas, ' & I feth I shall*e* the
    brynge

wher thowe shalte haue A yerls wagis of Jamy our skottish
    kynge.

thoue shalte haue thy Ransom fre, I hight the hear this
    thinge ; 70

for the manfullyste man yet art thowe that eu*er* I conqueryd
    In filde fighttyng*e*.'

' nay,' sayd the lorde p*er*se, ' I tolde it the beforne,

that I wolde neue*r* yeldyde be to no man of A woman born.'

w*ith* that ther cam An arrowe[1] hastely forthe off A myghtte wane,

hit hathe strekene the yerle duglas In at the brest-bane;   75

thoroue[2] lyvar & long*es* bathe the sharpe arrowe ys gane,

*tha*t neue*r* aft*er* In all his lyffe-days he spayke mo word*es* but ane,

*tha*t was, 'fyghte ye, my myrry men, whyllys ye may, for my lyff-days ben gan.'

the p*er*se leanyde on his brande, & sawe *the* duglas de;

he tooke the dede mane by the hande, & sayd, 'wo ys me for the !   80

to haue savyde thy lyffe, I wolde haue p*ar*tyde w*ith* my land*es* for years iij. ;

for a bett*er* man of hart nare of hande was nat In all *the* north contre.'

off all that se a skottishe knyght, was callyd s*er* hewe *the* monggo*m*byrry,

he sawe the duglas to the deth was dyght, he spendyd A spear a trusti tre,

he Rod vppone a corsiare throughe A hondrith archery,   85

he neue*r* stynttyde nar neue*r* blane tyll*e* he cam to *th*e good lord p*er*se.

he set vppone the lorde p*er*se A dynte that was full soare,

with a suar spear of a myghtte tre clean thorow the body he *th*e p*er*se ber,

athe tothar syde that a man myght se a large cloth-yard & mare.

towe bettar captayns wear not in cristiante then *that* day slan wear *ther*.   90

An archar[3] off northomb*er*londe say slean was *the* lord perse,

---

[1] MS. 'A narrowe.'   [2] MS. 'throrowe.'   [3] MS. 'A narchar.'

he bar A bende bowe In his hand was made off trusti tre,

an arow *that* A cloth-yarde was lang to*the* harde stele
      halyde[1] he,

a dynt *that* was both sad & soar he sat on *ser* hewe *the*
      monggombyrry,

the dynt yt was both sad & sar *that* he of monggomberry
      sete,   .   95

the swane-fethars *that* his arrowe bar w*ith* his hart-blood *the*
      wear wete.

ther was neu*er* a freake wone foot wolde fle, but still In stour
      dyd stand,

heawyng on yche othar whyll*e* the myghte dre, w*ith* many A
      balfull brande.

this battell begane In chyviat An owar[2] before the none,

& when even-songe bell was Rang the battell was nat half
      done.   100

the tocke [the fight] on ethar hande be the lyght off the
      mone ;

many hade no strenght for to stande In chyviat *the* hillys
      Abon.

of xvC archars of ynglonde went A-way but vij[x] & thre ;

of xxC spear-men off skotlonde but even five & fifti,

but all wear slayne cheviat w*ith*In, *the* hade no streng[th]e
      to stand on hy;   105

the chylde may Rue that ys vn-borne, it was *the* mor pitte.

thear was slayne, withe the lord p*er*se, ser Joh*a*n of ag*er*stone ;

ser Rogar the hinde hartly, *ser* Wyllyam the bolde hearone ;

ser Jorg the worthe lou*m*le, A knyghte of great Renowen ;

ser Raff the Ryche Rugbe, with dyn*tes* wear beaten dowene ;

for Wetharryngton my harte was wo, *that* eu*er* he slayne
      shulde be ;   111

[1] MS. 'haylde.'   [2] MS. 'A nowar.'

for when both his leggis wear hewyne In to, yet he knyled
     & fought on his kny.

ther was slayne, w*ith* *th*e dougheti duglas, s*er* hewe the
     mongg*o*mbyrry;

s*er* dauy lwdale, *tha*t worthe was, his sistars son was he;

s*er* charls a murre In that place, *tha*t neu*er* A foot wolde fle;

s*er* hewe maxwell*e*, A lorde he was, w*ith* *th*e doglas dyd he
     dey.   116

so on the morrowe the mayde them byears off birch & hasell
     so g[r]ay;

many wedous w*ith* wepyng tears cam to fache *ther* makys
     A-way;

tivydale may carpe off care, northo*m*barlond may mayk great
     mon,

for towe such captayns as slayne wear thear on the march
     p*ar*ti shall neu*er* be non.   120

word ys co*m*men to edden-burrowe to Jamy *th*e skottishe
     kynge,

that dougheti duglas, lyff-tenant of the m*ar*ches, he lay slean
     chyviat w*ith*In;

his handdes dyd he weal & wryng, he sayd, 'alas! & woe
     ys me!

such A-nothar captayn skotland w*ith*In,' he sayd, 'ye-feth
     shuld neu*er* be.'

wo*r*de ys co*m*myn to lovly londone, till *th*e iiij. harry our
     kynge,   125

*tha*t lord p*er*se, cheyff tenante of the m*ar*ches, he lay slayne
     chyviat w*ith*In;

'god haue m*er*ci on his soll*e*,' sayde kyng harry, 'good lord,
     yf thy will it be,

I haue a C. captayns In ynglonde,' he sayd, 'as good as eu*er*
     was he;

but, p*er*se, & I brook my lyffe, thy deth well quyte shall be.'

as our noble kynge mayde his A-vowe, lyke a noble prince **of**
    Renowen,   130

for the deth of the lord per*se* he dyde the battell of ho*m*byll-
    down,

wher syx & thritte skottishe knygh*tes* on a day wear beaten
    down,

glendale glytteryde on ther armor bryght ov*er* castill*e*, towar,
    & town.

this was the hontynge off the cheviat, that tear begane this
    spurn;

old men that knowen the grownde well ye-noughe, call it *the*
    battell of otter̄burn.   135

at otter̄burn begane this spurne, vppone A monnynday;

ther was the doughté doglas slean, *the* p*er*se neu*er* went
    A-way;

ther was neu*er* A tym on the marche p*ar*tes sen *th*e doglas
    & *th*e per̄se met,

but yt ys m*er*vele & the Rede blude Ro*n*ne not as the Reane
    doys In *th*e stret.

Ihesue crist our balys[1] bete, & to the blys vs brynge!   140

thus was the hountynge of the chivyat, god send vs all*e* good
    endyng!

Expliceth, quoth Rychard Sheale.

[1] MS. 'ballys.'

VIII.

SIR THOMAS MALORY.

A.D. 1469.

A FAMOUS book is 'Le Morte Darthur,' compiled from numerous French romances by Sir Thomas Malory, completed by him, as he tells us, in the ninth year of Edward IV (1469–1470), and first printed by Caxton at Westminster in 1485. The colophon of Caxton's book is as follows :—

'¶ Thus endeth thys noble and Ioyous book entytled le morte Darthur / Notwithstondyng it treateth of the byrth / lyf / and actes of the sayd kynge Arthur / of his noble knyghtes of the rounde table / theyr meruayllous enquestes and aduentures / thachyeuyng of the sangreal / & in thende the dolourous deth & departyng out of thys world of them al / Whiche book was reduced in to englysshe by syr Thomas Malory knyght as afore is sayd / and by me deuyded in to xxi bookes chapytred and enprynted / and fynysshed in thabbey westmestre the last day of Iuyl the yere of our Lord M/CCCC/lxxx/V/ ¶ Caxton me fieri fecit.'

Our extract relates the actual death of King Arthur, from which the whole work took its name. It is printed from Southey's reprint (1817) of Caxton's original edition (1485). An old Alliterative Poem called 'La Morte Arthure' was edited by Mr. Perry for the Early English Text Society, in 1865, from the Thornton MS. at Lincoln, and an old rimed version with the same title was edited from the Harleian MS. 2252, in the British Museum, by Mr. Furnivall in 1864. The latter most agrees with the account in Malory. The 'Globe' edition of Malory's book, edited by Sir E. Strachey, is modernized from Caxton.

Liber XXI. *Capitulum III.*

And thenne the kyng lete serche all the townes for his knyghtes that were slayne, and enteryd them, & salued them with softe salues that so sore were wounded. Thenne moche peple drewe vnto kynge Arthur. And thenne they sayd that sir Mordred warred vpon kyng Arthur with wronge, and thenne kynge Arthur drewe hym with his hoost doune by the see-syde westward toward Salysbury, and ther was a day assygned betwixe kyng Arthur and sire mordred that they shold mete vpòn a doune besyde Salysbury, and not ferre from the see-syde, and this day was assygned on a monday after Trynyte sonday, wherof kyng Arthur was passyng glad that he myghte be auengyd vpon sire Mordred. Thenne syr Mordred areysed moche peple aboute london, for they of Kente, Southsex and Surrey, Estsex and of Southfolke and of Northfolk helde the most party with sir Mordred, and many a ful noble knyghte drewe vnto syr Mordred and to the kynge, but they loued sir Launcelot drewe vnto syr Mordred. Soo vpon Trynyte sonday at nyghte kynge Arthur dremed a wonderful dreme, & that was this, that hym semed, he satte vpon a chaflet in a chayer, and the chayer was fast to a whele and therupon satte kynge Arthur in the rychest clothe of gold that myghte be made, and the kyng thoughte ther was vnder hym fer from hym an hydous depe blak water, and there-in were alle maner of serpentes and wormes and wylde bestes foule and horryble, and sodenly the kynge thoughte the whele torned vp-soo-doune, and he felle amonge the serpentys, & euery beest took hym by a lymme, and thenne the kynge cryed as he lay in his bedde and slepte, 'helpe !' And thenne knyghtes, squyers, and yomen awaked the kynge, and thenne he was soo amased that he wyst not where he was, & thenne he felle on slomberynge ageyn, not slepynge nor thorouly wakynge. So the kynge semed veryly, that there came syr Gawayne vnto hym with a nombre of fayre ladyes with hym.

35   And whan kynge Arthur sawe hym, thenne he sayd, 'welcome, my systers sone; I wende thou haddest ben dede, and now I see the on lyue, moche am I beholdynge vnto almyghty Jhesu. O fayre neuewe and my systers sone, what ben these ladyes that hydder be come with yow?' 'Sir,'
40 said sir Gawayne, 'alle these ben ladyes for whome I haue foughten whanne I was man lyuynge, and alle these are tho, that I dyd batail for in ryghteuous quarel, and god hath gyuen hem that grace at their grete prayer, by cause I dyd bataille for hem, that they shold brynge me hydder vnto
45 yow; thus moche hath god gyuen me leue for to warne yow of youre dethe, for and ye fyghte as to morne with syre Mordred, as ye bothe haue assygned, doubte ye not, ye must be slayne, and the moost party of your peple on bothe partyes; and for the grete grace and goodenes that almyghty
50 Jhesu hath vnto yow, and for pyte of yow and many moo other good men there shalle be slayne, God hath sente me to yow of his specyal grace to gyue yow warnynge, that in no wyse ye do bataille as to morne, but that ye take a treatyce for a moneth day and profer yow largely, so as to morne
55 to be putte in a delaye. For within a monethe shalle come syr launcelot with alle his noble knyghtes and rescowe yow worshipfully, and slee sir mordred and alle that euer wylle holde with hym.' Thenne syr Gawayne and al the ladyes vaynuysshed. And anone the kyng called vpon hys knyghtes,
60 squyres, and yemen, and charged them wyghtly to fetche his noble lordes and wyse bysshoppes vnto hym. And whan they were come, the kyng tolde hem his auysyon, what sir Gawayn had tolde hym, and warned hym that yf he faught

on the morne he shold be slayn. Than the kyng comaunded
syr Lucan de butlere And his broder syr Bedwere with two 65
bysshoppes wyth hem, and charged theym, in ony wyse &
they myght, take a traytyse for a monthe day wyth Syr
mordred. 'And spare not, proffre hym londes & goodes as
moche as ye thynke best.' So than they departed & came
to syr Mordred, where he had a grymme hoost of an hondred 70
thousand men. And there they entreted syr Mordred longe
tyme, and at the laste Syr mordred was agreyd for to haue
Cornwayl and kente by Arthures dayes; After, alle Englond,
after the dayes of kyng Arthur.

Capitulum IIII.

THAN were they condesended that Kyng Arthur and syr
mordred shold mete betwyxte bothe theyr hoostes and euer-
yche of them shold brynge fourtene persones. And they came
wyth thys word vnto Arthure. Than sayd he, 'I am glad
that thys is done.' And so he wente in to the felde. And 5
whan Arthure shold departe, he warned al hys hoost that,
and they see ony swerde drawen, 'look ye come on fyersly,
and slee that traytour syr Mordred; for I in noo wyse truste
hym.' In lyke wyse syr mordred warned his hoost that,
'and ye see ony swerde drawen, look that ye come on 10
fyersly & soo slee alle that euer before you stondeth; for in
no wyse I wyl not truste for thys treatyse. For I knowe wel
my fader wyl be auenged on me.' And soo they mette as
theyr poyntemente was & so they were agreyd & accorded
thorouly. And wyn was fette and they dranke. Ryght soo 15
came an adder oute of a lytel hethe busshe & hyt stonge
a knyght on the foot, & whan the knyght felte hym stongen
he looked doun and sawe the adder, & than he drewe his
swerde to slee the adder, & thought of none other harme.

20 And whan the hoost on bothe partyes saw that swerde
drawen, than they blewe beamous, trumpettes, and hornes,
and shouted grymly. And so bothe hoostes dressyd hem
to-gyders. And kyng Arthur took his hors and sayd, 'allas!
thys vnhappy day,' & so rode to hys partye. And syr mor-
25 dred in like wyse. And neuer was there seen a more dool-
fuller bataylle in no crysten londe. For there was but
russhyng & rydyng, fewnyng and strykyng, & many a grymme
worde was ther spoken eyder to other & many a dedely
stroke. But euer kyng Arthur rode thorugh-oute the ba-
30 taylle of syr Mordred many tymes, & dyd ful nobly as
a noble Kyng shold, & at al tymes he faynted neuer, & syr
Mordred that day put hym in deuoyr and in grete perylle.
And thus they faughte alle the longe day, & neuer stynted
tyl the noble knyghtes were layed to the colde erthe, & euer
35 they faught stylle tyl it was nere nyghte, & by that tyme was
there an hondred thousand layed deed vpon the down.
Thenne was Arthure wode-wrothe oute of mesure whan he
sawe his peple so slayn from hym. Thenne the kyng loked
aboute hym, & thenne was he ware, of al hys hoost & of al
40 his good knyghtes were lefte no moo on lyue but two
knyghtes, that one was Syr Lucan de butlere, & his broder
Syr Bedwere. And they were ful sore wounded. 'Jhesu,
mercy,' sayd the kyng, 'where are al my noble knyghtes
becomen? Allas, that euer I shold see thys dolefull day,
45 for now,' sayd Arthur, 'I am come to myn ende. But wolde
to god that I wyste where were that traytour Syr mordred,
that hath caused alle thys myschyef.' Thenne was kyng
arthure ware where syr Mordred lenyd vpon his swerde
emonge a grete hepe of deed men. 'Now gyue me my spere,'
50 sayd Arthur vnto Syr Lucan. 'For yonder I haue espyed
the traytour that alle thys woo hath wrought.' 'Syr, lete
hym be,' sayd Syr Lucan, 'for he is vnhappy. And yf ye

passe thys vnhappy day ye shalle be ryght wel reuengyd
vpon hym. Good lord, remembre ye of your nyghtes dreme,
& what the spyryte of Syr Gauwayn tolde you this nyght; 55
yet god of his grete goodnes hath preserued you hyderto.
Therfore, for goddes sake, my lord, leue of by thys; for,
blessyd be [1] god, ye haue wonne the felde. For here we ben
thre on lyue, and wyth syr Mordred is none on lyue. And
yf ye leue of now, thys wycked day of desteynye is paste.' 60
'Tyde me deth, betyde me lyf,' sayth the kyng, 'now I see
hym yonder allone, he shal neuer escape myn handes. For at
a better auaylle shall I neuer haue hym.' 'God spede you wel,'
sayd syr bedwere. Thenne the kyng gate hys spere in bothe his
handes & ranne toward syr Mordred, cryeng, 'traytour, now 65
is thy deth-day come.' And whan syr Mordred herde syr
Arthur, he ranne vntyl hym with his swerde drawen in his
hande. And there kyng Arthur smote syr mordred vnder
the shelde wyth a foyne of his spere thorughoute the body
more than a fadom. And whan syr Mordred felte that he 70
had hys dethes wounde, He thryst hym self wyth the myght
that he had vp to the bur of kyng Arthurs spere. And right
so he smote his fader Arthur wyth his swerde holden in
bothe his handes on the syde of the heed, that the swerde
persyd the helmet and the brayne-panne, and ther-wyth-all 75
syr Mordred fyl starke deed to the erthe. And the nobyl
Arthur fyl in a swoune to the erthe, and there he swouned
ofte tymes. And syr Lucan de butlere and syr Bedwere
oftymes houe [2] hym vp. And soo waykely they ledde hym
betwyxte them bothe to a lytel chapel, not ferre from the 80
see-syde. And whan the kyng was there, he thought hym
wel eased. Thenne herde they people crye in the felde.
'Now goo thou, syr Lucan,' sayd the kyng, 'and do me to

---

[1] Printed 'by.'   [2] Printed 'heue.'

G

wyte what bytokenes that noyse in the felde.'   So syr Lucan
85 departed, for he was greuously wounded in many places.
And so as he yede, he sawe and herkened by the mone-
lyght how that pyllars and robbers were comen in to the
felde to pylle and to robbe many a ful noble knyghte of
brochys and bedys, of many a good rynge, & of many a
90 ryche jewel, and who that were not deed al oute, there they
slewe theym for theyr harneys and theyr rychesse.   Whan
syr Lucan vnderstode thys werke, he came to the kyng
assone as he myght, and tolde hym al what he had herde
& seen.   'Therfore, be my rede,' sayd syr Lucan, 'it is
95 beste that we brynge you to somme towne.'   'I wolde it
were soo,' sayd the kyng.

Capitulum V.

'But I may not stonde, myn hede werches soo.   A! Syr
Launcelot,' sayd kyng Arthur, 'thys day haue I sore myst
the.   Alas that euer I was ayenst the, for now haue I my
dethe.   Wherof syr Gauwayn me warned in my dreme.'
5 Than syr lucan took vp the kyng the one parte And Syr
Bedwere the other parte, & in the lyftyng the kyng sowned;
and syr Lucan fyl in a sowne wyth the lyfte, that the parte of
his guttes fyl oute of his bodye.   And therwyth the noble
knyghtes herte braste.   And whan the kyng awoke, he be-
10 helde syr Lucan how he laye foomyng at the mowth, & parte
of his guttes laye at his feet.   'Alas,' sayd the kyng, 'thys is
to me a ful heuy syght, to see thys noble duke soo deye for
my sake; for he wold haue holpen me, that had more nede
of helpe than I.   Alas, he wold not complayne hym; hys
15 herte was so sette to helpe me.   Now Jhesu haue mercy
vpon hys soule!' than syr bedwere wepte for the deth of his
brother.   'leue thys mornyng & wepyng,' sayd the kyng,

'for al this wyl not auaylle me; for wyte thow wel, and I
myght lyue my self, the deth of syr Lucan wolde greue me
euer more; but my tyme hyeth fast,' sayd the kyng. Ther- 20
fore sayd Arthur vnto syr Bedwere, 'take thou Excalybur
my good swerde, and goo with it to yonder water syde; and
whan thou comest there, I charge the throwe my swerde in
that water, & come ageyn and telle me what thou there
seest.' 'My lord,' said Bedwere, 'your commaundement 25
shal be doon; & lyghtly brynge you worde ageyn.' So syr
Bedwere departed, & by the waye he behelde that noble
swerde, that the pomel & the hafte was al of precyous stones,
& thenne he sayd to hym self, 'yf I throwe this ryche swerde
in the water, therof shal neuer come good, but harme & 30
losse.' And thenne syr bedwere hydde excalybur vnder a
tree. And so as sone as he myght, he came ageyn vnto the
kyng, and sayd he had ben at the water and had throwen
the swerde in to the water. 'What sawe thou there?' sayd
the kyng; 'syr,' he sayd, 'I sawe no thynge but wawes and 35
wyndes.' 'That is vntrewly sayd of the,' sayd the kynge.
'Therfore goo thou lyghtelye ageyn and do my commaunde-
mente, as thou arte to me leef & dere; spare not, but throwe
it in.' Than syr bedwere retorned ageyn, & took the swerde
in hys hande, and than hym thought synne and shame to 40
throwe awaye that nobyl swerde, and so efte he hydde the
swerde, and retorned ageyn and tolde to the kyng that he
had ben at the water and done his commaundement. 'What
sawe thou there?' sayd the kyng. 'Syr,' he sayd, 'I sawe
no thynge but the waters wappe and wawes wanne.' 'A! 45
traytour vntrewe,' sayd kyng Arthur, 'now hast thou betrayed
me twyse. Who wold haue wente that thou that hast been
to me so leef and dere, and thou arte named a noble knyghte,
and wold betraye me for the richesse of the swerde? But
now goo ageyn lyghtly, for thy longe taryeng putteth me in 50

grete jeopardye of my lyf. For I haue taken colde, and but
yf thou do now as I byd the, yf euer I may see the I shal
slee the [wyth] myn owne handes, for thou woldest for my
ryche swerde see me dede.' Thenne Syr Bedwere departed,
55 and wente to the swerde and lyghtly took hit up, and wente
to the water syde and there he bounde the gyrdyl aboute the
hyltes, and thenne he threwe the swerde as farre in to the
water as he myght, & there cam an arme and an hande
aboue the water and mette it, & caught it and so shoke it
60 thryse and braundysshed, and than vanysshed awaye the
hande wyth the swerde in the water. So syr Bedwere came
ageyn to the kyng and tolde hym what he sawe. 'Alas!'
sayd the kyng,' helpe me hens, for I drede me I haue taryed
ouer longe.' Than syr Bedwere toke the kyng vpon his
65 backe and so wente wyth hym to that water syde, & whan
they were at the water syde, euyn fast by the banke houed
a lytyl barge wyth many fayr ladyes in hit, & emonge hem
al was a quene, and al they had blacke hoodes, and al they
wepte and shryked whan they sawe Kyng Arthur.

70   'Now put me in to the barge,' sayd the kyng, and so he
dyd softelye. And there receyued hym thre quenes wyth
grete mornyng, and soo they sette hem doun, and in one of
their lappes kyng Arthur layed hys heed, and than that
quene sayd, 'a dere broder! why haue ye taryed so longe
75 from me. Alas, this wounde on your heed hath caught ouer-
moche colde.' And soo than they rowed from the londe,
and syr bedwere behelde all tho ladyes goo from hym. Than
syr bedwere cryed, 'a! my lord Arthur, what shal become of
me now ye goo from me. And leue me here allone emonge
80 myn enemyes?' 'Comfort thy self,' sayd the kyng, 'and
doo as wel as thou mayst; for in me is no truste for to
truste in. For I wyl in to the vale of auylyon, to hele me
of my greuous wounde. And yf thou here neuer more of

me, praye for my soule;' but euer the quenes and ladyes
wepte and shryched that hit was pyte to here.　And assone 85
as syr Bedwere had loste the syght of the baarge, he wepte
and waylled and so took the foreste, and so he wente al that
nyght, and in the mornyng he was ware, betwixte two holtes
hore, of a chapel and an ermytage.

Capitulum VI.

THAN was syr Bedware glad, and thyder he wente; & whan
he came in to the chapel, he sawe where laye an heremyte
grouelyng on al foure, there fast by a tombe was newe
grauen.　Whan the Eremyte sawe syr Bedwere, he knewe
hym wel; for he was but lytel tofore bysshop of caunter- 5
burye, that syr Mordred flemed.　'Syr,' sayd Syr Bedwere,
'what man is there enterd, that ye praye so fast fore?'
'Fayr sone.' sayd the heremyte, 'I wote not verayly, but by
demyng.　But thys nyght at mydnyght here came a nombre
of ladyes, and broughte hyder a deed cors, and prayed me 10
to berye hym, and here they offeryd an hondred tapers and
they gaf me an hondred besauntes.'　'Alas,' sayd syr bedwere, 'that was my lord kyng Arthur, that here lyeth buryed
in thys chapel.'　Than syr bedwere swouned; and whan he
awoke, he prayed the heremyte he myght abyde wyth hym 15
stylle there, to lyue wyth fastyng and prayers.　'For from
hens wyl I neuer goo,' sayd syr bedwere, 'by my wylle, but
al the dayes of my lyf here to praye for my lord Arthur.'
'Ye are welcome to me,' sayd the heremyte, 'for I knowe
you better than ye wene that I doo.　Ye are the bolde bed- 20
were, and the ful noble duke Syr Lucan de butlere was your
broder.'　Thenne syr Bedwere tolde the heremyte alle as ye
haue herde tofore.　so there bode syr bedwere with the hermyte that was tofore bysshop of Caunterburye, and there syr

25 bedwere put vpon hym poure clothes, and seruyd the hermyte ful lowly in fastyng and in prayers.

Thus of Arthur I finde neuer more wryton in bookes that
ben auctorysed nor more of the veray certente of his deth
herde I neuer redde, but thus was he ledde aweye in a shyppe
30 wherin were thre quenes; that one was kyng Arthurs syster,
quene Morgan le fay, the other was the quene of North
galys, the thyrd was the quene of the waste londes. Also
there was Nynyue, the chyef lady of the lake, that had
wedded Pelleas the good knyght, and this lady had doon ·
35 moche for kyng Arthur; for she wold neuer suffre syr Pelleas
to be in noo place where he shold be in daunger of his lyf,
& so he lyued to the vttermest of his dayes wyth hyr in grete
reste. More of the deth of kyng Arthur coude I neuer fynde,
but that ladyes brought hym to his buryellys, & suche one
40 was buryed there that the hermyte bare wytnesse that somtyme was bysshop of caunterburye, but yet the heremyte
knewe not in certayn that he was verayly the body of kyng
Arthur; for thys tale syr Bedwer, knyght of the table rounde,
made it to be wryton.

Capitulum VII.

YET somme men say in many partyes of Englond that '
kyng Arthur is not deed. But had, by the wylle of our lord
Jhesu, in to another place, and men say that he shal come
ageyn & he shal wynne the holy crosse[1]. I wyl not say it
5 shal be so, but rather I wyl say here in thys world he chaunged
his lyf; but many men say that there is wryton vpon his
tombe this vers. *Hic iacet Arthurus, Rex quondam, Rex que
futurus.*

Thus leue I here syr Bedwere with the hermyte, that

---

[1] Printed 'crorse' in Southey's edition.

dwellyd that tyme in a chapel besyde glastynburye, & there 10
was his ermytage, & so they lyuyd in theyr prayers & fast-
ynges & grete abstynence; and whan quene Gueneuer vnderstood that kyng Arthur was slayn, & al the noble kny3tes,
syr Mordred & al the remenaunte, Than the quene stale
aweye & v ladyes wyth hyr, and soo she wente to almes- 15
burye; & there she let make hir self a Nonne, & ware whyte
clothes & blacke; & grete penaunce she toke as euer dyd
synful lady in thys londe, & neuer creature coude make hyr
mery, but lyued in fastyng, prayers, and almes dedes, that al
maner of peple meruaylled how vertuously she was chaunged. 20
Now leue we quene Gueneuer in Almesburye, a nonne in
whyte clothes & blacke, and there she was abbesse and rular
as reason wolde, and torne we from hyr, and speke we of
Syr Launcelot du lake.

IX.

WILLIAM CAXTON.

A.D. 1471.

A COLLECTION of Specimens like the present, would be incomplete without a genuine extract from a book printed by William Caxton. He was born in the Weald of Kent about 1422, and died in 1491 or 1492. He is chiefly celebrated for introducing printing into England in 1477, but he was also an author, and an indefatigable translator, there being upwards of twenty-two folio volumes among those printed by him, which he himself translated from French, Dutch, or Latin originals. The first book he printed (and the first ever printed in the English language) was his translation of a work entitled 'Le Recueil des Histoires de Troye, compose par Raoulle le Feure [Fevre], chapellein de Monseigneur le duc Philippe de Bourgoigne, en l'an de grace mil cccclxiiii' [1464]. This was a compilation from various romances on the subject of the Trojan war, made somewhat after the fashion of Sir Thomas Malory's 'Morte Darthur'; the chief foundation being the Latin romance of Guido de Colonna. Caxton made the translation of the first two parts in 1468 and 1471, and that of the third part shortly afterwards. The whole 'Recuyell' must have been printed before 1477, probably at Bruges. The extract (from a copy in the Cambridge University Library) is taken from near the end of the volume, and narrates the actual taking of Troy and the death of Priam. It may be compared with Surrey's translation of Virgil's second Æneid, printed below. I give the punctuation of the original, that the reader may see exactly what it is like.

—

[*From the ' Recuyell of the Historyes of Troye.'*]

**How the trayttre Anthenor bought of the preest the pal-
ladyum / and gaf hyt to Vlixes and of the horse of
brasse that was by the grekes brought to the temple
of Pallas beyng full of men of armes / And how the
cyte of Troye was taken and brente And the kynge
: pryant slayn &c.**

Whan Dyomedes and vlixes were retorned in to their oost.
Anthenor wente hym vnto the kynge pryant and said to hym
that he shold assemble all his folk to counceyll. And whan
they were alle comen. Anthenor sayd to hem that for to
come to þe peas of the grekes they muste nedes paye twenty 5
thousand marc of gold and of good poys / and as moche of
syluer / And also an honderd thousand quarters of whete.
And this muste be maad redy with in certayn terme. And
than whan they haue this / they shall sette sewrte to holde
the peas wyth out ony frawde or malengyne. There it was 10
ordeyned how this some shold be leueyed and whylis they
were besy ther abowtes. Anthenor wente to the preest þat
kepte the palladyum / the whiche preest had to name
Thoant / and bare to hym a grete quantite of gold. And
there were they two at counceill Anthenor sayd to hym that 15
he shold take this some of gold. wherof he shold be ryche
all hys lyf / and that he shold gyue to hym the palladyum /
and that noman shold knowe therof / ffor I haue. sayd he.
grete fere and as moche drede as thou. that ony man shold
knowe therof. And I shall sende hit to vlixes / and he 20
shall bere the blame vpon hym. and euery man shall saye
that vlixes shall haue stolen hyt / and we shall be quyte
therof bothe two &c.

THoant the preest resisted longe to the wordes of Anthe-
25 nor / but in the ende for couetyse of the grete some of gold
that anthenor gaf to hym.   He consentyd that he shold take
the palladyum and bere hyt away.   Than Anthenor toke hyt
anone and sente hyt vnto vlixes / the same nyght / And
after the voys ranne amonge the peple that vlixes by his
30 subtilite had taken and born awaye the palladyum out of troye
O what trayson was thys of a preest / that louyd better for
covetyse to betraye his cyte / than to leue the gold that was
gyuen hym.   Certes hyt is a foule vyce in a preest the synne
of couetyse / But fewe haue ben to fore thys tyme / and
35 fewe ben yet but yf they ben attaynte therwyth / wherof hyt
is grete pyte / syn hyt is so that auaryce is moder of all
vyces / Whilis that the troians gadryd to gyder their gold
and syluer and put hyt in the temple of mynerve to kepe
vnto the tyme that hyt was alle assemblid.   Hit playsid them
40 to offre & make sacrefyse to theyr god Appolyn / And whan
they hadd slayn many bestes for their sacrefyce and had put
them vpon the Awter / And hadd sette fyre on them for to
brenne them / Hit happend that ther cam there two mer-
uayllis / the fyrste was that the fyre wold not alyghte ne
45 brenne / for they began to make the fyre more than ten
tymes / And alway hyt quenchid and myght neuer brenne
the sacrefyce.   The seconde myracle or meruaylle was whan
they had appoynted the entraylles of the bestes for theyr
sacrefyce / A grete Eygle descended fro the ayer cryyng
50 gretly and toke wyth his feet the said entraylles and bare
hem in to the shyppes of the grekes.

Of these two thinges were the troians sore abasshid &
esmayed / And said that the goddes were wroth wyth hem.
And than they demanded of cassandra / what these thinges
55 signefied / and she sayd to them / that the god appolyn was
wroth with hem for theffusion of the blood of Achylles that

was shedde wherwith his temple was defowlid & violid / this
is þe firste / & ye muste go fecche fyre at the sepulture of
achilles And lighte your sacrefyce ther with / and than hit
shał quenche no more / And they dide so / and the sacre- 60
fyce brente cleer / And for the second myracle. she sayd to
hem that for certayn the trayson was maad of the cyte wyth
the grekes. Whan the grekes herde speke of these myracles.
they demaunded of Calcas what hyt signefyed. And he sayd
to hem that the tradicion of the cyte shold come shortly. 65
Amonge these thynges Calcas and Crisis the preest coun-
cellyd the grekes / that they shold make a grete hors of
brasse. And that muste be as grete as myght holde with in
hit a thousand knyghtes armed. And they sayd to them
that hyt was the playsir of the goddes. This hors made 70
a passyng wyse mayster as Apius was. Whos name was
synon / and he maad hyt so subtylly that wyth oute forth no
man coude parceyue ne see entree[1] ne yssue. But wythin
hyt apperyd to them that were closid ther in for to yssue
whan they wold &c. 75

Whan the hors was fułł maad. and the thousand knyghtes
therein by the counseył of Crysis / they prayed the kynge
pryant that he wold suffre thys hors entre in to the cyte : and
that hit myght be sette in the temple of Pallas / for as moche
as they sayd that they had maad hyt in the honour[2] of Pallas 80
for a vowe that they had maad for restytucion of the Palladyum that they hadd doon be taken oute of the same
temple &c.

Amonge these thynges the prynces that were yet in troye /
Whan they sawe that the kynge had so fowle and shame- 85
fully trayted with the grekes they wente oute of troye and
toke theyr men with them And the kyng philemenus ladde
no moo with hym but two honderd and fyfty men and sixty

---

[1] Caxton prints 'eɴtree.'   [2] Printed 'hanour.'

maydens of amazone that were lefte of a thousand that cam
90 wyth the quene panthasile And caryed the bodye of her with
hem And rood so moche that they cam vnto theyr contre.
Than cam the day that the grekes shold swere the peas
faynedly vpon the playn felde vpon the sayntuaryes. The
kynge pryant yssued out of the cyte and his peple And
95 sware there eche partye to holde the peas fermly fro than
forthon / And dyomedes swore fyrste for the grekes / after
whan they had broken the peas that they had treatid with
Anthenor of that thyng that they made after / And therfore
they mayntene that they were not forsworne by that colour /
100 And therfore me sayth in a proverbe / he that swerith by
cawtele or malicyously / he by malice forswerith hym self /
After diomedes sware in lyke wyse all the kynges and prynces
of grece. And than the kynge pryant and the troians swore
in good fayth as they that knewe no thynge of the grete
105 trayson And after theyr othes thus maad / The kynge pryant
delyueryd helayne to menelaus her husbond / and prayd
hym and other kynges and prynces of grece that they wold
pardoune helayne wyth oute suffryng to be doon to her ony
Iniurye or hurte / And they promysid hym faynedly that
110 they wold do to her no wronge.

Than prayd the grekes that they myghte sette the hors
of brasse wyth in the temple of pallas / ffor the restytucion
of [the] palladyum / to thende that the goddesse Pallas
myght be to them aggreable In their retourne. And as the
115 kynge pryant answerd not therto. Eneas and Anthenor sayd
to hym that hit shold be well doon / And that hit shold be
honour to the cyte / how be hyt the kynge pryant accorded
hyt wyth euyll wyll / Than the grekes receyuyd the gold
and siluer & the whete / that was promysid to them. And
120 sente hyt and putte hit in to their shyppis / After these
thynges they wente all in maner of procession and in deuo-

cyon wyth theyr prestis. And began with strength of cordes
to drawe the horse of brasse vnto tofore the gate of the cyte /
And for as moche as by the gate hyt myght not entre in to
the cyte / hit was so grete / therfore they brake the walle of 125
the cyte in lengthe and heyght in suche wyse as hyt entryd
with in the town And the troians receyuyd hyt wyth grete
Ioye. But the custome of fortune is suche that grete ioye
endeth in tristes[1] and in sorowe : The troians maad Ioye of
this hors / wherin was closid theyr deth. and knewe no- 130
thynge of hyt : In this hors was a subtill man named synon
that bare the keyes of the horse for to opene hyt. Whan
the troians were aslepe and restyd hem in the nyght. And
assone as they yssued out of the horse / they gaf a token of
fyre to them that were in the feldes to the ende that they 135
shold come in to the cyte for to putte hyt alle to de-
struccion.

Tнe same day the grekes fayneden to goo vnto Thenadon :
And sayd that they wolde resseyve Helayne and sette her in
saefte / be cause that the peple shold not renne vpon her for 140
the grete evyllys and hurtes that were fallen for her. And
thus they departyd from the porte of troyes wyth her saylles
drawen vp / and cam to fore the sonne goyng doun to
thenedon. Than had the troians grete Ioye whan they sawe
the grekes departe / And they sowped that euenyng wyth 145
grete gladnes / And the grekes as sone as they were come
to thenedon / they armed them in the euenyng / and wente
hem stylly and pryuely toward troye / whan the troians had
well sowped they wente to bedde for to slepe / than synon
opend the hors and wente oute and lyghte his fyre and 150
shewyd hit to them that were with oute / And anone with
oute delaye / they that were in a wayte entryd in to the cyte
by the gate that was broken for to brynge in the hors of

---

[1] Caxton prints ' tristres.'

brasse.   And the thousand knyghtes yssued out / and where
155 they fonde þe troians they slewe hem in their howsis / where
they slepte as they that thought on no thinge.

Thus entrid the grekes in to the cyte And slewe men and
women and chyldren wyth oute sparyng of ony and toke all
that they fonde in their howses / And slewe so many that er
160 hyt was daye they had slayn moo than twenty thousand /
they pylled and robbed the temples / the crye aroose moche
horryble of them that they slewe / Whan the kynge pryant
herde the crye / he knewe anone that eneas and anthenor
had betrayed hym he aroose anone hastely and wente hym
165 in to hys temple of Appolyn that was wythin hys palays / as
he that had no more esperance ne hope of hys lyf / And
knelid to fore the hyghe awter.   Cassandra fledde on that
other syde as one that had ben oute of her witte in to the
temple of mynerue / wepyng and demenyng grete sorowe.
170 And the other noble women abood styll in the palays in
wepynges and in teeris.

Whan hyt cam on the morn the grekes by the conduyte
of Eneas and of Anthenor that were open traytours vnto
theyr Cyte and also to theyr kynge and lord.   cam and
175 entrid in to the palays of ylyon where they fonde no deffence
and put to deth all them that they fonde.   Than pyrrus
entryd in to the temple of Appolyne and fonde there the
kynge pryant abidyng his deth / Than he ran vpon hym
with a nakyd swerd seeyng Eneas and Anthenor that guyded
180 hym   He slewe there the kynge pryant tofore the hyghe
awter / whiche was all bebledd of his blood.   The quene
hecuba and polixene fledde and wyste neuer whyder to goo /
and happend that she mette with Eneas.   And than sayd
hecuba to hym in a grete fureur Ha A felon trayttre / fro
185 whens is comen to the so grete cruelte / that thou hast
brought with the / them that haue slayn the kynge pryant /

that hath doon to the so moche good and hath sette the in magnyfycence: and also hast betrayed the contre where thou were born / and the Cyte that thou oughtest to kepe At the lest late hit suffise the And refrayne the now of thy corage: 190 and haue pyte of thys vnhappy polixene / to thende that amonge so many euyllis as thou haste done: thou mayst haue grace to haue doon one good dede as for to saue her fro deth er the grekes slee her / Eneas meuyd with pyte resseyuyd polixene in hys garde and putte her in a secrete 195 place.

X.

THE NUT-BROWN MAID.

ABOUT A.D. 1500.

THIS ballad is justly styled by Mr. Hales (Bishop Percy's Folio MS., vol. iii. p. 174) 'one of the most exquisite pieces of late mediæval poetry.' There is a late copy of it in the book just quoted; and another copy, from the Balliol MS. 354, is also there printed. But the oldest copy extant (here reprinted) is to be found in 'Arnold's Chronicle,' first printed at Antwerp about 1502, and reprinted by Douce in 1811. It must have been written some years earlier. From the tone of the last stanza, Bishop Percy conjectured that it was written by a woman. The fourth stanza is still more suggestive on this point. Prior's poem, entitled 'Edwin and Emma,' is imitated from 'The Nut-Brown Maid,' and is inferior to it. Warton has some excellent remarks upon it, and compares a part of it with Prior's poem in his 'History of English Poetry,' sect. xliv; vol. iii. p. 124, ed. 1840. He remarks:—'What degree of credit this poem maintained among our earlier ancestors, I cannot determine. I suspect the sentiment was too refined for the general taste. Yet it is enumerated among the popular tales and ballads by Laneham, in his narrative of queen Elizabeth's entertainment at Kenilworth Castle in 1575.' See also Mr. Hales' remarks in his 'Percy Folio MS.,' vol. ii. pp. xxvii and 334. A modernized version of a considerable part of it is in 'Chambers' Cyclopædia of English Literature,' vol. i. p. 57. The reader must observe that the poem takes the form of a dialogue between two lovers, in alternate stanzas; the knight begins, and, at the end of stanza 3, personates the hero of an imaginary love-tale. The lady replies in stanza 2, and personates the heroine in stanza 4.

[*Poem of 'The Nut-Brown Maid.'*]

1.

Be it right or wrong, these men among, on women do com-
      plaine,
Affermyng this, how that it is a labour spent in vaine
To loue them wele; for neuer a dele they loue a man
      agayne;
For lete a man do what he can, ther fauour[1] to attayne,
Yet yf a newe to them pursue, ther furst trew louer than   5
Laboureth for nought, and from her though[t] he is a ban-
      nisshed man.

2.

I say not nay, but that all day it is bothe writ and sayde
That womans fayth, is as who saythe, all vtterly decayed;
But neuertheles, right good witnes in this case might be
      layde
That they loue trewe, & contynew; recorde *the* Nutbr[o]wne
      maide,   10
Whiche from her loue, whan, her to proue, he cam to make
      his mone,
Wolde not departe, for in her herte she louyd but hym
      allone.

3.

Than betwene vs lete vs discusse, what was all the maner
Be-twene them too; we wyl also telle all the[2] peyne in-fere
That she was in; now I begynne, soo that ye me answere. 15

---

[1] Printed 'fouour' in the first edition.
[2] Printed 'they' in the first edition; the Balliol MS. has 'the.'

Wherfore alle[1] ye, that present be, I pray you geue an
    eare :—

I am the knyght, I cum be nyght, as secret as I can,

Sayng ;—'alas, thus stondyth the case[2], I am a bannisshed
    man.'

4.

And I, your wylle for to fulfylle, in this wyl not refuse,

Trusting to shewe, in wordis fewe, *tha*t men haue an ille
    vse   20

To ther owne shame, wyme*n* to blame, & causeles the*m*
    accuse ;

Therfore to you, I answere now, alle wymen to excuse :—

'Myn owne hert dere, w*ith* you what chiere? I prey you telle
    anoon,

For in my mynde, of all mankynde, I loue but you allon.'

5.

' It sto*n*dith so, a dede is do, wherfore moche harme shal
    growe,   25

My desteny is for to dey a shamful dethe, I trowe,

Or ellis to flee; the ton must bee, none other wey I knowe

But to w*ith*drawe, as an outlaw, and take me to my bowe;

Wherfore adew, my owne hert trewe, none other red[e]
    I can,

For I muste to the grene wode goo, alone, a bannysshed
    man.'   30

6.

'O Lorde, what is this worldis blisse, that chaungeth as *the*
    mone?

---

[1] ' alle' supplied from Balliol MS.

[2] ' cause' in Arnold; but ' case' in Percy MS.

My somers day, *in* lusty may, is derked before the none;
I here you saye 'farwel'; nay, nay, we departe not soo
    sone;
Why say ye so, wheder wyl ye goo, alas! what haue ye
    done?
Alle my welfare to sorow and care shulde chaunge, yf ye
    were gon;   35
For in my mynde, of all mankynde, I loue but you alone.'

7.

'I can beleue, it shal you greue, and somwhat[1] you dis-
    trayne;
But aftyrwarde, your paynes harde *with*in a day or tweyne
Shal sone a-slake, and ye shal take confort to you agayne.
Why shuld ye nought? for to take[2] thought your labur were
    in vayne,   40
And thus I do, & pray you, loo! as hertely as I can;
For I muste too *the* grene wode goo, alone, a banysshed
    man.'

8.

'Now syth that ye haue shewed to me *the* secret of your
    mynde,
I shalbe playne to you agayne, lyke as ye shal me fynde;
Syth it is so, that ye wyll goo, I wol not leue behynde,   45
Shal neuer[3] be sayd, the Nutbrowne mayd was to her loue
    vnkind;
Make you redy, for soo am I, all-though it were anoon,
For in my mynde, of all mankynde, I loue but you alone.'

---

[1] 'shomwhat' in Arnold.   [2] 'make' in Arnold; 'take' in Ball. MS.
    [3] Arnold 'neyer.'

9.

'Yet I you rede to[1] take good hede, what[2] men wyl thinke
     & sey;
Of yonge and olde it shalbe tolde, that ye be gone away,   50
Your wanton wylle for to fulfylle, In grene wood you to
     play,
And that ye myght from your delyte noo lenger make delay.
Rather than ye shuld thus for me be called an ylle woman,
Yet wolde I to the grene wodde goo, alone, a banyshed
     man.'

10.

'Though it be songe of olde and yonge, that I shuld be to
     blame,   55
Theirs be the charge, *that* speke so large in hurting of my
     name;
For I wyl proue that feythful loue, it is deuoyd of shame,
In your distresse and heuynesse, to parte wyth you the
     same;
And sure all thoo, that doo not so, trewe louers ar they
     noon;
But in my mynde, of all mankynde, I loue but you alone.' 60

11.

'I councel yow, remembre how it is noo maydens lawe
Nothing to dowte[3], but to renne out to wod *with* an out-
     lawe:
For ye must there In your hande bere, a bowe redy to[4]
     drawe,

---

[1] 'to' supplied from Balliol MS.   [2] 'whan' Arnold; 'what' Ball. MS.
[3] 'dowte' Ball. MS.; 'dought' Arnold.
[4] 'redy to' in Balliol MS.; Arnold has 'to bere and.'

And as a theef thus must ye lyue[1], euer in drede and awe,
By whiche to yow gret harme myght grow, yet had I leuer
  than   65
That I had too the grene wod goo, Alone, a banysshyd man.'

12.

'I thinke not nay, but as ye saye, it is noo maydens lore;
But loue may make me, for your sake, as ye haue said
  before,
To com on fote, to hunte and shote to get vs mete and
  store;
For soo that I your company may haue, I aske noo more; 70
From whiche to parte, it makith myn herte as colde as ony
  ston,
For in my mynde, of all mankynde, I loue but you alone.'

13.

'For an outlawe this is the lawe, that men hym take &
  binde
Wythout pytee, hanged to bee, and wauer with the wynde.
Yf I had neede, as god for-bede, what rescous coude ye
  finde?   75
For sothe I trowe, you and your bowe shul drawe for fere
  behynde;
And noo merueyle, for lytel auayle were in your councel
  than;
Wherfore I too the woode wyl goo, alone, a banysshd man.'

14.

'Ful wel knowe ye, that wymen bee ful febyl for to fyght[2],
Noo womanhed is it in deede, to bee bolde as a knight; 80

[1] Arnold 'lyeue.'   [2] Arnold 'fyght.'

Yet in suche fere yf that ye were, amonge enemys day and
      nyght,
I wolde wythstonde, *with* bowe in hande, to greue them as I
      myght,
And you to saue, as wymen haue, from deth [men] many
      one;
For in my mynde, of all man-kynde, I loue but you alone.'

15.

'Yet take good hede, for euer I drede, that ye coude not
      sustein   85
The thorney wayes, *th*e depe valeis, the snowe, *th*e frost, *th*e
      reyn,
The colde, the hete; for drye or wete, we must lodge on the
      playn;
And, vs aboue¹, noon other roue, but a brake, bussh, or
      twayne;
Whiche sone shulde greue you, I beleue, and ye wolde gladly
      than,   89
That I had too the grene wode goo, alone, a banysshyd man.

16.

'Syth I haue here ben partynere *with* you of Ioy & blysse,
I muste also parte of your woo endure, as reason is;
Yet am I sure of oo plesure, and shortly it is this,
That where ye bee, me semeth, perde, I coude not fare
      a-mysse;
Wythout more speche, I you beseche, that we were soon
      a-gone;   95
For in my mynde, of all mankynde, I loue but you alone.'

---

¹ 'above' Ball. MS.; 'a-bowe' Arnold.

17.

'Yef ye goo thidyr[1], ye must consider, whan ye haue lust·to
    dyne,
Ther shal no mete be for[2] to gete, nor drinke, bere, ale, ne
    win[e],
Ne shetis clene to lye betwene, made of thred and twyne;
Noon other house but leuys and bowes, to keuer your hed
    & myn :   100
Loo ! myn herte swete, this ylle dyet shuld make you pale
    & wan,
Wherfore I to the wood wyl goo, alone, a banysshid man.'

18.

' Amonge the wylde dere suche an archier as men say *that*
    ye bee
Ne may not fayle of good vitayle, where is so grete plente;
And watir cleere, of the ryuere, shalbe ful swete to me,   105
Wyth whiche in hele I shal right wele endure, as ye shal see;
And er we goo, a[3] bed or twoo I can prouide a-noon,
For in my mynde, of all mankynde, I loue but you alone.'

19.

' Loo yet, before, ye must doo more, yf ye wyl goo with me,
As cutte your here vp by your ere, your kirtel by the
    knee,   110
Wyth bowe in hande, for to withstonde your enmys, yf
    nede be :
And this same nyght, before day-lyght, to wood-ward wyl
    I flee ;

---

[1] 'thyder' Ball. MS.; 'thedyr' Arnold.
[2] So in Ball. MS.; Arnold has ' before.'   [3] ' a' supplied from MS.

And if[1] ye wyl all this fulfylle, doo it shortely as ye can,
Ellis wil I to the grene wode goo, alone, a banysshyd man.'

20.

'I shal as now do more for you *than*[2] longeth to woman-
hede[3],   115
To short my here, a bowe to bere, to shote in tyme of
nede.
O my swete mod*er*, before all other for you haue I most
drede ;
But now a-diew ; I must ensue wher fortune doth[4] me leede :
All this make ye ; now lete vs flee, the day cumeth[5] fast
vpon ;
For in my mynde, of all mankynde, I loue but you alone.' 120

21.

' Nay, nay, not soo, ye shal not goo, & I shal telle you
why ;
Your appetyte is to be lyght of loue, I wele aspie ;
For right as ye haue sayd to me, in lyke wyse hardely
Ye wolde answere, who-so-euer it were, in way of company.
It is sayd of olde, " sone hote, sone colde," and so is a
woman ;   125
Wherfore I too the woode wyl goo, alone, a banysshid man.'

22.

' Yef ye take hede, yet is noo nede such wordis to say bee
me,
For ofte ye preyd, and longe assayed, or I you louid, p*er*dee ;

---

[1] ' if' supplied from the copy in Percy's Folio MS.
[2] MS. 'than'; Arnold '*that*.'   [3]'So in MS.; Arnold 'womanhod.'
[4] So in MS.; Arnold 'dnth.'   [5] MS. 'com*m*eth'; Arnold 'cum.'

And though that I, of auncestry, a barons doughter bee,
Yet haue you proued how I you loued, a squyer of lowe
    ·degree,   130
And euer shal, what so befalle, to dey therfore a-noon;
For in my mynde, of al mankynde, I loue but you alone.'

23.

' A barons childe to be begyled, it were a curssed dede;
To be felow w*ith* an out-lawe, almyghty god for-bede !
Yet bettyr were the pore [1] squyer alone to forest yede,   135
Than ye shal saye, another day, that be my [2] wyked dede
Ye were betrayed; wherfore, good maide, the best red[e]
    that [3] I can,
Is, that I too the grene wode goo, alone, a banysshed man.'

24.

'Whatso-euer be-falle, I neuer shal of this thing you vpbraid,
But yf ye goo and leue me soo, than haue ye me be-
    traied;   140
Remembre you wele how that ye dele, for yf ye, as ye [4]
    sayde,
Be so vnkynde, to leue behynde your loue, the notbrowne
    maide,
Trust me truly that I shal [5] dey, sone after ye be gone,
For in my mynde, of all man-kynde, I loue but you alone.'

25.

'Yef that ye went, ye shulde repent, for in the forest now 145
I haue purueid me of a maide, whom I loue more tha*n* you.
Another fayrer than euer ye were, I dare it wel auowe;

---

[1] So in Ball. and Percy MSS.; Arnold has 'power.'
[2] 'my' supplied from Balliol MS.   [3] MS. 'that'; Arnold '*tbe*.'
[4] MS. 'ye'; Arnold 'the.'   [5] 'shal' supplied from Ball. MS.

And of you bothe, eche shuld be wrothe w*ith* other, as I
      trowe :
It were myn ease to lyue in pease; so wyl I, yf I can;
Wherfore I to the wode wyl goo, alone, a banysshid man.' 150

26.

' Though in the wood I vndirstode ye had a paramour,
All this may nought remeue my thought, but *that* I wil be
      your ;
And she shal fynde me softe and kynde, and curteis euery
      our,
Glad to fulfylle all that she wylle co*m*maunde me, to my
      power ;
For had ye, loo! an hondred moo, yet wolde I be that
      one ;   155
For in my mynde, of all mankynde, I loue but you alone.'

27.

' Myn owne dere loue, I see the proue that ye be kynde and
      trewe ;
Of mayde and wyf, in al my lyf, the best *that* euer I knewe.
Be mery and glad, be no more sad, the case is chau*n*ged
      newe ;
For it were ruthe, that for your trouth you shuld haue cause
      to rewe.   160
Be not dismayed; what-soeuer I sayd to you, whan I began,
I wyl not too the grene wod goo, I am noo banysshyd man.'

28.

'Theis tidingis be more glad to me, than to be made a
      quene,
Yf I were sure they shuld endure; but it is often seen,

When men wyl breke promyse, they speke the wordis on
    the splene. 165
Ye shape some wyle, me to begyle, and stele fro me, I
    wene;
Then were the case wurs than it was, & I more woo
    begone;
For in my mynde, of al mankynde, I loue but you alone.'

29.

'Ye shal not nede further to drede, I wyl not disparage
You, god defende, sith ye[1] descende of so grete a lynage: 170
Now vnderstonde, to Westmorelonde[2], whiche is my hery-
    tage,
I wyl you bringe, and wyth a rynge, be wey of maryage
I wyl you take, and lady make, as shortly as I can;
Thus haue ye wone an erles son, and not a banysshyd man!'—

30.

Here may ye see that wymen be in loue meke, kinde, &
    stable, 175
Late neuer man repreue them than, or calle them variable;
But rather prey god that we may to them be confortable,
Which somtyme prouyth suche as he[3] loueth, yf they be
    charitable:
For sith men wolde that wymen sholde be meke to them
    echeon,
Moche more ought they to god obey, and serue but hym
    alone. 180

[1] 'ye' in MS.; 'you' in Arnold; see note.
[2] 'Westmorelond' in MS.; 'westmerlande' in Arnold.
[3] 'he' supplied from the MS.

XI.

WILLIAM DUNBAR.

A.D. 1503.

WILLIAM DUNBAR was born about 1465, and educated at the University of St. Andrews. He entered the Franciscan order of Grey Friars, and travelled in the garb of the order in Scotland, England, and France. In 1500 he received a pension from the king, James IV. of Scotland. He is known to have survived the year 1517, and must have died about 1520, or later. His chief poems are 'The Golden Terge' (Targe, or Shield), 'The Thistle and the Rose,' and the 'Dance of the Seven Deadly Sins,' the last of which may be found in Chambers' 'Encyclopædia of English Literature,' vol. i. p. 51. All three of these poems are analysed by Warton, who remarks that 'The Thistle and the Rose was occasioned by the marriage of James the Fourth, king of Scotland, with Margaret Tudor, eldest daughter of Henry the Seventh, king of England; an event in which the whole future political state of both nations was vitally interested, and which ultimately produced the union of the two crowns and kingdoms. It was finished on the ninth day of May in the year 1503 [1], nearly three months before the arrival of the queen in Scotland.' The only complete edition of Dunbar's works is that entitled, 'The Poems of William Dunbar, now first collected, with Notes, and a Memoir of his Life, by David Laing;' 2 vols. 8vo., Edinburgh, 1834. 'The Thistle and the Rose' is found in the Bannatyne MS. in the Advocate's Library at Edinburgh, from which it is here printed. I subjoin also, from Mr. Laing's edition, a short poem, which 'conveys nearly all the information we possess regarding the earlier period' of Dunbar's life.

[1] See the last line of the Poem.

[(A) *The Thrissill and the Rois.*]

1 Quhen merch wes with variand windis past,
  And appryll had, with hir siluer schouris,
  Tane leif at nature with ane orient blast,
  And lusty may, that muddir is of flouris,
  Had maid the birdis to begyn thair houris,
  Amang the tendir odouris reid and quhyt,
  Quhois armony to heir it wes delyt:

2 In bed at morrow, sleiping as I lay,
  Methocht aurora, with hir cristall ene,
  In at the window lukit by the day,
  And halsit me, with visage paill and grene;
  On quhois hand a lark sang fro the splene,
  'Awalk, luvaris, out of ȝour slomering,
  Se how the lusty morrow dois vp-spring!'

3 Me thocht, fresche may befoir my bed vp-stude,
  In weid depaynt of mony diverss hew,
  Sobir, benyng, and full of mansuetude,
  In brycht atteir of flouris forgit new,
  Hevinly of color, quhyt, reid, broun, and blew,
  Balmit in dew, and gilt with phebus bemys;
  Quhill all the houss illumynit of hir lemys.

4 'Slugird,' scho said, 'awalk annone for schame,
  And in my honour sum thing thow go wryt;
  The lark hes done the mirry day proclame, ‑
  To raiss vp luvaris with confort and delyt;
  ȝit nocht incressis thy curage to indyt,
  Quhois hairt sum tyme hes glaid and blisfull bene,
  Sangis to mak undir the leuis grene.'

5 'Quhairto,' q*uod* I, ' sall I upryss at morrow,
   For in this may few birdis herd I sing;
   Thai haif moir causs to weip and plane thair sorrow,
   Thy air it is no*ch*t holsum nor benyng;
   Lord Eolus dois in thy sessone ring :
   So busteous ar the blastis of his horne,
   Ama*n*g thy bewis to walk I haif forborne.'

6 W*ith th*at this lady sobirly did smyll,
   And said, 'upryss, and do thy obseruance;
   Thow did promyt, in mayis lusty quhyle,
   For to discryve the Ross of most plesance.
   Go se the birdis how thay sing and dance,
   Illumynit oure w*ith* orient skyis brycht,
   A*n*namyllit richely w*ith* new asure lycht.'

7 Quhen this wes said, depa*r*tit scho, this quene,
   And enterit in a lusty gairding gent;
   And tha*n*, metho*ch*t, full hestely besene,
   In serk and mantill [eftir hir][1] I went
   In-to *th*is garth, most dulce and redolent
   Off herb and flour, and tendir pla*n*tis sueit,
   And grene levis, doing of dew doun fleit.

8 The purpour sone, w*ith* tendir bemys reid,
   In orient bricht as angell did appeir,
   Throw goldin skyis putting vp his heid,
   Quhois gilt tressis schone so wondir cleir,
   That all *the* world tuke confort, fer and neir,
   To luke vpone his fresche and blisfull face,
   Doing all sable fro the hevy*n*nis chace.

   [1] The MS. has ' full haistely,' repeated from above.

9 And as *the* blisfull soune of cherarchy,
  The fowlis song throw confort of the licht;
  The birdis did w*ith* oppin vocis cry,
  ' O luvaris fo, away thow dully nycht,
  And welcum day *th*at confortis every wicht;
  Haill may, haill flora, haill aurora schene,
  Haill princes nature, haill venus, luvis quene!'

10 Dame nature gaif ane inhibitioun thair
  To ferss neptunus, and Eolus the bawld,
  No*ch*t to perturb *the* wattir nor the air,
  And *th*at no schouris [snell]¹ nor blastis cawld
  Effray suld flouris nor fowlis on *the* fold:
  Scho bad eik Iuno, goddes of the sky,
  That scho *the* hevin suld keip amene and dry.

11 Scho ordand eik that every bird and beist
  Befoir hir hienes suld a*n*none compeir,
  And every flour of vertew, most and leist,
  And every herb be feild, fer and neir,
  As thay had wont in may, fro ȝeir to ȝeir,
  To hir thair makar to mak obediens,
  Full law incly*n*na*n*d w*ith* all dew reuerens.

12 W*ith* *th*at a*n*none scho send the suyft ro
  To bring in beistis of all conditioun;
  The restles suallow co*m*mandit scho also
  To feche all foull of small and greit renown;
  And to gar flouris compeir of all fassoun
  Full craftely conjurit scho the ȝarrow,
  Quhilk did fur*th* swirk als swift as ony arrow.

¹ Omitted in MS.

13 All p*res*ent wer in twynkling of ane E,
   Baith beist, and bird, and flour, befoir the quene;
   And first the lyone, gretast of degre,
   Was callit thair, and he, most fair to sene,
   W*ith* a full hardy contena*n*ce and kene,
   Befoir dame nature come, and did inclyne,
   With visage bawld, and curage leonyne.

14 This awfull beist full t*er*rible wes of cheir,
   Persing of luke, and stout of countena*n*ce,
   Ry*ch*t strong of corpis, of fassoun fair, but feir,
   Lusty of schaip, lycht of deliuerance,
   Reid of his cullour, as is the ruby glance;
   On feild of gold he stude full mychtely,
   W*ith* flour-de-lycis sirculit lustely.

15 This lady liftit vp his cluvis cleir,
   And leit him listly lene vpone hir kne,
   And crownit him w*ith* dyademe full deir,
   Off radyous stonis, most ryall for to se;
   Saying, 'the king of beistis mak I the,
   And the cheif protector in woddis and schawis;
   Onto *th*i leigis go fur*th*, and keip the lawis.

16 Exerce justice w*ith* m*er*cy and conscience,
   And lat no small beist suffir skaith na scornis,
   Of greit beistis *th*at bene of moir piscence;
   Do law elyk to aipis and unicornis,
   And lat no bowgle w*ith* his busteous hornis
   The meik pluch-ox oppress, for all his pryd,
   Bot in *the* yok go peciable him besyd.'

17 Quhen this was said, w*it*h noyis and soun of joy,
    All kynd of beistis in-to thair degre,
    At-onis cryit lawd, ' *Vive le Roy,*'
    And till his feit fell w*it*h humilite;
   'And all thay maid him homege and fewte;
    And he did thame ressaif w*it*h princely laitis,
    Quhois noble yre is *parcere*[1] *prostratis.*

18 Syne crownit scho *th*e egle king of fowlis,
    And as steill dertis scherpit scho his pe*n*nis,
    And bawd him be als just to awppis and owlis,
    As unto pacokkis, papingais, or cre*n*nis,
    And mak a law for wycht fowlis and for wre*n*nis;
    And lat no fowll of ravyne do effray[2],
    Nor devoir birdis bot his awin pray.

19 Than callit scho all flouris *th*at grew on feild,
    Discirny*n*g all *th*air fassionis and effeiris;
    Upone *th*e awfull Thrissil scho beheld,
    And saw him kepit w*it*h a busche of speiris;
    Considering him so able for *th*e weiris,
    A radius crown of rubeis scho him gaif,
    And said, ' In feild go fur*th*, and fend the laif:

20 And sen thow art a king, thow be discreit;
    Herb w*ith*out vertew thow hald nocht of sic pryce
    As herb of vertew and of odor sueit;
    And lat no nettill, vyle and full of vyce,
    Hir fallow to *th*e gudly flour-de-lyce;
    Nor latt no wyld weid, full of churlicheness,
    Compair hir till the lilleis nobilness:

[1] Indistinct in MS.   [2] MS. ' efferay.'

I

21 Nor hald non udir flour in sic denty
    As the fresche ross, of cullour reid and quhyt:
    For gife thow dois, hurt is thyne honesty;
    Considdering *th*at no flour is so p*er*fyt,
    So full of vertew, plesans, and delyt,
    So full of blisful angeilik bewty,
    Imperiall birth, hono*u*r and dignite.'

22 Than to the ross scho turnit hir visage,
    And said, 'O lusty dochtir most benyng,
    Aboif *th*e lilly, Illustare of ly*n*nage,
    Fro *th*e stok ryell rysing fresche and ying,
    But ony spot or macull doing spring:
    Cum, blowme of joy, with jemis to be cround,
    For oure the laif thy bewty is renownd.'

23 A coistly croun, with clarefeid stonis brycht,
    This cumly quene did on hir heid incloiss,
    Quhill all *th*e land Illumynit of the licht;
    Quhairfoir, me tho*ch*t, all flouris did rejoiss,
    Crying attonis, ' Haill be thow, richest ross !
    Haill hairbis Empryce, haill freschest quene of flouris,
    To the be glory and hono*u*r at all houris.'

24 Thane all *th*e birdis song w*ith* voce on hicht,
    Quhois mirthfull soun wes m*er*velus to heir;
    The mavyss sang, ' haill ross, most riche and richt,
    That dois up-flureiss undir phebus speir;
    Haill plant of yowth, haill princes dochtir deir,
    Haill blosome breking out of *th*e blud royall,
    Quhois pretius vertew is Imperiall.'

25 The merle scho sang, ' haill roiss of most delyt,
   Haill of all flouris quene and souerane :'
   The lark scho sang, ' haill roiss, both reid and quhyt,
   Most plesand flour, of michty cullouris twane :'
   The nychtingaill sang, ' haill naturis suffragane [1],
   In bewty, nurtour, and every nobilness,
   In riche array, renown, and gentilness.'

26 The commoun voce upraiss of birdis small,
   Apon this wyss, ' O blissit be the hour
   That thow wes chosin to be our principall ;
   Welcome to be our Princes of honour,
   Our perle, our plesans, and our paramour,
   Our peax, our play, our plane felicite ;
   Chryst [2] the conserf frome all adversite.'

27 Than all the birdis song with sic a schout,
   That I annone awoilk quhair that I lay,
   And with a braid I turnyt me about
   To se this court ; bot all wer went away :
   Than up I lenyt, halflingis in affray [3],
   And thuss I wret as ye haif hard to-forrow,
   Off lusty may upone the nynt morrow.

   Explicit, quod Dumbar.

---

[1] MS. ' suffragene.'   [2] MS. ' Crhyst.'   [3] MS. ' affrey.'

[(B) *How Dunbar was desyred to be ane freir.*]

1 This [hindir]¹ nycht, befoir the dawing cleir,
  Me thocht Sanct Francis did to me appeir,
  With ane religiouse abbeit in his hand,
  And said, 'In this go cleith the, my servand,
  Refuiss the warld, for thow mon be a freir.'   5

2 With him and with his abbeit bayth I skarrit,
  Lyk to ane man that with a gaist wes marrit:
  Me thocht on bed he layid it me abone;
  But on the flure, delyverly and sone,
  I lap thair-fra, and nevir wald cum nar it.   10

3 Quoth he, 'quhy skarris thow with this holy weid?
  Cleith the thairin, for weir it thow most neid.
  Thow, that hes long done Venus lawis teiche,
  Sall now be freir, and in this abbeit preiche;
  Delay it nocht, it mon be done, but dreid.'   15

4 Quoth I, 'Sanct Francis, loving be the till,
  And thankit mot thow be of thy gude will
  To me, that of thy claithis are so kynd:
  Bot thame to weir it nevir come in my mynd;
  Sweit confessour, thow tak it nocht in ill.   20

5 In haly legendis haif I hard allevin
  Ma sanctis of bischoppis nor freiris, be sic sevin;
  Off full few freiris that hes bene sanctis I reid.
  Quhairfoir ga bring to me ane bischoppis weid,
  Gife evir thow wald my saule yeid unto hevin.'   25

---

¹ Omitted in the Bannatyne MS.; see note.

6 'My brethir oft hes maid the supplicationis
  Be epistillis, sermonis, and relationis,
  To tak this abbeit; bot thow did postpone.
  But furder process, cum on thairfoir anone,
  All circumstance put by and excusationis.'   30

7 'Gif evir my fortoun wes to be a freir,
  The dait thairof is past full mony a yeir.
  For in-to every lusty toun and place
  Off all Yngland, from Berwick to Kalice,
  I haif in-to thy habeit maid gud cheir.   35

8 In freiris weid full fairly haif I fleichit,
  In it haif I in pulpet gone and preichit
  In Derntoun kirk, and eik in Canterberry.
  In it I past at Dover oure the ferry,
  Throw Piccardy, and thair the peple teichit.   40

9 Als lang as I did beir the freiris style,
  In me, god wait, wes mony wrink and wyle,
  In me wes falset, with every wicht to flatter,
  Quhilk mycht be flemit with na haly watter;
  I wes ay reddy all men to begyle.'   45

10 The freir, that did Sanct Francis thair appeir,
  Ane feind he wes, in liknes of ane freir;
  He vaneist away with stynk and fyrrie smowk:
  With him, me thocht, all the house-end he towk,
  And I awoik, as wy that wes in weir.   50

XII.

STEPHEN HAWES.

A.D. 1506.

THE times of this poet's birth and death are alike uncertain, but he was alive throughout the reign of Henry VII. His chief poem is named the 'Passetyme of Pleasure,' of which Warton speaks highly, giving a complete analysis of its contents. But a short extract will probably suffice. The work describes how Graunde Amoure, the hero, who speaks in the first person, after many adventures, obtains the hand of La Belle Pucelle (literally 'the Beautiful Virgin'). It was composed about the year 1506, and printed by Wynkyn de Worde in 1517, by John Wayland in 1554, by Jhon Waley in 1555, and by Rychard Tottell in the same year. The last edition was reprinted by Mr. Wright for the Percy Society in 1845, and closely resembles that of Waley, which is here followed. Hawes took Lydgate for his model, and sometimes improved upon his teacher. The following stanzas are rather more lively than usual, and shew some imagination; indeed, they anticipate something of the manner of Spenser's 'Faerie Queene.'

Cap. XXXIII.

How graunde amoure dyscomfyted the giaunte with thre hedes, and was received of thre fayre ladies.

1 Whan golden Phebus in the Capricorne
   Gan to ascend fast unto Aquary,

And Janus Bifrons[1] the crowne had worne,
With his frosty berd, in January;
Whan clere Diana joyned with Mercury,
The cristall ayre and assure[2] firmament
Were all depured, without encumbrement.

2 Forth than I rode, at myne owne adventure,
Over the mountaynes and the craggy rockes[3];
To beholde the countrees I had great pleasure,
Where corall growed by right hye flockes[4];
And the popyngayes in the tre toppes;
Than as I rode, I sawe me beforne-
Besyde a welle hange both a shelde and horne[5].

3 Whan I came there, adowne my stede I lyght,
And the fayre bugle I ryght well behelde;
Blasynge the armes as well as I myghte
That was so graven upon the goodly shelde;
Fyrst all of sylver dyd appere the felde,
With a rampynge lyon of fyne golde so pure,
And under the shelde there was this scrypture:

4 'Yf ony knyght that is aduenturous
Of his great pride dare the bugle blowe,
There is a gyaunte bothe fyerce and rygorous[6]
That wyth his might shall hym soune[7] overthrowe.
This is the waye, as ye shall nowe knowe
To La Belle Pucell[8], but withouten fayle
The sturdy gyaunte wyll geve you batayle.'

[1] Old text 'bifrus.'   [2] Old text 'assured.'   [3] Old text 'roche.'
[4] Old text 'flackes.'   [5] Old text 'and a horne.'
[6] Old text 'rygoryous.'   [7] Old text 'sonne.'   [8] Old text 'pusell.'

5 Whan I the scripture ones or twyes hadde redde,
  And knewe therof all the hole effecte,
  I blewe the horne without ony drede,
  And toke good herte all f[e]are to abjecte,
  Makynge me redy, for I dyde suspecte
  That the great gyaunte unto me wolde hast,
  Whan he had herde me blowe so loude a blast.

6 I alyght anone upon my gentyll stede,
  Aboute the well then I rode to and fro,
  And thought ryght well upon the joyfull mede
  That I shoulde have after my payne and wo;
  And [on] my lady I dyd thynke also:
  Tyll at the last my varlet dyd me tell,
  ' Take hede,' quod he, ' here is a fende of hell.'

7 My greyhoundes leped and my stede did sterte,
  My spere I toke, and did loke aboute;
  Wyth hardy courage I did arme my[1] herte;
  At last I saw a sturdy giaunt stoute,
  Twelve fote of length, to fere a great route,
  Thre hedes he had, and he armed[2] was,
  Both hedes and body, all about with bras.

8 Upon his first head, in his helmet creest,
  There stode a fane of the silke so fyne,
  Where was wrytten, with letters of the best,
  ' My name is Falshed; I shall cause enclyne
  My neyghbours goods for to make them myne:
  Alway I get theyr lande or substaunce,
  With subtyll fraude, deceyte, or variaunce.

[1] Old text ' me.'   [2] Old text ' amed.'

9 And whan a knyght with noble chyvalry
   Of La Belle Pucell should attayne the grace,
   Wyth my great falshed I werke so subtylly
   That in her herte he [1] hath no [certayn] place:
   Thus of his purpose I do let the cace.
   This is I my power and my condicion,
   Love to remove by great illusion.'

10 And of the second head in a silken tassell,
   There I saw wrytten: ' Ymaginacion;
   My crafty wytte is withouten fayle
   Love for to bring in perturbacion;
   Where La Belle Pucell wold have affeccion
   To Graund Amour, I shall a tale devyse
   To make her hate him and him to dispyse.

11 By my false wytte, so muche imaginative,
   The trouth full ofte I bring in disease;
   Whereas was peace, I cause to be stryfe;
   I wyll suffer no man for to lyve in ease;
   For if by fortune he wyll me [2] displease,
   I shall of him ymagin such a tale,
   That out of joy it shall turne into bale.'

12 And on the thirde hede, in a stremer grene,
   There was written: ' My name is Perjury;
   In many a towne I am knowen, as I wene;
   Where as I lyst, I do great injury,
   And do forswere my selfe full wrongfully:
   Of all thinges, I do hate conscience,
   But I love lucre with all diligence.

[1] Old text 'she.'   [2] Old text · be.'

13 Betwene two lovers I do make debate;
   I will so swere, that they thinke I am true;
   For ever falshed with his owne estate
   To a lady cometh, and sayth, " to eschew
   An inconvenience, that ye do not rue;
   Your love is nought, ymaginacion knoweth;"
   I swere in lykewise and anon she troweth.

14 That we have sayd is of very trouth;
   Her love she casteth right clene out of minde;
   That with her love she is wonderly wroth;
   With fayned kindnes we do her so blynde,
   Than to her lover she is full unkinde.
   Thus our thre powers were joyned in one,
   In this mighty giaunt many dayes agone.'

15 And whan that I had sene every thinge,
   My spere I charged, that was very great,
   And to this giaunt so fyersly coming
   I toke my course, that I with him mette,
   Breking my spere upon¹ his first helmet,
   And right anone adowne my stede I lyght,
   Drawing my swerde that was fayre and bryght,

16 Iclyped Clara prudence, that was fayre and sure.
   At the giaunt I stroke with all my vyolence,
   But he my strokes might right well endure,
   He was so great and huge of puysaunce;
   His glave he did agaynst me advaunce,
   Whiche was foure fote and more of cuttyng;
   And as he was his stroke discharginge,

---

¹ Old text ' opon.'

17 Because his stroke was[1] hevy to beare,
   I lept asyde from hym full quickly,
   And to him I ran without any feare.
   Whan he had discharged agayne full lightly,
   He rored loude, and sware I should abye,
   But what for that?   I stroke at him fast,
   And he at me, but I was not agast.

18 But as he faught he had a vauntage,
   He was right hye and I under him low;
   Tyll at the last, with lusty courage,
   Upon the side I gave him such a blow
   That I right nere did him overthrow,
   But right anone he did his might enlarge,
   That upon me he did such a stroke discharge,

19 That unneth I might make resistaunce
   Agayn[2] his power, for he was so stronge.
   I dyd defend me agaynst his vyolence,
   And thus the battayll dured right longe;
   Yet evermore I did thinke amonge
   Of La Belle Pucell, whom I shold attayne
   After my battayles, to release my payne.

20 And as I loked I saw than onvale
   Fayre golden Phebus, with his beames read,
   Than up my courage I began to hale,
   Which nigh before was agone and dead.
   My swerde so entred that the giaunt blede,
   And with my strokes I cut of anone
   One of his legges, amiddes the thye bone.

[1] Old text 'wys.'   [2] Old text 'Agayng.'

21 Than to the ground he adowne did fall,
    And upon me he gan to loure and glum,
    Enforcing him so for to ryse withall,
    But that I shortly unto him[1] did cum;
    With his thre hedes he spytte all his venum;
    And I with my swerde, as fast as coude be,
    With all my force cut of his hedes thre.

22 Whan I had so obteyned the victory,
    Unto me than my verlet well sayd:
    'You haue demaunded well and worthely:'
    My greyhoundes lepte and my stede than brayde;
    And than from ferre I saw, well arayed,
    To me come ryding thre ladyes right swete;
    Forth than I rode and did wyth them mete.

23 The fyrst of them was called Veryte,
    And the second Good Operacion,
    And the thirde[2] cleped Fydelyte.
    All they at ones wyth good opinion
    Did geve to me great laudacion,
    And me besched with her hert entere
    Wyth them to rest and to make good chere.

24 I graunted them, and than backeward we rode
    The mighty giaunt to se and behold,
    Whose huge body was more than five carte-lode,
    Which lay there bleding, that was almost colde;
    They for his death did thanke me many a fold;
    For he to them was enmy mortall,
    Wherfore his thre hedes they toke in special.

---

[1] Old text 'hem.'   [2] Old text 'The thirde and.'

25 And than Verite, on the first fane,
    Did sette aloft of Falshoed the hede,
    And Good Operacion in lykewise had tane
    Of Ymaginacion, that full sore than bledde,
    His[1] hede alofte upon his baner rede.
    And in likewise Fydelite had served
    Perjuries hede, as he had well deserved.

26 And with swete songes and swete armony
    Before me they rode to their fayre castell;
    So forth I rode, with great joy and glory,
    Unto the place where these ladies did dwell,
    Sette on a rocke beside a spryng or[2] well,
    And fayre Observaunce, the goodly portres,
    Did us receyve with solemp[n]e gladnes.

   [1] Old text 'Upon his.'   [2] Old text 'or a.'

XIII.

GAWIN DOUGLAS.

A.D. 1513.

GAWIN DOUGLAS, born in 1474 or 1475, was the third son of Archibald, Earl of Angus, known in history by the nickname of Archibald Bell-the-Cat; see Note 2Y (59) to Sir Walter Scott's Marmion. He is described in the Trinity MS., mentioned below, as 'Master Gawyn Dowglas, provest of Sanct Gylys kyrk in Edinburgh, and person of lyntoun in louthiane, quhilk eftyr was bischop of Dunkeld.' He died of the plague in 1522, in London. The poems by which he is best known are 'King Hart,' 'The Palice of Honour,' and his translation of Virgil's Æneid. He not only translated the twelve books of Virgil, but also the thirteenth book of the Æneid, added by Maphæus Vegius, who died in 1458. This translation occupied him for sixteen months, as he himself informs us, and was finished in 1513. The whole of the work is of considerable merit, but the more interesting portions of it are the original Prologues which are prefixed to each book. The best of these is, on the whole, that to the twelfth book, here printed entire from an excellent MS. in Trinity College, Cambridge, marked O. 3. 12. A good edition of the entire work, from the same MS., was printed for the Bannatyne Club in 1839, and was to have been followed by a Glossary, which has, how-

ever, not even yet appeared. Most readers will remember the
description of the poet in Marmion, Canto VI, st. 11:—

> ' A bishop by the altar stood,
>   A noble lord of Douglas blood,
>   With mitre sheen, and rocquet white.
>   Yet show'd his meek and thoughtful eye
>   But little pride of prelacy ;
>   More pleased that, in a barbarous age,
>   He gave rude Scotland Virgil's page,
>   Than that beneath his rule he held
>   The bishopric of fair Dunkeld.'

The Proloug of the xii buk of Eneados.

Dyonea, ny*ch*t-hyrd, and wach of day,
*Th*e starnys chasyt of *th*e hevyn away,
Dame Cynthia dovn rollyng in *th*e see,
And venus lost *th*e bewte of hir E,
Fleand eschamyt within Cylenyus cave ;   5
Mars onbydrew, for all his grundyn glave,
Nor ſrawart Saturn from hys mortall speir
Durst langar in *th*e firmament appeir,
Bot stall abak ȝond in hys regioun far
Behynd *th*e circulat warld of Iupiter ;   10
Nycthemyne, affrayt of *th*e lyght,
Went ondir covert, for gone was *th*e ny*ch*t ;
As fresch Aurora, to myghty Tythone[1] spows,
Ischit of hir safron bed and evir hows,
In crammysyn cled and granyt violat,   15
With sangwyne cape, *th*e selvage purpurat,
Onschet *th*e wyndois of hir large hall,

---

[1] MS. ' Tytan.'

Spred all with rosys, and full of balm ryall,
And eik *the* hevynly port*is* cristallyne
Vpwarpis braid, *the* warld till Illumẏn.   20
The twynklyng stremowr*is* of *the* orient
Sched purpo*ur* sprang*is* with gold & asur*e* ment,
Persand *the* sabill barmkyn nocturnall,
Bet doun *the* skyis clowdy mantill wall :
Eous *the* steid, with ruby harnys red,   25
Abuf *the* sey lyftis furth hys hed,
Of cullo*ur* soyr, and su*m*deill brovn as berry,
Forto alichtyn and glaid our Emyspery,
The flambe owtbrastyng at his noyss-thyrlys ;
Sa fast pheton with *the* quhyp hym quhyrlys,   30
To roll Appollo hys fader*is* goldyn char,
*Th*at schrowdith all *the* hevy*n*nys & *the* ayr.
Quhill schortly, w*ith the* blesand torch of day,
Abilӡeit in hys lemand fresch array,
Furth of hys palyce ryall Ischit Phebus,   35
With goldyn crovn and vissage gloryus,
Crysp har*is*, bry*ch*t as chrisolyte or topace,
For quhais hew my*ch*t nane behald hys face ;
The fyry spark*is* brastyng from hys Eyn,
To purge *the* ayr, and gylt *the* tendyr greyn,   40
Defundand from hys sege etheryall
Glaid influe*n*t aspect*is* celicall ;
Befor*e* hys regale hie magnificens
Mysty vapour vpspryngand, sweit as sens,
In smoky soppys of donk dewis wak,   45
Moich hailsum stovys ourheldand *the* slak.
The aureat fanys of hys trone sou*e*rane
With glytrand glans ourspred *the* occiane,
The large flud*is* lemand all of ly*ch*t .
Bot with a blenk of hys sup*er*nale sy*ch*t.   50

Forto behald, It was a glore to se
The stablit wynd*is* and *the* cawmyt see,
The soft sesson, *the* firmame*n*t sereyn,
The lowne illumynat ayr, & fyrth ameyn;
The sylu*er* scalyt fyschis on the greit   55
Ourthwort cleir stremys sprynkland for *the* heyt,
With fynnys schynand brovn as synopar,
And chyssell talys, stowrand heir & *th*ar;
The new cullo*ur* alych̄tnyng all *the* land*is*,
Forgane *th*ir sta*n*nyr*is* schane *the* beriall stra*n*d*is*,   60
Quhil *the* reflex of *the* diurnal bemys
The beyn bonk*is* kest ful of variant glemys:
And lusty flora dyd hyr blomys spreid
Vnd*er* the feit of Phebus sulȝart steid;
The swardit soyll enbrovd w*ith* selcouth hewys,   65
Wod and forest obumbrat with *th*ar bewys,
Quhois blisfull branschis porturat on *the* grund;
W*ith* schaddoys schene schew rochis rubicund;
Towr*is*, turett*is*, kyrnellis, pynnaclys hie
Of kyrk*is*, castellis, and Ilke fair Cite,   70
Stude, payntit, eu*er*y fyall, fayn, & stage,
Apon *the* plane grund, by *th*ar awyn vmbrage.
Of Eolus north blast*is* havand no dreid,
The sulȝe spred her braid bosu*m* on breid,
Zephyrus confortabill Inspiratioun   75
Fortill ressaue law in hyr barm adoun;
The cornys croppis & *the* ber*is* new brerd
With glaidsu*m* garmont revestyng *the* erd;
So thik *the* plant*is* sprang in eu*er*y peyce,
The feild*is* ferleis of *th*ar fructuus fleyce;   80
Byssy dame Ceres, and provd pryapus,
Reiosyng of *the* planys ple*n*tuus,
Plenyst sa plesand & mast pr*o*pyrly,

K

By natur nurysyt wondir nobilly,
On *th*e fertill skyrt-lappys of *th*e grund   85
Strekyng on breid ondyr *th*e Cyrkyll rovnd;
*Th*e variand vestur of *th*e venust vaill
Schrowd*is* *th*e scherald fur, & euery faill
Ourfret w*ith* fulȝeis of figur*is* full diuerss.
*Th*e spray bysprent with spryngand sprowt*is* dispers, 90
For callo*u*r humo*u*r on *th*e dewy nyght,
Rendryng sum place *th*e gerss-pilis thar hy*ch*t,
Als far as catal, *th*e lang sy*m*myr*is* day,
Had in *th*ar pastur eyt & knyp away;
And blisfull blossu*m*mys in *th*e blomyt ȝard   95
Submitt*is* *th*ar hed*is* in *th*e ȝong so*n*nys salfgard:
Ive levys rank ourspred *th*e barmkyn wall,
*Th*e blomyt hawthorn cled hys pyk*is* all;
Furth of fresch burgionys *th*e wyne-grapis ȝyng
Endlang *th*e treilȝeis dyd on twyst*is* hyng;   100
*Th*e lowkyt buttonys on *th*e ge*m*myt treis
Ourspredand leyvis of natur*is* tapestreis;
Soft gresy verdo*u*r eftir balmy schowr*is*
On curland stalk*is* smylyng to *th*ar flowr*is*;
Behaldand *th*ame sa mony diuerss hew,   105
Sum perss, sum paill, su*m* burnet, and sum blew,
Sum greyce, su*m* gowlys, su*m* purpo*u*r, sum sangwane,
Blanchit or brovne, fawch-ȝallow mony ane,
Sum hevynly culloryt in celestiall gre,
Sum watry hewit as *th*e haw wally see,   110
And su*m* depart in freklys red and quhite,
Sum bry*ch*t as gold with aureat levys lyte.
The dasy dyd on breid hyr crownell smaill,
And eu*er*y flour onlappyt in *th*e daill;
In battill gyrss burgionys *th*e banwart wild,   115
*Th*e clavyr, catcluke, and *th*e ca*m*mamyld;

The flour-delyss furthspred hys hevynly hew,
Flour-dammes, and columby blank and blew;
Seir downys smaill on dent-de-lyon sprang,
The ȝyng greyn blomyt straberry levys amang;   120
Gymp gerraflouris *th*ar royn levys onschet,
Fresch prymross, and *the* purpour violet;
The Royss knoppys, tutand furth *th*ar hed,
Gan chyp, and kyth *th*ar vermel lippys red,
Crysp scarlet levis sum scheddand, baith at anys,   125
Kest fragrant smell amyd from goldyn granys;
Hevynly lylleis, with lokrand toppys quhyte,
Oppynnyt and schew *th*ar creistis redymyte,
The balmy vapour from *th*ar silkyn croppys
Distilland hailsum sugurat hunny droppys,   130
And syluer schakaris gan fra levys hyng,
With crystal sprayngis on *the* verdour ȝyng;
The plane pulderit with semly settis sovnd,
Bedyit full of dewy peirlys rovnd,
So *th*at Ilk burgioun, syon, herb, and flour,   135
Wolx all embalmyt of *the* fresh liquour,
And bathit hait dyd in dulce humouris fleyt,
Quharof *the* beys wro*ch*t *th*ar hunny sweit.
By myghty Phebus operatiouns,
In sappy subtell exhalatiouns,   140
Forgane *the* cummyn of *th*is prynce potent,
Redolent odour vp from rutis sprent,
Hailsum of smell as ony spicery,
Tryakill, droggis, or electuary,
Seroppys, sewane, sugur, & Synnamome,   145
Precyus Invnctment, salve, or fragrant pome,
Aromatik gummys, or ony fyne potioun,
Must, myr, aloes, or confectioun;
Ane paradyce It semyt to draw neir

Thir galȝart gardyng*is* and Ilke greyn herber*e*.   150
Maist amyabill walxis *the* amerant med*is*;
Swa*n*nys swouchis throw-owt *the* rysp and red*is*,
Our al *th*ir lowys and *the* flud*is* gray,
Seirsand by kynd a place quhar *th*ai suld lay:
Phebus red fowle hys corall creist can steir,   155
Oft strekyng furth hys hekkill, crawand cleir,
Amyd *the* wort*is* and *the* rutys gent,
Pykland hys meyt in alleis quhar he went;
Hys wif*is*, Coppa and P*a*rtelot, hym by,
As byrd al tyme *th*at hant*is* bigamy: 160
The pantyt povn, pasand with plomys gym,
Kest up his taill, a provd plesand quheill-rym,
Yschrowdyt in hys fedra*m*me·bry*ch*t & scheyn,
Schapand *the* prent of Argus hundreth Eyn:
Amang *the* brouys of *the* olyve twest*is*   165
Seir smaill fowlys wirkand crafty nest*is*,
Endlang *the* heggeis thyk, and on rank ak*is*,
Ilk byrd reiosyng with *th*ar myrthfull mak*is*.
In corner*is* and cleir fenystar*is* of glass
Full bissely Aragne wevand was,   170
To knyt hir nett*is* and hir wobbys sle,
*Th*arwith to caucht *the* myghe & litill fle:
So dusty puld*er* vpstowr*is* in eu*er*y streit,
Quhil corby gaspyt for *the* fervent heit.
Vnd*er* *the* bewys beyn in lusty valys,   175
Within fermans, and park*is* cloyss of palys,
The bustuus bukk*is* rak*is* furth on raw;
Heyrd*is* of hert*is* throw *the* thyk wod-schaw,
Baith *the* brokkett*is*, and w*ith* braid burnyst tynd*is*,
The sprutlyt calvys sowkand *the* red hynd*is*,   180
The ȝong fownys followand *the* dun days,
Kydd*is* skippand throw ro*n*nys eftir rays;

In lyssouris ånd on leys litill lammys
Full tayt & tryg socht bletand to thar dammys,
Tydy ky lowys, veilys by thame rynnys; 185
All snog & slekit worth thir bestis skynnys.
On salt stremys wolx doryda and thetis,
By rynnand strandis nymphes and naedes,
Sik as we clepe wenschis and damysellis,
In gresy gravys wandrand by spryng-wellis, 190
Of blomyt branchis and flowris quhite & red
Plettand thar lusty chaplettis for thar hed;
Sum [sang] ryng-sangis, dansys ledys, and rovndis,
With vocis schill, quhill all the dail resovndis;
Quharso thai walk into thar caralyng, 195
For amorus lays doith the Rochys ryng:
Ane sang, ' the schyp salys our the salt faym,
Will bryng thir merchandis and my lemman haym;'
Sum other syngis, ' I wilbe blyth and lycht,
Mine hart Is lent apon sa gudly wight.' 200
And thochtfull luffaris rowmys to and fro,
To lyss thar pane, and pleyn thar Ioly wo;
Eftir thar gyss, now syngand, now in sorow,
With hartis pensyve, the lang symmyris morow;
Sum ballettis lyst endyte of hys lady, 205
Sum levis in hoip, and sum aluterly
Disparit Is, and sa quyte owt of grace,
Hys purgatory he fyndis in euery place.
To pleyss his lufe sum thocht to flat & feyn,
Sum to hant bawdry and onlesum meyn; 210
Sum rownys to hys fallow, thame betwene,
Hys myrry stouth and pastans lait ȝisterevin:
Smyland says ane, ' I couth in previte
Schaw the a bovrd.' ' Ha, quhat be that?' quod he;
' Quhat thyng? that most be secrete,' said the tother. 215

'Gud lord! mysbeleif ȝe ȝour verray broder?'
'Na, neuer a deill, bot harkis quhat I wald;
*Th*ou mon be prevy:'—'lo, my hand vphald.'
'*Th*an sal *th*ou walk at evin:' q*uod* he, 'quhidd*er*?'
'In sik a place heir west, we baith togydd*er*,   220
Quhar scho so freschly sang *th*is hyndyr ny*ch*t;
Do choyss *th*e ane, and I sal quynch *th*e ly*ch*t.'
'I salbe *th*ar, I hope,' q*uod* he, and lewch;
'ȝa, now I knaw *th*e mater weill eneuch.'
Thus oft dywlgat Is *th*is schamefull play,   225
Na thyng accordyng to our hailsu*m* may,
Bot rathar co*n*tagius and infective,
And repugna*n*t *th*at sesşon nutrytyve,
Quhen new curage kytlys all gentill hart*is*,
Seand throu kynd Ilk thyng spryng*is* & revert*is*.   230
Dame natur*is* me*n*stralis, on *th*at o*ther* part,
*Th*ar blysfull bay entonyng eu*er*y art,
To beyt thir amorus of *th*ar ny*ch*t*is* baill.
*Th*e merl, *th*e mavyss, and *th*e nychtyngale,
With mery notis myrthfully furth brest,   235
Enforcyng *th*ame quha my*ch*t do clynk it best:
*Th*e cowschet crowd*is* [&] pyrk*is* on *th*e ryss,
*Th*e styrlyng chang*is* diuerss stevy*n*nys nyss,
*Th*e sparrow chyrmys in *th*e wallis clyft,
Goldspynk and lyntquhite fordy*n*nand *th*e lyft;   240
*Th*e Gukgo galys, & so quytt*er*is *th*e quaill,
Quhill ryver*is* rerdit, schawis, & eu*er*y vaill,
And tend*er* twyst*is* trymlyt on *th*e treis,
For byrd*is* sang, and bemyng of *th*e beys;
In wrablis dulce of hevynly armonyis   245
The lark*is* lowd, releschand in *th*e skyis,
Lovys *th*ar lege with tonys curyus,
Baith to dame natur, & *th*e fresch venus,

Rendryng hie lawd*is* in *th*ar obs*er*uance;
Quhais suguryt throt*is* maid glaid hart*is* danss,   250
And al smail fowlys syng*is* on *th*e spray:
'Welcu*m* *th*e lord of lyc*h*t, and lamp of day,
Welcu*m* fostyr of tendir herbys grene,
Welcu*m* quyknar of floryst flowr*is* scheyn,
Welcu*m* support of eu*er*y rute and vayn,   255
Welcu*m* confort of alkynd fruyt & grayn,
Welcu*m* *th*e byrd*is* beild apon *th*e brer,
Welcu*m* mast*er* and rewlar of *th*e 3er,
Welcu*m* weilfar of husband*is* at *th*e plewys,
Welcu*m* reparar of wodd*is*, treis, & bewys,   260
Welcu*m* depayntar of *th*e blomyt med*is*,
Welcu*m* *th*e lyfe of eu*er*y thyng *th*at spred*is*,
Welcu*m* storour of alkynd bestiall,
Welcu*m* be thy bryc*h*t bemys, gladyng all,
Welcu*m* celestial myrro*u*r and aspy,   265
Attechyng all *th*at hant*is* sluggardy!'
And w*ith* *th*is word, in chalm*er* quhar I lay,
*Th*e nynt morow of fresch temp*er*it may,
On fut I sprent into my bair sark,
Wilfull fortill compleit my langsu*m* wark   270
Twichand *th*e lattyr buke of dan virgill,
Quhilk me had tareit al to lang a quhile;
And to behald *th*e cu*m*myng of *th*is kyng,
That was sa welcu*m* tyll all warldly thyng,
With sic tryu*m*phe and pompos curage glaid   275
*Th*an of hys souerane chy*m*mys, as Is said,
Newly aryssyn in hys estait ryall,
That, by hys hew, but orleger or dyall,
I knew It was past four hour*is* of day,
And thoc*h*t I wald na langar ly in may,   280
Less Phebus suld me losanger attaynt:

For progne had, or *th*an, sung hir co*m*playnt,
And eik hir dreidfull systir philomeyn
Hyr lays endyt, and in wodd*is* greyn
Hyd hir-selvyn, eschamyt of hir chance;   285
And Esacus complet*is* hys pe*n*nance
In Ryver*is*, flud*is*, and on eu*er*y laik:
And Peristera bydd*is* luffar*is* awaik;—
'Do serve my lady venus heir with me,
Lern *th*us to, mak ʒo*ur* obs*er*uance,' q*uod* sche,   290
'Into myne hart*is* ladeis sweit presens
Behald*is* how I beynge, and do reuerens.'
Hyr nek .scho wrynklys, trasyng mony fold,
With plomys glitt*er*and, asur apon gold,
Rendryng a cullo*ur* betwix greyn & blew,   295
In purpo*ur* glans of hevynly variant hew;
I meyn o*u*r awyn natyve byrd, ge*n*till dow,
Syngand in hyr kynd, 'I come hydd*er* to wow;'
So pryklyng hyr greyn curage forto crowd
In amorus voce and wowar sound*is* lowd,   300
*Th*at, for *th*e dynnyng of hir wanton cry,
I Irkyt of my bed, and my*ch*t not ly.
But gan me blyss, syne in my wed*is* dress,
And, for It was ayr morow, or tyme of mess,
I hynt a scripto*ur* and my pen furth tuke: 305
Syne *th*us begouth of virgill *th*e twelt buke.

        Explicit scitus prologus ;
        Quharof *th*e auto*ur* says *th*us.

*Th*e lusty crafty p*r*eambill, perle of may
I *th*e entitil, crownyt quhil domysday;   310
And al w*ith* gold, in syng of stait ryall,
Most beyn illu*m*nyt thy lett*er*is capital.

XIV.

JOHN SKELTON.

A.D. 1522.

JOHN SKELTON was born about A.D. 1460, and died June 21, 1529. He was created poet laureate in the University of Oxford (as Caxton expresses it), before the year 1490, was afterwards admitted to a degree at Cambridge, and promoted to the rectory of Diss in Norfolk before 1504. Many accusations of misbehaviour have been made against him, but they do not seem to be sustained by proof; no doubt his habit of indulging without restraint in satirical invective made him many enemies. His chief poems are, 'The Bowge of Courte,' 'Magnyfycence,' 'The Boke of Colyne Cloute,' 'Ware the Hauke,' 'Phyllyp Sparowe' (a beautiful elegy on the death of a pet bird, from which I give an extract describing the beauty of Jane, the bird's mistress), and others. One of the best is entitled 'Why come ye nat to Courte?'—an extract from which is also here printed. It contains a bitter satirical attack on Cardinal Wolsey, and was written about A.D. 1522. It can hardly be wondered at that Wolsey resented the attack, and even went so far as to order Skelton to be arrested. The poet took sanctuary at Westminster, where he was protected by Abbot Islip. He lived in retirement there during the remainder of his life, and was buried in the church of Saint Margaret, adjoining the Abbey.

Few editions of any English poet's works are so thoroughly satisfactory as that of Skelton's poems, by the Rev. A. Dyce, printed in 1843. I therefore take the extracts below from Mr. Dyce, without alteration. The text of 'Why come ye nat to

Courte' was taken by Mr. Dyce chiefly from an old undated edition by Kele, collated with the editions by Wyght and Kytson (also undated), and with Marshe's edition of Skelton's 'Workes,' printed in 1568. 'Phyllyp Sparowe' is also chiefly from Kele's edition.

[(A) *From 'Why come ye nat to Courte?'*]

The Erle of Northumberlande
Dare take nothynge on hande :
Our barons be so bolde,
Into a mouse-hole they wolde   290
Rynne away and crepe,
Lyke a mayny of shepe ;
Dare nat loke out at dur
For drede of the mastyue cur,
For drede of the bochers dogge   295
Wold wyrry them lyke an hogge.
    For and this curre do gnar,
They must stande all a far,
To holde vp their hande at the bar.
For all their noble blode,   300
He pluckes them by the hode,
And shakes them by the eare,
And brynge[s] them in suche feare ;
He bayteth them lyke a bere,
Lyke an oxe or a bull :   305
Theyr wyttes, he saith, are dull ;
He sayth they haue no brayne
Theyr astate to mayntayne ;
And maketh them to bow theyr kne
Before his maieste.   310

Juges of the kynges lawes,
He countys them foles and dawes;
Sergyantes of the coyfe eke,
He sayth they are to seke
In pletynge of theyr case 315
At the Commune Place,
Or at the Kynges Benche;
He wryngeth them such a wrenche,
That all our lerned men
Dare nat set theyr penne 320
To plete a trew tryall
Within Westmynster hall;
In the Chauncery where he syttes,
But suche as he admyttes,
None so hardy to speke; 325
He sayth, ' thou huddypeke,
Thy lernynge is to lewde,
Thy tonge is nat well thewde,
To seke before our grace;'
And openly in that place 330
He rages and he raues,
And cals them cankerd knaues:
Thus royally he dothe deale
Vnder the kynges brode seale;
And in the Checker he them cheks; 335
In the Ster Chambre he noddis and beks,
And bereth him there so stowte,
That no man dare rowte,
Duke, erle, baron, nor lorde,
But to his sentence must accorde; 340
Whether he be knyght or squyre,
All men must folow his desyre.
  What say ye of the Scottysh kynge?

That is another thyng.
He is but **an** yonglyng, 345
A stalworthy stryplyng:
There is a whyspring and a whipling,
He shulde be hyder brought;
But, and it were well sought,
I trow all wyll be nought, 350
Nat worth a shyttel-cocke,
Nor worth a sowre calstocke.
There goth many a lye
Of the Duke of Albany,
That of shulde go his hede, 355
And brought in quycke or dede,
And all Scotlande owers
The mountenaunce of two houres.
But, as some men sayne,
I drede of some false trayne 360
Subtelly wrought shall be
Vnder a fayned treatee;
But within monethes thre
Men may happely se
The trechery and the prankes 365
Of the Scottyshe bankes.
  What here ye of Burgonyons,
And the Spainyardes onyons?
They haue slain our Englisshmen
Aboue threscore and ten: 370
For all your amyte,
No better they agre.
  God saue my lorde admyrell!
What here ye of Mutrell?
There-with I dare nat mell. 375
  Yet what here ye tell

Of our graunde counsell?
I coulde say some-what,
But speke ye no more of that,
For drede of the red hat   380
Take peper in the nose;
For than thyne heed of gose!

.   .   .   .   .

Ones yet agayne
Of you I wolde frayne,
Why come ye nat to court?—
To whyche court?
To the kynges courte,   400
Or to Hampton Court?—
Nay, to the kynges court:
The kynges courte
Shulde haue the excellence;
But Hampton Court   405
Hath the preemynence,
And Yorkes Place,
With my lordes grace,
To whose magnifycence
Is all the conflewence,   410
Sutys and supplycacyons,
Embassades of all nacyons.
Strawe for lawe canon [1],
Or for the lawe common,
Or for lawe cyuyll!   415
It shall be as he wyll:
Stop at law tancrete,
An obstract [2] or a concrete;

[1] 'conon' in Kele's ed.; 'canon' in others.
[2] So; for 'abstract.'

Be it sowre, be it swete,
His wysdome is so dyscrete,   420
That in a fume or an hete—
'Wardeyn of the Flete,
Set hym fast by the fete !'
And of his royall powre
Whan hym lyst to lowre,   425
Than, ' haue him to the Towre,
Saunz aulter remedy !
Haue hym forthe by and by
To the Marshalsy,
Or to the Kynges Benche !'   430
He dyggeth so in the trenche
Of the court royall,
That he ruleth them all.
So he dothe vndermynde,
And suche sleyghtes dothe fynde,   435
That the kynges mynde
By hym is subuerted,
And so streatly cöarted
In credensynge his tales,
That all is but nutshales   440
That any other sayth;
He hath in him suche fayth.
    Now, yet all this myght be
Suffred and taken in gre,
If that that he wrought   445
To any good ende were brought ;
But all he bringeth to nought,
By God, that me dere bought !
He bereth the kyng[1] on hand,

---

[1] Kele's ed. has ' dkeyng'; other eds. ' kyng.'

That he must pyll his lande, 450
To make his cofers ryche;
But he layth all in the dyche,
And vseth suche abusyoun,
That in the conclusyoun
All commeth to confusyon. 455
Perceyue the cause why,
To tell the trouth playnly,
He is so ambicyous,
So shamles, and [1] so vicyous,
And so supersticyous, 460
And so moche obliuyous
From whens that he came,
That he falleth into a *cæciam* [2],
Whiche, truly to expresse,
Is a forgetfulnesse, 465
Or wylfull blyndnesse,
Wherwith the Sodomites
Lost theyr inward syghtes,
The Gommoryans also
Were brought to deedly wo, 470
As Scrypture recordis:
A cæcitate cordis,
In the Latyne synge we,
Libera nos, Domine!
 But this madde Amalecke, 475
Lyke to a Mamelek [3],
He regardeth lordes
No more than potshordes;

---

[1] Kele's ed. has 'an'; other eds. 'and.'
[2] The eds. have 'Acisiam'; but see ll. 466-468, and l. 472. Cf. Gen. xix. 11.
[3] Printed 'Amamelek' in the old editions.

He is in suche elacyon
Of his exaltacyon,   480
And the supportacyon
Of our souerayne lorde,
That, God to recorde,
He ruleth all at wyll,
Without reason or skyll: 485
How be it the primordyall
Of his wretched originall,
And his base progeny,
And his gresy genealogy,
He came of the sank royall,   490
That was cast out of a bochers stall.
    Bot how euer he was borne,
Men wolde haue the lesse scorne,
If he coulde consyder
His birth and rowme togeder,   495
And call to his mynde
How noble and how kynde
To him he hathe founde
Our souereyne lorde, chyfe grounde
Of all this prelacy,   500
And set hym nobly
In great auctoryte,
Out from a low degre,
Whiche he can nat se:
For he was, parde,   505
No doctor of deuinyte,
Nor doctor of the law,
Nor of none other saw:
But a poore maister of arte,
God wot, had lytell parte   510
Of the quatriuials,

Nor yet of triuials,
Nor of philosophy,
Nor of philology,
Nor of good pollycy,   515
Nor of astronomy,
Nor acquaynted worth a fly
With honorable Haly,
Nor with royall Ptholomy,
Nor with Albumasar,   520
To treate of any star
Fyxt or els mobyll;
His Latyne tonge dothe hobbyll,
He doth but cloute and cobbill
In Tullis faculte,   525
Called humanyte;
Yet proudly he dare pretende
How no man can him amende:
But haue ye nat herde this,
How an one-eyed man is   530
Well-syghted when
He is amonge blynde men?
   Than, our processe for to stable,
This man was full vnable
To reche to suche degre,   535
Had nat our prynce be
Royall Henry the eyght,
Take him in suche conceyght,
That he set him on heyght,
In exemplyfyenge   540
Great Alexander the kynge,
In writynge as we fynde;
Whiche of his royall mynde,
And of his noble pleasure,

L

Transcendynge out of mesure,　　　545
Thought to do a thynge
That perteyneth to a kynge,
To make vp one of nought,
And made to him be brought
A wretched poore man,　　　550
Whiche his lyuenge wan
With plantyng of lekes
By the dayes and by the wekes,
And of this poore vassall
He made a kynge royall,　　　555
And gaue him a realme to rule,
That occupyed a showell,
A mattoke and a spade,
Before that he was made ·
A kynge, as I haue tolde,　　　560
And ruled as he wolde.
Suche is a kynges power,
To make within an hower,
And worke suche a myracle,
That shall be a spectacle　　　565
Of renowme and worldly fame :
In lykewyse now the same
Cardynall is promoted,
Yet with lewde condicyons cotyd,
As herafter ben notyd,　　　570
Presumcyon and vayne glory,
Envy, wrath, and lechery,
Couetys and glotony,
Slouthfull to do good,
Now frantick, now starke wode.　　　575

Allmyghty God, I trust,

Hath for him dyscust
That of force he must
Be faythfull, trew, and iust
To our most royall kynge,   750
Chefe rote of his makynge;
Yet it is a wyly mouse
That can bylde his dwellinge-house
Within the cattes eare   755
Withouten drede or feare.

[(B) *From 'Phyllyp Sparowe.'*]

How shall I report
All the goodly sort
Of her fetures clere,
That hath non erthly pere?   1000
The[1] fauour of her face
Ennewed all with grace,
Confort, pleasure, and solace,
Myne hert doth so enbrace,   1005
And so hath rauyshed me
Her to behold and se,
That, in wordes playne,
I cannot me refrayne
To loke on her agayne: 1010
Alas, what shuld I fayne?
It wer a plesaunt payne
With her aye to remayne.
Her eyen gray and stepe
Causeth myne hert to lepe;   1015
With her browes bent
She may well represent

---

[1] The editions have 'Her' by mistake; cf. l. 1035.

Fayre Lucres, as I wene,
Or els fayre Polexene,
Or els Caliope,   1020
Or els Penolope;
For this most goodly floure,
This blossome of fresshe coloure,
So Jupiter me socoure,
She florisheth new and new   1025
In beautye and vertew:
Hac claritate gemina
O gloriosa fœmina,
Memor esto verbi tui servo tuo!
Servus tuus sum ego.   1030
    The Indy saphyre blew
Her vaynes doth ennew;
The orient perle so clere,
The whytnesse of her lere;
Her[1] lusty ruby ruddes   1035
Resemble the rose-buddes;
Her lyppes soft and mery
Emblomed lyke the chery,
It were an heuenly blysse
Her sugred mouth to kysse.   1040
    Her beautye to augment,
Dame Nature hath her lent
A warte vpon her cheke,
Who so lyst to seke
In her vysage a skar,   1045
That semyth from afar
Lyke to the radyant star,
All with fauour fret,
So properly it is set:

---

[1] The editions wrongly have ' The'; cf. l. 1002.

She is the vyolet, 1050
The daysy delectable,
The columbine [1] commendable,
The ielofer amyable;
[For] [2] this most goodly floure,
This blossom of fressh colour, 1055
So Jupiter me succour,
She florysheth new and new
In beaute and vertew:
Hac claritate gemina
O gloriosa fœmina, 1060
Bonitatem fecisti cum servo tuo, domina,
Et ex præcordiis sonant præconia !
  And whan I perceyued
Her wart, and conceyued,
It cannot be denayd 1065
But it was well conuayd,
And set so womanly,
And nothynge wantonly,
But ryght conuenyently,
And full congruently, 1070
As Nature cold deuyse,
In most goodly wyse;
Who so lyst beholde,
It makethe louers bolde
To her to sewe for grace, 1075
Her fauoure to purchase;
The sker upon her chyn,
Enhached on her fayre skyn,
Whyter than the swan,
It wold make any man 1080

[1] So in other editions; Kele has 'calumbyn.'
[2] Omitted by accident; see l. 1021.

To forget deadly syn
Her fauour to wyn;
For this most goodly floure,
This blossom of fressh coloure,
So Jupiter me socoure,   1085
She flouryssheth new and new
In beaute and vertew;
Hac claritate gemina
O gloriosa fœmina,
Defecit in salutare tuum[1] anima mea;   1090
Quid petis filio, mater dulcissima ? babœ[2]!
  Soft, and make no dyn,
For now I wyll begyn
To haue in remembraunce
Her goodly dalyaunce,   1095
And her goodly pastaunce:
So sad and so demure,
Behauynge her so sure,
With wordes of pleasure
She wold make to the lure,   1100
And any man conuert
To gyue her his hole hert.
She made me sore amased
Vpon her whan I gased,
Me thought min hert was crased,   1105
My eyne were so dased;
For this most goodly flour,
This blossom of fressh colour,
So Jupyter me socour,
She flouryssheth new and new   1110
In beauty and vertew:

[1] Mr. Dyce corrects this, but unnecessarily; see note to l. 1061.
[2] Printed ' ba ba ' in the old editions.

Hac claritate gemina,
O gloriosa fœmina,
Quomodo dilexi legem tuam, domina!
Recedant vetera, nova sint omnia.   1115
    And to amende her tale,
Whan she lyst to auale,
And with her fyngers smale,
And handes soft as sylke,
Whyter than the mylke,   1120
That are so quyckely vayned—
Wherwyth my hand she strayned,
Lorde, how I was payned!
Vnneth I me refrayned;
How she me had reclaymed,   1125
And me to her retayned,
Enbrasynge therwithall
Her goodly myddell small
With sydes longe and streyte!
To tell you what conceyte   1130
I had than in a tryce,
The matter were to nyse,
And yet there was no vyce,
Nor yet no villany,
But only fantasy;   1135
For this most goodly floure,
This blossom of fressh coloure,
So Jupiter me succoure,
She floryssheth new and new
In beaute and vertew: 1140
Hac claritate gemina,
O gloriosa fœmina,
Iniquos odio habui!
Non calumnientur me superbi.

But whereto shulde I note   1145
How often dyd I tote
Vpon her prety fote?
It raysed myne hert rote
To se her treade the grounde
With heles short and rounde.   1150
She is playnly expresse
Egeria, the goddesse,
And lyke to her image,
Emportured with corage,
A louers pylgrimage;   1155
Ther is no beest sauage,
Ne no tyger so wood,
But she wolde chaunge his mood,
Such relucent grace
Is formed in her face;   1160
For this most goodly floure,
This blossome of fresshe coloure,
So Jupiter me succour,
She flouryssheth new and new
In beaute and vertew: 1165
Hac claritate gemina
O gloriosa fœmina,
Mirabilia testimonia tua!
Sicut novellæ plantationes in juventute sua.
So goodly as she dresses,   1170
So properly[1] she presses
The bryght golden tresses
Of her heer so fyne,
Lyke Phebus beames shyne.
Whereto shuld I disclose   1175
The garterynge of her hose?

[1] So in other eds.; Kele's ed. has 'propeeyly.'

It is for to suppose
How that she can were
Gorgiously her gere;
Her fresshe habylementes   1180
With other implementes
To serue for all ententes,
Lyke dame Flora, quene
Of lusty somer grene;
For this most goodly floure,   1185
This blossom of fressh coloure,
So Jupiter me socoure,
She florisheth new and new
In beautye and vertew:
Hac claritate gemina   1190
O gloriosa fœmina,
Clamavi in toto corde, exaudi me!
Misericordia tua magna est super me.

. . . .

My pen it is vnable,
My hand it is vnstable,   1220
My reson rude and dull
To prayse her at the full;
Goodly maystres Jane,
Sobre, demure Dyane;
Jane this maystres hyght,   1225
The lode-star[1] of delyght,
Dame Venus of all pleasure,
The well of worldly treasure;
She doth excede and pas
In prudence dame Pallas;   1230
[For] this most goodly floure,
This blossome of fresshe colour,

---

[1] So in other eds.; Kele has 'lode stare.'

So Jupiter me socoure,
She floryssheth new and new
In beaute and vertew :   1235
Hac claritate gemina
O gloriosa fœmina !
　Requiem æternam dona eis, Domine !
With this psalme, *Domine probasti me,*
Shall sayle ouer the see,   1240
With *Tibi, Domine, commendamus,*
On pylgrimage to saynt Jamys
For shrympes and for pranys,
And for stalkynge[1] cranys ;
And where my pen hath offendyd,   1245
I pray you it may be amendyd
By discrete consyderacyon
Of your wyse reformacyon ;
I haue not offended, I trust,
If it be sadly dyscust.   1250
It were no gentle gyse
This treatyse to despyse
Because I haue wrytten and sayd
Honour of this fayre mayd ;
Wherefore shulde I be blamed,   1255
That I Jane haue named,
And famously proclamed ?
She is worthy to be enrolde
With letters of golde.
　Car elle vault.   1260

---

[1] So in other eds.; Kele's ed. 'stalke.'

XV.

LORD BERNERS.

A.D. 1523.

JOHN BOURCHIER, Lord Berners, was born about A.D. 1464[1], and was the eldest son of Sir Humphrey Bourchier, a Yorkist, who was killed at the battle of Barnet in 1471. He was with Henry VII. at the siege of Boulogne in 1492, and was appointed Chancellor of the Exchequer under Henry VIII. about 1515. He died on the 19th of March, 1532. He is best remembered by his excellent translation of Froissart's 'Chronicles,' which was undertaken by the King's command, the first volume being printed by Pynson in 1523, and the second in 1525. The language of his time was exceedingly well suited to render the chivalrous pages of Froissart with picturesque effect, and his translation from this point of view is preferable to the modern one by Mr. Johnes. Mr. Marsh says—'This translation is doubtless the best English prose style which had yet appeared, and, as a specimen of picturesque narrative, it is excelled by no production of later periods.'—Student's Manual of the English Language, ed. Smith; Lect. V. p. 84. The first extract describes the sea-fight off Sluys, in which Edward III. gained a victory over the French fleet; and the second extract gives an account of the battle of Creçy.

[1] This is conjectural; the date generally given is 1474, three years after his father's death.

[(A) *The Sea-fight off Sluys.*]

**Of the batell on the see before Sluse in Flaunders, by-
twene the kynge of England and the frenchmen. Ca. 1.**

Nowe let vs leaue som-what to speke of therle of Henalt
and of the duke of Normandy: and speke of *th*e kyng of
England, who was on *th*e see to the intent to arryue in
Flaunders, and so into Heynalt to make warr*e* agaynst the
5 fre*n*chmen.   This was on mydsomer euyn, in the yer*e* of our
lorde M.CCC.xl. al thenglyssh flete was departed out of the
ryuer of Tames, and toke the way to Sluse.   And the same
tyme, bytwene Blanqueberque and Sluse on the see, was
sir Hewe Kyryell, sir Peter Bahuchet, and Barbnoyr: and
10 mo than sixscore great vessels besyde other, and they wer*e*
of normayns, bydaulx, genowes, and pycardes: about the
no*m*bre of .xl.M.   Ther*e* they were layd by the french
kyng, to defend *th*e kyng of Englandes passage.   The kyng
of England and his, came saylyng tyll he ca*m*e before
15 Sluse: and whan he sawe so great a nombre of shippes
*tha*t their mastes semed to be lyke a gret wood, he de-
mau*n*ded of the maister of his shyp what peple he thought
they were: he answered and sayd, 'sir, I thynke they be
normayns layd here by *th*e frenche kyng, and hath done gret
20 dyspleasur*e* in Englande, brent your towne of Hampton, and
taken your great shyppe the Christofer:' 'a!' q*uod* the kyng,
'I haue long desyred to fyght with the fre*n*chmen: and
nowe shall I fyghte with some of the*m*, by the grace of god
and saynt George; for truly they haue done me so many
25 dysplesurs *tha*t I shall be reuenged, & I may.'   Than the
king set all his shyppes in order; the grettest befor*e*, well
furnysshed with archers, .& euer bytwene two shyppes of

archers he had one shyppe with men of armes; & than he
made an-other batell to ly a-lofe with archers, to confort euer
them that were moost wery, yf nede were. And there were 30
a great nombre of countesses, ladyes, knyghtes wyues, &
other damosels, *that* were goyng to se the quene at Gaunt:
these ladyes *the* kyng caused to be well kept · with thre
hundred men of armes, and .v.C. archers.

When the kyng, and his marshals had ordered his batayls, 35
he drewe vp the seales & cam with a quarter wynde, to haue
the vauntage of the sonne. And so at last they tourned a
lytell to get the wynde at wyll: and whan the normayns sawe
them recule backe, they had maruell why they dyde so. And
some sayd, ' they thynke them selfe nat mete to medyll with 40
vs: wherfore they woll go backe;' they sawe well howe the
kyng of England was there personally, by reason of his
baners. Than they dyd appareyle their flete in order, for
they were sage and good men of warre on the see: and dyd
set the Christofer, the which they had won the yere before, 45
to be formast, with many trumpettes and instrumentes: and
so set on their ennemies. There began a sore batell on bothe
partes: archers and crosbowes began to shote, and men of
armes aproched and fought hande to hande; and the
better to come togyder, they had great hokes, & grapers of 50
yron to cast out of one shyppe into an-other; And so tyed
them fast togyder; there were many dedes of armes done,
takyng and rescuyng agayne. And at last, the great Christofer was first won by thenglysshmen, and all that were within
it taken or slayne. Than there was great noyse and cry, and 55
thenglysshmen aproched and fortifyed the Christofer with
archers, and made hym to passe on byfore to fyght with the
genoweys. This batayle was right fierse and terryble: for
the batayls on the see ar more dangerous and fierser, than the
batayls by lande. For on the see there is no reculyng nor 60

fleyng, there is no remedy but to fight, and to abyde fortune :
and euery man to shewe his prowes.   Of a trouthe sir
Hewe Kyriell, and sir Bahuchet, and Barbe Noyer, were
ryght good and expert men of warre.   This batayle en-
65 dured fro the mornyng tyll it was noone, & thenglysshmen
endured moche payne, for their ennemies were foure agaynst
one, and all good men on the see.   There the king of
England was a noble knight of his owne handes; he was
in the flouer of his youthe[1].   In like wyse so was the erle
70 of Derby, Pembroke, Herforde, Huntyngdon, Northampton,
and Glocester[2]: sir Raynolde Cobham, sir Rycharde Staf-
forde, the lorde Percy, sir water of Manny, sir Henry of
Flaunders, sir John Beauchamp: the lorde Felton, *the* lorde
Brasseton, sir Chandos, the lorde Dalawarre, the lorde of
75 Multon, sir Robert Dartoys, called erle of Rychmont: and
dyuerse other lordes and knyghtes, who bare themselfe so
valyantly with some socours that they had of Bruges, and
of the countrey there about, that they obtayned the vyctorie.
So that the frenchmen, normayns, and other, were dyscon-
80 fetted, slayne, and drowned; there was nat one that scaped:
but all were slayne.   Whanne this vyctorie was atchyued, the
kyng all that nyght abode in his shyppe before Sluse, with
great noyse of trumpettes and other instrumentes.   Thyder
came to se the kynge dyuers of Flaunders, suche as had herde
85 of *th*e kynges comming: and than the kyng demaunded of
the burgesses of Bruges, howe Jaques Dartuell dyd.   They
answered, that he was gone to *th*e erle of Heynalt agaynst
the duke of Normandy with .lx.M. flemynges.   And on the
next day, *th*e which was mydsomer day, the kyng and all
90 his toke lande; and the kyng on fote went a pylgrimage

---

[1] So in Myddylton's edition; Pynson has 'yongh.'
[2] Printed ' Glocetter.'

to our lady of Ardenbourge, and there herd masse and dyned, and thanne toke his horse and rode to Gaunt, where the quene receyued hym with great ioye: and all his caryage came after, lytell and lytell. Than the kyng wrote to therle of Heynault, and to theym within the castell of Thyne, certy- 95 fieng them of his arryuall. And whan therle knewe therof, & that he had dysconfyted the army on the see: he dysloged, and gaue leaue to all the souldyours to depart. And toke with hym to Valencennes al the great lordes, and there feasted them honourably, and specially the duke of Brabant, 100 and Jaques Dartuell. And there Jaques Dartuell, openly in the market place, in the presence of all the lordes, and of all such as wold here hym, declared what right the kyng of Englande had to the crowne of France, and also what puyssaunce the thre countreis were of, Flaunders, Heynault, 105 and Brabant, surely ioyned in one alyance. And he dyde so by his great wysedom and plesaunt wordes, that all people that harde hym praysed hym moche, and sayd howe he had nobly spoken, & by great experyence. And thus he was greatly praysed, & it was sayd *that* he was well worthy 110 to gouerne *the* countrey[1] of Flaunders. Than the lordes departed, and promysed to mete agayne within .viii. dayes at Gaunt to se the kyng of England, and so they dyd. And the kyng feasted them honorably, and so dyd the quene, who was as than nuly purifyed of a sonne called John, who was 115 after duke of Lancastre, by his wyfe, doughter to duke Henry of Lancastre. Than there was a counsell set to be at Vylleuort[2], and a day lymitted.

[1] So in Myddylton's edition; Pynson has ' countie.'
[2] Printed ' Vyllenort.'

[(B) *The Battle of Creçy.*]

Of the batayle of Cressy bytwene the kyng of England and the frenche kyng. Cap. C.xxx.

Tʜᴇ*n*glysshmen who were in thre batayls lyeng on the
grounde to rest them, assone as they saw the frenchmen
aproche, they rose vpon their fete fayre and easely, without
any hast, and aranged their batayls.   The first, which was
5 the princes batell, the archers ther stode in maner of a herse,
and the men of armes in the botome of the batayle; Therle
of Northa*m*pton & therle of Arundell with the second batell
were on a wyng in good order, redy to confort the princes
batayle, if nede were.   The lord*es* & knygh*tes* of France
10 ca*m*e nat to the assemble togyder in good order, for some
ca*m*e before and some came after, in such hast and yuell order,
*th*e one of the*m* dyd trouble another.   Whan the french
kyng sawe the englysshmen, his blode chaunged, and sayde
to his marshals, 'make the genowayes go on before, and
15 begynne the batayle in the name of god and saynt Denyse:'
ther*e* were of the genowayes crosbowes about a fiftene thousand, but they were so wery of goyng a fote that day a six
leages armed with their crosbowes, that they sayde to their
constables, 'we be nat well ordred to fyght this day, for we
20 be nat in the case to do any great dede of armes, we haue
more nede of rest.'   These wordes came to the erle of
Alanson, who sayd, 'a man is well at ease to be charged
w*ith* suche a sorte of rascalles, to be faynt and fayle nowe
at moost nede !'   Also the same season there fell a great
25 rayne and a clyps, with a terryble thonder; and before the
rayne, ther*e* came fleyng ouer bothe batayls a great nombre
of crowes, for feare of the tempest co*m*mynge.   Than anone

the eyre beganne to waxe clere, and the sonne to shyne fayre
and bright: the which was right in the frenchmens eyen,
and on the englysshmens backes. Whan the genowayes were 30
assembled toguyder and beganne to aproche, they made a
great leape and crye to abasshe thenglysshmen, but they
stode styll and styredde nat for all that; thanne the genowayes agayne the seconde tyme made a-nother leape and a
fell crye, and stepped forwarde a lytell, and thenglysshmen 35
remeued nat one fote: thirdly agayne they leapt and cryed,
and went forthe tyll they came within shotte; thanne they
shotte feersly with their crosbowes. Than thenglysshe
archers stept forthe one pase and lette fly their arowes so
holly and so thycke that it semed snowe; whan the geno- 40
wayes felte the arowes persynge through heedes, armes, and
brestes, many of them cast downe their crosbowes and dyde
cutte their strynges, and retourned dysconfited. Whan the
frenche kynge sawe them flye away, he sayd, 'slee these
rascals, for they shall lette and trouble vs without reason;' 45
than ye shulde haue sene the men of armes dasshe in among
them, and kylled a great nombre of them. And euer styll the
englysshmen shot where as they sawe thyckest preace; the
sharpe arowes ranne into the men of armes, and into their
horses: and many fell, horse and men, amonge the genowayes: 50
and whan they were downe, they coude nat relyue agayne;
the preace was so thycke, that one ouerthrewe a-nother.
And also amonge the englysshemen there were certayne
rascalles that went a fote, with great knyues, and they went
in among the men of armes, and slewe and murdredde'55
many as they lay on the grounde, bothe erles, barownes,
knyghtes, and squyers; wherof the kyng of Englande was
after dyspleased, for he had rather they had bene taken
prisoners. The valyant kyng of Behaygne, called Charles
of Luzenbourge, sonne to the noble emperour Henry of 60

Luzenbourge, for all that he was nyghe blynde, whan he
vnderstode the order of the batayle, he sayde to them
about hym, 'where is the lorde Charles my son?' his men
sayde, 'sir, we can nat tell, we thynke he be fightynge;'
65 than he sayde, 'sirs, ye are my men, my companyons and
frendes in this iourney. I requyre you, bring me so farre
forwarde, that I may stryke one stroke with my swerde;'
they sayde they wolde do his commaundement, and to the
intent that they shulde nat lese hym in the prease, they tyed
70 all their raynes of their bridelles eche to other and sette
the kynge before, to acomplysshe his desyre, and so thei
went on their ennemyes; the lorde Charles of Behaygne
his sonne, who wrote hymselfe kyng of Behaygne and bare
the armes, He came in good order to the batayle; but
75 whanne he sawe that the matter wente a-wrie on their partie,
he departed, I can nat tell you whiche waye; the kynge his
father was so farre forewarde, that he strake a stroke with
his swerde, ye, and mo than foure, and fought valyantly.
And so dyde his company, and they aduentured themselfe
80 so forwarde, that they were there all slayne, and the next day
they were founde in the place about the kyng, and all their
horses tyed eche to other. The erle of Alansone came to
the batayle right ordynatly and fought with thenglysshmen,
and the erle of Flaunders also on his parte; these two
85 lordes with their companyes coosted the englysshe archers,
and came to the princes batayle and there fought valyantly
longe. The frenche kynge wolde fayne haue come thyder
whanne he sawe their baners, but there was a great hedge
of archers before hym. The same daye the frenche kynge
90 hadde gyuen a great blacke courser to sir Iohan of Heynault,
and he made the lorde Iohan of Fussels to ryde on hym
and to bere his banerre; the same horse tooke the bridell in
the tethe, and brought hym through all the currours of

the*n*glysshmen; and as he wolde haue retourned agayne, he
fell in a great dyke, and was sore hurt, and had ben ther*e* deed 95
& his page had nat ben, who folowed hym through all the
batayls, and sawe wher*e* his maister lay in the dyke, and had
none other lette but for his horse, for thenglysshmen wolde
nat yssue out of their batayle, for takyng of any prisoner;
than*n*e the page alyghted and relyued his maister; than he 100
went nat backe agayn *th*e same way that they came, there
was to many in his way. This batayle bytwene Broy and
Cressy, this saturday, was ryght cruell and fell, and many
a feat of armes done that came nat to my knowlege; in
the night dyuerse knyghtes and squyers lost their maisters, 105
and somtyme came on thenglysshmen, who receyued theym
in suche wyse, that they were euer nighe slayne; for there
was none taken to mercy nor to raunsome, for so the
englysshmen were determyned. in the mornyng, the day of
the batayle, certayne frenchemen and almaygnes perforce 110
opyned the archers of the princes batayle, and came and
fought with the men of armes hande to hande. Than the
seconde batayle of thenglysshmen came to socour the
princes batayle, the whiche was tyme, for they had as than
moche a-do, and they with *th*e prince sent a messanger to 115
the kynge, who was on a lytell wyndmyll hyll; than the
knyght sayd to the kyng, 'sir, therle of Warwyke, and therle
of Ca*m*fort, sir Reynolde Cobham, and other suche as be
about the prince your sonne, ar feersly fought with-all and are
sore handled; wherfore they desyre you that you and your 120
batayle wolle come and ayde them; for if the frenchmen
encrease as they dout they woll, your sonne and they shall
haue moche a-do.' Than the kynge sayde, 'is my sonne
deed or hurt, or on the yerthe felled?' 'no, sir,' q*uod* the
knyght, 'but he is hardely matched, wherfore he hathe nede 125
of your ayde.' 'Well,' sayde the kyng, 'retourne to hym and

to them that sent you hyther, and say to them that they
sende no more to me for any aduenture that falleth, as long
as my sonne is a-lyue : and also say to them that they suffre
130 hym this day to wynne his spurres ; for if god be pleased, I
woll this iourney be his, and the honoure therof, and to
them that be aboute hym.'   Than the knyght retourned
agayn to them, and shewed the kynges wordes, the which
gretly encouraged them, and repoyned in that they had
135 sende to the kynge as they dyd.   Syr Godfray of Harecourt
wolde gladly that the erle of Harecourt his brother myght
haue bene saued, for he hard say by them that sawe his baner
howe that he was there in the felde on the frenche partie,
but sir Godfray coude nat come to hym betymes ; for he was
140 slayne or he coude come at hym, and so was also the erle of
Almare his nephue.   In another place the erle of Alenson
and therle of Flaunders fought valyantly, euery lorde vnder
his owne baner, but finally they coude nat resyst agaynst
the puyssaunce of the englysshemen ; and so there they were
145 also slayne, & dyuers other knyghtes and squyers. Also therle
Lewes of Bloyes, nephue to the frenche kyng, and the duke
of Lorayne fought vnder their baners, but at last they were
closed in among a company of englysshmen and wallshemen,
& there were slayne for all their prowes.   Also there was
150 slayne the erle of Ausser, therle of saynt Poule, and many
other ; in the euenynge the frenche kynge, who had lefte
about hym no mo than a threscore persons, one and other ;
wherof sir Iohan of Heynalt was one, who had remounted
ones the kynge, for his horse was slayne with an arowe ; than
155 he sayde to the kynge, 'sir, departe hense, for it is tyme ; lese
nat your selfe wylfully ; if ye haue losse at this tyme, ye
shall recouer it agayne another season.'   And soo he toke
the kynges horse by the bridell and ledde hym away in a
maner perforce ; than the kyng rode tyll he came to the

castell of Broy; the gate was closed bycause it was by that 160
tyme darke. Than the kynge called the capytayne, who
came to the walles and sayd, 'who is that calleth there this
tyme of nyght?' than the kynge sayde, 'opyn your gate
quickely, for this is the fortune of Fraunce.' The captayne knewe than it was the kyng, and opyned the gate and 165
let downe the bridge; than the kyng entred, and he had
with hym but fyue barownes, syr Iohan of Heynault, sir
Charles of Momorency, the lorde of Beauiewe, the lorde
Dabegny, and the lorde of Mountfort; the kynge wolde nat
tary there, but dranke and departed thense about mydnyght, 170
and so rode by suche guydes as knewe the countrey tyll he
came in the mornynge to Amyense, and there he rested.
This saturday the englysshemen neuer departed fro their
batayls, for chasynge of any man; but kept styll their felde
and euer defended themselfe agaynst al such as came to 175
assayle them; this batayle ended aboute euynsonge tyme.

XVI.

WILLIAM TYNDALE.

A.D. 1528.

WILLIAM TYNDALE was born about 1477, or later, and was burnt at Antwerp in October 1536, after a long imprisonment, for heresy. His beautiful translation of the New Testament is one of the finest works in our language: our present Authorized Version owes very much to it. His tracts, such as his 'Obedience of a Christian Man,' his dissertation on the parable of 'The Wicked Mammon,' and his 'Practice of Prelates,' are written in a clear, bold, vigorous style. The extract here printed is from the first of these, viz. 'The Obedience of a Christen man, and how Christen rulers ought to governe,' printed in 1528. It is a very interesting passage, and contains a splendid defence of the wisdom of translating the Scriptures into a tongue 'understanded of the people.' This piece should be carefully compared with the extracts from the works of Sir Thomas More, Tyndale's great opponent. Tyndale's version of the New Testament was printed in quarto in 1525, and in octavo in 1525 or January 1526. A facsimile edition of the latter was produced in 1862, by Mr. Fry, of Bristol; and of the extant fragment of the former, by Mr. Arber, in 1871. See 'The Gothic and Anglo-Saxon Gospels in parallel columns, with the versions of Wycliffe and Tyndale,' edited by Dr. J. Bosworth, 1865, pp. xxiii–xxix, and p. 584: also the remarks on Tyndale's version by Mr. Marsh, in the 'Student's Manual of the English Language,' ed. Smith, pp. 84 and 446; and Mr. Arber's Preface.

[On the translation of the Scriptures.   Fol. xii.]

Tʜᴀᴛ thou maist perceave how *that the* scripture ought
to be in *the* mother toɴge, and *that the* reasoɴs
which oure sprites make for *the* coɴtrary are but
sophistry & false wiles, to feare the[1] from *the*

That the scrip-
ture oughte to
be in the
english tonge.

5 lighte, *that* thou mighteste folowe them blyndefolde & be
their captive / to honoure their cerimonies & to offer to
their bely.

Fyrst god gave *the* childeʀne of israel a lawe by *the* hoɴde
of moyses in their mother toɴge, & al *the* prophetes wrote iɴ
10 their mother toɴge.   & all the psalmes were in *the* mother
tonge.   And there was Christe but fygured and described
in cerimonies / in redles / in parables and in darke prophesies.   What is the cause that we maye not have the olde
testamente with the newe also, which is *the* lighte of the
15 olde, and wherin is openly declared before the eyes that
there was darkely prophesied?   I can imagen no cause
veryly, excepte it be that we shulde not se the worke of
Antychrist and iugulynge of ypocrites.   what shulde be the
cause that we which walke in the brode daye / shulde not
20 se as well as they that walked in the night / or that we
shulde not se as well at none / as they dyd in the twylighte?
Came Christe to make the worlde moare blynde?   By this
meanes, Christe is the darkenes of the worlde and not the
light / as he saith hym selfe, Iohn .viij.
25 Moare over, Moyses saith, Deutro .vj. ' Heare, Israel, let
these wordes which I commaunde the this daye steke fast
in thine herte / aɴd whette them on thy childerne & talke

---

[1] Printed ' yᵉ,' as if it were the definite article.

of the*m* as thou sittest in thine house / and as thou walkest
by the waye / & when thou liest doune / & whe*n* thou risest
vppe / & bynde the*m* for a token to thine ha*n*de / & let the*m* 30
be a reme*m*brau*n*ce betwene thine eyes / & write the*m* on
*th*e postes & gates of thine house.'   This was commau*n*ded
generally vnto all me*n*.   how cometh it that Gods worde
perteneth lesse vnto vs tha*n* vnto the*m*?   Yee, how cometh
it that oure Moyseses forbydde vs and commau*n*de vs the 35
contrary / & threate vs yf we doo / & will not that we once
speake of Gods worde?   How can we whette gods worde
(that is, put it in practyse / vse, and exercise) apon oure
childerne & housholde / whe*n* we are violently kepte from
it & know it not?   How can we (as Peter comma*n*deth) geve 40
a reason of oure hope, when we wote not what it is that
God hath promysed or what to hope?   Moyses also comma*n*deth in *th*e said chapter : yf the sonne aske what the
testimonies lawes and obseruau*n*ces of the lorde meane, that
No ner syr Iohn
his goostly chil-
derne.   *th*e father teach him.   Yf oure childerne aske 45
what oure cerimonies (which are mo the*n* the
Ieweses ware) meane, No father ca*n* tell his
sonne.   And in the .xj. chapter, he repeteth all agayne, for
feare of forgettynge.

     They will saye happly / '*th*e scripture requireth a pure 50
mynde & a quiete mynde.   And therfore *th*e laye-ma*n*,
because he is altogether co*m*bred with wordly busynes / ca*n*
not vnd*er*sto*n*de the*m*.'   Yf *th*at be the cause / the*n* it is
a playne case / that oure prelates vndersto*n*de not the scriptures them-selues.   For no laye-ma*n* is so tangled with 55
wordly busynes as they are.   The greate thi*n*ges of *th*e
worlde are ministred by them.   Nether do *th*e laye People
any greate thinge / but at their assignemente.

     'Yf the scripture were in the mother to*n*ge,' they will
saye / ' then wolde the laye people vndersto*n*de it every ma*n* 60

after his awne wayes.' Wher-fore serveth the curate / but
to teach them the righte way? Wher-fore were
the holydayes made / but that the people shulde
come and lerne? Are ye not abhomynable scolemasters /
65 in that ye take so greate wages / yf ye wyll not
teach? If ye wolde teach, how coulde ye do it so
well and with so great profitt / as when the laye
people have the scripture before them in their mother tonge?
For then shulde they se by the order of the texte / whether
70 thou iugledest or not. And then wolde they beleve it / because it is the scripture of God / though thy lyvinge be
never so abhominable. Where now, because youre
lyvinge and youre preachinge are so contrary /
and because they grope out in every sermone
75 youre open and manyfest lyes / & smell youre
vnsaciable covetousnes, they beleve you not / when you
preach trouth. But alas / the curates them-selves
(for the most parte) wote no moare what the
newe or olde testamente meaneth / then do the
80 turkes. Nether know they of any moare then that they
reade at masse / matens and evensonge, which yet they
vnderstonde not. Nether care they but even to mumble
vp so moch every daye (as the pye & popyngay speake
the[y] wote not what) to fyll their belyes with all. Yf they
85 will not lat the laye man have the worde of God in his
mother tonge / yet let the prestes have it /
which, for a greate parte of them, doo vnderstonde no latine at all: but synge & saye and
patter all daye / with the lyppes only / that which the herte
90 vnderstondeth not.

Christ commaundeth to sherch the scriptures, Iohn .v.
Though that miracles bare recorde vnto his doctrine / yet desyred he no fayth to be geven ether

Marginal notes:

Holidayes.

Oure scolemas-
ters take greate
wages but teach
not.

Why the
preachers ar
not beleved
when they saye
trouth.

The curates
wotte not
what a bibyll
meaneth.

The prestes
vnderstonde
no laten.

Sherch the
scriptures.

vnto his doctrine or vnto his miracles / without recorde of
the scripture. When Paul preached / Actes .xvij. the other 95
sherched *the* scriptures dayly / whether they were as he
alleged the*m*. Why shal not I lyke-wise se / whether it be
the scripture *tha*t thou allegest? yee, why shall I not se the
scripture and the circumsta*n*ces and what goeth before and
after / that I maye know whether thyne interpretacio*n* be 10c
the right sence / or whether thou iuglest˙ and drawest the
scripture violently vnto thy carnall and fleshly purpose? or
whether thou be aboute to teach me or to disceave me?

Christ saith, ' that there shall come false prophetes in his
name and saye that they them-selves are Christe' / that ys / 105
they shall so preach Christe, that men must beleve in them,
in their holines and thinges of their imaginacion, without
Gods worde: yee, and that agenst-Christ, or Antichriste, that
shall come, is no thinge but soch false prophetes that shall
iuggle with the scripture, and begile the people with false 110
interpretacions, as all the false prophetes / scribes a*n*d pha-
rises did in *th*e olde testame*n*te. How shal I knowe whether
ye are that agenste-christe, or false prophetes, or no / seinge
ye will not let me se how ye allege the scriptures?

*Age*n*st-Christ
is knowen by
his deades.*

Christ saith: ' By their deades ye shall know 115
them.' Now when we loke on youre deades /
we se that ye are all sworne to-gether and have separated

*A severell king-
dom. Seuerell
lawes. what
christ lowseth
frely, the pope
byndeth, to
lowse it agayne
for money.*

youreselves from the laye people / & have a severall ki*n*gdome amo*n*ge youre-selves and severall
lawes of youre awne makynge / where-with ye 120
violently bynde the laye people, that never co*n*-
sented vnto the makynge of the*m*. A thowsande
thynges forbydde ye which christ made free / and dispe*n*se

*A secret coun-
sell.*

with them agayne for money. Nether is ther any
excepcio*n* at all / but lacke of money. Ye have 125
a secret councell by youre-selves. All other me*n*s councels

and secretes knowe ye and no man yours. ye seke but
honoure / ryches / promocion / auctorite, and to regne over
all / and will obeye no man.   Yf the father geve you ought
130 of curtesie / ye will compell the sonne to geve it violently,
whether he will or not, by craft of youre awne lawes.   These
deades are agenst-Christ.

¶ When an hole parysh of vs hyre a scolemaster to teach
oure childerne / what reason is it that we shulde be com-
135 pelled to paye this scolemaster his wages / and he shulde
have lycens to goo where he wyll, and to dwell in a-nother
contre, and to leve oure childerne on-taught?   Doeth not *the*
Pope so?   Have we not geven vp oure tythes, of curtesy,
vnto one, for to teach vs Gods worde?   And cometh not
140 the Pope and compelleth vs to paye it violently to them that
never teach?   Maketh he not one person which
cometh never at vs? yee, one shall have .v. or .vj.   Person.
or as many as he can get, and wotteth oftentymes where
never one of them stondeth.   A-nother is made   Vicar.
145 vicare / to whome he geveth a dispensacion to
goo where he will, and to set in a parish-preste   Parish-prest.
which can but mynister a sorte of dome cerimonies.   And
he, because he hath most laboure and leest profit, polleth on
his parte, and fetteth here a masse-peny, there a trentall /
150 yonder dirige-money, and for his beyderoule, with a con-
fession-peny, and soch lyke.   And thus are we never taughte,
and are yet neverthelesse compelled: ye, compelled[1] to hyre
many costly scolemasters.   Thes deades are veryly agenst-
Christ.   Shall we therfore iudge you by youre deades / as
155 Christe commaundeth?   So are ye false prophetes and *the*
disciples of Antichriste or of agenst-Christe.

The sermons which thou readist in the Actes of *the*

---

[1] Printed ' compolde.'

apostles & all *tha*t the apostles preached were no doute
preached in the mother to*n*ge. Why the*n* mighte they not
be writte*n* in the mother tonge? As yf one of vs preach 160
a good sermon, why maye it not be written? Saynt hierom
also tra*n*slated the bible in-to his mother tonge. Why maye
not we also? They will saye, 'it can not be translated in-to
our tonge, it is so rude.' It is not so rude as they are false
lyers. For the greke tonge agreeth moare with the english then 165
with the latyne. And the propirties of the hebrue

The propirties
of the hebrue
to*n*ge agre
withe the
english.

tonge agreth a thousande tymes moare with the
english then with the latyne. The maner of speak-
ynge is both one, so *tha*t in a thousande places
thou neadest not but to tra*n*slate it in-to *th*e english worde for 170
worde, whe*n* thou must seke a compasse in the latyne / and
yet shalt have moch worke to tra*n*slate it wel-faveredly / so
that it have the same grace a*n*d swetnesse / sence and pure
vnderstandinge with it in the latyne / as it hath in the
hebrue. A thousande partes better maye it be translated in- 175
to the english then in-to the latyne. Yee, and excepte my
memory fayle me and that I have forgotten what I redde
when I was a childe, thou shalt fynd in the englesh cronycle

Kinge Adel-
ston.

how that kynge Adelstone caused the holy scripture to be tra*n*slated in-to the to*n*ge that then was 180
in Englo*n*de, and how the prelates exhorted him there-vnto.

Moareover, seinge *tha*t one of you ever preacheth con-

Co*n*trary
preachinge.

trary to a-nother. And whe*n* two of you mete /
the one disputeth and bravleth with the other /
as it were two scoldes. And for as moch as one holdeth 185

Contrari doc-
tours.

this doctoure, and a-nother that. One foloweth
duns, a-nother saynte Thomas / a-nother Bonaventure / alexander de hales / raymo*n*de / lyre / brygot /
dorbell / holcott / gorra*n* / tru*m*bett / hugo de sancto vic-
tore / de monte regio / de nova villa / de media villa, & soch 190

lyke out of nu*m*bre.   So *that* if thou haddest but of every
auctor one boke, thou coudest not pyle the*m* vp in any warehouse in londo*n* / and every auctor is one co*n*trary vnto
a-nother.   In so greate diversite of sprites, how shall I know
195 who lyeth, and who saith trouth?   Wherby shall I trye the*m*
& iudge the*m*?   Verely, by gods worde, which o*n*ly is true.
But how shal I *that* doo whe*n* thou wilt not let me se the
scripture?

'Naye,' saye they / 'the scripture is so harde, that thou
200 coudest never vnderstande it but by *the* doctours.'   That is,
I must measure the mete-yarde by the cloth.   Here be twe*n*ty
clothes of divers lengthes and of divers bredthes.   How shall
I be sure of the length of the mete-yarde by them?   I suppose rather I must be fyrst sure of the length of the mete-
205 yarde / and there-by measure & iudge the clothes.   Iff I
must fyrst beleve the doctoure / then is the doctoure fyrst
true, & the trueth of the scripture dependeth of his trueth,
and so the trueth of God springeth of *th*e trueth of man.
Thus Antichriste turnith the rotes of the trees   Antichrist
210 vppwarde.   What is *th*e cause that we damme   turneth the
rotes of the tre
some of Origenes workes, and alowe some?   How   vpward.
know we that some is heresy and some not?   By the scripture, I trowe.   How knowe we *tha*t saint Augustine (which
is the best or one of the best that ever wrot apon the scrip-
215 ture) wrot many thi*n*ges amysse at *th*e begynnynge / as
many other doctours doo?   Verely, by the scrip-
tures / as he him-selfe well perceaved afterwarde,   The scripture
is the triall of   .
all doctrine a*n*d
whe*n* he loked moare diligently apo*n* them / and   the righte
twich-ston.
revoked many thynges agayne.   He wrote of
220 many thynges which he vnderstode not when he was newly
converted / yer he had thorowly sene the scriptures / and
folowed the opinions of Plato and the commune persuasio*n*s
of mans wisdome *that* were then famouse.

They will saye yet moare shamefully / 'that no man can
vnderstonde the scriptures without philautia / that 225

Philosophy.

is to saye, philosophy. A man must fyrst be well
sene in Aristoteles yer he can vnderstonde the scripture,' saye

Aristotell.

they. Aristoteles doctrine is / that the worlde was
without begynnynge, and shalbe without ende /
and that the fyrst man never was, and the last shall never 230
be. And that God doeth all of necessite, nether careth what
we doo, nether will aske any accomptes of that we doo.

Scripture.

Without this doctrine, how coulde we vnderstonde the scripture, that sayeth / God created
the worlde of nought / and God worketh all thinge of his 235
fre will and for a secret purpose / and that we shall all ryse
agayne / and that God will have acomptes of all that we

Aristotell.

have done in this lyfe? Aristotle saith. Geve
a man a lawe, and he hath power of hym-selfe
to doo or fulfyll *the* lawe, and becometh righteous with 240

Paul.

workynge righteously. But Paul and all the
scripture saith / that the lawe doeth but vtter
synne only, and helpeth not. Nether hath any man power
to doo the lawe / tyll the sprite of God be geven hym
thorow fayth in Christ. Is it not a madnes then to saye 245
that we coulde not vnderstonde the scripture without Aris-

Aristotell.

totle? Aristotles righteousnes & all his vertues
springe of a mans fre will. And a turke and
every infidele and ydolater maye be righteous and vertuous
. with that righteousnes and those vertues. Moare-over, Aris- 250
toteles felicite and blessednes stondeth in avoydinge of all
tribulacions / and in riches / health / honoure / worshepe /
frendes & autorite / which felicite pleaseth our spiritualty

Scripture.

well. Now without these and a thousande soch
lyke poyntes / couldest thou not vnderstande 255
scripture, which sayeth, *that* righteousnes cometh by christe &

not of ma*n*s wil, and how that vertues are the frutes and the
gifte of gods sprite, and that Christe blesseth vs in tribulacions / persecucion, & adversite?   How / I saye / coudest
260 thou vndersto*n*de the scripture without Philo-   Philosophi.
sophy / in as moch as Paul / in the seconde to   Paul.
the Collosie*n*s, warned them to beware lest any man shulde
spoyle them (that is to say / robbe them of their fayth in
Christe) thorowe Philosophy and disceytfull vanytes / and
265 thorow the tradicions of men & ordinaunces, after the
worlde, and not after Christe?

'By this meanes then / thou wilt that no man teach a-
nother / but that every man take the scripture & lerne by
hym-selfe.' Naye, verely / so saye I not. Never-   When no man
will teach, yf
we desyre, god
will teach.
270 *the*-lesse / seinge that ye will not teach / yf any
man thyrste for the trueth / & reade the scripture
by hym-selfe, desyringe God to open *the* dore of knowlege
vn-to hi*m* / God for his truethes sake will & must teach hym.
How be it, my meani*n*ge is, *tha*t as a master teacheth his
275 pre*n*tyse to knowe all *the* poyntes of the mete-yarde / first
how many enches / how many fote & the halfe[1] yarde / *the*
quarter & the naile / & the*n* teacheth hi*m* to mete other
thinges therby: eve*n* so will I that ye teach the   The order of
teachinge.
people Gods lawe / & what obedience God re-
280 quyreth of vs, vnto father and mother / master / lorde /
ki*n*ge & all superiours / and with what frendly love he co*m*-
maundeth one to love a-nother. And teach the*m* to know
that naturall vename & byrth-poyson which moveth the very
hertes of vs to rebelle agenste the ordinaunces and will of
285 God / and prove that no man is righteous in the sight of
God / but that we are all damned by the lawe. And then
(when thou hast meked them and feared them with the lawe)

---

[1] Printed ' halse.'

teach them the testamente and promises which God hath made vnto vs in Christe / & how mercyfull and kynde he is / and how moch he loveth vs in Christe.   And teach 290 them the principles and the grounde of the fayth, and what the sacramentes signifye, and then shall the sprite worke with thy preachinge and make them feale.   So wolde it come to passe / that as we know by naturall witte what foloweth of a true principle of naturall reason : even so by 295 the principles of the fayth and by the playne scriptures and by the texte / shulde we iudge all mens exposicion and all mens doctrine / and shulde receave the best and refuse the worst.   I wolde have you to teach them also the propirties and maner of speakinges of the scripture / and how to ex- 300 pounde proverbes and similitudes.   And then if they goo abroade, and walke by the feldes and medowes of all maner doctours and philosophers, they coulde catch no harme. They shulde dyscerne the poyson from the hony, and bringe whome no thinge but that which is holsome.   305

But now do ye clene contrary.   Ye dryve them from Gods

The disorder or overwarte order of oure scolemen.

worde and will let no man come there-to / vntyll he have byn two yeres master of arte.   First they nosell them in sophistry and in benefundatum.

The scole doctrine : as they call it : corrupteth the iudgementes of youth.

And there corrupte thei their iudgementes with 310 apparente argumentes and with alleginge vnto them textes of logycke / of naturall philautia / of methaphisick and morall philosophy, and of all maner bokes of Aristotle, and of all maner doctours which they yet never sawe.   Moare-over, one holdeth this, a-nother that. 315

Dreames.

One is a reall / a-nother a nominall.   What won- derfull dreames have they of their predicamentes / vniversales / seconde intencions / quidities, hecseities, & re- latives !   And whether *species fundata in chimera* be *vera species.*   And whether this proposicion be true, *non ens est* 320

aliquid. Whether *ens* be *equivocum* or *vnivocum. Ens* is a voyce only, saye some. *Ens* is *vnivocum,* saith a-nother, and descendeth in-to *ens creatum* and in-to *ens increatum per modos intrinsecos.* when they have this wise brauled viij. x.
325 or xij. or moo yeres, and after that their iudgementes are vtterly corrupte: then they beginne their Devinite.

Not at the scripture: but every man taketh a sondry doctoure / which doctours are as sondry and as dyvers / the one contrary vnto the other /
330 as there are divers facions and monstrous shappes / none lyke a-nother / amonge oure sectes of religion. Every religion / every vniversite, & all most every man, hath a sondry dyvinite. Now what-so-ever opinions every man fyndeth
335 with his doctoure / that is his Gospell, and that only is true with him, and that holdeth he all his lyfe longe / and every man, to mayntene his doctoure withall / corrupteth the scripture, & facioneth it after his awne imaginacion, as a Potter doeth his claye. Of what
340 texte thou provest hell / will a-nother prove purgatory / a-nother *lymbo patrum* / and a-nother the assumpcion of oure ladi: And a-nother shall prove of the same texte that an Ape hath a tayle. And of what texte the graye frere proveth *that* oure lady was without originall
345 sinne / of the same shall the blacke frere prove *that* she was conceyved in originall synne. And all this doo they with aparente reasons, with false similitudes, and likenesses / and with argumentes and persuasions of mans wisdome. Now there is no other division or heresy
350 in the worlde save mans wisdome, and when mans folish wisdome interpreteth[1] *the* scripture. Mans wisdome scatereth /

Scole diuinite. yet in this they all agre: that no man is saved by Christ but by holy werkes. And that christe hath geven vp his godhed to the pope, And all his power, and that the pope maye geve christes merites to whom he will, and take them from whom he will.

Potters: ye, mockers, or rather iugulars.

False similitudes.

---

[1] Printed 'intetpreteth.'

N

divideth, and maketh sectes / while the wisdome of one

Mans wisdome heresy. is that a white Cote is best to sarve God in / and a-nother saith, a blacke / a-nother, a

Cotes. grey / [a]nother, a blew : And while one saith 355

that God will heare youre prayer in this place / a-nother

Place. saith in *that* place : And while one saith this place is holier / and a-nother that place is

One religion is holier then another : holier / and this religion is holyer then that /

and this saynte is greater with God then that / 360

and an hundred thousande lyke thinges.   Mans wisdome

Mans wisdome is ydolatry. is playne ydolatry / nether is there any other ydolatry then to imagen of God after mans wis-

dome.   God is not mans imaginacion / but that only which

What God ys. he saith of hym-selfe.   God is no thinge but 365 his law and his promyses / that is to saye /

that which he biddeth the doo, and that which he biddeth the beleve and hope. God is but his worde : as Christ saith, John .viij. ' I am that I saye vnto you' / that is to saye / that which I preach am I. ' My wordes are spirite and lyfe.' 370 God is that only which he testifieth of hym-selfe and to imagen any other thinge of God then that / is damnable ydolatry.   Therfore saith the .cxviij. Psalme, ' happy are they which sherch *the* testimonies of the lorde' / that is to saye / that which God testifieth and witteneseth vnto vs. 375 But how shall I that doo, when ye will not let me have his testimonies or wittenesses in a tonge which I vnderstonde ? Will ye resist god ? Will ye forbidde hym to geve his spirite vnto the laye as well as vnto you ? Hath he not made the english tonge ? Why forbidde ye hym to speake 380 in the english [1] tonge then / as well as in the latyne ?

Fynally, that this thretenynge and forbiddynge the laye

---

[1] Printed 'enhlish.'

people to reade the scripture is not for love of youre soules
(which they care for as *the* foxe doeth for *the* gysse) is
385 evide*n*te & clerer the*n* the sonne / in-as-moch as they permitte & sofre you to reade Robyn hode & bevise
of ha*m*pto*n* / hercules / hector, a*n*d troylus, with
a t[h]ousande histories & fabies of love & wa*n*-
tones & of rybaudry, as fylthy as herte ca*n* thinke /

Reade what
thou wilt : ye,
a*n*d saye what
thou wylt, save
the trueth.

390 to corrupte *the* myndes of youth with-all / clene co*n*trary
to the doctrine of christ & of his apostles. For Paul (Ephes.
v.) sayeth : ' se that fornicacion and all vnclenes or covetousnes be not once named amo*n*ge you / as it becometh
sayntes : nether fylthines / nether folysh talkynge / nor gest-
395 inge, which are not comly. For this ye know, that no whore-
monger other vnclene person or covetous persone (which is
the worsheper of images) hath any enheritaunce in the kyngdome of Christ & of God.' And after / sayeth he / ' thorow
soch thinges cometh the wrath of God apon the childerne of
400 vnbelefe.' Now, seinge they permitte you frely to reade
those thinges which corrupte youre mi*n*des & robbe you of
the kyngdome of god & christe, & brynge *the* wrath of god
apo*n* you, how is this forbyddi*n*ge for love of youre soules ?

A thousande reasons moo myght be made (as thou maist
405 se in *paraclesis Erasmi* & in his preface to *the paraphasis* of
Mathew) vnto which they shulde be compelled to holde their
peace or to geve shamfull answares. But I hope that these
are sufficient vnto them that thirst [for] the trueth. God for
his mercy and trouth shall well open the*m* moo : ye, and other
410 secretes of his Godly wisdome / yf they be diligent to crye
vnto him / which grace graunte God. AMEN.

XVII.

SIR THOMAS MORE.

A.D. 1528.

SIR THOMAS MORE was born in London in 1480, educated at Oxford, and, after holding several important offices, appointed Lord Chancellor, Oct. 25, 1529. He continued to be Chancellor till May 16, 1532. He was afterwards accused of high treason, and beheaded on the 6th of July, 1535. His earliest productions were chiefly poems. About the year 1509, according to Hallam, he wrote his 'History of Edward V. and Richard III.' His most famous work is his 'Utopia'; but this was written in Latin: it was first published in 1516. His 'Dialogue concerning Heresies' was written in 1528, and contains some very interesting passages, some of which are here given. His arguments are chiefly directed against those advanced by William Tyndale, and his opinions concerning the translation of the Bible into English should be compared with Tyndale's in Section XVI. above. In another work, entitled 'A Confutacioun of Tyndales aunswere, made Anno 1532,' he accuses Tyndale of not distinguishing aright between the words 'no' and 'nay,' but commits the singular mistake of misstating his own rule. This curious passage is here printed; see p. 191. The English works of Sir Thomas More were collected and published at London in 1557, and from this edition my extracts are made.

[(A) *From 'A Dialogue concernynge Heresyes;'*
Book III. ch. 14; 'Workes,' p. 233.]

For ye shal vnderstande that the great arche-heretike wickliffe, whereas *the* hole bybble was lo*n*g before his dayes by
vertuous & wel lerned men tra*n*slated into *the* english tong, & by good & godly people w*ith* deuo-   Wickliffes
                                                     translacion of
                                                     the bybble.
5 cion & sobrenes wel and reuerently red, toke vpon
hym of a malicious purpose to translate it of new.   In which
tra*n*slacio*n*, he purposely corrupted *the* holye text, malici-
ously planting therein suche wordes, as might in *the* reders
eres serue to *the* profe of such heresies as he went about to
10 sow, which he not only set furth with his own tra*n*slacio*n* of
the bybble, but also w*ith* certain prologes & glosis whiche he
made thereupon.   And these thinges he so ha*n*dled (which
was no great maistry) w*ith* reasons p*r*obable & likely to ley
peple & vnlerned, *that* he corrupted in his time many folke
15 in this realme.

[(B) *From the same;* Book III. ch. 15; p. 234.]

. . . . . . but my-self haue seen and can shew you
bybbles fayre and old writen in englishe, whiche haue been
knowen & seen by the byshop of the dyoces, & left in
leye mens handes & womens, to suche as he knewe for
5 good and catholike folke, that vsed it with deuocion &
sobrenes.   But of truth al such as are founde*n* in *the*
handes of heretikes, they vse to take away.   But they
doe cause none to be burned as farre as euer I coulde

wit, but onely suche as be founden faultie. Wherof many
be sette foorth with euill prologes or gloses, maliciouslye 10
made by Wickliffe and other heretikes.   For no good
manne would (I wene) be so mad to burne vp the byble,
wherin they founde no faulte, nor anye lawe that letted it
to be looked on & read.

[(C) *From the same;* Book III. ch. 16; p. 243.]

Nor I neuer yet heard any reason layd, why it were not
conuenient to haue the byble translated into the
englishe tong, but al those reasons, semed they
neuer so gay & glorious at the first sight : yet when
they were well examined, they myght in effect, 5

There can be
no reson why
the byble
should not be
translated into
englishe.

for ought that I can see, as wel be layde against *the* holy
writers that wrote the scripture in the Hebrue tongue, and
against the blessed euangelistes *tha*t wrote the scripture in
Greke, and against all those in likewise that translated it
oute of euery of those tonges into latine, as to their charge 10
that would well & faithfully translate it oute of latine into
our englishe tong.   For as for that our tong is called bar-
barous, is but a fantasye.   For so is, as euery lerned man
knoweth, euery straunge language to other.   And if they
would call it barayn of wordes, there is no doubte but it is 15
plenteous enough to expresse our myndes in anye thing
wherof one man hath vsed to speke with another.   Nowe,
as touchynge the difficultie which a translatour fyndeth in
expressing well and liuely the sentence of his author, whiche
is hard alwaye to doe so surely but that he shall sometime 20
minyshe eyther of the sentence or of the grace that it bereth
in the formar tong : that poynt hath lyen in their lyght that
haue translated the scrypture alreadye, eyther out of greke

into latiné, or out of hebrue into any of them both; as, by
25 many translaciōns which we rede already, to them that be
learned. appereth. Now as touching the harme that may
growe by suche blynde bayardes as will, whan they reade
the byble in englishe, be more busy than will become them :
They that touche that poynt harpe vpon the right string, &
30 touche truely the great harme that wer likely to growe to
some folke : howe be it, not by the occasion yet of the
english translacion, but by the occasion of theyr own lewdnes and foly, whiche yet were not in my mynde a sufficiente
cause to exclude the translacion, and to put other folke from
35 the benefite therof : but rather to make prouision agaynste
such abuse, & let a good thing goe furth. No wise manne
wer there that woulde put al weapoͧns away because manquellers misuse them. Nor this letted not, as I
sayd, the scripture to be first writen in a vulgare
40 tong. For scripture, as I said before, was not
writen but in a vulgare tonge, suche as the whole

No good thing
ought to be put
awaye because
of the missevse
therof.

people vnderstode, nor in no secrete cyphers, but such
common letters as almost euery man could rede. For neither
was the hebrue nor the greke tong nor the laten, neither
45 any other speche, than such as all *th*e peple spake. And
therfore, if we shold lay that it wer euil done to translate *th*e
scripture into our tong, because it is vulgare and comen to
euery englishe man, than had it been as euill done to translate it into greke or into latin, or to wryte the new testament
50 first in greke, or the old testament in hebrew, because both
those tonges wer as verye vulgare as ours. And yet should
there, by this reason also, not onely the scripture be kepte
out of oure tong, but, ouer that, shoulde the reading therof
be forboden, both al such ley people and all suche priestes
55 too, as can no more than theyr grammer, and verye scantly
that. All which compͧanye, though they can vnderstande

the wordes, be yet as farre from the perceiuing of the sentence in harde and doubtefull textes, as were our weomen if
the scripture were translated to oure own language.	How
be it, of trouth, seldome hath it been seen that any secte of 60
heretikes hath begonne of suche vnlearned folke as nothynge
coulde elles but the language wherein they reead the scripture : but there hathe alway comonly these sectes sprongen
of the pryde of such folke, as had, with the knowledge of *the*
to*n*g, some high persuasion in themselfe of their owne lern- 65
ing beside.	To whose authoritie some other folke haue
soone after, parte of malice, parte of symplenesse, and muche
parte of pleasure and delighte in new-fanglenesse, fallen in,
and encreased the faccion.	But *the* head hath euer comonly
been eyther some prowde learned man, or at the least, beside 70
*th*e language, some proude smaterer in learning.	So *that*
if we should, for feare of heretikes that might hap to growe
thereby, kepe the scripture out of any to*n*g, or out of vnlerned mens ha*n*des, we should for like feare be fayne to
kepe it out of al to*n*ges, & out of vnlerned me*n*s handes to, 75
and wot not who*m* we mighte trust therwith.	Wherfore ther
is, as me thinketh, no remedie but if any good thi*n*g shall
goe foreward, some what must nedes be aduentured.	And

some folke will not fayle to be naughte. Agaynst
A commoditie
ought not to be which thinges prouision must bee made, that as 80
kepte backe for
the harme that muche good maye growe, and as litle harme
may come of it.
come as canne bee deuysed, and not to kepe
the whole commoditie from any hole people, because of
harme that by their owne foly and faulte may come to some
part; as thoughe a lewde surgion woulde cutte of the legge 85
by the knee to kepe the toe from the goute, or cut of a mans
head by the shoulders to kepe him from the toothe-ache.
There is no treatice of scripture so hard but *that* a good vertuous man, or woman eyther, shal somewhat find therin

that shall delyte and encreace their deuocion, besydes this,
that euerye preachinge shall be the more pleasant and fruit-
full vnto the*m* whan they haue in their mind the place of
scrypture that they shall there heare expowned. For though
it bee, as it is in dede, great[1] wisedome for a
preacher to vse discrecion in hys preachyng and
to haue a respecte vnto the qualities and capaci-
ties of his audience, yet letteth *that* nothinge, but that the
whole audience maye without harme haue read & haue
readye the scrypture in mynde, that he shall, in hys preachyng, declare and expowne. For no doute[2] is there, but that
god & his holye spirite hath so prudentlye tempered theyr
speche thorowe the whole corps of scripture, that euery ma*n*
may take good therby & no man harme, but he that wil in
the study therof leane proudly to the foly of hys own wit.
For albeit that Chryst did speake to the people in parables,
and expowned them secretly to hys especiall disciples, &
sometime forbare to tell some thynges to the*m* also, because
they were not as yet hable to beare them : and the apostles,
in lykewyse, didde sometyme spare to speake to some people
the thinges that they dydde not let playnly to speake to
some other, yet letteth all thys nothing the translacion of the
scripture into our own tong no more than in the latine. Nor
it is no cause to kepe the corps of scripture out of the handes
of anye christen people, so many yeres fastly confyrmed in
fayth, because Christ & hys apostles vsed suche prouision in
their vtterance of so stra*n*ge and vnherd misteries, either vnto
Iewes, Paynims, or newly christened folk ; except we would
say that all the exposicions which Chryst made himself vpon
hys owne parables vnto hys secret seruauntes and disciples
withdrawen fro*m* the people, shoulde nowe at thys day be

A precher in his preaching must vse dyscrecion.

---

[1] Printed 'gteat.' [2] Printed 'noute.'

kept in lykewyse from the comons, and no man suffred to
reade or heare them, but those that in hys churche represent
the state & office of hys apostles, whiche ther will (I wote
well) no wyse manne say; consideryng *that* those thinges
which were than comonly most kept from the people, be 125
now most necessary for *the* people to knowe. As it well
appeareth by al such things in effect as our sauiour at *the*
tyme taught his apostles a part. Wherof I would not, for
my mynde, witholde the profite that one good deuoute vnlerned ley man might take by the reading, not for the harme 130
that an hundred heretikes would fall in by theyr own wilful
abusion, no more than oure sauiour letted, for the weale of
suche as woulde bee with hys grace of hys little chosen flock,

i. Peter. ii. to come into thys world and be *lapis offensionis &
petra scandali*, the stone of stumbling and the stone 135
of falling, and ruine to all the wilful wretches in the world beside. Finally, me thynketh that the constitucion prouincial of
whiche we spake right now, hath determined thys question alreadye. For whan the cleargie therein agreed that the englyshe
bybles should remayne whiche were translated afore Wick- 140
liffes dayes, they consequentlye dydde agree that to haue the
byble in englishe was none hurte. And in that they forbade
any new translacion to be read till it wer approued by the
bishoppes: it appeareth well therby, that theyr intent was
that the byshop should approue it if he found it faultlesse, 145
and also of reason amend it where it wer faultye; but if the
manne wer an heretike that made it, or the faultes such and
so many, as it were more eth to make it all newe than mend
it. As it happed for bothe poyntes in the translacion of
Tyndall. Now if it so be that it woulde happely be thought 150
not a thyng metely to be aduentured to set all on a flushe at
ones, and dashe rashelye out holye scrypture in euerye lewde
felowes teeth: yet thynketh me ther might such a modera-

cion be taken therein, as neither good vert[u]eous ley folke
155 shoulde lacke it, nor rude and rashe braynes
abuse it. For it might be, w*it*h diligence, well
and truelye translated by some good catholike and well
learned man, or by dyuers diuiding the labour among them,
and after conferring theyr seueral parties together eche with
160 other. And after that might the worke be alowed and approued by the ordinaries, and by theyr authorities so put
vnto prent, as all the copies should come whole vnto the
bysshoppes hande. Which he may, after his discrecion and
wisedom, deliuer to such as he perceiueth honest, sad, & ver-
165 teous, with a good monicion & fatherly cou*n*sell to vse it
reuerently with humble heart & lowly mind, rather sekyng
therin occasion of deuocion than of despicion. And pro-
uiding as much as may be, that the boke be, after *th*e de-
cease of the partie, brought again & and reuerently restored
170 vnto *th*e ordinarye. So that, as nere as maye be deuised, no
man haue it but of *th*e ordinaries hande, & by hym thought
& reputed for such as shalbe likly to vse it to gods honor
& merite of his own soule. Amo*n*g who*m* if any be proued
after to haue abused it, tha*n* *th*e use therof to be forbode*n*
175 him, eyther for euer, or till he be waxe*n* wyser. 'By our
lady,' q*uod* your fre*n*d, 'this way misliketh not me. But
who should sette the price of the booke?' Forsoth, q*uod* I,
that reke*n* I a thing of litle force. For neither wer it a great
matter for any man in maner to giue a grote or twain aboue
180 the mene price for a boke of so greate profite, nor for the
bysshoppe to geue them all free, wherin he myght serue his
dyoces with the cost of x.li., I thynke, or xx. markes. Which
summe, I dare saye, there is no bishop but he wold be glad
to bestow about a thing *that* might do his hole dyoces so
185 special a pleasure w*it*h such a spirituall profit. 'By my
trouth,' q*uod* he, 'yet wene I *that* *th*e peple would grudge to

Good cou*n*sel.

haue it on this wise deliuered the*m* at *th*e bishops hande, &
had leuer pay for it to *th*e pri*n*ter, tha*n* haue it of the byshop
free.'   It might so happen w*i*t*h* some, q*uod* I.   But yet in
myne opinion ther wer in that maner more wilfulnes tha*n* 190
wisedom or any good mind, in suche as would not be conte*n*t so to receiue the*m*.   And therfore I wold think, in good
faith, *tha*t it wold so fortune in few.   But, for god, the more
dout would be, lest they would grudge & hold themself sore
greued, that wold require it & wer happely denied it: which 195
I suppose would not often happe*n* vnto any honest hous-
holder, to be by his discrecio*n* reuere*n*tly red in his house.
But though it wer not taken to euery lewde lad in his own
ha*n*des to rede a litle rudely wha*n* he list, & than cast the
boke at his heles, or amo*n*g other such as himselfe, to kepe 200

A pot parlia-
ment.   a *quotlibet* & a pot parlame*n*t vpo*n*, I trow there
wil no wise ma*n* find a faulte therin.   'Ye spake
right now of *th*e Iewes, among whom *th*e hole peple haue,
ye say, the scripture in their ha*n*ds.   And ye thought it no
reason *tha*t we shold reken christe*n* me*n* lesse worthy therto 205
than the*m*.   Wherin I am as ye see of your own opinion.'
But yet wold god we had *th*e like reuere*n*ce to *th*e scripture
of god *tha*t they haue.   For I assure you I haue heard very
worshipfull folke say which haue been in their houses, *tha*t a
man could not hyre a Iewe to sit down vpon his byble of *th*e 210

How reue-
rentlye the
Iewe doeth vse
the scripture.   olde testame*n*t, but he taketh it w*i*t*h* gret reuerence in ha*n*d whan he wil rede, & reuerently
layeth it vp agayn whan he hath doone.   Wheras
we (god forgeue vs) take a litle regarde to sit down on our
byble, w*i*t*h* the old testament & the new too.   Which homely 215
handeling, as it pro*c*edeth of litle reuere*n*ce, so doth it more
& more enge*n*dre in *th*e mind a neglige*n*ce & contempt of
gods holi words. We find also *tha*t among *th*e Iewes, though
al their whole byble was write*n* in their vulgare to*n*g, & those

220 bokes therof, wherin their lawes wer write*n*, wer vsuall in euerye mans handes, as thinges *that* God wold haue commonly knowen, repeted, & kept in reme*m*brance : yet wer ther again certain parts therof which *the* co*m*mon peple of *the* Iewes of old time, both of reuerence & for the difficultie,

225 did forbeare to medle w*ith*. But now, sith *the* veyle of the te*m*ple is broke*n* asunder, *that* diuided, among *th*e Iewes, *the* peple from *the* sight of *the* secretes, and *that* god had se*n*t his holy spirit to be assistent w*ith* his hole church to teche all necessary trouth ; though it

The vayle of the temple is broken asunder.

230 maye therfore be *the* better suffred *that* no part of holy scripture wer kept out of honest ley me*n*s ha*n*des, yet wold I *that* no part therof shoulde co*m*e in theirs, which, to their own harme & happely their neybours to, would ha*n*dle it ouer homely, & be to bold and busy therw*ith*. And also

235 though holye scripture be, as ye saide whyleere, a medicine for him *that* is sick, & fode for him *that* is hole : yet sith the*r* is many a body sore soule-sicke *that* taketh himself for hole, & in holy scripture is a̗n whole feast of so much diuers vyand, that after *th*e affection & state of so*n*dry stomakes,

240 one may take harme by *th*e selfsame that shall do another good ; and sicke folke often haue such a corrupt tallage in their tast, *that* they most like *that* mete that is most vnholesome for the*m* ; it were not therfore, as me thinketh, vnreasonable that *th*e ordinary who*m* god hath in the dyoces

245 appointed for *th*e chief phisicio*n*, to discerne betwene *th*e hole & the sicke, & betwene disease & disease, should after hys wisedom & discrecio*n* appoynt euery body their part, as he shoülde p*er*ceiue to bee good & holesome for the*m*. And therfore, as he should not fayle to find many a man to

250 who*m* he might commit all *the* hole, so, to say *the* trouth, I can see none harme therin, though he shold co*m*mit vnto some ma*n* the gospel of Mathew, Marke, or Luke, whome

he shoulde yet forbydde the gospell of S. Iohn, and suffer
some to reade *the* actes of *the* apostles, who*m* he woulde not
suffer to medle w*ith* the Apocalips.   Manye wer there, I 255
thinke, *that* shoulde take much profit by saint Paules epistle
ad Ephesios, wherin he geueth good counsaile to euery kind
of people, & yet should find litle fruit for their vnderstanding

The epistle to
the Romanes
conteyneth
hygh diffi-
culties.
in hys epystle *ad Romanos,* conteynyng suche
hygh dyfficulties as verye fewe lerned men can 260
very wel attayne.   And in likewise would it be
in diuers other partes of the byble, aswell in the
olde testame*n*t as the newe: so that, as I say: though the
bishop might vnto some ley man betake and commit with
good aduise & instruccion ·the hole byble to rede: yet might 265
he to some manne well and with reason restrayne the read-
yng of some parte, and from some busy-body the medling
with any parte at al, more than he shal heare in sermons
sette out and declared vnto hym; and in lykewise to take the
byble away from such folke agayn, as be proued by their 270
blynde presumpcion to abuse the *o*ccasyon of their profitte
vnto theyr owne hurte and harme.   And thus may the bishoppe order the scripture in our handes, with as good
reason as the father doeth by his discrecion appoynte which
of his childre*n* may, for hys sadnes, kepe a knife to cut his 275
meate, and which shal, for his wanto*n*nes, haue his knife
taken fro*m* him for cutting of hys fyngers.   And thus am I
bold w*ith*out preiudice of other mens iudgement, to shew
you my mind in this matter; how the scripture might, without great perill, & not without great profite, be brought into 280
oure tong, & taken to ley men & women both, not yet meaning therby but *that* the whole byble might for my minde be
suffered to be spred abrode in englishe.   But if that wer
so·much douted, *that* percase al might thereby be letted:
th*e*n woulde I rather haue vsed such moderacion as I speake 285

of, or some such other as wyser men can better deuise.
Howbeit, vpon that I read late in the pistle that the kinges
highnes translated into english of his own, which hys grace
made in latine, aunsweryng to the letter of Luther : my mind
190 geueth me that his maiestie is of his blessed zele so mynded
to mooue thys matter vnto *the* prelates of the clergie, among
whom I haue perceiued some of the greatest and of the best
of their own mindes well inclinable thereto alredy, that we
ley people shal in this matter, ere long time passe, except
195 the faulte be founde in oure-selfe, be well and fully satisfyed
and content. ‘In good fayth,’ quod he, ‘that will in my
mynde be very well done. And now am I for my mind
in al this matter fully content & satisfied.’ Wel, q*uod* I,
than wil we to diner, & the remenant wil we finishe after
300 diner. And therw*ith* went we to meate.

¶ The end of the thirde boke.

[(D) *From ‘The Confutacion of Tyndales aunswere, made*
Anno 1532;’ Book III ; ‘Workes,’ p. 448.]

I shall shew you fyrst an example therof in the fyrst
chapiter of the ghospell of saint Ihon, whych place Tyndall
hath wronge translated also ; for what cause, the deuyll and
he knoweth. For Tyndall is not ignorant of that article,
5 neither the greke nor the englishe, and maketh hymself as
though he translated the new testament out of greke. These
wordes be the wordes of the ghospell in that place, after
Tyndalles translacion.
. ¶ Thys is the recorde of Iohn, when the Iewes sent

priestès and leuites fro*m* Hierusalem to aske him what art 10
thou, and he confessed and denyed not & sayed playnely,
' I am not Christ.' And thei asked him, ' what the*n*, art thou
Helias ?' And.he sayd, ' I am not.' ' Arte thou a prophete ?'
And he aunswered, ' no.'

¶ I woulde not here note by. the way, that Tyndal here 15
tra*n*slateth *no* for *nay*, for it is but a trifle and mistaking
of *th*e englishe worde : sauing that ye shoulde see *th*at he,
whych in two so plain englishe wordes, and so commen as
is *naye* and *no*, can not tell when he should take the tone,
and whe*n* the tother, is not, for tra*n*slating into englishe, 20
a man very mete. For the vse of those two wordes in
au*n*swerring to a question is this. *No*[1] aunswereth the
question framed by the affirmatiue. As for ensample, if a
manne should aske Tindall hymselfe : ' ys an heretike mete
to translate holy scripture into englishe ?' Lo, to thys 25
question, if he will aunswere trew englishe, he muste aunswere *nay* and not *no*. But and if the question be asked
hym thus, lo : ' Is not an heretyque mete to translate holy
scripture into english ?' To this questio*n*, lo, if he wil
au*n*swer true english, he must au*n*swere *no* & not *nay*. 30
And a lyke difference is there betwene these two ad-
uerbes, *ye* and *yes*. For if the questeion bee framed
vnto Tindall by thaffirmatiue in thys fashion : ' If an
heretique falsely translate the newe testament into englishe,
to make hys false heresyes seeme *th*e worde of Godde, be 35
hys bookes worthy to be burned ?' To this question asked
in thys wyse, yf he wil aunswere true englishe, he must
aunswere *ye* and not *yes*. But nowe if the question be
asked hym thus, lo, by the negatiue : ' If an heretike falsely
translate the newe testament in-to englishe, to make hys 40

---

[1] Read ' nay '; but the mistake is More's own.

false heresyes seme the word of God, be not his bokes well
worthy to be burned?' To thys question in thys fashion
framed, if he wyll aunswere trew englyshe, he maye not
aunswere *ye*, but he must aunswere *yes*, and say, ' yes, mary,
45 be they, bothe the translacion and the translatour, and al
that wyll holde wyth them.' And thys thing, lo, though it
be no great matter: yet I haue thought it good to giue
Tindall warning of, because I would haue him write true
one way or other, *tha*t though I ca*n* not make him by no
50 meane to write true matter, I would haue him yet at the
lest wise write true englishe.

XVIII.

SIR THOMAS ELYOT.

A.D. 1531.

SIR THOMAS ELYOT, an eminent physician of the reign of Henry VIII, was born about 1495, and died in 1546. His principal works are 'The Castle of Health,' on the subjects of diet, regimen, and exercise, and 'The Governour,' the first edition of which appeared in 1531. For the rest, I may quote the words of Hallam, in his 'Introduction to the Literature of Europe,' Pt. I. ch. vii. § 31: 'The author was a gentleman of good family, and had been employed by the king in several embassies. ... The plan of Sir Thomas Elyot in his "Governor," as laid down in his dedication to the king, is bold enough. It is "to describe in our vulgar tongue the form of a just public weal, which matter I have gathered as well of the sayings of most noble authors Greek and Latin, as by mine own experience, I being continually pained in some daily affairs of the public weal of this most noble realm almost from my childhood." But it is far from answering to this promise. After a few pages on the superiority of regal over every other government, he passes to the subject of education, not of a prince only, but any gentleman's son, with which he fills up the rest of his first book,' &c. See the whole passage. The 'Governour' is divided into three books, and has been frequently reprinted. I give the seventeenth chapter of the first book entire, and a part of the eighteenth chapter, from the rare first edition of 1531. The mark / answers nearly to our modern comma.

[From ' The firste boke' of the ' Gouernour.']

Cap. XVII. Exercises / whereby shulde growe both recreation and profite.

WRastlynge is a very good exercise in the begynnynge of youthe / so that it be with one that is equall in strengthe / or some-what vnder / & that the place be softe / that in fallinge theyr bodies be nat brused.

5   There be diuers maners of wrastlinges / but the beste / as well for helthe of body / as for exercise of   wrastlynge. strengthe is: whan layeng mutually their handes   Galenus. one ouer a-nothers necke / with the other hande they holde faste eche other by the arme / and claspyng theyr legges 10 to-gether / they inforce them-selfes with strengthe & agilitie / to throwe downe eche other / whiche is also praysed by Galene.   And vndoubtedly it shall be founde profitable in warres / in case that a capitayne shall be constrayned to cope with his aduersary hande to hande / hauyng his weapon 15 broken or loste.   Also it hath ben sene / that the waiker persone / by the sleight of wrastlyng / hath ouerthrowen the strenger / almost or he coulde fasten on the other any violent stroke.   Also rennyng is bothe a good exercise and a laudable solace.   It is written of   Rennynge. 20 Epaminondas the valiant capitayne of Thebanes / who as well in vertue and prowesse / as in leringe surmounted all noble-men of his tyme.: that daily he exercised him-selfe in the mornyng with rennyng and leapyng: in the euening in wrastling : to the intent that likewise in armure he mought 25 the more strongly / embracinge his aduersary / put hym in daunger.   And also that in the chase rennyng and leaping /

he mought either ouertake his enemye : or beyng pursued /
if extreme nede required / escape him.   Semblably before
him dyd the worthy Achilles / for whiles his shippes laye
at rode / he suffred nat his people to slomber in ydle- 30
nesse / but daily exercised them and him-selfe in rennyng /
wherin he was moste excellent and passed all other : and
therfore Homere throughout all his warke / calleth hym
swifte-foote Achilles.   The great Alexander beyng a childe /
excelled all his companions in rennyng.   wherfore on a 35
tyme / one demaunded of hym / if he wolde renne at the
great game of Olympus : wherto out of all partes of Grece /
came the most actife and valiant persons to assay maistries :
whervnto Alexander answered in this fourme : I wold very
gladly renne ther / if I were sure to renne with kinges : for 40
if I shulde contende with a priuate person / hauing respect
to our bothe astates / our victories shulde nat be equall.
Nedes muste rennynge be taken for a laudable exercise /
sens one of the mooste noble capitaynes of all the Romanes /
toke his name of rennyng / and was called *Papirius Cursor:* 45
which is in englisshe / Papirius the Renner.   And also the
valiant Marius the Romane / whan he had bene seuen tymes
Consul / and was of the age of foure score yeres / exercised
him-selfe dayly amonge the yonge men of Rome / in suche
wyse / that there resorted people out of ferre partes / to 50
beholde the strength & agilitie of that olde Consul / wherin
he compared with the yonge and lusty soudiours.

    There is an exercise / whiche is right profitable in ex-
treme daunger of warres / but by cause there
Swymmynge.
semeth to be some perile in the lernynge ther-of : 55
And also it hath nat bene of longe tyme moche vsed / specially amonge noble-men : perchance some reders wyll litle
esteme it : I meane swymmynge.   But nat-withstandyng / if
they reuolue the imbecilitie of our nature / the hasardes and

60 daungers of batayle : with the examples / which shall herafter be showed / they wyll (I doubt nat) thinke it as necessary to a capitayne or man of armes / as any that I haue
yet rehersed. The Romanes / who aboue all thinges / had
moste in estimation martiall prowesse : they had a large and
65 spaciouse felde withoute the citie of Rome / whiche was
called Marces felde / in latine *Campus Martius.* wherin the
youth of the citie was exercised : this felde adioyned to the
ryuer of Tyber to the intent that as well men as children
shulde wasshe and refresshe them in the water after their
70 labours / as also lerne to swymme : And nat men & children only / but also the horses : that by suche vsaige they
shulde more aptly and boldly passe ouer great riuers / and
be more able to resist or cutte the waues / & not be aferde
of pirries or great stormes. For it hath ben often tymes
75 sene / that by the good swimminge of horse / many men
haue ben saued / and contrary wise / by a timorouse royle /
where the water hath vneth come to his bely / his legges
hath foltred : wherby many a good and propre man hath
perisshed. what benefite receiued the hole citie
80 of Rome / by the swymmynge of Oratius Cocles!   Oratius Cocles.
whiche is a noble historie / and worthy to be remembred.

   After the Romanes had expelled Tarquine their kynge / as
I haue before remembred / he desired ayde of Porsena /
kynge of Thuscanes / a noble and valiant prince / to re-
85 couer eftsones his realme and dignitie : who with a great
and puissant hoste / besieged the citie of Rome / and so
sodaynely and sharpely assaulted it / that it lacked but litle /
that he ne had entred in-to the citie with his host / ouer the
bridge called *Sublicius :* where encountred with hym this
90 Oratius with a fewe Romanes : And whiles this noble capitayne being alone / with an incredible strengthe resisted all
the hoste of Porcena / that were on the bridge / he com-

maunded the bridge to be broken behynde hym / where-
with-all the Thuscanes theron standyng fell in-to the great
riuer of Tiber / but Oratius all armed lepte in-to the water 95
& swamme to his company / al-be-it that he was striken
with many arowes & dartes / & also greuouslye wounded.
Nat-withstandynge by his noble courage and feate of swymmyng / he saued the citie of Rome from perpetuall seruitude /
whiche was likely to haue ensued by the returne of the 100
proude Tarquine.

Howe moche profited the feate in swymmynge to the
Julius Cæsar swymmyng. valiant Julius Cesar! who at the bataile of Alex-
andri / on a bridge beinge abandoned of his
people for the multitude of his enemyes / whiche oppressed 105
them / whan he moughte no lenger sustaine the shotte of
dartes and arowes / he boldly lepte in-to the see / and
diuynge vnder the water / escaped the shotte / and swamme
the space of .CC. pasis to one of his shyppes / drawynge his
cote-armure with his teethe after hym / that his enemies 110
shulde nat attayne it.   And also that it moughte some-what
defende hym from theyr arowes: And that more meruaile
was / holdynge in his hande aboue the water / certayne
lettres / whiche a litle before he had receyued from the
Senate.   115

Before hym Sertorius / who of the spanyardes was named
Sertorius. the seconde Anniball for his prowesse / in the
bataile that Scipio faughte agayne the Cimbres /
which inuaded Fraunce / Sertorius when by negligence of
his people / his enemyes preuailed / and put his hoste to 120
the warse / he beinge sore wounded / and his horse beinge
lost / armed as he was in a gesseron / holdyng in his
handes a tergate / and his sworde / he lepte in-to the
ryuer of Rone / whiche is wonderfull swyfte / and swymmyng agayne the streme / came to his company / nat 125

XVIII. THE FIRSTE BOKE OF THE GOUERNOUR. 199

withoute greate[1] wondryng of all his enemies / whiche stode
and behelde hym.

The great kynge Alexander lamented / that he had nat
lerned to swimme : For in Inde whan he wente agayne the
130 puissaunt kynge Porus / he was constrayned / in folowynge
his entreprise / to conuay his hoste ouer a ryuer of wonderfull greatnesse : than caused he his horse-men to gage the
water / wherby he firste perceiued / that it came to the
brestis of the horsis / and in the myddle of the streme / the
135 horsis wente in water to the necke : wherwith the fotemen
beinge aferde / none of them durst auenture to passe ouer
the ryuer : That perceiuynge Alexander / with a dolorouse
maner in this wyse lamented : 'O howe moste vnhappy am
I of all other / that haue nat or this tyme lerned to swymme!'
140 And therwith he pulled a tergate from one of his souldiours /
and castynge it in-to the water / standynge on it / with his
spere conuaied hym-selfe with the streme / and gouernyng the
tergate wysely / broughte hym-selfe vnto the other side of the
water : wherof his people beinge abasshed / some assayed
145 to swymme / some holdyng faste by the horses / other by
speares / and other lyke weapons / many vpon fardels & trusses /
gate ouer the ryuer : in so moche as nothinge was perisshed
saue[2] a litle bagage / and of that no great quantitie lost.

what vtilitie was shewed to be in swymmynge at the firste
150 warres / whiche the Romanes had agayne the Carthagi-
nensis! it happened a bataile to be on the see betwene
them / where they of Carthage / beinge vainquisshed /
wolde haue sette vp their sailes to haue fledde / but that
perceiuynge diuers yonge Romanes / they threw them-selfes
155 in-to the see / & swymmynge vnto the shippes / they enforced theyr ennemies to stryke on lande / and there assaulted

---

[1] Printed 'greatte.'   [2] Printed 'sauue.'

them so asprely / that the capitaine of the Romanes / called
Luctatius / mought easily take them.

Nowe beholde what excellent commoditie is in the feate
of swymmyng / sens no kyng / be he neuer so puissaunt or 160
perfecte in the experience of warres / may assure hym-selfe
from the necessities / whiche fortune sowethe amonge men
that be mortall. And sens on the helth and saulfe garde of
a noble capitayne / often tymes dependeth the weale of a
realme / nothing shulde be kepte from his knowlege / wherby 165
his persone may be in euery ieoperdie preserued.

Amonge these exercises / it shall be conuenient to lerne
to handle sondrye waipons / specially the sworde
and the batayle-axe : whiche be for a noble-man
moste conuenient.   170

Defence with
waipons.

But the moste honorable exercise in myne opinion / and
that besemeth the astate of euery noble persone /
is to ryde suerly & clene / on a great horse and
a roughe / whiche vndoubtedly nat onely im-
porteth a maiestie & drede to inferiour persones / beholding 175
him aboue the common course of other men / dauntyng a
fierce and cruell beaste / but also is no litle socour / as well
in pursuete of enemies & confoundyng them / as in escapyng
imminent daunger / whan wisedome therto exhorteth. Also
a stronge and hardy horse dothe some-tyme more domage 180
vnder his maister / than he with al his waipon : and also
setteth forwarde the stroke / and causethe it to lighte with
more violence.

Rydynge and
vauntynge of
horsis.

Bucephal / the horse of great kynge Alexander / who
suffred none on his backe saulfe onely his maister 185
/ at the bataile of Thebes beinge sore wounded /
wolde nat suffre the kinge to departe from hym to a-nother
horse / but persistyng in his furiouse courage / wonderfully
continued out the bataile / with his fete & tethe betyng

Bucephal.

·90 downe & destroyenge many enemies. And many semblable
maruailes of his strength be shewed. wherfore Alexander /
after the horse was slayne / made in remembrance of hym a
citie in the countray of India / and called it Bucephal / in
perpetual memorie of so worthy a horse : which in his lyfe
95 had so well serued hym.

what wonderfull enterprises dyd Julius Cesar achieue by
the helpe of his horse ! whiche nat onely dyd excell all other
horsis in fiercenesse and swyfte rennynge / but also was in
some parte discrepant in figure from other horsis / hauing
100 his fore hoeues like to the feete of a man. And in that
figure Plinius writeth / that he sawe hym kerued before the
temple of Venus. Other remembrance there is of diuers
horsis / by whose monstruous power / men dyd exploite
incredible affaires : but by cause the reporte of them con-
105 tayneth thinges impossible / and is nat writen by any approued autour : I will nat in this place reherce them : sauyng
that it is yet supposed / that the castell of Arun-
dell in Sussex / was made by one Beauuize /   Arundell.
erle of South-hamton / for a monument of his horse called
210 Arundell : whiche in ferre countrayes had saued his maister
from many periles. Nowe considerynge the vtilitie in rydynge greate[1] horses / hit shall be necessary (as I haue
sayd) that a gentilman do lerne to ride a great and fierce
horse whiles he is tender and the brawnes and sinewes of his
215 thighes nat fully consolidate.

There is also a ryght good exercise / which is also expedient to lerne : whiche is named the vauntynge of a horse :
that is to lepe on him at euery side withoute stiroppe or
other helpe / specially whiles the horse is goynge. And
220 beinge therin experte / than armed at all poyntes to assay

[1] Printed ' greatte.'

the same / the commoditie wherof is so manifest / that I
nede no further to declare it.

Cha. XVIII. The auncient huntyng of Greekes and Romanes.

BVt nowe wyll I procede to write of exercises / whiche be
nat vtterly reproued of noble auctours / if they be vsed
with oportunitie and in measure / I meane huntyng / hauking / and daunsyng.

  .   .   .   .

Al-be-it Pompei / Sertorius / & diuers other noble Romanes / 5
whan they were in Numidia / Libia / & suche other countrayes / which nowe be called Barbary & Morisco / in the
vacation season from warres / they hunted lions / liberdes /
& suche other bestis / fierce and sauage : to thentent therby
to exercise them-selfes & their souldiours. But all-myghty 10
god be thanked / in this realme be no suche cruel bestis to
be pursued. Not-withstandyng in the huntyng of redde
dere and falowe / mought be a great parte of semblable
exercise / vsed by noble-men / specially in forestis / which
be spaciouse : if they wold vse but a fewe nombre of 15
houndes / onely to harborowe or rouse the game : and by
their yornyng to gyue knowlege / whiche way it fleeth : the
remenant· of the disporte to be in pursuyng with iauelyns
and other waipons / in maner of warre. And to them /
whiche in this hunting do shewe moste prowesse and acty- 20
uytie : a garlande or some other lyke token / to be gyuen
in signe of victorie / and with a ioyfull maner to be broughte
in the presence of him that is chiefe in the company : there
to receiue condigne prayse for their good endeuour. I dispraise nat the huntynge of the foxe with rennynge houndes : 25

but it is nat to be compared to the other hunting in commoditie of exercise. Therfore it wolde be vsed in the deepe wynter / whan the other game is vnseasonable.

Huntyng of the hare with grehoundes / is a righte good
30 solace for men that be studiouse : or them to whom nature hath nat gyuen personage or courage apte for the warres. And also for gentilwomen / which fere neither sonne nor wynde for appairing their beautie. And perauenture they shall be there-at lasse idell / than they shulde be at home
35 in their chambres.

Kylling of dere with bowes or grehundes serueth well for the potte (as is the commune saynge) and therefore it muste of necessitie be some-tyme vsed. But it contayneth therin no commendable solace or exercise / in comparison to the
40 other fourme of hunting / if it be diligently perceiued.

As for haukyng / I can finde no notable remembrance / that it was vsed of auncient tyme amonge noble princes. I call auncient tyme before a thousande yeres passed / sens which tyme vertue and noblenesse hath rather decayed than
45 increased. Nor I coulde neuer knowe who founde firste that disporte.

Plinius makethe mention in his .viij. boke of the historie of nature / that in the partes of grece / called Thracia / men and haukes / as it were by a confederacie / toke byrdes to-
50 gether in this wyse : The men sprange the birdes out of the busshes / and the haukes sorynge ouer them / bete them doune : so that the men mought easily take them. And than dyd the men departe equally the praye with the faukons : whiche beinge well serued / eftsones and of a cus-
55 tome repayred to suche places / where beinge a-lofte / they perceyued men to that purpose assembled. By which rehersall of Plinius / we may coniecte / that from Thracia came this disporte of hauking. And I doubt nat but many other /

as wel as I haue sene a semblable experience of wilde hobies /
whiche in some countrayes that be champaine / wyll sore 60
and lie a-lofte / houeringe ouer larkes and quailes / & kepe
them downe on the grounde / whiles they / whiche awayte
on the praye do take them.   But in what wise / or where-
so-euer the beginninge of hauking was / suerly it is a right
delectable solace / thoughe ther-of commeth nat so moche 65
vtilitie (concerning exercise) as there dothe of huntinge.
But I wolde our faukons mought be satisfied with the diui-
sion of their pray / as the faukons of Tracia were / that they
neded nat to deuour and consume the hennes of this realme /
in suche nombre / that vnneth it be shortly considred / & that 70
faukons be brought to a more homely diete / it is right likely
that within a shorte space of yeres / our familiar pultrie shall
be as scarce / as be nowe partriche and fesaunt.   I speake
nat this in dispraise of the faukons: but of them whiche
kepeth them like coknayes.   75

XIX.

LORD SURREY.

ABOUT A.D. 1540.

HENRY HOWARD, Earl of Surrey, was born about A.D. 1518[1].
His grandfather had the command of the English army at the
battle of Flodden Field, and his father, Thomas Howard, third
Duke of Norfolk, was uncle to the Catharine Howard who is
found in the list of the wives of Henry VIII. Father and son
were arrested on the 12th of December, 1546, and lodged in the
Tower, on the charge of having quartered the royal arms with
their own. The young poet was executed Jan. 19, 1547, but his
father's life was saved by a reprieve, and by the opportune death
of the king a few days later, Jan. 28. Surrey's chief praise is that
he was the earliest writer of decasyllabic blank verse, into which
metre he rendered parts of the Æneid, with much success. His
sonnets and other similar writings are natural and graceful, and
are in general beautifully melodious. The first extract is from
' Certain Bokes of Virgiles Aenæis turned into English meter by
the right honorable lorde, Henry Earle of Surrey,' and the rest
are from ' Songes and Sonettes, written by the ryght honorable
Lorde Henry Haward [*sic*] late Earle of Surrey, and other,' both
of which were first printed by Richard Tottell in the year 1557;
the former on the 21st of June, and the latter (generally known
as ' Tottell's Miscellany') on the 5th of the same month.

[1] Some say 1516; but the portrait by Titian, engraved in ' Lodge's Por-
traits,' has the inscription ' Anno domini 1526, ætatis sve 29.'

[(A) *Part of Book II of the Æneid.*]

Us caitifes then a far more dredful chaunce
Befell, that trobled our vnarmed brestes.
Whiles Laocon, that chosen was by lot   255
Neptunus priest, did sacrifice a bull
Before the holy Altar, sodenly
From Tenedon, behold ! in circles great
By the calme seas come fletyng adders twaine,
Which plied towardes the shore (I lothe to tell)   260
With rered brest lift vp aboue the seas :
Whoes bloody crestes aloft the waues were seen :
The hinder parte swamme hidden in the flood :
Their grisly backes were linked manifold :
With sound of broken waues they gate the strand,   265
With gloing eyen, tainted with blood and fire :
Whoes waltring tongs did lick their hissing mouthes.
We fled away, our face the blood forsoke.
But they with gate direct to Lacon ran.
And first of all eche serpent doth enwrap   270
The bodies small of his two tender sonnes :
Whoes wretched limmes they byt, and fed theron.
Then raught they hym, who had his wepon caught
To rescue them, twise winding him about,
With folded knottes, and circled tailes, his wast.   275
Their scaled backes did compasse twise his neck,
Wyth rered heddes aloft, and stretched throtes.
He with his handes straue to vnloose the knottes :
Whose sacred fillettes all be-sprinkled were
With filth of gory blod and venim rank.   280
And to the sterres such dredfull shoutes he sent,

Like to the sound the roring bull fourth loowes,
Which from the halter wounded doth astart,
The swaruing axe when he shakes from his neck.
The serpentes tw[a]ine with hasted traile they glide   285
To Pallas temple, and her towres of heighte:
Under the feete of which, the Goddesse stern,
Hidden behinde her targettes bosse, they crept.
New gripes of dred then pearse our trembling brestes.
They sayd, Lacons desertes had derely bought   290
His hainous dede, that pearced had with stele
The sacred bulk, and throwen the wicked launce:
The people cried with sondry greeing shoutes,
To bring the horse to Pallas temple bliue,
In hope thereby the Goddesse wrath tappease.   295
We cleft the walles and closures of the towne;
Wherto all helpe, and vnderset the feet
With sliding rolles, and bound his neck with ropes.
This fatall gin thus ouerclambe our walles,
Stuft with armd men: about the which there ran   300
Children and maides, that holly carolles sang.
And well were they whoes hands might touch the cordes.
With thretning chere thus slided through our town
The subtil tree, to Pallas temple ward.
O natiue land, Ilion, and of the Goddes   305
The mansion place!   O warrlik walles of Troy!
Fowr times it stopt in thentrie of our gate:
Fowr times the harnesse clattred in the womb.
But we goe on, vnsound of memorie,
And blinded eke by rage perseuer still.   310
This fatal monster in the fane we place.

    Cassandra then, inspired with Phebus sprite,
Her prophetes lippes, yet neuer of vs leeued,
Disclosed eft, forespeking thinges to come.

We wretches, loe, that last day of our life,   315
With bowes of fest the town and temples deck.
    With this the skie gan whirle about the sphere:
The cloudy night gan thicken from the sea,
With mantells spred that cloked earth and skies,
And eke the treason of the Grekish guile.   320
The watchemen lay disperst, to take their rest,
Whoes werried li*m*mes sound slepe had then opprest:
When well in order comes the Grecian fleet,
From Tenedon toward the costes well knowne,
By frendly silence of the quiet moone.   325
When the Kinges ship put fourth his mark of fire,
Sinon, preserued by froward destinie,
Let fou[r]th the Grekes enclosed in the womb,
The closures eke of pine by stealth vnpind.
Whereby the Grekes restored were to aire,   330
With ioy down hasting from the hollow tree.
With cordes let down did slide vnto the ground
The great captaines, Sthenel, and Thesander,
The fierce Ulisses, Athamas and Thoas,
Machaon first, and then King Menolae,   335
Opeas eke that did the engin forge.
By cordes let fal fast gan they slide adown:
And streight inuade the town yburied then
With wine and slepe.   And first the watch is slain,
Then gates vnfold to let their fellowes in.   340
They ioyne them-selues with the coniured bandes.
It was the time, when graunted from the godds
The first slepe crepes most swete in wery folk.
Loe! in my dreame before mine eies, me thought,
With rufull chere I sawe where Hector stood: 345
Out of whoes eies there gushed streames of teares,
Drawn at a cart as he of late had be:

Distained with bloody dust, whoes feet were bowlne
With the streight cordes wherwith they haled him.
Ay me! what one! that Hector how vnlike,   350
Which erst returnd clad with Achilles spoiles:
Or when he threw into the Grekish shippes
The Troian flame!   So was his beard defiled,
His crisped lockes al clustred with his blood:
With all such wounds, as many he receiued   355
About the walls of that his natiue town.
Whome franckly thus, me thought, I spake vnto,
With bitter teres and dolefull deadly voice,
'O Troyan light, O only hope of thine:
What lettes so long thee staid? or from what costes, 360
Our most desired Hector, doest thou come?
Whom, after slaughter of thy many frends,
And trauail[1] of the people and thy town,
Alweried (lord) how gladly we behold!
What sory chaunce hath staind thy liuely face?   365
Or why see I these woundes (alas) so wide?'
He answeard nought, nor in my vain demaundes
Abode: but from the bottom of his brest
Sighing he sayd: 'flee, flee, O Goddesse son,
And saue thee from the furie of this flame.   370
Our enmies now ar maisters of the walles:
And Troye town now falleth from the top.
Sufficeth that is done for Priams reigne.
If force might serue to succor Troye town,
This right hand well mought haue ben her defense.   375
But Troye now commendeth to thy charge
Her holy reliques, and her priuy Gods.
Them ioyne to thee, as felowes of thy fate.

---

[1] Old text 'trauaiil.'

Large walles rere thow for them.   For so thou shalt,
After time spent in thouerwandred flood.'   380
This sayd, he brought fourth Vesta in his hands,
Her fillettes eke, and euerlasting flame.

. . . .

To Priams palace crye did cal vs then.   570
Here was the fight right hideous to behold:
As though there had no battail ben but there,
Or slaughter made els-where throughout the town.
A fight of rage and furie there we saw.
The Grekes toward the palace rushed fast,   575
And couerd with engines the gates beset,
And rered vp ladders against the walles,
Under the windowes scaling by their steppes,
Fenced with sheldes in their left hands, wheron
They did receiue the dartes, while their righthands   580
Griped for hold thembatel of the wall.
The Troyans on the tother part rend down
The turrets hye, and eke the palace roofe:
With such weapons they shope them to defend,
Seing al lost, now at the point of death.   585
The gilt sparres and the beames then threw they down,
Of old fathers the proud and royal workes.
And with drawn swerds some did beset the gates,
Which they did watch and kepe in routes full thick.
Our sprites restorde to rescue the kings house,   590
To help them, and to geue the vanquisht strength.
    A postern with a blinde wicket there was,
A common trade to passe through Priams house:
On the backside wherof wast houses stood.
Which way eftsithes, while that our kingdome dured,   595
Thinfortunate Andromache alone
Resorted to the parentes of her make,

With yong Astyanax, his grandsire to see.
Here passed I vp to the hyest toure,
From whense the wretched Troyans did throw down   600
Dartes spent in wast.   Unto a turret then
We stept: the which stood in a place aloft,
The top wherof did reache wellnere the sterres,
Where we were wont all Troye to behold,
The Grekish nauie, and their tentes also.   605
With instrumentes of iron gan we pick,
To seke where we might finde the ioyning shronk
From that high seat: which we razed, and threw down;
Which falling gaue fourthwith a rushing sound,
And large in breadth on Grekish routes it light.   610
But sone an other sort stept in theyr stede.
No stone vnthrown, nor yet no dart vncast.
    Before the gate stood Pyrrhus, in the porche,
Reioysing in his dartes, with glittring armes,
Like to the adder with venimous herbes fed,   615
Whom cold winter all bolne hid vnder ground,
And shining bright when she her slough had slong,
Her slipper back doth rowle with forked tong,
And raised brest lift vp against the sun.
With that together came great Periphas,   620
Automedon eke, that guided had somtime
Achilles horse, now Pyrrhus armure bare.
And eke with him the warlike Scyrian youth
Assayld the house, and threw flame to the top.
And he an axe before the formest raught: 625
Wherwith he gan the strong gates hew, and break.
From whens he bet the staples out of brasse:
He brake the barres, and through the timber pearst
So large a hole, wherby they might discerne
The house, the court, and secret chambers eke   630

P 2

Of Priamus, and auncient kings of Troy,
And armed foes in thentrie of the gate.
  But the palace within confounded was
With wayling, and with rufull shrikes and cryes.
The hollow halles did howle of womens plaint.   635
The clamor strake vp to the golden sterres.
The frayd mothers, wandring through the wide house,
Embracing pillers, did them hold and kisse.
Pyrrhus assaileth with his fathers might,
Whom the closures ne kepers might hold out.   640
With often pushed ram the gate did shake,
The postes beat down remoued from their hookes.
By force they made the way, and thentrie brake.
And now the Grekes, let in, the formest slew:
And the large palace with soldiars gan to fill.   645
Not so fercely doth ouerflow the feldes
The foming flood, that brekes out of his bankes:
Whoes rage of waters beares away what heapes
Stand in his way, the coates, and eke the herdes:
As in thentrie of slaughter furious   650
I saw Pyrrhus, and either Atrides.
  There Hecuba I saw with a hundred moe
Of her sons wyues, and Priam at the altar,
Sprinkling with blood his flame of sacrifice.
Fiftie bedchambers of his childrens wyues,   655
With losse of so great hope of his ofspring;
The pillers eke proudly beset with gold,
And with the spoiles of other nations,
Fell to the ground: and whatso that with flame
Untouched was, the Grekes did all possesse.   660
  Parcase yow wold ask what was Priams fate.
When of his taken town he saw the chaunce,
And the gates of his palace beaten down,

His foes amid his secret chambers eke:
Thold man in vaine did on his sholders then,   665
Trembling for age, his curace long disused:
His bootelesse swerd he girded him about:
And ran amid his foes, redy to dye.
Amid the court vnder the heuen all bare
A great altar there stood, by which there grew   670
An old laurel tree bowing therunto,
Which with his shadow did embrace the Gods.
Here Hecuba, with her yong daughters all,
About the altar swarmed were in vaine:
Like Doues, that flock together in the storme: 675
The statues of the Gods embracing fast.
But when she saw Priam had taken there
His armure, like as though he had ben yong:
'What furious thought, my wretched spouse,' (quod she)
'Did moue thee now such wepons for to weld?   680
Why hastest thow?   This time doth not require
Such succor, ne yet such defenders now,
No, though Hector my son were here againe.
Come hether: this altar shall saue vs all:
Or we shall dye together.'   Thus she sayd.   685
Wherwith she drew him back to her, and set
The aged man down in the holy seat.
   But loe Polites, one of Priams sons,
Escaped from the slaughter of Pyrrhus,
Comes fleing through the wepons of his foes,   690
Searching all wounded the long galleries,
And the voyd courtes: whom Pyrrhus all in rage
Followed fast, to reache a mortal wound:
And now in hand wellnere strikes with his spere,
Who fleing fourth, till he came now in sight   695
Of his parentes, before their face fell down,

Yelding the ghost, with flowing streames of blood.
Priamus then, although he were half ded,
Might not kepe in his wrath, nor yet his words,
But cryeth out: 'for this thy wicked work,   700
And boldnesse eke such thing to enterprise,
If in the heauens any iustice be,
That of such things takes any care or kepe,
According thankes, the Gods may yeld to thee,
And send thee eke thy iust deserued hyre,   705
That made me see the slaughter of my childe,
And with his blood defile the fathers face.
But he, by whom thow fainst thy self begot,
Achilles, was to Priam not so stern.
For loe he, tendring my most humble sute,   710
The right and faith, my Hectors bloodlesse corps
Rendred, for to be layd in sepulture,
And sent me to my kingdome home againe.'
Thus sayd the aged man: and therewithall
Forcelesse he cast his weake vnweldy dart,   715
Which, repulst from the brasse, where it gaue dint,
Without sound hong vainly in the shieldes bosse.
Quod Pyrrhus, ' then thow shalt this thing report.
On message to Pelide my father go:
Shew vnto him my cruel dedes, and how   720
Neoptolem is swarued out of kinde.
Now shalt thou dye,' quod he. And with that word
At the altar him trembling gan he draw,
Wallowing through the blodshed of his son:
And, his lefthand all clasped in his heare,   725
With his right arme drewe fourth his shining sword,
Which in his side he thrust vp to the hilts.
Of Priamus this was the fatal fine,
The wofull end that was alotted him.

When he had seen his palace all on flame,   730
With ruine of his Troyan turrets eke;
That royal prince of Asie, which of late
Reignd ouer so many peoples and realmes,
Like a great stock now lieth on the shore:
His hed and sholders parted ben in twaine,   735
A body now without renome and fame.

(B) *Descripcion of the restlesse state of a louer, with sute to*
his ladie, to rue on his diyng hart.

THE sonne hath twise brought furth his tender grene,
And [1] clad the earth in liuely lustinesse:
Ones haue the windes the trees despoiled clene,
And new [2] again begins their cruelnesse,
Since I haue hid vnder my brest the harm   5
That neuer shall recouer healthfulnesse.
The winters hurt recouers with the warm,
The parched grene restored is with [3] shade.
What warmth (alas) may serue for to disarm
The frosen hart that mine in flame hath made?   10
What colde againe is able to restore
My fresh grene yeares, that wither thus and fade?
Alas, I se, nothing hath hurt so sore,
But time in time reduceth a returne:
In time my harm increaseth more and more,   15
And semes to haue my cure alwaies in scorne.
Strange kindes of death in life that I doe trie,
At hand to melt, farre of in flame to burne.
And like as time list to my cure aply,

---

[1] Second ed. ' Twise.'   [2] Second ed. ' ones.'
[3] First ed. ' with the'; but second ed. omits ' the.'

So doth eche place my comfort cleane refuse.   20
All thing aliue, that seeth the heauens with eye,
With cloke of night may couer, and excuse
It-self from trauail of the dayes vnrest,
Saue I, alas, against all others vse,
That then stirre vp the tormentes of my brest,   25
And curse eche sterre as causer of my fate.
And when the sonne hath eke the dark opprest,
And brought the day, it doth nothing abate
The trauailes of mine endles smart and payn.
For then, as one that hath the light in hate,   30
I wish for night, more couertly to playn,
And me withdraw from euery haunted place,
Lest by my chere my chance appere to playn :
And in my minde I measure pace by pace,
To seke the place where I my-self had lost,   35
That day that I was tangled in the lace,
In semyng slack that knitteth euer most :
But neuer yet the trauaile of my thought
Of better state coulde catche a cause to bost.
For if I found sometime that I haue sought,   40
Those sterres by whome I trusted of the porte,
My sayles doe fall, and I aduance right nought.
As ankerd fast, my sprites[1] doe all resorte
To stande agazed, and sinke in more and more
The deadly harme which she dothe take in sport.   45
Lo, if I seke, how I doe finde my sore :
And yf I flee, I carie with me still
The venomde shaft, whiche dothe his force restore
By hast of flight ; and I may plaine my fill
Vnto my-selfe, vnlesse this carefull song   50

---

[1] So second ed.; first ed. ' spretes.'

Printe in your harte some parcell of my tene.
For I, alas, in silence all to long,
Of myne olde hurte yet fele the wounde but grene.
Rue on my life : or els your cruell wronge
Shall well appere, and by my death be sene.   55

(C) *Description of Spring, wherin eche thing renewes, saue*
onelie the louer.

THE soote season, that bud and blome furth bringes,
With grene hath clad the hill and eke the vale :
The nightingale with fethers new she singes :
The turtle to her make hath tolde her tale :
Somer is come, for euery spray nowe springes,   5
The hart hath hong his olde hed on the pale :
The buck in brake his winter cote he flinges :
The fishes flete [1] with newe repaired scale :
The adder all her sloughe awaye she slinges :
The swift swalow pursueth the flies smale :   10
The busy bee her honye now she minges :
Winter is worne, that was the flowers bale :
And thus I see among these pleasant thinges
Eche care decayes ; and yet my sorow springes.

(D) *A complaint by night of the louer not beloued.*

ALAS, so all thinges nowe doe holde their peace.
Heauen and earth disturbed in nothing :
The beastes, the ayer, the birdes their song doe cease :
The nightes chare the starres aboute dothe bring :
Calme is the Sea, the waues worke lesse and lesse :   5

---

[1] First ed. 'flote'; second ed. 'flete.'

So am not I, whom loue, alas! doth wring,
Bringing before my face the great encrease
Of my desires, whereat I wepe and syng,
In ioye and wo, as in a doutfull ease.
For my swete thoughtes sometyme doe pleasure bring,   10
But by and by the cause of my disease
Geues me a pang, that inwardly dothe sting,
When that I thinke what griefe it is againe,
To liue and lacke the thing should ridde my paine.

(E) *Vow to loue faithfully, howsoeuer he be rewarded.*

Set me whereas the sunne doth parche the grene.
Or where his beames do not dissolue the yse :
In temperate heate where he is felt and sene :
In presence prest of people madde or wise.
Set me in hye, or yet in lowe degree :   5
In longest night, or in the shortest daye :
In clearest skye, or where clowdes thickest be :
In lusty youth, or when my heeres are graye.
Set me in heauen, in earth, or els in hell,
In hyll, or dale, or in the fomyng flood :   10
Thrall, or at large, aliue where so I dwell :
Sicke, or in health : in euyll fame, or good :
Hers will I be, and onely with this thought
Content my-selfe, although my chaunce be nought.

(F) *Prisoned in windsor, he recounteth his pleasure there
passed.*

So cruell prison how coulde betide, alas,
As proude Windsor? where in lust and ioye,
With a kinges sonne, my childishe yeres did passe,

In greater feastes[1] than Priams sonnes of Troy:
Where eche swete place returns a taste full sower.   5
The large grene courtes, where we were wont to houe,
With eyes cast vp into the maydens tower,
And easie sighes, suche as folke drawe in loue :
The stately seates, the ladies bright of hewe :
The daunces shorte, longe tales of great delight ?   10
With wordes and lokes, that tygers coulde but rewe,
Where eche of vs did pleade the others right :
The palme-play, where, dispoyled for the game,
With dazed eies oft we by gleames of loue,
Haue mist the ball, and got sight of our dame,   15
To baite her eyes, whiche kept the leads aboue :
The grauell-grounde, with sleues tyed on the helme,
On fomynge horse, with swordes and frendlye hartes:
With cheare, as though one should another whelme,
Where we haue fought, and chased oft with dartes :   20
With siluer droppes the meade yet spred for ruthe,
In actiue games of nimblenes and strength,
Where we did straine, trayned with swarmes of youth,
Our tender lymmes, that yet shot vp in length:
The secrete groues, which oft we made resounde   ·25
Of pleasaunt playnt, and of our ladies prayse,
Recordyng ofte what grace eche one had founde,
What hope of spede, what dreade of long delayes :
The wilde forest, the clothed holtes with grene :
With rayns auailed, and swift ybreathed horse,   30
With crye of houndes, and mery blastes betwene,
Where we did chase the fearfull harte of force :
The wide [walles][2] eke, that harborde vs ech night,
Wherwith (alas) reuiueth in my brest

---

[1] First ed. 'feast'; second ed. 'feastes.'   [2] Old text 'vales.'

The swete accorde : such slepes as yet delight,   35
The pleasant dreames, the quiet bed of rest,
The secrete thoughtes imparted with such trust,
The wanton talke, the diuers change of play,
The frendship sworne, eche promise kept so iust,
Wherwith we past the winter nightes [1] away.   40
And, with this thought, the bloud forsakes the face
The teares berayne my chekes of deadly hewe :
The whiche as sone as sobbyng sighes (alas)
Vpsupped haue, thus I my plaint renewe :
' O place of blisse, renuer of my woes,   45
Geue me accompt, where is my noble fere,
Whom in thy walles thou [didst] [2] eche night enclose,
To other leefe, but vnto me most dere ?'
Eccho (alas) that dothe my sorow rewe,
Returns therto a hollow sounde of playnte.   50
Thus I alone, where all my fredome grewe,
In prison pyne with bondage and restrainte :
And with remembrance of the greater greefe,
To banishe the lesse I find my chief releefe.

[1] First ed. 'night'; second ed. ' nightes.'   [2] Old text ' doest.'

XX.

SIR THOMAS WIAT.

ABOUT A.D. 1540.

SIR THOMAS WIAT, or Wyatt, called 'the Elder,' to distin-
guish him from his son, was born in 1503. In 1515, at the age
of twelve, he was entered at St. John's College, Cambridge. In
1537 he was appointed minister at the Spanish Court, and remained at Madrid till the beginning of 1538. His death was
occasioned by his excess of zeal: being summoned to attend the
king, he overheated himself in his journey, and died at Sherborne
on the 11th of October, 1542. His son, Sir Thomas Wiat 'the
Younger,' is well known as the leader of an insurrection against
Queen Mary, for which he was beheaded April 11, 1554. Our
poet tried two forms of composition, song and satire. His songs
are an inferior imitation of Surrey's, and of no very great merit;
but his *Satires* are not only the earliest examples in the modern
polished style, but are exceedingly well written, and evidently
suited to his genius. Unfortunately there are but three of them,
and they are but short. I therefore take the opportunity of
printing *the whole of them*. They were printed by Richard
Tottell in 1557, at the end of 'Songes and Sonettes, written by
the ryght honorable Lorde Henry Haward [*sic*] late Earle of
Surrey, and other.' I add two Sonnets, and four other poems,
from the same source. It may be noted that the spelling *Wiat*
is that which appears in the poet's autograph.

(A) *Of the meane and sure estate, written to John Poins.*

My mothers maides, when they do sowe and spinne,
They sing a song made of the feldishe[1] mouse;
That, forbicause her liuelod was but thinne,
Would nedes go se her townish sisters house;
She thought her-selfe endured to greuous payne,   5
The stormy blastes her caue so sore did sowse,
That, when the furrowes swimmed with the rayne,
She must lie colde, and wet in sory plight.
And worse then that, bare meat there did remaine
To comfort her, when she her house had dight;   10
Sometime a barly-corne, sometime a beane,
For which she laboured hard both day and night,
In haruest tyme, while she might go and gleane.
And when her store was stroyed with the floode,
Then weleaway, for she vndone was cleane;   15
Then was she faine to take, in stede of fode,
Slepe, if she might, her honger to begyle.
'My sister' (quod she) 'hath a liuyng good,
And hence from me she dwelleth not a myle.
In colde and storme, she lieth warme and dry,   20
In bed of downe; the durt doth not defile
Her tender fote, she labours not as I,
Richely she fedes, and at the richemans cost;
And for her meat she nedes not craue nor cry.
By sea, by land, of delicates the most   25
Her cater sekes, and spareth for no perill;
She fedes on boyle-meat, bake-meat, and on rost;
And hath therfore no whit of charge nor trauell.

[1] Printed 'seldishe'; but the second ed. has 'feldishe.'

And, when she list, the licour of the grape
Doth glad her hart, till that her belly swell.'   30
And at this iourney makes she but a iape :
So forth she goes, trusting of all this wealth
With her sister her part so for to shape,
That, if she might there kepe her-self in health,
To liue a Lady while her life doth last.   35
And to the dore now is she come by stealth,
And with her fote anone she scrapes full fast.
Thother, for fear, durst not well scarse appere ;
Of euery noyse so was the wretch agast.
At last, she asked softly, who was there ;   40
And, in her language as well as she could,
'Pepe' (quod the other) 'sister, I am here.
'Peace' (quod the towne mouse) 'why speakest thou so
        loude ?'
And by the hand she toke her fayre and well.
'Welcome' (quod she) 'my sister, by the rode.'   45
She feasted her, that ioye it was to tell
The fare they hadde ; they dranke the wine so clere,
And, as to purpose now and then it fell,
She chered her, with 'how, sister, what chere ?'
Amid this ioye be-fell a sory chance,   50
That (weleaway) the stranger bought full dere
The fare she had.   For, as she lookt a-scance,
Under a stole she spied two stemyng eyes
In a rounde head, with [two] sharpe eares : in Fraunce
Was neuer mouse so ferde, for the vnwise   55
Had not ysene such a beast before.
Yet had nature so taught her, after her gise,
To know her fo, and dread him euermore.
The townemouse fled, she knew whither to go :
The other had no shift, but wonders sore ;   60

Ferde of her life, at home she wisht her tho,
And to the dore (alas) as she did skippe,
The heauen it would, lo! and eke her chance was so,
At the threshold her sely fote did trippe;
And ere she might recouer it agayne,   65
The traytour cat had caught her by the hippe,
And made her there against hir will remayne,
That had forgot her power, surety, and rest,
For semyng welth, wherin she thought to raine.
Alas (my Poyns) how men do seke the best,   70
And finde the worst, by errour as they stray;
And no maruell, when sight is so opprest,
And blindes the guide, anone out of the way
Goeth guide and all, in seking quiet life.
O wretched mindes, there is no golde that may   75
Graunt that you seke, no warre, no peace, no strife.
No, no, although thy head were hoopt with golde,
Sergeant with mace, with hawbart, sword, nor knife,
Can not repulse the care that folow should.
Ech kinde of life hath with him his disease.   80
Liue in delite, euen as thy lust would,
And thou shalt finde, when lust doth most thee please,
It irketh straight, and by it-selfe doth fade.
A small thing is it, that may thy minde appease.
None of you al there is, that is so madde,   85
To seke for grapes on brambles or on bryers;
Nor none, I trow, that hath his witte so badde,
To set his haye for conies ouer riuers;
Nor ye set not a dragge-net for an hare;
And yet the thing, that most is your desire,   90
You do misseke, with more trauell and care.
Make plaine thine hart, that it be not knotted
With hope or dreade, and so thy will be bare

From all affectes, whom vice hath euer spotted;
Thy-selfe content with that is thee assinde,   95
And vse it well, that is to thee alotted.
Then seke no more out of thy-selfe to finde
The thing that thou hast sought so long before;
For thou shalt feele it stickyng in thy minde.
Madde, if ye list to continue your sore,   100
Let present passe, and gape on time to come,
And depe your-selfe in trauell more and more.
Henceforth (my Poins) this shalbe all and summe,
These wretched foles shall haue nought els of me,
But [bow] to the great God and to his dome.   105
None other paine pray I for them to be,
But when the rage doth leade them from the right,
That, lokyng backward, Vertue they may se,
Euen as she is, so goodly fayre and bright.
And whilst they claspe their lustes in armes a-crosse,   110
Graunt them, good Lord, as thou maist of thy might,
To freate inward, for losyng such a losse.

(B) *Of the Courtiers life, written to* John Poins.

MYne owne Iohn Poyns, sins ye delite to know
　　The causes why that homeward I me draw,
And fle the prease of courtes, where so they go,
Rather then to liue thrall, vnder the awe
Of lordly lokes, wrapped within my cloke,   5
To will and lust learnyng to set a law:
It is not that [1] because I scorne or mocke
The power of them, whom fortune here hath lent
Charge ouer vs, of ryght to strike the stroke:

---

[1] The word 'that' is inserted in second ed. The first ed. omits it.

Q

But true it is, that I haue alwayes ment   10
Lesse to esteme them then the common sort,
Of outward thinges that iudge in their entent,
Without regard what inward doth resort.
I graunt, sometime of glory that the fire
Doth touch my hart.   Me list not to report   15
Blame by honour, and honour to desire.
But how may I this honour now attaine,
That can not dye the colour blacke a lyer?
My Poyns, I can not frame my tune to fayne,
To cloke the truth, for prayse without desert   20
Of them that list all uice[1] for to retaine.
I can not honour them that set their part
With Venus and Bacchus, all their life long;
Nor holde my peace of them, although I smart.
I can not crouch nor knele to such a wrong;   25
To worship them like God on earth alone,
That are as wolues these sely lambes among.
I can not with my wordes complaine and mone,
And suffer nought; nor smart without complaynt;
Nor turne the worde that from my mouth is gone.   30
I can not speake and loke like as a saynt,
Vse wiles for wit, and make disceyt a pleasure;
Call craft counsaile, for lucre still to paint.
I can not wrest the law to fill the coffer,
With innocent bloud to fede my-selfe fatte,   35
And do most hurt, where that most helpe I offer.
I am not he, that can alowe the state
Of hye Ceasar, and damne Cato to dye;
That with his death did scape out of the gate
From Ceasars handes, if Liuye doth not lye,   40

---

[1] Printed 'nice' first ed.; 'vice' second ed.

And would not liue where libertie was lost,
So did his hart the common-wealth apply.
I am not he, such eloquence to bost,
To make the crow in singyng as the swanne;
Nor call the lyon of coward beastes the most,   45
That can not take a mouse, as the cat can;
And he that dieth for honger of the golde,
Call him Alexander; and say that Pan
Passeth Appollo in musike manifold:
Praise 'syr Topas' for a noble tale,   50
And scorne the story that the knight tolde:
Prayse him for counsell, that is dronke of ale:
Grinne when he laughes, that beareth all the sway:
Frowne, when he frownes, and grone, when he is pale:
On others lust to hang both night and day.   55
None of these poyntes would euer frame in me,
My wit is nought, I can not learne the way.
And much the lesse of thinges that greater be,
That asken helpe of colours to deuise;
To ioyne the meane with ech extremitie,   60
With nearest vertue ay to cloke the vice:
And, as to purpose likewise it shall fall,
To presse the vertue that it may not rise;
As, dronkennesse 'good felowship' to call:
The frendly foe, with his faire double face,   65
Say, he is gentle and curties therewithall:
Affirme, that fauell hath a goodly grace
In eloquence: And cruelty to name
Zeale of Iustice: And change in time and place:
And he that suffreth offence withoutt blame,   70
Call him pitifull; and him true and plaine,
That rayleth rechlesse vnto ech mans shame:
Say, he is rude, that can not lye and faine:

The letcher a louer; and tyranny
To be the [trew] right of a Prynces rayghne :   75
I can not, I; no, no, it will not be.
This is the cause that I could neuer yet
Hang on their sleues, that weygh (as thou mayst se)
A chippe of chance more then a pounde of wit.
This maketh me at home to hunt and hauke,   80
And in fowle wether at my boke to sit;
In frost and snow, then with my bow to stalke.
No man doth marke where so I ride or go,
In lusty leas at libertie I walke;
And of these newes I fele nor weale nor wo,   85
Saue that a clogge doth hang yet at my heele.
No force for that, for it is ordred so,
That I may leape both hedge and dike full wele.
I am not now in Fraunce, to iudge the wine,
With savry sauce those delicates to fele;   90
Nor yet in Spaine, where one must him incline,
Rather then to be, outwardly to seme;
I meddle not with wyttes that be so fine.
Nor Flaunders chere lettes not my syght to deme
Of blacke and white, nor takes my wittes away   95
With beastlinesse; such do those beastes esteme.
Nor I am not, where truth is geuen in pray
For money, poyson, and treason, of some
A common practise, vsed nyght and day;
But I am here, in kent and christendome,   100
Among the Muses, where I reade and ryme;
Where, if thou list, myne owne Iohn Poyns, to come,
Thou shalt be iudge, how I do spende my time.

(C) *How to vse the court and him-selfe therin, written to* *syr* Fraunces Bryan.

A Spendyng hand, that alway powreth out,
  Had nede to haue a bringer in as fast.
And, on the stone that styll doth turne about,
There groweth no mosse.   These prouerbes yet do last;
Reason hath set them in so sure a place,   5
That length of yeres their force can neuer waste.
When I remember this, and eke the case
Wherin thou standst, I thought forthwith to write,
Brian, to thee, who knowes how great a grace
In writyng is to counsaile man the right.   10
To thee therfore, that trottes still vp and downe,
And neuer restes, but runnyng day and night
From realme to realme, from citye, strete, and towne,
Why doest thou weare thy body to the bones?
And mightest at home slepe in thy bedde of downe,   15
And drinke good ale, so nappy[1] for the nones,
Fede thy-selfe fatte, and heape vp pounde by pounde.
Likest thou not this? 'No.' Why? 'For swine so
      grones[2]
In stye, and chaw dung moulded on the ground,
And driuell on pearles with head styll in the manger;   20
So of the harpe the asse doth heare the sound;
So sackes of durt be filde.   The neate courtier
So serues for lesse then do these fatted swine.
Though I seme leane and drye, withouten moysture,
Yet will I serue my prince, my lord and thine,   25

[1] Printed 'noppy' first ed.; 'nappy' second ed.
[2] Printed 'groines.'

And let them liue, to fede the paunch, that lyst,
So I may liue to fede both me and myne.'
By God, well said!   But what and if thou wist
How to bring in, as fast as thou doest spend?
'That would I learne.'   And it shall not be mist,   30
To tell thee how.   Now harke what I intende.
Thou knowest well first, who so can seke to please,
Shall purchase frendes, where trouth shall but offend.
Flee therefore truth; it is both welth and ease.
For though that trouth of euery man hath prayse,   35
Full neare that winde goeth trouth in great misease.
Vse vertue, as it goeth now a dayes,
In worde alone to make thy language swete,
And, of the dede, yet do not as thou saies.
Els, be thou sure, thou shalt be farre vnmete   40
To get thy bread, ech thing is now so skant.
Seke still thy profite vpon thy bare fete.
Lende in no wise, for feare that thou do want;
Vnlesse it be, as to a calfe a chese;
By which returne be sure to winne a cant   45
Of halfe at least.   It is not good to leese.
Learne at the ladde that in a long white cote,
From vnder the stall, withouten landes or feese,
Hath lept into the shoppe; who knowes by rote
This rule that I haue told thee here before.   50
Sometime also riche age beginnes to dote,
Se thou when there thy gaine may be the more ;
Stay him by the arme, where-so he walke or go ;
Be nere alway, and if he coughe to sore,
What he hath spit treade out, and please him so.   55
A diligent knaue that pikes his masters purse
May please him so, that he withouten mo
Executour is.   And what is he the wurs ?

But, if so chance thou get nought of the man,
The wydow may for all thy charge deburs[1];   60
A riueld skynne, a stinkyng breath; what than?
A tothelesse mouth shall do thy lippes no harme,
The golde is good, and, though she curse or banne,
Yet, where thee list, thou mayest lye good and warme;
Let the olde mule bite vpon the bridle,   65
Whilst there do lye a sweter in thine arme.
In this also se thou be not idle;
Thy nece, thy cosyn, thy sister, or thy daughter,
If she bee faire, if handsome be her middle,
If thy better hath her loue besought her,   70
Auaunce his cause, and he shall helpe thy nede.
It is but loue; turne thou[2] it to a laughter.
But ware, I say, so gold thee helpe and spede,
That in this case thou be not so vnwise
As Pandar was in such a like dede.   75
For he, the fole! of conscience was so nice,
That he no gaine would haue for all his payne.
Be next thy-selfe, for frendshyp beares no price.
Laughest thou at me? why? do I speake in vaine?
'No, not at thee, but at thy thrifty iest.   80
Wouldest thou, I should for any losse or gayne,
Change that for golde that I haue tane for best
Next godly thinges: to haue an honest name?
Should I leaue that? then take me for a beast.'
Nay then, farewell, and if thou care for shame;   85
Content thee then with honest pouertie;
With free tong, what thee mislikes, to blame,
And, for thy trouth, sometime aduersitie.

[1] Second ed. 'disburse.'
[2] The second ed. inserts 'thou,' but omits 'a' in this line.

And therwithall this thing I shall thee giue,
In this world now litle prosperitie,   90
And coyne to kepe, as water in a siue.

(D) *A renouncing of loue.*

FArewell, Loue, and all thy lawes for euer !
     Thy bayted hokes shall tangle me no more.
Senec and Plato call me from thy lore
To parfit wealth my wit for to endeuer.
In [my] blinde errour when I dyd perseuer,   5
Thy sharp repulse, that pricketh aye so sore,
Taught me, in trifles that I set no store,
But scape forth thence, since libertie is leuer.
Therfore, farewell ; go trouble yonger hartes,
And in me claime no more auctoritie.   10
With ydle youth go vse thy propartie,
And theron spend thy many brittle dartes.
For, hytherto though I haue lost my tyme,
Me lyst no longer[1] rotten bowes to clime.

(E) *The louer forsaketh his vnkinde loue.*

MY hart I gaue thee ; not to do it pain,
     But to preserue, lo, it to thee was taken.
I serued thee not that I should be forsaken,
But, that I should receiue reward again,
I was content thy seruant to remain,   5
And not to be repayd after this fashion.
Now, since in thee is there none other[2] reason,

---

[1] Printed 'lenger'; but a copy, printed by Tottell in 1574, has 'longer.'
[2] Printed 'nother.'

Displease thee not if that I do refrain,
Vnsaciat of my wo and thy desyre,
Assured by craft for to excuse thy fault.   10
But since it pleaseth thee to fain defaut,
Farewell, I say, departing from the fire.
For he that doth beleue bearyng in hand
Ploweth in the water, and soweth in the sand.

(F) *The louer determineth to serue faithfully.*

SYnce loue wyll nedes that I shall loue,
   Of very force I must agree;
And since no chance may it remoue,
In welth and in aduersitie
I shall alway my-self apply   5
To serue, and suffer paciently.
   Though for good will I finde but hate,
And cruelty, my life to wast,
And though that still a wretched state
Should pine my dayes vnto the last,   10
Yet I professe it willingly
To serue, and suffer paciently.
   For since my hart is bound to serue,
And I not ruler of mine owne,
What so befall, tyll that I sterue,   15
By proofe full well it shall be knowne,
That I shall still my-selfe apply
To serue, and suffer paciently.
   Yea, though my grief finde no redresse,
But still increase before mine eyes,   20
Though my reward be cruelnesse,
With all the harme, happe can deuise,

Yet I professe it willingly
To serue, and suffer paciently.
    Yea, though fortune her pleasant face   25
Should shew, to set me vp a-loft,
And streight, my wealth for to deface,
Should writhe away, as she doth oft,
Yet would I styll my-self apply
To serue, and suffer paciently.   30
    There is no grief, no smart, no wo
That yet I fele, or after shall,
That from this mynde may make me go;
And, whatsoeuer me befall,
I do professe it willingly   35
To serue, and suffer paciently.

(G) *A description of such a one as he would loue.*

A Face that should content me wonderous well
    Should not be faire, but louely to beholde;
Of liuely loke, all griefe for to repell
With right good grace; so would I that it should
Speake, without word, such wordes as none can tell.   5
The tresse also should be of crisped gold.
With wit and these perchance I might be tryde,
And knit againe with knot that should not slide.

(H) *Comparison of loue to a streame falling from the*
Alpes.

F Rom these hie hilles as when a spring doth fall,
    It trilleth downe with still and suttle course,
Of this and that it gathers ay, and shall,
Till it haue iust downflowed to streame and force,

Then at the fote it rageth ouer all.   5
So fareth loue, when he hath tane a sourse;
Rage is his raine, Resistance vayleth none.
The first eschue is remedy alone.

(I) *Of his loue that pricked her finger with a nedle.*

SHe sat, and sowed, that hath done me the wrong
   Wherof I plain, and haue done many a day:
And, whilst she herd my plaint in piteous song,
She wisht my hart the samplar, thar[1] it lay.
The blinde maister whom I haue serued so long,   5
Grudgyng to heare that he did heare her say,
Made her owne weapon do her finger blede,
To fele if pricking wer so good in dede.

Old text 'that,' which gives no sense. Read 'thar,' which is often used to mean 'where.'

XXI.

HUGH LATIMER.

A.D. 1549.

HUGH LATIMER, the son of a farmer in Leicestershire, was born A.D. 1491. He was, as a young man, to use his own expression, 'as obstinate a papist as any in England,' but altered his opinions in consequence of his acquaintance with Thomas Bilney, a celebrated defender of the doctrines of Luther. He was educated at Cambridge, it is said at Clare Hall, was elected fellow of his college, and in 1516 was Professor of Greek in the University. In 1535 he was appointed Bishop of Worcester by Henry VIII, but resigned his bishopric in 1539, owing to the passing of 'The Act of Six Articles.' In 1548 he resumed preaching, and frequently preached at St. Paul's Cross. He suffered at the stake beside Bishop Ridley at Oxford, Oct. 16, 1555. We have no very correct copies of his remarkably popular sermons, as they have been chiefly preserved by the diligence of others, especially of Thomas Some, who calls himself the 'humble and faithful oratour' of the Duchess of Suffolk, and of Augustine Bernher, Latimer's Swiss servant and faithful friend. One of the most 'notable' of his sermons is that which has been called the 'Sermon on the Ploughers,' preached at St. Paul's on Friday, Jan. 18, 1548-9 (i.e. 1548, according to the Old Style, when the year began on the 1st of March, but 1549 according to our modern reckoning). An extract from this sermon is here given, from the first edition, published within a few weeks of the day of its delivery. See Mr. Arber's reprint of the whole sermon.

[*From the 'Sermon on the Ploughers.'*]

Here haue I an occasion by the way somwhat to saye vnto you, yea, for the place that I alledged vnto you before oute of Hieremy the xlviii. Chapter[1]. And it was spoken of a spirituall worcke of God, a worke that was commaunded to be done; & it was of sheddynge bloude, and of destroy- 5 ing the cities of Moab. For (sayeth he) ' curssed be he *that* kepeth backe hys sworde frome sheddynge of bloud[2].' As Saule when he kepte backe the sworde from shedding of bloude, at what tyme he was sent agaynst Amalech, was refused of God for beinge disobedient to Goddes commaunde- 10 mentes, in that he spared Agag *the* kyng. So that, that place of *the* prophet was spoken of them that wente to the distruction of the cityes of Moab, amonge the which there was one called Nebo, whyche was muche reproued for idola- trie, supersticion, pryde, auarice, crueltie, tiranny, and for 15 hardenes of herte, and for these sinnes was plaged of God and destroyed. Nowe what shall we saye of these ryche citizens of London? What shall I saye of them? shal I cal them proude men of London, malicious men of London, mercylesse men of London? No, no, I may not saie so, 20 they wil be offended wyth me than. Yet must I speake. For is there not reygning in London as much pride, as much coueteousnes, as much crueltie, as much oppression, as much supersticion, as was in Nebo? Yes, I thynke & muche more to. Therfore I saye, repente O London! 25 Repent, repente! Thou heareste thy faultes tolde the;

---

[1] 'Cursed be he that doeth the work of the Lord deceitfully.' Jer. xlviii. 10.   [2] Jer. xlviii. 10.

amend the*m*, amend the*m*. I thinke if Nebo had had the
preachynge *that* thou haste: they wold haue conuerted.
And you, rulers and officers, be wise & circu*m*spect, loke
30 to your charge and see you do your dueties and rather be
glad to amend your yll liuyng then to be angrye when you
are warned or tolde of your faulte. What a-do was there,
made in London at a certein ma*n* because he sayd, & in
dede at that time, on a iust cause, 'Burgesses,' quod he,
35 'nay, butterflies!' Lorde! what a-do there was for *that*
worde! And yet would God they were no worse then
butterflies. Butterflyes do but theyre nature, the butterflye
is not couetouse, is not gredye of other mens goodes, is not
ful of enuy and hatered, is not malicious, is not cruel, is
40 not mercilesse. The butterflye gloriethe not in hyr owne
dedes, nor preferreth the tradicions of men before Gods
worde; it committeth not idolatry nor worshyppeth false
goddes. But London can not abyde to be rebuked; suche
is the nature of man. If they be prycked, they wyll kycke.
45 If they be rubbed on the gale, they wil wynce. But yet
they wyll not amende theyr faultes, they wyl not be yl
spoke*n* of. But howe shal I speake well of them? If you
could be conte*n*te to receyue and folowe the worde of god
and fauoure good preachers, if you coulde beare to be toulde
50 of youre faultes, if you coulde amende when you heare of
them: if you woulde be gladde to reforme that is a-misse:
if I mighte se anie suche inclinacion in you, that leaue to be
mercilesse and begynne to be charytable, I would the*n* hope
wel of you, I woulde then speake well of you. But London
55 was neuer so yll as it is now. In tymes past men were full
of pytie and compassion, but nowe there is no pitie; for
in London their brother shal die in the streetes for colde,
he shall lye sycke at theyr doore betwene stocke & stocke,
I can not tel what to call it, & peryshe there for hunger;

was there any more vnmercifulnes in Nebo? I thinke not. 60
In tymes paste when any ryche man dyed in London, they
were wonte to healp the pore scholers of the vniuersitye
wyth exhibition. When any man dyed, they woulde bequeth
greate summes of money towarde the releue of the pore.
When I was a scholer in Cambrydge my selfe, I harde verye 65
good reporte of London, & knewe manie that had releue
of the rytche men of London, but nowe I can heare no such
good reporte, and yet I inquyre of it, & herken for it, but
nowe charitie is waxed colde, none helpeth the scholer nor
yet the pore. And in those dayes what dyd they whan 70
they helped the scholers? Mary, they maynteyned & gaue
them liuynges that were verye papists and professed the
popes doctrine; & nowe that the knowledge of Gods word
is brought to lyght, and many earnestelye studye and laboure to set it forth, now almost no man healpeth to mayn- 75
teyne them. Oh! London! London! repente, repente, for
I thynke God is more displeased wyth London then euer he
was with the citie of Nebo. Repente, therfore, repent, London, and remembre that the same God liueth nowe *that*
punyshed Nebo, eue*n* the same god & none other, and 80
he wyl punyshe synne as well nowe as he dyd then, and
he will punishe the iniquitie of London as well as he did
then of Nebo. Amende therfore; and ye that be prelates
loke well to your office, for right prelatynge is busye labour-
ynge & not lordyng. Therfore preache and teach and 85
let your ploughe be doynge; ye lordes, I saye, that liue
lyke loyterers, loke well to your office; the ploughe is your
office & charge. If you lyue idle & loyter, you do not your
duetie, you folowe not youre vocation; let your plough therfore be going & not cease, that the ground maye brynge 90
foorth fruite. But nowe, me thynketh I heare one saye vnto
me, wotte you what you say? Is it a worcke? Is it a

labour? how then hath it happened *that* we haue had so
manye hundred yeares so many vnpreachinge prelates, lord-
95 ing loyterers, and idle ministers?   Ye woulde haue me here
to make answere and to showe the cause thereof.   Nay,
thys land is not for me to ploughe, it is to stonye, to thorni,
to harde for me to plough.   They haue so many thynges
*tha*t make for them, so many things to laye for them-selues,
100 that it is not for my weake teame to plough them.   They
haue to lay for them-selues longe customes, Cerimonyes,
and authoritie, placyng in parliamente, & many thynges
more.   And I feare me thys lande is not yet rype to be
ploughed.   For as the saying is, it lacketh wethering, this
105 geare[1] lacketh wetheringe; at leaste way it is not for me to
ploughe.   For what shall I loke for amonge thornes but
prickyng and scrachinge?   what among stones but stum-
blyng?   What (I had almost sayed) among serpenttes but
stingyng?   But thys muche I dare say, that sence lording
110 and loytrying hath come vp, preaching hath come downe,
contrarie to the Apostells times.   For they preached and
lorded not.   And nowe they lorde & preache not.

For they that be lordes wyll yll go to plough.   It is no
mete office for them.   It is not semyng for their state.   Thus
115 came vp lordyng loytere[r]s.   Thus crept in vnprechinge prelates, and so haue they longe continued.

For howe many vnlearned prelates haue we now at this
day?   And no meruel.   For if *the* plough-men *tha*t now be
were made lordes, they woulde cleane gyue ouer ploughinge,
120 they woulde leaue of theyr labour & fall to lordyng out-
right, & let the plough stand.   And then bothe ploughes not
walkyng, nothyng shoulde be in the common weale but
honger.   For euer sence the Prelates were made Loordes

[1] Old text 'greare.'

and nobles, the ploughe standeth, there is no worke done,
the people sterue.   125

Thei hauke, thei hunt, thei card, they dyce, they pastyme
in theyr prelacies with galaunte gentlemen, with theyr daun-
singe minyons, and with theyr freshe companions, so that
ploughinge is set a-syde.   And by the lordinge and loytryng,
preachynge & ploughinge is cleane gone.   And thus if 130
the ploughemen of the countrey were as negligente in theyr
office as prelates be, we shoulde not longe lyue for lacke
of sustinaunce.   And as it is necessarie for to haue thys
ploughinge for the sustentacion of the bodye : so muste we
haue also the other for the satisfaction of the soule, or elles 135
we canne not lyue longe gostly.   For as the bodie wasteth
& consumeth awaye for lacke of bodily meate : so doeth
the soule pyne a-way for default of gostly meate.   But there
be two kyndes of inclosynge, to lette or hinder boeth these
kyndes of plougheinge.   The one is an inclosinge to let or 140
hinder *the* bodily ploughynge, and the other to lette or hynder
the holi-day ploughyng, the church ploughinge.   The bodylye
plougheyng is taken in and enclosed thorowe singulare commoditie.   For what man wyll lette goe or deminishe hys
priuate commoditie for a commune welth ? and who wyll 145
susteyne any damage for the respecte of a publique commoditie ?   The other plough also no man is diligent to sette
forward, nor no man wyll herken to it, but to hinder and let
it al mennes eares are open, yea, and a great meany of this
kynde of ploughmen whiche are very busie and woulde seme 150
to be verie good worckmen.   I feare me some be rather
mocke gospellers then faythful ploughmen.   I knowe many
my-selfe that professe the gospel, and lyue nothyng thereafter.   I knowe them, and haue bene conuersant wyth some
of them.   I knowe them, and I speake it wyth an heauy herte, 155
there is as litle charitye & good liuinge in them as in any

R

other, accordyng to that which Christe sayed in the Gospel
to the greate numbre of people that folowed hym, as thoughe
they had had an earneste zeale to his doctrine, wher as in
160 deede they had it not. '*Non quia Vidistis signa, sed quia come-
distis de panibus*[1]. Ye folowe me (sayth he) not because ye
haue seene the sygnes and myracles that I haue done, but
because ye haue eaten the breade and refreshed your bodyes.'
Therefore you folowe me, so that I thynke manye one nowe
165 a-dayes professeth the gospel for the lyuynge sake, not for
the loue they beare to gods word. But they that wil be true
ploughmen muste worke faythfullye for Goddes sake, for the
edifiynge of theyr brethrene[2]. And as diligentelye as the
husband-man plougheth for the sustentacion of the bodye:
170 so diligently muste the prelates and ministers labour for the
fedinge of the soule: boeth the ploughes muste styll be
doynge, as mooste necessarye for man. And wherefore are
magistrates ordayned, but that the tranquillitie of the commune weale maye be confirmed, limiting both ploughes.
175   But nowe for the defaulte of vnpreaching prelates, me
thinke I coulde gesse what myghte be sayed for excusynge
of them: They are so troubeled wyth Lordelye lyuynge,
they be so placed in palacies, couched in courtes, ruffelynge
in theyr rentes, daunceynge in theyr dominions, burdened
180 wyth ambassages, pamperynge of theyr panches lyke a monke
that maketh his Iubilie, mounchynge in their maungers, and
moylynge in their gaye manoures and mansions, and so
troubeled wyth loyterynge in theyr Lordeshyppes[3]: that they
canne not attende it. They are otherwyse occupyed, somme
185 in the Kynges matters, some are ambassadoures, some of
the pryuie counsell, some to furnyshe the courte, some are

[1] 'Not because ye saw the miracles, but because ye did eat of the loaves.
John vi. 26.
[2] Old text 'bretherne.'   [3] Old text 'Lordeshyypes.'

Lordes of the Parliamente, some are presidentes, and some comptroleres of myntes. Well, well.

Is thys theyr duetye? Is thys theyr offyce? Is thys theyr callyng? should we haue ministers of the church to be 190 comptrollers of the myntes? Is thys a meete office for a prieste that hath cure of soules? Is this hys charge? I woulde here aske one question? I would fayne knowe who comptrolleth the deuyll at home at his parishe, whyle he comptrolleth the mynte? If the Apostles mighte not leaue 195 the office of preaching to be deacons, shall one leaue it for myntyng?

I can not tell you, but the sayinge is, that since priests haue bene minters, money hath bene wourse then it was before. And they saye that the euylnes of money hath made 200 all thinges dearer. And in thys behalfe I must speake to England.

Heare, my contrey England, as Paule sayed in his firste epistle to the Cor. vi. Chap. for Paule was no sittynge bi- shoppe, but a walkinge and a preachynge byshop. But 205 when he wente from them, he lefte there behind hym the ploughe goynge styll; for he wrotte vnto them and rebuked them for goynge to lawe and pleadynge theyr causes before heathen Iudges : 'is there,' (sayeth he) 'vtterlye amonge you no wyse manne, to be an arbitratoure in matters of iudgement? 210 What? not one [amonge] all, that canne iudge betwene brother and brother? But one brother go[eth] to lawe wyth an other, and that vnder heathen Iudges? *Constituite contemptos qui sunt in ecclesia : et cete[ra]* [1], Appoynte them Iudges that are moost abiecte, and vyle in the congregation;' whyche he 215 speaketh in rebukynge them; for (sayth he) '*Ad erubescen- ciam vestram dico*—I speake it to youre shame.' So, England,

---

[1] ' Set them to judge who are least esteemed in the church.' 1 Cor. vi. 4.

I speake it to thy shame. Is there neuer a noble-man to
be a Lorde-president, but it muste be a prelate? Is there
220 neuer a wyse man in the realme to be a comptroller of the
minte? I speake it to your shame, I speake it to youre
shame. Yf there be neuer a wyse man, make a water-
bearer, a tinker, a cobler, a slaue, a page, comptroller of the
mynte. Make a meane gentylman[1], a groome, a yeoman,
225 make a poore begger Lorde-president: Thus I speake not
that I would haue it so, but to your shame: Yf there be
neuer a gentleman meete nor able to be Lorde-presidente.
For whye are not the noble-men and yong gentlemen of
England so brought vp in knoweledge of God and in learn-
230 ynge that they maye be able to execute offices in the commune weale? The Kynge hath a greate meanye of wardes,
and I trowe there is a courte of wardes; why is there not
a schole for the wardes, as well as there is a courte for their
landes? Whye are they not set in scholes, where they maye
235 learne? Or why are they not sent to the vniuersities, that
they maye be able to serue the kyng when they come to
age? Yf the wardes and yonge gentlemen were well brought
vp in learnyng and in the knowledge of God, they woulde
not when they come to age, so muche geue them-selues to
240 other vanities.

And if the nobilitie be wel trayned in godly learnynge, the
people would folowe *the* same traine. For truly such as the
noble-men be, suche wyll the people be. And nowe the
onely cause, why noble-men be not made Lorde-presidentes,
245 is because they haue not bene brought vp in learninge.
Therefore, for the loue of God, appoynte teachers &
s[c]holemaisters, you that haue charge of youth, and giue
the teachers stipendes worthy their paynes, that they maye

---

[1] Old text 'gentylmam.'

brynge them vp in grammer, in Logike, in rethorike, in
Philosophe, in the ciuile lawe, and in that whiche I can not 250
leaue vnspoken of, the word of God. Thankes be vnto God,
the nobilitie other-wyse is verie well broughte vp in learninge
and godlines, to the great ioye and comfort of England ; so
that there is nowe good hope in the youth, that we shal an
other day haue a florishinge common-welth, considering 255
theyr godly education. Yea, & there be al ready noble-
men ynough (though not so many as I woulde wishe) able
to be Lorde-presidentes[1], & wyse men ynough, for the
mynte. And as vnmeete a thynge it is for byshoppes to be
Lorde presidentes or priestes to be mynters, as it was for the 260
Corrhinthians to pleade matters of variaunce before heathen
Iudges. It is also a sclaunder to the noble-men, as thoughe
they lacked wysedome, and learninge to be able for suche
offices, or elles were no men of consciences, or elles were
not meete to be trusted, and able for suche offices : And 265
a prelate hath a charge & cure other wyse, and therfore he
can not discharge his dutie, and be a Lorde-president to.
For a presidentshippe requireth a whole man, and a by-
shoppe can not be two menne. A bishoppe hath his office,
a flocke to teache, to loke vnto, and therfore he can not 270
meddle wyth an other office, which alone requireth a whole
man. He should therfore gyue it ouer to whome it is meete,
and laboure in his owne busines, as Paule writeth to the
Thessalonians. ' Lette euerie man do his owne busines, and
folow his callying[2].' Let the priest preache, and the noble- 275
men handle the temporal matters. Moyses was a meruelous
man, a good man. Moyses was a wonderful felowe, and
dyd his dutie beinge a maried man. We lacke suche as
Moyses was. Well, I woulde al men woulde loke to their

---

[1] Old text ' Lolde presidentes.'   [2] 1 Thess. iv. 11

280 dutie, as God hath called them, and then we shoulde haue
a florishyng christian commune-weale. And nowe I would
aske a straung question. Who is the most diligent bishoppe
and prelate in al England, that passeth al the reste in doinge
his office? I can tel, for I knowe him, who it is; I knowe
285 hym well. But nowe I thynke I se you lysting and hearken-
ing, that I shoulde name him. There is one that passeth al
the other, and is the most diligent prelate & precher in al
England. And w[y]l ye knowe who it is? I wyl tel you.
It is the Deuyl. He is the moste dyligent preacher of al
290 other, he is neuer out of his dioces, he is neuer from his
cure, ye shal neuer fynde hym vnoccupyed, he is euer in his
parishe, he keepeth residence at al tymes, ye shall neuer
fynde hym out of the waye; cal for him when you wyl, he is
euer at home, the diligenteste preacher in all the Realme; he
295 is euer at his ploughe, no lordynge nor loytringe can hynder
hym; he is euer appliynge his busynes, ye shal neuer fynde
hym idle, I warraunte you. And his office is, to hinder religion, to mayntayne supersticion, to set vp Ido[l]atrie, to teache
al kynde of popetrie; he is readye as can be wished for to
300 sette forthe his ploughe, to deuise as manye wayes as can
be, to deface and obscure Godes glory. Where the Deuyl
is residente and hath his plough goinge: there awaye wyth
bokes, and vp wyth candelles; awaye wyth Bibles and vp
wyth beades; awaye wyth the lyg[h]te of the Gospel, & vp
305 wyth the lyghte of cand[e]lles, yea, at noone-dayes. Where the
Deuyll is residente, that he maye preuaile, vp wyth al superstition and Idolatrie, sensing, peintynge of ymages, candles,
palmes, asshes, holye water, & newe seruice of me[n]nes
inuenting, as though man could inuent a better waye to
310 honoure God wyth then God him-selfe hath apointed.
Downe with Christes crosse, vp with purgatory picke-purse,
vp wyth hym, the popishe pourgatorie, I meane. Awaye wyth

clothinge the naked, the pore & impotent, vp wyth deck-
ynge of ymages and gaye garnishinge of stockes and stones,
vp wyth mannes traditions and his lawes, Downe wyth Gods 315
traditions and hys most holy worde, Downe wyth the olde
honoure dewe to God, and vp wyth the new gods honour,
let al things be done in latine.   There muste be nothynge
but latine, not as much as '*Memento, homo, quod cinis es, et in
cinerem reuerteris*—Remembre, man, that thou arte asshes, 320
and into asshes thou shalte returne,' Whiche be the wordes
that the minister speaketh to the ignoraunte people when he
gyueth them asshes vpon asshe wensdaye, but it muste be
spoken in latine.   Goddes worde may in no wyse be translated into englyshe.   Oh that our prelates woulde be as dili- 325
gente to sowe the corne of good doctrine, as Sathan is to
sowe cockel and darnel!   And this is the deuilyshe ploughinge, the which worcketh to haue thinges in latine, and letteth
the fruteful edification.

XXII.

SIR DAVID LYNDESAY.

A.D. 1552.

SIR DAVID LYNDESAY (generally surnamed 'of the Mount,' from the name of an estate in Fifeshire, in the parish of Moni- mail) was born about 1490, and educated at the university of St. Andrew's. He was the companion of the young Scottish prince, afterwards James V, whose course he watched from his earliest days till his death in 1542. He was knighted by James, and made Lord Lyon King-at-Arms in 1530, though Sir Walter Scott confers that title upon him seventeen years earlier, by a poetical license, as he tells us; see Marmion, canto iv. st. 7, and the note. Lyndesay retired in his latter days to the Mount, where he died about 1557. His principal works are 'The Dreme,' written about 1528; 'The Complaynt,' 1529; 'The Complaynt of the Kingis Papyngo' (Parrot), 1530; 'Ane Satyre of the Thrie Estaits,' 1535; 'The Historie of William Meldrum, Squyer,' be- fore 1550; and 'The Monarche' (i. e. Monarchie or Monarchy), 1552. The last and longest is an account of the most famous monarchies that have flourished in the world. It commences with the Creation, and ends with the Day of Judgment. It was first printed by Jhon Skott in 1552, and has lately been reprinted for the Early English Text Society, edited by Fitz- edward Hall. I follow this edition, and number the lines as they are there numbered. The reader will see that Lyndesay was a fierce Protestant.

From 'The Monarche'; Book III.

[*Pride of the Popes.*]

All men may knaw quhow popis ryngis,
In Dignitie abufe all kyngis,   4500
Als weill in temporalitie
As in-to Spiritualitie.
Thow may se, be experience,
The popis Princely preheminence,
In Cronicles geue thow lyst to luke,   4505
Quhow Carion wryttis, in his buke,
Ane Notabyll Narratioun:
The ȝeir of oure Saluatioun
Alewin hundreth and sax and fyftie,
Pope Alexander, presumptuouslie,   4510
Quhilk wes the thrid pope of that name,
To Fredrike Empriour did diffame:
In Veneis, that tryumphand town,
That nobyll Empriour gart ly down
Apone his wambe, with schame and lake,   4515
Syne tred his feit apone his bake,
In toknyng of obedience.
Thare he schew his preheminence,
And causit his Clergy for to syng
Thir wourdis efter following: 4520
'*Super Aspidem & basiliscum ambulabis,*
Et conculcabis leonem & draconem.'
Than said this humyll Empriour:
'I do to Peter this honour.'

The Pope answerit, with wordis wroith :   4525
' Thow sall me honour, and Peter, boith.'
   Christ, for to schaw his humyll spreit,
Did wasche his pure Disciplis feit :
The Popis holynes, I-wys,
Wyll suffer Kyngis his feit to kys.   4530
Birdis had thare nestis, and toddis thare den ;
Bot Christ Iesus, Saiffer of men,
In erth had nocht ane penny-breid
Quhare-on he mycht repose his heid.
   Quhowbeit, the Popis excellence   4535
Hes Castellis of Magnifycence ;
Abbottis, Byschoppis, and Cardinallis
Hes plesand palyces royallis :
Lyke Paradyse ar those prelattis places,
Wantyng no plesoure of fair faces.   4540
Ihone, Androw, Iames, Peter, nor Paull
Had few housis amang thame all :
Frome tyme thay knew the veritie
Thay did contempne all propertie,
And wer rycht hartfully content   4545
Off meit, drynk, and Abilȝement.
   To saif Mankynde, that wes forlorne,
Christ bure ane creuell crown of thorne ;
The Pope, thre crownis, for the nonis,
Off gold, poulderit with pretious stonis.   4550
   Off gold and syluer, I am sure,
Christ Iesus tuke but lytill cure,
And left nocht, quhen he ȝald the spreit,
To by hym-self ane wynding scheit.
Bot his Successoure, gude Pope Iohne,   4555
Quhen he deceisit in Auinione,
He left behynd hym one treassoure

Off gold and syluer, by mesoure,
Be one Iuste computatioun,
Weill fyue and twentye myllioun, 4560
As dois Indyte Palmerius :
Reid hym, and thow sall fynd it thus.
   Christis Disciplis wer weill knawin
Throuch vertew, quhilk wes be thame schawin
In speciall feruent charitie, 4565
Gret pacience, and humylite :
The popis floke, in all regionis,
Ar knawin best be thare clyppit crounis.
   Christ, he did honour Matromony
In-to the Cane of Galaly, 4570
Quhare he, be his power Diuyne,
Did turne the walter in-to Wyne ;
And, als, chesit sum Maryit men
To be his seruandis, as ȝe ken :
And Peter, duryng all his lyfe, 4575
He thocht no Syn to haif ane wyfe.
Ȝe sall nocht fynd, in no passage,
Quhare Christ forbiddith mariage ;
Bot leifsum tyll ilk man to marye,
Quhilk wantis the gyft of Chaistitye. 4580
   The Pope hes maid the contrar lawis
In his kyngdome, as all men knawis :
None of his preistis dar marye wyfis,
Vnder no les paine nor thare lyfis.
Thocht thay haif Concubynis fyftene, 4585
In-to that cace thay ar ouersene.
Quhat chaistytie thay keip in Rome
Is weill kend ouer all christindome.
   Christ did schaw his obedience
Onto the Empriouris excellence, 4590

And causit Peter for to pay
Trybute to Cesar for thame tway.
Paull biddis ws be obedient
To Kyngis, as the most excellent.

The contrar did Pope Celistene,   4595
Quhen that his Sanctytude serene
Did crown Henry the Empriour:
I thynk he did hym small honour;
For with his feit he did hym crown,
Syne with his fute the crown dang doun,   4600
Sayand: 'I haif Auctoritie
Men tyll exalt to dignitie,
And to mak Empriouris and kyngis,
And Syne depryue thame of thare Ryngis.'
Peter, be my Opinioun,   4605
Did neuer vse sic Dominioun.
Apperandlye, be my Jugement,
That Pope red neuer the new Testament:
Gyf he had lernit at that lore,
He had refusit sic vaine glore,   4610
As Barnabas, Peter, and Paull,
And, rycht so, Christis Disciplis all.

[*Titles of Nuns and Priests.*]

The seilye Nun wyll thynk gret schame,
Without scho callit be Madame;
The pure Preist thynk*is* he gett*is* no rycht,   4665
Be he nocht stylit lyke ane Knycht,
And callit 'schir' affore his name,
As 'schir Thomas' and 'schir Wilȝame.'
All Monkrye, ȝe may heir and se,
Ar callit Denis, for dignite: 4670

Quhowbeit his mother mylk the kow,
He man be callit Dene Androw,
Dene Peter, dene Paull, and dene Robart.
With Christ thay tak ane painfull part,
With dowbyll clethyng frome the cald,   4675
Eitand and drynkand quhen thay wald;
With curious Countryng in the queir:
God wait gyf thay by heuin full deir!
My lorde Abbot, rycht venerabyll,
Ay marschellit vpmoste at the tabyll;   4680
My lord Byschope, most reuerent,
Sett abufe Erlis, in Parliament;
And Cardinalis, duryng thare ryngis,
Fallowis to Princis and to Kyngis;
The Pope exaltit, in honour,   4685
Abufe the potent Empriour.

The proude Persone, I thynk trewlye,
He leidis his lyfe rycht lustelye;
For quhy he hes none vther pyne,
Bot tak his teind, and spend it syne.   4690
Bot he is oblyste, be resoun,
To preche on-tyll perrochioun:
Thoucht thay want precheing sewintene ʒeir,
He wyll nocht want ane boll of beir.

[The Cruelty of Vicars.]

And als the Vicar, as I trow,
He wyll nocht faill to tak ane kow,   4710
And vmaist claith, thoucht babis thame ban,
From ane pure selye housband-man.
Quhen that he lyis for tyll de,
Haiffeing small bairnis two or thre,

And hes thre ky, withouttin mo,   4715
The Vicare moist haue one of tho,
With the gray cloke that happis the bed,
Howbeit that he be purelye cled.
And gyf the wyfe de on the morne,
Thocht all the babis suld be forlorne,   4720
The vther kow he cleik*is* awaye,
With hir pure coit of roploch graye.
And gyf, within tway dayis or thre,
The eldest chyild hapnis to de,
Off the thrid kow he wylbe sure.   4725
Quhen he hes all, than, vnder his cure,
And Father and Mother boith ar dede,
Beg mon the babis, without remede :
Thay hauld the Corps at the kirk-style,
And thare it moste remane ane quhyle,   4730
Tyll thay gett sufficient souerte
For thare kirk-rycht and dewite.
Than cumis the Landis Lord, perfors,
And cleiks tyll hym ane herield hors.
Pure laubourars wald that law wer doun,   4735
Quhilk neuer was fundit be resoun.
I hard thame say, onder confessioun,
That law is brother tyll Oppressioun.

From ' The Monarche'; Book IV.

[*The Signs of the Day of Judgment.*]

The Scripture sayis, efter thir signis   5450
Salbe sene mony maruellous thyngis :
Than sall ryse trybulationis

In erth, and gret mutationis,
Als weill heir vnder as aboue,
Quhen vertewis of the heuin sall moue.   5455
Sic creuell weir salbe, or than,
Wes neuer sene sen the warld began,
The quhilk sall cause gret Indigence,
As darth, hunger, and pestilence.
The horribyll soundis of the sey   5460
The peple sall perturbe and fley.
Ierome sayis, it sall ryse on heycht
Abone montanis, to mennis sycht;
Bot it sall nocht spred ouir the land,
Bot, lyke ane wall, ewin straycht vpstand,   5465
Syne sattell doun agane so law
That no man sall the walter knaw.
Gret Quhalis sall rummeis, rowte, and rair,
Quhose sound redound sall in the air;
All fysche and Monstouris maruellous   5470
Sall cry, with soundis odious,
That men sall wydder on the erd,
And, wepyng, wary sall thare weird,
With lowde allace and welaway,
That euer thay baid to se that day;   5475
And, speciallye, those that dwelland be
Apone the costis of the see.
Rycht so, as Sanct Ierome concludis,
Sall be sene ferleis in the fludis:
The sey, with mouyng maruellous,   5480
Sall byrn with flammis furious:
Rychtso sall byrn fontane and flude;
All herb and tre sall sweit lyk blude;
Fowlis sall fall furth of the air;
Wylde beistis to the plane repair,   5485

And, in thare maner, mak gret mone,
Gowland with mony gryslye grone.
The bodeis of dede creaturis
Appeir sall on thare Sepulturis:
Than sall boith men, wemen, and bairnis   5490
Cum crepand furth of howe Cauernis,
Quhare thay, for dreid, wer hyd affore,
With seych, and sob, and hartis sore;
Wandryng about as thay war wode,
Affamysit for falt of fude.   5495
Non may mak vtheris confortyng,
Bot dule for dule, and Lamentyng.
Quhat may thay do bot weip and wounder,
Quhen thay se roches schaik in schounder,
Throw trimlyng of the erth and quakyng?   5500
Off sorrow, than, salbe no slakyng.
Quho that bene leuand, in those dayis,
May tell of terrabyll affrayis;
Thare ryches, rentis, nor tressour,
That tyme, sall do thame small plesour.   5505
Bot, quhen sic wonderis dois appeir,
Men may be sure the day drawis neir,
That Iuste men pas sall to the glore,
Iniuste, to pane for euer-more.

COVRTIOVR.

Father, said I, we daylie reid   5510
One Artekle, in-to our creid,
Sayand that Christe Omnipotent,
In-to that generall Iugement,
Sall Iuge boith dede and quik also.
Quharefore, declare me, or ʒe go,   5515
Geue thare sall ony man or wyue
That day be funding vpon lyue?

EXPERIENCE.

Quod he : as to that questione,
I sall mak, sone, solutione.
The Scripture planelye doith expone,   5520
Quhen all tokynnis bene cum and gone,
3itt mony one hundreth thousand
That samyn day salbe leuand :
Quhowbeit, thare sall no Creature
Nother of day nor hour be sure ;   5525
For Christ sall cum so suddantlye,
That no man sall the tyme espye ;
As it wes in the tyme of Noye,
Quhen God did all the warld distroye.
Sum on the feild salbe lauborand ;   5530
Sum, in the templis Mariand ;
Sum, afore Iugis makand pley ;
And sum men, saland on the sey.
Those that bene on the feild-going
Sall nocht returne to thare luging.   5535
Quho bene apone his hous aboue
Sall haif no laser to remoue.
Two salbe in the Myll grindyng,
Quhilke salbe taking, but warnyng ;
The one, tyll euerlestyng glore,   5540
The vther, loste for euer-more.
Two salbe lying in one bed ;
The one, to plesour salbe led,
The vther, salbe left allone,
Gretand with mony gryslie grone.   5545
And so, my Sonne, thow may weill trow,
The warld salbe as it is now,—
The peple vsyng thare besynes,
As holy Scripture doith expres.

S

Sen no man knawis the hour, nor day, 5550
The Scripture biddis ws walk and pray,
And for our Syn be penitent,
As Christ wald cum Incontinent.

FINIS.

The Maner quhow Christ sall cvm to his Iugement.

EXPERIENCE.

Qvhen al takinnis bene brocht till end,
Than sall ye sone of god discend: 5555
As fyreflaucht haistely glansyng,
Discend sall ye most heuinly kyng.
As Phebus, in the Orient,
Lychtnis, in haist, the Occident,
So plesandlye he sall appeir 5560
Amang the heuinlye cluddis cleir,
With gret power and Maiestie,
Aboue the cuntrie of Iudee,
As Clerkis doith concludyng haill,
Direct aboue the lustye vaill 5565
Off Iosaphat and Mont Olyueit:
All Prophesie thare salbe compleit.
The Angellis of the Ordoris Nyne
Inueron sall that throne Diuyne
With heuinlye consolatioun, 5570
Makand hym Ministratioun.
In his presens thare salbe borne
The signis of Cros, and Croun of thorne,
Pillar, Nalis, Scurgis, and Speir,
With euerilk thyng that did hym deir, 5575
The tyme of his grym Passioun;
And, for our consolatioun,
Appeir sall, in his handis and feit,

And in his syde, the prent compleit
Off his fyue Woundis Precious,   5580
Schynand lyke Rubeis Radious,
Tyll Reprobatt confusioun;
And, for fynall conclusioun,
He, Sittand in his Trybunall,
With gret power Imperiall.   5585
There sall ane Angell blawe a blast
Quhilk sall mak all the warld agast,
With hydous voce, and vehement—
' Ryse, dede folk, cum to Iugement.'
With that, all Reasonabyll Creature   5590
That euer wes formit be Nature
Sall suddantlye start vp attonis,
Coniunit with Saull, Flesche, Blude, & Bonis.
That terribyll Trumpat, I heir tell,
Beis hard in Heuin, in erth, and hell: 5595
Those that wer drownit in the sey,
That boustious blast thay sall obey;
Quhare-euer the body buryet wase,
All salbe fundyng in that plase.
Angellis sall passe in the four airtis   5600
Off erth, and bryng thame frome all partis,
And, with one instant diligence,
Present thame to his excellence.
　　Sanct Ierome thoucht continuallye
On this Iugement, so ardentlye,   5605
He said, 'quhidder I eit, or drynk,
Or walk, or sleip, forsuth me thynk
That terrabyll Trumpat, lyke ane bell,
So quiklye in my eir doith knell,
As Instantlye it wer present,—   5610
Ryse, dede folk, cum to Iugement !'

Geue Sanct Ierome tuke sic ane fray,
Allace! quhat sall we Synnaris say?
    All those quhilk funding bene on lyue
Salbe Immortall maid belyue;   5615
And, in the twynkling of one Ee,
With fyre thay sall translatit be,
And neuer for to dee agane,—
As Diuine scripture schawis plane,—
Als reddy, boith for pane and glore,   5620
As thay quhilk deit lang tyme affore.
    The scripture sayis, thay sall appeir
In aige of thre and thretty ʒeir,
Quhidder thay deit ʒoung or auld,
Quhose gret nummer may nocht be tauld.   5625
That day sall nocht be myst one man
Quhilk borne wes sen the warld began.
The Angellis sall thame separate,
As Hird the Scheip doith frome the Gate;
And those quhilk bene of Baliallis band   5630
Trymling apone the erth sall stand,
On the left hand of that gret Iuge,
But espirance to gett refuge.
    Bot those quhilk bene Predestinate
Sall frome the erth be Eleuate;   5635
And that moste happy cumpanye
Sall ordourit be tryumphantlye
Att the rycht hand of Christe, our kyng,
Heych in the air, with loude louyng.

XXIII.

NICHOLAS UDALL.

BEFORE A.D. 1553.

WHILST Lyndesay was employed upon his 'Monarche,' Nicholas Udall was probably at work upon his 'Roister Doister,' which is the earliest English play extant, and is divided into Acts and Scenes. Udall was born in Hampshire, about 1504, educated at Corpus Christi College, Oxford, master of Eton College from 1534 to 1543, vicar of Braintree from 1537 to 1544, and master of Westminster School in 1555 and 1556. He died in December 1556, and was buried in St. Margaret's, Westminster. The proof that the comedy of 'Ralph Roister Doister' was written before 1553 lies in the fact that it was quoted from in that year in Sir Thomas Wilson's 'Rule of Reason,' third edition; though the second edition, dated 1552, has *not* the quotation. There is but *one* copy of Udall's comedy in existence, having no title-page; but it was probably printed in 1566. It is now in the library of Eton College, and has been reprinted several times, the last reprint being by Mr. Arber in 1869. I extract the last three Scenes of the third Act from Mr. Arber's edition. Udall wrote several other dramas, but they are all lost. He also published a translation of the third and fourth books of Erasmus' 'Apophthegms,' and assisted in translating Erasmus' 'Paraphrase of the New Testament.'

Our extract tells how Ralph Roister Doister, a silly town-rake, having sent his friend Matthew Merygreeke with a poetical

epistle to Dame Christian Custance, in which he asks the widow
to marry him, receives the answer 'No.' Ralph persists in his
suit, but Dame Custance refers him to his own letter. This
letter, it appears, was read out by Merygreeke so as to destroy
the meaning. It is a fair specimen of comedy.

Actus iij.   Scæna iij.

Mathew Merygreeke.   Roister Doister.

M. Mery. Nowe that the whole answere in my deuise
  doth rest,
I shall paint out our wower in colours of the best.
And all that I say shall be on Custances mouth,
She is author of all that I shall speake forsoth.
But yond commeth Roister Doister nowe in a traunce. 5
R. Royster. Iuno sende me this day good lucke and good
  chaunce.
I can not but come see how Merygreeke doth speede.
M. Mery. I will not see him, but giue him a iutte in
  deede.
I crie your mastershyp mercie.
R. Royster.   And whither now?
M. Mery. As fast as I could runne, sir, in poste against
  you. 10
But why speake ye so faintly, or why are ye so sad?
R. Royster. Thou knowest the prouerbe, bycause I can
  not be had.
Hast thou spoken with this woman?
M. Mery.   Yea, that I haue.
R. Royster. And what will this geare be?
M. Mery.   No; so God me saue.
R. Royster. Hast thou a flat answer?

M. Mery.   Nay, a sharp answer.

R. Royster.   What?

M. Mery. Ye shall not (she sayth) by hir will, marry hir
    cat.   16

Ye are such a calfe, such an asse, such a blocke,

Such a lilburne, such a hoball, such a lobcocke,

And bicause ye shoulde come to hir at no season,

She despised your ma*ster*ship out of all reason.   20

Beware[1] what ye say (ko I) of such a ientman,—

Nay, I feare him not (ko she) doe the best he can.

He vaunteth him-selfe for a man of prowesse greate,

Where-as a good gander I dare say may him beate.

And where he is louted and laughed to skorne,   25

For the veriest dolte that euer was borne,

And veriest lubber, slouen, and beast,

Liuing in this worlde from the west to the east:

Yet of himselfe hath he suche opinion,

That in all the worlde is not the like minion.   30

He thinketh eche woman to be brought in dotage

With the onely sight of his goodly personage:

Yet none that will haue hym: we do hym loute and flocke,

And make him, among vs, our common sporting-stocke,

And so would I now (ko she) saue onely bicause,—   35

Better nay (ko I) I lust not medle with dawes;

Ye are happy (ko I) that ye are a woman,

This would cost you your life in case ye were a man.

    R. Royster. Yea, an hundred thousand pound should not
        saue hir life.

    M. Mery. No, but that ye wowe hir to haue hir to your
        wife.   40

But I coulde not stoppe hir mou∫h.

---

[1] Old text 'Bawawe.'

R. Royster.   Heigh how, alas,—

M. Mery. Be of good cheere, man, and let the worlde
    passe.

R. Royster. What shall I doe or say nowe that it will not
    bee?

M. Mery. Ye shall haue choise of a thousande as good as
    shee,

And ye must pardon hir, it is for lacke of witte.   45

R. Royster. Yea, for were not I an husbande for hir fitte?
Well, what should I now doe?

M. Mery.   In faith I can not tell.

R. Royster. I will go home and die.

M. Mery.   Then shall I bidde toll the bell?

R. Royster. No.

M. Mery.   God haue mercie on your soule, ah good
    gentleman,

That er ye shuld th[u]s dye for an vnkinde woman.   50
Will ye drinke once ere ye goe?

R. Royster.   No, no, I will none.

M. Mery. How feele [ye] your soule to God?

R. Royster.   I am nigh gone.

M. Mery. And shall we hence streight?

R. Royster.   Yea.

M. Mery.   *Placebo dilexi.*

Maister Roister Doister will streight go home and die.

R. Royster. Heigh how, alas, the pangs of death my
    hearte do breake.   55

M. Mery. Holde your peace for shame, sir, a dead man
    may not speake.

Nequando: What mourners and what torches shall we haue?

R. Royster. None.

M. Mery.   *Dirige.*   He will go darklyng to his graue,
Neque lux, neque crux, neque mourners, *neque* clinke,

He will steale to heauen, vnknowing to God, I thinke.   60

A porta inferi : who shall your goodes possesse ?

   R. Royster. Thou shalt be my sectour, and haue all, more

       and lesse.

   M. Mery. Requiem æternam.   Now God reward your

       mastershyp.

And I will crie halfepenie doale for your worshyp.

Come forth, sirs, heare the dolefull newes I shall you tell. 65

                       (*Euocat seruos militis.*)

Our good maister here will no longer with vs dwell,

But in spite of Custance, which hath hym weried,

Let vs see his ma*ster*shyp solemnely buried.

And while some piece of his soule is yet hym within,

Some part of his funeralls let vs here begin.   70

Audiui vocem.   All men take heede by this one gentleman,

Howe you sette your loue vpon an vnkinde woman.

For these women be all such madde pieuishe elues,

They will not be wonne except it please them-selues.

     ·   ·   ·   ·   ·   ·   ·

And will ye needes go from vs thus in very deede?

   R. Royster. Yea, in good sadnesse.

   M. Mery.   Now Iesus Christ be your speede.

Good night, Roger olde knaue, farewell, Roger olde knaue,

Good night, Roger, olde knaue, knaue, knap.   80

Pray for the late maister Roister Doisters soule,

And come forth parish Clarke, let the passing bell toll.

Pray for your mayster, sirs, and for hym ring a peale.

                       (*Ad seruos militis.*)

He was your right good maister while he was in heale.

Qui Lazarum.

   R. Royster.   Heigh how.

   M. Mery.   Dead men go not so fast. 85

In Paradisum.

R. Royster.   Heihow.

M. Mery.   Soft, heare what I haue cast.

R. Royster. I will heare nothing, I am past.

M. Mery.   Whough, wellaway.

Ye may tarie one houre, and heare what I shall say;

Ye were best, sir, for a while to reuiue againe,

And quite them er ye go.

R. Royster.   Trowest thou so ?

M. Mery.   Ye, plain.   90

R. Royster. How may I reuiue, being nowe so farre past ?

M. Mery. I will rubbe your temples, and fette you againe
          at last.

R. Royster. It will not be possible.

M. Mery.   Yes, for twentie pounde.

R. Royster. Armes, what dost thou ?

M. Mery.   Fet you again out of your sound.

By this crosse, ye were nigh gone in deede, I might feele 95

Your soule departing within an inche of your heele.

Now folow my counsell.

R. Royster.   What is it ?

M. Mery.   If I wer you,

Custance should eft seeke to me, ere I woulde bowe.

R. Royster. Well, as thou wilt haue me, euen so will
          I doe.

M. Mery. Then shall ye reuiue againe for an houre or
          two.   100

R. Royster. As thou wilt ; I am content for a little space.

M. Mery. Good happe is not hastie : yet in space com[e]th
          grace ;

To speake with Custance your-selfe shoulde be very well,

What good therof may come, nor I, nor you can tell.

But now the matter standeth vpon your mariage,   105

Ye must now take vnto you a lustie courage.

Ye may not speake with a faint heart to Custance,
But with a lusty breast and countenance,
That she may knowe she hath to answere to a man.

R. Royster. Yes, I can do that as well as any can.   110

M. Mery. Then bicause ye must Custance face to face
    wowe,
Let vs see how to behaue your-selfe ye can doe.
Ye must haue a portely bragge after youre estate.

R. Royster. Tushe, I can handle that after the best rate.

M. Mery. Well done, so loe, vp, man, with your head and
    chin,   115
Vp with that snoute, man: so loe, nowe ye begin;
So, that is somewhat like, but prankie cote, nay whan,
That is a lustie brute, handes vnder your side, man:
So loe, now is it euen as it should bee,
That is somewhat like, for a man of your degree.   120
Then must ye stately goe, ietting vp and downe,
Tut, can ye no better shake the taile of your gowne?
There loe, suche a lustie bragge it is ye must make.

R. Royster. To come behind, and make curtsie, thou must
    som pains take.

M. Mery. Else were I much to blame, I thanke your mas-
    tershyp;   125
The lorde one day all to begrime you with worshyp.
'Backe, sir sauce, let gentlefolkes haue elbowe-roome,
Voyde, sirs, see ye not maister Roister Doister come?
Make place, my maisters.'

R. Royster.   Thou iustlest nowe to nigh.

M. Mery. 'Back, al rude loutes.'

R. Royster.   Tush.

M. Mery.   I crie your ma*s*ter*s*hip mercy.
Hoighdagh, if faire fine mistresse Custance sawe you now,
Ralph Royster Doister were hir owne, I warrant you.   132

R. Royster. Neare an M by your girdle?

M. Mery.   Your good mastershyps
Maistershyp were hir owne Mistreshyps mistreshyps;
Ye were take vp for haukes, ye were gone, ye were gone; 135
But now one other thing more yet I thinke vpon.

R. Royster. Shewe what it is.

M. Mery.   A wower, be he neuer so poore,
Must play and sing before his bestbeloue[d]s doore;
How much more than you?

R. Royster.   Thou speakest wel, out of dout.

M. Mery. And perchaunce that woulde make hir the sooner
    come out.   140

R. Royster. Goe call my Musitians, bydde them high
    apace.

M. Mery. I wyll be here with them ere ye can say trey
    ace.   *Exeat.*

R. Royster. This was well sayde of Merygreeke, I lowe
    hys wit;
Before my sweete hearts dore we will haue a fit,
That if my loue come forth, that I may with hir talke, 145
I doubt not but this geare shall on my side walke.
But lo, how well Merygreeke is returned sence.

[Re-enter Merygreeke.]

M. Mery. There hath grown no grasse on my heele since
    I wente hence,
Lo, here haue I brought [them] that shall make you pastance.

R. Royster. Come, sirs, let vs sing to winne my deare loue
    Custance.   150

Cantent.

M. Mery. Lo where she commeth, some countenaunce to
    hir make,
And ye shall heare me be plaine with hir for your sake.

Actus iij. Scæna iiij.

Custance. Merygreeke. Roister Doister.

C. Custance. What gaudying and foolyng is this afore my
  doore?

M. Mery. May not folks be honest, pray you, though they
  be pore?

C. Custance. As that thing may be true, so rich folks may
  be fooles.

R. Royster. Hir talke is as fine as she had learned in
  schooles.

M. Mery. Looke partly towarde hir, and drawe a little
  nere.   5

C. Custance. Get ye home, idle folkes.

M. Mery.   Why may not we be here?
Nay and ye will haze, haze : otherwise I tell you plaine,
And ye will not haze, then giue vs our geare againe.

C. Custance. In deede I haue of yours much gay things,
  God saue all.

R. Royster. Speake gently vnto hir, and let hir take all. 10

M. Mery. Ye are to tender-hearted : shall she make vs
  dawes?
Nay dame, I will be plaine with you in my friends cause.

R. Royster. Let all this passe, sweete heart, and accept
  my seruice.

C. Custance. I will not be serued with a foole in no wise;
When I choose a husbande I hope to take a man.   15

M. Mery. And where will ye finde one which can doe that
  he can?
Now thys man towarde you being so kinde,

You ought[1] to make him an answere somewhat to his
    minde.

C. Custance. I sent him a full answere by you, dyd I not?

M. Mery. And I reported it.

C. Custance.   Nay, I must speake it againe.

R. Royster. No, no, he tolde it all.

M. Mery.   Was I not metely plaine?

R. Royster. Yes.

M. Mery.   But I would not tell all, for faith, if I had,
With you, dame Custance, ere this houre it had been bad,
And not without cause: for this goodly personage
Ment no lesse than to ioyne with you in mariage.   25

C. Custance. Let him wast no more labour nor sute about
    me.

M. Mery. Ye know not where your preferment lieth, I see,
He sending you such a token, ring, and letter.

C. Custance. Mary here it is, ye neuer sawe a better!

M. Mery. Let vs see your letter.

C. Custance.   Holde, reade it if ye can,
And see what letter it is to winne a woman. [*Gives a letter.*]

M. Mery. [*reads*] 'To mine owne deare [darling] birde,
    swete heart, and pigsny,
Good Mistresse Custance, present these by and by,'—
Of this superscription do ye blame the stile?

C. Custance. With the rest as good stuffe as ye redde a
    great while.   35

M. Mery. 'Sweete mistresse, where as I loue you nothing
    at all,
Regarding your substance and richesse chiefe of all,
For your personage, beautie, demeanour, and wit,
I commende me vnto you neuer a whit.

---

[1] Old text 'not.'

Sorie to heare report of your good welfare.   40
For (as I heare say) suche your conditions are,
That ye be worthie fauour of no liuing man,
To be abhorred of euery honest man ;
To be taken for a woman enclined to vice ;
Nothing at all to Vertue gyuing hir due price.   45
Wherfore concerning mariage, ye are thought
Suche a fine Paragon, as nere honest man bought.
And nowe by these presentes I do you aduertise
That I am minded to marrie you in no wise.
For your goodes and substance, I can¹ bee contente   50
To take you as ye are.   If ye will² bee my wyfe,
Ye shall be assured for the tyme of my lyfe,
I will keepe you³ ryght well from good rayment and fare ;
Ye shall not be kepte but in sorowe and care.
Ye shall in no wyse lyue at your owne libertie,   55
Doe and say what ye lust, ye shall neuer please me ;
But when ye are mery, I will be all sadde ;
When ye are sory, I will be very gladde.
When ye seeke your heartes ease, I will be vnkinde,
At no tyme in me shall ye muche gentlenesse finde.   60
But all things contrary to your will and minde
Shall be done : otherwise I wyll not be behinde
To speake.   And as for all them that woulde do you wrong,
I will so helpe and mainteyne, ye shall not lyue long.
Nor any foolish dolt shall cumbre you but I.   65
I, who ere—say nay—wyll sticke by you tyll I die⁴.
Thus, good mistresse Custance, the lorde you saue and kepe
From me Roister Doister, whether I wake or slepe ;
Who fauoureth you no lesse, (ye may be bolde)
Than this letter purporteth, which ye haue vnfolde.'   70

¹ Old text 'coulde'; but see p. 278.   ² Old text 'mynde to'; cf. p. 278.
³ Old text 'you.'   ⁴ This line is omitted here ; but see p. 278.

C. Custance. Howe by this letter of loue? is it not fine?

R. Royster. By the armes of Caleys, it is none of myne.

M. Mery. Fie, you are fowle to blame; this is your owne
hand.

C. Custance. Might not a woman be proude of such an
husbande?

M. Mery. Ah that ye would in a letter shew such despite!

R. Royster. Oh I would I had hym here, the which did it
endite!   76

M. Mery. Why, ye made it your-selfe, ye tolde me, by this
light.

R. Royster. Yea, I ment I wrote it myne owne selfe yes-
ternight.

C. Custance. Ywis, sir, I would not haue sent you such a
mocke.

R. Royster. Ye may so take it, but I ment it not so, by
cocke.   80

M. Mery. Who can blame this woman to fume and frette
and rage?

Tut, tut, your-selfe nowe haue marde your own marriage.

Well, yet mistresse Custance, if ye can this remitte,

This gentleman other-wise may your loue requitte.

C. Custance. No; God be with you both, and seeke no
more to me.   *Exeat.*

R. Royster. Wough, she is gone for euer, I shall hir no
more see.   86

M. Mery. What? weepe? fye for shame, and blubber?
for manhods sake,

Neuer lette your foe so muche pleasure of you take.

Rather play the mans parte, and doe loue refraine.

If she despise you, een despise ye hir againe.   • 90

R. Royster. By gosse, and for thy sake I defye hir in
deede.

M. Mery. Yea, and perchaunce that way ye shall much
     sooner speede;
For one madde propretie these women haue in fey,
When ye will, they will not: Will not ye, then will they.
Ah foolishe woman, ah moste vnluckie Custance,   95
Ah vnfortunate woman, ah pieuishe Custance,
Art thou to thine harmes so obstinately bent,
That thou canst not see where lieth thine high preferment?
Canst thou not lub dis man, which coulde lub dee so well?
Art thou so much thine own foe?

R. Royster.   Thou dost the truth tell.

M. Mery. Wel I lament.

R. Royster.   So do I.

M. Mery.   Wherfor?

R. Royster.   For this thing,
Bicause she is gone.

M. Mery.   I mourne for an other thing.   102

R. Royster. What is it, Merygreeke, wherfore thou dost
     griefe take?

M. Mery. That I am not a woman myselfe for your
     sake;
I would haue you my-selfe, and a strawe for yond Gill,   105
And make [1] much of you though it were against my will.
I would not, I warrant you, fall in such a rage,
As so to refuse suche a goodly personage.

R. Royster. In faith, I heartily thanke thee, Merygreeke.

M. Mery. And I were a woman—

R. Royster.   Thou wouldest to me seeke.

M. Mery. For though I say it, a goodly person ye bee.   111

R. Royster. No, no.

M. Mery.   Yes, a goodly man as ere I dyd see.

---

[1] Old text 'mocke.'

T

R. Royster. No, I am a poore homely man as God made
mee.

M. Mery. By the faith that I owe to God, sir, but ye bee.
Woulde I might, for your sake, spende a thousande pound
land.   115

R. Royster. I dare say thou wouldest haue me to thy husbande.

M. Mery. Yea: And I were the fairest lady in the shiere,
And knewe you as I know you, and see you nowe here.
Well, I say no more.

R. Royster.   Gramercies, with all my hart.

M. Mery. But since that can not be, will ye play a wise
parte?   120

R. Royster. How should I?

M. Mery.   Refraine from Custance a while now,
And I warrant hir soone right glad to seeke to you:
Ye shall see hir anon come on hir knees creeping,
And pray you to be good to hir, salte teares weeping.

R. Royster. But what and she come not?

M. Mery.   In faith, then farewel she!
Or else, if ye be wroth, ye may auenged be.   126

R. Royster. By cocks precious potsticke, and een so I shall.
I wyll vtterly destroy hir, and house and all,
But I woulde be auenged, in the meane space,
On that vile scribler, that did my wowyng disgrace.   130

M. Mery. Scribler (ko you) in deede he is worthy, no
lesse.
I will call hym to you, and ye bidde me doubtlesse.

R. Royster. Yes, for although he had as many liues,
As a thousande widowes, and a thousande wiues,
As a thousande lyons, and a thousand rattes,   .   135
A thousande wolues, and a thousand cattes,
A thousand bulles, and a thousande calues,

And a thousande legións diuided in halues,
He shall neuer scape death on my swordes point,
Though I shoulde be torne therfore ioynt by ioynt.   140
   M. Mery. Nay, if ye will kyll him, I will not fette him,
I will not in so much extremitie sette him;
He may yet amende, sir, and be an honest man,
Therfore pardon him, good soule, as muche as ye can.
   R. Royster. Well, for thy sake, this once with his lyfe he
      shall passe,   145
But I wyll hewe hym all to pieces, by the Masse.
   M. Mery. Nay fayth, ye shall promise that he shall no
      harme haue,
Else I will not fet him.
   R. Royster.   I shall, so God me saue.
But I may chide him a good.
   M. Mery.   Yea, that do hardely.   149
   R. Royster. Go then.
   M. Mery.   I returne, and bring him to you by and by.
                    Ex.

Actus iij. Scæna v.

Roister Doister. Mathewe Merygreeke. Scriuener.

   R. Royster. What is a gentleman but his worde and his
      promise?
I must nowe saue this vilaines lyfe in any wise;
And yet at hym already my handes doe tickle.
I shall vneth holde them, they wyll be so fickle.
But lo, and Merygreeke haue not brought him sens!   5
   M. Mery. [*to Scriv.*] Nay, I woulde I had of my purse
      payde fortie pens.
   Scriuener. So woulde I too: but it needed not that
      stounde.

M. Mery. But the ientman had rather spent fiue thousande pounde,

For it disgraced him at least fiue tymes so muche.

Scriuener. He disgraced hym-selfe, his loutishnesse is suche.   10

R. Royster. Howe long they stande prating? Why comst thou not away?

M. Mery. Come nowe to hymselfe, and hearke what he will say.

Scriuener. I am not afrayde in his presence to appeere.

R. Royster. Arte thou come, felow?

Scriuener. How thinke you? am I not here?

R. Royster. What hindrance hast thou done me, and what villanie?   15

Scriuener. It hath come of thy-selfe, if thou hast had any.

R. Royster. All the stocke thou comest of, later or rather,

From thy fyrst fathers grandfathers fathers father,

Nor all that shall come of thee to the worldes ende,

Though to three score generations they descende,   20

Can be able to make me a iust recompense

For this trespasse of thine and this one offense.

Scriuener. Wherin?

R. Royster. Did you not make me a letter, brother?

Scriuener. Pay the like hire, I will make you suche an other.

R. Royster. Nay, see and these [wretched] Phariseys and Scribes   25

Doe not get their liuyng by polling and bribes.

If it were not for shame—

Scriuener. Nay, holde thy hands still.

M. Mery. Why? did ye not promise that ye would not him spill?

Scriuener. Let him not spare me.

R. Royster. Why? wilt thou strike me again?

Scriuener. Ye shall haue as good as ye bring of me, that
    is plaine.   30

M. Mery. I can not blame him, sir, though your blowes
    wold him greue.

For he knoweth present death to ensue of all ye geue.

R. Royster. Well, this man for once hath purchased thy
    pardon.

Scriuener. And what say ye to me? or else I will be gon.

R. Royster. I say the letter thou madest me was not
    good.   35

Scriuener. Then did ye wrong copy it of likelyhood.

R. Royster. Yes, out of thy copy worde for worde I wrote.

Scriuener. Then was it as ye prayed to haue it, I wote;

But in reading and pointyng there was made some faulte.

R. Royster. I wote not, but it made all my matter to
    haulte.   [*Shews the original.*]   40

Scriuener. Howe say you, is this mine originall or no?

R. Royster. The selfe same that I wrote out of, so mote
    I go.

Scriuener. Loke you on your owne fist, and I will looke
    on this,

And let this man be iudge whether I reade amisse.

'To myne owne dere [darling] birde, sweete heart, and
    pigsny,   45

Good mistresse Custance, present these by and by.'

How now? doth not this superscription agree?

R. Royster. Reade that is within, and there ye shall the
    fault see.

Scriuener. 'Sweete mistresse, where as I loue you, nothing
    at all

Regarding your richesse and substance: chiefe of all,   50

For your personage, beautie, demeanour, and witte

I commende me vnto you: Neuer a whitte

Sory to heare reporte of your good welfare.
For (as I heare say) suche your conditions are,
That ye be worthie fauour: Of no liuing man   55
To be abhorred: of euery honest man
To be taken for a woman enclined to vice
Nothing at all: to vertue giuing hir due price.
Wherfore concerning mariage, ye are thought
Suche a fine Paragon as nere honest man bought.   60
And nowe by these presents I doe you aduertise,
That I am minded to marrie you: In no wyse
For your goodes and substance: I can be content
To take you as you are: yf ye will be my wife,
Ye shall be assured for the time of my life,   65
I wyll keepe you right well: from good raiment and fare
Ye shall not be kept: but in sorowe and care
Ye shall in no wyse lyue: at your owne libertie,
Doe and say what ye lust: ye shall neuer please me
But when ye are merrie: I will bee all sadde   70
When ye are sorie: I wyll be very gladde
When ye seeke your heartes ease: I will be vnkinde
At no time: in me shall ye muche gentlenesse finde.
But all things contrary to your will and minde
Shall be done otherwise: I wyll not be behynde   75
To speake: And as for all them[1] that woulde do you wrong,
(I wyll so helpe and maintayne ye) shall not lyue long.
Nor any foolishe dolte shall cumber you, but I,
I, who ere say nay, wyll sticke by you tyll I die.
Thus, good mistresse Custance, the lorde you saue and
        kepe.   80
From me, Roister Doister, whether I wake or slepe,
Who fauoureth you no lesse, (ye may be bolde)

---

[1] Old text 'they'; but see p. 271.

Than this letter purporteth, which ye haue vnfolde.'
Now sir, what default can ye finde in this letter?

    R. Royster. Of truth, in my mynde, there can not be a
      better.   • 85

    Scriuener. Then was the fault in readyng, and not in
      writyng,
No, nor I dare say in the fourme of endityng;—
But who read this letter, that it sounded so nought?

    M. Mery. I redde it in deede.
    Scriuener.   Ye red it not as ye ought.

    R. Royster. Why, thou wretched villaine, was all this same
      fault in thee?   90

    M. Mery. I knocke your costarde if ye offer to strike me.

    R. Royster. Strikest thou in deede? and I offer but in iest?

    M. Mery. Yea, and rappe you againe except ye can sit in
      rest.
And I will no longer tarie here, me beleue.

    R. Royster. What, wilt thou be angry, and I do thee
      forgeue?   95
Fare thou well, scribler, I crie thee mercie in deede.

    Scriuener. Fare ye well, bibbler, and worthily may ye
      speede!   [*Exeat.*]

    R. Royster. If it were an other but thou, it were a knaue.

    M. Mery. Ye are an other your-selfe, sir, the lorde vs both
      saue;
Albeit in this matter I must your pardon craue.   100
Alas, woulde ye wyshe in me the witte that ye haue?
But as for my fault, I can quickely [it] amende,
I will shewe Custance it was I that did offende.

    R. Royster. By so doing, hir anger may be reformed.

    M. Mery. But if by no entreatie she will be turned,   105
Then sette lyght by hir and bee as testie as shee,
And doe your force vpon hir with extremitie.

R. Roister. Come on therefore, lette vs go home in sad-
    nesse.

M. Mery. That if force shall neede, all may be in a readi-
    • nesse;

And as for thys letter, hardely let all go,   110
We wyll know where she refuse you for that or no.

                                   Exeant am[bo].

XXIV.

THOMAS SACKVILLE, LORD BUCKHURST.

A.D. 1563.

THOMAS SACKVILLE, the first Lord Buckhurst and Earl of
Dorset, only son of Sir Richard Sackville, was born in 1536, at
Buckhurst in Sussex. He is alike celebrated as a poet and a
statesman. After the death of his political enemy, the Earl of
Leicester, he was taken into Elizabeth's confidence, and, on the
death of Burghley in 1598, was made Lord Treasurer, which
office he held till his death in the reign of James, April 19, 1608.
He is best known as joint author, with T. Norton, of 'Gorboduc,'
otherwise called 'Ferrex and Porrex.' 'The Mirrour for Magistrates,' a collection of narratives by several poets on the misfortunes of the great men in English history, was planned by
him; and he contributed to it 'The Induction' or poetical
preface, and 'The Complaint of the Duke of Buckingham.'
'The Induction' is an extraordinary poem, and too little known.
It describes how the poet, being in a melancholy frame of mind,
beheld the personification of Sorrow, who undertook to guide
him to the infernal regions, as Virgil guided Dante, and shewed
him there the figures of Remorse, Dread, Revenge, Misery,
Greed, Sleep, Old Age, Malady, Famine, Death, and War, and
many of the unfortunate heroes of history, as Darius, Hannibal,
Pompey, Marius, Cyrus, Xerxes, and Priam. The reader should
peruse this with patience. The beginning is purposely sombre,

monotonous, and somewhat prolix, but the latter portion is sub-
lime and majestic, and not inferior to Spenser. In the opinion
of Hallam, it 'forms a link which unites the school of Chaucer
and Lydgate with the Fairy Queen.' It is here printed *entire*,
from 'A Myrrovr for Magistrates' [Second Part; by William
Baldwyne], London, 1563, quarto; fol. cxiiii, back. The short
prose Prologue is of course not by Sackville, but by William
Baldwyne.

[*Induction to 'The Mirrour for Magistrates.'*]

Prologue.

WHEN I had read this, one sayd it was very darke, and
hard to be vnderstood: excepte it were diligently and very
leasurely considered. 'I like it the better' (q*uod* an other)
'For that shal cause it to be the oftener reade, and the
5 better remembred. Considering also that it is written for
the learned (for such all Magistrates are or should be), it
can not be to hard, so long as it is sound and learnedly
wrytten.' Then sayd the reader: 'The next here whom I
finde miserable are king Edwards two sonnes, cruelly mur-
10 dered in the tower of London: Haue you theyr tragedy?'
'No surely' (q*uod* I) 'The Lord Vaulx vndertooke to penne
it, but what he hath done therein I am ńot certayne, &
therfore I let it passe til I knowe farder. I haue here *the*
duke of Buckingha*m*, king Richardes chyefe instrument,
15 wrytten by mayster Thomas Sackuille.' 'Read it, we pray
you,' sayd they: 'with a good wyl' (q*uod* I) 'but fyrst you
shal heare his preface or Induction.' 'Hath he made a
preface' (q*uod* one), 'what meaneth he thereby, seeing none
other hath vsed the like order?' 'I wyl tell you the cause
20 thereof' (q*uod* I) 'which is thys: After that he vnderstoode

that some of the counsayle would not suffer the booke to
be printed in suche order as we had agreed and determined,
he purposed with him-selfe to haue gotten at my handes
al the tragedies that were before the duke of Buckinghams,
Which he would haue preserued in one volume. And from 25
that time backeward euen to the time of William the con-
querour, he determined to continue and perfect all the story
him-selfe, in such order as Lydgate (folowing Bocchas) had
already vsed. And therfore to make a meete induction into
the matter, he deuised this poesye: which in my iudgement 30
is so wel penned, that I woulde not haue any verse therof
left out of our volume. Nowe that you knowe the cause
and meanyng of his doing, you shal also heare what he
hath done. His Induccion beginneth thus.'

The Induction.

1 THe wrathfull winter, prochinge on a-pace,
  With blustring blastes had al ybared the treen,
  And olde Saturnus with his frosty face
  With chilling colde had pearst the tender green:
  The mantels rent, wherein enwrapped been
  The gladsom groves that nowe laye ouerthrowen,
  The tapets torne, and euery blome downe blowen.

2   The soyle that earst so seemely was to seen
  Was all despoyled of her beauties hewe:
  And soot freshe flowers (wherwith the sommers queen
  Had clad the earth) now Boreas blastes downe blewe.
  And small fowles flocking, in theyr song did rewe
  The winters wrath, wherwith eche thing defaste
  In woful wise bewayld the sommer past.

3   Hawthorne had lost his motley lyverye,
The naked twigges were shivering all for colde:
And dropping downe the teares abundantly,
Eche thing (me thought) with weping eye me tolde
The cruell season, bidding me withholde
My-selfe within, for I was gotten out
Into the feldes, where as I walkte about.

4   When loe! the night with mistie mantels spred
Gan darke the daye, and dim the azure skyes,
And Venus in her message Hermes sped
To bluddy Mars, to wyl him not to ryse,
While she her-selfe approcht in speedy wise:
And Virgo hiding her disdaineful brest
With Thetis nowe had layd her downe to rest.

5   Whiles Scorpio, dreading Sagittarius dart,
(Whose bowe, prest bent in sight, the string had slypt),
Downe slyd into the Ocean-flud aparte,
The Beare, that in the Iryshe seas had dipt
His griesly feete, with spede from thence he whypt:
For Thetis, hasting from the Virgines bed,
Pursued the Bear, that ear she came was fled.

6   And Phaeton nowe neare reaching to his race
With glistering beames, gold-streamynge where they bent,
Was prest to enter in his resting-place.
Erythius, that in the cart fyrste went,
Had euen nowe attaynde his iourneyes stent,
And fast declining, hid away his head;
while Titan couched him in his purple bed.

7   And pale Cinthea, with her borowed light
Beginning to supply her brothers place,
was past the Noonesteede syxe degrees in sight,
when sparklyng starres amyd the heauens face
with twinkling light shone[1] on the earth apace,
That, whyle they brought about the nightes chare,
The darke had dimmed the daye ear I was ware.

8 And sorowing I to see the sommer flowers,
The liuely greene, the lusty leas forlorne,
The sturdy trees so shattered with the showers,
The fieldes so fade that floorisht so beforne,
It taught me wel all earthly thinges be borne
To dye the death, for nought long time may last.
The sommers beauty yeeldes to winters blast.

9   Then looking vpward to the heauens leames
with nightes starres thicke powdred euery where,
which erst so glistened with the golden streames
That chearefull Phebus spred downe from his sphere,
Beholding dark oppressing day so neare :
The sodayne sight reduced to my minde
The sundry chaunges that in earth we fynde.

10 That, musing on this worldly wealth in thought,
which comes and goes more faster than we see
The flyckering flame that with the fyer is wrought,
My busie minde presented vnto me
Such fall of pieres as in this realme had be :
That ofte I wisht some would their woes descryue,
To warne the rest whom fortune left aliue.

---

[1] Printed 'shoen.'

11   And strayt forth stalking with redoubled pace
      For that I sawe the night drewe on so fast,
      In blacke all clad there fell before my face
      A piteous wight, whom woe had al forwaste;
      Furth from her iyen the cristall teares outbrast,
      And syghing sore, her handes she wrong and folde,
      Tare al her heare, that ruth was to beholde.

12   Her body small, forwithered and forespent,
      As is the stalke that sommers drought opprest,
      Her wealked face with woful teares besprent,
      Her colour pale, and (as it seemd her best)
      In woe and playnt reposed was her rest.
      And as the stone that droppes of water weares,
      So dented were her cheekes with fall of teares.

13   Her iyes swollen with flowing streames aflote,
      Wherewith her lookes throwen vp full piteouslye,
      Her forceles handes together ofte she smote,
      With dolefull shrikes, that eckoed in the skye:
      Whose playnt such sighes dyd strayt accompany,
      That in my doome was neuer man did see
      A wight but halfe so woe-begon as she.

14   I stoode agast, beholding all her plight,
      Tweene dread and dolour so distreynd in hart,
      That, while my heares vpstarted with the sight,
      The teares out-streamde for sorowe of her smart:
      But when I sawe no ende that could aparte
      The deadly dewle, which she so sore dyd make,
      With dolefull voice then thus to her I spake :—

5   'Vnwrap thy woes, what euer wight thou be,
And stint betime to spill thy-selfe wyth playnt;
Tell what thou art, and whence, for well I see
Thou canst not dure wyth sorowe thus attaynt.'
And with that worde, of sorrowe all forfaynt,
She looked vp, and prostrate as she laye,
With piteous sound loe! thus she gan to saye:—

6   'Alas, I wretche, whom thus thou seest distreyned
With wasting woes that neuer shall aslake,
Sorrowe I am, in endeles tormentes payned,
Among the furies in the infernall lake:
Where Pluto, god of Hel so griesly blacke,
Doth holde his throne, and *Letheus* deadly taste
Doth rieue remembraunce of eche thyng forepast;

7   Whence come I am, the drery destinie
And luckeles lot for to bemone of those,
Whom Fortune in this maze of miserie
Of wretched chaunce most wofull myrrours chose,
That when thou seest how lightly they did lose
Theyr pompe, theyr power, & that they thought most sure,
Thou mayest soone deeme no earthly ioye may dure.'

8   Whose rufull voyce no sooner had out-brayed
Those wofull wordes, wherewith she sorrowed so,
But 'out! alas!' she shryght, and never stayed,
Fell downe, and all to-dasht her-selfe for woe.
The colde pale dread my lyms gan overgo,
And I so sorrowed at her sorowes eft,
That, what with griefe and feare, my wittes were reft.

19 I strecht my-selfe, and strayt my hart reuiues,
That dread and dolour erst did so appale,
Lyke him that with the feruent feuer stryves,
When sickenes seekes his castell health to skale :
With gathered spirites so forst I feare to auale.
And rearing her with anguishe all fordone,
My spirits returnd, and then I thus begonne.

20 'O Sorrowe, alas, sith Sorrowe is thy name,
And that to thee this drere doth well pertayne,
In vayne it were to seeke to ceas the same :
But, as a man hym-selfe with sorrowe slayne,
So I, alas ! do comfort thee in payne,
That here in sorrowe art forsonke so depe,
That at thy sight I can but sigh and wepe.'

21 I had no sooner spoken of a stike,
But that the storme so rumbled in her brest
As Eolus could neuer roare the like,
And showers downe rayned from her iyen so fast,
That all bedreynt the place, till at the last
Well eased they the dolour of her minde,
As rage of rayne doth swage the stormy wynde.

22 For furth she paced in her fearfull tale :
'Cum, cum,' (quod she) 'and see what I shall shewe ;
Cum heare the playning, and the bytter bale
Of worthy men, by Fortune ouerthrowe.
Cum thou and see them rewing al in rowe.
They were but shades that erst in minde thou rolde,
Cum, cum with me, thine iyes shall them beholde.'

23 What could these wordes but make me more agast,
To heare her tell whereon I musde while-eare?
So was I mazed therewyth, tyll at the last,
Musing vpon her wurdes, and what they were,
All sodaynly well lessoned was my feare:
For to my minde returned howe she telde
Both what she was, and where her wun she helde.

24 Whereby I knewe that she a Goddesse was,
And therewithall resorted to my minde
My thought, that late presented me the glas
Of brittle state, of cares that here we finde,
Of thousand woes to silly men assynde:
And howe she nowe byd me come and beholde,
To see with iye that erst in thought I rolde.

25 Flat downe I fell, and with al reuerence
Adored her, perceyuing nowe that she,
A Goddesse sent by godly prouidence,
In earthly shape thus showed her-selfe to me,
To wayle and rue this worldes vncertayntye:
And while I honourd thus her godheds might,
With playning voyce these wurdes to me she shryght:

26 'I shal the guyde first to the griesly lake,
And thence vnto the blisfull place of rest,
Where thou shalt see and heare the playnt they make,
That whilom here bare swinge among the best.
This shalt thou see, but great is the vnrest
That thou must byde before thou canst attayne
Vnto the dreadfull place where these remayne.

U

27 And with these wurdes as I vpraysed stood,
  And gan to folowe her that strayght furth paced,
  Eare I was ware, into a desert wood
  We nowe were cum : where, hand in hand imbraced,
  She led the way, and through the thicke so traced,
  As, but I had bene guyded by her might,
  It was no waye for any mortall wight.

28 But loe ! while thus, amid the desert darke,
  We passed on with steppes and pace vnmete :
  A rumbling roar, confusde with howle and barke
  Of Dogs, shoke all the ground vnder our feete,
  And stroke the din within our eares so deepe,
  As halfe distraught vnto the ground I fell,
  Besought retourne, and not to visite hell.

29 But she forth-with vplifting me apace
  Remoued my dread, and with a steadfast minde
  Bad me come on, for here was now the place,
  The place where we our trauayle[s] ende should finde.
  Wherewith I arose, and to the place assynde
  Astoynde I stalke, when strayt we approched nere
  The dredfull place, that you wil dread to here.

30 An hydeous hole al vaste, withouten shape,
  Of endles depth. orewhelmde with ragged stone,
  Wyth ougly mouth, and grisly Iawes doth gape,
  And to our sight confounds it-selfe in one.
  Here entred we, and yeding forth, anone
  An horrible lothly lake we might discerne
  As blacke as pitche, that cleped is Auerne.

31 A deadly gulfe where nought but rubbishe growes,
With fowle blacke swelth in thickned lumpes *that* lyes,
Which vp in the ayer such stinking vapors throwes,
That ouer there may flye no fowle but dyes,
Choakt with the pestilent sauours that aryse.
Hither we cum, whence forth we styll did pace,
In dreadfull feare amid the dreadfull place.

32 And first within the portche and iawes of Hell
Sate diepe Remorse of conscience, al besprent
With teares : and to her-selfe oft would she tell
Her wretchednes, and cursing neuer stent
To sob and sigh : but euer thus lament
With thoughtful care, as she that all in vayne
Would weare and waste continually in payne.

33 Her iyes vnstedfast, rolling here and there,
Whurld on eche place, as place that ve[n]geauns brought,
So was her minde continually in feare,
Tossed and tormented with the tedious thought
Of those detested crymes which she had wrought :
With dreadful cheare and lookes throwen to the skye,
Wyshyng for death, and yet she could not dye.

34 Next sawe we Dread, al tremblyng how he shooke,
With foote vncertayne profered here and there :
Benumde of speache, and with a gastly looke
Searcht euery place al pale and dead for feare,
His cap borne vp with staring of his heare,
Stoynde and amazde at his owne shade for dreed,
And fearing greater daungers than was nede.

35   And next within the entry of this lake
Sate fell Reuenge, gnashing her teeth for yre,
Deuising meanes howe she may vengeaunce take,
Neuer in rest tyll she haue her desire :
But frets within so farforth with the fyer
Of wreaking flames, that nowe determines she
To dye by death, or vengde by death to be.

36   When fell Reuenge with bloudy foule pretence
Had showed her-selfe as next in order set,
With trembling limmes we softly parted thence,
Tyll in our iyes another sight we met :
When fro my hart a sigh forthwith I fet,
Rewing alas ! vpon the wofull plight
Of Miserie, that next appered in sight.

37   His face was leane, and sumdeale pyned away,
And eke his handes consumed to the bone,
But what his body was I can not say,
For on his carkas rayment had he none
Saue cloutes & patches, pieced one by one.
With staffe in hand, and skrip on shoulders cast,
His chiefe defence agaynst the winters blast.

38   His foode, for most, was wylde fruytes of the tree,
Unles sumtime sum crummes fell to his share,
Which in his wallet long, God wote, kept he.
As on the which full dayntlye would he fare ;
His drinke the running streame : his cup the bare
Of his palme closed, his bed the hard colde grounde.
To this poore life was Miserie ybound.

39   Whose wretched state when we had well behelde
With tender ruth on him and on his feres,
In thoughtful cares, furth then our pace we helde.
And by and by, an other [1] shape apperes
Of Greedy care, stil brushing vp the breres,
His knuckles knobd, his fleshe deepe dented in,
With tawed handes, and hard ytanned skyn.

40   The morrowe graye no sooner hath begunne
To spreade his light euen peping in our iyes,
When he is vp and to his worke yrunne ;
But let the nightes blacke mistye mantels rise,
And with fowle darke neuer so much disguyse
The fayre bright day, yet ceasseth he no whyle,
But hath his candels to prolong his toyle.

41   By him lay Heauy slepe, the cosin of death,
Flat on the ground, and stil as any stone,
A very corps, save yelding forth a breath.
Small kepe tooke he whom Fortune frowned on,
Or whom she lifted vp into the trone
Of high renowne ; but as a liuing death,
So dead alyve, of lyef he drewe the breath.

42   The bodyes rest, the quyete of the hart,
The travayles ease, the still nightes feer was he.
And of our life in earth the better parte,
Reuer of sight, and yet in whom we see
Thinges oft that tide, and ofte that neuer bee.
Without respect esteming equally
Kyng Cresus pompe, and Irus pouertie.

[1] Printed ' ohter.'

43   And next in order sad Olde age we found,
His beard all hoare, his iyes hollow and blynde,
With drouping chere still poring on the ground,
As on the place where nature him assinde
To rest, when that the sisters had vntwynde
His vitall threde, and ended with theyr knyfe
The fleting course of fast declining life.

44   There heard we him with broken and hollow playnt
Rewe with him-selfe his ende approching fast,
And all for nought his wretched minde torment
With swete remembraunce of his pleasures past,
And freshe delites of lusty youth forwaste.
Recounting which, how would he sob & shrike,
And to be yong againe of Ioue beseke !

45   But and the cruell fates so fixed be
That time forepast can not retourne agayne,
This one request of Ioue yet prayed he :
That in such withered plight, and wretched paine
As elde (accompanied with his lothsom trayne)
Had brought on him, all were it woe and griefe,
He myght a while yet linger forth his lief,

46   And not so soone descend into the pit :
Where death, when he the mortall corps hath slayne,
With retcheles hande in grave doth couer it,
Thereafter neuer to enioye agayne
The gladsome light, but, in the ground ylayne,
In depth of darkenes waste and weare to nought,
As he had neuer into the world been brought.

47   But who had seene him, sobbing howe he stoode
Vnto him-selfe, and howe he would bemone
His youth forepast, as though it wrought hym good
To talke of youth, al wer his youth foregone,
He would haue mused, & meruayld muche whereon
This wretched age should life desyre so fayne,
And knowes ful wel life doth but length his payne.

48   Crookebackt he was, toothshaken, and blere-iyed,
Went on three feete, and sometime crept on fower,
With olde lame bones, that ratled by his syde,
His skalpe all pilde, & he with elde forlore:
His withered fist stil knocking at deathes dore,
Fumbling and driueling as he drawes his breth,
For briefe, the shape and messenger of death.

49   And fast by him pale Maladie was plaste,
Sore sicke in bed, her colour al forgone,
Bereft of stomake, sauor, and of taste,
Ne could she brooke no meat but brothes alone.
Her breath corrupt, her kepers euery one
Abhorring her, her sickenes past recure,
Detesting phisicke and all phisickes cure.

50   But oh ! the doleful sight that then we see ;
We turnde our looke, and on the other side
A griesly shape of Famine mought we see,
With greedy lookes, and gaping mouth that cryed,
And roard for meat as she should there haue dyed ;
Her body thin and bare as any bone,
Wherto was left nought but the case alone.

51 And that, alas! was gnawen[1] on euery where,
All full of holes, that I ne mought refrayne
From teares, to se how she her armes could teare,
And with her teeth gnashe on the bones in vayne:
When all for nought she fayne would so sustayne
Her starven corps, that rather seemde a shade
Then any substaunce of a creature made.

52 Great was her force, whom stonewall could not stay,
Her tearyng nayles snatching at all she sawe:
With gaping Iawes, that by no meanes ymay
Be satisfyed from hunger of her mawe,
But eates her-selfe as she that hath no lawe:
Gnawyng, alas! her carkas all in vayne,
Where you may count eche sinow, bone, and vayne.

53 On her while we thus firmely fixt our iyes,
That bled for ruth of such a drery sight,
Loe, sodaynelye she shryght in so huge wyse,
As made hell-gates to shyver with the myght.
Wherewith a darte we sawe howe it did lyght
Ryght on her brest, and therewithal pale death
Enthryllyng it, to reve her of her breath.

54 And by and by a dum dead corps we sawe,
Heauy and colde, the shape of death aryght,
That dauntes all earthly creatures to his lawe:
Agaynst whose force in vayne it is to fyght.
Ne piers, ne princes, nor no mortall wyght,
No townes, ne realmes, cities, ne strongest tower,
But al perforce must yeeld vnto his power.

---

[1] Old text 'knawen'; cf. st. 52, l. 6.

55   His Dart anon out of the corps he tooke,
And in his hand (a dreadfull sight to see)
With great tryumphe eftsones the same he shooke,
That most of all my feares affrayed me :
His bodie dight with nought but bones, perdye,
The naked shape of man there sawe I playne,
All save the fleshe, the synowe, and the vayne.

56   Lastly stoode Warre, in glitteryng armes yclad,
With visage grym, sterne lookes, and blackely hewed ;
In his right hand a naked sworde he had,
That to the hiltes was al with blud embrewed :
And in his left (that kinges and kingdomes rewed)
Famine and fyer he held, and therewythall
He razed townes, and threwe downe towers and all.

57   Cities he sakt, and realmes, that whilom flowred
In honor, glory, and rule above the best,
He overwhelmde, and all theyr fame deuowred,
Consumed, destroyed, wasted, and neuer ceast,
Tyll he theyr wealth, theyr name, and all opprest.
His face forhewed with woundes, and by his side
There hunge his targe with gashes depe and wyde.

58   In mids of which depaynted there we founde
Deadly debate, al ful of snaky heare,
That with a blouddy fillet was ybound,
Outbrething nought but discord euery-where.
And round about were portrayd here and there
The hugie hostes, Darius and his power,
His kynges, prynces, his pieres, and all his flower,

59   Whom great Macedo vanquisht there in fight[1]
With diepe slaughter, dispoylyng all his pryde,
Pearst through his realmes, and daunted all his might.
Duke Hanniball beheld I there beside,
In Cannas field, victor howe he did ride,
And woful Romaynes that in vayne withstoode,
And Consull Paulus covered all in blood.

60   Yet sawe I more the fight at Trasimene,
And Trebye[2] fyeld, and eke when Hanniball
And worthy Scipio last in armes were seene
Before Carthago gate, to trye for all
The worldes empyre, to whom it should befal.
There sawe I Pompeye, and Cesar clad in armes,
Theyr hostes alyed and al theyr civil harmes;

61   With conquerours hands forbathde in their owne blood,
And Cesar weping ouer Pompeyes head.
Yet sawe I Scilla and Marius where they stoode,
Theyr great crueltie, and the diepe bludshed
Of frendes: Cyrus I sawe and his host dead,
And howe the Queene with great despyte hath flonge
His head in bloud of them she overcome.

62   Xerxes the Percian kyng yet sawe I there,
With his huge host, that dranke the riuers drye,
Dismounted hilles, and made the vales vprere,
His hoste and all yet sawe I slayne, perdye.
Thebes I sawe all razde howe it dyd lye
In heapes of stones, and Tyrus put to spoyle,
With walles and towers flat euened with the soyle.

---

[1] Printed 'sight.'   [2] Printed 'Trebery.'

63   But Troy, alas! (me thought) aboue them all,
It made myne iyes in very teares consume :
When I beheld the wofull werd befall,
That by the wrathfull wyl of Gods was come :
And Ioues vnmooved sentence and foredoome
On Priam kyng, and on his towne so bent.
I could not lyn, but I must there lament,

64   And that the more, sith destinie was so sterne
As, force perfor[c]e, there might no force auayle,
But she must fall : and by her fall we learne,
That cities, towres, wealth, world, and al shall quayle.
No manhoode, might, nor nothing mought preuayle,
Al were there prest ful many a prynce and piere,
And many a knight that solde his death full deere :

65   Not wurthy Hector, wurthyest of them all,
Her hope, her ioye : his force is nowe for nought.
O Troy, Troy, there is no boote but bale,
The hugie horse within thy walles is brought :
Thy turrets fall ; thy knightes, that whilom fought
In armes amyd the fyeld, are slayne in bed,
Thy Gods defylde, and all thy honour dead.

66   The flames vpspring, and cruelly they crepe
From wall to roofe, till all to cindres waste,
Some fyer the houses where the wretches slepe,
Sum rushe in here, sum run in there as fast.
In euery-where or sworde or fyer they taste.
The walles are torne, the towers whurld to *the* ground,
There is no mischiefe but may there be found.

67   Cassandra yet there sawe I howe they haled
From Pallas house, with spercled tresse vndone,
Her wristes fast bound, and with Greeks rout empaled:
And Priam eke in vayne howe he did runne
To armes, whom Pyrrhus with despite hath done
To cruel death, and bathed him in the bayne
Of his sonnes blud before the altare slayne.

68   But howe can I descryve the doleful sight,
That in the shylde so liue-like fayer did shyne?
Sith in this world I thinke was neuer wyght
Could haue set furth the halfe, not halfe so fyne.
I can no more but tell howe there is seene
Fayer Ilium fal in burning red gledes downe,
And from the soyle great Troy, Neptunus towne.

69   Herefrom when scarce I could mine iyes withdrawe,
That fylde with teares as doeth the spryngyng well,
We passed on so far furth tyl we sawe
Rude Acheron, a lothsome lake to tell,
That boyles and bubs vp swelth as blacke as hell,
Where grisly Charon, at theyr fixed tide,
Stil ferreies ghostes vnto the farder side;

70   The aged God no sooner sorowe spyed,
But hasting strayt vnto the banke apace
With hollow call vnto the rout he cryed,
To swarve apart, and geue the Goddesse place.
Strayt it was done, when to the shoar we pace,
Where hand in hand as we then linked fast,
Within the boate we are together plaste.

71   And furth we launch, ful fraughted to the brinke,
Whan with the vnwonted weyght the rustye keele
Began to cracke as if the same should sinke.
We hoyse vp mast and sayle, that in a whyle
We set the shore, where scarcely we had while
For to arryve, but that we heard anone
A thre-sound barke, confounded al in one.

72   We had not long furth past, but that we sawe
Blacke Cerberus, the hydeous hound of hell,
With bristles reard, and with a thre-mouthed Iawe,
Foredinning the ayer with his horrible yel,
Out of the diepe darke cave where he did dwell;
The Goddesse strayt he knewe, and by and by
He peaste and couched, while that we passed by.

73   Thence cum we to the horrour and the hel,
The large great kyngdomes, and the dreadful raygne
Of Pluto, in his trone where he dyd dwell,
The wyde waste places, and the hugye playne:
The waylinges, shrykes, and sundry sortes of payne,
The syghes, the sobbes, the diepe and deadly groane,
Earth, ayer, and all resounding playnt and moane.

74   Here pewled the babes, and here the maydes vnwed
with folded handes theyr sory chaunce bewayled,
Here wept the gyltles slayne, and louers dead,
That slewe them-selues when nothyng els auayled:
A thousand sortes of sorrowes here that wayled
with sighes and teares, sobs, shrykes, and all yfere,
That (oh! alas!) it was a hel to heare.

75   we stayed vs strayt, and wyth a rufull feare
Beheld this heauy sight, while from mine eyes
The vapored teares downstilled here and there,
And Sorowe eke, in far more woful wyse,
Tooke on with playnt, vp heauing to the skyes
Her wretched handes, that with her crye the rout
Can all in heapes to swarme vs round about.

76   'Loe here' (q*uod* Sorowe) 'Prynces of renowne,
That whilom sat on top of Fortunes wheele,
Nowe layed ful lowe, like wretches whurled downe,
Euen with one frowne, that stayed but with a smyle;
And nowe behold the thing that thou erewhile
Saw only in thought, and what thou now shalt heare,
Recompt the same to Kesar, King, and Pier.'

77   Then first came Henry duke of Buckingham,
His cloke of blacke al pilde and quite forworne,
Wringing his handes, and Fortune ofte doth blame,
Which of a duke hath made him nowe her skorne.
With gastly lookes, as one in maner lorne,
Oft spred his armes, stretcht handes he ioynes as fast,
With ruful chere, and vapored eyes vpcast.

78   His cloke he rent, his manly breast he beat,
His heare al torne about the place it laye;
My hart so molte to see his griefe so great,
As felingly, me thought, it dropt awaye:
His iyes they whurled about withouten staye:
With stormy syghes the place dyd so complayne,
As if his hart at eche had burst in twayne.

79   Thryse he began to tell his doleful tale,
     And thrise the sighes did swalowe vp his voyce,
     At eche of which he shryked so wythal
     As though the heauens rived with the noyse :
     Tyll at the last, recovering his voyce,
     Supping the teares that all his brest beraynde,
     On cruel Fortune weping thus he playnde.

XXV.

ROGER ASCHAM.

A.D. 1570.

ROGER ASCHAM was born in 1515, at Kirby Wiske, near North-allerton, Yorkshire. He was educated at St. John's College, Cambridge, where he was elected Fellow March 23, 1534. In 1544 he was chosen University Orator. In 1545 appeared his 'Toxophilus,' a treatise on archery, with many incidental remarks on things connected with it; see Mr. Arber's reprint of the first edition. In 1548, he was appointed instructor to the Lady (afterwards Queen) Elizabeth, but resigned his duties in 1550. After Elizabeth's accession he regained her favour, and was her tutor in Greek. He was also Latin secretary to Edward VI, Mary, and Elizabeth successively. He died on the 30th of December, 1568, universally regretted, and by few more than by the Queen. Dr. Johnson wrote a life of him, which was prefixed to a collected edition of his works by Mr. J. Bennet in 1761. His greatest work is 'The Scholemaster,' published post-humously by his widow in 1570, and again in 1571. There is an excellent reprint of it by the Rev. J. E. B. Mayor, published in 1863, to which are appended many useful explanatory notes; and it has since been again reprinted by Mr. Arber, in his cheap and useful series. The following extracts are from the original first edition of 1570, which is exactly followed, excepting that several needless commas have been omitted.

[*From 'The Scholemaster'; Book I.*]

[*Lady Jane Grey; leaf 11, back.*]

Therfore, to loue or to hate, to like or contemne, to plie
this waie or that waie, to good or to bad, ye shall haue as ye
vse a child in his youth.

And one example, whether loue or feare doth worke more
5 in a child, for vertue and learning, I will gladlie report:
which maie be hard with some pleasure, and folowed with
more profit. Before I went into *Germanie*, I came to Brode-
gate in Lecetershire, to take· my leaue of that
noble Ladie *Iane Grey*, to whom I was exceding $\quad$ Lady Iane Grey.
10 moch beholdinge. Hir parentes, the Duke and the Duches,
with all the houshould, Gentlemen and Gentlewomen, were
huntinge in the Parke: I founde her in her Chamber, read-
inge *Phædon Platonis* in Greeke, and that with as moch
delite, as som ientleman wold read a merie tale in *Bocase*.
15 After salutation and dewtie done, with som other taulke, I
asked hir, whie she wold leese soch pastime in the Parke?
smiling she answered me: 'I-wisse, all their sporte in the
Parke is but a shadoe to that pleasure that I find in *Plato*:
Alas good folke, they never felt what trewe pleasure ment.'
20 'And howe came you, Madame,' quoth I, 'to this deepe
knowledge of pleasure, and what did chieflie allure you vnto
it: seinge not many women, but verie fewe men have at-
teined thereunto?' 'I will tell you,' quoth she, 'and tell you
a troth, which perchance ye will meruell at. One of the
25 greatest benefites that euer God gaue me, is, that he sent
me so sharpe and seuere Parentes, and so ientle a scholemaster. For when I am in presence either of father or
mother, whether I speake, kepe silence, sit, stand, or go,

x

eate, drinke, be merie, or sad, be sowyng, plaiyng, dauncing, or doing anie thing els, I must do it, as it were, in soch ₃₀ weight, mesure, and number, euen so perfitelie as God made the world, or els I am so sharplie taunted, so cruellie threatened, yea presentlie some tymes, with pinches, nippes, and bobbes, and other waies, which I will not name for the honor I beare them, so without mesure misordered, that I ₃₅ thinke my-selfe in hell, till tyme cum that I must go to *M. Elmer,* who teacheth me so ientlie, so pleasantlie, with soch faire allurements to learning, that I thinke all the tyme nothing, whiles I am with him. And when I am called from him, I fall on weeping, because, what soever I do els, but ₄₀ learning, is ful of grief, trouble, feare, and whole misliking vnto me: And thus my booke hath bene so moch my pleasure, & bringeth dayly to me more pleasure & more, that in respect of it, all other pleasures, in very deede, be but trifles and troubles vnto me.' I remember this talke gladly, ₄₅ both bicause it is so worthy of memorie, & bicause also, it was the last talke that euer I had, and the last tyme that euer I saw that noble and worthie Ladie. • • • • •

[Leaf 14.]

For wisedom and vertue, there be manie faire examples in this Court, for yong Ientlemen to folow. But they ₅₀ be like faire markes in the feild, out of a mans reach, to far of to shote at well. The best and worthiest men, in deede, be sometimes seen, but seldom taulked withall: A yong Ientleman may sometime knele to their person, [but] smallie vse their companie, for their better instruction. ₅₅

But yong Ientlemen ar faine commonlie to do in the Court, as yong Archers do in the feild: that is, take soch markes as be nie them, although they be neuer so foule to shote at. I meene, they be driuen to

Ill companie marreth youth.

60 kepe companie with the worste: and what force ill companie
hath to corrupt good wittes, the wisest men know best.

And not ill companie onelie, but the ill opinion also of the
most part, doth moch harme, and namelie of those, which shold be wise in the trewe de-
65 cyphring of the good disposition of nature, of
cumlinesse in Courtlie maners, and all right doinges of
men.

The Court judgeth worst of the best natures in youth.

But error and phantasie do commonlie occupie the place
of troth and iudgement. For if a yong ientleman be de-
70 meure and still of nature, they say, he is simple and lacketh
witte: if he be bashefull and will soon blushe, they call him
a babishe and ill brought vp thyng, when *Xeno-*
phon doth preciselie note in *Cyrus*, that his bash-
fulnes in youth was *the* verie trewe signe of his vertue &
75 stoutnes after: If he be innocent and ignorant of ill, they
say, he is rude and hath no grace, so vngra-
ciouslie do som gracelesse men misuse the faire
and godlie word GRACE.

Xen. in 1 Cyr. Pæd.

The Grace in Courte.

But if ye would know what grace they meene, go, and
80 looke, and learne emonges them, and ye shall see that it is:
First, to blush at nothing. And blushyng in youth, sayth
Aristotle, is nothyng els but feare to do ill: which feare
beyng once lustely fraid away from youth, then foloweth, to
dare do any mischief, to contemne stoutly any goodnesse,
85 to be busie in euery matter, to be skilfull in euery thyng,
to acknowledge no ignorance at all. To do
thus in Court is counted of some the chief and
greatest grace of all: and termed by the name of a vertue,
called Corage & boldnesse, whan *Crassus* in
90 *Cicero* teacheth the cleane contrarie, and that
most wittelie, saying thus: *Audere, cum bonis*
etiam rebus coniunctum, per seipsum est magnopere fugiendum.

Grace of Courte

Cic. 3. de Or.

Boldnes yea in a good matter, not to be praised.

Which is to say, to be bold, yea in a good matter, is for itself greatlie to be exchewed.

Moreouer, where the swing goeth, there to follow, fawne, 95
Iore Grace of flatter, laugh and lie lustelie at other mens liking.
Iourte. To face, stand formest, shoue backe: and to the
meaner man, or vnknowne in the Court, to seeme somwhat
solume, coye, big, and dangerous of looke, taulk, and answere:
To thinke well of him-selfe, to be lustie in contemning of 100
others, to haue some trim grace in a priuie mock. And in
greater presens, to beare a braue looke: to be warlike, though
he neuer looked enimie in the face in warre: yet som warlike signe must be vsed, either a slouinglie busking, or an
ouerstaring frounced hed, as though out of euerie heeres 105
toppe should suddenlie start out a good big othe, when
Men of warre, nede requireth; yet praised be God, England hath
best of condi- at this time manie worthie Capitaines and good
tions. souldiours, which be in deede so honest of behauiour, so cumlie of conditions, so milde of maners, as they 110
may be examples of good order to a good sort of others,
which neuer came in warre. But to retorne, where I left:
In place also, to be able to raise taulke, and make discourse
Palmistrie. of euerie rishe: to haue a verie good will, to heare
him-selfe speake: To be seene in Palmestrie, 115
wherby to conueie to chast eares som fond or filthie
taulke:

And, if som Smithfeild Ruffian take vp som strange going:
som new mowing with the mouth: som wrinchyng with the
shoulder, som braue prouerbe: som fresh new othe, that is 120
not stale, but will rin round in the mouth: som new disguised garment or desperate hat, fond in facion or gaurish
in colour, what soeuer it cost, how small soeuer his liuing be,
by what shift soeuer it be gotten, gotten must it be, and vsed
with the first, or els the grace of it is stale and gone: som 125

part of this gracelesse grace was discribed by me, in a litle
rude verse long ago.

> *To laughe, to lie, to flatter, to face :*
> *Foure waies in Court to win men grace.*
130   *If thou be thrall to none of thiese,*
> *Away, good Peek-goos, hence, Iohn Cheese :*
> *Marke well my word, and marke their dede,*
> *And thinke this verse part of thy Crede.* . . . .

[Leaf 18, *back.*]

It is a notable tale, that old Syr *Roger Chamloe,*
135 sometime cheife Iustice, wold tell of him-selfe.   *Syr Roger*
Whan he was Auncient in Inne of Courte,   *Chamloe.*
Certaine yong Ientlemen were brought before him, to be
corrected for certaine misorders : And one of the lustiest
saide : 'Syr, we be yong ientlemen, and wise men before vs
140 have proued all facions, and yet those haue done full well:'
this they said because it was well knowen, that Syr *Roger*
had bene a good feloe in his yougth. But he aunswered
them verie wiselie. ' In deede,' saith he, ' in yougthe, I was,
as you ar now: and I had twelue feloes like vnto my-self,
145 but not one of them came to a good ende. And therfore,
folow not my example in yougth, but folow my councell in
aige, if euer ye thinke to cum to this place, or to thies
yeares, that I am cum vnto, lesse ye meete either with pouertie
or Tiburn in the way.' . . . . .

[Leaf 19.]

150   And I do not meene, by all this my taulke, that
yong Ientlemen should alwaies be poring on   Diligent learn-
a booke, and by vsing good studies shold   inge ought to be
                                     ioyned with
lease honest pleasure and haunt no good pas-   pleasant pas-
                                     times, namelie
time, I meene nothinge lesse: For it is well   in a ientleman.
155 knowne that I both like and loue, and haue alwaies, and do

yet still vse, all exercises and pastimes, that be fitte for my
nature and habilitie. And beside naturall disposition, in
iudgement also, I was neuer either Stoick in doctrine, or
Anabaptist in Religion, to mislike a merie, pleasant, and
plaifull nature, if no outrage be committed against lawe, 160
mesure, and good order. . . . . .

[Leaf 19, *back.*]

Therefore, to ride cumlie : to run faire at the tilte or

The pastimes that be fitte for Courtlie Ientle-men. ring : to plaie at all weapones : to shote faire
in bow, or surelie in gon : to vaut[1] lustely :
to runne : to leape : to wrestle : to swimme : 165
To daunce cumlie : to sing, and playe of instrumentes
cunnyngly : to Hawke : to hunte : to playe at tennes, & all
pastimes generally, which be ioyned with labor, vsed in
open place, and on the day-light, conteining either some
fitte exercise for warre, or some pleasant pastime for peace, 170
be not onelie cumlie and decent, but also verie necessarie,
for a Courtlie Ientleman to vse. . . . . .

[Leaf 21.]

Present examples of this present tyme I list not to

Queene Elisabeth. touch : yet there is one example, for all the
Ientlemen of this Court to folow, that may 175
well satisfie them, or nothing will serue them, nor no example moue them to goodnes and learnyng.

It is your shame, (I speake to you all, you yong Ientlemen of England) that one mayd should go beyond you all,
in excellencie of learnyng and knowledge of diuers tonges. 180
Pointe forth six of the best giuen Ientlemen of this Court,
and all they together shew not so much good will, spend
not so much tyme, bestow not so many houres, dayly,

---

[1] Printed 'vant.'

orderly, & constantly, for the increase of learning & know-
185 ledge, as doth the Queenes Maiestie her-selfe. Yea I beleue,
that beside her perfit readines in *Latin, Italian, French,* &
Spanish, she readeth here now at Windsore more Greeke,
euery day, than some Prebendarie of this Chirch doth read
Latin in a whole weeke. And that which is most praise-
190 worthie of all, within the walles of her priuie chamber, she
hath obteyned that excellencie of learnyng, to vnderstand,
speake & write, both wittely with head, and faire with
hand, as scarse one or two rare wittes in both the Uniuer-
sities haue in many yeares reached vnto. Amongest all the
195 benefites *that* God hath blessed me with-all, next the knowledge of Christes true Religion, I counte this the greatest,
that it pleased God to call me to be one poore minister in
settyng forward these excellent giftes of learnyng in this
most excellent Prince. Whose onely example if the rest of
200 our nobilitie would folow, than might England be, for learnyng and wisedome in nobilitie, a spectacle to all
the world beside. But see the mishap of men:
The best examples haue neuer such forse to
moue to any goodnes, as the bad, vaine, light and fond, haue
205 to all ilnes.

Ill Examples haue more force then good examples.

 And one example, though out of the compas of learning,
yet not out of the order of good maners, was notable in this
Courte, not fullie xxiiij. yeares a-go, when all the actes of
Parlament, many good Proclamations, diuerse strait com-
210 maundementes, sore punishment openlie, speciall regarde
priuatelie, cold not do so moch to take away one misorder,
as the example of one big one of this Courte did, still to
kepe vp the same. The memorie whereof doth yet remaine,
in a common prouerbe of Birching lane.

XXVI.

GEORGE GASCOIGNE.

A.D. 1576.

GEORGE GASCOIGNE was the eldest son of Sir John Gascoigne of Cardington in Bedfordshire, and was born about 1525. He was educated at Trinity College, Cambridge, and afterwards entered at Gray's Inn as a law-student; but after some time spent in idleness and extravagance, he embarked for Holland, and served as a soldier under William, Prince of Orange. He returned to England in 1573, and nominally resumed the study of law, but spent much of his time in writing verses. In July, 1575, we find him at Kenilworth, reciting verses before Queen Elizabeth, and writing an account of the pageantries with which she was there entertained. He died at Stamford, Oct. 7, 1577. A complete collection of his poems has very lately been printed by W. C. Hazlitt, for the 'Roxburghe Library.' His best poem is certainly 'The Steel Glas,' lately reprinted (with a few others) by Mr. Arber, and from which I give extracts. The *Steel Glas* is, in fact, a mirror, in which the poet sees a reflection of various estates of men, whom he describes with severe exactness and some fine satirical touches. Our extracts refer to the Gentlemen, the Merchants, the Priests, and the Ploughmen; with an Epilogue upon Women. The poem was commenced in April, 1575, and printed in April, 1576. It was dedicated to his patron, Arthur, Lord Gray of Wilton, whom he frequently addresses as 'my lord' in the poem.

[*From ' The Steel Glas.'*]

The Gentleman, which might in countrie keepe
A plenteous boorde, and feed the fatherlesse
VVith pig and goose, with mutton, beefe and veale,   420
(Yea now and then, a capon and a chicke)
VVil breake vp house, and dwel in market townes,
A loytring life, and like an *Epicure*.

But who (meane while) defends the common welth?
VVho rules the flocke, when sheperds so are fled?   425
VVho stayes the staff, which shuld vphold the state?
Forsoth, good Sir, the Lawyer leapeth in,
Nay, rather leapes both ouer hedge and ditch,
And rules the rost, but fewe men rule by right.

O Knights, O Squires, O Gentle blouds yborne,   430
You were not borne al onely for your selues:
Your countrie claymes some part of al your paines.
There should you liue, and therin should you toyle,
To hold vp right and banish cruel wrong,
To helpe the pore, to bridle backe the riche,   435
To punish vice, and vertue to aduaunce,
To see God servde and *Belzebub* supprest.
You should not trust lieftenaunts in your rome,
And let them sway the scepter of your charge,
VVhiles you (meane while) know scarcely what is don, 440
Nor yet can yeld accompt if you were callde.
The stately lord, which woonted was to kepe
A court at home, is now come vp to courte,
And leaues the country for a common prey
To pilling, polling, brybing, and deceit: 445

(Al which his presence might haue pacified,
Or else haue made offenders smel the smoke.)
And now the youth which might haue serued him
In comely wise, with countrey clothes yclad,
And yet thereby bin able to preferre　　　　　450
Vnto the prince, and there to seke aduance :
Is faine to sell his landes for courtly cloutes,
Or else sits still, and liueth like a loute,
(Yet of these two the last fault is the lesse :)
And so those imps which might in time haue sprong　455
Alofte (good lord) and servde to shielde the state,
Are either nipt with such vntimely frosts,
Or else growe crookt, bycause they be not proynd.

These be the Knights which shold defend the land,
And these be they which leaue the land at large.　　460
Yet here, percase, it wilbe thought I roue
And runne astray, besides the kings high-way,
Since by the Knights, of whom my text doth tell,
(And such as shew most perfect in my glasse,)
Is ment no more, but worthy Souldiours　　　　465
Whose skil in armes, and long experience
Should still vphold the pillers of the worlde.
Yes, out of doubt, this noble name of Knight,
May comprehend both Duke, Erle, lorde, Knight, Squire,
Yea, gentlemen, and euery gentle borne.　　　　470

　　　·　　·　　·　　·　　·　　·　　·

Art thou a Gentle? liue with gentle friendes,
VVhich wil be glad thy companie to haue,
If manhoode may with manners well agree.　　　630

Art thou a seruing man? then serue againe,
And stint to steale as common souldiours do.

Art thou a craftsman? take thee to thine arte,
And cast of slouth, which loytreth in the Campes.

Art thou a plowman pressed for a shift?   635
Then learne to clout thine old cast cobled shoes,
And rather bide at home with barly bread, ·
Than learne to spoyle, as thou hast seene some do.

. . . .

Merchants.

And master Merchant, he whose trauaile ought   750
Commodiously to doe his countrie good,
And by his toyle the same for to enriche,
Can finde the meane to make *Monopolyes*
Of euery ware that is accompted strange,
And feeds the vaine of courtiers vaine desires   755
Vntil the court haue courtiers cast at heele,
Quia non habent vestes Nuptiales.

O painted fooles, whose harebrainde heades must haue
More clothes attones than might become a king :
For whom the rocks in forain Realmes must spin,   760
For whom they carde, for whom they weaue their webbes,
For whom no wool appeareth fine enough,
(I speake not this by english courtiers,
Since english wool was euer thought most worth)
For whom al seas are tossed to and fro,   765
For whom these purples come from *Persia,*
The crimosine and liuely red from *Inde :*
For whom soft silks do sayle from *Sericane,*
And all queint costs do come from fardest coasts :
Whiles, in meane while, that worthy Emperour,   770
Which rulde the world and had all welth at wil,
Could be content to tire his wearie wife,

His daughters and his neipces eueryehone,
To spin and worke the clothes that he shuld weare,
And neuer carde for silks or sumpteous cost,   775
For cloth of gold or tinsel figurie,
For Baudkin, broydrie, cutworks, nor conceits.
He set the shippes of merchantmen on worke
VVith bringing home oyle, graine, and savrie salt,
And such like wares as serued common vse.   78ɔ

Yea, for my life, those merchants were not woont
To lend their wares at reasonable rate,
(To gaine no more but *Cento por cento,*)
To teach yong men the trade to sel browne paper,
Yea, Morrice-bells, and byllets too sometimes,   785
To make their coyne a net to catch yong frye.
To binde such babes in father Derbies bands,
To stay their steps by statute-Staples staffe,
To rule yong roysters with *Recognisance*
To read *Arithmeticke* once euery day   790
In VVoodstreat, Bredstreat, and in Pultery,
(VVhere such schoolmaisters keepe their counting-house,)
To fede on bones when flesh and fell is gon,
To keepe their byrds ful close in caytiues cage,
(Who being brought to libertie at large,   795
Might sing, perchaunce, abroade, when sunne doth shine,
Of their mishaps, & how their fethers fel,)
Vntill the canker may their corpse consume.

These knackes (my lord) I cannot cal to minde,
Bycause they shewe not in my glasse of steele.   800
But holla: here I see a wondrous sight,
I see a swarme of Saints within my glasse:
Beholde, behold, I see a swarme in deede
Of holy Saints, which walke in comely wise,

Not deckt in robes, nor garnished with gold, 805
But some vnshod, yea, some ful thinly clothde,
And yet they seme so heauenly for to see,
As if their eyes were al of Diamonds,
Their face, of Rubies, Saphires, and Iacincts,
Their comly beards and heare, of siluer wiers. 810
And, to be short, they seeme Angelycall.
What should they be, (my Lord) what should they be ?

Priest.

O gratious God, I see now what they be.
These be my priests, which pray for evry state.
These be my priests, deuorced from the world, 815
And wedded yet to heauen and holynesse,
Which are not proude, nor couet to be riche.
Which go not gay, nor fede on daintie foode,
VVhich enuie not, nor knowe what malice meanes,
Which loth all lust, disdayning drunkenesse, 820
Which cannot faine, which hate hypocrisie :
Which neuer sawe Sir *Simonies* deceits :
Which preach of peace, which carpe contentions,
Which loyter not, but labour al the yeare,
Which thunder threts of gods most greuous wrath, 825
And yet do teach that mercie is in store.

Lo these (my Lord) be my good praying priests,
Descended from *Melchysedec* by line,
Cosens to Paule, to Peter, Iames, and Iohn :
These be my priests, the seasning of the earth, 830
VVhich wil not leese their Savrinesse, I trowe.

Not one of these (for twentie hundreth groats)
VVil teach the text that byddes him take a wife,
And yet be combred with a concubine.

Not one of these wil reade the holy write   835
Which doth forbid all greedy vsurie,
And yet receiue a shilling for a pounde.

Not one of these wil preach of patience,
And yet be found as angry as a waspe.

Not one of these can be content to sit   840
In Tauerns, Innes, or Alehouses all day,
But spends his time deuoutly at his booke.

Not one of these will rayle at rulers wrongs,
And yet be blotted with extortion.

Not one of these will paint out worldly pride,   845
And he himselfe as gallaunt as he dare.

Not one of these rebuketh auarice,
And yet procureth proude pluralities.

Not one of these reproueth vanitie
Whiles he him-selfe, (with hauke vpon his fist,   850
And houndes at heele,) doth quite forget his text.

Not one of these corrects contentions
For trifling things: and yet will sue for tythes.

Not one of these (not one of these, my Lord)
Wil be ashamde to do euen as he teacheth.   855

My priests haue learnt to pray vnto the Lord,
And yet they trust not in their lyplabour.

My priests can fast and vse al abstinence
From vice and sinne, and yet refuse no meats.

My priests can giue in charitable wise,   860
And loue also to do good almes-dedes,
Although they trust not in their owne deserts,

My priestes can place all penaunce in the hart,
VVithout regard of outward ceremonies.

My priests can keepe their temples vndefyled, 865
And yet defie all Superstition.

Lo now, my Lorde, what thinke you by my priests?
Although they were the last that shewed themselues,
I saide at first their office was to pray,
And since the time is such euen now a dayes 870
As hath great nede of prayers truely prayde,
Come forth my priests, and I wil bydde your beades:
I wil presume, (although I be no priest)
To bidde you pray as Paule and Peter prayde.

The poets Beades.

Then pray, my priests, yea, pray to god himselfe, 875
That he vouchsafe, (euen for his Christes sake)
To giue his word free passage here on earth,
And that his church (which now is Militant)
May soone be sene triumphant ouer all,
And that he deigne to ende this wicked world, 880
VVhich walloweth stil in Sinks of filthy sinne.

For Princes.

Eke pray, my priests, for Princes and for Kings,
Emperours, Monarks, Duks, and all estates,
VVhich sway the sworde of royal gouernment,
(Of whom our Queene which liues without compare 885
Must be the chiefe, in bydding of my beades,
Else I deserue to lese both beades and bones)
That God giue light vnto their noble mindes,
To maintaine truth, and therwith stil to wey
That here they reigne not onely for themselues, 890

.And that they be but slaues to common welth,
Since al their toyles and al their broken sleeps
Shal scant suffize to hold it stil vpright.

.   .   .   .

For the Cominaltie.

Now these be past, (my priests) yet shal you pray   1010
For common people, eche in his degree,
That God vouchsafe to graunt them al his grace.
Where should I now beginne to bidde my beades?
Or who shal first be put in common place?
My wittes be wearie, and my eyes are dymme,   1015
I cannot see who best deserues the roome.
Stand forth, good *Peerce*, thou plowman by thy name,
Yet so the Sayler saith I do him wrong:
That one contends, his paines are without peare;
That other saith, that none be like to his;   1020
In dede they labour both exceedingly.
But since I see no shipman that can liue
Without the plough, and yet I many see
(Which liue by lande) that neuer sawe the seas:
Therefore I say, stand forth *Peerce* plowman first,   1025
Thou winst the roome, by verie worthinesse.

The plovvman.

Behold him (priests) & though he stink of sweat,
Disdaine him not: for shal I tel you what?
Such clime to heauen before the shauen crownes.
But how? forsooth, with true humilytie.   1030
Not that they hoord their grain when it is cheape,
.Not that they kill the calfe to haue the milke,
Nor that they set debate betwene their lords
By earing vp the balks that part their bounds:
Nor for because they can both crowche & creep   1035

(The guilefulst men, that euer God yet made)
VVhen as they meane most mischiefe and deceite;
Nor that they can crie out on landelordes lowde,
And say they racke their rents an ace to high,
VVhen they themselues do sel their landlords lambe   1040
For greater price then ewe was wont be worth.
I see you, *Peerce*, my glasse was lately scowrde.
But for they feed with frutes of their gret paines
Both King and Knight, and priests in cloyster pent:
Therefore I say, that sooner some of them   1045
Shall scale the walles which leade vs vp to heauen,
Than cornfed beasts whose bellie is their God,
Although they preach of more perfection.

    And yet (my priests) pray you to God for *Peerce*,
As *Peerce* can pinch it out for him and you.   1050
And if you haue a *Paternoster* spare,
Then shal you pray for Saylers (God them send
More mind of him when as they come to lande,
For towarde shipwracke many men can pray)
That they once learne to speake without a lye,   1055
And meane good faith without blaspheming othes :
That they forget to steale from euery fraight,
And for to forge false cockets, free to passe:
That manners make them giue their betters place,
And vse good words, though deeds be nothing gay.   1060

    But here, me thinks, my priests begin to frowne,
And say, that thus they shal be ouerchargde,
To pray for al which seme to do amisse :
And one I heare more saucie than the rest,
VVhich asketh me, ' when shal our prayers end?'   1065
I tel thee (priest) when shoomakers make shoes
That are wel sowed, with neuer a stitch amisse,
And vse no crafte in vttring of the same :

                 Y

VVhen Taylours steale no stuffe from gentlemen,
VVhen Tanners are with Corriers wel agreede,   1070
And both so dresse their hydes, that we go dry:
when Cutlers leaue to sel olde rustie blades,
And hide no crackes with soder nor deceit:
when tinkers make no more holes than they founde,
when thatchers thinke their wages worth their worke, 1075
when colliers put no dust into their sacks,
when maltemen make vs drinke no firmentie,
when Dauie Diker diggs and dallies not,
when smithes shoo horses as they would be shod,
when millers toll not with a golden thumbe,   1080
when bakers make not barme beare price of wheat,
when brewers put no bagage in their beere,
when butchers blowe not ouer al their fleshe,
when horsecorsers beguile no friends with Iades,
when weauers weight is found in huswiues web: 1085
(But why dwel I so long among these lowts?)
VVhen mercers make more bones to swere and lye,
VVhen vintners mix no water with their wine,
VVhen printers passe none errours in their bookes,
VVhen hatters vse to bye none olde cast robes,   1090
VVhen goldsmithes get no gains by sodred crownes,
When vpholsters sel fethers without dust,
When pewterers infect no Tin with leade,
When drapers draw no gaines by giuing day,
When perchmentiers put in no ferret-Silke,   1095
When Surgeons heale al wounds without delay,
(Tush, these are toys, but yet my glas sheweth al:)—
When purveyours prouide not for themselues,
VVhen Takers take no brybes, nor vse no brags,
When customers conceale no covine vsde,   1100
VVhen Sea[r]chers see al corners in a shippe,

(And spie no pens by any sight they see),
VVhen shriues do serue al processe as they ought,
VVhen baylifes strain none other thing but strays,
VVhen auditours their counters cannot change,   1105
VVhen proude surveyours take no parting pens,
VVhen Siluer sticks not on the Tellers fingers,
And when receiuers pay as they receiue,
When al these folke haue quite forgotten fraude :—

(Againe, my priests, a little, by your leaue)—   1110
VVhen Sicophants can finde no place in courte,
But are espied for *Ecchoes,* as they are :
When roysters ruffle not aboue their rule,
Nor colour crafte by swearing precious coles :
When Fencers fees are like to apes rewards,   1115
A peece of breade, and therwithal a bobbe :
VVhen *Lays* liues not like a ladies peare,
Nor vseth art in dying of hir heare :
When al these things are ordred as they ought,
And see themselues within my glasse of steele,   1120
Euen then (my priests) may you make holyday,
And pray no more but ordinarie prayers.
   And yet therin, I pray you (my good priests)
Pray stil for me, and for my Glasse of steele,
That it (nor I) do any minde offend,   1125
Bycause we shew all colours in their kinde.
And pray for me, that (since my hap is such
To see men so) I may perceiue myselfe.
O worthy words, to ende my worthlesse verse,
Pray for me, Priests, I pray you, pray for me.   1130

EPILOGVS.

Alas (my lord) my hast was al to hote,
I shut my glasse before you gasde your fill,

And, at a glimse, my seely selfe haue spied
A stranger trowpe than any yet were sene:
Beholde (my lorde) what monsters muster here,   1135
With Angels face, and harmefull helish harts,
With smyling lookes, and depe deceitful thoughts,
With tender skinnes, and stony cruel mindes,
With stealing steppes, yet forward feete to fraude.
Behold, behold, they neuer stande content,   1140
With God, with kinde, with any helpe of Arte,
But curle their locks with bodkins & with braids,
But dye their heare with sundry subtill sleights,
But paint and slicke til fayrest face be foule,
But bumbast, bolster, frisle, and perfume: 1145
They marre with muske the balme which nature made,
And dig for death in dellicatest dishes.
The yonger sorte come pyping on apace,
In whistles made of fine enticing wood,
Til they haue caught the birds for whom they birded. 1150
The elder sorte go stately stalking on,
And on their backs they beare both land and fee,
Castles and Towres, revenewes and receits,
Lordships and manours, fines, yea, fermes and al.
What should these be? (speake you, my louely lord) 1155
They be not men: for why? they haue no beards.
They be no boyes, which weare such side long gowns.
They be no Gods, for al their gallant glosse.
They be no diuels, (I trow) which seme so saintish.
What be they? women? masking in mens weedes?   1160
With dutchkin dublets, and with Ierkins iaggde?
With Spanish spangs, and ruffes fet out of France,
With high-copt hattes, and fethers flaunt-a-flaunt?
They be so sure, euen *VVo* to *Men* in dede.
Nay then (my lorde) let shut the glasse apace,   1165

High time it were for my pore Muse to winke,
Since al the hands, al paper, pen, and inke,
Which euer yet this wretched world possest,
Cannot describe this Sex in colours dewe !
No, no (my Lorde) we gased haue inough,   1170
(And I too much, God pardon me therfore)
Better loke of, than loke an ace to farre :
And better mumme, than meddle ouermuch.
But if my Glasse do like my louely lorde,
VVe wil espie, some sunny Sommers day,   1175
To loke againe, and see some semely sights.
Meane while, my Muse right hu*m*bly doth besech,
That my good lorde accept this ventrous verse,
Vntil my braines may better stuffe deuise.

FINIS.

Tam Marti, quam Mercurio.

XXVII.

JOHN LYLY.

A.D. 1579.

JOHN LYLY, a native of the Weald of Kent, was born probably in 1553, and died in 1606. He studied at Magdalen College, Oxford, where he took his degree of B.A. in 1573. His nine plays, published between 1584 and 1601, are named ' Alexander and Campaspe,' 'Sappho and Phao,' 'Endimion,' 'Galathea,' ' Midas,' 'Mother Bombie,' 'The Woman in the Moon,' 'The Maid's Metamorphosis,' and 'Love's Metamorphosis.' But he is best remembered by his two works named respectively ' Euphues : the Anatomy of Wit,' first printed in the spring of 1579, and ' Euphues and his England,' 1580. He seems also to have been the author of the anonymous tract called ' Pap with a Hatchet,' written during the ' Martin Mar-prelate' controversy. The works of Lyly gave rise to the name of ' Euphuism,' a term applied to a then fashionable pedantic style, and over-strained method of expression, of which many examples are to be found in ' Euphues.' On this account, Lyly's works have been frequently decried and ridiculed, but it deserves to be remarked that he sometimes exhibits strong common sense; and Charles Kingsley, in his ' Westward Ho,' is right in calling Euphues, 'in spite of occasional tediousness and pedantry, as brave, righteous, and pious a book as man need look into.' I believe it will be difficult for any one to read the following extract without feeling the better for it; which is

—

my reason for quoting it. It is taken from that part of the first volume which is entitled 'Euphues and his Ephœbus,' and contains some excellent advice given by Euphues to young men. Both volumes of 'Euphues' were reprinted by Mr. Arber in 1868.

[*From 'Euphues aud his Ephœbus.'*]

'WISE Parents ought to take good heede, especially at this time, *th*at they frame their sonnes to modestie, either by threats or by rewards, either by faire promises or seuere practises; either shewing the miseries of those that haue ben ouercome with wildnesse, or *th*e happinesse of them 5 that haue conteined themselues within the bandes of reason: these two are as it wer the ensignes of vertue, the hope of honour, the feare of punishment. But chiefly parents must cause their youths to abandon the societie of those which are noted of euill liuing and lewde behauiour, which *Pi*- 10 *thagoras* seemed somwhat obscurely to note in these his sayings :—

First, that one should abstein from the tast of those things that haue blacke tayles : That is, we must not vse the company of those whose corrupt manners doe as it were make 15 their lyfe blacke. Not to goe aboue the ballaunce ; that is, to reuerence Iustice, neither for feare or flatterie to leane vnto any one partially. Not to lye in idlenesse ; that is, that sloth shoulde be abhorred. That we should not shake euery man by *th*e hand : That is, we should not con- 20 tract friendshippe with all. Not to weare a straight ring : that is, that we shoulde leade our lyfe, so as wee neede not to fetter it with chaynes. Not to bring fire to a slaughter : that is, we must not prouoke any that is furious with words. Not to eate our heartes : that is, that wee shoulde not vexe 25 our-selues with thoughts, consume our bodies with sighes, with sobs, or with care to pine our carcasses. To absteine from beanes, that is, not to meddle in ciuile affaires or businesse of the common weale, for in the old times the election 30 of Magistrates was made by the pullyng of beanes. . . . Not to retire when we are come to the ende of our race: that is, when we are at the poynt of death we should not be oppressed with griefe, but willingly yeeld to Nature.

But I will retourne to my former precepts: that is, that 35 young men shoulde be kept from the company of those that are wicked, especially from the sight of *th*e flatterer. For I say now as I haue often times before sayde, that there is no kinde of beast so noysome as the flatterer, nothing that will sooner consume both the sonne and the father and all honest 40 friendes.

When the Father exhorteth the sonne to sobrietie, the flatterer prouoketh him to Wine: when the Father warneth[1] them to continencie, the flatterer allureth them to lust: when the Father admonisheth them to thrifte, the flatterer haleth 45 them to prodigalytie: when the Father incourageth them to labour, the flatterer layeth a cushion vnder his elbowe, to sleepe, bidding him[2] to eate, drinke, and to be merry, for that the lyfe of man is soone gone, and but as a short shaddowe, and seeing that we haue but a while to lyue, who 50 woulde lyue lyke a seruant? They saye that now their fathers be olde, and doate through age like *Saturnus*.

Heeroff it commeth that young men, giuing not only attentiue eare but ready coyne to flatterers, fall into such misfortune: heereoff it proceedeth that they . . . mary before 55 they be wise, and dye before they thriue. These be the beastes which liue by the trenchers of young Gentlemen,

---

[1] Ed. 1579 'weaneth'; ed. 1581 'warneth.'
[2] Ed. 1579 'them'; ed. 1581 'him.

and consume the treasures of their reuenewes; these be
they that sooth young youths in al their sayings, that vphold
them in al their doings, with a yea, or a nay; these be they
that are at euery becke, at euery nod, freemen by fortune, 60
slaues by free will.

Wherfore if ther be any Father[1] that would haue his
children nurtured and brought vp in honestie, let him expell
these Panthers which haue a sweete smel, but a deuouring
minde : yet would I not haue parents altogether precise, or 65
too seuere in correction, but lette them with mildenesse forgiue light offences, and remember that they themselues haue
ben young : as *the* Phisition, by minglyng bitter poysons with
sweete lyquor, bringeth health to the body, so the father
with sharpe rebukes, sesoned with louing lookes, causeth a 70
redresse and amendement in his childe. But if the Father
bee throughly angry vppon good occasion, let him not continue his rage, for I had rather he should be soone angry
then hard to be pleased; for when the sonne shall perceiue
that the Father hath conceiued rather a hate then a heat 75
agaynst him, hee becommeth desperate, neither regarding
his fathers ire, neither his owne duetie.

Some lyght faults lette them dissemble as though they
knew them not, and seeing them, let them not seeme to see
them, and hearing them, lette them not seeme to heare. 80
We can easely forget *the* offences of our friendes, be they
neuer so great, and shall wee not forgiue the escapes of our
children, be they neuer so small? Wee beare oftentimes
with our seruaunts, and shal we not sometimes with our
sonnes : the fairest Iennet is ruled as well with the wande 85
as with the spurre, the wildest child is as soone corrected
with a word as with a weapon. If thy sonne be so stub-

---

[1] Original ‘Fathers.’

burne obstinately to rebel against thee, or so wilful to perseuer in his wickednesse, *th*at neither for feare of punishment,
90 neither for hope of reward, he is any way to be reclaymed,
then seeke out some mariage fit for his degree, which is the
surest bond of youth, and the strongest chayne to fetter
affections *th*at can be found.   Yet let his wife be such a one
as is neither much more noble in birth or far more richer in
95 goods, but according to the wise saying : choose one euery
way, as neere as may be, equal in both : for they that do
desire great dowryes do rather mary themselues to the wealth
then to their wife. ⹀ But to returne to the matter, it is most
requisite that fathers, both by their discreete counsayle, and
100 also their honest conuersation, be an example of imitation
to their children, *th*at they seing in their parents, as it were
in a glasse, the perfection of manners, they may be encouraged by their vpright liuing to practise the like pietie.   For
if a father rebuke his child of swearing, and he himselfe
105 a blasphemor, doth he not see that in detecting his sons
vice, hee also noteth his owne ?   If the father counsaile the
sonne to refrayne wine as most vnwholsome, and drinke
himselfe immoderately, doth hee not as well reproue his
owne folly, as rebuke his sonnes ?   Age alway ought to
110 be a myrrour for youth, for where olde age is impudent,
there certeinly youth must needes be shamelesse ; where the
aged haue no respect of their honorable and gray haires,
there the young gallants haue little regard of their honest
behauiour : and in one worde to conclude al, wher age is
115 past grauity, ther youth is past grace.   The sum of al wherwith I would haue my *Ephœbus* endued, and how I would
haue him instructed, shal briefly appeare in this following·
First, that he be of honest parents, nursed of his mother,
brought vp in such a place as is incorrupt, both for the ayre
120 and manners, with such a person as is vndefiled, of great

zeale, of profound knowledge, of absolute perfection, *th*at be
instructed in Philosophy, whereby he may atteine learning,
and haue in al sciences a smacke, whereby he may readily
dispute of any thing. That his body be kept in his pure
strength by honest exercise, his wit and memory by diligent 125
study.

. . . .

There is nothing more swifter then time, nothing more
sweeter : wee haue not, as *Seneca* saith, little time to liue,
but we leese muche ; neither haue we a short life by Nature,
but we make it shorter by naughtynesse ; our life is long 130
if we know how to vse it. Follow *Appelles*, that cunning
and wise Painter, which would lette no day passe ouer his
head without a lyne, without some labour. It was pretely
sayde of *Hesiodas*, lette vs endeauour by reason to excell
beastes, seeinge beasts by nature excell men ; although, 135
strick[t]ely taken, it be not so, (for that man is endewed with
a soule), yet taken touching their perfection of sences in their
kind, it is most certeine. Doth not the Lyon for strength,
the Turtle for loue, the Ante for labour, excell man? Doth
not the Eagle see cleerer, the Vulter smel better, the Mowle 140
heare lyghtlyer? Let vs therefore endeauour to excell in
vertue, seeing in qualities of *th*e body we are inferiour to
beastes. And heere I am most earnestly to exhort you to
modesty in your behauiour, to duetye to your elders, to dyl-
ligence in your studyes. I was of late in *Italy*, where mine 145
eares gloed, and my heart was galled to heare the abuses
that reygne in *Athens* : I cannot tell whether those things
sprang by the lewde and lying lippes of the ignoraunt, which
are alwayes enimyes to learning, or by the reports of such
as saw them and sorrowed at them. It was openly reported 150
of an olde man in *Naples*, that there was more lightnesse in
Athens then in all *Italy;* more wanton youths of schollers,

then in all *Europe* besids ; more Papists, more *Atheists*, more
sects, more schi[s]mes, then in all the Monarchès in the
155 world; which thinges although I thincke they be not true,
yet can I not but lament that they shoulde be deemed to be
true, and I feare me they be not altogether false ; ther can
no great smoke arise, but there must be some fire, no great
reporte without great suspition.   Frame therefore your lyues
160 to such integritie, your studyes to atteininge of such perfection, that neither the might of the stronge, neyther the mal-
lyce of the weake, neither the swifte reportes of the ignoraunt
be able to spotte you wyth dishonestie, or note you of vn-
godlynesse.   The greatest harme that you can doe vnto the
165 enuious, is to doo well; the greatest corasiue that you can
giue vnto the ignoraunte, is to prosper in knowledge; the
greatest comforte that you can bestowe on your parents, is to
lyue well and learne well; the greatest commoditie that you
can yeelde vnto your Countrey, is with wisedome to bestowe
170 that talent, that by grace was giuen you.

   And here I cannot choose but giue you that counsel that
an olde man in *Naples* gaue mee most wisely, although I
had then neither grace to followe it, neyther will to giue
eare to it, desiring you not to reiect it bicause I did once
175 dispise it.   It was this, as I can remember, word for word.

   " Descende into your owne consciences, consider with
your-selues the great difference between staring and starke-
blynde, witte and wisedome, loue and lust : Be merry, but
with modestie : be sober, but not too sullen : be valiaunt, but
180 not too venterous : let your attire be comely, but not too
costly : your dyet wholesome, but not excessiue : vse pastime
as the word importeth, to passe *the* time in honest recrea-
tion : mistrust no man without cause, neither be ye credulous
without proofe : be not lyght to follow euery mans opinion,
185 neither obstinate to stande in your owne conceipts : serue

God, feare God, loue God, and God will blesse you, as either
your hearts can wish, or your friends desire."

This was his graue and godly aduise, whose counsel I
would haue you all to follow; frequent lectures, vse disputa-
cions openly, neglect not your priuate studies, let not degrees 190
be giuen for loue but for learning, not for mony, but for
knowledge, and bicause you shall bee the better incouraged
to follow my counsell, I wil be as it were an example my-
selfe, desiring you al to imitate me.'

Euphues hauing ended his discourse, and finished those 195
precepts which he thought necessary for the instruction of
youth, gaue his minde to the continual studie of Philosophie,
insomuch as he became publique Reader in the Vniuersitie,
with such commendation as neuer any before him, in the
which he continued for the space of tenne yeares, only 200
searching out the secrets of Nature and the hidden misteries
of philosophy; and hauing collected into three volumes his
lectures, thought for the profite of young schollers to sette
them foorth in print, which if he had done, I would also in
this his *Anatomie* haue inserted; but he, altering his determi- 205
nation, fell into this discourse with himselfe.

'Why *Euphues*, art thou so addicted to the studie of the
Heathen, that thou hast forgotten thy God in heauen? shal
thy wit be rather employed to the atteining of humaine wisedome then diuine knowledge? Is *Aristotle* more deare to 210
thee with his bookes, then Christ with his bloud? What
comfort canst thou finde in Philosophy for thy guiltie conscience? What hope of the resurrection? What glad tidings
of the Gospell?

Consider with thy-selfe that thou art a gentleman, yea, and 215
a Gentile; and if thou neglect thy calling, thou art worse
then a *Iewe*. Most miserable is the estate of those Gentlemen, which thinke it a blemmish to their auncestours and a

blot to their owne gentrie, to read or practize Diuinitie.
220 They thinke it now sufficient for their felicitie to ryde well
vppon a great horse, to hawke, to hunt, to haue a smacke in
Philosophie, neither thinking of the beginning of wisedome,
neither the ende, which is Christ: onely they accompt diuinitie most contemptible, which is and ought to be most
225 notable.   Without this there is no Lawyer, be he neuer so
eloquent, no Phisition, be he neuer so excelent, no Philosopher, bee hee neuer so learned, no King, no Keysar, be he
neuer so royall in birth, so polytique in peace, so expert in
warre, so valyaunt in prowesse, but he is to be detested and
230 abhorred.   Farewell therefore the fine and filed phrases of
Cicero, the pleasaunt *Eligues* of *Ouid*, the depth and profound knowledge of *Aristotle*.   Farewell Rhethoricke, farewell Philosophie, farewel all learning which is not sprong
from the bowells of the holy Bible.

235   In this learning shal we finde milke for the weake and
marrow for the strong, in this shall we see how the ignoraunt
may be instructed, the obstinate confuted, the penitent com-
forted, the wicked punished, the godly preserued.   Oh! I
would Gentlemen would some times sequester themselues
240 from their owne delights, and employ their wits in searching
these heauenly and diuine misteries.   It is common, yea,
and lamentable to see, that if a young youth haue the giftes
of Nature, as a sharpe wit, or of Fortune, as sufficient wealth
to mainteine him[1], he employeth the one in the vayne inuen-
245 tions of loue, the other in the vile brauerie of pride: the one
in the passions of his minde and prayses of his Lady, the
other in furnishing of his body and furthering of his lust.
Heeroff it commeth that such vaine ditties, such idle sonnets,
such enticing songs, are set foorth to the gaze of the world
250 and griefe of the godly.   I my-selfe know none so ill as

---

[1] Original ' them.'

my-selfe, who in times past haue bene so supersticiously addicted, *th*at I thought no Heauen to *th*e Paradise of loue, no Angel to be compared to my Lady; but as repentaunce hath caused me to leaue and loath such vaine delights, so wisdome hath opened vnto me the perfect gate to eternall 255 lyfe.

Besides this, I my-selfe haue thought that in Diuinitie there could be no eloquence, which I might imitate; no pleasaunt inuention which I might follow, no delycate phrase that might delight me; but now I see that, in the sacred 260 knowledge of Gods will, the onely eloquence, the true and perfect phrase, the testimonie of saluation doth abide; and seeing without this all learning is ignoraunce, al wisdome mere [1] folly, all witte plaine bluntnes, al Iustice iniquitie, al eloquence barbarisme, al beautie deformitie—I will spend all 265 the remainder of my life in studying the olde Testament, wherin is prefigured the comming of my Sauiour, and the new testament, wherin my Christ doth suffer for my sinnes, and is crucified for my redemption; whose bitter agonyes should cast euery good christian into a sheeuering ague to 270 remember his anguish; whose sweating of water and bloud should cause euery deuout and zealous Catholique to shedde teares of repentaunce, in remembraunce of his torments.'

Euphues hauing discoursed this with himselfe, did immediately abandon all lyght company, all the disputations in 275 schooles, all Philosophie, and gaue himselfe to the touchstone of holinesse in diuinitie, accompting all other things as most vyle and contemptible.

---

[1] Original 'more.'

XXVIII.

EDMUND SPENSER.

A.D. 1579.

OF Edmund Spenser, one of the greatest names in English poetry, little need be said here; I refer the reader to the Globe edition of his works, edited by Dr. Morris, with a Memoir by Mr. Hales. He was born in London in 1552, educated at Pembroke Hall, Cambridge, and went to Ireland in 1580 as private Secretary to the Lord Lieutenant, Lord Grey of Wilton, residing part of the time at Kilcolman Castle, in the county of Cork, and occasionally visited England. In October, 1598, Kilcolman Castle was burnt during Tyrone's rebellion, and the poet and his family barely escaped. He never recovered this sad blow, but died shortly afterwards, in a tavern in King-street, Westminster, Jan. 16, 1599. His first important work was the 'Shepheardes Calender,' published in the winter of 1579–80, which I quote from here, because it fairly marks an era in English poetry. It was soon perceived that a new and true poet had arisen. The poem consists of twelve eclogues, one for each month in the year. The eleventh, that for November, is an elegy upon 'the death of some maiden of great blood, whom he calleth Dido.' The twelfth, for December, is one of the three in which he treats of his own disappointment in love. The poems were accompanied by some copious 'Glosses' or explanations, written by E. K., who was doubtless Edward Kirke, the poet's college friend. The text is that of the *first* edition, 'imprinted at London by Hugh Singleton, dwelling in Creede lane, at the signe of the gylden Tunn neere vnto Ludgate.' The punctuation has been slightly modified.

(A) *Nouember.   Ægloga vndecima.*

Argument.—IN this xi. Æglogue he bewayleth the death
of some mayden of greate bloud, whom he calleth Dido.
The personage is secrete, and to me altogether vnknowne,
albe of him-selfe 1 often required the same.   This Æglogue
is made in imitation of Marot his song, which he made vpon
the death of Loys the frenche Queene; But farre passing his
reache, and in myne opinion all other the Eglogues of this
booke.

Thenot.   Colin.

[*The.*] *Colin,* my deare, when shall it please thee sing,
As thou were wont, songs of some iouisaunce?
Thy Muse to long slombreth in sorrowing,
Lulled a-sleepe through loues misgouernaunce;
Now somewhat sing, whose endles souenaunce   5
Emong the shepeheards swaines may aye remaine,
Whether thee list thy loued lasse aduaunce,
Or honor *Pan* with hymnes of higher vaine.

Colin.

Thenot, now nis the time of merimake,
Nor *Pan* to herye, nor with loue to playe: 10
Sike myrth in May is meetest for to make,
Or summer shade vnder the cocked haye.
But nowe sadde Winter welked hath the day,
And *Phœbus,* weary of his yerely taske,
Ystabled hath his steedes in lowlye laye,   15
And taken vp his ynne in *Fishes* haske.
Thilke sollein season sadder plight doth aske,
And loatheth sike delightes, as thou doest prayse:

z

The mornefull Muse in myrth now list ne maske,
As shee was wont in youngth and sommer dayes. 20
But if thou algate lust light virelayes
And looser songs of loue to vnderfong,
Who but thy-selfe deserues sike Poetes prayse?
Relieue thy Oaten pypes, that sleepen long.

Thenot.

The Nightingale is souereigne of song, 25
Before him sits the Titmose silent bee:
And I, vnfitte to thrust in skilfull thronge,
Should *Colin* make iudge of my fooleree?
Nay, better learne of hem, that learned bee,
And han be watered at the Muses well: 30
The kindlye dewe drops from the higher tree,
And wets the little plants that lowly dwell.
But if sadde winters wrathe, and season chill,
Accorde not with thy Muses meriment,
To sadder times thou mayst attune thy quill, 35
And sing of sorrowe and deathes dreeriment.
For deade is Dido, dead, alas, and drent,
Dido, the greate shepehearde his daughter sheene:
The fayrest May she was that euer went,
Her like shee has not left behinde, I weene. 40
And if thou wilt bewayle my wofull tene,
I shall thee giue yond Cosset for thy payne:
And if thy rymes as rownd and rufull bene,
As those that did thy *Rosalind* complayne,
Much greater gyfts for guerdon thou shalt gayne 45
Then Kidde or Cosset, which I thee bynempt:
Then vp, I say, thou iolly shepeheard swayne,
Let not my small demaund be so contempt.

Colin.

Thenot, to that I choose, thou doest me tempt,
But ah, to well I wote my humble vaine,   50
And howe my rymes bene rugged and vnkempt:
Yet, as I conne, my conning I will strayne.

Vp then, *Melpomene*, thou mournefulst Muse of nyne,
Such cause of mourning neuer hadst afore:
Vp, grieslie ghostes, and vp, my rufull ryme,   55
Matter of myrth now shalt thou haue no more.
For dead shee is, that myrth thee made of yore.
　　Dido, my deare, alas! is dead,
　　Dead, and lyeth wrapt in lead:
　　　　O heauie herse;   60
Let streaming teares be poured out in stoie:
　　　　O carefull verse.

Shepheards, that by your flocks on Kentish downes abyde,
Waile ye this wofull waste of Natures warke:
Waile we the wight, whose presence was our pryde: 65
Waile we the wight, whose absence is our carke.
The sonne of all the world is dimme and darke:
　　The earth now lacks her wonted light,
　　And all we dwell in deadly night,
　　　　O heauie herse.   70
Breake we our pypes, that shrild as lowde as Larke,
　　　　O carefull verse.

Why doe we longer liue, (ah why liue we so long),
Whose better dayes death hath shut vp in woe?
The fayrest floure our gyrlond all emong   75

Z 2

Is faded quite, and into dust ygoe.
Sing now, ye shepheards daughters, sing no moe
 The songs that *Colin* made you [1] in her prayse,
 But into weeping turne your wanton layes,
  O heauie herse.   80
Now is time to dye: Nay, time was long ygoe,
  O carefull verse.

Whence is it, that the flouret of the field doth fade,
And lyeth buryed long in Winters bale:
Yet, soone as spring his mantle hath displayd [2], 85
It floureth fresh, as it should neuer fayle?
But thing on earth that is of most availe,
 As vertues braunch and beauties budde,
 Reliuen not for any good.
  O heauie herse.   90
The braunch once dead, the budde eke needes must quaile,
  O carefull verse.

She, while she was, (that was, a woful word to sayne),
For beauties prayse and plesaunce had no pere:
So well she couth the shepherds entertayne 95
With cakes and cracknells and such country chere.
Ne would she scorne the simple shepheards swaine,
 For she would cal hem often he[a]me,
 And giue hem curds and clouted Creame.
  O heauie herse.   100
Als *Colin cloute* she would not once disdayne.
  O carefull verse.

But nowe sike happy cheere is turnd to heauie chaunce,
Such pleasaunce now displast by dolors dint.

[1] First ed. omits ' you.' [2] Printed ' doth displaye' in first edition.

All Musick sleepes, where death doth leade the daunce, 105
And shepherds wonted solace is extinct.
The blew in black, the greene in gray is tinct,
 The gaudie girlonds deck her graue,
 The faded flowres her corse embraue.
  O heauie herse. 110
Morne nowe, my Muse, now morne with teares besprint.
  O carefull verse.

O thou greate shepheard *Lobbin*, how great is thy griefe!
Where bene the nosegayes that she dight for thee:
The colour[e]d chaplets wrought with a chiefe, 115
The knotted rushrings, and gilte Rosemaree?
For shee deemed nothing too deere for thee.
 Ah, they bene all yclad in clay,
 One bitter blast blewe all away.
  O heauie herse. 120
Thereof nought remaynes but the memoree.
  O carefull verse.

Ay me, that dreerie death should strike so mortall stroke,
That can vndoe Dame natures kindly course:
The faded lockes fall from the loftie oke, 125
The flouds do gaspe, for dryed is theyr sourse,
And flouds of teares flowe in theyr stead perforse.
 The mantled medowes mourne[1],
 Theyr sondry colours tourne[1],
  O heauie herse. 130
The heauens doe melt in teares without remorse.
  O carefull verse.

---

[1] Printed 'morune,' 'torune.'

The feeble flocks in field refuse their former foode,
And hang theyr heads, as they would learne to weepe :
The beastes in forest wayle as they were woode,   135
Except the Wolues, that chase the wandring sheepe,
Now she is gon that safely did hem keepe.
　　The Turtle on the bared braunch
　　Laments the wound that death did launch.
　　　　O heauie herse.   140
And *Philomele* her song with teares doth steepe.
　　　　O carefull verse.

The water-Nymphs, that wont with her to sing and daunce,
And for her girlond Oliue-braunches beare,
Nowe balefull boughes of Cypres doen aduaunce :   145
The Muses, that were wont greene bayes to weare,
Now bringen bitter Eldre-braunches seare ;
　　The fatall sisters eke repent,
　　Her vitall threde so soone was spent.
　　　　O heauie herse.   150
Morne now, my Muse, now morne with heauie cheare.
　　　　O carefull verse.

O trustlesse state of earthly things, and slipper hope
Of mortal men, that swincke and sweate for nought,
And shooting wide, doe misse the marked scope :   155
Now haue I learnd (a lesson derely bought)
That nys on earth assuraunce to be sought :
　　For what might be in earthlie mould,
　　That did her buried body hould.
　　　　O heauie herse.   160
Yet saw I on the beare when it was brought :
　　　　O carefull verse.

But maugre death, and dreaded sisters deadly spight,
And gates of hel, and fyrie furies forse,
She hath the bonds broke of eternall night,   165
Her soule vnbodied of the burdenous corpse.
Why then weepes Lobbin so without remorse?
   O Lobb, thy losse no longer lament,
   Dido nis dead, but into heauen hent.
     O happye herse.   170
Cease now, my Muse, now cease thy sorrowes sourse,
     O ioyfull verse.

Why wayle we then? why weary we the Gods with playnts,
As if some euill were to her betight?
She raignes a goddesse now emong the saintes,   175
That whilome was the saynt of shepheards light:
And is enstalled nowe in heauens hight.
   I see thee, blessed soule, I see,
   Walke in *Elisian* fieldes so free.
     O happy herse.   180
Might I once come to thee (O that I might!)
     O ioyfull verse.

Vnwise and wretched men, to weete whats good or ill,
We deeme of Death as doome of ill desert:
But knewe we, fooles, what it vs bringes vntil,   185
Dye would we dayly, once it to expert.
No daunger there the shepheard can astert:
   Fayre fieldes and pleasaunt layes there bene,
   The fieldes ay fresh, the grasse ay greene:
     O happy herse.   190
Make hast, ye shepheards, thether to reuert,
     O ioyfull verse.

Dido is gone afore (whose turne shall be the next?)
There liues shee with the blessed Gods in blisse,
There drincks she[1] *Nectar* with *Ambrosia* mixt,   195
And ioyes enioyes, that mortall men doe misse.
The honor now of highest gods she is,
  That whilome was poore shepheards pryde,
  While here on earth she did abyde.
   O happy herse.   200
Ceasse now, my song, my woe now wasted is.
   O ioyfull verse.

Thenot.

Ay, francke shepheard, how bene thy verses meint
With doolful pleasaunce, so as I ne wotte
Whether reioyce or weepe for great constrainte!   205
Thyne be the cossette, well hast thow it gotte.
Vp, *Colin*, vp, ynough thou morned hast,
Now gynnes to mizzle, hye we homeward fast.

   Colins Embleme.

   La mort ny mord.

GLOSSE.

[N.B. *The explanations marked with an asterisk are not quite correct.*
   See the Notes.]

2. *Iouisaunce*) myrth.
5. *Souenaunce*) remembraunce.
10. *Herie*) honour. [*Rather*, praise.]
13. **Welked*) shortned or empayred. As the Moone, being in
the waine, is sayde of Lidgate *to welk.*
15. *In lowly lay*) according to the season of the moneth Nouember, when the sonne draweth low in the South toward his
Tropick or returne.
16. **In fishes baske*) the sonne reigneth, that is, in the signe

   [1] First edition 'the.'

Pisces all Nouember: *a baske* is a wicker pad, wherein they vse to cary fish.

21. *Virelaies*) a light kind of song.

30. *Bee watred*) For it is a saying of Poetes, that they haue dronk of the Muses well Cast[a]lias, whereof was before sufficiently sayd.

36. *Dreriment*) dreery and heauy cheere.

38. *The great shepheard,* is some man of high degree, and not, as some vainely suppose, God Pan. The person both of the shephearde and of Dido is vnknowen and closely buried in the Authors conceipt. But out of doubt I am, that it is not Rosalind, as some imagin: for he speaketh[1] soone after of her also.

38. *Shene*) fayre and shining.

39. *May*) for mayde.

41. *Tene*) sorrow.

45. *Guerdon*) reward.

46. *Bynempt*) bequethed.

46. *Cosset*) a lambe brought vp without the dam.

51. *Vnkempt*) Incompti. Not comed, that is, rude & vnhansome.

53. *Melpomene*) The sadde and waylefull Muse, vsed of Poets in honor of Tragedies: as saith Virgile—Melpomene Tragico proclamat mæsta boatu.

55. *Vp griesly gosts*) The maner of Tragicall Poetes, to call for helpe of Furies, and damned ghostes: so is Hecuba of Euripides, and Tantalus brought in of Seneca. And the rest of the rest.

60. **Herse*) is the solemne obsequie in funeralles.

64. *Wast of*) decay of so beautifull a peece.

66. *Carke*) care.

73. *Ah why*) an elegant Epanorthosis: as also soone after, 'nay time was long ago' (l. 81).

83. *Flouret,* a diminutiue[2] for a little floure. This is a notable and sententious comparison, *A minore ad maius.*

89. *Reliuen not*) liue not againe. s[cilicet,] not in theyr earthly bodies: for in heauen they enioy their due reward.

91. *The braunch*) He meaneth Dido, who being, as it were, the mayne braunch now withered, the buddes, that is, beautie (as he sayd afore) can no more flourish.

96. *With cakes*) fit for shepheards bankets.

98. *Heame*) for home, after the northerne pronouncing.

107. *Tinct*) deyed or stayned.

108. *The gaudie*) the meaning is, that the things, which were the ornaments of her lyfe, are made the honor of her funerall, as is vsed in burialls.

---

[1] Printed 'speakerh.'   [2] Printed 'dimumtine.'

113. *Lobbin*) the name of a shepherd, which seemeth to haue bene the louer & deere frende of Dido.

116. *Rushrings*) agreeable for such base gyftes.

125. *Faded lockes*) dryed leaues. As if Nature her-selfe bewayled the death of the Mayde.

126. *Sourse*) spring.

128. *Mantled medowes*) for the sondry flowres are like a Mantle or couerlet wrought with many colours.

141. *Philomele*) the Nightingale: whome the Poetes faine once to haue bene a Ladye of great beauty, till being rauished by hir sisters husbande, she desired to be turned into a byrd of her name: whose complaintes be very well set forth of Ma. George Gaskin, a wittie gentleman, and the very chefe of our late rymers, who, and if some partes of learning wanted not (albee it is well knowen he altogyther wanted not learning) no doubt would haue attayned to the excellencye of those famous Poets. For gifts of wit and naturall promptnesse appeare in hym aboundantly.

145. *Cypresse*) vsed of the old Paynims in the furnishing of their funerall Pompe, and properly the [signe] of all sorow and heauinesse.

148. *The fatall sisters*) Clotho, Lachesis, and Atropos, daughters[1] of Herebus and the Nighte, whom the Poetes fayne to spinne the life of man, as it were a long threde, which they drawe out in length, till his fatal howre & timely death be come; but if by other casualtie his dayes be abridged, then one of them, that is, Atropos, is sayde to haue cut the threde in twain. Hereof commeth a common verse,

Clotho colum baiulat, lachesis trahit, Atropos occat.

153. *O trustlesse*) a gallant exclamation moralized with great wisedom and passionate wyth great affection.

161. *Beare*) a frame, wheron they vse to lay the dead corse.

164. *Furies*) of Poetes be feyned to be three, Persephone Alecto and Megera, which are sayd to be the Authours of all euill and mischiefe.

165. *Eternall night*[2]) Is death, or darknesse of hell.

174. *Betight*) happened.

178. *I see*) A liuely Icon, or representation, as if he saw her in heauen present.

179. *Elysian fieldes*) be deuised of Poetes to be a place of pleasure like Paradise, where the happye soules doe rest in peace and eternal happynesse.

186. *Dye would*) the very e[x]presse saying of Plato in Phædone.

---

[1] Printed 'Atropodas, ughters.   [2] Printed 'might.'

187. *Astert) befall vnwares.

195. *Nectar and Ambrosia*) be feigned to be the drink and foode of the gods : Ambrosia they liken to Manna in scripture, and Nectar to be white like Creme, whereof is a proper tale of Hebe, that spilt a cup of it, and stayned the heauens, as yet appeareth. But I haue already discoursed that at large in my Commentarye vpon the dreames of the same Authour.

203. *Meynt*) Mingled.

Embleme. Which is as much to say, as *death biteth not.* For although by course of nature we be borne to dye, and being ripened with age, as with a timely haruest, we must be gathered in time, or els of our-selues we fall like rotted ripe fruite fro the tree : yet death is not to be counted for euil, nor (as the Poete sayd a little before) as doome of ill desert. For though the trespasse of the first man brought death into the world, as the guerdon of sinne, yet being ouercome by the death of one, that dyed for al, it is now made (as Chaucer sayth) the grene path-way to lyfe. So that it agreeth well with that was sayd, that Death byteth not (that is) hurteth not at all.

(B) *December. Ægloga Duodecima.*

Argument. This Æglogue (euen as the first beganne) is ended with a complaynte of Colin to God Pan : wherein, as weary of his former wayes, he proportioneth his life to the foure seasons of the yeare, comparing hys youthe to the spring time, when he was fresh and free from loues follye. His manhoode to the sommer, which, he sayth, was consumed with greate heate and excessiue drouth caused throughe a Comet or a blasinge starre, by which hee meaneth loue, which passion is comenly compared to such flames and immoderate heate. His riper yeares hee resembleth to an vnseasonable harueste wherein the fruites fall ere they be rype. His latter age to winters chyll & frostie season, now drawing neare to his last ende.

THE gentle shepheard satte beside a springe,
All in the shadowe of a bushye brere,
That *Colin* hight, which wel could pype and singe,
For he of *Tityrus* his songs did lere.
    There as he satte in secreate shade alone,   5
    Thus gan he make of loue his piteous mone.

O soueraigne *Pan*, thou God of shepheards all,
Which of our tender Lambkins takest keepe:
And when our flocks into mischaunce mought fall,
Doest saue from mischiefe the vnwary sheepe: 10
    Als of their maisters hast no lesse regarde
    Then of the flocks, which thou doest watch and ward:

I thee beseche (so be thou deigne to heare
Rude ditties tund to shepheards Oaten reede,
Or if I euer sonet song so[1] cleare   15
As it with pleasaunce mought thy fancy feede)
    Hearken awhile, from thy greene cabinet,
    The rurall song of carefull Colinet.

Whilome in youth, when flowrd my ioyfull spring,
Like Swallow swift I wandred here and there: 20
For heate of heedlesse lust me so did sting,
That I of doubted daunger had no feare.
    I went the wastefull woodes and forest wyde,
    Withouten dreade of Wolues to bene espyed.

I wont to raunge amydde the mazie thickette,   25
And gather nuttes to make me Christmas game:
And ioyed oft to chace the trembling Pricket,
Or hunt the hartlesse hare, til shee were tame.
    What wreaked I of wintrye ages waste?
    Tho deemed I, my spring would euer laste.   30

[1] First edition 'to.'

How often haue I scaled the craggie Oke,
All to dislodge the Rauen of her neste :
Howe haue I wearied with many a stroke
The stately Walnut tree, the while the rest
    Vnder the tree fell all for nuts at strife :   35
    For ylike to me was libertee and lyfe.

And for I was in thilke same looser yeares,
(Whether the Muse so wrought me from my birth,
Or I to much beleeued my shepherd peres),
Somedele ybent to song and musicks mirth.   40
    A good olde shephearde, *Wrenock* was his name,
    Made me by arte more cunning in the same.

Fro thence I durst in derring-doe [1] compare
With shepheards swayne, what-euer fedde in field :
And if that *Hobbinol* right iudgement bare,   45
To *Pan* his owne selfe pype I neede not yield.
    For if the flocking Nymphes did folow *Pan*,
    The wiser Muses after *Colin* ranne.

But ah, such pryde at length was ill repayde,
The shepheards God (perdie, God was he none)   50
My hurtlesse pleasaunce did me ill vpbraide,
My freedome lorne, my life he lefte to mone.
    Loue they him called, that gaue me checkmate,
    But better mought they haue behote him Hate.

Tho gan my louely Spring bid me farewel,   55
And Sommer-season sped him to display
(For loue then in the Lyons house did dwell)
The raging fyre, that kindled at his ray.
    A comett stird vp that vnkindly heate,
    That reigned (as men sayd) in *Venus* seate.   60

      [1] Printed ' derring to '; but see the ' Glosse.'

Forth was I ledde, not as I wont afore,
When choise I had to choose my wandring waye :
But whether luck and loues vnbridled lore
Would leade me forth on Fancies bitte to playe.
   The bush my bedde, the bramble was my bowre, 65
   The Woodes can witnesse many a wofull stowre.

Where I was wont to seeke the honey-Bee,
Working her formall rowmes in Wexen frame :
The grieslie Todestoole growne there mought I se,
And loathed Paddocks lording on the same. 70
   And where the chaunting birds luld me a sleepe,
   The ghastlie Owle her grieuous ynne doth keepe.

Then as the springe giues place to elder time,
And bringeth forth the fruite of sommers pryde :
Also my age, now passed youngthly pryme, 75
To thinges of ryper reason selfe applyed.
   And learnd of lighter timber cotes to frame,
   Such as might saue my sheepe and me fro shame.

To make fine cages for the Nightingale,
And Baskets of bulrushes, was my wont : 80
Who to entrappe the fish in winding sale
Was better seene, or hurtful beastes to hont ?
   I learned als the signes of heauen to ken,
   How *Phœbe* fayles, where *Venus* sittes, and when.

And tryed time yet taught me greater thinges ; 85
The sodain rysing of the raging seas :
The soothe of byrds by beating of their wings,
The power of herbs, both which can hurt and ease :
   And which be wont tenrage the restlesse sheepe,
   And which be wont to worke eternall sleepe. 90

But ah, vnwise and witlesse *Colin cloute*,
That kydst the hidden kinds of many a wede:
Yet kydst not ene to cure thy sore hart-roote,
Whose ranckling wound as yet does rifelye bleede.
   Why liuest thou stil, and yet hast thy deathes wound?
   Why dyest thou stil, and yet aliue art founde?   96

Thus is my sommer worne away and wasted,
Thus is my haruest hastened all to rathe:
The eare that budded faire, is burnt & blasted,
And all my hoped gaine is turnd to scathe.   100
   Of all the seede, that in my youth was sowne,
   Was nought but brakes and brambles to be mowne.

My boughes with bloosmes that crowned were at firste,
And promised of timely fruite such store,
Are left both bare and barrein now at erst: 105
The flattring fruite is fallen to grownd before,
   And rotted, ere they were halfe mellow-ripe:
   My haruest wast, my hope away dyd wipe.

The fragrant flowres, that in my garden grewe,
Bene withered, as they had bene gathered long;   110
Theyr rootes bene dryed vp for lacke of dewe,
Yet dewed with teares they han be euer among.
   Ah, who has wrought my *Rosalind* this spight
   To spil the flowres, that should her girlond dight?

And I, that whilome wont to frame my pype   115
Vnto the shifting of the shepheards foote,
Sike follies nowe haue gathered as too ripe,
And cast hem out, as rotten and vnsoote.
   The loser Lasse I cast to please no more,
   One if I please, enough is me therefore.   120

And thus of all my haruest-hope I haue
Nought reaped but a weedye crop of care:
Which, when I thought haue thresht in swelling sheaue,
Cockel for corne, and chaffe for barley, bare.
  Soone as the chaffe should in the fan be fynd, 125
  All was blowne away of the wauering wynd.

So now my yeare drawes to his latter terme,
My spring is spent, my sommer burnt vp quite:
My harueste hasts to stirre vp winter sterne,
And bids him clayme with rigorous rage hys right. 130
  So nowe he stormes with many a sturdy stoure,
  So now his blustring blast eche coste doth scoure.

The carefull cold hath nypt my rugged rynde,
And in my face deepe furrowes eld hath pight:
My head besprent with hoary frost I fynd, 135
And by myne eie the Crow his clawe dooth wright.
  Delight is layd abedde, and pleasure past,
  No sonne now shines, cloudes han all ouercast.

Now leaue, ye shepheards boyes, your merry glee,
My Muse is hoarse and weary of thys stounde: 140
Here will I hang my pype vpon this tree,
Was neuer pype of reede did better sounde.
  Winter is come, that blowes the bitter blaste,
  And after Winter dreerie death does hast.

Gather together, ye[1] my little flocke, 145
My little flock, that was to me so liefe:
Let me, ah, lette me in your folds ye lock,

---

[1] Printed 'ye together' in first edition; but 'together ye' in 1597.

Ere the breme Winter breede you greater griefe.
  Winter is come, that blowes the balefull breath,
  And after Winter commeth timely death.   150

Adieu delightes, that lulled me asleepe,
Adieu my deare, whose loue I bought so deare:
Adieu my little Lambes and loued sheepe,
Adieu ye Woodes that oft my witnesse were:
  Adieu good *Hobbinol*, that was so true,   155
  Tell *Rosalind*, her *Colin* bids her adieu.

COLINS EMBLEME.

[*Vivitur ingenio: cætera mortis erunt.*][1]

GLOSSE.

4. *Tityrus*) Chaucer, as hath bene oft sayd.
8. *Lambkins*) young lambes.
11. *Als of their*) Semeth to expresse Virgils verse—
      Pan curat oues ouiumque magistros.
13. *Deigne*) voutchsafe.
17. *Cabinet*) *Colinet*) diminutiues.
25. *Mazie*) for they be like to a maze whence it is hard to get out agayne.
39. *Peres*) felowes and companions.
40. *Musick*) that is Poetry, as Terence sayth—Qui artem tractant musicam—speking of Poetes.
43. *Derring doe*) aforesayd[2].
57. *Lions house*) He imagineth simply that Cupid, which is loue, had his abode in the whote signe Leo, which is in the middest of somer; a pretie allegory, whereof the meaning is, that loue in him wrought an extraordinarie heate of lust.
58. *His ray*) which is Cupides beame or flames of Loue.
59. *A Comete*) a blasing starre, meant of beautie, which was the cause of his whote loue.

[1] Not in first edition.
[2] 'Manhoode and chevalrie'; Glosse to *October.*

A a

60. *Venus*) the goddesse of beauty or pleasure. Also a signe in heauen, as it is here taken. So he meaneth that beautie, which hath alwayes aspect to Venus, was the cause of all his vnquietnes in loue.

67. *Where I was*) a fine discription of the chaunge of hys lyfe and liking; for all things nowe seemed to hym to haue altered their kindly course.

70. *Lording*) Spoken after the manner of Paddocks and Frogges sitting, which is indeed Lordly, not remouing nor looking once a-side, vnlesse they be sturred.

73. *Then as*) The second part. That is, his manhoode[1].

77. *Cotes*) sheepecotes: for such be the exercises of shepheards.

81. *Sale*) or Salow, a kinde of woodde like Wyllow, fit to wreath and bynde in leapes to catch fish withall.

84. *Phœbe fayles*) The Eclipse of the Moone, which is alwayes in Cauda, or Capite Draconis, signes in heauen.

Venus) s[cilicet,] Venus starre, otherwise called Hesperus and Vesper and Lucifer, both because he seemeth to be one of the brightest starres, and also first ryseth and setteth last. All which skill in starres being conuenient for shepheardes to knowe, as Theocritus and the rest vse.

86. *Raging seaes*) The cause of the swelling and ebbing of the sea commeth of the course of the Moone, sometime encreasing, sometime wayning and decreasing.

87. *Sooth of byrdes*) A kind of sooth-saying vsed in elder tymes, which they gathered by the flying of byrds; First (as is sayd) inuented by the Thuscanes, and from them deriued to the Romanes, who (as is sayd in Liuie) were so supersticiously rooted in the same, that they agreed that euery Noble man should put his sonne to the Thuscanes, by them to be brought vp in that knowledge.

88. *Of herbes*) That wonderous thinges be wrought by herbes, as well appeareth by the common working of them in our bodies, as also by the wonderful enchauntments and sorceries that haue bene wrought by them; insomuch that it is sayde that Circe, a famous sorceresse, turned men into sondry kinds of beastes & Monsters, and onely by herbes: as the Poete sayth—Dea sæua potentibus herbis, &c.

92. *Kidst*) knewest.

99. *Eare*) of corne.

100. *Scathe*) losse, hinderaunce.

109. *The flagraunt flowres*) sundry studies and laudable partes of learning, wherein our Poete is seene, be they witnesse which are priuie to this study.

---

[1] The second part really begins at l. 55.

112. *Euer among*) Euer and anone.

97. *This is my*[1]) The thyrde parte, wherein is set forth his ripe yeres as an vntimely haruest, that bringeth little fruite.

127. *So now my yeere*) The last part, wherein is described his age, by comparison of wyntrye stormes.

133. *Carefull cold*) for care is sayd to coole the blood.

139. *Glee*) mirth.

135. *Hoary frost*) A metaphore of hoary heares scattered lyke to a gray frost.

148. **Breeme*) sharpe and bitter.

151. *Adiew delights*) is a conclusion of all; where in sixe verses he comprehendeth briefly all that was touched in this booke. In the first verse, his delights of youth generally. In the second, the loue of Rosalind. In the thyrd, the keeping of sheepe, which is the argument of all [the] Æglogues. In the fourth, his complaints. And in the last two, his professed frendship and good will to his good friend Hobbinoll.

Embleme.—The meaning whereof is, that all thinges perish and come to theyr last end, but workes of learned wits and monuments of Poetry abide for euer. And therefore Horace of his Odes, a work though ful indede of great wit & learning, yet of no so great weight and importaunce, boldly sayth—

Exegi monimentum ære perennius,
Quod nec imber [edax] nec aquilo vorax, &c.

Therefore let not be enuied, that this Poete in his Epilogue sayth he hath made a Calendar, that shall endure as long as time, &c. folowing the ensample of Horace and Ouid in the like.

Grande opus exegi, quod[2] nec Iouis ira nec ignis,
Nec fer[r]um poterit nec edax abolere vetustas, &c.

[*Epilogue.*]

Loe, I haue made a Calender for euery yeare,
That steele in strength, and time in durance shall outweare:
And if I marked well the starres reuolution,
It shall continewe till the worlds dissolution.
To teach the ruder shepheard how to feede his sheepe,   5
And from the falsers fraud his folded flocke to keepe.

---

[1] Wrongly cited. He means ' Thus is my,' &c.
[2] Printed ' quae.'

Goe, lyttle Calender, thou hast a free passeporte,
Goe but a lowly gate emongste the meaner sorte.
Dare not to match thy pype with Tityrus his style,
Nor with the Pilgrim that the Ploughman playde awhyle: 10
But followe them farre off, and their high steppes adore,
The better please, the worse despise, I aske no more.

Merce non mercede.

NOTES.

I. PERES THE PLOWMANS CREDE.

THE reader should bear in mind that the poem called 'The Complaint of the Ploughman,' or the 'Plowmans Tale,' printed in early editions of Chaucer and in Mr. Wright's edition of Political Poems, is by the author of the 'Crede,' and is therefore frequently quoted here in illustration of it.

Line 153. *Foure ordirs.* See Massingberd, Hist. of Reformation, chap. vii., on ' The Mendicant Orders; their Rise and History.' A few of the most useful facts about the four orders of friars are here collected for convenience. They were,

(1) The Minorites, Franciscans, or *Gray* Friars, called in France *Cordeliers.* Called Franciscans from their founder, St. Francis of Assisi; Minorites (in Italian *Fratri Minori,* in French *Frères Mineurs*), as being, as he said, the humblest of the religious foundations; Gray Friars, from the colour of their habit; and *Cordeliers,* from the hempen cord with which they were girded. For further details, see Monumenta Franciscana (ed. J. S. Brewer), which tells us that they were fond of physical studies, made much use of Aristotle, preached pithy sermons, exalted the Virgin, encouraged marriages, and were the most popular of the orders, but at last degenerated into a compound of the pedlar or huckster with the mountebank or quack doctor. See Mrs. Jameson's Legends of the Monastic Orders, and the Life of St. Francis in Sir J. Stephen's Ecclesiastical Biography. They arrived in England in A.D. 1224. Friar Bacon was a Franciscan.

(2) The Dominicans, Black Friars, Friars Preachers, or Jacobins. Founded by St. Dominick, of Castile; order confirmed by Pope Honorius in A.D. 1216; arrived in England about 1221. Habit, a white woollen gown, with white girdle; over this, a white scapular; over these, a *black* cloak with a hood, whence their name. They were noted for their fondness for preaching, their great knowledge of scholastic theology, their excessive pride, and the splendour of their buildings. The Black *Monks* were the Benedictines.

(3) The Augustine or Austin Friars, so named from St. Augustine of Hippo. They clothed in black, with a leathern girdle. They were first congregated *into one body* by Pope Alexander IV, under one Lanfranc, in 1256. They are distinct from the Augustine *Canons*.

(4) The Carmelites, or *White* Friars, whose dress was white, over a dark-brown tunic. They pretended that their order was of the highest antiquity and derived from Helias, i. e. the prophet Elijah; that a succession of anchorites had lived in Mount Carmel from his time till the thirteenth century; and that the Virgin was the special protectress of their order. Hence they were sometimes called 'Maries men,' as at l. 48, with which cf. l. 384.

As the *priority* of the foundation of the orders is discussed in the poem, I add that the dates of their *first* institution are, Augustines, 1150; Carmelites, 1160; Dominicans, 1206; Franciscans, 1209.

153. *The first,* i.e. the Dominicans, as being the wealthiest, proudest, and most learned. In the next line they are called the *Preachers*.

157. 'It was a singular change when the friars began to dwell in palaces and stately houses. . . . Richard Leatherhead, a grey friar from London, having been made bishop of Ossory, in A.D. 1318, pulled down three churches to get materials for his palace. But the conventual buildings, especially of the Black Friars, are described by the author of Pierce Plowman's Creed, a poet of Wycliffe's time, as rivalling the old monasteries in magnificence.'—Massingberd, Hist. Eng. Reform. p. 119. The following remark on this subject is striking: 'Swilk maner of men bigging (*building*) thus biggings semen to turn bred into stones; that is to sey, the bred of the pore, that is, almis beggid, into hepis of stonis, that is, into stonen howsis costly and superflew, and therfor they semen werrar (*worse*) than the fend, that askid stonis into bred.'—Apology attributed to Wyclif, p. 49 (Camden Soc.). Compare also,

'Hi domos conficiunt miræ largitatis,
Politis lapidibus, quibusdam quadratis;
Totum tectum tegitur lignis levigatis;
Sed transgressum regulæ probant ista satis.
   With an O and an I, facta vestra tabent,
   Christus cum sic dixerat, "foveas vulpes habent."'
            Political Poems (ed. T. Wright), vol. i. p. 255.

Pecock, bishop of Chichester, in his Repressor (ed. Babington, p. 543), complains that the Wyclifites blamed the friars for having 'grete, large, wijde, hiȝe, and stateli mansiouns for lordis and ladies ther-yn to reste, abide, and dwelle.'

158. *Say I,* saw I. We generally find seȝ, seiȝ. See ll. 208, 421.

159. *Y ȝemede,* I gazed with attention; ȝerne, eagerly, earnestly.

161. *Knottes;* see Glossary.

165. *Posternes in pryuytie.* 'These private posterns are frequently alluded to in the reports of the Commissioners for the Dissolution of the Monasteries in the Reign of Henry VIII. One of them, speaking of the abbey of Langden, says, "Wheras, immediately descendyng fro my horse, I sent Bartlett, your servant, with all my servantes to circumcept the abbay and surely to kepe *all bake-dorres and startyng-hoilles*, and I myself went alone to the abbottes logeyng joyning upon the feldes and wode. *evyn lyke a cony-clapper full of startyng-hoilles.*"—(MS. Cotton. Cleop. E. iv. fol. 127.) Another commissioner (MS. Cotton. Cleop. E. iv. fol. 35), in a letter concerning the monks of the Charter-house in London, says, "These charter-howse monkes wolde be called solytary, but to the cloyster-dore ther be above xxiiij. keys in the handes of xxiiij. persons, and hit is lyke my [many?] letters, unprofytable tayles and tydinges and sumtyme perverse concell commythe and goythe by reason therof. Allso to the buttrey-dore ther be xij. sundrye keyes in xij. [mens] hands, wherein symythe to be small husbandrye."' Quoted from Mr. Wright's notes to the 'Crede.'

166. *Euesed*, bordered. This verb is formed from the A.S. *efese*, the modern English *eaves*, which (it ought to be remembered) is, strictly, a noun in the *singular* number.

167. *Entayled*, carved, cut. This word occurs in Spenser, Faerie Queene, Bk. ii. c. 3, st. 27, and c. 6, st. 29.

168. *Toten*, to spy; a *tote-hyll* is a hill to spy from, now shortened to Tothill. Cf. ll. 219, 339.

169. 'The price of a carucate of land would not raise such another building.' Warton's note, in History of English Poetry, vol. ii. p. 97, ed. 1840.

172. *Awaytede a woon*, beheld a dwelling; *ybeld*, built.

174. *Crochetes*, crockets (see Glossary). They were so named from their resembling bunches or locks of hair, and we find the word used in the latter sense in the Complaint of the Plowman.

'They kembe her *crokettes* with christall.'

Political Poems, vol. i. p. 312.

175. *Ywritten full thikke*, inscribed with many texts or names.

176. *Schapen scheldes*, 'coats of arms of benefactors painted in the glass.' Warton's note; which see, for examples of them.

177. *Merkes of marchauntes*, 'their symbols, cyphers, or badges, drawn or painted in the windows.... Mixed with the arms of their founders and benefactors stand also the *marks* of tradesmen and merchants, who had no arms, but used their marks in a shield like Arms. Instances of this sort are very common.'—Warton's note, where he also says they

were still found, in his day, in Great St. Mary's, Cambridge, in Bristol cathedral, and in churches at Lynn.

180. *Rageman.* Alluding to the Ragman Rolls, originally 'a collection of those deeds by which the nobility and gentry of Scotland were tyrannically constrained to subscribe allegiance to Edward I of England, in 1296, and which were more particularly recorded in four large rolls of parchment, consisting of thirty-five pieces, bound together, and kept in the Tower of London.'—Jamieson's Scottish Dictionary. See also Halliwell's Dictionary, where it is explained that several kinds of written rolls, especially those to which many seals were attached, were known by the name of *Ragman* or *Ragman-roll*. In the Prologue to Piers the Plowman (l. 75) the name is given to a papal bull. The modern *rigmarole* is a curious corruption of this term.

181. *Tyld opon lofte*, set up on high. It means that the tombs were raised some three or four feet above the ground.

182. *Housed in hirnes*, enclosed in corners or niches.

183. In the church of the Grey Friars, near Newgate, were buried, in all, 663 persons of quality. Stowe says 'there were nine tombs of alabaster and marble, invironed with strikes of iron, in the choir.' See preface to the Chronicle of the Grey Friars of London; (Camden Soc., 1852), p. xxi.

184, 185. The Trinity MS. omits these lines, obviously owing to the repetition of *clad for the nones*. They are found in MS. Reg. 18. B. xvii. in the British Museum, and in the old printed editions.

185. 'In their *cognisances* or surcoats of arms.'—Warton.

188. *Gold-beten*, adorned with beaten gold.

194. *Peynt til*, painted tiles.

> 'And yit, God wot, unnethe the foundement
> Parformed is, ne of oure *pavyment*
> Is nought a *tyle* yit withinne our wones.'
>
> Chaucer, Sompnoures Tale, l. 403.

197. I trow the produce of the land in a great shire would not furnish that place (hardly) one bit towards the other end; a stronger phrase than 'from one end to the other,' as Warton explains it. *Oo* properly = one.

199. *Chaptire-hous.* 'The chapter-house was magnificently constructed in the style of church-architecture, finely vaulted, and richly carved.'—Warton.

201. With 'a seemly ceiling, or roof, very lofty.'—Warton.

202. *Y-peynted*, painted. Before tapestry became fashionable, the walls of rooms were painted. For proofs, see Warton's long note.

203. *Fraytour*, refectory.

209. *Chymneyes*, fireplaces.   Langland complains bitterly that the rich often despise dining in the hall, and eat by themselves 'in a privy parlour, or in a chamber with a chimney.' Piers Plowman, B-text, Pass. x. 98, ed. Skeat (Early English Text Society); or ed. Wright, p. 179.

211. *Dortour*, dormitory.

212. *Fermery*, infirmary; *fele mo*, many more.   Chaucer uses *fermerere* for the person who had charge of the infirmary; Sompnoures Tale, l. 151; *dortour* occurs in the same passage, just four lines above.

216. Compare

> 'Yif us a busshel whet, or malt, or reye,
> A Goddes kichil, or a trip of chese,
> Or elles what yow list, we may not chese,' &c.
>
> Sompnoures Tale, l. 38.

217. *Onethe*, with difficulty.

219. *Ytoted*, investigated, espied; see note to l. 168.

220. Friars are also accused of fatness in the following :—

> 'I have lyued now fourty ȝers,
> And fatter men about the neres
> Ȝit sawe I neuer then are these frers
> In contreys ther thai rayke.

Meteles, so *megre* are thai made, and penaunce so *puttes ham doun*, That ichone is an *hors-lade*, when he shal trusse of toun!'[1]

> Political Poems, i. 264.

222. 'With a face as fat as a full bladder that is blown quite full of breath; and it hung like a bag on both his cheeks, and his chin lolled (or flapped) about with a jowl (or double-chin) that was as great as a goose's egg, grown all of fat; so that all his flesh wagged about like a quick mire (quagmire).'

228. The line, 'with double worsted well ydight,' occurs also in the Complaint of the Ploughman; Political Poems, i. 334.

229. The *kirtle* was the under-garment, which was worn *white* by the Black Friars.   The outer *black* garment is here called the *cope*, and was made, very comfortably, of double worsted, reaching down to his heels. The *kirtle* was of clean white, cleanly sewed, and was good enough in its *ground* or texture to admit of its being dyed *in grain*, i. e. of a *fast* colour.   See Smith's Student's Manual of the English Language, p. 55, and cf. Collier's Eccl. Hist. i. 612.   The kirtle 'appears to have been a kind of tunic or surcoat, and to have resembled the hauberk or coat of mail; it seems, in some instances, to have been worn next the shirt, if

---

[1] *Neres*, kidneys; cf. German *Niere*. *Rayke*, wander about; cf. l. 72 of the 'Crede.' *Hors-lade*, a horse-load. *Trusse of toun*, pack off out of the town.

not to serve the purpose of it, and was also used as an exterior garment by pages when they waited on the nobility.'—Strutt, Dress and Habits, 349. When Jane Shore did penance, she was 'out of all array save her *kirtle* only.'—Holinshed, p. 1135; ed. 1577. But the word *kirtle* seems to have been really used in two distinct senses, sometimes for the jacket, and sometimes for the train or upper petticoat attached to it. See Gifford's note to Ben Jonson's Cynthia's Revels (Jonson's Works, ii. 260), and Dyce's note in Skelton's Works, ii. 149.

242. *Euelles*, evil-less; but there seems little force in this epithet, and I suspect the reading is corrupt. The other readings are no better.

247. 'It is merely a pardoner's trick; test and try it!'

252. An allusion to the reputation of the Dominicans for scholastic learning.

256. 'Three popes, John XXI, Innocent V, and Benedict XI, were all taken from the order of Black Friars, between A.D. 1276-1303.'—Massingberd, Eng. Ref. p. 117.

263. *In lyknes*, by way of parable.

342. *On leuest*, believest in.

345. *Halt*, holdeth; so we find *rit* for rideth, *fynt* for findeth, &c.

347. *Letten but werchen*, prevent him from working.

350. *For thei ben*, whether they be; *on to trosten*, to trust in.

351. 'I would requite thee with thy reward, according to my power.'

355. 'They are as disdainful as Lucifer, that (for his pride) falls from heaven.' Perhaps we should read *droppede*.

356. 'With their hearts (full) of haughtiness, (see) how they hallow churches, and deal in divinity as dogs treat bones.'

358. 'He had i-made ful many a *mariage*.'—Chaucer, Prol. l. 212.

360. In the Complaint of the Ploughman, it is said of the Pope that
> 'He maketh bishops for *earthly thanke*,
> And no thing at all for Christ[e]s sake.'
>   Political Poems, vol. i. p. 315.
The context shews that *earthly thanke* means a *bribe*.

361. 'They wish for honours :—only look at their deeds (and you'll see proofs of it).'

362. I have no doubt, from the context, that these goings-on of the friars at Hertford mean that they cajoled Richard II and his relatives into granting them money. There was no house of the Black Friars at Hertford itself (there was one of Black *Monks*), but the allusion is doubtless to their famous convent at King's Langley, in Hertfordshire, the richest (says Dugdale) in all England. Richard II made no less than three grants to it, and it received large sums from Edmund de Langley (who was born in that town), and from Edmund's first wife. 'And 'tis

said that this great Lady, having been somewhat wanton in her younger years, became an *hearty Penitent*, and departed this life *anno* 1394, 17 R. II, and was *buried in this church*' (the church of the Black Friars' convent).—Chauncy's Hertfordsh., p. 545. Edmund de Langley was also buried here, and so was the king himself. The custom was, to bequeath one's body to a convent for burial, and to bequeath a large sum of money to it at the same time; see ll. 408–417. It should be noted, too, that Richard often held a royal Christmas at Langley; he did so certainly in 1392, and again in 1394; see Stow's and Capgrave's Chronicles. This, doubtless, gave the Friars excellent opportunities.

365. See Glossary, s. v. Claweþ.

366. 'God grant they lead them well, in heavenly living, and cajole them not for their own advantange, to the peril of their (the kings') souls.'

374. *Lefte*, remained.

375. *Digne*, disdainful; hence, repulsive; but there is not often much logical sequence or connection in proverbs of this sort. Yet that this is the right explanation is evident from Chaucer; see the Glossary.

378. *Als as*, all so as, i. e. just as if.

379. *Leesinges lyeth*, lies his lies, utters them.

383. See note to l. 153. The friar in the Sompnoures Tale seems to have been a Carmelite; see Somp. Tale, l. 416.

387. *By lybbeth*, live by.

388. 'We know of no subtlety, Christ knows the truth.'

393. *And*, if. See note to Sect. VIII. iii. 46.

401. *To wynnen withe my fode*, to earn my food with.

402. *Lerne*, teach; common in provincial English.

405. 'Catus amat pisces, sed non vult tingere plantam;' see Macbeth, act. i. sc. 7, l. 45. The proverb is also alluded to in Chaucer, Ho. of Fame, iii. 683, Gower, Conf. Amantis, vol. ii. p. 39.

4c6. *So—parted*, are not given away in that manner.

409. Carefully compare the death-bed scene described fully in Massingberd's Eng. Ref. pp. 165–168; and see also Chaucer's Sompnoures Tale.

'Si dives in patria quisquis infirmetur,
Illuc frater properans et currens monetur;
Et statim cum venerit infirmo loquetur,
Ut cadaver mortuum fratribus donetur.'

Political Poems, vol. i. p. 257.

415. 'It is God's forbidding but that she die while she is in a mind to share her wealth among us; God let her live no longer, for our letters (of confraternity) are so numerous.' Rich people could buy letters or charters of fraternization; see Massingberd, Eng. Ref. p. 118. It was

of course inconvenient that those who had obtained these letters should live long afterwards.   Or *letteres* may mean 'hinderers,' as in P. Plowman, B. i. 69; but this hardly improves the sense.

421. 'I saw near me a simple man hang upon (bend over) his plough.'

I here venture to quote the *whole* of the *Prologue* to the Ploughman's Tale, from an early undated edition.   It is much to the point, and was certainly written by the author of the 'Crede,' though inserted in early editions of Chaucer.

'Here endeth the Manciples Tale, and here beginneth the Plow-mannes Prologue.

> The Plowman plucked vp his plowe
>   Whan Midsomer Moone was comen in,
> And saied his bestes shuld eate inowe,
>   And lige in the Grasse vp to the chin.
> Thei been feble bothe Oxe and Cowe,
>   Of hem nis left but bone and skinne,
> He shoke of her shere and coulter ofdrowe,
>   And honged his harnis on a pinne.
>
> He toke his tabarde and his staffe eke,
>   And on his hedde he set his hat,
> And saied he would sainct Thomas seke,
>   On pilgremage he goth forth plat.
> In scrippe he bare bothe bread and lekes,
>   He was forswonke and all forswat;
> Men mi3t haue sen through both his chekes,
>   And euery wang-toth and where it sat.
>
> Our hoste behelde well all about,
>   And sawe this men was Sunne ibrent,
> He knewe well by his senged snout,
>   And by his clothes that were to-rent,
> He was a man wont to walke about,
>   He nas not alwaie in cloister ipent;
> He could not religiousliche lout,
>   And therefore was he fully shent.
>
> Our hoste him axed, "what man art thou?"
>   "Sir" (q*uod* he) "I am an hine;
> For I am wont to go to the plow,
>   And earne my meate er[1] that I dine;

---

[1] Old copy 'yer.'

To swette and swinke I make auowe,
 My wife and children therewith to finde;
And serue God and I wist how,
 But we leude men been full blinde.

For clerkes saies we shullen be fain
 For her liuelod swette and swinke,
And thei right nought vs giue again, .
 Neither to eate ne yet to drinke.
Thei mowe by lawe, as thei sain,
 Vs curse and dampne to hell[e] brinke;
Thus thei putten vs to pain
 With candles queint and belles clinke.

Thei make vs thralles at her lust,
 And sain we mowe not els be saued;
Thei haue the corne and we the dust,
 Who speaketh there-again, thei saie he raued."

[*Four lines lost.*]

"What? man," (q*uod* our hoste) "canst thou preache?
 Come nere and tel vs some holy thing."
"Sir," q*uod* he, " I heard ones teache
 A priest in pulpit a good preaching."
"Saie one," q*uod* our hoste, "I thee beseche."
 " Sir, I am redy at your bidding;
I praie you that no man me reproche
 While that I am my tale telling."

Thus endeth the Prologue, and here foloweth the first parte of the tale.'

425. It means that his shoes were so worn and tight that his toes
peeped out as he walked along, whilst his hose, being ungartered, hung
down round and over the tops of his gaiters, and so became bedaubed
with mud. Gaiters made of old stockings with the feet cut off are
called *hoeshins* in Ayrshire. See *Hoeshins, Hushions,* and *Hoggers,* in
Jamieson's Scottish Dictionary.

428. *As mete,* as tight, scanty, close-fitting as the shoes were. It is
the A. S. *mǽte,* moderate, small. The true sense is given by the inele-
gant but expressive term 'skinny,' i.e. insufficient. Mr. Wedgwood sent
me a quotation from an old ballad—

 'There's no room at my side, Margaret,
  My coffin's made so *meet.*'

The word also occurs in Bishop Percy's Folio MS. (ed. Hales and Furnivall, vol. iii. p. 225).

431. *Worthen*, become. In Layamon's Brut, the past participle of the verb *worthen*, to become, takes the forms *iwurðen, iwurden, iworðen, iworþe;* and is sometimes used in the exact sense here required, as in 'for alle ure heðene-scipe hæne is iwurðen'—'for all our heathendom is become base.'—Layamon, vol. ii. p. 279. Cf. l. 492.

432. *Reufull*, sorry-looking; a great improvement on the old reading *rentfull.*

436. Compare, 'As two of them [Minorites] were going into a neighbouring wood, picking their way along the rugged path over the frozen mud and rigid snow, whilst the blood lay in the track of their naked feet without their perceiving it,' &c.—Monumenta Franciscana, p. 632.

443. 'At heighe pryme peres · lete þe plowe stonde.'—Piers Plowman (ed. Skeat), B. vi. 114.

445. 'If livelihood (i.e. means of living) fail thee, I will lend thee such wealth as God hath sent; come, dear brother.' *Go we* (= come along) was a common exclamation; cf. 'gowe dyne, gowe,' Piers Pl. B. prol. 226.

452. 'For there I expected to have known (it).'

456. 'Attendite a falsis prophetis, qui veniunt ad vos *in vestimentis ovium*, intrinsecus autem sunt lupi rapaces.'—Matt. vii. 15 (Vulgate).

459. *Werwolves*, lit. man-wolves, Fr. *loupgarous*, from the Teutonic *wer*, a man, which was modified into *gar* in Norman-French. For a full discussion of the etymology, see Glossary to Sir F. Madden's edition of 'William and the Werwulf,' reprinted in 'William of Palerne,' ed. Skeat, p. xxv. For a full discussion of the very prevalent mediæval superstition, that men could be turned into peculiarly ferocious wolves, see 'A Book on Werwolves,' by S. Baring Gould, and Thorpe's Northern Mythology.

462. *Curates*, parish-priests with a cure of souls. The friars were continually interfering with and opposing them.

'unnethe may prestes seculers
Gete any service, for thes frers,' &c.

Political Poems, i. 267.

468. *Confessions*, i.e. the right of hearing confessions, and being paid for so doing.

469. *Sepultures*, burials. They used to get people to order in their wills that they should be buried in a convent-church, and then they would be paid for the singing of masses for them.

471. *He loketh*, they look for, look out for.

478. 'I trow that some wicked wight wrought these orders through the subtlety of the tale called Golias; or else it was Satan,' &c. A satire on the monkish orders, called 'Apocalypsis Goliae,' may be found

among the poems by Walter Mapes, &c, edited by Mr. Wright for the Camden Society. The idea expressed in l. 479 is this :—perhaps, after all, that satire of Golias was written as an artful contrivance for bringing about the disrepute of the monks, and the rise of the mendicant orders. It is certain that the friars succeeded at first because the monks had become so dissolute, but it is not likely that this particular poem had much to do with it. *Gleym* = bird-lime, and hence subtlety, craft, guile. It is a strong metaphor, but explained by our author's own words in l. 564, 'I liken it to a limed twig, to draw men to hell.'

486. Cain's name was generally spelt *Caim* or *Caym* in Early English : whence Wyclif declared that the letters C, A, I, M meant the Carmelites, Augustines, Jacobins, and Minorites, and he delighted in calling the convents 'Caim's castles,' an idea which appears below, at l. 559. It was common to call wicked people Cain's children or Judas's children ; see Piers Pl. A. prol. 35, and x. 149.

> 'Nou se the sothe whedre it be swa,
> That frere Carmes came of a K,
> The frer Austynes come of A,
> Frer Jacobynes of I,
> Of M comen the frer Menours ;
> Thus grounded *Caym* thes four ordours
> That fillen the world ful of errours,
> And of ypocrisy.'—Political Poems, i. 266.

487. The Wyclifites were never tired of comparing the friars to *Pharisees* : ll. 487-502 and 546-584 are entirely devoted to this comparison, which, as well as that in 457, may be found in the Apology attributed to Wyclif. *feyned for gode*, feigned to be good men.

489. *Kynde ypocrites*, natural hypocrites, hypocrites by nature.

492. *Wo worthe you*, woe happen to you ; *worthe* is the imperative of *worthen*, to become, to happen ; see the next line.

498. 'Now *maister* (quod this lord) I yow biseke.—
> No *maister*, sir (quod he) but servitour,
> Though I have had in scole such honour.
> God likith not that *Raby* men us calle
> Neyther in market, neyther in your large halle.'
> > Sompnoures Tale, l. 484.

So too in the Comp. of the Ploughman ; Political Poems, i. 337.

499. Compare
> 'Priestes should for no catell plede,
> But chasten hem in charitè ;
> Ne to no battaile should men lede,
> For inhaunsing of her own degree ;

> Nat wilne sittings in high see,
> Ne soueraignty in house ne hall;
> All wordly worship defie and flee;
> For who willeth highnes, foule shal fall.'
>
> Ploughman's Complaint, Political Poems, i. 306.

550. *Chapolories*, scapulars. The writer cleverly substitutes the *scapulars* of the friars for the *phylacteries* of the Pharisees. The scapular (Fr. *scapulaire*, Ital. *scapulare*) was so called because thrown over the *shoulders*. Compare the words of Jack Upland, 'What betokeneth your great hood, your *scaplerie*, your knotted girdle, and your wide cope?'— Political Poems, ii. 19. The word has been oddly misunderstood; Richardson thought it meant a *chapelry*, and inserted this line in his dictionary under 'Chapel.' But the spellings *scaplory* and *scapelary* are both given in the Promptorium Parvulorum, and the alteration into *chapolory* is less remarkable than the spelling of *chaff* in l. 663, viz. *schaf.*

559. See note to l. 486.

562. 'In the bodili chirche ben had and vsid signes of greet curiosite, preciosite, and cost, and in greet multitude and dyuersite, as bellis, *baners*, and suche othere.'—Pecock's Repressor, ed. Babington, ii. 562.

564. So in Piers Plowman, 'For leccherye in likyng is lyme-yerde of helle;' ed. Skeat, B. ix. 179; or ed. Wright, p. 170.

744. 'Now must each cobbler set his son to school.'

748. *Bychop*, bishop. The alliteration requires this word, but the old printed text has *abbot*. Such an alteration must have been made by the printer *of set purpose*. Compare

> 'For to lords they woll be liche,
>   An harlots sonne not worth an hawe!'
>
> Ploughman's Complaint, Political Poems, i. 312.

750. Compare

> 'Lords also mote to them loute,' &c.
>
> Ploughman's Complaint, Political Poems, i. 308.

758. *Faytoures*, deceivers. Mr. Wrights edition has *forytoures*, which is a misprint.

761. 'No one could sit down to meat, high or low, but he must ask a friar or two, who when they came would play the host to themselves, and carry away bread and meat besides.'—Quoted in Massingberd, Eng. Ref. p. 110.

763. *Randes*, strips, slices. The old printed text has *bandes*. This improves the alliteration, but it does not appear that there is any such word. See the Glossary.

764. Compare
> ' With chaunge of many manner meates,
> With song and solas sitting long,' &c.
>> Ploughman's Complaint, Political Poems, i. 307.

785. Compare
> 'Had they been out of religion,
> * They must have hanged at the plowe,
> Threshing and diking fro toune to toune
> With sorrie meat, and not halfe ynowe.'
>> Ploughman's Complaint, Political Poems, i. 335.

786. 'And receive for their food common mixed-corn bread.'

787. 'And vegetables cooked (lit. wrought) without meat.'

808. When Christ descended into hell, he fetched out Adam and the patriarchs, and led them with him to heaven. This was called the Harrowing of Hell. The story is given in the apocryphal gospel of Nicodemus, and is repeated at great length in Piers Plowman, B. xviii.

816. *Generall*, i.e. Catholic, universal. So in p. 1 of the Apology attributed to Wyclif, we find the *general feith*, meaning the Catholic faith.

817–821. Here occur five *spurious* lines, only found in the early printed edition, and not in the MSS.

822. 'And I believe in the sacrament too, that the very God is in, both flesh and blood fully, who suffered death for us.'

On = upon, in; A.S. *on*. Cf. the phrases *on leuest*, believest in, l. 342; *leue on*, believe in, l. 795. The word *in* in l. 815 is exactly equivalent to the word *on* in l. 799.

As we know the author of the Crede to have written the Complaint of the Ploughman, we find his views concerning the Eucharist expressed thus :—

> 'On our Lords body I doe not lie,
> I say sooth through true rede,
> His flesh and blood through his misterie
> Is there, in the forme of brede :

> How is it there it needeth not strive,
> Whether it be subget or accident,
> But as Christ was when he was on-live,
> So is he there verament.'—Political Poems, i. 341.

Such was the position of the Wyclifites. They denied the *extreme* form of the doctrine as declared by the friars, maintaining that whilst Christ was *bodily* present, the bread *never ceased to remain bread;* how this could be was a thing, they said, not to be explained. See Wyclif's Works, ed. Arnold, i. 125, iii. 483, 500, 502.

B b

II. THOMAS OCCLEVE, *or* HOCCLEVE.

The first extract is quoted by Warton, Hist. Eng. Poetry, ii. 262, ed. 1840; iii. 46, ed. 1871.

Since printing the first edition of this book, I have collated the text of this piece with a MS. in St. John's College, Cambridge. In many places it has inferior readings, but some variations are worthy of note, and are given below.

Stanza 281. *Fructuous entendement,* fruitful understanding.

Science. This may seem to have some reference to Chaucer's treatise on the Astrolabe. But *science* was formerly a general term, as *knowledge* is still; cf. Gray's Elegy, st. 20.

Bequethe. This is a clear instance of the pronunciation of a final *e,* since the word rimes to *sle the;* yet the MS. omits it.

282. *Harme singuler,* individual harm. *Herteth,* encourages.

298. *Hir.* Here and afterwards Occleve makes death feminine (as in French), although in st. 281 it is masculine (as in Anglo-Saxon). But perhaps we ought in the former instance to read *why wold she sle the.* The Royal MS. omits *the* before *swetnesse,* but it occurs in MS. Arundel 38.

Tullius; i. e. Marcus Tullius Cicero. The St. John's Coll. MS. has *for vnto Tullius* instead of *fro vs to Tullius.*

Amonges; so in Arundel MS.; the Royal MS. has *amonge.*

299. *Combreworld.* This refers to death. It means that death is an encumbrance to or troubler of the world. The word is used more explicitly by Occleve in another passage, l. 225 of La Male Regle de T. Hoccleve, printed in Shorter English Poems, ed. Morley, p. 61. It is copied from Chaucer, Troilus and Creseide, Bk. iv. st. 36—

'I combre-world, that may of nothing serve.'

But Chaucer does not use it in quite the same sense, since he here makes Troilus describe himself as an encumbrance of the world, in the sense that he wishes to leave it. The sentence appears to mean, 'That cumber-world, death, who slew thee, my master (would I were slain!), was too hasty, to run on thee and bereave thee of thy life as she did.' The word þee is omitted in the Royal MS., but retained in the Arundel MS. Cf. the phrase 'Why *cumbereth* it the ground?' Luke xiii. 7.

301. The Arundel MS. has *forth brynge;* in the Royal MS. it is *bryng forthe.* The word *as,* after *truste,* is also from the Arundel MS.; the other MS. omits it.

598. Mr. Wright says that the story here related is a common one, in

different forms, in the Middle Ages. He observes that it resembles in some respects the well-known story of King Lear and his three daughters.

Note, know not; better spelt *noot*.

Canace. Occleve says that he does not know in what country this place is. Neither do I, unless it be *Canosa* in the south-east of Italy.

600. *Haunted in partie*, used in part.

In this stanza, MS. J. [St. John's Coll.] has *mekill* for *muche*, *as that* for *as* in l. 2, *so vp* for *up* in l. 3, and *of his* for *of* in l. 5; all improvements to the metre.

601. *Outrage*, extravagance; cf. *outrageous* in st. 600.

In this stanza, MS. J. has *And whan* for *And* in l. 3, and *aswage* for *swage* in the same line; line 4 runs—'They wexid vnkynde to hym anoon;' and in l. 6, it has *weren* for *were*.

602. *Cheuyce of*, provide with.

605. *Not but*, only; *nobbut* is still common in the North. Several passages in our older authors shew that the partitions between bed-chambers were often of very slight make. Thus in the romance of Sir Tristram we read,

> 'A borde he tok oway
> Of her bour.'—p. 114.

On which Sir W. Scott remarks, 'The bed-chamber of the queen was constructed of wooden boards, or shingles, of which one could easily be removed.' See also Havelok, ed. Skeat, l. 2076.

606. In l. 1, MS. J. has *slepten* for *slept*. In l. 4, it has *shulden* for *shuld*. In l. 7, *writhid* for *wrestede*.

608. *Dresse hem vpward*, lit. make themselves ready (or direct themselves) upwards, i. e. rise from their beds.

611. *Also*, as. Etymology tells us that *as* is simply a contraction of *also*.

612. *Me dresse*, turn, or direct myself, return.

615. *In-fere*, together.

Assoile, resolve, answer.

616. *Tolde*, counted.

618. *Prechours*, the Preachers or Dominican Friars.

Freres grey, the Franciscan Friars.

Karmes, the Carmelites or White Friars. See note on Sect. I. p. 357. Mr. Wright notes that, in London, the house and church of the Carmelites stood on the South side of Fleet Street, between the Temple and Salisbury Court.

619. *Of hem*, from them, the friars.

Taketh, take ye. *By*, concerning.

620. *Her berdes shaued he both smothe and clene*, shaved their beards neatly and cleanly.   To shave or make the beard was a proverbial expression, signifying to cheat.   Compare

> 'Yet can a miller make a clerkes beard.'
>
> Chaucer, Reeves Tale, 176.

Tyrwhitt says, '*Faire la barbe*, Fr., is to shave, or trim the beard; but Chaucer translates the phrase literally . . . Boccace has the same metaphor, Decam. viii. 10.   Speaking of some exorbitant cheats, he says, that they applied themselves "*non a radere ma a scorticare huomini;*" and a little lower, "*si a soavemente* la barbiera *saputo menare il rasoio.*"'

621. *Do*, done.

Dressen hem, direct themselves, i.e. go.

Where as, where that.

Or, ere.

Pekked moode, pecked mud; or, as we should now say, ate dirt.

623. Here, having ended his story, Occleve proceeds to apply the moral to his own case.   Having spent all his money, and not knowing how to appear rich like John of Canace, he finds no man to care for him; all he can do is to appeal to King Henry V for payment of the annuity promised him.

Sette, miswritten for *set*, the contracted form of *setteth*, 3rd pers. sing. indicative.   MS. J. reads—'The indigent men men settyn nothing by.' Clearly the right reading is—'The indigent men setten nothing by;' i.e. the indigent (person) men set no store by; no one cares for the poor.

So seith, so says Poverty, who justifies himself in the case of every man who is foolishly extravagant.

Here *foole-large* is a coined compound word, like *foole-largely* above. *Large* in Old English commonly means 'profuse,' 'lavish.'

624. In l. 4, MS. J. has *sore, and don* for *and do*; an improvement.

Stanzas 624-626 should be compared with La Male Regle de T. Hoccleve, a poem printed in Shorter English Poems, ed. Morley, p. 57.

625. *Gane*, yawn; cf. *gone* in Gower, l. 238, in Specimens II. sect. 20.

His small stuffe, its small contents.   In l. 4, MS. J. has *Isworn* for *sworne*.

My lord, i.e. Henry V, to whom the poem is addressed.   In like manner, Chaucer addressed his 'Compleynt to his Purse' to Richard II, praying him to 'have mind upon his supplication.'

III. JOHN LYDGATE.

(A) *London Lyckpeny.*

This piece has been several times printed; see Strutt's Manners and Customs of the People of England, vol. iii. p. 59; A Chronicle of London (printed in London, 1827), p. 265; and vol. ii. of the Percy Society's publications, p. 103. The two MSS. of it are the Harleian MSS. 367 and 542 in the British Museum; *both* of them are printed in 'A Chronicle of London,' which was edited by Sir H. Nicolas.

Mention is made of the Court of King's Bench, the Court of Common Pleas, and the Rolls Court. 'The three courts of the King's Bench, the Common Pleas, and the Exchequer, had each of them a perfectly distinct and separate existence. The Court of King's Bench had the control of all the inferior tribunals and the cognizance of all trespasses against the king's peace; the Court of Exchequer had cognizance of all cases relating to the revenue; and the Court of Common Pleas was the only tribunal for causes of a purely civil nature between private persons. The Courts of King's Bench and Exchequer still retain each of them its peculiar jurisdiction; and the Common Pleas is still the only court in Westminster in which a real action can be tried; but the great mass of causes between party and party may now be brought indiscriminately in any of the three courts.'—English Cyclopædia, s. v. Courts; iii. 301. It must be remarked, however, that the Courts of King's Bench and Exchequer often contrived to secure business which properly belonged to the Court of Common Pleas; and hence Lydgate represents himself as carrying his complaint from one court to another.

The word *Lyckpeny* has been explained as being an epithet of London. London is said to be a *lickpenny* in the sense that it licks up the pence that come near it. I believe this explanation to be the true one. Mr. Halliwell suggests 'lackpenny,' with reference to the situation in which the poet found himself; but this would require an article before it, as—*The* London Lackpenny. Moreover, Mr. Halliwell has entirely overlooked the fact that this expression would signify—*a Londoner without pence;* whereas the poet describes himself as a *countryman*, a man of Kent, who had come to London *for the day*, with the hope of succeeding in some litigation; hence he begins by saying,

'To London *once* my steppes I bent.'

We must therefore conclude that the poet did not intend to describe the experiences of a country lack-penny, but his adventures whilst wandering through London the lick-penny. In confirmation of this, Mr. G.

Ellis quotes from Howell's Londinopolis, p. 406, the following:—'Some call London a *lick-penny* (as Paris is called, by some, a *pick-purse*) because of feastings, with other occasions of expense and allurements, which cause so many unthrifts among country gentlemen, and others, who flock into her in such excessive multitudes.' Besides all which, Lydgate *had* a penny; see st. 14.

The poet describes his peregrinations; from his description he seems to have crossed the Thames and landed at Westminster, where he first went to the Court of King's Bench, then to the Court of Common Pleas, then to the Court of Chancery, Westminster Hall, and Westminster Gate. He next bent his steps towards London, passing up Cheapside, out of which he turned aside to Cannon Street and East Cheap; and then retraced his steps towards Cornhill, where he spent his penny on a pint of wine. Being by this time tired of London he made the best of his way to Billingsgate, and so at last returned to Kent.

Stanza 1. *Faynt*, weak, nearly extinct. He expected to find truth flourishing in London, but was certainly disappointed.

Spede, thrive, succeed.

3. *Rychard*, &c. Mr. Todd, in his Illustrations of Gower and Chaucer, p. 249, quotes from a commentary on Fortescue by Waterhous, explaining the condition of the Franklins in olden time, in the course of which he says:—' Of this race of men, who were and are but plain *Good Man*, and *John*, and *Thomas*, many in *Kent* and Middlesex especially, besides *sparsim* in every severall County, have been men of Knights' estate, who could dispend many hundreds a year, and yet put up to raise daughters' portions,' &c. A good deal of their money was, doubtless, often spent in going to law.

4. *Common place*, Common Pleas. I find the same spelling used in Stow's Survey of London. It also occurs below, sect. XIV (A). 316.

Sylken hoode. The law-sergeants used to wear hoods of white silk. See note to Piers the Plowman (Clar. Press Series), Prol. 210.

Mum, i.e. the least possible sound made with closed lips. The whole of this stanza appears to be copied from Piers the Plowman, Prol. 210-215:—

> '3it houed þere an hondreth in houues of selke,
> Seriauntz it semed þat serueden atte barre,
> Plededen for penyes and poundes þe lawe,　·
> And nou3t for loue of owre lorde vnlese here lippes onis.
> þow my3test better mete þe myste on maluerne hulles
> þan gete a *momme* of here mouthe, but money were shewed.'

5. *Rolles*, the Court of Chancery.

6. *Raye,* striped cloth. *Ray* means properly a *ray, streak, stripe;* but was commonly used in the above sense. See note to Piers the Plowman, v. 211.

Of help, for help; the usual phrase. Cf. Shakespeare, Othello, iii. 3. 212.

7. *Flemynges.* The Flemish tradesmen in London were noted for their weaving, dyeing, wool-combing, hat manufacture, and the like.

Copen. This is simply the old Flemish word for 'to buy'; the modern Dutch word is *koopen.*

8. *Hyghe pryme.* I believe this to mean the end of the first quarter of the artificial day, or day according to the sun. This would be about 9 a.m. at the equinoxes. See note to Piers the Plowman, vi. 114, a line cited in the note to Sect. I. l. 443 above. And see note to Sect. IV. l. 171 below. It must be remembered that our ancestors were early risers.

Cookes. This is again copied from Piers the Plowman, prol. 225:—

'Cokes and here knaues crieden, "Hote pies, hote!
Gode gris [*pigs*] and gees, gowe dyne, gowe!"
Tauerners vntil hem tolde þe same,
"White wyn of Oseye and red wyn of Gascoigne,
Of þe Ryne and of þe Rochel, þe roste to defye."'

It was the practice for tradesmen thus to tout for custom, standing outside their shop-doors. See Chambers' Book of Days, i. 349.

9. *In the ryse,* on the bough. So in Chaucer, Milleres Tale, 138:—
'As whyt as is the blosme *upon the rys.*'

Bede, offer.

10. *Chepe,* West Cheap or Cheapside. Mr. Riley remarks that a great portion of the northern side, as far as Guildhall, was formerly open ground.

11. *London stone.* A fragment of London stone is still preserved in Cannon Street, formerly Canwick or Candlewick Street. It is built into the street wall of the Church of St. Swithin. In Riley's Liber Albus, Canewykestrete is mentioned at p. 478; and John de Londoneston occurs as a proper name at p. 91. Cf. Shakespeare, 2 Hen. VI. iv. 6.

Met I. Altered to *comes me* in the MS., though perhaps with little reason.

Ryshes, rushes: misprinted *ryster* by Halliwell. *Greete,* cry aloud.

12. *By cock,* a vulgar corruption, answering to the old French *parde,* i.e. *par dieu.*

Jenken and Julyan, evidently the subjects of street-ballads. Possibly *Julian* is the St. Julian whose life is narrated in Caxton's Golden Legende, and in an old MS. metrical Lives of the Saints. Chaucer

compares his Franklin to St. Julian, and Sir John Mandeville identifies
the saint with Simon the leper. See Warton, Hist. Eng. Poetry, i. cxlviii.
(ed. 1840): i. 247 (ed. 1871).

There mede, their reward. They sang to get pence.

14. *Taverner;* see note to st. 8.

Yede, went. In st. 13 we have *yode;* cf. A. S. *ge-eode.*

`15. *I lyst not;* the true reading is probably *me list not,* it does not
please me. *List* in Old English is commonly an impersonal verb. The
boatman tells him that it is not yet his pleasure to bestow an alms.

16. *Convayd me,* conveyed myself, made my way. Lydgate does not
tell us *how* he got across the Thames. Probably he went over London
Bridge; if so, there could have been, in his day, no toll to be paid by
foot passengers.

Of the law, with the law.

Dyght me, prepared myself, resolved; he resolved to do as he had
ever done, i. e. to put up with grievances, and get on as well as he could.
We may compare Lydgate's experience with a piece which Warton
quotes as a specimen of Sir Thomas More's juvenile poetry :—

> ' A man of lawe that never sawe
>   The wayes to bye and sell,
> Wenyng to ryse by marchaundyse,
>   I praye God spede hym well!
> A marchaunt eke, that wyll goo seke
>   By all the meanes he may,
> To fall in sute tyll he dispute
>   His money cleane away,
> Pletyng the lawe for every strawe,
>   Shall prove a thrifty man
> With bate and strife; but, by my life,
>   I cannot tell you whan!'

(B) *From the Storie of Thebes.*

Besides the Arundel and Trinity MSS., there are several others, of
which the best seem to be MS. Addit. 18632 and the Royal MS. 18 D ii.
both in the British Museum. In the black-letter edition of 1561, our
extract begins on fol. ccclxvi. Warton gives a long account of this poem.
He says: 'Our author's originals are Guido Colonna, Statius, and
Seneca the tragedian. . . . Lydgate, in this poem, often refers to *myne
auctor,* who, I suppose, is either Statius or Colonna. He sometimes
cites Boccaccio's Latin tracts; particularly the Genealogiæ Deorum,
a work which at the restoration of learning greatly contributed to

familiarise the classical stories; De Casibus Virorum Illustrium, the groundwork of the Fall of Princes; and De Claris Mulieribus, in which Pope Joan is one of the heroines. . . . He also characterises Boccaccio for a talent, by which he is not now so generally known, for his poetry; and styles him, "among poetes in Itaile stalled." But Boccaccio's Theseid was yet in vogue.' With respect to the execution of the poem, he says: 'This poem is the Thebaid of a troubadour. The old classical tale of Thebes is here clothed with feudal manners, enlarged with new fictions of the Gothic species, and furnished with the descriptions, circumstances, and machineries, appropriated to a romance of chivalry.' He also thus refers to the story of Tydeus: 'Tydeus having a message to deliver to Eteocles, king of Thebes, enters the hall of the royal palace, completely armed and on horseback, in the midst of a magnificent festival. This palace, like a Norman fortress, or feudal castle, is guarded with barbicans, portcullises, chains, and fosses.' And again: 'Tydeus, being wounded, sees a castle on a rock, whose high towers and crested pinnacles of polished stone glitter by the light of the moon: he gains admittance, is laid in a sumptuous bed of cloth of gold, and healed of his wound by a king's daughter.' The latter passage will be found in the extract, lines 1217-1379.

Line 1065. *His massage*, his message. The argument of the preceding part of the story is as follows: Eteocles and Polynices, having dethroned their father Œdipus, king of Thebes, agree to reign alternately, each for a year. Eteocles is chosen to reign the first year; at the expiration of which he refuses to resign. Polynices therefore goes to Adrastus, king of Argos, to solicit aid against his brother. He there chances to meet Tydeus, and, to quote Warton, 'Tydeus and Polymite [Polynices] tilt at midnight for a lodging, before the gate of the palace of King Adrastus; who is awakened with the din of the strokes of their weapons, which shake all the palace, and descends into the court with a long train by torch-light. He orders the two combatants to be disarmed, and clothed in rich mantles studded with pearls; and they are conducted to repose by many a stair to a stately tower, after being served with a refection of hypocras from golden goblets. The next day they are both espoused to the king's two daughters, and entertained with tournaments, feasting, revels, and masques.' A triple alliance being thus formed between Adrastus, Polynices, and Tydeus, the last-mentioned undertakes to deliver a message to Eteocles, claiming the crown of Thebes for Polynices. The message being met by a refusal, Tydeus denounces war, and makes the best of his way out of Thebes. At this point our extract commences. See Statius, Thebaidos lib. ii. 467. A translation of Statius into English verse, by T[homas] S[tephens], was printed in 1648; a translation by Lewis will be found in vol. xiv. of Anderson's British Poets.

1067. *As he that list*, like one who chose. *List* is properly an impersonal verb, but in the fifteenth century it began to be used personally. See l. 1130.

1076. *Arge*, Argos, then governed by King Adrastus.

1079. *Kyng*, i.e. Eteocles, king of Thebes.

1081. *Euel apayd*, ill pleased. The first foot in the line consists of the single word *In*.

1085. *See*, seat, throne.

1089. The word *The* seems required at the beginning of the line, by the sense even more than by the metre. It is not unusual to find lines in which the first foot consists of but *one* syllable, as in l. 1081 above. Most of Lydgate's lines scan much better than they *appear* to do at first sight, if they be read *out loud*, with a *slow* and *measured* pronunciation, sounding all the lighter syllables fully, and with an *even* intonation. Much of the difference between his metre and our modern verses is due to the change of pronunciation and intonation; for these have altered, in many words, more than the spelling has done.

1090. *Fast* requires a final *e*, being an *adverb*, both here and in l. 1074. In both places, read *faste*.

1091. *Chooce*, chosen men; cf. Gk. ἐκλογή.

1095. *Vp peyn*, upon pain; so in Chaucer, Cant. Tales, l. 7853. *Up* is used in Old English where a penalty is implied; see Mätzner, Eng. Gram. ii. 1. 320.

Her hede, their heads.

1098. *Myn autour*, probably Statius; for although Statius does not here mention the number, he does so in other passages: Thebaidos lib. iii. 76, 363.

Vnwarly, unawares.

Tencombre, to encumber, overwhelm by numbers.

1101. *Rubric.* At the end of the rubric ed. 1561 adds—*in his repaire*, i.e. on his return.

1102. *Geyn*, convenient, short.

1104. *Only of*, purely out of treason, &c. So in l. 1106, *of cruel malys*.

1107. *Thorgh a forest*, &c. Cf. Statius, Theb. ii. 496:—

> ' Fert uia per dumos propior, qua calle latenti
> Praecelerant, densaeque legunt compendia siluae.
> Lecta dolis sedes : gemini procul urbe malignis
> Faucibus urgentur colles, quos umbra superni
> Montis, et incuruis claudunt iuga frondea siluis:
> Insidias natura loco, caecamque latendi

    Struxit opem : medias arcte secat aspera rupes
    Semita, quam subter campi, deuexaque latis
    Arua iacent spatiis.'
There is a very similar description in Virgil, Æn. xi. 522 :—
   ' Est curuo anfractu uallis, accommoda fraudi
    Armorumque dolis ; quam densis frondibus atrum
    Urget utrinque latus ; tenuis quo semita ducit,
    Angustaeque ferunt fauces, aditusque maligni.'

 1112. *Spynx*, the Sphinx. When Œdipus solved her riddle, the Sphinx threw herself from a cliff of the mountain and perished.

 1113. *Nothing war*, in no degree aware in his thoughts.

 1118. *Wisse*, teach him, viz. to teach him the way.

 1137. *Be compas envyroun*, by a compass around, i.e. on all sides at once.

 1143. *In euery half*, on every side.

 1145. *Founde*, with a final *e*, because it is plural. Ed. 1561 inserts *it* after *founde*.

 1146. *Was mad*, was made to alight on foot, to dismount. So *grounded*, in the next line, means brought upon the ground, thrown down.

 1153. *Took*, i.e. entered.

 Of ful high prudence, because of his great prudence.

 1164. *With water turned doun*, detached by (the effect of) water.

 1165. This hurling of a stone by a warrior is described by Homer, Il. v. 302, &c. ; and by Virgil, Æn. xii. 896.

 1167. *For the nonys,* for the occasion. This is the exact meaning of the expression, which is here used quite correctly.

 1174. *Left*, remained. So also in Sect. II. st. 607.

 1182. *Saue oon*, save one. His name, according to Statius, was Mæon, the son of Hæmon.

 1186. *For a wedde*, for a pledge. *Spedde* is miswritten for *sped*, the past participle of *speed* ; it rimes with *wed*.

 1200. *Spede*, succeed.

 1201. *Tendure*, to endure ; cf. *tenforme*, l. 1207.

 1202. *Record I take*, I take as an example or proof (of this). There is a passage in Barbour's account of Bruce, in which he describes the Scottish king as fighting single-handed against no less than *two hundred* enemies in a narrow pass. Barbour compares this exploit with that of Tydeus, in the course of which comparison he gives a full account of the latter, telling the story better than Lydgate does ; see Barbour's Bruce, ed. Skeat (Early English Text Society), bk. vi. 179-284.

 1213. *Worthed vp*, got up ; literally *became* up ; it is the past tense of the verb *worthen* (Germ. *werden*), to become.

1215. 'And verily, in his imagination, he was still all the while afraid of (further) treason.'

1219. *Lygurgus*, Lycurgus. In Statius, there is not a word about this part of the story; he makes Tydeus return to Argos immediately after the combat.

1226. *Be nyght*, by night, shone against the moon, i.e. by reflecting the light thrown on it by the moon.

1244. *Grene* requires a final *e*; but in *white* and *rede* the final *e* is omitted, because *elided*, since they occur before vowels. See *grene* and *rede* in l. 1260.

1245. *Beste* and *reste* require each a final *e*; but I leave them out, because they are left out in the MS., and the use of them in Lydgate is far less regular than in Chaucer. Ed. 1561 has the full forms (*reste, beste*) correctly. The final *e*, in a plural adjective, is seen in *newe*, l. 1251.

1250. *To*, unto, till; i.e. till daybreak. Lydgate probably remembered Chaucer's lines in the Knightes Tale, l. 633:—

> 'The busy larke, messager of daye,
> Salueth in hire song the morwe graye;
> And fyry Phebus riseth vp so brighte
> That al the orient laugheth of the lighte,
> And with his stremes dryeth in the greues
> The siluer droppes, honging on the leues.'

From this passage Lydgate borrows the word *stremes* for sunbeams (l. 1254), and the expression *syluer dewe*.

1259. *That*, &c., that painted the soil, by means of the green being mingled with the red.

1262. The description of Lycurgus' daughter is clearly influenced by Lydgate's reminiscences of Chaucer's Emelye, in the Knightes Tale, who was 'fresscher than the May with *floures newe*,' and of whom Chaucer says that

> 'in the gardyn at the sonne vpriste
> Sche walketh vp and doun wher as hire liste.'

1267. *Allures*. Warton says (Hist. Eng. Poetry, ii. 300) that Lydgate, in his description (in his Troyboke) of the city of Troy, relates how 'the sides of every street were covered with fresh *alures* of marble, or cloisters, crowned with rich and lofty pinnacles, and fronted with tabernacular or open work, vaulted like the dormitory of a monastery, and called *deambulatories*, for the accommodation of travellers in all weathers.' In a footnote we find it explained by 'allies [alleys] or covert-ways; Lat. *Alura*; as in "*Alura* quae ducit a coquina conventus usque ad cameram prioris;" Hearne's Otterb. Praef. Append. p. cxi. Hearne derives it from *Ala*, a wing or side. Rather from [French] *Aller*, whence

Allée, alley.   Robert of Gloucester mentions the ladies standing "upe [upon] the *alurs* of the castle" to see a tournament.'   In the last instance, the expression no doubt means that the ladies stood upon the leads with which the covered ways were protected; hence we find Lord Surrey speaking of the ladies *upon the leads*.   See Sect. XIX. (F), 16, p. 219.

1268. *Goo*, gone; cf. *ago*.   So also we find *do* for *done*, Sect. II. st. 621.

1274. 'Fell into a kind of fear.'   Ed. 1561 has *fere*.

1276. *Aboute* certainly has a final *e*, fully pronounced; this *e* is a remnant of the *an* in the Saxon form *onbútan*.

1293. 'And have pity on him, by reason of her womanhood.'   In l. 1296, *of* means *by*; in l. 1302 it means *upon*.

1336. *Her thoghte*, it seemed to her.

1349. *Leches*, physicians.

1352. *Taswage*, to assuage.

Tapese, to appease.

1359. *Taken kep*, take care, watch.

1360. *Anyghtes*, on nights, every night.   So also *aday*, daily.

Slep, slept.   The A.S. pt. t. is *ic slép*.

1367. *Bywelde hym*, &c., exercise his limbs in any way he liked.

1377. 'While he lives, in anything she might command him to do.'

1378. *Arge*, Argos.   The return of Tydeus to Argos is told in Statius, Theb. iii. 324 :—

'Iamque remensus iter fesso Danaëia Tydeus
    Arua gradu, uiridisque legit deuexa Prosymnae.'

1381. *Repeir*, repairing homewards, return.

1390. *Polymytes*, Polynices.

1392. *Vnsounded*, unhealed.   Our extract goes as far as l. 406, lib. iii. of Statius.

IV.   JAMES I (OF SCOTLAND).

JAMES I was murdered on the 20th of February, 1437, in the forty-fourth year of his age, and the thirteenth of his actual reign.   For an account of his life and poetry see particularly Irving's Lives of the Scottish Poets, i. 287–335.   In the appendix to the first volume of Pinkerton's History of Scotland will be found 'A full lamentable Cronycle of the Dethe and false Murdure of James Stewarde, last Kynge of Scottys.'   This account differs in many particulars from that given by Bower and other Scottish historians.   In an edition of the Mirrour for Magistrates, printed in 1563, there is a legend written by Baldwyn, and entitled ' How Kyng James the First, for breaking his othes and bondes, was by God's suffraunce miserably murdered of his owne Subiectes;' but this was omitted in later editions.

There are other editions of the Kingis Quair, besides those by Tytler and Chalmers, as e.g. one printed at Perth in 1786; and an edition, with notes and glossary, by E. Thompson, of Ayr, in 1824. In 1884, I edited it myself for the Scottish Text Society. Warton has a note upon the poem in his Hist. of Eng. Poetry, sect. xxv., note the first; ii. 328, ed. 1840; iii. 121, ed. 1871.

The word *quair*, our modern *quire*, was originally applied to any small book. Thus Lydgate begins the last stanza of his Chorle and Bird with the line—

'Goo, litell *quayer*, and recomande me,' &c.

Roxburghe Club edition, 1818.

Again, in the colophon to the Paternoster, Ave, and Credo, printed by Wynkyn de Worde in 1509, we are told that Thomas Betson 'drewe and made the contentes of this litell *quayer* and exhortation.' See also Skelton's Works, ed. Dyce, i. 422.

The extract here given may be compared with the edition of the Kingis Quair, in 'The Poetic Remains of some of the Scottish Kings,' by G. Chalmers, 1824; p. 84. The text given by Chalmers is modernized throughout, except in the case of such words as he prints in italics. It is consequently not very correct, neither are the notes quite to be depended upon. I quote a few of them, which I mark with the letter C.

Stanza 152. *Endlang*, along; A.S. *andlang*, Germ. *entlang*.

Maner soun, kind of sound.

153. *Sonne*; the final *e* is sounded, being preserved from elision by cæsura. Chalmers prints *sun*, to the injury of the metre.

154. 'I found a way which seemed to be a highway.' The final *e* in *hye* should, perhaps, be sounded, but an extra word seems to be required. It must be carefully borne in mind that this poem is by no means written in pure Lowland-Scotch; the influence of Chaucer was then so supreme that his Scottish imitators frequently copied, not only his words, but his dialect and mode of pronunciation.

155. *Fere*, companion, mate. 'As Orpheus and Eurydice his *fere*;' Chaucer, Troilus, b. iv. l. 791.

Smaragdyne, emerald or green-coloured stone. Mr. Chalmers is puzzled to know how a panther can be like an emerald; but we must remember that the poet of course follows the usual descriptions given in the old so-called 'Bestiaries,' or descriptions of beasts. These contain some of the wildest notions, quite at variance with all facts. An old

English Bestiary is printed in Wright and Halliwell's Reliquiæ Antiquæ, vol. i. p. 208, and is reprinted in Mätzner's Altenglische Sprachproben. The Bestiary of Philip de Thaun, in old Norman-French, is printed in Mr. Wright's Popular Treatises on Science. Again, there is a description of the panther in the Codex Exoniensis, or collection of Anglo-Saxon poetry from a MS. at Exeter, edited by Mr. Thorpe, 1842. The latter describes the panther as of various colours, *like Joseph's coat.* All the descriptions agree in assigning to the panther a deliciously sweet odour; see note to Sect. XXVII. 64.

Slawe ass, slow ass, the drudging beast of pain; i. e. of painful toil.

' *Werely* or *warlike* porcupine, armed with quills.'—C.

Lufar vnicorne. Lufar, i. e. lover. Why the unicorn is called a *lover*, is sufficiently clear from the description in Philippe de Thaun. When a hunter wishes to catch a unicorn, he instructs a young girl to entice it; the unicorn goes to sleep on the girl's lap, and then the hunter has him fast. 'The unicorn humbleth himself to a maid;' Calisto and Meliboea; in Old Plays, ed. Hazlitt, i. 81. His 'ivory horn' was supposed to dispel poison. Thus Alviano (Venetian general, died 1515) took the device of a unicorn putting his horn into water before drinking, with the motto—*Venena pello* (I dispel poisons). See Mrs. Palliser's Devices, Badges, &c. p. 21.

156. *Fery*, fiery. Not ' active.'

Standar oliphant, elephant that always stands. The elephant was said to have only one joint in his legs, and so could not lie down. He used to lean against a tree to go to sleep. See Philippe de Thaun; p. 101.

The wedowis Inemye, the widow's enemy; because he steals her chickens. An evident allusion to Chaucer's Nonne Prestes Tale, which see.

Clymbare gayte, goat that climbs.

Alblastrye, warlike weapon for shooting. An *arblast* or *alblast* (Lat. *arcubalista*) is any kind of catapult or crossbow. Mr. Chalmers suggests that the sinews of the elk may have been used for bow-strings.

Herknere bore, listening boar, boar with keen hearing.

Holsum grey for hortis, badger, wholesome for hurts or wounds. Badgers' teeth, &c., were a charm against all things harmful; Cockayne's Leechdoms, i. 327. Mr. Chalmers is hopelessly wrong here, and frequently elsewhere. He supposes it to mean a greyhound, wholesome for the gardens; *why* it is so, he leaves to the reader's ingenuity.

157. *Bugill, drawar*, ox, who draws. The *Bugle*, or wild ox, is described in Topsell's Four-footed Beasts, ed. 1658, p. 45.

Martrik, marten. *Poynȝee*, probably the beech-marten.

Tippit as the Iete, tipped like jet, i. e. on its tail.

Nocht say ho, never says *stop!* The word *ho* is an interjection, meaning 'stop!' 'cease!' See Chaucer. For *say*, read *sayis*.

157. *Lesty*, lusty; i. e. pretty, as usual.

Ravin, ravenous.

158. *To purpose*, to my purpose, to my story.

Furth, forth, along; the Scottish trilled *r* makes this word almost dissyllabic—*fur-r-th*.

In hye, in haste; a mere expletive. Used by Barbour some hundred times.

159. *Spide* is evidently a mistake of the scribe for *espide*, or rather *aspide*, the usual Middle English form. See Chaucer.

Cleuering, clinging; holding on as a cat holds on by its *claws*, which are called in Middle English *clivers*.

160. *Glewis;* a word is here omitted, probably because the scribe did not understand it. The right word is certainly *glewis*. The old Eng. *glew*, modern *glee*, meant a game or sport, but was used with particular reference to the tricks of fortune; so that *glewis* answers in sense to our modern *freaks*. See *Glew* in Jamieson's Dict.; and Barbour's Bruce, ed. Skeat, i. 90, vi. 658. Instead of &, the usual abbreviation for *and*, Mr. Chalmers prints an italic Q upside down, and supposes it to mean *askew is* (*as Q is*)!

Anewis, probably *rings*, from Lat. *annulus*, O. Fr. *anel*, also spelt *aniau, aigniau*, &c. See Roquefort.

161. *Degoutit*, spotted.

Self, same; alluding to the black tails with which white ermine is ornamented.

Chiere, cheer, demeanour.

Alyte, put for *a lyte*, a little.

Slake, i. e. slacken or leave off frowning, and so begin to smile.

And, if. *For* must be inserted.

At ane contenance, in one aspect.

162. We must either read *pitte*, or insert *as*.

163. *Weltering*, rolling, turning. Fortune's wheel is represented as turning on a horizontal axis, whilst numbers of men cling on to it. As some suddenly clutch at it, or fall off into the pit beneath, it as suddenly turns round.

164. 'And, on the wheel (viz. near the highest point), there was a small vacant space, nearly stretched across (like an arch) from the lower to the higher part of it; and they must be clever who long sat in their place there, so unsteadily, at times, she caused it to go on one side.

There was nothing but climbing up and immediately hurrying down; and there were some too who had fallen so sorely, that their courage for climbing up again was gone.'

Fallyng is for *fallen*, the past participle. This singular spelling occurs several times in the Scottish MS. of Lancelot of the Laik, ed. Skeat; so also in Sect. XXII. 5517, below.

So must be supplied before *sore;* it was omitted owing to the repetition of the letters *s, o.*

165. We must supply *thame*.

Ythrungin, thrust. We must supply *thought*, i. e. hoped, tried, l. 6.

167. *Lyis the on hert*, lies upon thy heart.

Stant, stands, is.

For lufe, for love, viz. love of Lady Jane Beaufort.

Endlang and ouerthwert, along and across (clearly copied from Chaucer, Knightes Tale, 1133); 'through my whole frame.'—C.

168. *Bring* should probably be *bringen*, the Chaucerian form; *bring*, being the Scottish infinitive, would naturally be used by a northern scribe, who could not see the use of the ending *-e*, or *-en*, which James probably used owing to his habit of affecting Anglicisms. In the word *slokin* in this stanza, the ending *-in* is no sign of a mood, but an integral part of the verb itself, from the Icelandic *slokna*, Middle English *sloknen*.

In poynt to mate, on the point of being defeated; with allusion to chess. See *Mate* in Nares, and observe the next note.

169. *Fundin stale*, (perhaps) found or experienced a stale-mate. An allusion to chess, as in the last stanza. Jamieson explains *stale* by *stall*, i. e. prison; but this would have been spelt *stall*; see st. 170, l. 3.

Clymben. See note on the last stanza; and cf. st. 164, l. 5.

Wantis, lackest. *Veray hertis hele*, health (or safety) of thy very heart. I. e. thou lackest thy *queen*, who would save the *king* (thyself) from being mated.

170. *Ycallit.* Here again, James probably used the non-Scottish form, as he uses *ythrungin* in st. 165. The scribe would naturally set it right, as he supposed. *Sulde* = which should; that should, the omission of the relative being usual. *Hert* becomes dissyllabic by trilling the letter *r*, just as *farls* is so in Burns' Holy Fair. So also *turne* at the end of the stanza.

Stallit, placed, kept within thine own heart. 'Kept in your own mind, without the comfort of communication with your friends.'—C.

Be froward opposyt, by means of the perverse men opposite you. This seems to refer to the idea of the wheel; the king is prevented from

C C

climbing up by enemies, but as for these enemies, fortune prophesies that 'now shall they turn, and look upon the dirt.' But this does not explain the hopelessly difficult phrase, *quhare till aspert*, the explanation of which is uncertain. The best explanation is that in Murray's New Eng. Dictionary. He gives—'*aspert*, from O. F. *espert*, variant of *apert*, probably mixed with *espert* [expert], apt, ready, clever.' I further suspect that *quhartill* should be *thartill*, thereto. 'Though thy beginning has been retrograde, by means of the froward (ones) opposite, whereunto they were ready'; or, 'owing to the froward ones opposite, who were apt for such doings.' The metaphor is strained because the poet, whilst talking of the turning wheel of fortune, brings in the astrological terms *retrograde* and *opposite*, as if he were casting a horoscope.

171. *Prime.* 'In ancient times, the hours, according to the times of devotion, were divided into two parts. From six in the morning till nine was called the *spatium orationum primarum*, or the hour of prime. Thus Milton:

"praise him in thy sphere,
While day arises, that sweet hour of *prime*."

Par. Lost, v. 170.'—C.

But the fact is, that *prime* is used in more senses than one in Early English, and it is doubtful whether Chalmers' quotation from Milton is to the point. The context shews that *prime* has *here* the meaning of the first quarter of the day, which is from 6 a.m. to 9 a.m. at the equinoxes. An hour or more *over* prime comes to something past 10 o'clock, and causes half of the day to be *near away.*

172. If *be* is here equivalent to *may be*, the sense is 'Take warning of this (or, by these) before that thou be rolled from my wheel like a ball.' *Be* is generally the subjunctive mood, and pronouns such as *thou* are sometimes omitted. Or, for *That*, read *Thou.*

Vale, sink. This dream of the king's may be compared to the dream of King Arthur, described in Malory's Morte Darthur (see p. 77, l. 20), and in the alliterative Morte Arthure, ed. Perry, ll. 3251–3393.

173. *Goste,* spirit. *Artow drest,* art thou treated.

Walking, waking. It may be remarked that this stanza is evidently imitated from Chaucer. Compare

'O wery ghost, that errest to and fro,
Why nilt thou flien out of the wofulleste
Body, that ever might on grounde go?
O soule, lurking in this wofull neste,
Fly forthout mine herte, and let it breste.'

Troilus and Creseide (ed. Tyrwhitt), bk. iv. l. 302.

V. REGINALD PECOCK.

(A) *Many things are allowable that are not prescribed in Scripture.*

THIS first extract will be found at p. 117 of Mr. Babington's first volume. It has been carefully collated with the MS. itself, but I have not deemed it necessary to denote by italics the letters signified by marks of abbreviation. These marks are throughout simple, and not to be mistaken; but, as almost every *n* is denoted by a stroke over the preceding vowel, the pages would have been inconveniently crowded with italic *n*'s.

The language of the 'Repressor' is so clear as to require but little explanation. The spelling is especially worth notice, as the reader who will observe it attentively may perhaps be led to think it better, in many cases, than the spelling in present use, when allowance has been made for the changes in the language.

Some remarks upon Pecock will be found in Milman's Annals of St. Paul's, pp. 92–97, and in Massingberd's Hist. of the Reformation, p. 213.

1. *þat þou.* This is addressed to a Wyclifite. The Wyclifites or Lollards adopted the opinion that no ordinance is to be esteemed a law of God, which is not grounded in Scripture; from which they proceeded to argue against the use of images, going on pilgrimages, and the like. Pecock, on the other hand, maintains that many excellent practices, which may be considered to be the 'law of God' in that they are truly lawful, are not so much as named in Scripture at all.

6. *Lay man, not preest.* Pecock was doubtless thinking of Exod. xxviii. 42, where garments are ordained for the sons of Aaron, but nothing is said about the laity.

7. *Cloke.* But *cloaks* are certainly mentioned in Scripture, especially in Matt. v. 40, 'let him have thy *cloak* also,' and in 2 Tim. iv. 13, where St. Paul speaks of leaving his *cloak* at Troas. Pecock generally quotes from the Wyclifite later version. For 'cloak' in Matt. v. 40, Wyclif has 'ouer-cloth' or 'mantil'; and 'cloth' in 2 Tim. iv. 13.

8. *Die woollen cloþ.* But 'dyed garments' are mentioned in Isaiah lxiii. 1, and 'dyed attire' in Ezekiel xxiii. 15; not to mention the 'rams' skins dyed red,' used for the tabernacle, Exod. xxv. 5.

10. *Ovyn.* The mention of an *oven* in Scripture generally refers to the baking of *bread.* The 'meat-offering baken in the oven' in Lev. ii. 4 is no exception; for *meat* here means food prepared from corn.

13. *Orologis.* From Fr. *orloges.* Pecock here refers to the ' dial of Ahaz,' Isaiah xxxviii. 8.

22. *Poul.* 'See 1 Cor. xi. 3–10. It need hardly be added that Pecock has committed an error in this sentence, the ἐξουσία of ver. 10 being certainly *a veil.* Veils are also several times mentioned in the Old Testament. See Kitto, Cycl. Bibl. Lit. s. v. *Veil.*'—Babington.

28. *Schulde not growe.* On the other hand, we may recall the story of Samson.

29. *As wijs;* i. e. as wise as thou (a Bible-man) considerest thyself to be in the Bible. Alluding to the name of Bible-man, frequently given to Lollards.

33. *It may be founde ;* i. e. still, it *may* be found, and can so be proved that thou shalt not be able to deny it.

43. *The book of worschiping.* This work by Pecock, to which he also gives the name of *The Book of signis in the chirche,* is believed to be no longer extant.

54. *Opere place.* 'Probably we should read *placis.*'—Babington. He frequently handles the same subject in other parts of the 'Repressor.'

56. *Berdis,* beards. The shaving of the beard is, however, expressly mentioned in Scripture. It was a sign of mourning, as in the case of 'fourscore men, having their *beards shaven,* and their clothes rent.' Jer. xli. 5.

63. *Lauȝwe,* laugh. This is expressly recognised in Scripture in the text, 'a time to weep, and a time to *laugh ;*' Eccl. iii. 4. So in Luke vi. 21, ' Blessed are ye that weep now; for ye shall *laugh.*' Compare Gen. xxi. 6, 'And Sarah said, God hath made me to *laugh,* so that all that hear will *laugh* with me ;' also Ps. xxxvii. 13, 'The Lord shall *laugh* at him,' and the like. Pecock is not happy in his instances.

69. *Pleie in word bi bourding,* play verbally in jesting, i.e. jest amongst themselves. But certainly some case might be made out in favour of jesting, running, &c. from Scripture. Elijah's reproof of the prophets of Baal (1 Kings xviii. 27) partakes much of the nature of jesting; the sun is spoken of as rejoicing ' as a strong man to *run a race,*' Ps. xix. 5 ; whilst, as to *shooting,* there is the well-known story of David and Jonathan (1 Sam. xx. 35–40), which Pecock seems to have forgotten. See the English editor's preface to 'The Biglow Papers'; Trübner, 1861.

76. *Esement,* i. e. pleasure. But cf. Eccles. ii. 8, where Solomon says: ' I gathered me also silver and gold, and the peculiar treasure of kings and of the provinces; I gat me men singers and women singers, and the

delights of the sons of men, as musical instruments, and that of all sorts.' This is clearly an allusion to other than *sacred* singing; Solomon intended it for his own *esement.*

84. *Ale or beer. Strong drink* is frequently mentioned in the Bible as distinct from wine, but the use of it is condemned. In Solomon's Song viii. 2, we read, 'I would cause thee to drink of spiced wine of the juice of my pomegranate,' which alludes to some drink not made from grapes. But the chief point of interest is Pecock's use of the word *beer*, as it is a very uncommon word in early English, whilst *ale* is very common. Six examples of the former word are given in Stratmann's Early English Dictionary, two of them being *beore* in Layamon, l. 13542, and *ber* in King Horn, ed. Lumby, l. 1112. Pecock also mentions *cider* and *mead*.

93. *And ȝit þou wolte seie.* Here Pecock draws inferences which his opponents would hardly have admitted.

104. *Englisch tunge or langage.* 'After this follows [in the MS.] *neither latyn tunge or langage*, but a later (?) hand has drawn a pen through it, rightly. See Luke xxiii. 38. But very possibly Pecock wrote it, since he was capable of making such a blunder as to say that a cloak is not mentioned in Scripture.'—Babington.

(B) *A defence of images and pictures.*

See Babington's edition, vol. i. p. 212. The Wyclifites attacked pictures and images in churches, and the practice of going upon pilgrimage. Pecock defends images on the score of the ease with which they recall the stories of the saints represented.

10. *Purtenancis*, i.e. the special emblems by which various saints are known. St. Catharine has her *wheel*, St. Barbara her *tower*, St. Margaret her *dragon*, St. Sebastian his *arrow*, St. Lawrence his *gridiron*, and so on. See Mrs. Jameson's excellent and most interesting book on Sacred and Legendary Art. As to those mentioned by Pecock, St. Peter has his *keys*, St. Paul commonly a *sword*, whilst St. Nicholas is often found in company with three very young boys standing in a tub, in allusion to the story of his bringing to life three children who had been slain, cut up, and placed in a pickle-tub.

54. *Dressid and lad*, directed and led, or guided.

78. *Dai of seint Kateryn*, November 25. But just below, he says that the pilgrimage to St. Catharine's College took place on the *vigil*, i.e. on the evening of Nov. 24. St. Catharine's College was more commonly known as St. Catharine's Hospital, and was close to the Tower of London. It was founded by Matilda, wife of King Stephen. See Stow's

Survey of London, ed. Strype, bk. i. p. 204. It is now, as I am informed, in Regent's Park.

94. *Gravyseende.* 'Stephen Gravesend was bishop of London from A. D. 1319-1338.'—Babington. See Milman's Annals of St. Paul's, p. 70.

97. *Chaunceler.* The Chancellor in olden times was commonly an archbishop or bishop. A list of chancellors is given in Haydn's Book of Dates, but it only goes back to the year 1487.

103. *De Profundis,* i.e. Ps. cxxx., called Ps. cxxix. in the Vulgate. In the Officium Mortuorum in the Sarum Missal occurs the rubric: 'In anniuersariis et trigesimis et in omnibus aliis missis pro defunctis dicitur sequens tractus *De Profundis* a toto choro alternatim,' &c.

113. *Cheyned,* chained; alluding to the practice of fastening books by an iron chain to the reading-desk, that they might not be stolen.

VI. HENRY THE MINSTREL.

LINE 181. *Will3ham Wallace, or,* &c.; William Wallace, ere he was a man capable of bearing arms. The following apt remarks occur in the English Cyclopædia; 'The life and exploits of this most popular national hero of the Scots have been principally preserved in a legendary form by poetry and tradition, and are only to a very small extent matter of contemporary record or illustrated by authentic documents. . . .

'The history of Wallace down to the year 1297 is entirely legendary, and only to be found in the rhymes of Henry the Minstrel; though many of the facts which Harry relates also still live as popular traditions in the localities where the scenes of them are laid, whether handed down in that way from the time when they happened, or only derived from his poem, which long continued to be the chief literary favourite of the Scottish peasantry. Harry, who, it may be observed, professes to translate from a Latin account written by Wallace's intimate friend and chaplain, John Blair, makes him to have been carefully educated by his uncle, a wealthy churchman, who resided at Dunipace, in Stirlingshire[1], and to have been afterwards sent to the grammar-school of Dundee. Here his first memorable act is said to have been performed, his slaughter of the son of Selby, the English governor of the castle of Dundee, in chastisement of an insult offered him by the unwary young man: Wallace struck him

---

[1] This is a slight error. Harry makes Wallace to have been educated by an uncle who lived at Gowrie. Besides him, Harry mentions *three* more of Wallace's uncles, viz. a 'wealthy churchman' or parson named Wallace who lived at Dunipace (l. 300), Sir Raynald Crawford, who lived at Crosby (l. 316), and Sir Richard Wallace of Riccartoun (l. 355).

dead with his dagger on the spot [as told in our extract]. This must have happened, if at all, in the year 1291, after Edward I had obtained possession of all the places of strength throughout Scotland on his recognition as Lord Paramount by the various competitors for the crown, which had become vacant by the death of the infant Margaret, the Maiden of Norway, in September, 1290. This bold deed committed by Wallace, who in making his escape is asserted to have laid several of young Selby's attendants as low as their master, was immediately followed by his outlawry.'

Wallace was born probably about 1270. His two chief battles against the English were the battle of Stirling Bridge, Sept. 11, 1297, which for a time freed Scotland, and the battle of Falkirk, July 22, 1298, where the Scots were completely routed. Wallace was hung in Smithfield, August 23, 1305.

The account of Wallace given in the book entitled 'The Greatest of the Plantagenets,' differs widely from that given by Henry the Minstrel, and should be consulted.

184. *Wyss.* In the MS. we frequently find a character like the German *sz*, which generally signifies *ss*, but is sometimes an abbreviation for *sis* in such words as *howsis*, *plesis* (pleases).

185. *Gowry*, Gowrie. The district called the Carse of Gowrie extends along the north bank of the Firth of Tay, between Perth and Dundee.

Worthy man, viz. the uncle who lived at Gowrie, as appears from the context, bk. i. l. 152; cf. l. 269.

187. *In-till*, in, within. Both *intill* and *into* are freely used in Lowland Scotch where we should use *in*.

189. *Mayne*, moan. Observe how the Scottish long *a* corresponds to our long o or *oa*.

194. *Thaim*, them, i.e. the English; see l. 190.

195. *Ane*, one Englishman alone, without the presence of others. This *ane* is the antecedent to *his* and *him* in l. 197.

200. 'For there could no man assign their deaths (lit. say them) entirely to him.'

207. *Hecht*, hight, was named.

Owtrage is here an adjective, *outrageous*.

209. *Vsyt*, used (to go).

216. 'Who the devil clothes thee in so gay a garb? It should be thy nature to wear an Erse mantle, to bear a Scotch whittle under thy belt, and have rough shoes (of undressed hide) on thy scoundrel feet. Give me thy knife; what means thy gear so fine?'

233. *Eyme*, uncle; viz. the one at Gowrie. The reader must observe the foot-note on p. 390, or he will get much confused about Wallace's uncles.

234. *Wyn*, get, i.e. go.

236. *For him*, for the sake of Him who died on the tree.

240. *At*, that. Observe this word, which is a clear mark of a northern dialect. It is the Swedish *att*, Danish *at*. *The layff*, the rest.

241. 'A soiled kerchief (she) let fall over his head and neck, and fastened on him withal a woven white hat (or cap).'

244. *Rok*, a distaff; Germ. *Rocken*.

249. *Nocht leryt lang*, had not long learnt; a jesting expression.

267. 'Unsufferable are those people of England.'

282-284. This passage is so punctuated in Jamieson's edition as to be unintelligible. It means: 'Whoever asked her, she said that they were going to St. Margaret (i.e. to St. Margaret's shrine at Dunfermline, in Fifeshire); whoever served *her*, such people always found great friendship with Southern people; since she (St. Margaret) was of England.' The allusion is to St. Margaret of Scotland, the wife of Malcolm Canmore, who died Nov. 16, 1093, aged 47, and was buried at Dunfermline. She was canonized by Pope Innocent IV in 1251. She was 'of England,' as being the granddaughter of Edmund Ironside, and niece of Edward the Confessor. See a sketch of her life in Chambers' Book of Days, vol. ii. p. 584.

285, 286. By 'Landoris' is meant Lindores, near Newburg, on the south bank of the Tay. The travellers crossed the Tay, and travelled southwards, crossing the Ochill Hills, to Dunfermline.

290. *Lithquhow*, Linlithgow, between Edinburgh and Falkirk.

291. *Pilgramage*, pilgrimage; viz. to St. Margaret's shrine.

296. *Quhill south our forth*, till, southwards, over the Forth.

298. Dunipace, in Stirlingshire, not far from Falkirk.

300. *Persone*, parson, called Wallace by name.

303. 'Caused him to know the land all a-stir.'

307. *Westermar*, more to the westward we will go.

310. *Will god*, if God wills that I may live. *On part*, in part.

313. 'Why should I speak of (this), useless as regards the present time?' I.e. Why should I say more about Wallace's wish, which, for this time, came to nothing.

315. *Elrisle*. Wallace's father was Sir Malcolm Wallace of Ellerslie or Elderslie, in the neighbourhood of Paisley.

317. Understand the word *who*; who dwelt in Corsby, i.e. Crosby, between Largs and Ardrossan.

318. *Hyr fadyr*. Wallace's mother was Margaret, daughter of Sir Raynald (some say Sir Hugh) Crawfurd, who was sheriff of Ayr, as his son was after him. Her name, *Margaret*, no doubt enabled her to make the better pretence of going to St. Margaret's shrine.

319. *Hyr husband*, viz. Sir Malcolm Wallace, killed at Lowdoun-hill, near Galston, not far from Kilmarnock, Ayrshire; so says our poet.

320. *Hyr eldest sone.* She had two sons, Malcolm and William. Malcolm, says the poet, was wounded in the sinews of the hock, &c.

324. 'To him (against him) there came more fighters then anew.'

328. *Schir Ranald*, i.e. Sir Raynald Crawfurd, son of the Sir Raynald mentioned in note to l. 318.

331. *Yrk of wer*, tired of war, harassed by the state of warfare.

342. 'For he knew great peril was appearing there; for they (the English) had all the strongholds of Scotland.

348, 349. 'He that offered him any scorn got a blow for it, whether he were lad or lord.'

355. 'Riccartoun is evidently a corruption of Richardtoun. It is generally supposed to have been so called from a Sir Richard Wallace, who lived in the vicinity of the village, and who is said to have been uncle to the celebrated patriot Sir William Wallace. Of his house no vestige now remains; the place, however, where it stood, is well known. The village of Riccartoun is within one English mile of the market-place of Kilmarnock.' Quoted by Jamieson, who adds, 'v. Riccartoun, Stat. Acc. V. 117.' It is now called Riccarton.

369. *Erewyn*, Irvine. The river Irvine flows past Galston, Kilmarnock, and Irvine, into the Firth of Clyde.

372. *Or nowne*, ere noon. Cf. l. 377.

383. *Martyns fysche*, fish to feast upon. St. Martin's day, Nov. 11, was especially set apart as a festival on which all good things might be eaten. A cow or ox fattened up was often killed about this time and salted for consumption at Christmas, and such meat hence received the name of *mart* in Scotland and the north of England. St. Martin's day itself was devoted to the consumption of fat geese and plenty of new wine. Fish might serve as an introduction to such a feast. See Chambers' Book of Days, ii. 567; and see *Martlemas* in Nares' Glossary.

386. *Waith*, spoil, prey, things caught.

389. *Our small*, over small, too little.

393. *Serwis our lady*, serves our Lady. This seems to mean, eats fish to-day, out of reverence to our Lady.

399. 'Whom dost thou *thou*?' i.e. to whom dost thou use the word *thou*? In addressing a superior, it was proper to say *ye*; *thou* savoured of familiarity or contempt. The Englishman began it; see l. 389. Before that, Wallace had 'meekly' said *ye*; see l. 385. Many examples of the difference between *thou* and *ye* are given in William of Palerne, ed. Skeat, p. xli, and in Abbott's Shakespearian Grammar, third ed. p. 153.

Serwis, deservest. The verb *serue* in Old English does duty both for *serve* and *deserve*.

402. To *pout* is to *poke about*. A *poutnet* is a round net fastened to two poles, by means of which the fishers poke the banks of rivers, and force the fish out of their holes. A *poutstaff* is one of the poles thus used.

404. 'With such goodwill, that he shook (was thrown) off his feet.'

407. *Awkwart*, athwart, crosswise, as in Bk. ii. l. 109 :—'Ane othir *awkwart* a large straik tuk he thar;' i.e. he hit another crosswise a severe blow.

Gawe, gave, sc. a blow. In Scottish we often find *w* for *v*; so in the next line *drawe* is for *drave*, and in l. 369 we have *Erewyn* for *Irvine*.

409. *Be that*, by that, by that time.

416. *Quhill*, till. *Can ly*, did lie, lay.

418. *Was last*, who was last.

430. *Foule mote зow fall*, may evil befall you !

433. *Beis*, shall be. This northern form of the verb generally has a *future* sense, as in Anglo-Saxon.

435. ' He took their horses and the gear that was left there, and gave over that craft, and went to fish no more.' *Hors* is the same both in the singular and plural in Old English; hence our phrase, *a troop of horse*; to match which, we further speak of *a company of foot*, though this may be short for *foot-soldiers*.

437. *Dede*. The MS. has *drede*, but the old editions have *deid* or *deed*. 'This is more in character, than to suppose that Wallace, after so chivalrous an achievement, should run to his uncle and tell him in what terror he was for the vengeance of the English. The term here used, indeed, seems to reduplicate on the phrase which occurs in l. 434, *this worthi werk*.'—Jamieson.

438. 'And he, for woe, well near began to go mad.'

446. *Gud*, good, i.e. money. *Cum*, come fetch enough from me, borrow what you like.

The reader may find more specimens of the 'Wallace' in Warton's History of English Poetry, vol. ii. pp. 113-120, ed. 1840; vol. iii. p. 256, ed. 1871. Warton puts the poem a century too early, having been misled by a statement by Dempster and others, who assigned to it the date 1361. I suspect that 3 is here a mere slip for 4, and I therefore adopt the date 1461 as probably the correct one. Most writers say, *about* 1460. Several passages from Henry the Minstrel are quoted in the notes to the poem of 'William Wallace' by Joanna Baillie.

VII. CHEVY CHASE.

THE whole of the Ashmole MS. 48, in which the oldest copy of 'Chevy Chase' occurs, was printed by Mr. T. Wright for the Roxburghe Club, with the title 'Songs and Ballads of the Reign of Philip and Mary.' Several of these have the name of Richard Sheale attached to them, shewing that he was the person from whose recitation most of them were written down. Some lines of his own composition are extant, of a lugubrious character and without merit, so that we are not surprised to find him complaining of the neglect which he suffered. The MS. itself is a mere scribble, and the spelling very unsatisfactory; but I have thought it best to reproduce it, nevertheless, as exactly as possible, since it is the sole authority. It is very probable that the original ballad was a good deal better than appears from this copy. Many of the lines, as they here stand, will hardly scan, and are manifestly faulty, so that the true form of what must once have been a most spirited and well-written poem has wellnigh perished. The 'more modern' version is often smoother, but at the same time weaker, and is of small assistance in helping us to imagine what the original ballad was like.

I am bound to say that I entirely reject the piece of guesswork which suggests that *Chevy Chase* is a corruption of O. F. *chevauchée*, a raid. If allowed to guess in this way, we may assert anything we please. See l. 31 of the poem itself.

Line 1. *An avowe*, a vow; see l. 130. In old English the form *avow* is very common, as e. g. in Chaucer (Knightes Tale, 1379)—
> 'That make I myn *avow*, so ye me helpe'—
whereas the form *vow* is unusual. Richard Sheale, who had probably learnt the ballad by ear, very naturally turned *an avow* into *and a vow*, which is nonsense. It is very likely that the popularity of this ballad has induced many to believe that *and* could sometimes be thrown in as an expletive at the beginning of a sentence, but this is merely an impression, and not borne out by the usage of good writers. If any other instances occur, they are ignorant imitations. This remark does not apply to Byron's poem, beginning '*And* thou art dead, as young and fair'—which is a natural expression enough.

3. *In the magger*, a mistake for *in maugre*, more frequently *maugre* (without *in*); i. e. in spite of, Fr. *mal gré*. *Dogles*, Douglas.

4, 5. These lines are too long, and clearly corrupt. The fourth line should almost certainly be
> 'The fattest hartes in all cheviat he said that he wold sle.'

To restore this ballad to its true old form is hopeless; we must be thankful for what we have, and make the best of it.

6. *Banborowe*, Bamborough, on the coast of Northumberland.

Meany, company, suite.

7. *XV.C*, fifteen hundred.

Shyars iij, three shires. This has been explained to mean three districts in Northumberland, called *shires*, all in the neighbourhood of Cheviot; viz. *Islandshire*, named from Holy Island, *Norhamshire*, named from Norham, and *Bamboroughshire*, from Bamborough.

8. *He*, high.

9. In Nos. 70 and 74 of the Spectator, there is a curious critique by Addison upon the Ballad of Chevy Chase, which the reader should by all means consult. A few of his most striking remarks I shall here quote for convenience, in their proper places. It must be remembered, however, that they apply to the later form of the poem. For instance, he remarks (Spect, No. 74), 'What can be greater than either the thought or the expression in that stanza?

> " To drive the deer with hound and horn
> 　　Earl Piercy took his way;
> The child may rue that is unborn
> 　　The hunting of that day!"

This way of considering the misfortunes which this battle would bring upon posterity, not only on those who were born immediately after the battle, and lost their fathers in it, but on those also who perished in future battles which took their rise from this quarrel of the two earls, is wonderfully beautiful, and conformable to the way of thinking among the ancient poets;

> "Audiet pugnas uitio parentum
> 　　Rara iuventus."—Hor. [Carm. i. 2].'

10–13. These four lines form a complete stanza, with the rimes *dear, cleare, shear, dear* at the end, and the rimes *went, bent, went, glent* in the middle. To this standard the whole poem may have been intended to conform, but the difficulty was too great; or our copy is sadly imperfect.

11. *Byckarte*, bickered. Falsely spelt; it should be *bikkered*; but I think it best to leave the utterly vicious spelling alone.

13. *Greahondes*, should be *grehondes*, i.e. greyhounds.

Grevis, groves; so in Chaucer.

14. *Ther*, probably an error for *thei*, they.

The hyls abone, above the hills; *abone* is the northern English form, to rime with *none*. It must not be printed *aboue*; cf. l. 102.

Yerly, early. This peculiarity of prefixing *y* pervades the whole poem. In some parts of the North an oak is called a *yaik.* Cf. *yaäle* for *ale*, in Tennyson's 'Northern Farmer.'

16. *Blewe a mort*, blew a blast to celebrate the death (*mort*) of the deer; the usual phrase; see Nares. Or the MS. reading *a mot*, i. e. a blast on the horn, may be quite right.

The is written for *thei*, they, here and throughout the poem. Addison compares the preceding passage to Virgil—

> 'Uocat ingenti clamore Cithaeron,
> Taygetique canes, domitrixque Epidaurus equorum;
> Et uox assensu nemorum ingeminata remugit.'
>
> Georg. lib. iii. 43.

17. *Quyrry*, miswritten for *quarry*, heap of dead game.

21. The word *ath* is a corruption of *of the*; see note to l. 51. But this would give *the* twice over, so that we must read *of*.

22. The singular word *brylly* is clearly an error for *bylle*, i. e. bill. The insertion of *r* after *b* is due to the confusion with *brande*.

24. *Feale*, an error for *fayle*, fail.

25. *The wear*, they were.

Yth, contracted from *in the*; as in the name Strongitharm.

Tividale, Teviotdale. Here the later version has

> 'All men of pleasant Tivydale,
> Fast by the riuer Tweede'—

on which Addison remarks—'The country of the Scotch warriors, described in these two last verses, has a fine romantic situation, and affords a couple of smooth words for verse. If the reader compares the foregoing six lines of the song with the following Latin verses, he will see how much they are written in the spirit of Virgil.

> " Aduersi campo apparent, hastasque reductis
> Protendunt longè dextris, et spicula uibrant":—

> " Quique altum Praeneste uiri, quique arua Gabinae
> Iunonis, gelidumque Anienem, et roscida riuis
> Hernica saxa colunt," &c.—Virg. Æn. xi. 605; vii. 682.'

26. *Boys*, miswritten for *bowys*, bows. See l. 60.

Lock, for *loke*, i. e. look.

29. *Glede*, glowing coal. Compare (says Addison)

> 'Turnus ut anteuolans tardum praecesserat agmen,' &c.

> 'Uidisti, quo Turnus equo, quibus ibat in armis
> Aureus?'—[Æneid ix. 47, 269.]

31. *Chyviat Chays*, hunting-ground upon the Cheviot hills; hence the name of the poem. *Chase* is thus shewn to be the *place* of hunting, not the *act*. See l. 34. *Chace* is common in local names.

36. *The ton*, that one, the one, one. Speaking of Douglas, Addison says, 'His sentiments and actions are every way suitable to an hero. One of us two, says he, must die: I am an Earl as well as yourself, so that you can have no pretence for refusing the combat: however, says he, 'tis pity, and indeed would be a sin, that so many innocent men should perish for our sakes; rather let you and I end our quarrel in single fight.'

39. *Yerle*, earl; cf. note to l. 14.

40. *Vppone a parti*, upon a side, aside. *Do*, let us do.

41. *Cors*, curse. *Crowne*, head.

44. *And*, if; if the good fortune may chance to me.

On man for on, one man to one, man to man.

46. *Sothe*, south.

Herry the iiij, Harry the Fourth; began to reign 1399, died March, 1413.

Jamy (mentioned in l. 121) began to reign in 1406. This period (1406–13) being the assigned date of the event, we may be sure that the poem was composed some time later.

47. *Wat*, for *wot*, know.

Twaw, for *twa* or *tweye*, two.

48. Addison says, 'We meet the same heroic sentiment in Virgil—
" Non pudet, O Rutuli, cunctis pro talibus unam
Obiectare animam? numerone an uiribus aequi
Non sumus?"'—Æn. xii. 229.

49. We must insert *fayle*.

50. *First fit*, first portion or canto of the poem. *Fynde*, a corruption of *fyne*, i.e. I finish, end.

51. *And*, if. *Here*, hear. *Athe*, for *of the*, twice.

52. *Ye-bent*, for *ybent*, i.e. bent.

Yenoughe, for *enough*, like *yerle* for *erle*, l. 39.

55. *Hom*, for *hem*, them.

Wouche; also spelt *wough* and *wowe*; it is from the A.S. *woh*, error, wrong, and quite distinct from *woe*, A.S. *wá*.

57. *Suar*, sure, trusty. Cf. l. 84. *Tre*, wood.

The cum In, they come in, invade, attack.

58. *Gave*, i.e. *they* gave.

59. *Doughete*, doughty man. *The garde*, they caused.

60. *Let thear boys be*, let their bows alone, abandoned them.

62. *Myne-ye-ple*, evidently a corruption. It has always been explained by *many folds*, an explanation to which we may reasonably demur, on the ground that *myne* does not mean *many*, and *ple* is not a *fold*. The context would lead us to suppose that it is some part of a man's body-

armour, and we may reasonably guess it to be a corruption of *manople*, a French term for a large gauntlet protecting the hand and the whole fore-arm. Roquefort's Glossaire gives—' *Manoples*, Gantelets, armes préservatrices des mains et de l'avant-bras ; de *manualis, manipulus.*'

Many sterne, &c. ; many stern ones they struck down straight.

65. *Myllan*, Milan steel.

66. *Worthe freckys*, for *worthi frekes*, worthy men.

67. *Sprente*, spurted. *Heal or ran*, hail or rain.

68. *I feth*, in faith.

74. *Wane*, the Northern form of O. Eng. *wone*, a quantity, multitude; it means a single arrow out of a vast quantity. ' Æneas,' says Addison, ' was wounded after the same manner by an unknown hand in the midst of a parley—

> " Has inter uoces, media inter talia uerba,
> Ecce uiro stridens alis allapsa sagitta est,
> Incertum quâ pulsa manu." '—Æn. xii. 318.

78. ' Merry men, in the language of those times, is no more than a cheerful word for companions and fellow-soldiers. A passage in the eleventh book of Virgil's Æneids is very much to be admired, where Camilla, in her last agonies, instead of weeping over the wound she had received, as one might have expected from a warrior of her sex, considers only (like the hero of whom we are now speaking) how the battle should be continued after her death—

> " Tum sic expirans, &c."—[Æn. xi. 820].'—Addison.

80. ' Earl Piercy's lamentation over his enemy is generous, beautiful, and passionate ; I must only caution the reader not to let the simplicity of the style, which one may well pardon in so old a poet, prejudice him against the greatness of the thought. That beautiful line, taking the dead man by the hand, will put the reader in mind of Æneas's behaviour towards Lausus, whom he himself had slain as he came to the rescue of his aged father—

> " At uero ut uultum uidit morientis, et ora,
> Ora modis Anchisiades pallentia miris :
> Ingemuit miserans grauiter, dextramque tetendit."
> [Æn. x. 821.].'—Addison.

83. *Mongomberry ;* in the later version, Mountgomerye.

84. *A trusti tre*, of trusty wood. The second *a* in this line probably means *of*; cf. note to l. 51, and see l. 92.

89. *Athe tother*, on the other; *a* is a short form both of *on* and *of*; thus *alive* is for *on lyue*, on or in life, whilst *adown* is for *of dune*, off a hill.

91. *Say slean*, saw (how) slain.

93. *Stele*, steel head. *Halyde*, hauled, pulled.

94. *Sat*, an error for *set*; see l. 87. So also, in l. 95, *sete* should be *set*.

95. *Sad and sar*, heavy and sore; cf. 'as *sad* As lump of lead;' Spenser, F. Q. ii. 1. 45.

96. This is even better than the more familiar line in the later version—
   'The grey goose winge than was there-on in his harts bloode
       was wett.'

97. *Freake*, man. *Wone*, for *one*, pronounced *wun*. *Stour*, combat.

98. *Whylle*, &c., whilst they could hold out.

99. *An owar*, an hour; see l. 15.

100. *Evensonge*, the English name for *vespers*.

101. *The tocke*, they took: after which some words are missing. I add *the fight*, because *to take the fight* is an expression found in Middle English, and suits the context.

105. *Hy*, miswritten for *he*; see l. 8.

106. Repeated from l. 9.

107. *Agerstone*. Sir W. Scott supposes Agerstone or Haggerston to have been one of the Rutherfords, barons of Edgerston [or Edgerstown, between Jedburgh and the Cheviot Hills], a warlike family long settled on the Scottish border, and retainers of the house of Douglas. This is, however, clearly wrong, for 'Agerstone' is called a companion of Lord Percy. There is a place called Haggerston, a little way inland, nearly opposite to Holy Island. Two of the 'Akerstons' are mentioned in the Ballad of Bosworth Feilde, Percy Folio MS. iii. 245.

108. *The hinde*, put for *the hende*, i.e. gentle, courteous. Hartley is near the Northumbrian coast, just north of Tynemouth.

   Hearone, Heron. Sir W. Scott, in Note L. to Marmion, speaks of Sir William Heron, of Ford, and refers us to Sir Richard Heron's Genealogy of the Heron Family. There is a place called Ford not far to the south-west of Haggerston.

109. *Loumle*, Lumley; always hitherto printed *louele* (and explained Lovel), though the MS. cannot be so read, the word being written 'loūle.' 'My Lord Lumley' is mentioned in the Ballad of Scotish Feilde, Percy Fol. MS. i. 226, l. 270; and again, in the Ballad of Bosworth Feilde, id. iii. 245, l. 250.

110. *Rugbe;* the later version has *Sir Ralph Rebby*, whom Sir W. Scott identifies with Ralph Neville, of Raby Castle, son of the first Earl of Westmoreland, and cousin-german to Hotspur.

111. *Wetharryngton:* later version, Witherington. There is a place called Widrington, in Northumberland, near the east coast, to the north of Morpeth.

112. *Kny*, miswritten for *kne*. The curious alteration in the latter version is well-known—

'For Witherington needs must I wayle as one in too full[1] dumpes,

For when his leggs were smitten of, he fought vpon his stumpes.'

On which Addison remarks—' In the catalogue of the English who fell, Witherington's behaviour is in the same manner particularised very artfully, as the reader is prepared for it by that account which is given of him in the beginning of the battle: though I am satisfied your little buffoon readers, who have seen that passage ridiculed in Hudibras, will not be able to take the beauty of it: for which reason I dare not so much as quote it.'

114. *Lwdale.* This seems to be the 'Sir David Lambwell' of the later version.

115. *A murre*, of Murray; later version, Sir Charles Morrell.

116. *Dey*, miswritten for *de*, die.

117. *The mayde them byears*, they made for them biers or litters.

118. *Wedous*, widows.

Fache ther makys, fetch their mates.

120. *March parti*, part of the country called the Marches, the Border-land; see l. 122.

121. *Jamy*, James I, born 1394; began to reign, 1406; died 1437.

Eddenburrowe, Edinburgh.

123. We should perhaps read *wringe and wayle*; cf. Chaucer, Clerkes Tale, last line.

124. *Yefeth*, for *y faith*, in faith.

129. *And I brook*, if I enjoy, if I have the use of. See note to VIII. iii. 46.

Quyte, quit, requited. ' The poet has not only found out an hero in his own country, but raises the reputation of it by several beautiful incidents. The English are the first who take the field, and the last who quit it. The English bring only 1500 to the battle, and the Scotch 2000. The English kept the field with fifty-three; the Scotch retire with fifty-five: all the rest on each side being slain in battle. But the most remarkable circumstance of this kind, is the different manner in which the Scotch and English kings receive the news of this fight, and of the great men's deaths who command it.'—Addison.

131. *Hombyll-down*, Homildon or Humbleton, near Wooler, in

---

[1] Altered by Percy to *doleful*, which is probably right; for Butler has the expression—

'As Widdrington, in *doleful* dumps,

Is said to fight upon his stumps.' Hudibras, pt. i. c. 3.

D d

Northumberland, where the Earl of Northumberland, his son Hotspur, and the Scotch Earl of March, defeated about 10,000 Scots under the Earl Douglas, who was taken prisoner, A.D. 1402. By comparing the note to l. 46, we see that the three dates thus assigned are not reconcileable; for the battle of Homildon was fought before the first James began to reign, indeed when he was but eight years old. Again, in l. 136 we are told it was called the battle of Otterburn; but this is impossible, seeing that the battle of Otterburn, in which Hotspur was taken prisoner, and Earl Douglas slain, took place in 1387 or 1388, and is celebrated in a ballad quite distinct from the present one; added to which, Otterbourne is not over the border, being only half way between Newcastle and Teviotdale. Hence, it has been proposed to identify the battle in Chevy Chase with the conflict at Pepperden in 1436, between the Earl of Northumberland and Earl William Douglas, with a small army of about 4000 each. In any case, we may conclude that the ballad was written after all these events, and therefore later than 1436.

133. *Glendale;* Homildon is situated within the district called Glendale Ward. It is a village one mile to the north-west of Wooler. The spot where the battle was fought has ever since been called the *Red Riggs.*

134. *That tear,* &c. This is said to be a proverb, meaning 'that tear or pull brought about this kick.'

136. *Monnynday,* Monday.

138. 'There was never a time, on the Border-land, since the Douglas and Percy thus met, but it is a marvel if the red blood ran not as rain does in the street.'

140. *Bete our balys,* make better or remedy our misfortunes. There is a common old English proverb, 'When bale is hext, then bote is next,' meaning 'When grief is highest (i. e. greatest), then the remedy is nearest.' It occurs among the Proverbs of Hendyng.

141. *Expliceth,* miswritten for *explicit,* here endeth; *quoth* signifies that Richard Sheale either dictated or wrote out this copy of the poem.

VIII. SIR THOMAS MALORY.

THE twenty-first book of Malory's Romance begins with describing how, during King Arthur's absence abroad, his nephew Sir Modred attempted to make himself King of England, and to marry queen Guinevere, his uncle's wife. Guinevere shut herself up in the Tower of London, where Modred failed to gain entrance; but he succeeded in raising a large host to oppose Arthur's landing on his return. Arthur effected his landing at Dover, but one of his best knights, Sir Gawain, was killed in the fray, and buried in a chapel in Dover castle. Sir Modred then withdrew with his host to Canterbury. At this point our extract commences.

Cap. III. 1. *Lete serche,* caused to be searched. This use of *lete* is very common in Malory. It is still a common idiom in German.

20. *Chaflet,* a small scaffold or platform. In the old alliterative poem called the 'Morte Arthure,' edited by Mr. Perry for the Early English Text Society in 1865, this dream of Arthur's is told in another place, and at great length; see ll. 3228-3394 in that edition. In that account also, the final battle is said to take place in Cornwall, whither Arthur had driven Modred or Mordred, after burying Gawain, not at Dover, but at Winchester.

36. *Systers sone.* Gawain was son of King Lot, who married a sister of Arthur's by the mother's side. Lot's sons were Gawain, Agravayn, Gaheret, and Gaheries; see 'Merlin,' a Prose Romance, ed. H. B. Wheatley, p. 179. Gawain's courtesy was proverbial, and is alluded to in Chaucer's Squyeres Tale, l. 87.

46. *And ye fyghte,* if ye fight. It is common to find *and* written instead of *an,* if; and conversely, the copulative *and* is often written *an.* The two words are, in fact, identical. The use of *and* in the sense of ' if ' is Scandinavian; see Cleasby and Vigfusson's Icelandic Dictionary, s. v. *enda*; but it also arose in English independently.

53. *As to morne*; this curious idiom is still imitated in the colloquial phrase 'as it may be to-morrow.'

66. *Charged theym,* 'charged them (to do so), if in any wise they might,' &c.

73. *By Arthures dayes,* 'whilst Arthur lived; and afterwards,' &c.

Cap. IIII. 21. *Beamous,* an error for *beamus,* a West-country form of *beames* or *bemes,* the plural of *beme,* a trumpet, from the A.S. *béme or býme,* a trumpet.

22. *Dressyd hem to-gyders,* arrayed themselves against each other.

44. *Becomen,* gone to. In Middle English we find *to be becomen* where we now say *to be gone to.*

59. *On lyue,* lit. *in life*; hence our modern *alive.*

79. *Waykely,* weakly, with difficulty.

83. *Do me to wyte,* cause me to know, bring me word.

Cap. V. 1. *Werches,* aches; lit. works. Common in the North.

7. *The lyfte,* the effort of lifting him.

The parte, a part.

13. *For he wold,* 'for he, who had more need of help than I had, would fain have helped me.'

21. *Excalibur.* Cf. 'Thou therefore take my brand *Excalibur*,' and the whole of the rest of Tennyson's poem entitled 'Morte d'Arthur.' The famous sword, also called Caliburn, was drawn by Arthur out of a stone in which it had been miraculously inserted, and from which no other man could draw it. This was the sign that he was the rightful king, and he was accordingly so proclaimed. The golden letters on the sword shone so brightly as to dazzle all his enemies. According to the English metrical romance of ' Merlin,' the inscription on it was

> ' Ich am y-hote [*called*] Escalibore,
> Unto a king a faire tresore.'

And it is added, in explanation—

> ' On Inglis [*in English*] is this writing
> " Kerue steel and yren and al thing."'

See Wheeler's Noted Names of Fiction. But the English prose romance gives the inscription thus,—' Who taketh this swerde out of this ston sholde be kynge by the election of Ihesu criste;' Merlin. ed. Wheatley, p. 98. It was also named *Brown Steel*, possibly from reading the name as *Staliburn;* for *c* is hardly distinguishable from *t* in old MSS. Roquefort gives the forms *Escalibor, Escalibourne,* and adds—'Ce mot est tiré de l'Hébreu, et veut dire tranchefer.' This reminds us of *Taillefer* (i.e. cut iron), the name of the Norman minstrel who is said to have struck the first blow at the Battle of Hastings. Other famous swords are likewise known by name; Charlemagne's was called *Joyeuse,* Roland's *Durindana,* Oliver's *Alta Clara,* and St. George's *Ascalon.*

41. *Efte,* again, a second time.

45. *Wappe,* beat; *wanne,* probably for *wane,* to ebb. It probably refers to the breaking of a wave followed by the usual reflux. Tennyson has—

> ' I heard the ripple washing in the reeds,
> And the wild water *lapping on the crag.*'

47. *Wente,* weened, believed, thought; from M. E. *wenen,* to ween.

82. *Auylyon,* Avilion, Avalon, or Avelon. 'This fair Avalon is the Isle of the Blessed of the Kelts. Tzetze and Procopius attempt to localize it, and suppose that the Land of Souls is Britain; but in this they are mistaken; as also are those who think to find Avalon at Glastonbury. Avalon is the Isle of Apples—a name reminding one of the Gardens of the Hesperides, in the far western seas, with its tree of golden apples in the midst;' *The Fortunate Isles,* in Baring-Gould's Curious Myths of the Middle Ages. In Welsh, *afal* is an *apple,* and *afallwyn* is an orchard. The name is spelt *Aualun* in Layamon, vol. iii. p. 124. Avalon is fully described, says Wheeler, in the old French romance of Ogier le Danois.

88. *Holtes hore,* hoary woods, gray groves.

Cap. **VI**. 3. *Was newe grauen,* which was lately dug.

8. *But by demyng,* except by judging or guessing.

31. *Morgan le fay,* Morgaine la Fée, i.e. the fairy. Arthur's sister, who revealed to him the intrigues of Lancelot and Guinevere. She was married to Sir Uriens. *North galys* is North Wales.

33. *Nynyue;* called *Nimue* in lib. iv. cap. i.; but the name is also written *Uyuyen* or *Vivien;* she is Tennyson's 'Vivien' in the 'Idylls of the King.'

Cap. **VII**. 1. The notion that Arthur is not dead is thus alluded to in Heywood's Life of Merlin, p. 43 (quoted by Southey):—'Where it is said that his [Arthur's] end shall be doubtful, he that shall make question of the truth of Merlin's prophecy in that point, let him to this day but travel into Armorica or little Britain, and in any of their cities proclaim in their streets that Arthur expired after the common and ordinary manner of men, most sure he shall be to have a bitter and railing language asperst upon him, if he escape a tempestuous shower of stones and brickbats.' A similar legend was current concerning Holger Danske, or Ogier le Danois, one of Charlemagne's twelve peers, as is so well told by Hans Andersen in his Stories for Children. See also Rückert's ballad on 'Barbarossa,' Southey's poem of 'Roderick the Last of the Goths,' &c. Harold was by some believed to have long survived the battle of Hastings, and Richard II. to have lived for many years in obscurity after his deposition.

7. *Hic iacet.* Compare the following account. 'A leaden cross, bearing the inscription, *Hic jacet sepultus inclitus rex Arthurus in insula Avallonia,* was found under a stone [at Glastonbury] seven feet beneath the surface; and nine feet below this, an oaken coffin, inclosing dust and bones, was discovered. Of this discovery [or trick], which took place in the time of Henry II., and is recorded by Giraldus Cambrensis, who was an eye-witness, there can be no doubt, though the genuineness of the remains has been questioned.'—The Imperial Cyclopædia; British Empire; art. Glastonbury. Glastonbury is in Somersetshire, and is celebrated for its abbey, and the great antiquity of its ecclesiastical traditions. Amesbury is in Wiltshire, on the river Avon, and is the parish wherein Stonehenge is situated. Compare the concluding passage with Tennyson's 'Guinevere.'

IX. WILLIAM CAXTON.

THE date of Caxton's birth is generally given as 1412; for the correction of this date, and for an account of him and his books, see the exhaustive work by Mr. W. Blades. A good popular biography of him was published by Charles Knight, with the title 'The Old Printer.' A list of most of the books printed by him is given at p. 170 of that volume. Caxton's translation of Le Fevre's 'Recueil' was made at the command of Margaret Plantagenet, who was married to the Duke of Burgundy at Bruges, July 3, 1468, shortly after Caxton commenced his task (March 1, of the same year). For some useful remarks on the Trojan romance of Colonna and others, see Knight's 'Old Printer,' pp. 118, 119.

Remarks on the verse Troy Boke by Lydgate, will be found in Warton, Hist. Eng. Poetry, ii. 292; cf. p. 299. Raoul le Fevre, like Lydgate, chiefly follows Guido de Colonna; and Colonna borrowed freely from Benoit de Sainte-Maure, who pretended to follow Dares Phrygius and Dictys Cretensis, rather than Homer, who was generally considered a prejudiced writer, as he too much favoured the Greeks. The western nations prided themselves upon being descended from the Trojans, and thought it their duty to speak, as far as they could, in favour of Troy.

Palladyum, the Palladium, a statue of the goddess Pallas or Minerva, which represented her as sitting with a spear in her right hand, and in her left a distaff and spindle. On the preservation of this statue by the Trojans depended the safety of their city.

Vlixes, Ulysses. *Pryant*, Priam.

6. *Marc.* The English mark was 13s. 4d. *Poys*, weight.

15. *And there*, and where. *There* often means *where* in Old English.

69. *A thousand knyghtes armed.* In order to enclose this number, the horse must indeed have been, as Virgil describes it, *instar montis*, as big as a mountain. Gower also describes the horse as made of *brass*; Conf. Amant, lib. i. Compare Chaucer's steed of brass, Squyeres Tale, 107.

71. *Apius*; this is a corruption of *Epeus* (Gk. Ἐπειός). Epeus was really the maker of the wooden horse, and not Sinon; cf. 'ipse doli fabricator Epeus;' Virg. Æn. ii. 264. Caxton (or Le Fevre) has wrongly attributed the work to Sinon, at the same time calling him 'as skilful as Apius.' It looks like a confusion of the name of Epeus with that of the Censor Appius Claudius, who made the Appia Via, and founded Appii Forum.

90. *Panthasile*, Penthesilea, Queen of the Amazons, slain by Achilles.

99. *By that colour*, by that pretext. The word *colour* is thus used in the Bible, Acts xxvii. 30. Compare the similar use of the Lat. *color*.

117. *Accorded hyt wyth euyll wyll*, gave his consent against his will. *Euyll wyll* is here put for the French words *mal grè*.

138. *Thenadon*, the island of Tenedos, off the coast of Troas. Caxton also prints it *thenedon*. See note to Sect. XXII. 4506.

152. *Were in a-wayte*, were in await, were watching.

184. *Ha A felon trayttre*, ah! ah! felonious traitor! The interjection *ah*, when repeated in Middle English, is occasionally writren *ha A*, as here. The form *A ha* occurs in a passage quoted in Dyce's edition of Skelton, ii. 168; and in Chaucer, C. T. 15387, Cf. Isaiah xliv. 16.

X. THE NUT-BROWN MAID.

THE last reprint of Arnold's Chronicle was edited, with an introduction, by F. Douce. The editor compares the poem of the Nut-brown Maid with the Latin poem called 'Vulgaris Cantio,' translated by Bebelius, poet laureate to the emperor Maximilian I, from a German ballad, and printed at Paris in 1516. He supposes that the English poem may also have been derived from the German. He also likens parts of it to some poems by Tibullus, referring us in particular to the fourth book, containing the ode *Ad amicam*. I must confess that I do not quite see why the poem may not have been, after all, purely English, and not under much obligation either to the German or the Latin.

In vol. ii. pp. 334–337, of the Percy Folio MSS., edited by Hales and Furnivall, there is a piece called 'A Jigge,' which is clearly a poor imitation of 'The Nut-brown Maid.' The word *jigge* or *jig* meant originally not only a dance but a *ballad*. In Mr. Hazlitt's Early Popular Poetry of England, vol. ii. p. 271, our ballad is handled so as to have a religious sense, and bears the title, 'The New Not-browne Mayd upon the Passion of Christ.' In Cotgrave's French Dictionary we find the word '*Brunette*, a nut-browne girle,' to which he appends the proverb '*Fille brunette est de nature gaye et nette*, A nut-browne girle is neat and blith by nature.'

Stanza 1. The poem appears to have been written by a woman; hence the slightly sarcastic expression *these men*. Still, it is *the knight* who is supposed to be speaking in this (and every alternate) stanza.

Among, i.e. at intervals, sometimes. So in the old poem of The Owl and the Nightingale, l. 6, we find 'sum wile softe, and lud *among*,' i.e. sometimes soft, and *sometimes* loud again.

On women, we should now say, 'of women.'

Neuer a dele, not a bit, in no degree.

A newe, a new lover. So Chaucer has *a fair* for a fair one; Prologue, l. 165. *Than*, then.

A bannisshed man; observe that this forms the refrain of every other stanza, alternating with the burden, *love but him alone.*

2. *I say not nay* must be connected with the words immediately following; thus it means, 'I admit that it is often affirmed that woman's faith is decayed.' It is now *the lady* who replies.

Sayde; this word, like *saythe* and *layde* below, and many others in this piece, is wrongly spelt, as it has no right to a final *e.*

Contynew, remain constant.

Recorde, let (her) bear witness.

3. The knight now proposes to argue the matter. *Too,* two.

In-fere, in company, together; i. e. together with her lover. 'For we be fewe briddes her *in-fere*'; Poem of the Cuckow and Nightingale, 273.

I am the knyght; here the knight begins to personate one of two characters in an imaginary story.

4. *And I;* this continues the *lady's* reply; she begins to personate the heroine in l. 23.

5. *Do,* done; cf. note to Sect. II. st. 621; p. 372.

The ton, the one; *the ton* and *the tother* are respectively corruptions of *that one* and *that other,* the word *that* being originally used as the neuter of the *definite article.*

Rede I can, counsel I know; as in stanza 23.

6. *Lusty,* pleasant.

Departe, part, separate, divide. The phrase 'till death us *do par*,' in the present Marriage Service, was 'till death us *depart*' in the Sarum Manual and in the reformed Prayer Book, until the last review. The word *depart* occurs in this sense 'as late as 1578 in the English version of the Bible; but it was no longer used in that sense at the Restoration; and it was altered in 1661, in consequence of an objection made to it by the dissenters at the Savoy Conference.'—Humphrey on the Book of Common Prayer, p. 261.

Wheder, whither; the Ball. MS. has *whether.*

7. *Take thought,* be over-anxious; cf. Matt. vi. 25.

8. *Leue,* remain; cf. note to Sect. III. (B), l. 1174; p. 379.

Soo am I; i.e. I am ready myself.

Anoon, immediately, this instant; as in Shakespeare, I Henry IV, ii. 1. *By and by* had formerly a similar sense; see *By and by* in the Glossary.

9. *Of yonge,* i.e. *by* young; see stanza 10, l. 55.

11. *Lawe;* here used for *custom* or *rule.*

Dowte, fear. *Than,* then.

Goo, gone; cf. *do,* in stanza 5.

12. *I thinke not nay,* I admit (it is as you say); cf. note to stanza 2.

13. *Yf I,* &c.; if I were in danger, which God forbid.

14. *As I myght*, as well as I could.

15. *Roue*, roof; the Balliol MS. has *roffe*.

18. *In hele*, in good health. *Endure*, remain.

19. *As* is often used where we now generally say *as for instance*; hence *as cutte* is equivalent to 'as, for instance, you must cut.'

To wood-ward, toward the wood; the word *toward* is often thus separated. Cf. 'to us-ward;' Eph. i. 19.

Shortely, quickly, soon.

20. *As now*, immediately, at the present moment.

Instead of *other*, the Ball. MS. has *oder*, to rime with *moder*.

Ensue, follow.

All this make ye, you are the cause of all this. She here addresses her lover. The word *ye* is used instead of *thou*, both here, and in the next stanza. See note to Sect VI. l. 399.

The day cumeth fast vpon, daylight is fast approaching; the knight had come to her *by night*, as we learn from stanza 3.

21. *Soon hot, soon cold* occurs in Heywood's Proverbs, &c., 1562.

22. *Bee me*, by me, i. e. with reference to me; this is certainly the right reading, and not *to me*, as in the Balliol MS. '*By* occurs in 1 Cor. iv. 4, where the Greek shews that it must mean "against," "with reference to": "I know nothing *by* myself," i. e. "am not conscious of guilt in the things laid against me, yet am I not justified by that consciousness of rectitude, &c."'—The Bible Word-Book, by J. Eastwood and W. Aldis Wright; where other examples are given.

To dey therfore anoon, though I were to die on that account immediately.

23. The rime shows that *felow* should be *felawe*; indeed, *felawe* is the older and more correct spelling. See the Glossary.

25. *It were myn ease*, i. e. I would rather live in peace, and so do not want a second love to quarrel with the first.

26. *Your*, yours. See the Glossary.

Our, hour; spelt 'owre' in the Balliol MS.

To my power, as far as in me lies.

That one, one of them, one amongst them.

27. *Proue*, proof. The lover is now satisfied, and begins to confess the true state of the case.

28. *On the splene*, in the haste of the moment. *Spleen*, in the sense of *extreme haste*, occurs twice in Shakespeare's King John, ii. 1. 448, and v. 7. 50. So *in a spleen*, in a moment; Mids. Night's Dr. i. 1. 146.

The phrase arose from the fact that the spleen was 'once regarded as the source of anger and melancholy, and thence associated with hasty and variable conduct;' as remarked by Prof. Morley in a note upon this passage. The word is very common in Shakespeare; see Schmidt's Shak. Lexicon, where the word is explained to mean (1) fire, heat, impetuosity, eagerness, (2) hate, malice, (3) a sudden motion, a fit, (4) a fit of passion, (5) a caprice. Shak. also has *splenitive, spleenful,* and *spleeny.*

29. *God defende,* God forbid! *Ye* is the nominative, and *you* the accusative, according to correct usage.

30. The last stanza contains the author's moral, and a very noble one it is; see the last line. It is the moral of The Tale of Griselda, as told by Petrarch; and (after him) by Chaucer. See Chaucer's Prioress's Tale, &c., ed. Skeat; Group E, 1149. The expression *that we may* means 'that we men may,' but it does not prove that the author was a man. Other expressions render it probable that the author was a woman, and in this case she may have remembered to speak in a man's character. The word *which* means *who* (as in the Lord's Prayer), and refers to God in the preceding line. Indeed the Balliol MS. reads—'God sumtyme provith such as he lovith;' but this alteration is unnecessary.

XI. WILLIAM DUNBAR.

(A) *The Thrissil and the Rois.*

DUNBAR has been highly praised by Warton, Hist. Eng. Poetry, sect. xxx.; G. Ellis, Specimens of English Poetry, i. 377; Pinkerton, Ancient Scottish Poetry, i. pref. p. xciv.; and others. Dr. Langhorne says of him—

'In nervous strains Dunbar's bold music flows,
And time yet spares *The Thistle and the Rose.*'

The reader may consult with advantage an article on Dunbar's writings in Mr. Wright's Essays on the Middle Ages, vol. ii. p. 291.

The poems of Dunbar are chiefly contained in two MSS., of which one, called the Bannatyne MS., is described in 'Memorials of George Bannatyne, 1546-1698;' Edinburgh, 1829. This MS. was written out by Bannatyne in 1548. The second, or Maitland MS., is in the Pepysian Library at Cambridge, and is described by Pinkerton in his 'Ancient Scottish Poems.'

Some account of the marriage of James IV is given in Leland's Collectanea, vol. iii. p. 265, ed. 1770; see also Irving's Lives of Scottish Poets, i. 203.

Stanza 1. *Thair houris,* their orisons. In the poem called The Court of Love, wrongly attributed to Chaucer, the different parts of a morning service are sung by various birds. See Warton's note.

2. *Window.* This reminds us of Milton's L'Allegro, l. 46—
'And at my window bid good morrow.'
Awalk. Here *lk* = *kk*, as elsewhere in Scotch. Cf. Lancelot of the Laik (ed. Skeat, Early Eng. Text Society), l. 1049—
'Saying, "*Awalk!* it is no tyme to slep."'

3. *Weid,* &c., 'garment, painted with many diverse hues.'

5. *Ring,* reign; i. e. the wind blows so strongly in the season of May.

6. *Ross,* the Rose, i. e. Margaret Tudor; it is a very appropriate symbol, as it is the emblem both of England and of the houses of Lancaster and York. The second line of the stanza is copied from Chaucer's Knightes Tale, l. 187, which see.

7. *Doing fleit* is the same as *fleitand,* i. e. flowing; just as *doing chace* in the next stanza merely means *chasing.* Hence the phrase means flowing down, or dripping, with dew.

9. 'And, like the blissful sound of a hierarchy;' cf. Job xxxviii. 7. The angels were divided into three *hierarchies,* each containing three *orders.*

14. *But feir,* without mate or peer.
Feild of gold. An allusion to the arms of Scotland, viz. a lion rampant, gules, in a field or, surrounded by a tressure, which is borne double, and ornamented flory and counterflory with fleurs-de-lis.

16. *Bowgle,* wild ox. See the Kingis Quhair, p. 43, st. 157.

17. *Yre,* anger; but *vre,* custom, would perhaps make better sense.
Parcere; the complete line is—'Parcere prostratis uult nobilis ira leonis'; see Fisher's Works, ed. Mayor, p. 19. Cf. Vergil, Æn. vi. 853; Ovid, Trist. iii. 5. 33.

18. *Als just,* &c.; as just to curlews and owls as unto peacocks, &c.
Fowll of ravyne, bird of prey. Cf. Chaucer, Assembly of Foules, l. 323:—
'That is to say, the *foules of ravine*
Were highest set, and than the foules smale.'
Do efferay (MS.), for *do effray,* i. e. cause terror.

19. *Thrissil,* Thistle, the Scottish emblem. Burns says, in The Author's Earnest Cry and Prayer, &c.—
'Paint Scotland greetin owre her *thrissle.*'
Kepit with, guarded by. *Fend the laif,* defend the rest.

20. *Hir fallow,* fellow herself, make herself fellow.

22. *But ony,* &c.; springing up without any spot or blemish. Observe how Dame Nature is made to consider the Rose of England superior to the Lily of France.

25. *Cullouris twane,* i. e. Red and White Roses, the emblems of Lancaster and York.

26. *Princes*, princess.

Paramour, object of chivalrous affection and devotion. Observe the alliteration. *Peax*, peace. *The conserf*, keep thee.

27. *With a braid*, in a moment; we sometimes find *at a braid* in the same sense, as in The Romaunt of the Rose, l. 1336.

Haif hard to-forrow, have heard previously, have heard already.

Nynt morow, ninth day; the very day of the year mentioned in Sect. XIII. l. 268. But it is ten years earlier.

(B) *Dunbar desyred to be ane Freir.*

The second extract is entitled by Mr. Laing 'The Visitation of St. Francis.' The title 'How Dunbar was desyred to be ane Freir,' is found in the Bannatyne MS. There is an apparent contradiction in the idea of the poet's being asked to become a Franciscan friar, when he states in st. 7 that he had worn the habit already. This may be reconciled by supposing that he had never completed the year of his noviciate, and that he was now called upon to do so. A novice might leave the order at any time within the first year, but not afterwards.

Stanza 1. *This hindir nycht*, this night past; answering to our modern phrase 'the other night.' It is evident that the word *hindir* has been omitted by accident, as it is not the only poem by Dunbar which begins with this expression. The habit of St. Francis was gray, and the Franciscans were called Gray Friars. See p. 357.

2. *Skarrit*, felt scared.

With him I skarrit, I shrank from him in terror, was frightened at him.

3. *Hes long done teiche*, hast long been engaged in teaching.

Mon, must. *But dreid*, without fear; hence, certainly.

4. *Loving*, praise. *The till*, to thee. *Mot*, mayest.

5. *Sic sevin*; probably a corrupt passage. The word *sic* would be better omitted; then *be sevin* would mean *by seven*, i. e. by seven times. Mr. Wright quotes a paraphrase of this stanza in the Somnium of George Buchanan, which ends thus:—

> 'Quod si tanta meae tangit te cura salutis,
> Vis mihi, vis animae consuluisse meae?
> Quilibet hac alius mendicet veste superbus,
> At mihi da mitram purpureamque togam.'

7. *Kalice*, Calais, which was *in England* in the sense that it belonged to the English.

8. *Derntoun;* possibly Dirrington, near Greenlaw, in Berwickshire.

9. *As wy that wes in weir*, like a man that was in distress.

XII. STEPHEN HAWES.

I HAVE corrected a few errors in Mr. Wright's edition by Waley's edition of 1555, a copy of which is in the Bodleian Library at Oxford. There are also two other copies in the same library, of the same date, with the imprint of R. Tottell in the colophon. There is no appreciable difference between Waley's and Tottell's editions of the above year. One of the latter is in the Douce collection, and contains the following MS. notes by Douce. 'The *first* edition of this book was printed by W. de Worde, 1517, 4to.; the *second* by Wayland, 1554, 4to... This is the *third* edition... See some account of Hawes, the author, in Wood's Athenæ Oxoniensis, i. col. 5, and in Warton, Hist. Eng. Poetry, ii. 219. See Bridges' Censura Literaria, iii. 225, and iv. 7. The first edition was sold at the Duke of Roxburgh's sale for £81.'

For a notice of Stephen Hawes and his writings see Warton, Hist. Eng. Poetry, ii. 397 (sect. xxviii.), ed. 1840. Warton gives an analysis of the Passetyme of Pleasure. His analysis of the canto which I have selected is as follows :—'He now continues his expedition, and near a fountain observes a shield and a horn hanging. On the shield was a lion rampant of gold in a silver field, with an inscription, importing, that this was the way to La Bell Pucell's habitation, and that whoever blows the horn will be assaulted by a most formidable giant. He sounds the horn, when instantly the giant appeared, twelve feet high, armed in brass, with three heads, on each of which was a streamer, with the inscriptions, Falsehood, Imagination, Perjury. After an obstinate combat, he cuts off the giant's three heads with his sword Claraprudence. He next meets three fair ladies, Verity[1], Good Operation, Fidelity. They conduct him to their castle with music ; where, being admitted by the portress Observance, he is healed of his wounds by them.'

Stanza 1. *The Capricorne;* the sign of Capricorn. On entering this sign, the sun passes through the southern or winter solstitial point, and begins to *ascend* northwards ; on leaving the sign, it passes into *Aquarius.* The sun now enters Aquarius about the 19th of January, but, in the time of Hawes, it was about a week earlier.

Janus Bifrons; the epithet *bifrons* (double-faced) as applied to Janus, occurs in Virgil's Æneid twice, in lib. vii. 180 and lib. xii. 198. It is explained in Ovid's Fasti, lib. i. 133-144. He was the guardian deity of gates, and hence is commonly represented with two heads,

---

[1] Misprinted 'Vanity' in Warton.

because every door looks two ways. He opened the year and the seasons, and hence the first month was named after him *Januarius.* I do not quite see the force of *the crowne had worne,* unless it means had ruled or presided in his turn, during his month of January.

1. *Joyned with,* was in conjunction with; i.e. the Moon and Mercury were seen in conjunction.

Assure, azure; *assured* is clearly a misprint.

Depured, made pure or clear, without the encumberment of clouds.

2. The rimes *rockes, flockes, toppes* are not very good ones; *roches* is an old spelling of *rocks,* but *rockes* is here the better form.

Corall; where coral grew in quite tall masses. This seems to be said at random, without any knowledge of the real mode of growth of *coral.*

Popyngayes, parrots. *Me beforne,* before me.

3. *Adowne,* off from; incorrectly used.

Lyght, alighted. *Blasynge,* blazoning, or describing. Cotgrave's French Dictionary has: ' *Blasonner,* to blaze armes.'

As well as I myghte, as well as I can. This is not very well after all, for metal upon metal, *or* upon *argent,* is false heraldry.

Scrypture, writing.

5. *All feare to abjecte,* to cast away all fear.

6. *Mede,* meed, reward. *Varlet,* squire.

7. *To fere,* (large enough) to frighten a great number of men.

8. *Fane,* pennon, a kind of flag. The giant has three heads, representing Falsehood, Evil Imagination, and Perjury. Spenser describes the giant Gerioneo, who had three bodies springing out of one waist, and six arms and legs; see Faerie Queene, v. 10. 8. He was destroyed by Prince Arthur. But the passage in the Faerie Queene which most closely approaches Hawes's description is the description of the combat between Arthr and the giant Orgoglio, Bk. i. canto 8.

9. *Let the cace,* prevent the chance of fulfilment. *Is I,* is aye.

13. *For ever,* &c. 'For Falsehood ever comes, with his own condition, to a lady, and says, to avoid an inconvenience (it is best) that ye should not have pity (on your lover); Imagination knows that your lover is of no value; I swear the same, and at once she believes (that all that we have said is the truth).' Here all three evils, Falsehood, Evil Imagination, and Perjury, conspire to destroy love.

15. *Charged,* prepared for the charge, or, made ready for service.

16. *Iclyped Clara prudence,* called Clara Prudentia, i.e. bright prudence, or, as Hawes explains it, ' fayre and sure. The paladin Oliver's sword was called Alta Clara, or tall and bright.

Glave, sword; from O. F. *glaive,* 'a gleave, or sword'; Cotgrave.

16. *Of cutting*, in the cutting part, or blade.

17. *Discharged*, discharged or dealt his blow without effect.

Abye, buy it dearly, now corrupted into *abide*.

20. *Onvale*, unveil, become free from clouds.

And with, &c. Compare Spenser—

> 'His sparkling blade about his head he blest,
> And smote quite off his right leg by the knee,
> That downe he tombled, &c.'—F. Q. i. 8. 22.

21. *Enforcing him*, forcing or exerting himself. Compare Spenser—

> 'Through all three bodies he him strooke attonce,
> That all the three attonce fell on the plaine.'
>
> F. Q. v. 11. 14.

22. *Demaunded*, required, asked; but it is probably an error for *demeaned*, i. e. borne yourself.

Brayde, either 'started off,' or 'neighed'; probably the latter.

23. The three ladies are Verity, Good Operation, and Fidelity; these are intended to be the exact opposites of the three evil qualities already mentioned, viz. Falsehood, Evil Imagination, and Perjury.

Her hert entere, their whole hearts.

25. *First fane*, viz. the streamer already mentioned in st. 8. This was an ornament upon the helmet, so that Verity must have taken the head out of its helmet, and then placed it on the spike with the silken streamer.

Of Ymaginacion, i. e. the head on which was the helmet, bearing the ornament inscribed 'Imagination.'

26. The three ladies have a faint resemblance to Spenser's Fidelia, Speranza, and Charissa (Faith, Hope, and Charity), in Bk. i. canto 10. Instead of a portress, 'fayre Observaunce,' Spenser has a porter named Humilta (Humility), a franklin named Zele (Zeal), and a squire called Reverence. However inferior Hawes is to Spenser, it is very likely that Spenser took a few hints from him, although the poet to whom the author of the Faerie Queene was really indebted to a far larger extent was Sackville. See Extract XXIV.

XIII. GAWIN DOUGLAS.

For a sketch of the life of Gawin or Gawain Douglas, see Warton Hist. Eng. Poetry, sect. xxxi. and Irving's Lives of the Scottish Poets, vol. ii. At p. 61 of the latter work, the author bids us remark, that 'in many instances Douglas has been guilty of modernizing the notions of his original. The Sibyl, for example, is converted into a nun, and admonishes Æneas, the Trojan baron, to persist in counting his beads'! The reader should also consult the complete edition of Douglas's Poems, by J. Small (1874).

1. *Dyonea,* Dionæa; an epithet of Venus, from the name of her mother Dione. As Venus is mentioned separately in l. 4, Dione herself may here be intended. Dione was a daughter of Oceanus and Tethys, or of Uranus and Ge, or of Aether and Ge. The poet here assigns to her the epithet of *night-herd,* or guardian of the night, and represents her as chasing the stars from the sky.

3. *Cynthia,* the Moon. In old times, the seven planets, supposed to revolve round the Earth, were the Moon, Mercury, Venus, the Sun, Mars, Jupiter, and Saturn. The poet mentions all of these, giving to Mercury the name of *Cyllenius,* and to the sun that of *Phœbus.*

5. *Cyllene* was the highest mountain in Peloponnesus, on the frontiers of Arcadia and Achaia, sacred to Mercury, who had a temple on the summit, and was hence called Cyllenius. There is a passage much like this in Chaucer—

> ' Now fleeth Venus into *Ciclinius* toure ...
> Within the gate she *fledde* into a *cave.*'
>
> Complaynt of Mars and Venus, st. xvii.

Here *Ciclinius* is an evident mistake for *Cyllenius,* as was pointed out by Mr. Brae, in Notes and Queries, in 1851, and *Cyllenius toure* means the mansion or house of Mercury, which, according to the old astrology, is the sign Gemini. It is clear that Douglas has here imitated Chaucer.

7. Saturn was a *froward* or inauspicious planet in the old astrology. The words *from hys mortal speir* seem to indicate the reason of his being called *frawart,* viz. because he was supposed to portend death.

10. *Circulat warld,* orbit. The orbit of Saturn was *behind,* i.e. *beyond* that of Jupiter.

11. *Nycthemyne,* Nyctimene, i.e. the owl. It refers to the owl seeking her daily hiding-place. *Nyctimene* was daughter of Epopeus, king of Lesbos, or, according to others, of Nycteus. Pursued by her amorous father, she concealed herself, and was changed by Athene into *an owl.* See Ovid, Metam. ii. 590.

13. A considerable portion of ll. 13-242 of this Prologue is written out by Warton into modern English prose, somewhat paraphrastically, and with a few omissions; nor is it free from mistakes. I therefore take the liberty to rewrite a part of it here, correcting Warton's mistakes by words in italics, and filling up the omissions between square brackets.

'Fresh Aurora, the wife of [mighty] Tithonus, issued from her saffron bed and ivory house. She was clothed in a robe of crimson and violet-colour [dyed in grain]; the cape vermilion, and the border purple: she opened the windows of her ample hall, overspread with roses, and filled with [royal] balm or nard. At the same time, (20) *she draws up* the crystal gates of heaven, to illumine the world: The glittering streamers of the orient diffused purple streaks mingled with gold and azure, [piercing the sable nocturnal rampart, and beatr down the sky's cloudy mantle-wall.] *Eous the steed,* in red harness of rubies, of colour [like sorrel, and somewhat] brown as the berry, *lifts its head* above the sea, to [enlighten and] glad our hemisphere: the *flame bursting out* from *his* nostrils; (30) [so quickly Phaethon by means of his whip makes him whirl round, to roll his father Apollo's golden chariot, that shrouds all the heavens and the air.] *Till* shortly, apparelled in his luminous [fresh] array, Phœbus, bearing the blazing torch of day, issued from his royal palace; with a golden crown, glorious visage, curled locks bright as the chrysolite or topaz, and with a radiance intolerable. The fiery sparks bursting from his eyes, (40) *to purge* the air, and gild the new verdure; [shedding down from his ethereal seat fortunately-influential aspects of the heavens; the misty vapour springing up, sweet as incense, before his kingly high magnificence, in smoky moisture of dank and humid dews, whilst moist wholesome mists conceal the hollow.] The golden vanes of his [sovereign] throne covered the ocean with a glittering glance, and the broad waters were all in a blaze, (50) at the first glimpse of his appearance. It was glorious to see the winds appeased, the sea becalmed, the soft season, the serene firmament, the still [illumined] air, and the *pleasant frith.* The silver-scaled fishes, on the gravel, gliding hastily, as it were, from the heat or sun, through clear streams, with fins shining brown as cinnabar, and chisel-tails, dartled here and there. The new lustre enlightening all the land, (60) *the beryl-like streams shone over against those gravelly beds, till* the reflection of the beams [of day] *filled the pleasant* banks *with* variegated gleams; and [sweet] Flora threw forth her blooms under the feet of the sun's brilliant *steed.* The bladed soil was embroidered with various hues. Both wood and forest were darkened with boughs, *whose pretty branches were depicted on the ground; the red rocks appeared distinct, with clearly-marked shadows.* Towers, turrets, battlements, and high pinnacles, (70) of churches, castles, and every fair city *stood depicted,* every *finial* (?) *vane and* story, *upon the plain country, by their own shadow.* The glebe, fearless of the northern blasts of [Eolus], spread *out* her broad bosom [in order to receive low down in her lap the comforting inspiration of Zephyrus.] The corn-*tops* and the new-sprung barley reclothe the earth with a gladsome garment. [So thick the plants sprang in every plot, (80) that the fields wonder at their fertile covering. Busy dame Ceres, and proud Priapus,

E e

rejoice in the fertile plains, replenished so pleasantly and most fittingly, nourished wondrously nobly by nature, stretching abroad, under the round circle, upon the fertile skirt-laps of the ground]. The variegated vesture of the [beauteous] valley covers the *turfy* furrow, and *every sod was* diversified with *leaves of very various shapes.* (90) *Each spray was sprinkled dispersedly with springing shoots; because of* the fresh moisture of the dewy night, restoring [partially] *its former height to* the herbage, *as far as* the cattle [in the long summer's day], had [eaten and] cropped [it away in their pasture]. The [pretty] blossoms in the blowing garden trust their heads to the protection of the young sun. Rank ivy-leaves overspread the wall of the rampart. The blooming hawthorn clothed all his thorns in flowers.'

The latter part of Warton's paraphrase is so sketchy, and, in many places, so hopelessly incorrect, that the reader could only glean a general idea of the sense from it, and it is hardly worth consulting. Some of his errors are extraordinary, and serve as instances of the fact that many a scholar who can translate Latin and Greek with ease is helplessly at sea as to the meaning of many words in Old English. In the part which I have already quoted, the tenses are sometimes confused. It must be observed, however, that the grammar in the original also shows signs of confusion. This was owing to the great influence of Chaucer's writings. His Scotch imitators sometimes went so far as to imitate his grammar. Thus the true Scottish pres. participle ends in *-and*, as in *persand*, piercing, l. 23; but in l. 21 we have the Chaucerian participle in *-yng*, as *twynklyng.* The Scotch infin. mood is seen in *behald*, l. 38; but the Chaucerian infinitive, which sometimes ends in *-en*, is imitated in the word *alichtyn*, l. 28. Hence Douglas's writings are not to be regarded as pure Scottish, but as Scottish much affected by Anglicisms.

99. 'Out of fresh buds, the young vine-grapes along the trellises hung on their stalks.' Warton is very wrong here, and actually translates *endlang* by *end-long*, which is very misleading.

101. *Lowkyt*, locked, closed. Warton wrongly has *unlocking.*'

103. *Gresy*, grassy.

113. *Dyd on breid*, did abroad, opened out. *Crownell*, corolla.

115. *Battill*, rich, luxuriant; not *embattelled*, as in Warton.

124. *Gan chyp, and kyth*, did break their covering, and show. *Chip* is used much as when a bird *chips open* its egg. *Kyth* is to show, manifest; nothing to do with *kissing*, as in Warton.

141. *Forgane*, against. *Prynce*, i. e. Phœbus.

154. *Seirsand by kynd*, searching for, according to their nature.

157. *Rutys gent*, gentle, i. e. fine or trim roots or herbs.

159. *Coppa* is printed *Toppa* in the Bannatyne Club edition. Mr. Small reads the MS. as *Toppa,* but I do not. It is a variation of *Coppell,* which is the name of a hen in 'The Tournament of Tottenham,' printed in Percy's 'Reliques.' A bird with a tuft of feathers on its head is called *copple-crowned;* see Halliwell's Dictionary. Cf. Du. *kop,* head, pate; Welsh *cop,* a top, *copa,* a tuft or crest. The fact is, that the name is borrowed from the old story of Reynard the Fox.

Pertelote occurs in Chaucer's Nonne Prestes Tale; see *Partlette* in Nares's Glossary.

160. *Hantis,* practises, uses.

161. *Pantyt povn,* painted peacock.

170. *Aragne,* Arachne, the spider.

'Laxos in foribus suspendit aranea casses.'

Virgil, Georg. iv. 247.

173. *So dusty,* i.e. such a dusty powder.

181. *Days,* does; so *rays* for *roes,* in l. 182.

187. *Wolx* = *woux*; *l* put for *u.* 'In salt streams were Doris and (her mother) Thetis, and nymphs and Naiads beside running rills.'

Wolx is waxed, became, were; not *walked,* as in Warton !

193. *Sang* is inserted from the editions; the Trinity MS. omits it. It is clearly wanted. As to 'ring-dances,' see The Complaint of Scotland, ed. J. A. H. Murray, p. xciii.

Dansys ledys, lead dances.

201. *Thocktfull,* anxious. *Rowmys,* roam.

205. 'It pleases one to endite ballads.' *Sum* is frequently singular in our early writers; see Chaucer, Knightes Tale, l. 397. And see below, l. 211.

212. *ʒisterevin;* this is practically a dissyllable here, like the modern *yestreen.*

217. *Neuer a deill,* not a bit.

Harkis, &c.; listen to what I would (tell you).

222. 'Do you choose one (of the girls whom we shall meet).'

225. *Dywlgat,* divulged. In Scottish MSS. we often find *w* in place of *v* or *u.* It here stands for *double u;* i.e. *dywlgat* is put for *dyuulgat,* where the first *u* has the sound of *v.*

226. 'In no way suitable to our wholesome May.'

232. 'Intone their blissful song on every side.'

Art is more commonly spelt *airt,* as in Burns's poems; cf. VI. 309.

233. 'To recover those lovers of their night's sorrow.'

244. *For byrdis sang,* because of the song of the birds.

252. This song of the birds was possibly suggested by the concluding stanzas of Chaucer's Assembly of Foules.

256. *Alkynd fruyt*, fruit of every kind. In l. 263, *alkynd bestiall* means every kind of thing that is bestial, i.e. all kinds of beasts.

268. He gives us here the date, viz. May 9; the year was 1513.

269. 'Being on my feet, I jumped into my bare shirt.' That is, a shirt and nothing more. It was then usual to sleep naked.

270. *Wilfull*, willing, desirous.

271. *Latter*, last or twelfth book. The epithet *Dan*, from the Old Fr. *dans*, Latin *Dominus*, was a title of respect. So Spenser speaks of *Dan Chaucer*, F. Q. iv. 2. 32; so also Tennyson, in 'A Dream of Fair Women.'

273. *This kyng*, viz. Phœbus, or the sun.

276. *As is said*, as has been said already.

277. The poet speaks of the sun as 'newly aryssyn.' On the 9th of May, at that date, and in the latitude of London, where he then probably was, the sun rose soon after four o'clock.

282. *Progne*, Procne, the swallow.

283. *Dreidfull*, full of dread, timid.

Philomeyn, Philomela. Philomela and Procne were sisters, of whom the former was turned into a nightingale, and the latter into a swallow, though some writers just reverse these changes. See Ovid, Metam. lib. vi.; Virgil, Georg. iv. 13, Eclog. vi. 79.

286. Æsacus, son of Priam, threw himself into the sea upon the death of his love Hesperia, and was changed into an aquatic bird; Ovid, Metam. xi. 791.

288. *Peristera*, the dove, sacred to Venus; see next line.

291. *Into*, in. *Into* continually has this sense in Scottish writers.

298. *In hyr kynd*, according to her nature. So also *after his kind* means according to his nature; Gen. i. 21.

304. *Ayr morow*, early morning, before the time of mass.

307. 'Here endeth the witty prologue,' &c. The author commends it as being his best, and deserving of having its capital letters illuminated with gold. This is not done in the Trinity MS., which merely has a red capital at the beginning.

XIV. JOHN SKELTON.

(A) '*From Why come ye nat to Courte?*'

MANY of the notes below are copied from Mr. Dyce's edition. These are marked with D.

Line 287. '*The Erle of Northumberlande*, i.e. Henry Algernon Percy, fifth earl of Northumberland. In 14 Henry VIII he was made warden of the whole Marches, a charge which, for some reason or other, he soon after resigned: vide Collins's Peerage, ii. 305, ed. Brydges. That he found himself obliged to pay great deference to the Cardinal is evident from Cavendish's Life of Wolsey, where (pp. 120–128, ed. 1827) see the account of his being summoned from the north when his son Lord Percy (who was then, according to the custom of the age, a "servitor" in Wolsey's house) had become enamoured of Anne Boleyn. This nobleman, who encouraged literature, and appears to have patronised our poet, died in 1527.'—D.

292. *Mayny,* flock. ℞. ᵐᵃʸⁿⁱ.

293. *Loke out at dur,* look out at the door.

295. *Bochers dogge.* 'Skelton alludes to the report that Wolsey was the son of a butcher. Compare too Roy's satire against Wolsey, "Rede me, and be not wrothe," &c,

"*The mastif curre,* bred in Ypswitch towne...

Wat. He cometh then of some noble stocke?

Jeff. His father coulde snatche a bullock,
    A *butcher* by his occupation.'

                    Harl. Miscell. ir. 3. 31. ed. Park,
and a poem "Of the Cardnalle Wolse;"

"To se a churle *a Bochers curre*
To rayne & rule in soche honour," &c.

                    MS. Harl. 7252, fol. 156.
Cavendish says that Wolsey "was an honest poor man's son;" and the will of his father (printed by Fiddes) shews that he possessed some property; but, as Mr. Sharon Turner observes, that Wolsey was the son of a butcher, "was reported and believed while he lived."—Hist. of Reign of Hen. the Eighth, i. 167, ed. 8vo.'—D.

312. *Dawes,* jackdaws. The daw was reckoned as a silly bird, and a *daw* meant a simpleton. So in Shakespeare—'Then thou dwellest with daws too;' Coriolanus, iv. 5. 48.

313. *Of the coyfe.* See note to Piers the Plowman, Prol. l. 210; ed. Skeat (Clar. Press Series).

316. '*Commune Place,* i.e. Common Pleas.'—D. See note to Piers the Plowman, Prol. l. 92; and cf. note to st. 4 of Lydgate's London Lyckpeny, p. 374 above.

326. *Huddypeke.* Skelton has *hoddypeke,* in the phrase 'can he play well at the *hoddypeke,*' Poem on Magnificence, l. 1176. It clearly here means a simpleton. It has not, hitherto, been well explained. Nares supposes it to be the same as *hodmandod,* a snail, of which there is no proof. Mr. Wedgwood takes it to be the Dutch word *hoddebek,* a stammerer, where *hodden* means to jolt or jog, and *bek* is a beak or

mouth. Both are guesses, and both are wrong. The word is clearly the same as *hudpik*, of which the plural *hudpikis* occurs in Dunbar's Dance of the Seven Deadly Sins, l. 59—

> ' Cativis, wretchis, and ockeraris,
> *Hudpikis*, hoarders, and gadderaris.'

Seeing that Dunbar also uses *purspik*, equivalent to Chaucer's *pikepors*, and our *pickpurse*, the word certainly means a *hoodpick* or *pickhood*, one who would thieve even out of a man's hood. This explains Skelton's line at once. *Crafty Conveyance* is the character who puts the question, cited above from Skelton's Magnificence, which simply means—' can he thieve in a small way?' The word being once established as a word of reproach, easily degenerated into the sense of simpleton. Skelton uses it twice, spelt *huddypeke*, in this latter sense also.

327. *To lewde*, too full of ignorance. *Lerned and lewde* meant originally *learned and ignorant*. ' So in our author's "Speke, Parrot," we find "*lewdlye* ar they *lettyrd*," l. 296.'—D.

328. ' *Well thewde*, i.e. well mannered.'—D.

335. *Checker*, the Court of Exchequer; see note on p. 373.

338. *Rowte*, snore, make a snoring noise, snort. ' I may just observe that Palsgrave not only gives *rowte* in that sense, but also " *I rowte*, . . . *Je roucte*."'—D.

343. *Scottysh kynge*, James the Fifth, born 1512; began to reign, 1513; died, 1542, aged only thirty.

347. ' *Whipling*, perhaps the same as *pippling*, i.e. piping—"the blast of the moche vayne glorious *pipplyng* wynde;" vol. i. p. 207.'—D. Compare *whiffler* in Shakespeare. Another similar word is *fipple*, to whimper. ' He *fippilit* like a fatherless foal;' Peebles to the Play, l. 239; printed in Shorter English Poems, ed. Morley, p. 69.

354. ' This passage relates to the various rumours which were afloat concerning the Scottish affairs in 1522, during the regency of John, Duke of Albany. The last and disastrous expedition of Albany against England in 1523 had not yet taken place; its failure called forth from Skelton a long and furious invective against the Duke. In 1522, when Albany, with an army 80,000 strong had advanced to Carlisle, Lord Dacre, by a course of able negotiations, prevailed on him to accept a truce for a month and to disband his forces; see Hist. of Scotl. v. 156 sqq. by Tytler,—who defends the conduct of Albany on this occasion from the charge of cowardice and weakness.'—D.

357. *Owers*; shall be *ours* for the space of two hours. Cf. the phrase, *the mountenance of an houre*, in Chaucer, Troil. and Cres. b. ii. l. 1707.

367. *Burgonyons*, Burgundians.

368. *Spainyardes onyons*, Spanish onions, i.e. Spanish people, whom

Skelton calls Spanish onions for the sake of a rime, and because there
are onions well-known by the name *Spanish.*

374. '*Mutrell* is Montreuil [in the extreme north of France, not far
from Creçy and Agincourt]; and the allusion must be to some attack intended or actual on that town, of which I can find no account agreeing
with the date of the present poem.'—D.

380. 'I.e. for dread that the Cardinal, Wolsey, take offence.

"He *taketh pepper in the nose*, that I complayne
Vpon his faultes."

Heywood's Dialogue, &c. sig. G.; Workes, ed. 1598.'—D.
The phrase is an old one, and occurs in Piers Plowman, B. xv. 197.

382. *Hede of gose*, head goes off.

401. *Hampton Court;* 'the palace of Wolsey, which he afterwards,
with all its magnificent furniture, presented to the king.'—D.

407. *Yorkes Place;* 'the palace of Wolsey, as Archbishop of York,
which he had furnished in the most sumptuous manner: after his disgrace, it became a royal residence under the name of Whitehall.'—D.

417. *Tancrete*, transcript. Roquefort has '*Tancrit:* Transcrit, copié.'

425. *Hym lyst*, it pleases him.

427. *Saunz*, i.e. *sans*, without.

Aulter is the Old Fr. *aultre*, now spelt *autre*, other.

429. *Marshalsy.* 'The highway from St. Margaret's Hill to Newing-
ton Causeway is called *Blackman Street*, on the east side of which is the
Marshalsea, which is both a court of law and a prison.'—Hughson's
Walks through London, p. 325. 'At the south-west corner of Blackman-
street, in the road to the obelisk, St. George's Fields, is situated the
King's Bench Prison, for debtors, and every one sentenced by the Court
of King's Bench.'—Ib. p. 327. See Dickens's 'Little Dorrit.'

434. *Vndermynde*, undermine. Cf. *sound* for Old Eng. *sowne*, Fr. *son.*

438. '*Coarted*, i.e. coarcted, confined.'—D.

Streatly means *narrowly, closely, strictly.*

449. '*Bereth on hand*, i.e. leads on to a belief, persuades. See Chaucer,
Wif of Bathes Prol. ll. 232, 382, 393, &c. "He is my countre man: as
he *bereth me an hande*—vti mihi vult persuasum." Hormanni Vulgaria,
sig. X viii. ed. 1530.'—D.

463. *Cæciam*, probably another form of *cæcitatem*. Mr. Dyce quotes
from Du Cange, '*Cæcia, σκοτοδινία*,' i. e. a vertigo with loss of sight.

A cæcitate, &c. This refers to the phrase in the Litany, 'From all
blindness of heart,' &c.

475. *Amalecke*, Amalekite; cf. 1 Sam. xv. 3.

476. *Mameluk*, i.e. a Mameluke. The *Mamelukes* were mercenary
horse-soldiers employed by the Turks. They afterwards made them-

selves masters of Egypt, but were murderously suppressed by Mehemet Ali in 1811. A body of them was defeated by Napoleon at the battle of the Pyramids, July 21, 1798. See an account of them in 'The History of Napoleon,' third ed. 1835, vol. i. p. 131.

483. '*God to recorde*, i. e. God to witness.'—D.

485. *Reason or skyll.* Mr. Dyce considers these words as nearly synonymous; but *skyll* in Old English generally means *discernment*, or power to separate, whereas *reason* implies rather a power of combining.

486. 'Notwithstanding, the first beginning.'

490. *Sank royall*, royal blood, where *royal* is applied derisively. We find the same phrase, spelt *saunke realle*, in Morte Arthure, ed. Perry (Early Eng. Text Soc.) l. 179.

495. '*Rowme*, i. e. room, place, office.'—D. Cf. Luke xiv. 7, and Shakespeare, Taming of Shrew, iii. 2. 252.

508. '*Saw*, i. e. saying, branch of learning.'—D.

511. 'The *trivials* were the first three sciences taught in the schools, viz. grammar, rhetoric, and logic; the *quatrivials* were the higher set, viz. astrology (or astronomy), geometry, arithmetic, and music. See Du Cange's Gloss. in vv. *Trivium, Quadrivium;* and Hallam's Introd. to Lit. of Europe, i. 4.'—D. Hence the common old phrase, *the Seven Sciences.*

Mr. Dyce remarks that Skelton's depreciation of Wolsey's talents is very unjust.

517. Cf. Chaucer, 'The goos seyde tho, al thys *nys worthe a flye*,' Assembly of Foules, l. 501.

518. '*Haly*, a famous Arabian; "claruit circa A.C. 1110." Fabr. Bibl. Gr. xiii. 17.'—D. Cf. Chaucer, Prol. l. 431.

519. *Ptholomy*, Claudius Ptolemy, the celebrated astronomer and geographer, who flourished between A.D. 139 and A.D. 161.

520. *Albumasar*, an Arabian astronomer, who died about A.D. 885.

522. *Mobyll*, moveable. The moveable stars are the planets.

526. '*Humanyte*, i. e. *humaniores literæ*, polite literature.'—D.

533. 'Then, to make good our story.'

538. *Take*, taken. '*Conceyght*, i. e. good opinion, favour.'—D.

540. '*Exemplyfyenge*, i. e. following the example of.'—D.

550. 'Abdalonimus or Abdolonimus, whom Alexander made king of Sidon; see Justin, xi. 10.'—D.

557. *Occupyed a showell*, i. e. used a shovel.

569. '*Cotyd*, i. e. quoted, noted, marked, with evil qualities.'—D. Skelton uses *coted* elsewhere in the phrase 'Howe scripture shulde be *coted*,' Colin Cloute, l. 758.

571–574. Here Skelton mentions all the Seven Deadly Sins. See Piers the Plowman, ed. Skeat (Clar. Press), note to l. 62 of Passus v.

752. 'Chief root or cause of his making or success.'

753. 'This proverbial saying occurs in a poem attributed to Lydgate:

> " An hardy mowse that is bold to breede
> In cattis eeris."
>
> The Order of Foles—MS. Harl. 2251, fol. 304.

And so Heywood:

> "I haue heard tell, it had need to bee
> A wylie mouse that should breed in the cats eare."
>
> Dialogue, &c., sig. G 4; Workes, ed. 1598.'—D.

'*Demaunde.* What thynge is it that never was nor never shall be? R[*esponse*]. Never mouse made her nest in a cattes ere;' Reliquiæ Antiquæ, ii. 73; cited from the Demaundes Joyous, 1511; and see Lyly's Euphues, 1580, repr. 1868, p. 233.

(B) *From 'Phyllyp Sparowe.'*

'*Phyllyp Sparowe* must have been written before the end of 1508; for it is mentioned with contempt in the concluding lines of Barclay's " Ship of Fooles," which was finished in that year. The "Luctus in morte Passeris" of Catullus no doubt suggested the present production to Skelton, who, when he calls on "all maner of byrdes" to join in lamenting Philip Sparrow, seems also to have had an eye to Ovid's elegy " In mortem Psittaci," Amor. ii. 6. Another piece of the kind is extant among the compositions of antiquity,—the " Psittacus Atedii Melioris" of Statius, Silv. ii. 4. In the " Amphitheatrum Sapientiæ Socraticæ Joco-seriæ," &c., of Dornavius, i. 460 sqq. may be found various Latin poems on the deaths, &c., of sparrows by writers posterior to the time of Skelton. See too Herrick's lines "Upon the death of his Sparrow," Hesper. 1648, p. 117; and the verses entitled " Phyllis on the death of her Sparrow," attributed to Drummond, Works. 1711, p. 50.'—D. Coleridge (Remains, iii. 163) speaks of 'Old Skelton's Philip Sparrow, an exquisite and original poem.'

In my larger edition of Piers the Plowman (B-text), I have noted that in Pass. xv. 119, where other MSS. have a totally different line, the Oriel MS. has the line—

> ' Schulden go synge seruyseles with *sire philip the sparwe.*'

In the extract here given, Skelton sings the praises of Jane Scroupe, the maiden whose sparrow was dead.

Line 999. '*Sort*, i. e. set, assemblage.'—D. So in Rich. III, v. 3. 316.

1002. *Fauour*, beauty; see l. 1048.

1014. *Stepe* probably means *shining, bright*, as in Chaucer, Prol. 201—

> ' His eyen *steepe*, and rollyng in his heed.'

Mr. Cockayne, in his edition of 'Seinte Marherete,' gives (at p. 108) several other instances, of which the most decisive is—'Schinende and schenre then eni gimstanes, *steapre* then is steorre,' i.e. shining and sheener than any gemstones, *brighter* than is a star; St. Cáth. 2661.

1018-1021. Lucretia, wife of L. Tarquinius Collatinus, who stabbed herself, according to the well-known story, B.C. 510. Polyxena, daughter of Priam, beloved by Achilles, slain by Neoptolemus on the tomb of Achilles. Calliope, the muse of epic poetry. Penelope, wife of Ulysses.

1027. 'O woman, famous for this double beauty, remember thy word to thy servant. Thy servant am I.' Cf. Psalm cxix. 49, 125; and see note to l. 1061.

1031. '*Indy* may perhaps be used here for *Indian;* but I believe the expression is equivalent to the *azure blue sapphire;* Skelton, in his Garlande of Laurell, has *saphiris indy blew.* Tyrrwhit has "*Inde*, Fr. azure-coloured" [see Rom. Rose, l. 67], in his Glossary to Chaucer. Cf. "Inde, *ynde;* couleur de bleu foncé, d'azur, *indicum*." Roquefort's Gloss. de la Lang. Rom. . . . Sir John Mandeville says that the beak of the Phœnix "is coloured blew as *ynde*."'—D. Mr. Dyce gives several other examples.

1035. '*Ruddes,* i.e. ruddy tints of the cheek, complexion.'—D.

1048. '*Fret,* not fraught, . . . but wrought, adorned, in allusion to fretwork; so in our author's Garlande of Laurell—"*Fret* all with orient perlys of Garnate."'—D. See *Fretted* in my Gloss. to Piers Plowman (Clar. Press Ser.)

1053. '*Ielofer* is perhaps what we now call gilly-flower; but it was formerly the name for the whole class of carnations, pinks, and sweet-williams. So Graunde Amoure [in Hawes's Pastime of Pleasure] calls La Bell Pucell—

"The gentyll *gyllofer*, the goodly *columbyne*."'—D.

1061. 'Thou hast dealt well with thy servant, O lady, and out of the heart sound thy praises!' This looks like a parody of David's Psalms; and by referring to Ps. cxix. (cxx. in the Vulgate), we observe that the various portions into which the Psalm is divided begin with the verses which Skelton has parodied, both here, and before and after. Thus the portion 'Zain' begins, '*Memor esto verbi tui servo tuo,* in quo mihi spem dedisti;' see above, l. 1029. The same Psalm has *Servus tuus sum ego,* in verse 125. The next portion but one (Teth) begins, '*Bonitatem fecisti cum servo tuo, domine,* secundum verbum tuum.' Again, the next portion but one (Caph) begins, '*Defecit in salutare tuum anima mea,*' &c.; which shows that *salutare tuum,* as in the old edition, is right. Mr. Dyce changes it into *salutatione tua,* in l. 1090. In like manner, the portions named Mem, Samech, Pe, and Koph, begin with passages which are imitated in ll. 1114, 1143, 1168, and 1192.

1081. *Deadly syn,* i. e. the recompense of deadly sin. Skelton uses the phrase elsewhere.

1091. 'My soul hath fainted for thy salvation. What askest thou for thy son, sweetest mother? Oh strange!' The last line is probably a hexameter, but with two false quantities.

1096. *Pastaunce,* a corruption of *passetemps,* pastime.

1097. '*Sad,* i. e. serious, grave, sober; so afterwards, "*sobre,* demure Dyane," l. 1224.'—D. See l. 1250.

1114. 'Oh how I love thy law, O lady! Let old things give place, let all things become new.' See Psalm cxix. 97.

1116. *To amende her tale,* to increase her number, or list, of perfections. *Tale* is used here as in Exod. v. 8.

1117. '*Auale* is generally to let down, to lower; but I know not how to explain the present passage, which appears to be defective.'—D. I take *auale* to be put for *auale herself,* i. e. to condescend. I think the defect only arises from a sudden change of construction; the poet was going to say, 'when she was pleased to condescend, and with her fingers small, &c., *to strain my hand,*' when he suddenly altered it to *wherwyth my hand she strayned.* The sense is clear, though the grammar is at fault. But there is certainly some deficiency in ll. 1124, 1125, which hardly agree.

1125. '*Reclaymed,* a metaphor from falconry. "*Reclaming* is to tame, make gentle, or bring a hawk to familiarity with the man." Latham's Faulconry (Explan. of Words of Art), 1658.'—D.

1143. Ps. cxix. 113. The Vulgate has *Iniquos odio habui,* I hate evil men; but our version has 'I hate vain thoughts.'

1148. *Hert rote,* heart-root, 'ground of the heart.' A common phrase.

1152. Ægeria, the goddess who is said to have instructed Numa Pompilius in religious rites. See Juvenal, iii. 12; Livy, i. 21.

1154-5. Mr. Dyce gives up these two lines as inexplicable. The only way to make some sense of them is to suppose *a* put for *on,* as frequently in Middle English; we may then translate 'Like her image, depicted (as going) with courage on a lover's pilgrimage;' i. e. going to meet Numa. *Emportured* is formed like the word *porturat* in Sect. XIII. l. 67.

1168. Ps. cxix. 129; see the Vulgate (Ps. cxviii).

1169. Ps. cxliv. 12; see the Vulgate (Ps. cxliii).

1192. Ps. cxix. 145; see the Vulgate (Ps. cxviii).

1193. Ps. lxxxvi. 13; lxxxv. 13 in the Vulgate.

1225. *Jane.* Her name was Jane or Johanna Scroupe, and she was probably a boarder at, and educated in, the nunnery at Carow, in the suburbs of Norwich.

1239. Psalm cxxxix. (cxxxviii. in the Vulgate) is known as *Domine, probasti me,* from the first three words in it.

1240. *Shall.* There is no nominative. Possibly, *they* shall sail; the *they* being implied in the preceding *eis.* Yet it looks as if Skelton makes three of the Psalms to be the pilgrims.

1242. St. James of Compostella. 'The body of St. James the Great having, according to the legend, been buried at Compostella in Galicia [Spain], a church was built over it. Pilgrims flocked to the spot; several popes having granted the same indulgences to those who repaired to Compostella, as to those who visited Jerusalem.'—D. See note to Piers the Plowman (Clar. Press. Ser.) Prol. l. 47.

1243. *Pranys*, prawns. *Cranys*, cranes. Skelton suggests contemptuously that all one gets by going to Spain is the opportunity of catching shrimps, &c. The mention of *cranes* is made, perhaps, only for the sake of the rime. But the whole passage is obscure.

1250. *Sadly*, seriously. See l. 1097.

1260. 'For she is worthy.' *Vault* (Lat. *valet*) is now spelt *vaut.*

XV. LORD BERNERS.

(A)   *The Sea-fight off Sluys.*

A SHORT account of this engagement may be found in most histories, See, e.g. Longman's Life and Times of Edward III, cap. ix.; a book to which I shall, for convenience, refer. Mr. Longman says that a full account of the battle is given in Nicolas's British Navy, vol. ii. chap. i. On the 22nd of June, 1340, Edward set sail from Orwell, in Suffolk, with a fleet of 200 vessels. He met with the enemy's fleet near the port of Sluys on the coast of Flanders, at the mouth of the West Scheldt. It is said that the enemy lost about 25,000 men and nearly the whole of the fleet. The battle was fought on Saturday, June 24, 1340, being Midsummer day.

Another translation of this passage from Froissart is given in Strutt, Manners and Customs, ii. 75.

Line 1. *Therle,* the earl. Hainault is now a province of Belgium.

8. *Blanqueberque*, Blankenberg, near Ostend.

11. *Normayns,* &c., men of Normandy, light-armed soldiers, Genoese, and Picards. *Bydaulx* is from the Low Lat. *bidaldus* or *bidardus,* a light-armed soldier. See Roquefort, who says they were armed with lances.

13. *Defend,* forbid, dispute, oppose.

20. *Hampton.* 'Southampton was pillaged and burnt by a body of Normans and Genoese, who landed on a Sunday while the inhabitants

were at mass.' Longman, p. 144. This was either in the end of 1338, or the beginning of 1339.

21. *Chrystofer;* the 'Christopher,' a large ship taken from the English in 1339, but retaken in the battle here described.

25. *& I may,* if I can be.

29. *Batell,* a squadron; common in this sense. See *batayls* below, l. 35.

32. *Gaunt,* Ghent. John of Gaunt was born there, just before this time; see p. 159, l. 115.

57. *Hym,* i.e. the vessel.

58. *Genoweys,* Genoese.

72. *Water,* another spelling of Walter, which was then commonly pronounced *Water.* Hence the abbreviation *Wat,* and the pun in Shakespeare on the name; 2 Hen. VI, iv. 1. 35.

74. *Brasseton;* spelt Bradestan in Johnes's translation.

Chandos; read *Sir [John] Chandos.*

86. *Jaques Dartuell,* Jaques, James, or Jacob van Arteveldt, called 'the brewer of Ghent,' and father to Philip van Arteveldt.

87. *The erle of Heynalt.* 'William, Count of Hainault, Holland, and Zealand, Edward's brother-in-law, who had so chivalrously adhered to Philip's side, when Edward invaded France [in 1339], but had since incurred Philip's anger by accompanying Edward into the Cambresis and Thierasche.' Longman's Edward III, p. 173.

91. *Ardenbourge,* Aardenburg, not far to the south-east of Sluys.

93. *Caryage,* baggage; as in Acts xxi. 15.

94. *Lytell and lytell,* gradually; also *lytlum and lytlum,* as in P. Plowman, B. xv. 599.

95. *Thyne,* according to Johnes, is Thin-l'evêque. It is described in the preceding chapter as being situated on the Scheldt.

97. *Dysloged,* broke up his encampment.

118. *Vyllenort* is a misprint for *Vylleuort,* i.e. Vilvorde, between Brussels and Malines, where Tyndale was imprisoned at a later date. 'When Edward landed in Flanders after defeating the French fleet at Sluys, he went to Ghent, where he held a council, and afterwards went with Van Artevelde to Vilvoorde, to arrange the plan of the intended campaign with his allies.' Longman's Edward III, p. 175.

(B) *The Battle of Crecy.*

This celebrated battle took place on Saturday, Aug. 26, A.D. 1346. The English were at the time in a very critical position.

Line 1. *Batayls,* squadrons, companies.

5. *In maner of a herse*, in a triangular form. On the word *hearse*, Mr. Wedgwood remarks, in his Etymological Dictionary—'The origin is the French *herce*, a harrow, an implement which in that country is made in a triangular form, not square as with us. Hence the name *herce* or *herche* was given to a triangular framework of iron used for holding a number of candles at funerals and church ceremonies. . . . The quantity of candles, being the great distinction of the funeral, the name of the frame which bore them came to be used for the whole funeral obsequies, or for the cenotaph at whose head the candles were placed, and finally for the funeral carriage.'

17. *A six leages*, i.e. a distance of six leagues, about sixteen to eighteen miles.

22. *Alanson*, Alençon, to the south of Caen, and west of Paris.

25. *Clyps*, eclipse; but it only signifies that the sky was darkened. See the description in Longman's Edward III, p. 258.

40. *Holly*, wholly, thickly.

51. *Relyue*, lift themselves up again; see below, l. 100.

53. *Rascalles*, rabble; Johnes says 'some Cornish and Welshmen.'

59. *Behaygne*, Bohemia; it is commonly so called in Early English, and occurs frequently in The Romans of Partenay, ed. Skeat, Early Eng. Text Soc. There is a very early allusion to this incident in Piers the Plowman, B-text (Early Eng. Text Soc.) Pass. xii. 107,—

'And as a blynde man in bataille bereth wepne to fighte.'

The duke's blindness was supposed to have been caused by poison, given to him when engaged in the wars of Italy.—Bonamy, Mém. de l'Académie, vol. xxiii. See Johnes's translation.

85. *Coosted*, went round, or by the side of.

96. *& his page had nat ben*, had it not been for his page. The old and modern English idioms are different.

102. *Broy*, La Broye or La Broyes, a village in Picardy

110. *Almaygnes*, Germans. The French call Germany *Allemagne* still. *Almain* occurs in Othello, ii. 3. 86.

118. *Camfort*: Johnes has 'Stafford.'

131. *I woll this iourney be*, I intend that this day may be.

150. *Ausser*, Auxerre, on the Yonne, south-east of Paris.
Saynt Poule, St. Pol, to the north-west of Arras.

152. *A threscore*, a number amounting to three score; cf. the phrase *a six leages* above; l. 17.
One and other, i.e. one with another, all told.

153. *Remounted ones*, once mounted the king again on a new horse.

158. *In a maner perforce*, in some degree forcibly.

160. *Broy*, La Broye. But this seems to be a mistake, unless there

were two places of the same name; for Froissart has already mentioned La Broye (which he describes as a castle situate on the river Authie) as the place where *Edward* slept on the night but one before the battle.

164. *For this,* &c. This phrase is probably due to a wrong reading. Buchon's edition of Froissart has a phrase of which the English is—'it is the unfortunate king of France.' Mr. Longman says—'in all previously printed editions of Froissart, this phrase is given as *cest la fortune de France,* but Buchon states that he did not find it in that form in any MSS. he examined, besides which he considers it to be in complete contradiction to the circumstances of the day and of the epoch.'

XVI. WILLIAM TYNDALE.

LINE 3. *Oure sprites,* our spiritual advisers; it is clear that *sprite* is here used in the sense of a spiritual teacher or adviser; this interpretation will alone suit the context, which says that the object of these *sprites* is to induce men *to honoure their cerimonies and to offer to their bely,* i.e. to attend their ministrations, and to supply their appetites by payment of mass-pence, &c., as expressed below.

4. *To feare the,* to frighten thee. *Feare* is an active verb frequently, as in Shakespeare, &c. *The* is printed *thee* in the edition of 1572.

11. Ed. 1572 has a comma after *figured,* but none after *Christ.* The meaning is—there was Christ *only* figured, &c. The *commas* are all mine, and may therefore be altered at the reader's pleasure. The slanting strokes, answering to marks of punctuation, are in the original.

14. *With the newe,* i.e. together with the new.

22. *By this meanes,* at this rate. So in l. 267.

24. *The light;* see John viii. 12.

25. *Moyses saith;* see Deut. vi. 4–9; xi. 18–21.

27. *Whette them;* the marginal reading in Deut. vi. 7, answering to *teach them diligently,* is *whet,* or *sharpen.*

35. *Oure Moyseses,* our Moseses, our teachers; cf. Matt. xxiii. 2.

40. *Peter;* see 1 Pet. iii. 15.

43. *In the said chapter;* see Deut. vi. 20.

46. *Then the Ieweses ware,* than were the ceremonies of the Jews. The side-note continues the sentence 'No father can tell his son' and means, 'no, nor [can] Sir John (i.e. the priest) tell his spiritual sons.' *Ner* is bad spelling for *nor,* and is corrected in ed. 1572.

56. *Wordly,* worldly. A common old spelling. It is certainly astonishing how much of the business of the realm was formerly performed by ecclesiastics. Wolsey, for instance, was Lord Chancellor,

Wyclif had said the same as Tyndale long before;—'But our Priests ben so busie about wordlie (*sic*) occupation, that they seemen better Baylifs or Reues, than ghostlie Priests of Jesu Christ.'—Two Treatises against Friars, ed. James, p. 16. This passage from Wyclif is quoted also in my edition of Piers the Plowman (Clar. Press Ser.), note to Prol. l. 95, which see.

58. *But at their assignemente*, but by their direction.

83. *As the pye*, &c., as the pie and parrot speak they know not what. A parrot was also called a *papingo*.

89. *Patter*, repeat over and over again. So in Pierce the Ploughman's Crede, l. 6.

91. *Sherch*, search; see John v. 39.

95. *Sherched*, searched; see Acts xvii. 11.

104. *Christ saith;* Luke xxi. 8.

108. *Agenst-Christ*, an Anglicised form of *Antichrist*.

115. *Christ saith;* Matt. v. 16, 20.

119. *Severall*, separate, different.

141. *One person*, i. e. one man a parson. Ed. 1572 has *one Parson*.

146. *Set in*, introduce, employ in his place.

147. *Dome*, dumb, i. e. inefficacious. Cf. '*dumb* dogs,' Isaiah lvi. 10.

148. *Polleth on his parte*, cheats or robs on his own account.

149. *Masse-peny*, money for saying mass.

Trentall, money for thirty masses.

161. *Saynt hierom*, St. Jerome, who translated the Scriptures into Latin. He died A.D. 420. His translation is known as the Vulgate version.

164. *Not so rude*, not rude in such a degree as that in which they are false liars. This idiomatic sentence is of unsurpassable vigour.

171. *Seke a compasse*, go round about; cf. Acts xxviii. 13.

179. Whether the translation of parts of the Bible into Anglo-Saxon was made by the direction of Ælfred or Æthelstan is uncertain; but Anglo-Saxon MSS. of the Psalms, Gospels, and part of the Old Testament, belonging to the latter part of the tenth century, *still exist*.

185. *Holdeth this doctoure*, i. e. holds *this* doctor's opinion to be correct.

187. *Duns*, Duns Scotus, schoolman; died A.D. 1308.

Thomas, St. Thomas Aquinas, called *the Angelic Doctor;* died A.D. 1274.

Bonaventure, St. Bonaventure, cardinal, called *the Seraphic Doctor;* died A.D. 1274.

188. *Hales*, Alexander Hales, called *the Infallible Doctor;* died A.D. 1245.

Raymonde, St. Raymond de Pegnafort, a Spanish Dominican; died A.D. 1275.

Lyre, Nicolas de Lyra, biblical commentator; died A.D. 1340.

189. *Gorran*, Nicholas de Gorran, French divine; died A.D. 1295.

Hugo, Hugh de St. Victor, divine; died about A.D. 1141. (The foregoing dates are from Hole's Brief Biographical Dictionary.)

210. *Damme*, condemn. *Alowe*, approve.

221. *Yer*, ere, before. St. Augustine of Hippo was born A.D. 354, died A.D. 430: Origen preceded him by nearly two hundred years.

225. *Philautia*, φιλαυτία, means properly *self-love*, or *self-regard*.

226. *Be well sene in*, be well skilled in, have *evident* skill in.

262. *Collosiens;* see Col. ii. 8.

267. *By this meanes*, at this rate; as before, l. 22. This is supposed to be spoken by an objecter.

287. *Meked them and feared them*, made them meek and fearful.

305. *Whome*, home; the pronunciation *whome* is provincial, and heard in many parts of England. Tyndale was born in Gloucestershire.

309. *Benefundatum*, lit. that which is well founded; I suppose it to mean rudiments of logic.

316. *Reall*. The disputes between the Realists and Nominalists were endless. The *Realists* contended that *things* (res), and not names or words (*nomina*), were the true subjects of dialectics. The *Nominalists* said the contrary.

317. *Predicamentes*, classes of ideas, called by the Greeks *categories*, and by the Romans *predicaments;* but I do not pretend to explain all these school terms, which Tyndale justly ridicules. In Milton's 'Vacation Exercise,' written at the age of nineteen, *Ens* is represented as the father of the *Predicaments*, his two sons, whereof the eldest stood for *Substance*, &c. On the whole subject, see Milman, Hist. of Latin Christianity, bk. xiv. c. iii.

318. 'There were three kinds of *Universals*, one abstract, self-existing, one in the object, one in the mind'; note in Milman, Latin Christianity, ed. 1855; vi. 456.

330. *Facions*, fashions, not factions; see *facioneth* below, l. 338.

339. *Of what texte*, by whatever text.

341. *Lymbo patrum;* see Milton, Par. Lost, iii. 495.

342. *Assumpcion;* the Assumption, or taking up into heaven, of the Virgin Mary, is said to have taken place August 15, A.D. 45. The festival was kept on Aug. 15.

344. *Graye frere*, Franciscan; *blacke frere*, Dominican. See notes to Pierce the Ploughman's Crede; p. 357.

369. *John viii.;* i. e. John viii. 25, where Tyndale's translation has

F f

—'And Jesus sayde vnto them, "Even the very same thynge that I saye vnto you."' The next quotation, 'My wordes, &c.,' is from John vi. 63.

373. *cxviij. Psalme.* This probably means Ps. cxix.; see Ps. cxix. 1–5. Psalm cxix. is called cxviii. in the Vulgate version.

386. *Robyn hode.* See, in the Percy Folio MSS., ed. Hales and Furnivall, the 'Robin Hood Ballads;' and the exploits of Sir Bevis of Southampton, in the second book of Drayton's 'Polyolbion.' Hercules, Hector, and Troilus all figure in the old Histories of Troy, which follow Guido de Colonna rather than Homer.

391. *Paul.* See Eph. v. 3–5; also verse 6.

405. *Erasmus*, born at Rotterdam, October 28, 1467; died at Basel, July 12, 1536. A complete edition of his works was printed in 1703–1706; in vol. v. (p. 138) is the piece entitled 'Desiderii Erasmi Roterodami Paraclesis, id est, adhortatio ad Christianiae philosophiae studium.' Near the beginning of vol. vi. is his 'In Annotationes Novi Testamenti praefatio, primae editionis, quae fuit An. M.D.xv., cui tamen post admixta sunt quaedam,' &c.

XVII. SIR THOMAS MORE.

(A) (B) *A Dialogue concerning Heresies.*

'It is a remarkable and important fact, that the style which Wycliffe himself employs in his controversial and other original works, is a very different one from that in which he clothed his translation. This circumstance seems to give some countenance to the declaration of Sir Thomas More, otherwise improbable, that there existed English Bibles long before Wycliffe; and hence we might suppose that his labours, and those of his school, were confined to the revision of still earlier versions. But although English paraphrases, mostly metrical, of different parts of the Bible were executed at the very commencement of our literature, yet there is no sufficient ground to believe that there were any prose translations of such extent and fidelity as to serve for a basis of revision; and the oldest known complete translation of the Old Testament, the earlier text in the late Oxford edition of the Wycliffe versions, has very much the aspect of a first essay.'—Marsh's Lectures, published in the 'Student's Manual of English Language,' ed. Smith, p. 446. The simplest solution of the difficulty is to suppose that Sir Thomas More had actually seen some copies of the Anglo-Saxon Gospels or Psalters; these he would of course call *englishe,* as they should be called; and he may have made the mistake of supposing the MSS. to contain the whole Bible. In any case, he exaggerates the truth. Observe how he says (Extract C, p. 189) that 'the cleargie therein agreed that the englyshe bybles should remayne which were translated afore Wickliffes dayes.' This they would easily have consented to, supposing them to be Anglo-Saxon MSS., because they were well aware that scarcely any one could read them.

(C) *From the same.*

Line 46. *Lay,* i. e. lay it down, agree about it; cf. 'reason *layd,*' l. 1.

61. *As nothynge coulde elles,* as knew nothing else.

110. *Dydde not let to speake,* did not hinder or refrain themselves from speaking.

111. *Yet letteth all thys nothing,* yet all this nowise prevents.

134. *Lapis offensionis,* &c.; so in the Vulgate, 1 Pet. ii. 8.

148. *More eth,* easier; from A.S. *eáð,* easy.

151. *To set all on a flushe at ones,* to flood (men) all at once; a metaphor from the sudden opening wide of floodgates.

164. *Sad,* discreet, steady, settled.

176. *Quod your frend,* says your friend to me. This is as if he were writing a letter to a person whose friend is present with him. See the concluding words of the extract.

182. *X. li.,* i. e. *decem libræ,* ten pounds. Twenty marks would amount to a little more, viz. to about 13*l.* 6*s.* 8*d.*, reckoning a mark at 13*s.* 4*d.*

193. *For,* probably for *fore,* an abbreviation of *before. For god* answers to the older English *parde,* which is so plentifully sprinkled over the works of our old authors. It was probably a mere expletive, to which little meaning was really attached.

200. *To kepe a quotlibet,* &c. A *quotlibet* or *quodlibet* means *what you please,* and I take the phrase *to kepe a quotlibet upon* to mean 'to sit upon whilst discoursing about what you please;' or, as we should say, 'whilst talking about things in general.' It is certainly odd that men should choose a big book to sit upon, but this is distinctly asserted below. A *pot parliament* is probably a talk in which the speakers are assisted by something to drink.

275. *For his sadnes,* on account of his discreet and careful behaviour; so *for his wantonness* means on account of his carelessness.

For cutting, for fear of cutting. This use of *for* is common in Mid. English. Cf. 'for catching cold' in Two Gent. of Verona, i. 2. 136.

287. *Pistle,* epistle. Unless More here refers to some subsequent

letter, he must mean the book entitled ' Assertio Septem Sacramentorum adversus Martinum Luterum,' of which the first edition was printed in London, 1521, and the second at Antwerp, in 1522. It was drawn up in Henry's own name by his chaplain, Edward Lee. Luther replied to it in violent terms. 'Two years ago (he says) I published a little book called, The Captivity of the Church in Babylon. It horribly vexed and confounded the papists, who spared neither lies nor invective in replying to it ... And now, quite recently, the lord Henry, not by the grace of God king of England, has written in Latin against my treatise. There are some who believe that this pamphlet of the king's did not emanate from the king's own pen; but whether Henry wrote it, or Hal, or the devil in hell, is nothing to the point. He who lies is a liar; and I fear him not, be he who he may. This is my own notion about the matter: that Henry gave out an ell or two of coarse cloth, and that then this pituitous Thomist, Lee, this follower of the Thomist herd, who, in his presumption, wrote against Erasmus, took scissors and needle and made a cape of it,' &c. Life of Luther, by M. Michelet; translated by W. Hazlitt, 1846; p. 123.

(D) *From the 'Confutacioun of Tyndale.'*

9. *Thys is*, &c. The passage is thus printed in Dr. Bosworth's edition of the Mœso-Gothic, Anglo-Saxon, Wyclif, and Tyndale Gospels :—' And this is the recorde off Jhon, when the Iewes sent prestes and levites from Jerusalem, to axe hym, What arte thou? And he confessed, and denyed nott, and sayde playnly, I am nott Christ. And they axed hym, What then? arte thou Helias? And he sayde, I am nott. Arte thou a prophet? And he answered, Noo.' S. John i. 19–21.

15. *I woulde not.* This must be taken along with the word *sauing* following. It means ' I would not draw attention to this, &c. except to shew you,' &c.

19. *The tone*, a corruption of *that one*, i.e. the one; just as *the tother* is for *that other*. *That* was used as the neuter of the definite article by our oldest writers.

22. *No aunswereth*, &c. Here *No* should be *Nay*, as is easily seen by the context. See a long and exhaustive note upon this subject, and upon this very passage, in Marsh's Lectures (Lect. xxvi.) printed in the Student's Manual of the English Language, ed. Smith, pp. 414, 415, and 422–425.

XVIII. SIR THOMAS ELYOT.

From ‘ *The Governour.*’

Cap. XVII. The preceding (sixteenth) Chapter also has some in·teresting remarks upon the exercises then most in use. It agrees tolerably closely with a passage in The Castle of Health, by the same author, which may be found in Chambers’ Encyclopædia of English Literature, vol. i. p. 70. A modernised edition of The Governour was printed at Newcastle in 1834, edited by A. T. Eliot.

12. *Galene.* Claudius Galenus, the celebrated physician, born at Pergamum A.D. 130, died about A.D. 200 ; author of at least eighty-three treatises on medical and philosophical subjects.

20. *Epaminondas,* the celebrated Theban general and statesman, slain at the moment of victory at Mantinea, B.C. 362. The praise here given to him for his running should rather have been given to Pelopidas. ‘ Both seemed equally fitted by nature for all sorts of excellence ; but bodily exercises chiefly delighted Pelopidas, learning Epaminondas ; and the one spent his hours in hunting and the Palæstra, the other in hearing lectures or philosophizing.’ Plutarch’s Lives (Life of Pelopidas), ed. A. H. Clough, vol. ii. p. 204.

34. *Swifte-foote Achilles ;* alluding to Homer’s frequent phrase πόδας ὠκὺς ’Αχιλλεύς. See also the description of the funeral games in honour of Patroclus in the Iliad, bk. xxiii.

Alexander. ‘ When he was asked by some one about him, whether he would run a race in the Olympic games, as he was very swift-footed, he answered, he would, if he might have kings to run with him.’ Plutarch’s Lives, ed. A. H. Clough, vol. iv. p. 163.

45. *Lucius Papirius Cursor.* There were two Roman generals of this name, father and son, distinguished in the second and third Samnite wars respectively. It is very probable that the first of the Papiria gens who was named Cursor did actually obtain it from being distinguished in running, but it is by no means certain that the elder Lucius was the man.

47. *Marius* died on the eighteenth day of his seventh consulship, in his seventy-first year. He therefore never attained to the age of ‘ four-score’ years, nor was there ever a time when he had seven times *completed* his years of consulship. For other examples of bodily strength and swiftness, see Pliny, lib. vii. cap. xx.

74. *Pirries,* storms of wind, gusts. In a Pageant printed in T. Sharp’s Dissertation on Pageants, p. 90, a shepherd is made to say—‘ E l freyndis ! þer cam a *pyrie* of wynd with a myst suddenly.’

80. *Oratius.* The story of Horatius Cocles (i. e. the one-eyed) is popularly known amongst us from Macaulay's 'Lays of Ancient Rome.' It is told by Livy, Dionysius of Halicarnassus, and Polybius; but the last of these makes Horatius to have perished in the stream. The Sublician bridge is supposed to have been beneath the Mons Aventinus.

83. *Remembred,* called to mind, mentioned. Elyot had mentioned Tarquin in Book i. cap. 2 of his book.

102. *Cesar.* The story of Cæsar's escape at the battle near the Pharus (a small island in the bay of Alexandria, connected with the mainland by a mole) is told by Plutarch and Dion Cassius. See Plutarch's Select Lives, translated by G. Long; Life of Cæsar, ch. xlix. and the notes; also Plutarch's Lives, ed. A. H. Clough, vol. iv. p. 408.

116. *Sertorius.* 'Now, first of all, after the Cimbri and Teutones had invaded Gaul, he was serving under Cæpio [not *Scipio*] at the time when the Romans were defeated and put to flight [B.C. 105]; and though he lost his horse and was wounded in the body, he crossed the Rhone swimming in his cuirass and with his shield against the powerful stream—so strong was his body and disciplined by exercise.' Plutarch's Select Lives, translated by G. Long; Life of Sertorius, ch. iii.

128. *Alexander.* This story is told by Plutarch. 'At another time, seeing his men march slowly and unwillingly to the siege of the place called Nysa, because of a deep river between them and the town, he advanced before them, and standing upon the bank, "What a miserable man," said he, "am I, that I have not learned to swim!" and then was hardly dissuaded from endeavouring to pass it upon his shield.' Plutarch's Lives, ed. A. H. Clough, vol. iv. 234. Observe that Plutarch merely says that Alexander *wished* to cross the river.

158. *Luctatius.* This name is more commonly spelt Lutatius. The allusion is to C. Lutatius Catulus, consul in B.C. 242, the last year of the first Punic war. The great sea-fight which terminated this war was gained by the Romans on the 10th of March, B.C. 241. Sixty-three Carthaginian vessels were taken, and a hundred and twenty sunk.

184. *Bucephal.* After Alexander had defeated the Indian king Porus, he founded two towns, one on each bank of the Hydaspes; one called Bucephala, in honour of his horse Bucephalus, who died there, and the other Nicæa, in honour of his victory. The whole passage is taken from Pliny, lib. viii. cap. xlii. In Philemon Holland's translation of 'Plinies Naturall Historie,' it stands thus:—'The same *Alexander* the Great, of whom erewhile wee spake, had a very straunge and rare horse, whom men called Bucephalus, either for his crabbed and grim looke, or else of the marke or brand of a buls head, which was imprinted upon his shoulder. It is reported that *Alexander*, being but a child, seeing

this fair horse, was in love with him, and bought him out of the breed and race of *Philonicus* the Pharsalian, and for him paied sixteene talents. He would suffer no man to sit him, nor come upon his backe, but Alexander; and namely, when hee had the kings saddle on, and was also trapped with roiall furniture; for otherwise hee would admit any whomsoever. The same horse was of a passing good and memorable service in the warres; and namely, being wounded upon a time at the assault of Thebes, he would not suffer *Alexander* to alight from his backe, and mount upon another. Many other strange and wonderfull things hee did: in regard whereof, when he was dead, the king solemnized his funerals most sumptuously: erected a tombe for him, and about it built a citie that bare his name, Bucephalia. *Cæsar* Dictatour likewise had another horse, that would suffer no man to ride him but his maister; and the same horse had his forefeet resembling those of a man: and in that manner standeth he pourtraied before the temple of *Venus* Mother.' Butler, in his Hudibras, i. 1. 433, cleverly ridicules this story in the lines about

> ' Cæsar's horse, who, as fame goes,   .
> Had corns upon his feet and toes.'

210. *Arundell.* It is perhaps needless to say that Arundel Castle was connected with the legend of Sir Bevis of Southampton and his horse Arundel solely because of the similarity of the names. The exploits of Sir Bevis are narrated in the second book of Drayton's Polyolbion.

.

Chap. XVIII. 21. *A garlande, &c.* This is well illustrated by act iv. sc. 2. of As You Like It :—

'*Jaques.* Which is he that killed the deer?

A Lord. Sir, it was I.

Jaques. Let's present him to the Duke like a Roman conqueror,' &c.

47. *Plinius.* The reference is wrong; it should be to lib. x. cap. viii. The passage is thus translated by Holland :—'In a part of Thracia, somwhat higher in the countrey beyond Amphipolis, men and hawkes join in fellowship and catch birds together : for the men drive the woods, beat the bushes and reeds to spring the foule; then the hawks flying over their heads, seize upon them, and either strike or bear them to the ground fit for the hands. On the other side, the hawkers and foulers when they have caught the foule, divide the bootie with the hawkes; and by report, they let such birds flie again at libertie aloft into the aire, and then are the hawkes readie to catch for themselves. Moreover, when the time is of hawking, they will by their manner of crie and flying together, give signe to the faulconers that there

is good game abroad, and so draw them forth to hawking for to take
the opportunitie.'

75. *Coknayes*, pets. 'The original meaning of *cockney* is a child too
tenderly or delicately nurtured, one kept in the house and not hardened
by out-of-doors life; hence applied to citizens as opposed to the hardier
inhabitants of the country, and in modern times confined to the inhabitants of London. The Promptorium Parvulorum, and the authorities cited
in Mr. Way's notes, give "*Coknay*, carifotus, delicius, mammotrophus."
"To bring up like a *cocknaye, mignoter*." "Delicias facere, to play the
cockney." Cf. "Puer in deliciis matris nutritus, Anglice a *cokenay*;"
Halliwell. "*Cockney*, niais, mignot;" Sherwood.' I altogether dissent
from Mr. Wedgwood's connection of this word with the verb to *cocker*,
though I agree with his explanation, which I have just quoted. The
M. E. form is *cokeney*, which seems to me to answer to an O. F.
*coquiné, Low Lat. **coquinatus*, i.e. brought up or attached to a kitchen.
Cf. F. *coquin.*

XIX. LORD SURREY.

(A) *From his translation of the Æneid.*

'Surrey was not merely the poet of idleness and gallantry. He was
fitted, both from nature and study, for the more solid and laborious
parts of literature. He translated the second and fourth book of Virgil
into blank verse; and it seems probable, that his active situations of life
prevented him from completing a design of translating the whole Eneid.
This is the first composition in blank verse, extant in the English language. Nor has it merely the relative and accidental merit of being a
curiosity. It is executed with great fidelity, yet not with a prosaic ser-
vility. The diction is often poetical, and the versification varied with
proper pauses.'—Warton.

Roger Ascham, in the second book of his 'Scholemaster,' says :—
'The noble lord Th' Earle of Surrey, first of all English men, in
translating the fourth booke of Virgill, and Gonsaluo Periz that excellent learned man, and Secretarie to kyng Philip of Spaine, in translating
the Vlisses of Homer out of Greke into Spanish, haue both, by good
iudgement, auoyded the fault of Ryming, yet neither of them hath fullie
hit[t]e perfite and trew versifying. Indeed, they obserue iust numbers,
and euen feete: but here is the fault, that their feete be feete without
ioyntes, that is to say, not distinct by trew quantite of sillabes: And so,
soch feete be but numme feete; and be euen as vnfitte for a verse to

turne and runne roundly withall, as feete of brass or wood be vnweeldie to go well withall,' &c.; Arber's Reprint, p. 147.

Mr. Craik thinks that Surrey's translation was suggested by the earliest Italian example of blank verse, viz. a 'translation of the First and Fourth Books of the Æneid, by the Cardinal Hippolito di Medici, or as some say, by Molza, which was published at Venice in 1541.' It also seems probable that Surrey was in some degree indebted to the translation made by Gawin Douglas. See also Warton, Hist. Eng. Poetry, ed. 1840, vol. iii. p. 39; ed. 1871, iv. 38.

Line 253. The portion of Surrey's translation here printed begins at l. 199 of Virgil's second Book—

'Hic aliud maius miseris multoque tremendum.'

254. *Vnarmed,* Lat. 'improuida.' Professor Conington translates it by *unprophetic* in his verse translation, third ed. p. 43. But it is no part of my purpose to remark upon the accuracy or inaccuracy of the translation, since the original is sufficiently accessible.

255. *Laocon,* Laocoön. He was a son of Antenor (some say of Priam), and a priest of Apollo, or, according to others (including Virgil), of Poseidon, i. e. Neptune. In l. 269 below, Surrey spells the name *Lacon.* In the passage preceding our extract, Virgil relates how Laocoön hurled his spear into the side of the wooden horse, and thus very nearly revealed the secret of it, which would have saved Troy. Laocoön's death is then here related. The group of Laocoön and his two sons writhing within the folds of two enormous serpents, is well known as one of the master-pieces of ancient art, and is the subject of the German poet Lessing's prose work entitled 'Laokoön.' In was executed by Agesander of Rhodes and two other sculptors, as related by Pliny (xxxvi. 5). It originally decorated the baths of Titus, among the ruins of which it was found in the year 1506. It is now preserved in the museum of the Vatican at Rome. See the account in the English Cyclopædia (Div. Arts and Sciences, s. v. Laocoön).

258. *Tenedon,* Tenedos; an island off the coast of Troas. The form *Tenedon* is a striking instance of the common use of accusative forms; see note to Sect. XXII. 4506, and remarks in the Preface, § 16.

259. *Fletyng,* floating; Lat. 'incumbunt pelago.'

265. *Gate the strand,* attained the shore; Lat. 'arua tenebant.'

267. *Waltring,* rolling; Lat. 'linguis uibrantibus.'

269. *Gate direct,* direct path; Lat. 'agmine certo.'

282. *Fourth loowes,* lows forth, bellows out.

285. *Twaine,* misprinted *twine* in the old copy; Lat. 'gemini.'

287. *Which,* whom; Lat. 'sub pedibusque Deae.'

291. *Hainous dede,* odious act, viz. his piercing of the wooden horse; Lat. 'scelus.'

295. *Tappease,* to appease; see other instances in the Glossary.

298. *Rolles,* i. e. rollers.

301. *Children and maides,* boys and girls. See Warton's note.

Holly, holy, Lat. 'sacra canunt.'

304. *To* and *ward* are here separated; *toward* is meant. This separation or tmesis is common in Early English. See Chaucer, Clerkes Prol. 51. Cf. 'to the mercy-seatward,' Exod. xxxvii. 9.

307. *Thentrie,* the entry.

308. *Harnesse,* armour.

310. *Perséuer.* So in Shakespeare, Mids. Night's Dr. iii. 2. 237; &c.

313. 'Unclosed again her lips, that were those of a prophet, yet never believed by us.' Insert a comma after *lippes.*

317. Lat. 'Uertitur interea caelum.'

329. *Vnpind,* unpinned, loosened; Lat. 'laxat.'

333. *Thesander,* Tisandrus. Surrey omits the name of Neoptolemus, and writes *Menolae* and *Opeas* for Menelaus and Epeos.

347. *Be,* been. This is by no means a solitary instance of *be,* as a past participle. So also *broke, spoke,* for *broken, spoken.*

350. *What one,* what a being! Lat. 'qualis erat!'

359. *Thine,* i. e. thy nation.

'O lux Dardaniae! spes O fidissima Teucrûm!'

364. *Alweried,* utterly wearied, with reference to *we;* Lat. 'defessi.'

372. *Troye;* pronounced as a dissyllable, as in l. 374.

576. *Engines,* contrivances; accented on the latter syllable.

581. *Thembatel,* for *the embatel,* i. e. the battlement; Lat. 'fastigia.'

593. *Trade,* thoroughfare; lit. a *trodden* path; see Rich. II, iii. 3. 156.

640. *The closures ne kepers,* neither the bars nor the guards.

642. *Remoued,* started; used intransitively, as often elsewhere.

649. *Coates,* sheepcotes.

650. *Of slaughter,* with slaughter; Lat. 'furentem caede.'

665. *Thold,* The old.

Did on, put on, donned.

721. *Neoptolem,* &c.; Neoptolemus (i. e. Pyrrhus) has swerved from his natural disposition.

(B) *The Restless State of a Lover.*

With respect to the poems of Surrey and Wiat, the following remarks are made by Puttenham, in the 'Arte of English Poesie,' first printed in 1589. 'In the latter end of the same kings raigne [Henry VIII] sprong vp a new company of courtly makers, of whom Sir Thomas Wyat th' elder and Henry Earle of Surrey were the two chieftaines, who hauing trauailed into Italie, and there tasted the sweete and stately measures and stile of the Italian Poesie, as nouices newly crept out of the schooles of Dante, Arioste, and Petrarch, they greatly pollished our rude and homely maner of vulgar Poesie from that it had bene before, and for that cause may iustly be sayd the first reformers of our English meetre and stile.'—Arber's reprint, p. 74. This poem is in the metre called terza rima; see note to Wiat's Satires, p. 446.

14. *Reduceth,* brings again.
   Returne, return to former vigour.
18. *At hand,* when near.
19. *Time list,* lit. it pleases time; but used for *time pleases.*
24. *Against all others vse,* contrary to the custom of all others.
37. 'That, whilst appearing slack, ever most knits together.'
40. 'For if I sometimes have found that which I sought, viz. those stars by which I trusted to reach the port.'
43. *As,* as if; *as* is short for *al-so,* wholly so.
   Sprites, spirits.
48. *Whiche,* &c.; which recovers its power through the haste of my flight.
49. *Plaine,* complain.
50. *Carefull,* melancholy, sad.
51. Strictly, this line ought to rime to *fill,* but Surrey wished to make a complete set of three rimes (*tene, grene, sene*) at the end of the poem.

(C) *Description of Spring.*

This is one of the finest sonnets in the language.
6. The hart hath shed his horns. Cf. Ovid, Art. Amat. iii. 77, 78.
8. *Flete,* float or swim; see extract A, l. 259; p. 206.

(D) *A Complaint, &c.*

4. *Chare,* chariot. An allusion to the apparent revolution of the heavens.
11. *By and by,* immediately afterwards. Cf. Matt. xiii. 21; Luke xxi. 9.

(E) *Vow to loue faithfully.*

Imitated from Horace, Carminum lib. i. 22—
> 'Pone me, pigris ubi nulla campis,' &c.

(F) *Imprisonment in Windsor.*

The metre resembles that of Gray's Elegy. According to Warton, Surrey was imprisoned in Windsor Castle in 1543 for eating flesh in Lent, the prohibition concerning which had been renewed or strengthened by a recent proclamation of the king. Observe that the first forty lines form one long sentence.

1. 'What prison could be so miserable as the stately castle of Windsor?' Price, on Warton.

2. *Lust,* pleasure.

3. *Kinges sonne.* 'While a boy, he [Surrey] was habituated to the modes of a court at Windsor Castle; where he resided, yet under the care of proper instructors, in the quality of a companion to Henry Fitzroy, Duke of Richmond, a natural son of King Henry the Eighth, and of the highest expectations.' Warton, Hist. E. P. iii. 22, ed. 1840. Warton adds that Richmond married the Lady Mary Howard, Surrey's sister, but died in the year 1536, aged only seventeen.

4. Cf. Homer, Il. xxiv. 261—
> 'Whose days the *feast* and wanton dance employ.'
>
> Pope's translation.

7. *Maydens tower,* maiden-tower. Warton says—'The *maiden-tower* was common in other castles, and means the principal tower, of the greatest strength and defence.... The old Roman camp near Dorchester in Dorsetshire, a noble work, is called *Maiden Castle,* the capital fortress in those parts. We have Maiden Down in Somersetshire with the same signification.' He adds that a strong bastion in the old walls of the city of Oxford was likewise called the *Maiden-tower.* Ritson cites the instance of the Maiden Castle at Edinburgh. Warton would derive the word from the French *magne,* great; but Ritson, with greater plausibility, suggests that '*Mai dun* are two ancient British words signifying a *great hill.*' Cf. Gaelic *maith,* good, strong; Welsh *maith,* ample: also Gaelic *dun,* a hill, a fortress, Welsh *din,* a hill-fort. Nares, however, explains the *maiden-tower* as one that has never been taken, and shews that French writers call such a fort *La Pucelle.*

11. *Coulde but rewe,* could only pity (and not scorn).

13. *Palme-play*, hand-ball, the modern fives. The French *jeu de paume* now means tennis, but must once have meant hand-ball.

Dispoyled, stripped ; imitated from the Italian *spogliato.*

14. 'We, with eyes often dazed by loving glances ;' a curiously involved line. *We*, throughout the poem, means himself and Richmond.

16. 'To allure the eyes of her who stood upon the leads above us.' The ladies used to watch the players from the leads above.

17. *Grauell-grounde*, the area or arena, strewn with gravel, where the young knights practised tilting.

Sleues ; this tying of a lady's sleeve upon the helmet was a common practice. See Tennyson's Elaine, where Elaine gives Lancelot a red sleeve broidered with pearls, and Lancelot binds it on his helmet.

21. Having mentioned the palm-play and the gravel-ground, the poet now mentions the meadow where he joined in athletic sports ; and he speaks of it as sprinkled with dew-drops, that looked like tears shed in pity. This stanza (ll. 21–24) Warton omits to quote.

29. *Clothed holtes with grene*, groves clad in green. This inversion of the order of words is common where the preposition *with* is concerned. In his sonnet entitled 'Descripcion of the restlesse state of a louer,' Surrey has the line—

'My specled chekes with Cupides hewe,'

i.e. my cheeks speckled, &c. See Tottell's Miscellany, reprinted by Arber, p. 5.

30. *Auailed*, lowered, let drop, loosened ; used by Spenser ; also spelt *uailed* or *ualed.*

33. *Walles* is surely the true reading, as in l. 47. See Park's note on Warton.

44. *Vpsupped.* Ashby remarks, 'how can sighs sup up tears ?' The word is not well chosen.

46. *Accompt*, account. *Fere*, companion ; i. e. Richmond.

47. For *doest*, says Warton, we must read *didst.* This seems nearly certain, for Richmond was now dead. Yet, after all, there may be an allusion to his seeing him every night in his dreams.

48. 'Dear to others, but dearest of all to me.'

54. 'He closes his complaint with an affecting and pathetic sentiment, much in the style of Petrarch :—To banish the miseries of my present distress, I am forced on the wretched expedient of remembering a greater. This is the consolation of a warm fancy. It is the philosophy of poetry.'—Warton. Cf. Faerie Queene, i. 6. 37.

XX. SIR THOMAS WIAT.

The metre of Wiat's Satires should be noticed. It is the *terza rima,* in which the lines rime alternately by threes. This is the metre of Dante's Divina Commedia, and was adopted by Lord Byron in his poem entitled the Prophecy of Dante. In his preface to this, Lord Byron says:—'The measure adopted is the terza rima of Dante, which I am not aware to have seen hitherto tried in our language, except it may be by Mr. Hayley, of whose translation I never saw but one extract, quoted in the notes to Caliph Vathek; so that—if I do not err—this poem may be considered as a metrical experiment.' From this it appears that Lord Byron was unaware of, or had forgotten, the three satires here printed. Shelley's 'Prince Athanase' is also in this metre.

After some reflections on Wiat's poems, Warton adds:—'But Wyat appears a much more pleasing writer when he moralises on the felicities of retirement, and attacks the vanities and vices of a court, with the honest indignation of an independent philosopher, and the freedom and pleasantry of Horace. Three of his poetical epistles are professedly written in this strain, two to John Poines[1], and the other to Sir Francis Bryan; and we must regret that he has not left more pieces in a style of composition for which he seems to have been eminently qualified.'— Warton, Hist. Eng. Poetry, ed. 1840, iii. 46; ed. 1871, iv. 45.

(A) *Of the meane and sure estate.*

Of the first of these satires Warton says:—'In another epistle to John Poines, on the security and happiness of a moderate fortune, he versifies the fable of the City and Country Mouse with much humour. This fable appositely suggests a train of sensible and pointed observa- tions on the weakness of human conduct, and the delusive plans of life.' —Hist. Eng. Poetry, iii. 48. It may be observed that the fable of the mice is told by Horace, Sermonum Liber ii. Sat. vi. ll. 79–117; and also exceedingly well by the Scottish poet Robert Henryson; see Morley's Shorter Eng. Poems, p. 77; and Chambers's Encycl. Eng. Literature, i. 47. A curious Latin prose version of the same fable is printed in Reliquiæ Antiquæ, ed. Halliwell and Wright, i. 320.

Line 3. *Liuelod,* livelihood, means of subsistence; see the Glossary.

---

[1] He seems to have been a person about the court. See 'Life of Sir Thomas Pope,' p. 46. (Warton's note.)

31. *At this iourney:* she makes but a jest of the journey, thinks lightly of the trouble of going there.

42. *Pepe.* This seems to be like our modern 'Peep, bo!' It was said shrilly, to startle the other mouse playfully.

48. *As it fell to purpose,* as it happened suitably, at fitting times.

53. *Stemyng,* gleaming. Compare

> 'Of hise mouth it stod a *stem*
> Als it were a sunnebeam.'

'Out of his mouth there stood a *gleam,* like a sunbeam.' Havelok the Dane; ed. Skeat, l. 591. So, too, in the Promptorium Parvulorum, we find—'*Steem,* or lowe of fyre: *Flamma;*' and again, '*Stemyn,* or lowyn vp: *Flammo.*'

54. The insertion of *two* improves the metre.

58. Imitated from Chaucer:—

> 'For naturelly a beest desireth flee
> Fro his contrarie, if he may it see,
> Though he never er had seyn it with his ye [*eye*].'
>
> Nonne Prestes Tale, l. 459.

In fact, Wiat has, throughout these satires, much of Chaucer's manner.

78. *Sergeant with mace.* Wiat is thinking of the Roman *consularis lictor,* as the passage is clearly imitated from Horace:—

> 'Non enim gazas neque consularis
> Submovet lictor miseros tumultus
> Mentis, et curas laqueata circum
> Tecta uolantes.' Carm. ii. 16.

A *hawbart* is a halberd, which was a lance fitted at the end with a small battle-axe.

86. The words *bryers, riuers, desire,* form but an imperfect leash of rimes. Warton proposes to read *breeres* (which is certainly a commoner old spelling), in order to rime with *riuères;* but this does not tell us what to do with *desire.* The readings *on brere* and *on riuere* would be still better; but poets are not immaculate. See Extract C. 20.

88. *Haye for conies,* snare for rabbits.

97. Cf. 'nec te quaesiueris extra;' Persius, Sat. i. 7.

100. *Madde,* i.e. ye mad ones; he here addresses men's *wretched mindes;* see l. 75.

Continue; accented on the *first* syllable, as in Sect. X. l. 10. The sentence means—'Mad ones, if ye wish to keep your disease, let the present pass, and gape after the future, and so sink yourselves still deeper in toil.' Cf. l. 91.

103. *All and summe,* the whole matter (collectively and particularly); a phrase used by Chaucer, Wif of Bathes Prol. l. 91.

105. A word is clearly wanting here; I supply *bow* because it is monosyllabic; but the context rather requires *be answerable to, be responsible to.*

108. *Vertue.* 'These Platonic doctrines are closed with a beautiful application of Virtue personified, and introduced in her irresistible charms of visible beauty.'—Warton. 'Compare

"Uirtutem uideant, intabescantque relictâ."

Persius, Sat. iii.

If Surrey copies but little, Wyat doth plentifully.'—Ashby's note, in Warton. Cf. Dryden's translation of the Third Satire of Persius, l. 69.

112. *Freate inward*, fret inwardly, grieve. See last note.

(B) *Of the Courtier's life.*

This Satire 'is a free version from the Florentine poet Luigi Alemanni, who lived and wrote in Wyatt's time, and was only about eight years his senior;' Shorter Eng. Poems, ed. Morley, p. 153.

3. *Prease*, press, crowd. So in Chaucer's 'Good Counseil'—

' *Fle fro the pres*, and duell with sothfastnesse.'

6. 'Learning to set a limit to will and pleasure.'

9. *Of ryght*, with justice, legally.

15. *Me list not*, it is not my pleasure.

To report blame by honour, to speak disparagingly concerning honour. Warton explains it by 'to speak favourably of which is bad,' which is obviously quite wrong.

19. *Tune;* Warton suggests the reading *tongue*, but, in my opinion, unnecessarily. In one of Wiat's songs, he says—

' Blame not my *lute*, for he must *sound*
Of this or that, *as liketh me.*'

24. *Of them*, concerning them.

32. *Pleasure;* a very bad rime to *coffer* and *offer.*

37. *Alowe*, applaud.

38. *Damne*, condemn; see note to Sect. XVI. 210, p. 433.

39. *Out of the gate*, out of the way.

40. *Liuye.* I do not know why he refers us to Livy; since, of the 114th book of Livy, which spoke of Cato's death, only an epitome, or table of contents, has come down to us, the book itself being lost. He should rather have referred us to Plutarch. The story of Cato stabbing himself at Utica (whence his surname Uticensis) is well known; see e.g. North's translation of Plutarch, ed. 1612, p. 797. In Addison's play of 'Cato' may be founded the once famous soliloquy which commences—

' It must be so; Plato, thou reasonest well.'

After spending the greater part of a night in reading Plato's Phædo, Cato stabbed himself in the breast, and soon after expired, at the age of forty-nine, B.C. 46.

42. *Apply*, apply itself to, devote itself to.

45. *The most*, i. e. the most cowardly.

47. *For honger*, through avarice.

50. *Syr Topas*, i. e. the Tale of Sir Thopas, by Chaucer. So in the next line, *the story that the knight tolde*, in Chaucer's Knightes Tale, concerning Palamon and Arcite. Wiat says he cannot praise the former, nor blame the latter. He shews his good taste. Chaucer himself only tells the 'Tale of Sir Thopas' in order to ridicule the style of it.

62. See note to Sat. i. l. 48, p. 447.

67. *Fauell*, Flattery. *Fauell* is the impersonation of Flattery or Cajolery, and is so used by Langley or Langland (Piers the Plowm. B. ii. 6), by Occleve (De Regimine Principum, ed. Wright, pp. 106 and 111), and by Skelton (ed. Dyce, i. 35).

74, 75. Line 74 we must scan thus:—The létcher á louér, &c. In l. 75, I take the liberty of inserting *trew*, to make up ten syllables.

80. 'The poet's execration of flatterers and courtiers is contrasted with the following entertaining picture of his own private life and rural enjoyments at Allington castle, in Kent.'—Warton. See l. 100.

86. *A clogge.* 'Probably he alludes to some office which he still held at court; and which sometimes recalled him, but not too frequently, from the country.'—Warton.

94. *Flaunders chere*, i. e. drunkenness and debauchery.

Lettes, hinders.

(C) *How to use the court, &c.*

Line 4. 'A rolling stone gathers no moss.' In Latin, 'Saxum uolutum non obducitur musco.' In Greek, Λίθος κυλινδόμενος τὸ φῦκος οὐ ποιεῖ. In Italian, 'Pietra mossa non fa muschio:' or, 'Pietra che rotola non piglia ruggine.' In French, 'La pierre souvent remuée n'amasse pas volontiers mousse.' To which is parallel that of Quintus Fabius—'Planta quae saepius transfertur non coalescit;' a plant often removed cannot thrive. See Ray's Proverbs, ed. 1737. A similar proverb occurs in Piers the Plowman, A-text, Pass. x. l. 101.

'Selden moseth the marbel-ston that men ofte treden;'

i. e. seldom the marble-stone becomes mossy, that men often tread upon.

18. *Grones;* so, to rime with *bones* and *nones*. Formerly, plural verbs frequently ended in *es* or *s*; in fact, *-es* or *-is* was the regular

G g

present plural ending in the Northern dialect. But,' *besides* this, the Elizabethan dramatists and others did actually use the singular form instead of the plural, *when a singular noun or pronoun was near at hand.*

20. Wiat's double or feminine rimes are poor; he here rimes *manger, courtier, moysture.*

Driuell on pearles, alluding to Matt. vii. 6. Langland uses a similar phrase, saying it is not well to cast pearls before hogs, for 'thei don but *dryuele* ther-on;' Piers the Plowm. B. x. 11.

29. Compare lines 1 and 2.

34. *It is both welth,* i.e. to flee truth is both for your welfare and your ease. This passage is strongly ironical.

36. Yet, very near to that wind (made by the praises of men) truth goes about in great distress.

44. By giving a cheese to a calf, one might perhaps get at least a cheese and a half in return.

45. *Cant,* portion; Shakespeare uses *cantle,* 1 Henry IV, iii. 1. 100.

47. *Learne at,* learn from. Cf. 'ask at' in Marmion, iii. 29.

53. All this is much in the manner of Juvenal; see, for instance, his Third Satire.

65. A nine-syllable line; place an emphasis on *Let,* since the *first* syllable is the one missing. So also, in l. 87 below, place an emphasis on *With.*

72. Here *laughter* appears to rime with *besought her* and *daughter,* but we cannot be certain as to the sound; cf. note to l. 20.

75. *Pandar,* Pandarus, whose name has become proverbial; see Chaucer's or Shakespeare's Troilus and Cressida.

78. *Be next thyselfe,* be nearest (or most friendly to) thyself; for friendship (to others) is valueless.

(D) *A renouncing of loue.*

3. *Senec,* Seneca. The MSS. of Chaucer have the form *Senek.*

5. I have inserted *my,* as it improves the sense and rhythm.

7. *That I set,* that I ought to set no store by trifles.

14. *Me lyst,* it pleases me, I like.

(E) *The louer forsaketh his vnkinde loue.*

10. *Fault.* The *l* in this word was not sounded. In our older authors, it is frequently written *faute.* Even Pope sounds it without the l, riming it with *taught* in his Moral Essays, Epist. ii. 212.

13. *Bearyng in hand,* cajolery, persuasion to belief of an untruth.

(F) *The louer determineth to serue faithfully.*

6. *Serue and suffer.* The phrase, ' suffren and seruen' occurs in Piers the Plowman, B. prol. 131.

(H) *Comparison of loue to a streame, &c.*

' It was from the capricious and overstrained invention of the Italian poets, that Wyat was taught to torture the passion of love by prolix and intricate comparisons and unnatural allusions. At one time his love is a galley steered by cruelty through stormy seas and desperate rocks ; the sails torn by the blast of tempestuous sighs, and the cordage consumed by incessant showers of tears : a cloud of griefs envelops the stars, reason is drowned, and the haven is at a distance. At another [viz. in this extract], it is a spring trickling from the summit of the Alps, which, gathering force in its fall, at length overflows all the plain beneath.'— Warton ; Hist. Eng. Poetry, ed. 1840 ; vol. iii. p. 45.

8. 'To avoid it in the first instance is the only remedy.'

XXI. HUGH LATIMER.

Line 2. *The place ;* i. e. the text. He has, in the former part of the sermon, quoted the text, ' Maledictus qui facit opus dei fraudulenter'— ' Cursed be he that doeth the work of the Lord deceitfully.' He immediately afterwards quotes (l. 6) the rest of the verse, ' and cursed be he that keepeth back his sword from blood.'

9. *Amalech*, Amalek ; 1 Sam. xv.

14. *Nebo.* Latimer reverts to the chapter he has already quoted, Jer. xlviii., which begins—' Against Moab thus saith the Lord of hosts, the God of Israel, Woe unto *Nebo*, for it is spoiled,' &c.

58. *Betwene stocke and stocke*, between one post and another ; like the proverbial saying of being driven from pillar to post.

85. *Lordyng*, acting like a 'laesy loord,' as Spenser has it (F. Q. iii. 7. 12). The O. E. *loord* answers to It. *lordo*, impudent, dirty, which is certainly derived from Lat. *luridus*. There is also an O. E. form *lordein* or *lourdayn*, a lout, stupid fellow, from the same. See the odd explanation in the Glosse to December, Extract XXVIII. p. 354, l. 8.

143. *Singulare commoditie*, private advantage ; alluding to enclosures made by wealthy people for their own use.

278. *Beinge a maried man ;* i. e. although he was a married man : a palpable hit at the enforced celibacy of the clergy in the Romish Church.

XXII. SIR DAVID LYNDESAY.

Line 4499. *Popis ryngis*, popes reign. The ending -*is* is used in Lowland Scotch for the plurals both of nouns, and of verbs in the present indicative.

4502. *In-to.* The use of *into* for *in* is very common indeed in Lowland Scotch.

4506. *Carion*, Cario. 'Cario's Chronicle was originally composed about the beginning of the sixteenth century, by Ludovicus Cario, an eminent mathematician, and improved or written anew by Melancthon.' —Warton, Hist. Eng. Poetry, ii. 471; where much information is given about Lyndesay. The reader should notice how, in Early English, words and names borrowed from Latin follow the form of the *accusative* case. Thus *Carion* is from Lat. *Carionem*, not *Cario*; so in Surrey's Virgil (see the Extract from Surrey) we find the island of *Tenedon*, from Lat. *Tenedon*, not *Tenedos*. This is a most important principle, because it is of almost universal application throughout the French, Italian, Spanish, and other Romance languages.

4510. A.D. 1156 is the date which Lyndesay here gives, and the event to which he alludes occurred either in this year or the year before. But he has not got hold of quite the right story. Alexander III was not made pope till the year 1159; it was his predecessor, Adrian IV, who should have been mentioned. The usual account is that Frederick I, surnamed Barbarossa, at a meeting with Pope Adrian IV (who was no other than Nicholas Brakespeare, the only Englishman who ever was pope), consented to prostrate himself before him, to kiss his foot, to hold his stirrup, and to lead the white palfrey on which he rode. See Haydn, Book of Dates, under Pope Adrian IV.

4520. *Thir*, these; still in common use in Scotland.

4521. Psalm xc. 13 in the Vulgate, xci. 13 in the Authorised English Version:—'Thou shalt tread upon the lion and adder; the young lion and the dragon shalt thou trample under feet.'

4528. *Pure*, poor. See John xiii. 5.

4531. *Toddis*, foxes. See Matt. viii. 20.

4533. *Penny-breid*, breadth of a penny. It means a space of ground of the size of a penny.

4536. *Hes*, for *has*; used in the plural, for *have*, two lines lower.

4550. *Poulderit*, powdered, powdered over, i. e. ornamented with gems laid on as thick as dust. An allusion to the Papal triple tiara.

4561. *Palmerius*. Matteo Palmeri, or Matthaeus Palmerius, a learned

Florentine, A.D. 1450, wrote an Italian poem, called 'Citta di Vita,' The City of Life, in imitation of Dante's Divina Commedia. He also wrote a general chronicle from the fifth century to his own times, entitled De Temporibus, which was printed at Milan, 1475. The latter is no doubt the work referred to. See Warton, Hist. Eng. Poetry, ii. 467, 472. There have been twenty-three popes of the name of John ; but only one of these, viz. John XXII, resided at Avignon. He died A.D. 1334.

4568. *Clyppit crounis,* clipped heads ; i. e. the tonsure.

4573. *Maryit men.* St. Peter was married, and so were other of the apostles ; 1 Cor. ix. 5.

4586. *Ouersene,* overlooked, connived at.

4592. Matt. xvii. 27. See also Rom. xiii.

4595. *Celistene.* Possibly Celestine III, pope from 1191-1198, who crowned Henry VI emperor of Germany. Lyndesay omits a still more striking instance, viz. the degrading penance submitted to by Henry IV, emperor of Germany, in deference to Hildebrand (Gregory VII). The pope kept Henry waiting for several days outside the castle of Canossa, in Modena, exposed to the inclemency of the wintry weather, in January, 1077, till he was pleased to admit him to his presence.

4663. 'The simple nun will think it a great shame to her, unless she be called Madame.' Chaucer (Prol. 121) says of the 'Prioresse,' who was a 'Nonne,' that ' she was cleped *madame* Englentyne.'

4667. There are of course innumerable instances of the priests being styled 'Sir.' It occurs, e. g., in Shakespeare, where the clown personates Sir Topas the curate ; Twelfth Night, iv. 2.

4670. *Denis,* not *Deans,* but *Dans* ; see l. 4672. The title Dene, Den, Don, or (more usually) Dan, is a corruption of the Latin *dominus,* lord.

4674. *Painfull ;* this word is used ironically.

4675. 'With double clothing to protect them from the cold.'

4677. 'With florid singing in the choir.' To *counter* is to sing an extemporaneous part upon the plain chant ; Dyce's Skelton, ii. 92.

4678. 'God knows whether they buy heaven very dear, or not ! '

4687. *Persone,* parson. Lyndesay's description differs widely from Chaucer's.

4690. 'Except take his tithe, and afterwards spend it. But he is obliged, by reason, to preach to parishioners. Though they go without preaching seventeen years, he will not go without a head of barley.'

4711. *Vmaist,* upmost, outermost.

4715. *Ky,* the plural of *cow,* is still in use provincially.

4718. 'Although he be poorly clad.'

4734. *Herield hors,* a horse that is a *heriot.* The whole passage is written against the dues paid by the poor on the occasion of a death. The poor man has three cows; the first of these the vicar takes as a burial-fee for the man himself; the second, because the wife is buried, and the third because the eldest child dies. But, besides this, there is the heriot due to the landlord. Jamieson says—'the heriot primarily signified the tribute given to the lord of a manor for his better preparation for war; but came at length to denote the *best aucht*, or beast of whatever kind, which a tenant died possessed of, due to his superior after death.'

5450. *The Scripture;* see Matt. xxiv. 6; Mark xiii. 8; Luke xxi. 10.

5456. 'Such cruel war shall be, ere then.'

5462. *Jerome.* A very favourite subject in early English is 'The Fifteen Signs before the Day of Judgment.' Thus in Hampole's Pricke of Conscience, ed. Morris, l. 4738, we find—

> ' Yhit spekes the haly man Saynt Ierome
> Of fiften takens that sal come,' &c.

But *Jerome* is sometimes strangely changed into *Jeremiah;* thus, in the poem called 'Fifteen Toknes before the Day of Judgment,' attributed to Adam Davie by Warton (ii. 5), they are said to be from the book of *Jeremiah.* So too in the 'Quindecim Signa ante diem Judicii,' printed in Hymns to the Virgin and Christ, ed. Furnivall (Early English Text Society), p. 118, we find—

> ' XV. tokenys telle I may
> That shal come before doomys day,
> As it is seyde yn the prophecye,
> In the book of *Jeremye.'*

There is even a list of them extant in Old Friesic, printed in Richtofen's Friesische Rechtsquellen, p. 130, with the heading—'Thit send tha fiftine tekna ther er domes di koma skilun, ther sancte Ieronimus fand eskriuin an thera Iothana bokon;' i. e. 'These are the fifteen tokens that shall come ere doomsday, which Saint Jerome found written in the books of the Jews.' All these clearly come from one source. The following is the list of tokens.

1. The rising of the sea; l. 5462.
2. The sinking of the sea; l. 5466.
3. The sea becomes even, as at first (omitted by Lyndesay).
4. The fishes shall make a great noise; l. 5468.
5. The sea shall burn; l. 5480.
6. A dew like blood shall fall on herbs; l. 5483.
7. Buildings shall fall down.
8. Rocks shall strike against each other; l. 5499.
9. There shall be earthquakes; l. 5500.

10. The earth shall become a plain.
11. Men shall come out of caves; l. 5490.
12. The stars shall fall; l. 5330 (not printed here).
13. The dead shall rise; l. 5488.
14. The living shall die.
15. The world shall be burnt.

The above list is from Hampole's Pricke of Conscience, whence Lyndesay has borrowed largely. Lyndesay omits some of these purposely, because they are not (as he supposes) in the Bible. This he says expressly in another passage, ll. 5316–5323 :—

> ' And mony toknis dois appeir,
> As efter, schortlye, thou sall heir,
> Quhow that Sanct Iherome doith indyte,
> That he has red, in Hebrew wryte,
> Off fiftene signis in speciall
> Affore that Iugement Generall.
> Of some of thame I tak no cure,
> Quhilk I fynd nocht in the scripture.'

5473. 'And, weeping, shall curse their fortune.'

5510. The 'Monarche' is supposed to be a long dialogue between a Courtier and Experience, wherein the former asks short questions, and the latter gives long explanations. In like manner Gower's Confessio Amantis or Lover's Confession is written as a dialogue between a Lover and a Sage.

5517. *Funding;* put for *funden,* i. e. found. There are numerous instances in Lowland Scotch, where *-ing* is thus written for *-en* in verbal inflexions. Cf. *beholdinge* for *beholden* in Sect. XXV. 10 ; *fallyng* for *fallen* in Sect. IV. 164. And see notes to ll. 5564, 5614.

Vpon lyue, in life, alive.

5528. *Noye,* Noah; Matt. xxiv. 37.

5532. *Makand pley,* making a plea, pleading.

5534. *On the field-going,* on an expedition into the fields. *Going* is a noun; the pres. part. would be *goand* in old Lowland Scotch, or rather *gangand,* as the latter is the form really used.

5551. *Walk,* wake, watch ; Matt. xxiv. 42. *Walk = Wakk* (p. 411).

5553. 'As if Christ would come immediately.' The word *Finis* denotes the end of the section merely. It is not the end of a Book; but is followed by the title of a new section or chapter.

5554. 'The appearance of Christ coming to judgment is poetically painted, and in a style of correctness and harmony, of which few specimens were now [i. e. at that date] seen.'—Warton, ii. 469.

5556. *Fyreflaucht,* lightning ; Matt. xxiv. 27.

5564. *Doith concludyng*, do conclude. Here *concludyng* is the infinitive mood. See note to l. 5517 above.

Haill, the whole of them; i. e. learned men all alike say this.

5566. Christ's descent into the valley of Jehoshaphat is taken from Joel iii. 12. See Hampole, Pr. Çonsc. 5152.

5568. *Ordoris nyne*, nine orders. The angels were distributed into three hierarchies of three orders each, viz. seraphim, cherubim, and thrones; dominions, virtues, and powers; principalities, archangels, and angels. Hence the expressions *trinall triplicities* in Spenser, F. Q. i. 12, 39; and *triple degrees* in Milton, P. L. v. 750; also *angelic symphony* in Milton's Hymn on Christ's Nativity, st. 13, as agreeing with the *ninefold* harmony of the spheres. See a note in Warton, ii. 464.

5573. *Signis*, representations.

5595. *Beis hard*, shall be heard. The verb *beón*, to be, is generally used in Anglo-Saxon with a *future* signification.

5604. Hampole, in his Prick of Conscience, quotes the very words of St. Jerome—' Siue [1] comedam, siue [1] bibam, siue [1] aliquid aliud faciam, semper michi uidetur illa tuba resonare in auribus meis, " surgite mortui, uenite ad iudicium." '

5614. *Funding bene*, shall be found. See notes to ll. 5517, 5595.

5619. *Scripture*; viz. 1 Cor. xv. 51–53.

5622. *Scripture*, writing. He does not say the *divine* scripture, as in l. 5619. The corresponding passage in Hampole ascribes this opinion to St. Augustin, and moreover assigns the reason, viz. that all men shall be of the same age as Christ was at his death; this age Hampole gives as thirty-two years and three months. See Hampole's Pricke of Conscience, ed. Morris, p. 135.

5629. ' As a shepherd does the sheep from the goats ;' see Matt. xxv. Hampole has the line

' Als the hird the shepe dus fra the gayte ;' l. 6134.

which makes it abundantly clear that a part of Lyndesay's Monarche is borrowed directly from Hampole. The metre is the same in both, and there is of course much similarity in the dialect. Sir David Lyndesay must have seen a MS. of Hampole's work; this he may easily have done, as MS. copies of it are very numerous.

5630. *Baliallis*, Belial's.

5633. 'Without hope of obtaining refuge.'

5639. *Louyng*, praising. The two words thus spelt in Middle English signify *loving* and *praising* respectively. The former is from the A.S. *lufian*, to love, the latter from the A.S. *lófian*, to praise.

---

[1] Mr. Morris prints *sine* in his edition, p. 127.

XXIII. NICHOLAS UDALL.

Perhaps the reader will understand the Extract better from a brief argument of the whole play. Mathew Merygreeke explains, in a soliloquy, that he gains his living by hanging on to rich men. At this time he has attached himself to Ralph Roister Doister, a silly rake, who soon enters upon the stage, and instructs Merygreeke to help him in paying his addresses to Dame Christian Custance, a rich and sensible widow. Ralph then meets with three of the widow's maids, Mage Mumblecrust, Tibet Talkapace, and Annot Alyface, whom he tries to propitiate. He gives Mage Mumblecrust a letter, which she undertakes to convey to her mistress. Next Dobinet Doughtie, Doister's servant, is sent to the widow with a ring and a token, which he manages to deliver to Tibet Talkapace; but she is roundly reproved by her mistress for receiving them. Merygreeke then applies to the widow himself, but with small success. He tells Ralph Roister Doister how ill he has fared, and Ralph says he will ' go home and die.' Ralph and Merygreeke, however, make another attempt, and see the widow, who hands over Ralph's letter to Merygreeke, and tells him to read it out. Merygreeke does so, misplacing all the stops, and so making it mean quite the reverse of what was intended. Ralph is enraged, but throws all the blame on the scrivener who wrote the letter, which Ralph himself had merely copied out. Ralph and Merygreeke repair to the scrivener, to ask him what he meant by such conduct, but the scrivener takes the letter in hand, and so reads it as to render it very courteous; whereupon Ralph has to beg the scrivener's pardon, since the incorrect punctuation was Merygreeke's. The rest of the play describes the further attempts which Ralph makes to gain the widow, but they are all alike unsuccessful, and in the end Dame Christian Custance marries Gawyn Goodluck, who makes up all the quarrels arising out of the suit, and actually asks Ralph and Merygreeke to sup with him; so that all ends merrily, as a comedy should do.

An older specimen of the metre here employed will be found in Skelton's poem of Magnificence. It is very like that of The Tale of Gamelyn.

Act iii. Scene 3. Merygreeke, having bad news to communicate, begins by pretending not to see his patron.

Line 1. 'Now that the whole answer rests in my relation,
    I shall paint out our wooer in the best colours.'

7. 'I cannot refrain from coming to see.'

8. *A iutte*, a jut, i.e. a hit, a push; cf. Fr. *jéter*, to throw. Accordingly, Merygreeke runs up against Ralph, then turns round, and begs his pardon.

12. *The prouerbe.* I regret to say that I do *not* know the proverb. It appears to run 'I am sad, because I cannot be had.'

14. *This geare*, this matter, this business. He means 'How will this affair turn out?'

17. Observe how Merygreeke takes a notable opportunity to call his patron names.

20. *Mastership.* Printed *maship* by way of abbreviation, here and elsewhere.

21. If *Bawawe* is not a misprint, it must be an imitation of the contemptuous tone which Merygreeke wishes it to be supposed that he adopted.

Ko, colloquial for *quod* or *quoth*.

32. *Onely sight*, sight alone, mere appearance.

33. *Yet none*, i.e. yet there are none.

36. 'Better not, quoth I; I wish not to meddle with daws.' The jackdaw was a proverbially foolish bird with our forefathers.

37. *Happy*, lucky. 'It's lucky for you you're a woman.'

49. *Toll the bell*, i.e. for your funeral. Here Merygreeke begins to pretend that Ralph is dead, and goes on to sing a dirge, &c.

51. I suppose this to refer to the custom of offering something to drink to a criminal on his way to execution. Hence 'will you drink?' is equivalent to saying 'you are on your way to death.' Criminals on their way from Newgate to Tyburn, were presented at the hospital of St. Giles with a large bowl of ale, as their last refreshment. See Chambers' Book of Days, ii. 558.

53. *Placebo; dilexi;* words from the Burial Service. The *Placebo* was the office for the dead at Vespers, which began—'*Placebo* domino in regione uiuentium;' Psalm cxvi. 9 (called cxv. 9 in the Vulgate). Skelton's Lament upon Phyllyp Sparowe begins with similar allusions—

> '*Placebo*
> Who is there, who?
> *Dilexi*,
> Dame Margery,' &c.

At the end of the play of Roister Doister there are some songs and additional lines that may be introduced if desired. At this point the lines entitled 'The Psalmodie,' may be sung:—

> '*Placebo: dilexi:*
> Maister Roister Doister wil streight go home and die;

Our Lorde Iesus Christ his soule haue mercie vpon;
Thus you see to-day a man, to-morrow John.
Yet, sauing for a womans extreeme crueltie,
He might haue lyued yet a moneth or two or three;
But in spite of Custance, which hath him weried,
His ma*ster*shyp shall be worshipfully buried.
And while some piece of his soule is yet hym within,
Some parte of his funeralls let vs here beginne.
Dirige.   He will go darklyng to his graue.
Neque lux, neque crux, nisi solum clinke.
Neuer gentman so went toward heauen, I thinke.'

The last three lines much resemble ll. 58–60.

58. *Darklyng,* in the dark.   The ending *-ling* is an adverbial ending ;
cf. *flatling.*   The *-long* in *head-long* is the same suffix.

59. ' Neither light, nor cross, nor mourners, nor the clink of a bell.'

60. *Vnknowing,* misused for *unknowen,* unknown.   Cf. note to XXII.
55^{17}.

63. The Anthem, or Officium, in the 'Missa pro Defunctis' (Mass for
the Dead) began with the words—' Requiem aeternam dona eis, Domine,
et lux perpetua luceat eis.'   Hence the term *requiem,* which is still
in use.

65. *Euocat,* &c.; he calls forward the knight's servants—a stage
direction.

67–70. See note to l. 53.

71. *Audiui vocem,* ' I heard a voice' (Rev. xiv. 13), still read in our
Burial Service.   At the end of the play, there are here again some
additional lines, to be sung by the actors if desired.   They are :—

> ' Yet, sirs, as ye wyll the blisse of heauen win,
>   When he commeth to the graue, lay hym softly in ;
>   And all men take heede by this one Gentleman,
>   How you sette,' &c. (as in the text).

83. *Ad seruos militis,* to the knight's servants—a stage direction.   At
the end of the play is the following extra passage :—

' The peale of belles rong by the parish Clerk, and Roister Doisters
foure men.

The first Bell, a Triple [Treble].
When dyed he?   When dyed he?

The seconde
We haue hym.   We haue him.

The thirde.
Royster Doyster.   Royster Doyster.

> *The fourthe Bell.*
> He commeth. He commeth.
> *The greate Bell.*
> Our owne. Our owne.'

84. *In heale,* in health.

90. *Quite,* requite.

94. *Fet,* fetch. *Sound,* swoon. Under pretence of 'rubbing his temples,' Merygreeke hits Ralph a smart blow.

106. *Courage.* It has been suggested that it should be *cariage,* for the sake of the rime. The suggestion is quite wrong and unnecessary ; for the rime, cf. p. 272, ll. 81, 82.

108. *Breast,* i. e. voice ; as in Shakespeare.

117. *Prankie cote,* fine coat. Merygreeke calls him *fine-coat,* to remind him how well he ought to carry himself. *Nay, whan,* when will you do it right ?

127–129. Here Merygreeke shews how he would behave to those who get in Ralph's way ; in so doing, he roughly jostles him.

133. 'Is there never an M at your girdle ?' i. e. have you no such word as *Master* at hand ? In l. 132 Merygreeke calls him plain Ralph, and Ralph reproves him. 'To have an M under the girdle, is to keep the term *Master* out of sight, to be wanting in proper respect.'—Halliwell. *M.* is an abbreviation for *Master.* Merygreeke then repeats what he said before, but in a very polite form.—'Your good mastership's mastership would be her own mistress-ship's mistress-ship's ;' i. e. you would be the widow's. Line 135 is obscure ; perhaps—' you would be a take-up (a prey) for hawks ;' you would soon be pounced upon.

141. *High,* hie, hasten.

142. *Trey, ace,* a three and an ace ; a call in playing dice, to signify that these two numbers are cast.

143. *Sayde of,* said by.

Lowe, allow, i. e. approve of.

144. *Fit ;* the old word *fytte,* for a portion or canto of a poem or ballad. So in Sect. VII. l. 50.

149. *Pastance,* a corruption of *passe-temps,* pastime. So in Skelton's Phyllyp Sparowe, 1096.

151. *Cantent,* let them sing—a stage direction.

Act iii. Sc. 4. 7. *Haze,* supposed to stand for *ha' us,* i. e. have us. This, at any rate, gives the sense.

11. *Dawes ;* see note to last scene, l. 36.

32. *Pigsny,* pig's eye, a term of endearment, the eyes of a pig being small. The letter *n* is prefixed to some words in a most curious manner

in Early English; thus it is very common to find *nale* for *ale*, and so also *ny* is often written for *eye*. The word *nale* arose from the phrase *at then ale*, afterwards *at the nale*, where *then* was originally the dative case of the article. The word *ny* arose from the phrases *min ey, thin ey*, afterwards corrupted into *my ney, thi ney*. See the quotation in Halliwell, 'turne *thi nye*,' s. v. *Nye*. Hence the explanation of the term *piggesnie* in Chaucer, which has so puzzled some editors. It is the same word as here. See note by me in Notes and Queries, 4 S. vi.

80. *By cocke*, a vulgar corruption, to avoid the use of God's name; so also *by gosse*, in l. 91.

99. *Lub*, a childish pronunciation, as though Merygreeke would soothe his friend as a nurse would a child. So also *dee* for *thee*.

110. *And I were*, if I were; so in l. 117. Cf. l. 125.

119. *Gramercies*, Fr. *grand merci*, great thanks.

131. *Ko you*, quoth you, ye say; Prov. Eng. 'says you.'

149. *A good*, a good deal. In Marlowe's Jew of Malta, A. ii. sc. 2, Ithamore says—'That I have laughed *a good* to see the cripples.'

Act iv. Sc. 5. 4. *Vneth*, scarcely, with difficulty.

5. *Lo and*, see if.

Sens, since, already.

7. *It needed*, &c., there was no necessity for it on that occasion.

42. *So mote I go*, so may I retain the power of walking!

43. 'Look on your own handwriting (that is, on your own copy), and I will look on this, the original which I wrote for you.'

92. Ralph had threatened to strike the scrivener, but now dares not strike Merygreeke.

98. 'If it were any one else but you, it would be a knave.' Excellent! So is Merygreeke's expostulation in l. 101.

XXIV. THOMAS SACKVILLE.

Prose Prologue. Line 1. *When I had read this*. Here *I* is William Baldwyne, and *this* is the preceding piece. This piece is the tragedy of Lord Hastings, betrayed by Catesby, and murdered in the tower by Richard Duke of Gloucester, in 1483; it was subscribed in Niccols's edition '*Master D.*' that is, John Dolman. It is therefore here supposed that Baldwyne had just been reading out Dolman's tragedy of Hastings, and was now expecting criticisms upon it. The chief criticism is that it was considered rather too *dark*, i. e. obscure and difficult. It was at first arranged that the tragedy of the murder of the two princes, to be written by Lord Vaulx, should succeed Dolman's piece, but no information about the tragedy was forthcoming.   Accordingly, the editors pass on to the next, which is Sackville's tragedy of Buckingham, whom Richard III so cruelly executed.   Then Baldwyne announces that Sackville had written a poetical Induction, or Introduction, which he had originally intended to serve as a Prologue to all the tragedies from William the Conqueror's time to the duke of Buckingham ; all which tragedies he had originally offered to write himself, although, in the sequel, he wrote but one.   On this account, the Induction was slightly modified, so as to serve for an introduction to the single tragedy of ' Buckingham ' instead of to the whole series, and was placed accordingly.

28. *Lydgate folowing Bocchas.*   The Mirror for Magistrates was professedly an imitation of Boccaccio's De Casibus Principum, which had been translated by Lydgate, with the title ' The Fall of Princes.'

The Induction.   There is a just estimate of this poem in Hallam's Introduction to the Literature of Europe, part ii. ch. v., where it is styled ' a link which unites the school of Chaucer and Lydgate to the Fairy Queen.'   It is indeed a magnificent poem, but the gloom and sadness of it no doubt deter many readers, and prevent us from wishing it longer.   Yet it is well worthy of careful and deliberate study.   Let it be remembered how highly Spenser esteemed it, and how much he possibly owed to the style of it.   Witness Spenser's own words, in a sonnet addressed ' To the Right honourable the Lord of Buckhurst, one of her Majesties privie Counsell' (Globe edition, p. 9):—

'In vaine I thinke, right honourable Lord,   .
By this rude rime to memorize thy name,
Whose learned Muse hath writ her owne record
In golden verse, worthy immortal fame.'

See the subject treated in Warton, Hist. Eng. Poetry, sect. xlix.

Stanza I. *Proching,* approaching; from Fr. *proche,* near; cf. Lat. *prope.*

Treen, trees; it occurs also in Fairfax's Tasso, vii. I.

Saturnus.   Cf. ' the pale Saturnus the colde' in Chaucer, Knightes Tale, 1585.

Mantels, i. e. foliage.

Tapets, properly *carpets;* but here it seems to mean the hanging tapestry of the groves, the green foliage.

It is clear that this first stanza was suggested by a similar stanza in Fabyan's Chronicle.   Fabyan mentions a Latin lament *said* to have been composed by Edward II. when in prison, beginning with the lines :—

'Dampnum michi contulit tempore brumali
Fortuna satis aspera vehementis mali.'

These lines Fabyan himself poorly paraphrases as follows :—

> ‘ Whan Saturne with his colde isy face
> The grounde with his frostys turnyth the grene to whyte,
> The tyme of wynter which trees doth deface
> And causyth all verdure to avoyde quyte :
> Than fortune, whiche sharpe was with stormys not a lyte
> Hath me assautyd with hir frowarde wyll,
> And me beclypped with daungeours right yll.’

2. *To seen,* the gerund, with the sense *for seeing,* i. e. *to sight.* Many moderns, utterly ignorant of Early English grammar, would suppose that *to be seen* is a more correct form; whereas the latter is a weak and inferior modern expedient.

3. *Withholde,* keep.

Where as, where that.

4. Here occur the favourite allusions to astronomical phenomena, expressed in astrological diction, which it is often so hard to follow or interpret. Hermes is Mercury, whose planetary orbit lies within that of Venus. The word *sped* refers to Mercury's rapid motion. Venus and Mars are the planets of those names. Venus is in the ascendant, but Mars is bidden not to rise. The epithet *bluddy* refers to the fiery red colour of the planet. As for the signs of the zodiac, Virgo had sunk beneath the western horizon, soon after followed by Scorpio; whilst Scorpio, in his turn, is pursued by Sagittarius, from whose dart he seems to flee.

5. *The Beare;* Ursa Major, a constellation which, in the latitude of London, never sets; yet a few scattered stars, near the supposed feet of the animal, just dip below the horizon for a few hours; hence the expression ‘had dipt his griesly feete’ is literally exact.

The *Iryshe Sea* means the sea on the *west* of England, still so called.

6. *Phaethon,* the sun. *Was prest,* &c., was ready to enter his resting-place; i. e. the *solstitium* or winter solstice. It was therefore very nearly midwinter. *Erythius* is put for *Erythraeus,* one of the four horses in the sun's chariot, so named from the redness of the dawn (Greek ἐρυθρός, red). *Titan* is also the sun; but probably Titan is imagined as reclining in the hinder part of the chariot, whilst Phaethon, his son or charioteer, stands in front to drive; see p. 128, l. 30. The *purple bed* is of course the glow of sunset.

7. *Cinthea,* the moon.

Noonesteede, place of noon, i. e. the southern meridian.

Syxe degrees; since fifteen degrees make an hour, six degrees are twenty-four minutes. The moon had southed twenty-four minutes before.

Chare, car. *Ear,* ere.

8. 'The altered scene of things, the flowers and verdure of summer deformed by the frosts and storms of winter, and the day suddenly overspread with darkness, remind the poet of the uncertainties of human life, the transient state of honour, and the instability of prosperity.'— Warton.

9. *Leames,* gleams, glowing lights.

Reduced, brought back, which is the original sense of the Latin *reducere.* Cf. note to Sect. XIX (B), 14; p. 443.

10. *Pieres,* peers. He alludes to Lydgate's 'Fall of Princes.'

11. 'Immediately the figure of Sorrow suddenly appears, which shows the poet in a new and bolder mode of composition.'—Warton.

12. *Forwithered and forespent,* utterly withered and utterly worn out. The proper spelling is *forspent.*

Wealked, withered; better spelt *welked,* as in Spenser, Sheph. Cal. November, l. 13. Nares is wrong in connecting it with the word *whelked* in King Lear, iv. 6. 71, which means 'covered with whelks or protuberances.'

13. *Doome,* opinion, judgment.

14. *Dewle,* mourning; Fr. *deuil.* Now spelt *dole.*

15. *Stint,* cease. *Spill,* destroy.

Of sorrowe, with sorrow.

16. *Letheus,* the water of Lethe or oblivion.

17. *Those,* the characters whose tragedies are related in the Mirror for Magistrates.

Whom, &c., 'whom, in this maze of misery, Fortune chose as most woeful mirrors of wretched chance.' Here *mirrors* is put instead of *examples,* in order to make a more direct allusion to the name of the work for which the Induction was intended.

18. *Out! alas!* a common exclamation; so in Romeo and Juliet, iv. 5. 25.

To-dasht, dashed herself down severely. The preceding *all* still further strengthens the intensive prefix *to-,* which is very common (both with and without *all*) in Middle English.

Eft, again, in my turn.

19. *Auale,* become low, decrease, diminish.

Her, viz. Sorrow.

All fordone, observe how *all* is used with the prefix *for-,* as well as with the prefix *to-*; in st. 21, it occurs before *be-.*

21. *Spoken of a stike,* spoken as much as a 'stich.' A stich is here a stanza; we still use the compound *distich* for a couple of verses. Nares observes that Sackville 'had exactly spoken a stanza (st. 20) before he

says this.' Compare the phrase *to sing a stave.* (I do not think that Prof. Morley's two guesses help us out here.)

22. *Overthrowe,* overthrown; so we find *be* for *been, do* for *done,* &c.

23. *While-eare,* a while before, formerly.

Telde, told : ungrammatical, but it secures a rime.

Wun, dwelling.

24. *Glas,* mirror; cf. Gascoigne's Steel *Glas.*

That erst, that which beforehand.

Rolde, meditated.

26. 'Sorrow then conducts the poet to the classical hell, to the place of torments and the place of happiness.'—Warton. So the Sibyl in Virgil conducted Æneas, and Virgil in La Divina Commedia conducted Dante.

Bare swinge, bore sway.

27. *Desert wood.* This is like Dante's *selva oscura* (gloomy wood) in the second line of the Inferno.

28. *I fell;* cf. Dante's Inferno, cant. iii. l. 136—

'E caddi, come l' uom, cui sonno piglia.'

I fell, as a man whom slumber seizes.

30. Compare Virgil, Æneid, vi.; Dante, Inf. iv. &c.

Yeding, going. There is really no such verb, since *yede* is properly used as the *past tense* of *go.* Hence to use *yede* as a new verb is altogether a mistake. But the truth is, that our poets, when purposely using obsolescent words, frequently use them wrongly; and Spenser has, in fact, carefully copied this very error in the line

'The whiles on foot was forced for to *yeed*;' F. Q. ii. 4. 2.

Auerne, Avernus.

'Inde ubi uenere ad fauces graueolentis Auerni.'

Virgil, Æneid, vi. 201.

31. *No fowle but dyes;* from Virgil, Æneid, vi. 239—

'Quam super haud ullae poterunt impune uolantes
Tendere iter pennis; talis sese halitus atris
Faucibus effundens supera ad conuexa ferebat.'

32. 'Our author appears to have felt and to have conceived with true taste that very romantic part of Virgil's Æneid which he has here happily copied and heightened. The imaginary beings which sate within the porch of hell are all his own.'—Warton. Virgil's description of these beings amounts to only nine lines; Æneid, vi. 273-281. It is possible that Sackville may have been acquainted with Dunbar's Dance of the Seven Deadly Sins, or with Passus v. of Piers the Plowman. He was at least acquainted with the description of the Temple of Mars

H h

in Chaucer's Knight's Tale. We find similar descriptions in Spenser; see the descriptions of Wrath and Avarice, F. Q. i. 4. 33 and 28.

34. *Benumde*, bereft. The use of this word is quite proper, as it is derived from the A.S. *niman*, to take away, to reave; M.E. *nim*, to steal. Hence it is exactly equivalent in sense to *bereft*.

Stoynde, astonied.

35. *Revenge* is masculine in Collins's Ode on the Passions.

So farforth, to such an extent.

41. *Slepe;* Virgil's 'consanguineus Leti Sopor,' Æneid, vi. 278. Cf. Spenser, i. 1. 40,

42. One of the finest stanzas in our language.

Feer, companion. Crœsus was king of Lydia; the story of his wealth is well-known.

Irus; the well-known beggar of Ithaca, slain by Ulysses, as told in the Odyssey. Cf.

'Irus et est subito qui modo Crœsus erat;'

Ovid, 3 Trist. vii. 42.

43. Virgil's 'Tristis Senectus;' Æn. vi. 275.

The sisters, the Fates—Clotho, Lachesis, and Atropos.

44. *Forwaste;* contracted from *forwasted*, i.e. totally misspent.

45. *And*, if.

Elde, old age.

His lothsome trayne; for these, see Milton, P. L. xi. 480.

Lief, life; yet in st. 43 it rimes with *knyfe*. The apparent contradiction is possibly to be explained by a change in our pronunciation since Sackville's time. This and similar changes can only be studied in Mr. Ellis's book on Early English Pronunciation.

46. *Ylayne*, laid.

As he, as if he.

47. *Al wer*, although (his youth) was.

Length, lengthen.

48. An allusion to the riddle propounded to Œdipus by the Sphinx.

Pilde, deprived of hair. In the Promptorium Parvulorum, ed. Way, we find '*Pyllyd*, depilatus;' see Mr. Way's long and curious note on the word.

For briefe, in short.

51. *Knawen on*, gnawed upon.

52. *Stonewall*. An allusion to the proverb 'Hunger pierceth stone walls,' which is quoted by Heywood, and alluded to in Coriolanus, i. 1. 210.

Ymay, may. In Anglo-Saxon we find *ge-* (afterwards softened into *y-*) prefixed to *all parts* of the verb; but in Sackville it is an affectation of archaic diction, as it was then only used with *past participles.*

54. *By and by*, immediately.　See Trench's Select Glossary.

Dauntes, tames, subdues.

55. *Affrayed*, terrified.

Shape, skeleton.

57. *Forhewed*, deeply cut.

Targe, target, shield.　It must be noted that all the things described in stanzas 58–68 are supposed to be depicted upon this shield.

59. *Macedo*, the Macedonian, Alexander the Great, who defeated the vast hosts of Darius Codomannus in the battle of Arbela, B.C. 331.　Hannibal defeated Lucius Æmilius Paulus in the battle of Cannæ, B.C. 216.

60. Hannibal defeated the Romans under Flaminius at Lake Trasimenus, B.C. 217; he had won the battle of Trebia in the preceding year. He was defeated by Scipio at Zama, B.C. 202.

61. Pompey the Great was assassinated B.C. 48, soon after his defeat by Julius Cæsar at Pharsalia.　Marius died B.C. 86, and Sulla B.C. 78. Cyrus the elder was slain in battle against the Massagetæ, a people of Scythia, B.C. 529.　Their queen Tomyris is said to have cast his head into a bag filled with human blood, that he might satiate himself therewith, as she expressed it.　In his ' Complaint of the Duke of Buckingham,' Sackville tells the story rather more at length.

62. Xerxes' fleet was defeated at Salamis by Themistocles, Oct. 20, B.C. 480.　His army was kept at bay at Thermopylæ by Leonidas for three days, August 7, 8, 9, in the same year.

Thebes, probably an allusion to the supposed capture of Thebes by Theseus; see Chaucer, Knightes Tale, 132.

Tyrus, Tyre, sacked by Alexander, B.C. 332.

63. *Werd*, weird, fate.

Ioves, &c.; cf. Iliad, i. 5—Διὸς δ' ἐτελείετο βουλή.

Lyn, cease; more common in the form *blin*, contracted from *be-lin*.

64. It is tolerably clear that Spenser has caught the tone of Sackville, in his piece called ' The Ruines of Time,' which is written in the same metre.

67. *Spercled*, scattered; from Virgil's ' passis crinibus;' Æn. ii. 403.

Bayne, bath.　For the death of Priam, see the Extracts from Caxton and Surrey.

69. ' From this scene Sorrow, who is well known to Charon, and to Cerberus the hideous hound of hell, leads the poet over the loathsome lake of rude Acheron, to the dominions of Pluto, which are described in numbers too beautiful to have been relished by his contemporaries, or equalled by his successors.'—Warton.

71. From Virgil, Æneid, vi. 413—

> ' Gemuit sub pondere cymba
> Sutilis, et multam accepit rimosa paludem.'

Hoyse up, hoist up. Cf. Acts xxvii. 40. Shakespeare has *hoised sail*, Richard III, iv. 4. 529.

Set, make.

Thre-sound, triple-sounding; from Virgil's 'latratu trifauci,' Æn. vi. 417.

72. See Virgil; also Dante, Inferno, vi. 22.

Foredinning, dinning greatly; it should be *fordinning*. This line is harsh, probably by intention.

Peaste, became quiet.

74. *Pewled;* Cotgrave's French Dictionary gives ' *Piauler*, to peep or cheep as a young bird, to *pule* or howl as a young whelp.'

Yfere, together.

75. *Tooke on with playnt*, took up her complaint.

Can, began to, did.

76. *Fortunes wheele;* see the description of it in the Extract from James I; p. 44.

Recompt, recount.

Kesar, Cæsar, emperor.

77. *Henry.* This is the subject of Sackville's own contribution to the 'Mirror.' The original 'Induction' probably ended at stanza 76, as we now have it; the rest, if any, was altered.

Ioynes, clasps.

78. *Molte*, melted; we still use *molten* in the past participle.

A large portion of Sackville's poem, in a modernized form, is quoted by Warton. This is followed by a short analysis of Dante's great work, in which, by the way, the Italian is very oddly spelt.

XXV. ROGER ASCHAM.

Line 4. 'In 1550, while on a visit to his friends in Yorkshire, he was recalled to court by a letter informing him that he had been appointed to accompany Sir Richard Morysine on his embassy to the court of the Emperor Charles V. It was on his way to London on this occasion that he had his well-known interview with Lady Jane Grey, at her father's seat at Broadgate [or Bradgate], in Leicestershire.' English Cyclopædia; s. v. Ascham.

13. *Phædon Platonis*, Plato's Phædo; the dialogue in which Plato's views concerning the immortality of the soul are developed.

14. *Bocase*, Boccaccio; the reference is to his Decamerone, which

contains one hundred tales, many of them more 'merie' than moral. For a specimen of one, see Keats's 'Isabella.'

Ascham also narrates his interview with Lady Jane in a Latin epistle to his friend Sturm. He there gives to her tutor, Mr. Elmer, the Christian name of John. See the notice of Bishop Aylmer in Athenæ Cantab. ii. 168, 547.

51. *Faire markes.* Ascham is fond of allusions to archery, in praise of which he wrote his 'Toxophilus.'

72. *Xenophon.* The passage is—'Ὡs δὲ προῆγεν αὐτὸν ὁ χρόνοs σὺν τῷ μεγέθει εἰs ὥραν τοῦ πρόσηβον γενέσθαι, ἐν τούτῳ δὴ τοῖs μὲν λόγοιs βραχυτέροιs ἐχρῆτο καὶ τῇ φωνῇ ἡσυχαιτέρᾳ, αἰδοῦs δ' ἐνεπίμπλατο, ὥστε καὶ ἐρυθραίνεσθαι ὁπότε συντυγχάνοι τοῖs πρεσβυτέροιs.—Cyropædia, bk. i. ch. 4, § 4.

82. *Aristotle;* Eth. N. iv. 9, §§ 2, 3. Cf. Diogenes Laert. vi. 2, § 54, with Ménage's note.—Mayor.

90. *Cicero;* De Oratore, iii. § 94.

113. *In place,* answering to our modern phrase 'in company.'

115. *To be seene,* to be experienced or skilful. Palmistry is divination by inspection of the lines and marks in the palm of the hand.

131. *Peekgoos* (also spelt Peak-goose, or corrupted into Pea-goose), a sickly goose. It is used also in Beaumont and Fletcher—''Tis a fine *peakgoose!*'—Prophetess, iv. 3. See Nares. Mr. Wedgwood explains *Peaking* as 'puling, sickly, from the pipy tone of voice of a sick person. Ital. *pigolare,* to peep as a chicken, to whine.' Hence *peaky, peakish,* means sickly. To *peak* also had the sense of prying about narrowly, or peeping. Cf. the double use of *Peep* (1) to pry, (2) to whine. Ascham here speaks ironically—'if you cannot laugh, lie, flatter, or face, you are of no use; and we must say to you, get away, silly fellow.' So also *John Cheese* means a rustic, a boor.

134. *Roger Chamloe.* 'Sir R. Cholmeley became Chief Baron of the Exchequer 11th Nov. 1545, Chief Justice of the King's Bench 21st March, 1552. See Foss, Judges of England, v. 293. "The date of his admission [at Lincoln's Inn] cannot be found; but the fact of his being re-admitted in 1509 gives some substance to the story that the embryo Chief Justice entered at first rather freely into the frolics of youth." For a letter of his see Calendar of State Papers (Mary), 88.'—Mayor.

I cannot mention the name of Sir Roger Cholmeley without gratitude, having spent three years at the Highgate Grammar School, which he founded in the year 1565. It is perhaps necessary to add that the article upon him and the school which appeared in the Gentleman's Magazine for April, 1834, turns out to be in many respects inaccurate, and the writer is wrong in questioning the date and in his description of the arms. My school prizes bear the right date and the right arms viz. 1565, and Gules, a sword in fess between a helmet in chief and a wolf's (not an eagle's) head erased in base. The latter perhaps refers to the fact of Sir Roger's descent from Hugh Lupus, first Earl of Chester and nephew of William the Conqueror, ancestor of the present Cheshire Egertons. His father, Sir Richard Cholmeley, Knight, was Lieutenant of the Tower, and his father's brother, also named Sir Roger, was knight of the body to Henry VIII. Sir Roger himself left no male heir, but had two daughters, Elizabeth and Frances. A pamphlet was published in 1822 entitled 'Some Account of the Free Grammar School at Highgate and of its founder, Sir Roger Cholmeley, Knight,' by J. N. [John Green]; which was followed by 'An Epistle to J. G. the author of a pamphlet entitled Some Account, &c.;' by A. Z. 1823. 8vo.

155. He here clearly refers to his ' Toxophilus,' or treatise on Archery.

174. *Queene Elisabeth.* 'See below, p. 105 [i. e. p. 105 of Mr. Mayor's edition, a passage near the beginning of Book ii. of the Scholemaster] and the Preface. [Also Ascham's] Epist. 51 (for her knowledge of Greek, Latin, Italian, and French); Epist. 53 (she was reading with Ascham Demosthenes and Æschines " of the crown," and shewed great intelligence, 14th Sept. 1555); Epist. 56, 57 (she in one day answered three ambassadors in Italian, French, and Latin respectively); Epist. 61 (20th Oct. 1562, she daily read with Ascham Greek or Latin); Whitaker's Richmondshire, i. 287 (Ascham to Leicester, 14th April, 1566): ' If I dye, all my thinges dye with me, and yett the poore service that I have done to Queene Elizabeth shall live still, and never dye soe long as her noble hand and excellent learneing in the Greeke and Latine tonge shalbe knowne to the world.'—Mayor.

206. *One example.* 'Strype (Stow, ed. 1720, bk. ii. p. 142) conjectures that this *disorder* may have been excess of apparel, and that the *big one of the court* was resident in Birchin-Lane about 1540. (Cf. Notes and Queries, Second Ser. i. 254).'—Mayor. It may be observed that Ascham proceeds to reprove absurdities of dress in the next page.

XXVI. GEORGE GASCOIGNE.

Line 429. *Rules the rost.* To *rule the roast* is to preside at the board, to assign what shares one pleases to the guests; hence it came to mean, to domineer, in which sense it is commonly used in our old authors. See Nares.

447. It means, 'Or else would have caused serious annoyance to offenders.'

458. *Proynd*, pruned. To *preen* is used of a bird setting its feathers in order; to *proine* is to trim, deck out, used by Chaucer. It is from the O.N. *prjon*, Sc. *preen*, a *pin*, used for neatness. *Prune* is the modern spelling of *proine*.

464. *Shew*, appear.

My glasse, my steel glass, my mirror, in which mankind are shewn as they are. Compare the title *Mirror* for Magistrates.

753. *Meane*, method. We now always use the plural *means*.

755. *The vaine*, the vein; i.e. the humour, particular temper.

757. 'Because they have not marriage-garments.' Cf. 'Amice, quomodo huc intrasti, non habens vestem nuptialem?'—St. Matt. xxii. 12.

760. *Rocks*, distaffs. The 7th of January was called *Rock-day* or St. Distaff's Day, because, the Christmas festivities having terminated on Twelfth Night, women were then supposed to return to their spinning.

763. *By*, with regard to, against, as in 1 Cor. iv. 4.

768. *Sericane.* He must mean China. The Chinese are called *Seres* in Latin, whence *Serica* means silken garments, and *Sericum* their fabric. From *Sericum* Mr. Wedgwood would derive the A.S. *seolc*, and the modern *silk* by the change of *r* into *l*. On the other hand, *silk* in Arabic and Persian means a *thread*; see Webster's Dictionary. Mr. Wedgwood's quotation from Holland's Pliny well illustrates the present passage: 'The first people of any knowledge and acquaintance be the *Seres*, famous for the fine *silke* that their woods doe yield.'

770. Against this line is printed what *looks* like August 9, but the 9 is put for the mark of contraction for *us* (see Preface, § 6), and the word meant is 'August*us*,' who is therefore the emperor here intended.

775. *Carde*, cared; cf. *rulde* for *ruled* in l. 771.

777. *Baudkin*, 'a very rich kind of stuff, the web being gold and the woof silk, with embroidery.'—Nares. It is derived from the Low Latin *Balderkinus*, an adjective formed from *Baldacca*, which again is formed from *Bagdad*, the Persian city, whence it came. It was first introduced into England in the thirteenth century.

Cutworks, fantastic patterns in lace, &c.

783. *Cento por Cento*, cent per cent; as much again. Gascoigne speaks ironically here, in saying that merchants are *not* wont to do the things which he enumerates.

784. *Browne paper.* 'First, here's young master Rash; he's in for

a commodity of *brown paper* and old ginger, nine-score and seventeen pounds;' Measure for Measure, iv. 3. In an excellent note upon this in Staunton's Shakespeare, we learn that it was the custom with money-lenders, then as now, to compel young spendthrift borrowers to take part of the loan in goods, frequently of the most worthless kind. In some cases, the commodity thus lent actually consisted, in part, of brown paper. This is clear from several passages; e. g. in Greene's Quip for an Upstart Courtier, 1592, we read :—' For the marchant delivered the yron, tin, lead, hops, sugars, spices, oiles, *browne paper,* or whatsoever else, from sixe moneths to sixe moneths : whiche when the poore gentleman came to *sell againe,* hee could not make three-score and ten in the hundred beside the usury.'

785. *Morrice-bells,* bells used for the morris-dance, in which mummers disported themselves. The 1st of May was a favourite day for such diversions.

Byllets, firewood; see note to l. 784.

787. *Father Derbies bands,* handcuffs. Why so called, I know not; but 'darbies' is still a slang term for the same.

788. 'To support their steps by the staff of statute-staple.' A certain kind of bond was named a *statute-merchant,* or a *statute-staple,* because it was sometimes acknowledged before one of the clerks of *statutes-merchant,* and the mayor of the *staple*; see the explanation in Blount's Νομολεξικον, which is quoted by Nares. Hence *statute-staple* means simply a *bond*; but in this particular passage it is (perhaps) jocularly applied to that particular *bond* which was exercised by fastening a prisoner by a chain to a *staple* in a wall; hence ' by statute-staples staffe' means here, by the support of a prison-wall staple. The true sense of *staple* was, an authorised place where only certain goods were allowed to be sold: see Longman, Hist. of Edward III, i. 340.

789. 'To compel young roysterers, by a legal recognisance or obligation, to read arithmetic daily ;' i. e. to learn accounts by being frequently dunned for payment of debts contracted.

791. Wood Street and Bread Street, which turn out of Cheapside, and Poultry, which is a continuation of it, each contained a prison called a *counter.* See next line; and see pref. to Ben Jonson's Every Man in his Humour, ed. Wheatley, p. lviii.

793. *Fell,* skin. It is the A.S. *fel,* equivalent to Lat. *pellis.*

817. *Are not,* said ironically; he means, they *are* proud, &c. The lines beginning *not one of these,* are equally ironical.

835. Lev. xxv. 36, 37. All usury was forbidden by the canon-law.

839. *A waspe.* This well illustrates a passage in Pierce the Ploughman's Crede, l. 648, where it is said of a friar—

'There is no waspe in this werlde that will wilfulloker [*more willingly*]
styngen.'

850. Chaucer (Prol. 190) says of the monk, that—

'Greyhoundes he hadde, as swifte as fowel in flight ;
Of prikyng and of huntyng for the hare
Was al his lust, for no cost wolde he spare.'

The hawks and hounds used by the clergy, even by bishops, furnished
a good subject for satire, of which our old poets frequently availed
themselves. Cf. Piers the Plowman, B. x. 308, and a note in Warton,
Hist. Eng. Poetry, ii. 57, ed. 1840 ; ii. 261, ed. 1871.

864. Shakespeare uses *ceremonies* at the end of a line in the same
manner ; Julius Cæsar, i. 1. 70.

874. *Bidde you pray.* Here the poet imitates the form of a bidding-
prayer, as it is called. *Beades* means *prayers*, and a *bidding-prayer*
signifies etymologically a *praying prayer*, and to *bid beads* is to *pray
prayers*.

876. *Christes sake*, the correct form, sometimes corrupted into *Christ
his sake*, as in our present Prayer Book.

1017. *Peerce.* The fame of the poem entitled 'Piers the Plowman'
made the phrase proverbial ; see l. 1025.

1018. *So*, in that case. *Sayler*, sailor.

1029. *Clime to heauen.* This looks as if Gascoigne had actually read
Piers the Plowman, viz. in the editions of 1550 or 1561. Compare—

'Ne none sonner saued ne sadder [*firmer*] of bileue
Than plowmen and pastoures and pore comune laboreres.
Souteres and shepherdes, such lewed iottes [*wretches*]
Percen with a *pater-noster* the paleys of heuene,' &c.—B. x. 458.

1034. 'By ploughing up the ridges which mark their boundaries.'

1039. *They racke*, they (the landlords) stretch, raise. A *rack-rent* is a
rent estimated at the *full* value. *An ace;* see l. 1172.

1058. *Cockets*, certificates that goods have paid duty. Also used in
the sense of a stamp for bread, and hence bread of a peculiar quality
was called *cocket*. See Piers the Plowman (Clar. Press Ser.), note to
Pass. vi. l. 306.

1066. *When*, &c. This, of course, means *never*.

1077. *Firmentie.* Nares says :—'Furmenty, Furmity, or Frumity.
Still a favourite dish in the north, consisting of hulled wheat boiled in
milk, and seasoned. It was especially a Christmas dish.' But Gascoigne
here uses it to denote adulterated malt.

1078. *Dauie Diker*, David the ditcher ; a proverbial name. It occurs
in Piers Plowman, B. v. 320.

1080. *Toll*, take toll, by stealing some of the corn sent to be ground.

Golden thumbe; see a long note in Mr. Morris's Chaucer's Prologue, &c. (Clar. Press. Ser.), on l. 563 of the Prologue.

1083. *Blowe,* blow out with a quill, to make it look plump.

1084. *Horsecorser,* sometimes corrupted into *horse-scorcer,* is an exchanger of or dealer in horses. See Nares, who wrongly regards *scorcer* as the original form.

1087. *Make more bones,* hesitate more. *To have a bone to pick* is to have plenty of occupation, and *to give a bone to pick* is to give one plenty to do; but *to make no bones* is to snap up without hesitation, to swallow whole, and hence, to do a thing at once, not to hesitate. Gascoigne has, in l. 565 of this very poem, the expression—'Yet never *made nor bones* nor brags therof.'

1094. *Giuing day,* assigning a future day of payment, giving credit.

1103. *Shriues,* sheriffs.

1104. *Strain,* distrain.

1114. *Coles,* possibly *deceits, lies.* A *cole-prophet* is a deceitful prophet. See the note by 'M. R.' in Notes and Queries, Fourth Series, iv. 358. Otherwise, 'precious coles' must be a minced oath.

1117. *Lays,* Laïs, a courtezan; a proverbial name in ancient Greece.

1135. *Monsters.* They turn out to be *women.*

1141. *Kinde,* nature, natural beauty.

1157. *Side,* ample, hanging down low. Occleve ridicules 'the *side* sleves of penyles groomes.' See Nares, who gives several examples. The A. S. *sid* means large, ample, vast.

1163. *Copt,* for *copped,* i. e. *topped,* from O. E. *cop,* a top, W. *cop.* Nares quotes 'Wearing long coates and *copped* caps, not unlike to our idiots;' Sandys, Travels, p. 47. Mr. Halliwell remarks, s. v. *Copatain,* 'According to Kennet, p. 54, "a hat with a high crown is called a *copped* crown hat."'

Flaunt-a-flaunt, 'an adverb of the author's own invention probably; but the sense is of course clear. The fashionable girls in Gascoigne's day wore tall hats with feathers.'—Hazlitt.

1172. *Loke of,* look off, look away. *An ace,* a jot.

1174. *Like,* please.

Tam Marti quam Mercurio, equally devoted to warfare and learning; Gascoigne's motto in all his works, and of frequent occurrence in them.

XXVII. JOHN LYLY.

Line 10. *Pithagoras.* Pythagoras, a native of Samos, flourished about B.C. 540–510. No writings of his are extant, but several spurious pieces are current in his name. In a Latin collection of apophthegms, entitled 'Symbola Pythagorae Philosophi,' we find some (but not all) of the precepts here referred to, viz.—' Ab eo, quod nigram caudam habet, abstine; terrestrium enim decorum est.' 'Stateram ne transilias.' 'Annulum ne feras.' 'Ignem gladio ne scalpas.' 'Cor ne vores' (a common proverb, quoted by Bacon in the form 'Cor ne edito '). ' Fabis abstine.'

64. *Panthers.* Panthers were supposed to have a very fragrant breath. This belief is found in Pliny (Hist. Nat. viii. 17, xxi. 7); in an old Anglo-Saxon poem on the Panther, in the Codex Exoniensis, and in most of the old Bestiaries, or descriptions of beasts. Cf. Dryden, The Hind and the Panther, pt. ii. 1. 228, and Mr. Christie's note (Clar. Press Series). Odet de Foix, marshal of France (died 1528) took for a device a panther, with the motto *Allicit ulterius,* he entices further. See Mrs. Palliser's Devices, Badges, and Warcries, p. 105.

68. *Phisition.* Cf. the lines in the third stanza of Tasso's Gerusalemme Liberata—

> ' Cosí all'egro fanciul porgiamo aspersi
> Di soave licor gli orli del vaso ;
> Succhi amari ingannato intanto ei beve,
> E dall' inganno suo vita riceve.'

115. *Grace.* Compare Ascham's remarks at p. 307.

131. *Appelles,* the most celebrated of Grecian painters, a contemporary and friend of Alexander the Great, is said never to have spent a day without practising his skill; whence the proverb, ' Nulla dies sine linea.'

134. *Hesiodas,* rather Hesiodus ('Ησίοδος), flourished about B.C. 735. The reference is to his Works and Days, 1. 276 :—

> τόνδε γὰρ ἀνθρώποισι νόμον διέταξε Κρονίων,
> ἰχθύσι μὲν, καὶ θηρσὶ καὶ οἰωνοῖς πετεηνοῖς,
> ἔσθειν ἀλλήλους, ἐπεὶ οὐ δίκη ἐστὶν ἐν αὐτοῖς,
> ἀνθρώποισι δ' ἔδωκε δίκην, ἣ πολλὸν ἀρίστη
> γίνεται.

The German poet Herder has an epigram, which I thus translate :—

> ' Over the race of brutes by *speech* man's race is exalted,
> If without *reason* he speak, brutes are more worthy than he.'

147. *Athens ;* doubtless intended by Lyly for England. At that time, Italy was regarded by Englishmen as a sink of iniquity ; hence the proverb, 'Inglese Italianato é un diavolo incarnato'—an 'Italianated' Englishman is a devil incarnate. See this proverb, and reflections upon it, in Ascham's Scholemaster, part i. near the end.

154. *Monarches,* old spelling for *monarchies ;* see p. 248.

176-187. The whole of this sentence is repeated from a passage very near the beginning of the book, where an old gentleman of Naples gives Euphues a long piece of excellent advice, to which he pays but little attention.

220. *To ryde well.* Cf. the remarks of Sir Thomas Elyot, p. 200.

XXVIII. EDMUND SPENSER.

(A) *The Shepheardes Calender. Nouember.*

Ægloga. This odd spelling of *eclogue* gave rise to a curiously wrong etymology. Kirke, who wrote the Arguments and Glosses to the Shepheardes Calender, derived the word from the Greek αἴξ (gen. αἰγός), a goat, as though they were *goatherd's* tales; though he admits that 'few Goteheards have to doe herein.' See the Generall Argument, prefixed by Kirke to Spenser's work.

Argument. Written by Kirke, who seems to have appreciated the eclogue as he ought. By Marot is meant Clément Marot, born 1495, died 1544. For a notice of him and his works, see Besant's Early French Poetry, ch. xii., and the lately published biography by Professor Morley, who shows that the whole of this eclogue is founded upon that of Marot on the death of Louise of Savoy, Queen-regent of France, mother of Francis I, who died September 29, 1531.

Colin is Spenser; *Thenot*, probably Sir Philip Sydney, at whose house, at Penshurst, this eclogue is said to have been written. The metre of this eclogue should be noticed. The first eight lines make a perfect stanza. In ll. 9–52 we have eleven stanzas of four lines each, in which each stanza begins with the rime with which the preceding one terminates; so that the stanzas are thus linked together throughout. In ll. 53–202 we have fifteen exquisitely constructed stanzas of ten lines each. At the end is a simple stanza of six lines.

Line 9. *Nis*, is not.

Merimake, merrymaking; a coined word.

13. *Welked*, shortened; the true meaning is *withered*; cf. Ger. *welken*, to wither, decay. Spenser's Old English is exceedingly incorrect.

15. *Laye*, clearly used for a *stall*; but there is apparently no other instance of it. Elsewhere in Spenser it means a *lea*, a *field*, as in l. 188 below. In Old English, a *lay-stall* is a place to deposit filth; hence Spenser takes the liberty of using *laye* as a place of deposit.

16. Literally, 'And taken up his abode in the Fishes' basket.' Spenser makes the very singular mistake of connecting November with the sign of Pisces, instead of with that of Sagittarius. See Nares, s. v. *Haske.*

21. 'But if thou by all means please to undertake light virelays,' &c.

26. *Sits*, it befits, becomes. It is *not* an error for *fits*, as might be supposed. The word is sufficiently common in Early English. In Morte Arthure, ed. Perry, l. 953, we have—

'He salu3ede that sorowfulle with *sittande* wordez'—

i. e. he saluted that sorrowful one with fitting words, where the alliteration makes us quite sure about the first letter. It occurs again in the Faerie Queene, i. 1. 30.

39. *May*, maiden ; no connection with the month. See the Glosse.

53. *Melpomene.* The line quoted by Kirke is not in the Eclogues, Georgics, or Æneid of Virgil. It is, in fact, from Ausonius, Idyll xx. 20.

55. Possibly, by Hecuba, Kirke means Polydorus; for his ghost appears with the very first line of the Hecuba of Euripides, saying—

Ἥκω νεκρῶν κευθμῶνα καὶ σκότου πύλας
λιπών, ἵν' Ἅιδης χωρὶς ᾤκισται θεῶν, κ.τ.λ.

The ghost of Tantalus appears in the first scene of Seneca's tragedy of Thyestes.

98. *Heame*, home. It is certain that the Shepheardes Calender contains many traces of Northern dialect, and the fact is important, as clearly indicating that he resided in Lancashire not only after going to Cambridge, as is known, but also for a considerable time *before* it. Compare his autobiographical statements in the eclogue for December. I should also conclude that *Dido* was a north-country girl, a Lancashire 'witch' probably. But her lover was 'Lobbin,' not 'Colin.'

105. An allusion to the famous Dance of Death, founded on some verses originally written by one Macaber in German. See Warton, ii. 271, ed. 1840 ; iii. 55, ed. 1871.

141. *Philomele.* Kirke, in mentioning Gascoigne, refers to an elegy composed by him, and printed in 1576, with the title 'The Complaynt of Phylomene.' It is worthy of remark that ll. 25 and 26 of this elegy well illustrate l. 26 above. The Nightingale is there thus spoken of—

'Now in good sooth, quoth she, sometimes I wepe
To see Tom Tyttimouse so much set by [*esteemed*].'

148. *Fatall sisters;* see note above, p. 461 ; and cf. l. 163 below.

186. E. K. refers us to Plato. There is a passage somewhat to this effect in Plato's Phædo, § v. where Socrates says that all who take a worthy view of the matter must wish for death, yet they may not lay violent hands upon themselves. Lucan (iv. 519) has the fine lines—

> ' Uicturosque dei celant, ut uiuere durent,
>   Felix esse mori.'

Expert, experience; a word coined by Spenser, and badly coined.

187. *Astert*, evidently intended to mean 'befall unawares,' as E. K. says. This is a good instance of the peril a poet incurs when using archaic terms which he does not well understand. The true meaning of *asterte* is to escape from, to start or get away, as in Chaucer, Knightes Tale, l. 737—

> ' Ches which thou wilt, for thou schalt not *asterte.*'

Thus Spenser's line, literally translated, means 'The shepherd can there escape from no danger,' which is just the opposite of what is intended. The fact is that Spenser, in using archaic words, frequently made mistakes, as e. g. when he took *yede* to be a verb in the infinitive mood; see note to Sect. XXIV. 30, p. 465.

194. Cf. Milton's Lycidas, l. 165, and Pope's Fourth Pastoral on Daphne.

195. The meaning of ' my Commentarye' in the Glosse upon this line is a little obscure, but we may easily guess it. It is clear that Kirke had written a commentary upon 'The Dreams' of Spenser. The only works to which this title is strictly applicable are 'The Visions of the World's Vanity,' ' Bellay's Visions,' and ' Petrarch's Visions.' But the work here referred to is certainly the Ruins of Time, a poem of much the same character, which must (like the poems above-mentioned) have been written at a very early period of the poet's life. L. 399 of the Ruins of Time is as follows:—

> ' On *Nectar* and *Ambrosia* do feede';

a line which is precisely parallel to 'There drincks she *Nectar* with *Ambrosia* mixt.'

Embleme (Glosse). The words 'as doome of ill desert' occur in l. 184 above. The reference to Chaucer I cannot verify. In Latin the same thought is epigrammatically expressed by *mors janua vitæ*.

(B)   *The Shepheardes Calender.   December.*

Argument. *Pan.* Evidently suggested by Clément Marot's poem, ' Eclogue au roy soubs les noms de Pan et Robin.' This Eclogue (as observed by Warton, and in Besant's Early French Poetry, pp. 254, 286) resembles Marot's poem very closely. See the comparison between the poems fully worked out in Professor Morley's ' Clément Marot,' vol. ii. ch. xi.

Line 4. *Tityrus* certainly means Chaucer. This is placed beyond doubt by the Epilogue at the end of the poem. *Colin* is Spenser.

7. Compare the lines in Marot (Besant, Early French Poetry, p. 255)—

> 'Que quelque jour je ferois des chansons
> À ta louenge, O Pan Dieu tressacré !'

11. The line cited by Kirke is in Eclogue ii. l. 33.

19. The lines at first sight seem to describe Spenser's early life, which he probably passed in the North. In fact, however, he here follows Marot pretty closely. I again quote from Mr. Besant.

> 'Sur le printemps de ma jeunesse folle,
> Je ressembloys l'arondelle qui vole,
> Puis çà, puis là ; l'aage me conduisoit
> Sans paour ne soing, où le cueur me disoit,
> En la forest, sans la craincte des loups,
> Je m'en allois souvent cueiller le houx, .
> Pour faire gluz a prendre oyseaulx ramaiges[1],
> Tous différens de chantz et de plumaiges ; .
> Ou me souloys[2], pour les prendre, entremettre
> À faire brics[3], ou caiges pour les mettre.
> Ou transnouoys[4] les rivières profondes,
> Ou r'enforçoys[5] sur le genoil les fondes[6],
> Puis d'en tirer droict et loing j'apprenois
> Pour chasser loups et abbatre des noix.
> O quantes foys aux arbres grimpé j'ay
> Pour desnicher ou la pie, ou la geay,
> Ou pour gecter des fruictz jà meurs et beaulx
> À mes compaings, qui tendoient leurs chappeaulx.'

38. This line is again like Marot's :—

> 'Ou la nature aux Muses inclinée.'

63. *Whether*, whither.

76. *Reason.* So in all the old editions. Hughes proposed to read *season.*

84. (Glosse.) I know no reason for the word 'alwayes.'

87. *Soothe of byrds*, soothsaying by observing the flights of birds. The words *augury* and *auspice* are both derived from the Lat. *auis*, a bird.

88. (Glosse.)

> 'Quos hominum ex facie Dea saeua potentibus herbis
> Induerat Circe in uultus ac terga ferarum.'—Virg. Æn. vii. 19.

---

[1] Wild. [2] Was accustomed. [3] Traps.
[4] Swam across. [5] Tied up. [6] Slings.

91. Compare

> 'Inuentum medicina meum est ; opiferque per orbem
> Dicor; et herbarum est subiecta potentia nobis.
> Hei mihi, quod nullis amor est medicabilis herbis,
> Nec prosunt domino, quae prosunt omnibus, artes.'
>
> Ovid, Met. i. 521.

98. *All to rathe,* all too soon.

105. *At erst,* lit. at first. But it is here made to express something else, viz. either *too soon* or *at last.* It is an instance of misuse of words.

113. *Rosalind,* whom he in the Eclogue for April terms 'the widdowes daughter of the glenne,' was some Northern beauty of unknown name, with whom Spenser fell deeply in love. She did not, however, return his love; and, after cherishing an affection for her for some years, he at length, in 1592, met an Elizabeth, whom, about a year and a half afterwards, he married.

116. *Shifting,* i. e. rapid movement, dancing.

118. *Unsoote,* unsweet, bitter.

121. Cf. Virgil, Ecl. v. 36, and Job xxxi. 38-40.

133. Spoken by poetical licence. Spenser was only twenty-seven years old.

Embleme (Glosse). 'Exegi,' &c.; Horace, Carm. iii. 50. 'Grande,' &c.; Ovid, Metam. xv. 871. The latter quotation is not quite correct. The usual reading is '*Jamque* opus,' &c.; also *ignes,* not *ignis.* The motto 'Vivitur ingenio,' &c., is paraphrased from Marot's motto.

Epilogue.

8. *A lowly gate,* a lowly way, in a humble manner.

9. *Tityrus.* Certainly Chaucer, because he is linked with his contemporary William Langley or Langland, the author of Piers the Plowman. Yet Spenser's description of the latter is not accurate, unless we take the word *playde* in a musical sense, i. e. take it to mean *played* or *piped* the story of the Ploughman. With this interpretation, however, it is strictly accurate to define Langland as a pilgrim, who sang of the Ploughman. This note is the more necessary, because it is a common mistake to suppose that Piers the Plowman is the name of an *author,* whereas it merely denotes the *subject* of the 'pilgrim' Langland's poem.

9-11. These lines are imitated from Statius, Thebaid xii. 816—

> 'Uiue precor, nec tu diuinam Aeneida tenta,
> Sed longe sequere, et uestigia semper adora.'

Merce, non Mercede, Thanks, not Reward (in money); it expresses the poet's object.

GLOSSARIAL INDEX.

Abbreviations employed, and List of Dictionaries referred to.

A. S. = Anglo-Saxon (Bosworth, Grein).
Dan. = Danish (Ferrall and Repp).
Du. = Dutch (Tauchnitz).
E. = English (Webster, revised by Goodrich, Porter, and Mahn).
F. = French (Pick's Etym. Dict.).
G. = German (Flügel).
Gael. = Gaelic (Macleod and Dewar).
Icel. = Icelandic (Egilsson, Möbius, Vigfusson).
It. = Italian (Meadows).
Low Lat. = Low Latin (Ducange).
M.E. = Middle English (Halliwell, Stratmann).
Mœso·Goth. = Mœso-Gothic (Skeat).
O.F. = Old French (Burguy, Roquefort).

O.H.G. = Old High German (Wackernagel).
P.Pl. = Piers the Plowman (ed. Skeat, or ed. Wright).
Prompt. Parv. = Promptorium Parvulorum, ed. Way (Camden Society).
Prov. E. = Provincial English (Halliwell).
Sc. = Scottish (Jamieson).
Sp. = Spanish (Meadows).
Sw. = Swedish (Tauchnitz).
Suio-Goth. = Suio-Gothic or Old Swedish (Ihre).
W. = Welsh (Spurrell).
Wedgwood = Wedgwood's Etymological English Dictionary.

Also *adj.* adjective; *adv.* adverb; *num.* numeral; *pres. part.* present participle; *pp.* past participle, &c.

The following abbreviations are used in a particular sense :—*v.* verb in the infinitive mood; *pr. s., pt. s.,* the *third person* singular of the present or past tense; *pr. pl., pt. pl.* the *third person* plural of those tenses, except when 1 *p.* or 2 *p.* is added; so also *imp. s.* the *second* person singular of the imperative; *imp. pl.* the *second* person plural of the same. S. or F. denotes that a word is of Saxon or French origin.

A.

A, *put for* of, 7. 84; *a trusti tre* = of trusty wood. Cf. l. 92. See Athe.

A, *prep.* on; a foote, on foot, 3 *b.* 1146.

Abasshe, *v.* F. to abash, terrify, 15 *b.* 32; *pp.* Abasshid, 9. 52; Abaist, 4. 166. O. F. *esbahir*, to

frighten, from *baer,* to open the mouth, to cry baa or bo.

Abhomynable, *adj.* abominable, 16. 64.

Abilʒeit, *pp.* apparelled, 13. 34. F. *habiller*, to dress.

Abilʒement, *sb.* habiliment, clothing, 22. 4546.

Abjecte, *v.* Lat. to cast aside, 12. 5.

Abone, *prep.* S. above, 7. 14, 22. 5564. A. S. *abúfan.*

Abye, *v.* S. pay, viz. for my rashness, 12. 17. A. S. *abicgan,* to buy back. To *abye* (pay) has often been corrupted into *abide.*

Accompt, *sb.* F. account, 19 *f.* 46, 26. 441; *pl.* Accomptes, 16. 232.

Accompted, *pp.* F. accounted, 26. 754. Lat. *computo,* I reckon.

Accorded, *pt. s.* F. granted, 9. 117. Lat. *ad,* to, and *cor,* gen. *cordis,* the heart.

Accordyng, *pres. part.* suiting, agreeing, 13. 226.

Ace, *sb.* a single bit, a jot, 26. 1039, 1172. Lat. *as,* one (on a die).

Adawed, *pp.* awakened, 3 *b.* 1287. Cf.

> 'And at the last he gan his breath to drawe,
> And of his *swough* sone after that *adawe.*'

Chaucer, Troil. and Cres. iii. 1126. From A.S. *dægian,* to become day, to dawn. See *Adaw* in Wedgwood.

A-do, to do, 15 *b.* 123. *A-do* stands for *at do,* i.e. to do, a Northern English idiom. In the Scandinavian languages, the sign of the infin. mood is not *to,* but *at.*

Aferde, *pp.* afraid, 18. xvii. 73. A. S. *afæran,* to frighten, from *fær, sb.* fear, wh. is related to *fær,* adj. sudden.

Affamysit, *pp.* famished, 22. 5495.

Afferde, *pp.* a-feared, frightened, 3 *b.* 1069.

Affray, *sb.* F. terror, fear, 3 *b.* 1294, 11 *a.* 27; *pl.* Affrayis, 22. 5503. F. *effroi,* terror. See **Effray.**

Affrayd, *pp.* F. terrified, afraid, 3 *b.* 1304; Affrayt, 13. 11. F. *effrayer,* to terrify. See **Affray.**

Agast, *adj.* terrified, 6. 230; 20 *a.*

39. Cf. Mœso-Goth. *usgaisjan,* to terrify. The modern spelling *aghast* is wrong.

Agayn, *prep.* S. against, 12. 19.

Agazed, *pp.* aghast, 19 *b.* 44. The mistake in using *agazed* for *aghast* is explained by Wedgwood. See **Agast.**

Agenst-Christ, *sb.* Antichrist, 16. 108.

Ageyn, *prep.* against, 3 *b.* 1179. A. S. *ongeán.*

Ageyns, *prep.* S. against, 3 *b.* 1199. Cf. Ageyn.

Aggreable, *adj.* F. favourable, 9. 114. Lat. *gratus.*

A-gone, *pp.* S. gone away, 10. 95. A. S. *ágán,* to pass away. Sometimes wrongly supposed to be a corruption of *ygone.*

A-hungerd, *pp.* pinched with hunger, 3 *a.* 14. A. S. *of-hingrian,* to hunger exceedingly.

Airtis, *sb. pl.* quarters, 22. 5600. Gael. *aird,* a quarter of the compass, *ard,* high, *ard,* a height, heaven. See **Art.**

Aisliche, *adv.* timorously, 1. 341. A. S. *egeslíce,* fearfully; O. H. G. *egesliche,* fearfully; from A. S. *egesa,* O. H. G. *egisa, egiso,* fear.

Akis, *sb. pl.* oaks, 13. 167. A.S. *ác.*

Alabaustre, *sb.* alabaster, 1. 183.

Alawe, *adv.* in the *low* ground, in the valley, 4. 154.

Alblastrye, *sb.* the use of crossbows, 4. 156. From Lat. *arcus* and *balista.*

Alewin, *num.* eleven, 22. 4509.

Algate, *adv.* by all means, wholly, 2. 604, 28 *a.* 21. M. E. *gate,* a way; A. S. *algeats,* altogether.

Alhool (*for* al hool), completely whole, 3 *b.* 1411.

Alichtyn, *v.* to enlighten, 13. 28.

Alkynd, i. e. of every kind, 13. 256. *Alkynd-fruyt* = fruit of every kind. *Alkynd bestiall* = beasts of every kind, 1. 263.

All, *adv.* completely, 23. iii. 126. *All* was frequently used before verbs beginning with the intensive prefix *to*; in course of time, this prefix was (by a mistake) separated from the verb, and used as if *all to* meant *altogether*.

Allevin, *pp.* admitted (?), 11 *b.* 21. See Jamieson's Dict. But it should mean *eleven*.

Allures, *sb. pl.* alleys, passages, walks, 3 *b.* 1267. See note.

Almaygnes, *sb. pl.* F. Germans, 15 *b.* 110.

A-lofe, *adv.* aloof, 15 *a.* 29. This shews the deriv. of *aloof* from *all off* (given in some books) to be absurd. Cf. Sw. *lof*, in *lofvart*, windward; Du. *loef*, weather-gauge, E. *luff*; connected with M. E. *lof*, a kind of rudder.

Aloute, *v.* to bow down, 1. 750. A. S. *hlútan*, to bow.

Alowe, *v.* F. to approve of, 16. 211, 20 *a.* 37. Lat. *ad*, to, and *laudare*, to praise.

Als, *adv.* also, 6. 230; as, 11 *a.* 18; als weill = as well, 22. 5454. Contr. from Also, q. v.

Als-as, *adv.* just as if, 1. 378. Contr. from *all-so-as*.

Also, *conj.* S. as, so, 2. 611. A. S. *eall swá*, all so, just so.

Aluterly, *adv.* all utterly, completely, 13. 206.

Alyctnyng, *pres. part.* illumining, 13. 59.

Alyte, *for* a lyte, *adv.* a little, 4. 161. A. S. *lyt*, a little.

Ambassages, *sb. pl.* F. embassies, 21. 180. Low Lat. *ambascia*, of Teutonic origin; Mœso-Goth. *andbahts*, a servant, whence G. *amt*, an office.

Amene, *adj.* pleasant, 11 *a.* 10; Ameyn, 13. 54. Lat. *amoenus*.

Amerant, *adj.* amaranth, 13. 151. Gk. ἀμάραντος, unfading, from ἀ, not, and μαραίνω, I wither.

Amonges, *prep.* S. amongst, 2. 298. A.S. *gemang*, among.

Amyabill, *adj.* lovely, 13. 151. Lat. *amare*, to love.

Ancient, *sb.* a senior, 25. 136.

And, *conj.* if, 1. 393, 2. 615, 7. 129, 14. 297; And if = an if, if, 20 *c.* 85. See note to 8. iii. 46.

Ane, *adj.* one, 6. 190. A. S. *án*.

Anew, *pl. adj.* enough, 6. 324. A. S. *genóh*, sufficient.

Anewis, *sb. pl.* lit. rings, perhaps buds or knops, 4. 160. O. F. *anel, aniau, aneau*, a ring; from Lat. *anellus*, dim. of *annulus*.

Annamyllit, *pp.* F. enamelled, 11 *a.* 6. O. F. *en*, prefix, and *esmail*, enamel; from the same root as E. *smelt*.

Anoon, *adv.* anon, immediately, 3 *b.* 1290. A. S. *on án*, in one.

Anuell, *sb.* a sum of money paid for a mass to be said *annually* (or perhaps, every day *throughout a year*), 1. 414.

Anyghtes (*for* on nyghtes), at night, nightly, 3 *b.* 1360.

Aparte, *v.* to part away, to interrupt, 24. 14.

Apayd, *pp.* F. pleased; hence, euel apayd = ill pleased, 3 *b.* 1081. O. F. *apaier*, to appease, from Lat. *pacare*.

Appairing, *sb.* injuring, lessening, 18. xviii. 33. From Lat. *ad*, and F. *pire*, Lat. *peior*, worse; hence *appair*, to make worse, *impair*.

Apperand, *pres. part.* appearing, 6. 342.

Apply, *v.* F. bend to, follow after, 20 *b.* 42.

Areysed, *pt. s.* raised, 8. iii. 13.

Armes, *interj.* arms! an oath, by God's arms (written *Gogs arms* in the same play, ed. Arber, p. 27), 23. iii. 3. 94.

Armony, *sb.* F. harmony, 4. 152; 11 *a.* 1. It. *armonia*.

Art, *sb.* quarter, direction, point of

the compass, 6. 309; *every art*, in every direction, on all sides, 13. 232. Gaelic *aird*, a height, point of the compass; hence, Sc. *airt*. See Airtis.

Artow, *for* art thou, 4. 173.

As, *prep*. as regards, 6. 313; 8. iii. 53.

Asaye, *imp. s.* test, try (it), 1. 247.

Aspectis, *sb. pl.* aspects, 13. 42. A term in astrology.

Aspert (?), *adj.* harsh, cruel, 4. 170. F. *aspre*, Lat. *asper*. So says Jamieson; but the passage is obscure. Perhaps *aspert = expert*; see note.

Aspie, *v.* to espy, 5 *a.* 31.

Asprely, *adv.* sharply, roughly, 18. xvii. 157. Lat. *asper*, rough.

Aspy, *sb.* spy, beholder, 13. 265.

Assay, *v.* F. make trial of, 3 *a.* 14: to attempt, try to do, essay, 18. xvii. 220. Lat. *exagium*, a balance, from *ex*, out, and *ago*, I put in motion.

Assay, *sb.* F. trial, proof, 5 *b.* 13.

Assoile, *v.* F. to answer, 2. 615. Lat. *absoluere*.

Assured, *pp.* bound by promise, 3 *b.* 1206.

Astart, *v.* to start aside, start from, 19 *a.* 283.

Astate, *sb.* F. state, 14. 308; *pl.* Astates, conditions, ranks, 18. xvii. 42.

Astert, *v.* to start from, shun, escape: *wrongly used in the sense* to startle, frighten, 28 *a.* 187; *pr. s.* Asterteth, starts aside, escapes, 2. 282; *pr. s. subj.* Asterte, may escape, may be missing, 3 *b.* 1361. See Astart.

Astoynde, *pp.* S. astounded, astonished, 24. 29. See Stoynde.

At, *conj.* that, 6. 240. Dan. *at*.

Athe, *put for* of the, 7. 51.

Attaynt, *pp.* F. attainted, marred, 24. 15. Lat. *tango*, I touch.

Attechyng, F. *pres. part.* attaching,

indicting, 13. 266. Cf. Bret. *tach*, a nail, *tack*.

Atteir, *sb.* F. attire, 11 *a.* 3.

Atteynt, *pp.* F. convicted of treason, proved to be traitors, 3 *b.* 1207. See Attaynt.

Attones, *adv.* at once, 26. 759; Attonis, 22. 5592; Attonys, 3 *b.* 1162.

Auale, *v.* F. to subside, 24. 19; to condescend, 14. 1117; *pp.* Auailed, lowered, 19 *f.* 30. O. F. *avaler*, M.E. *vail*, to lower; from *à val*, Lat. *ad uallem*, to the valley, downward. Cf. E. *avalanche*.

Auaunce, *imp. s.* F. advance, 20 *c.* 71. Lat. *ab*, from, *ante*, before; whence also E. *van*, *van*-guard.

Avauntagis, *sb. pl.* F. advantages, 5 *b.* 1.

Auchtene, *num.* eighteen, 6. 192.

Auctor, *sb.* Lat. an author, 16. 192.

Aventure, *sb.* F. adventure, chance, 3 *b.* 1232.

Auld, *adj.* old, 6. 192. A.S. *eald*.

Aunter, *sb.* adventure, chance; *an aunter 3if*, it is a chance if, 1. 789.

Auntrede, 1 *p. s. pt.* adventured (myself), 1. 341.

Avowe, *sb.* F. a vow, 7. 1, 130. Cf. 'That make I myn 'avow;' Chaucer, Kn. Ta. 1379.

Auowe, *v.* F. to maintain, 10. 147. Lat. *uouere*.

Aureat, *adj.* golden, 13. 47. Lat. *aurum*, gold.

Autorite, *sb.* F. authority, 16. 253.

Autour, *sb.* F. author, 18. xvii. 206.

Auysyon, *sb.* F. vision, 8. iii. 62.

Awalk, *imp. s.* S. awake, 11 *a.* 2. The substitution of *lk* for *kk* occurs in Scottish MSS. *Awalk = awakk*, put for *awak*.

Awance, *v.* F. to advance, 6. 366.

Awaytede, 1 *p. s. pt.* perceived,

beheld, 1. 172. O. F. *agaiter*, to watch; cf. E. *wait, wake, watch.*

Awin, *adj.* own, 11 *a.* 18; Awn, 6. 239; Awyn, 13. 72. A. S. *ágen*, own, from *ágan*, to possess.

Awkwart, *adv.* sideways, with a back stroke, 6. 407.

Awoik, 1 *p. s. pt.* awoke, 11 *b.* 50; *pt. s.* Awoilk, 11 *a.* 27. See **Awalk.**

Awppis, *sb.* curlews, 11 *a.* 18.

Awter, *sb.* F. altar, 9. 167.

Axed, *pt. pl.* S. asked, asked for, 2. 600; asked, 2. 610. A. S. *ácsian.*

Ay, *adv.* ever, continually. Icel. *ei.*

Ayer, *sb.* F. air, 24. 31.

Ayr, *sb.* F. an itinerant court of justice; *ane ayr* = in the court, 6. 275. Law French *eyre*, Lat. *iter.*

Ayr, *adj.* early, 13. 304. A. S. *ǽr*, ere.

Aӡenward, *adv.* S. on the contrary, 5 *b.* 53.

B.

Babelyng, *sb.* babbling, 1. 551.

Babishe, *adj.* babyish, 25. 72.

Backside, *sb.* back part, 19 *a.* 594.

Bade. See **Baid.**

Bagage, *sb.* dregs, refuse, 26. 1082. A quotation in Nares (ed. Halliwell, shews that *baggage* sometimes means *scum.*

Baid, *pt. pl.* abode, remained, lasted, lived, 22. 5475; Bade, abode, 6. 260. A. S. *bídan*, pt. t. *ic bád.*

Baill, *sb.* bale, sorrow, 13. 233.

Bair, *adj.* bare, worn alone, 13. 269.

Bairnis, *sb. pl.* bairns, children, 22. 4714. Mœso-Goth. *barn*, a child.

Baite, *v.* to feed, 19 *f.* 16. Icel. *beita*, to cause to *bite*, to feed.

Balks, *sb. pl.* S. ridges, 26. 1034. A. S. *balca*, a balk, heap.

Baly, *sb.* belly, 1. 763.

Balys, *sb. pl.* woes, ills, 7. 140. A. S. *bealu*, bale, evil.

Banne, *pr. s. subj.* may curse, 20 *c.* 63.

Banwart, *sb.* bonewort, 13. 115. A. S. *bánwort*, bonewort, a violet, perhaps the small knapweed (Bosworth).

Barayn, *adj.* F. barren, 17 *c.* 15

Barm, *sb.* bosom, 13. 76. A. S. *bearm.*

Barmkyn, *sb.* rampart, 13. 23. Certainly unconnected with E. *barm*, bosom; probably allied to G. *brame*, a *brim*, border, *verbrämen*, to border. It is equivalent to O. E. *barnekyn*, the outermost ward of a castle, which has been connected with *barn*, but doubtfully. I find no reason for connecting it with *barbican.*

Barmkyn-wall, *sb.* rampart-wall, 13. 97.

Barne, child, man, 7. 29. See **Bairnis.** (Or it may be for M. E. *burn*, A. S. *beorn*, a warrior.)

Barrat, *sb.* F. confusion, 6. 253. O. F. *barat*, fraud, confusion; Breton *barad*, treason (Burguy).

Basnetes, *sb. pl.* helmets, 7. 67. O. F. *bassinet*, dim. of *bassin*, a helmet in the form of a *basin.*

Batayls, *sb. pl.* F. battalions, corps, 15 *b.* 1. This use is common in Early English.

Battill, *adj.* rich for pasture, 13. 115.

Baudkin, *sb.* cloth of gold, 26. 777. It. *baldacchino*, a canopy of cloth of gold, from Baldacca, i. e. Bagdad.

Bauld, *adj.* S. bold, 6. 191. A. S. *bald.* See **Bawld.**

Bawd, *pt. s.* S. bade, 11 *a.* 18. See **Bede.**

Bawdry, *sb.* foul conversation, 13. 210.

Bawld, *adj.* S. bold, 11 *a.* 10, A. S. *bald*, Mœso-Goth. *balths.*

Bay, *sb.* noise made by the united songs of birds, din, 13. 232.

Bayardes, *sb. pl.* foolish people, 17 *c.* 27. Properly, a *blind bayard* is a blind horse of a bay colour.

Bayne, *sb.* F. bath, 24. 67. F. *bain.*

Be, *prep.* by, 3 *b.* 1147; be that = by the time that, 7. 15; *or* by that time, 6. 409.

Be. See **Beis.**

Beades, *sb. pl.* S. prayers, 26. 872. See **Bedes.**

Beamous, *sb. pl.* trumpets, 8. iv. 21. (It should rather be spelt *bemes.*) A. S. *béme,* a trumpet.

Beare, *sb.* bier, 28 *a.* 161.

Bearyng, *sb. in phr.* bearyng in hand, i.e. false assurances, 20 *e.* 13.

Beauuize, *prop. name,* Sir Bevis, 18. xvii. 208.

Bebledd, *pp.* covered with blood, 9. 181.

Becomen, *pp.* gone to, 8. iv. 44.

Bede, *v.* S. to offer, 3 *a.* 9; to bid, 3 *a.* 6; *pt. s.* Bawd, bade, 11 *a.* 18; *pt. pl.* Beden, 2. 621. A. S. *beódan,* to bid, to offer.

Bedes, *sb. pl.* prayers, 1. 389. A.S. *béd,* a prayer, *biddan,* to pray.

Bedreynt, *pt. pl.* completely drenched, 24. 21.

Been, *sb. pl.* bees, 1. 727. A. S. *beo,* pl. *beon.*

Beforne, *prep.* before, 7. 28. A. S. *beforan.*

Begouth, 1 *p. s. pt.* began, 13. 306.

Begrime, *pr. s. subj. as imp.* smear, daub, cover all over, 23. iii. 3. 126. The verb would properly have been *tobegrime* in older English, but the use of *to* as a prefix was no longer rightly understood.

Beheestyng, *pres. part.* promising, 3 *b.* 1375. But the spelling *Behoting* (Trin. MS.) is far preferable. A. S. *behátan,* to promise.

Beholdinge, *wrongly used for* Beholden, *pp.* indebted, 25. 10. 'Beholdyn, or bowndyn, *Obligor, teneor.*' Prompt. Parv. Old writers

use not only *beholding,* but even *beholdingness.*

Behote, *pp.* called, named, 28 *b.* 54. (*Misused.*)

Beild, *sb.* protection, 13. 257. O. Swed. *bylja,* to build; but see Murray's Dict.

Beir, *sb.* barley, 22. 4694. Sc. *bear,* Mœso-Goth. *barizeins,* of barley, John 6. 9.

Beis, *pr. s. as fut.* shall be, 6. 433, 22. 5595; *pr. pl.* Beþ, are, 1. 254; *imp. pl.* Beþ, be ye, 1. 442; Beth, 2. 627; *pp.* Be, been, 19 *a.* 347.

Beks, *pr. s.* beckons, gives a sign, gives a significant token or nod, 4. 336. Cf. 'nods and *becks*' in Milton's L'Allegro.

Belded, *pp.* built, 1. 548; Belt, 3 *b.* 1223.

Beldyng, *sb.* building, 1. 548; Beldinge, the act of building, 1. 501.

Belliche, *adv.* beautifully, 1. 173. O. F. *bel,* F. *beau.*

Belt. See **Belded.**

Belyue, *adv.* immediately, 22. 5615. M. E. *bi life,* with life, quickly.

Bemyng, *sb.* humming, 13. 244. Cf. Du. *bommen,* to give a sound like an empty barrel. Probably suggested by M. E. *beme,* a trumpet.

Benefundatum, *sb.* Lat. that which is well founded, premisses (a term in logic), 16. 309.

Benen, *sb. pl.* beans, 1. 762.

Bent, *sb.* coarse grass, grass-covered plain, 7. 11. Cf. G. *binse,* rush, bent-grass.

Benumde, *pp.* bereft, 24. 34. See note.

Benyng, *adj.* F. benign, 6. 202, 11 *a.* 3.

Berayne, *pr. pl.* be-rain, bedew, 19 *f.* 42; *pt. pl.* Beraynde, bedewed, wetted, 24. 74.

Berdes, *sb. pl.* 2. 620; shaued her

berdes = shaved their beards. See note.

Bereth, *pr. s.* bereth on hand = persuades, makes (him) believe, assures, 14. 448.

Beriall, *adj.* blueish-green, of the colour of beryl, 13. 60.

Beris, *sb. gen. sing.* of barley, 13. 77. Sc. *bear,* E. *bar-ley.* See **Beir.**

Besauntes, *sb. pl.* bezants, 8. v. 12. A gold coin worth 15*l.* sterling, first coined at *Byzantium.*

Beseyn, *pp.* S. arrayed, 3 *b.* 1337; Besene, equipped, 11'*a.* 7; Beseyne, decked, 6. 213. *Well beseen* is the common phrase for arranged in a sightly manner.

Beslombred, *pp.* beslobbered, bedaubed, 1. 427. Cf. G. *schlumpern,* to draggle.

Bespayke, *pt. s.* spake, 7. 45. A. S. *besprecan,* to speak to.

Besprent, *pp.* besprinkled, bedewed, 24. 32; Besprint, 28 *a.* 111. A. S. *sprengan,* (1) to spring, (2) to sprinkle.

Besynesse, *sb.* activity, 4. 155.

Bet, *pt. s.* beat, 13. 24; 19 *a.* 627.

Bete, 3 *p. s. imp.* make better, remedy, amend, 7. 140. A. S. *bétan,* to better; *bet,* better; *bót,* advantage, *boot,* remedy; cf. Sc. *beet,* kindle.

Beþ, Beth. See **Beis.**

Betight, *pp.* happened, befallen, 28 *a.* 174. (Should be *had betided.*)

Bewis, *sb. pl.* S. boughs, 11 *a.* 5; Bewys, 13. 66.

Beyderoule, *sb.* a bead-roll, i.e. a catalogue of persons for whom prayers are to be said, the prayers being counted on the beads of a chaplet, 16. 150.

Beyn, *adj.* fair, pleasant, 13. 62. Cf. Icel. *beini,* hospitality, *beinn,* straight.

Beynge, 1 *p. s. pr.* make obeisance,

13. 292. Formed from Icel. *beygja,* to bow; cf. Sw. *bugning,* bowing, *böjning,* bending.

Beyt, *v.* to heal, comfort, 13. 233. See **Bete.**

Biclypped, *pt. s.* embraced, enclosed, covered, 1. 227. M. E. *clip,* to embrace.

Biggeth, *pr. pl.* buy, 1. 360. A.S. *bicgan.*

Bild, *sb.* building, 1. 157.

Birde, *sb.* either *bird* as a term of endearment, or put for M. E. *birde,* a bride, 23. iii. 4. 32.

Birded, *pt. pl.* laid snares as a fowler does for birds, 26. 1150.

Blane, *pt. s.* ceased, stayed, 7. 86. See **Blyne.**

Blank, *adj.* white, 13. 118. F. *blanc.*

Blasynge, *pres. part.* blazoning, i.e. describing in proper heraldic terms, 12. 3. See note. F. *blason,* a coat-of-arms.

Bledder, *sb.* bladder, 1. 222.

Blenk, *sb.* blink, glance, 13. 50.

Blesand, *pres. part.* blazing, 13. 33.

Bleyk, *adj.* bleak, wan, 3 *b.* 1286.

Blive, *adv.* S. quickly, 2. 610; Bliue, 19 *a.* 294. See **Belyue.**

Blomys, *sb. pl.* blooms, 13. 63; Bloosmes, 28 *b.* 103.

Blomyt, *pp.* full of flowers, 13. 95. E. *bloom,* G. *blume.*

Blyne, *v.* S. to stop, 6. 422: *pt. s.* Blane, ceased, 7. 86. A.S. *blinnan, linnan,* to cease.

Blyss, *v.* to bless, 13. 303.

Blyve; as blyve = as quickly as possible, very soon, 3 *b.* 1173. See **Belyue.**

Bobbe, *sb.* a jerk, jog, knock, fillip, 26. 1116; *pl.* Bobbes, 25. 34. 'Bobbyd and betyn' = struck and beaten; Coventry Mysteries, ed. Halliwell, p. 332.

Bochers, *gen. sing.* F. butcher's, 14. 295.

Boistous, *adj.* F. boisterous, noisy, 2. 606. From W. *bwyst*, wild; *bwystus*, savage, ferocious.

Boll, *sb.* a head, rounded top, 22. 4694. Du. *bol*, a globe; cf. E. *bole*, *bowl*, *ball*, a *boil*. See **Bolne**.

Bolne, *pp.* bollen, swollen, 19 *a.* 616. Sw. *bulna*, Dan. *bolne*, to swell, *bulge*.

Bones, *sb. pl.* 26. 1087. To *make bones* is to *hesitate*. It is taken from the idea of wasting time in picking bones; *to make no bones* is to swallow whole.

Bonkis, *sb. pl.* banks, 13. 62.

Boote, *sb.* S. boot, remedy, 2. 627. See **Bete**.

Bootelesse, *adj.* S. useless, 19 *a.* 667. See **Bete**.

Bore, *pp.* born, 3 *a.* 16.

Borned, *pp.* F. burnished, polished, 3 *b.* 1123. See Warton, Hist. Eng. Poetry, ed. 1840, ii. 275. F. *brunir*, lit. to make *brown*.

Bot, *conj.* but, only, merely, 13. 50.

Boun, *adj.* ready, 2. 620; Boune, made ready, prepared to go; *also*, departed, gone on their way, 6. 253. Icel. *búinn*, pp. of *búa*, to prepare. See *Boun* in Glossary to Piers the Plowman.

Bountevous, *adj.* F. bounteous, kind, 3 *b.* 1372.

Bovrd, *sb.* a jest, 13. 214. O.F. *bourde*, a jest, confused with O.F. *bohort*, a tournament, game; from *horde*, a barrier, E. *hurdle*.

Bourding, *sb.* jesting, 5 *a.* 69.

Boustious, *adj.* boisterous, 22. 5597. See **Boistous**.

Bowes, *sb. pl.* S. boughs, 19 *a.* 316; 10. 100.

Bowgle, *sb.* F. wild ox, 11 *a.* 16. See **Bugill**.

Bowlne, *pp.* bollen, swollen, 19 *a.* 348. See **Bolne**.

Bownd, *pt. s.* prepared himself, got ready, 6. 364. See **Boun**.

Boys, *sb. pl.* bows, 7. 26, 60.

Bradit, *pt. s.* drew (used esp. of pulling out a knife or sword), 6. 223. A.S. *bredan*, to draw, *braid*.

Braid, *adv.* broad, wide open, 13. 20.

Braid, *sb.* sudden movement, 11 *a.* 27. Icel. *brægð*, a sudden movement; A.S. *bredan*, to weave, draw away, *braid*.

Brake, *sb.* bracken, brake-fern, 19 *c.* 7.

Brake, *sb.* a thicket, 10. 88; *pl.* Brakes, thorns, briars, 28 *b.* 102. Low Ger. *brake*, brushwood, Dan. *bregne*, fern, E. *bracken*, W. *brwg*, brushwood.

Brassit, *pt. s.* F. braced, i.e. fastened, 6. 242.

Brastyng, *pres. part.* bursting, 13. 39.

Breast, *s.* i.e. voice, 23. iii. 3. 108.

Brede, *sb.* breadth, 3 *b.* 1341; on breid = on breadth, abroad, 13. 74: *hence*, did on breid = did abroad, unfolded, 13. 113. A.S. *brædo*, breadth.

Breme, *adj.* furious, violent, rough, 28 *b.* 148. A.S. *bremman*, to rage, roar.

Brenne, *v.* S. to burn, 9. 43; *pp.* Brent, burnt, 14 *a.* 20.

Brer, *sb.* briar, 13. 257; Brere, 28 *b.* 2; *pl.* Breres, 24. 39. A.S. *brér*; the form *brere* occurs in Spenser.

Brerd, *sb.* surface, top, extent along the surface, 13. 77. A.S. *brerd*, brim, top. See **Croppis**.

Brest, *pt. pl.* burst, 13. 235.

Bretful, *adj.* brimful, 1. 223. Sw. *bräddfull*, brimful; from Sw. *brädd*, A.S. *brerd*, a brim. See **Brerd**.

Brethir, *sb. pl.* brethren, brothers, 11 *b.* 26.

Brokkettis, *sb. pl.* brockets, 13.

179. A *brocket* is a red deer of two years old.

Brol, *sb.* a brat, child, 1. 745. In Piers the Plowman, A-text, iii. 198, some MSS. read *brol* where others have *barn = bairn*, child.

Brooke, *v.* to endure, 24. 49; 1 *p. s. pr.* Brook, enjoy, continue to use, 7. 129. A.S. *brúcan*, to enjoy, cognate with Lat. *frui, fructus*; M.E. *brouke*, to enjoy, but afterwards, to endure, to *brook*.

Brouys, *sb.* small wood, small shoots like brushwood, 13. 165. Prov. E. *brouse*, brushwood, O.F. *broce*, small wood; cf. M.H.G. *broz*, a bud.

Broydrie, *sb.* embroidery, 26. 777.

Bryttlynge, *sb.* breaking up, cutting up, 7. 17. A.S. *brytan*, to break, Sw. *bryta*, Dan. *bryde*.

Bubs, *pr. s.* bubbles, 24. 69.

Bugill, *sb.* F. a young ox, bullock, 4. 157. O.F. *bugle*, Lat. *buculus*, a bullock.

Bumbast, *pr. pl.* stuff out, pad out, 26. 1145. Low Lat. *bombax*, It. *bombace*, cotton used for quilting or stuffing out.

Bur, *sb.* the broad ring of iron behind the place for the hand on a tilting-spear, 8. v. 72. Gaelic *borr*, a knob, bunch, swelling.

Burdenous, *adj.* burdensome, 28 *a.* 166.

Bure, *pt. s.* S. bore, 22. 4548.

Burgionys, *sb. pl.* buds, 13. 99. F. *bourgeon.*

Burgionys, *pr. s.* buds, 13. 115.

Burnet, *adj.* of a brown colour, 13. 106. F. *brun, brunette.*

Buryellys, *sb. pl. but miswritten for* Buryels, *sb. sing.* a sepulchre, 8. vi. 39. A.S. *byrgels*, a sepulchre.

Busking, *sb.* dressing, manner of dressing, 25. 104. Icel. *búask*, to prepare oneself, from *búa*, to prepare. See **Boun.**

Busshement, *sb.* an ambuscade, 3 *b.* 1108.

Busteous, *adj.* boisterous, rude, 11 *a.* 5, 16; Bustuus, huge, powerful, 13. 177. W. *bwyst*, wild. See **Boistous.**

But, *prep.* without, 11 *a.* 14, 11 *b.* 29, &c.: except, 2. 625; But yf, except, 2. 625.

Buttonys, *sb. pl.* small buds, 13. 101. F. *bouton*, from *bout*, an end; cf. E. *butt*-end.

By, *prep.* with regard to, 26. 763.

By and by, *adv.* immediately, 3 *b.* 1331; 23. iii. 4. 33. Used in the same sense in our Authorised Version of the Bible.

Byckarte, *pt. pl.* bickered, skirmished, 7. 11. W. *bicra*, to fight, skirmish.

Byears, *sb. pl.* S. biers, 7. 117.

Bynempt, *pt. s.* 1 *p.* promised, 28 *a.* 46. A.S. *benemnan*, to engage, declare.

Bysprent, *pp.* besprinkled, 13. 90. A.S. *springan*, to spring; also, to sprinkle, spread.

Bywelde, *v. refl.* S. wield himself, i.e. have full and free use of his limbs, 3 *b.* 1367.

C.

Cabinet, *sb.* small cabin, arbour, 28 *b.* 17.

Cæciam, *sb.* (*acc.* Lat.) blindness, 14. 463. A Low Latin word, used for *cæcitatem.*

Caitifes, *sb. pl.* F. wretches, unhappy men, 19 *a.* 253. F. *chétif*, It. *cattivo*, Lat. *captivus*, a captive.

Callour, *adj.* fresh, cool, 13. 91. Sc. *caller*, fresh; Icel. *kaldr*, cold.

Calstocke, *sb.* the centre of a stem of cabbage, 14. 352. Sc. *custock*, which occurs in Burns's Halloween, st. 5. A.S. *cál*, cole-wort, and *stoc*, a stock.

Cammamyld, *sb.* camomile, 13. 116.

Can, 1 *p. s. pr.* S. know, 10. 29; *pr. pl.* Can, know, ken, 17 *c.* 55.

Cankerd, *pp.* corrupted, malignant, 14. 332. Lat. *cancer.*

Cant, *sb.* a slice, piece, bit, 20 *c.* 45. O. E. *cantle,* O. F. *chantel,* Dan. *kant,* an edge, border; It. *canto,* a side, corner. It cannot be certainly connected with W. *cant,* a rim or edge of a circle.

Capitayne, *sb.* F. captain, 18. xvii. 62. Low Lat. *capitaneus,* from *caput,* a head.

Carde, *pr. pl.* card, comb or prepare wool, 26. 761. F. *carde,* the head of a thistle (used for carding), Lat. *carduus,* a thistle.

Carefull, *adj.* full of care, wretched, 1. 441, 19 *b.* 50, 28 *a.* 62.

Carke, *sb.* consuming sorrow, deep grief, 28 *a.* 66.

Carpe, *v.* to talk, 7. 119; *pr. pl.* Carpe, blame, rebuke, 26. 823. Icel. *karpa,* to boast.

Cary, *sb.* the name of a very coarse material, 1. 422. In Piers the Plowman, it is called *cauri-mauri;* A-text, v. 62; B-text, v. 79.

Cass, *sb.* F. case, mishap, 6. 263. From Lat. *cadere,* to fall.

Cast, 1 *p. pl. pr.* we intend, 7. 35; *pt. s.* Caste, designed, planned, 1. 486. Icel. *kasta,* to throw.

Catcluke, *sb.* trefoil, 13. 116. Named from some fanciful resemblance to a cat's paw; cf. Sc. *cleuk,* a claw.

Cater, *sb.* F. caterer, purveyor of food, 20 *a.* 26. F. *acheter,* to buy.

Caucht, *v.* to catch, 13. 172. An anomalous usage.

Cawmyt, *pp.* calmed, 13. 52.

Cawtele, *sb.* F. deceit, 9. 101. Lat. *cautela,* caution, from *cauere.*

Cayr, *sb.* S. anxiety, care, 6. 187. A. S. *cearu.*

Caytiues, *sb.* captives, 26. 794. See Caitifes.

Celicall, *adj.* heavenly, 13. 42. Lat. *caelum,* heaven.

Certis, *adv.* certainly, 5 *a.* 5.

Chaflet, *sb.* F. a small platform or scaffold, 8. iii. 20. Dim. from O.F. *eschaffaut,* a scaffold; which is from Old Span. *catar,* Lat. *captare,* to view, and It. *palco,* a planking; cf. F. *catafalque.*

Chalmer, *sb.* chamber, 13. 267.

Chamelot, *sb.* camlet, a stuff made of camel's hair, 4. 157.

Champaine, *adj.* flat, 18. xviii. 60. From *Campania,* used as the name of a country, from Lat. *campus.*

Chance, *sb.* lot, fate, 13. 285.

Chanpartye, *sb.* F. a divided field (sc. of battle), a drawn battle, equality of power, 3 *b.* 1198. F. *champ parti.*

Chapiter, *sb.* chapter, 17 *d.* 2.

Chapolories, *sb. pl.* scapulars, 1. 550. See Fairholt's Costume in England, p. 595. From Lat. *scapula,* the shoulder.

Chapyt, *pp.* escaped, 6. 427.

Char, *sb.* F. car, 13. 31; Chare, 19 *d.* 4; 24. 7. Lat. *carrus.*

Charchyng, *pres. part.* F. charging, 3 *b.* 1090.

Chays, *sb.* F. chase, i.e. hunting-ground, 7. 31.

Cheare, *sb.* F. outward look, carriage, deportment, 19 *f.* 19.

Checker, *sb.* court of exchequer, 14. 335.

Chepe, *sb.* market-place (now *Cheapside*), 3 *a.* 10.

Cherarchy, *sb.* hierarchy, i.e. choir, 11 *a.* 9. The allusion is to the singing of angels in their hierarchies or orders; cf. Spenser, F. Q. i. 12. 39. The form of the word is less removed from the original than is the It. *gerarchia.*

Chere, *sb.* F. countenance, 19 *a.* 345. Low. Lat. *cara,* face; cf. Gk. κάρα, head.

Cherte, *sb.* F. friendship, 5 *a.* 91. Lat. *carus,* dear.

Chesit, *pt. s.* chose, 22. 4573.

Cheuyce, *v.* F. to bargain, make a contract about a loan; *hence,* to lend, 2. 602. O. F. *chevir,* to accomplish, from *chef,* Lat. *caput,* head.

Chiere, *sb.* F. cheer, countenance, 4. 161. See **Chere.**

Childre, *sb. pl.* children, 1. 756.

Chol, *sb.* jowl; the part extending from ear to ear beneath the chin, 1. 224. A.S. *ceafl,* the jaw, *ceaflas,* jaws, chops.

Choyss, *imp. s.* choose, 13. 222.

Chrisolyte, *sb.* chrysolite, 13. 37. From χρυσός, gold, and λίθος, a stone.

Chymmys, *sb.* palace, chief mansion, 13. 276. O. F. *chefmez,* from Lat. *caput,* head, and *mansio,* dwelling.

Chymneyes, *sb. pl.* chimneys, 7. 209.

Chynnes, *sb. pl.* S. chinks, 2. 609.

Chynnyng, *sb.* a chink, 2. 605. A.S. *cinu,* a chink, nick. Cf. Prov. Eng. *chine,* a cleft.

Chyp, *v.* to chip (applied to the bursting open of buds), 13. 124.

Chyrmys, *pr. s.* chirrups, 13. 239. A. S. *cyrm,* a noise, cry.

Chyssell, *adj.* chisel-like, flat and sharp, 13. 58. O. F. *cisel,* a chisel.

Circulat, *adj.* going round in a circle, revolving (in an orbit), 13. 10.

Clavyr, *sb.* clover, 13. 116.

Clawep, *pr. pl.* stroke down, smooth down, 1. 365. '*Flateur,* a flatterer, gloser, fawner, soother, foister, smoother, a *clawback,* sycophant, pickthanke.'—Cotgrave's French Dict.

Cled, *pt. s.* clad, clothed, 13, 98; *pp.* Cled, 22. 4718.

Cleikis, *pr. s.* clutches, takes, 22. 4721. E. *clutch,* A.S. *gelæccan,* to seize. (Doubtful.)

Clepit, *pt. s.* called, 4. 166. A.S. *cleopian,* to call.

Cleuering, *pres. part.,* clinging, holding on as a cat by its claws, 4. 159. M. E. *cliver,* a claw.

Closures, *sb. pl.* enclosures, defences, 19 *a.* 296; fastenings, 19 *a.* 329. Lat. *claudere,* to shut.

Clout, *v.* S. to patch, 26. 636; Cloute, 14. 524; *pp.* Clouted, esp. said of strengthening a shoe with an iron plate, called in Norfolk a *cleat* or *clout,* 1. 424. A.S. *clút,* a patch.

Cloutes, *sb. pl.* clouts, patches, 1. 244, 428; rags, tattered clothes, 1. 438; patches, 24. 37.

Cloyss, *sb.* close, enclosure, 13. 176.

Cluddis, *sb. pl.* S. clouds, 22. 5561.

Clustred, *pp.* clustered, i. e. clotted, 19 *a.* 354.

Cluvis, *sb. pl.* S. claws, 11 *a.* 15. Icel. *klauf,* Dan. *klov,* Du. *klaauwe.*

Clymbare, *sb. used as adj.* climber, climbing, 4. 156.

Clynk, *v.* to make a ringing sound; *quha mycht do clynk it,* which might cause a merry sound, 13. 236. Cf. G. *klingen,* to ring.

Clyps, *sb.* an eclipse, 15 *b.* 25. The same spelling occurs in Piers the Plowman, B. xviii. 135.

Coarted, *pp.* co-arcted, constrained, 14. 438. Lat. *coarctare,* to contract, compress.

Coates, *sb. pl.* cotes, sheep-cotes, 19 *a.* 649. E. *cot.*

Cocke, a profane oath, 23. iii. 4. 80. See the note.

Cockel, *sb.* a weed among corn, 28 *b.* 124. Gaelic *cogall,* cockle, husks, *cogan,* a loose husk.

Cockets, *sb. pl.* certificates, 26. 1058. 'A *cocket* was a certificate that goods had paid duty;' Nares. It seems also to have meant a particular stamp for sealing or marking, as a certain kind of stamped bread was called *cocket.* See Gloss. to Piers the Plowman.

Cofred, *pt. s.* F. put into a coffer or box, 2. 609.

Coitis, *sb. pl.* quoits, 5 *a.* 71. Of F. origin.

Coknayes, *sb. pl.* pets, 18. xviii. 75. See the note.

Coles, *sb. pl.* falsehoods (?), 26. 1114. M.E. *cole, cold,* crafty; but see the note.

Colour, *sb.* F. pretence, 9. 99; *pl.* Colours, 20 *b.* 59.

Columby, *sb.* columbine, 13. 118.

Combren, *v.* to cumber, encumber, 1.461; Comeren, to gorge, 1.765. O.F. *combrer,* to hinder; Low Lat. *cumbrus,* Lat. *cumulus,* a heap.

Combreworld, *sb.* a cumberer or spoiler of the world, 2. 299.

Comen, *pp.* come, 9. 4.

Comeren. See Combren.

Commoditie, *sb.* F. advantage, profit, gain, 21. 143.

Compasse, *sb.* F. a roundabout method of expression, 16. 171.

Compeir, *v.* F. to appear, 11 *a.* 11.

Comptrollers, *sb. pl.* superintendents, overseers of accounts, 21. 191. F. *contrerolle,* a copy of a roll of accounts.

Conandly, *adv.* S. cunningly, skilfully, 6. 248.

Conceipts, *sb. pl.* conceits, imaginations, 27. 185.

Conceits, *sb. pl.* fantastic patterns, 26. 777.

Concludyng (*for* Concluden), *v.* to conclude, 22. 5564.

Condicyons, *sb. pl.* manners, 14. 569.

Conduyte, *sb.* F. conduct, guidance, 9. 172. Lat. *ducere.*

Coniecte, *v.* F. to conjecture, suppose, 18. xviii. 57.

Conies, *sb. pl.* rabbits, 20 *a.* 88. Cf. G. *kaninchen,* M.E. *conynge.*

Conisantes, *sb. pl.* badges of distinction, 1. 185.

Coniunit, *pp.* conjoined, conjoint, 22. 5593.

Coniured, *pp.* confederate, 19 *a.* 341. Lat. *iurare,* to swear.

Conne, *v.* to know, 1. 234; 2 *p. s. pr. subj.* know, 1. 395; *we connen on,* we know of, 388. A. S. *cunnan.*

Conpassed, *pp.* compassed, plotted, 3 *b.* 1114.

Conserf, *pr. s. subj.* F. conserve, keep, 11 *a.* 26.

Contempt, *pp.* contemned, 28 *a.* 48.

Conyng, *sb.* coney, rabbit, 4. 157. See Conies.

Coosted, *pt. pl.* F. went alongside of, passed beside, went past, 15 *b.* 85. F. *côté,* Lat. *costum.*

Copen, *v.* to barter for, buy, 3 *a.* 7. D. *koopen,* G. *kaufen,* to buy. Cf. E. *cheapen, chop, chapman.*

Corasiue, *sb.* lit. a *corrosive,* i.e. a caustic, a sharp remedy, a biting rebuke, 27. 165. This word, when corrupted (as it frequently is in M.E.) into *coresy, corsey, corsive,* has puzzled many.

Corby, *sb.* a raven, 13. 174. F. *corbeau,* Lat. *corvus,* a crow.

Cornys, *sb. gen. sing.* of corn, 13. 77.

Corpis, *sb.* F. body, 11 *a.* 14; Corps, body, whole extent, 17 *c.* 102. Lat. *corpus.*

Cors, *sb.* S. curse, 7. 41.

Coruen, *pp.* carved, 1. 200, 5 *b.* 10.

Cosset, *sb.* pet lamb, 28 *a.* 42. There is a somewhat similar word in Italian, *casiccio,* a tame lamb, der. from *casa,* a house.

Costarde, *sb.* head, pate, 23. iii. 5. 91. O.E. *costard,* an apple (hence an apple-shaped head); whence *costardmonger, costermonger,* an apple-seller.

Cote, *sb.* coat; prankie cote = fine coat, a term of admiration, 23. iii. 3. 117.

Cote-armure, *sb.* coat-armour, body-armour, 18. xvii. 110.

Cotes, *sb. pl.* sheep-cotes, sheepfolds, pens, 28 *b.* 77.

Cotyd, *pp.* coated, clothed, 14. 569.

Couetyse, *sb.* F. covetousness, 9. 25.

Coulde, *pt. s.* knew, 17 *c.* 62.

Countenance, *sb.* encouragement, or show of politeness, 23. iii. 3. 151.

Countryng, *sb.* countering, 22. 4677. Lat. *contra,* against. See the note.

Courche, *sb.* a kerchief, 6. 241. corrupted from F. *couvrechef.*

Couth, *pt. s.* S. could, 6. 200, 252; 2 *p.* Couþist, 5 *a.* 31; *also used as an auxiliary* = did, 6. 222; Couþe, knew how to, 1. 233.

Covine, *sb.* craft, deceit, trickery, 26. 1100. O. F. *covine,* a secret convention, from Lat. *conuenire.*

Cowart, *sb.* F. covert, hidden passage, 6. 258. Lat. *coopertus.*

Cowschet, *sb.* cushat, 13. 237. A. S. *cúsceote,* a ringdove.

Coyfe, *sb.* F. coif, cap, 14 *a.* 313. A sergeant-at-law was entitled to wear a skull-cap. See Strutt's Manners and Customs, iii. 76. Low Lat. *cofea,* a cap.

Crage, *sb.* neck, 6. 408. Sc. *craig,* E. *craw,* G. *kragen.*

Crammasyn, *adj.* crimson, 13. 15. See Crimosine.

Crased, *pp.* crazed; but lit. broken, 14. 1105. F. *écraser,* to shatter.

Crawand, *pres. part.* crowing, 13. 156.

Credensynge, *sb.* believing (of), 14. 439. Lat. *credere.*

Creistis, *sb. pl.* crests, 13. 128. Lat. *crista;* Gk. κάρα, head.

Crennis, *sb. pl.* cranes, 11 *a.* 18.

Crimosine, *sb.* crimson, 26. 767. F. *cramoisi,* from Ar. *qirmiz,* the dye from the cochineal insect, from Sanskrit *krimi,* a worm, which is cognate with Lat. *uermis,* E. **worm.**

Crisped, *pp.* curled in small curls, or rather, wavy through having been curled, 20 *g.* 6. A. S. *cirps,* Lat. *crispus.*

Cristalline, *adj.* made of crystal, 13. 19. Gk. κρύσταλλος, ice, from κρύος, cold, frost.

Cristiante, *sb.* F. Christendom, 7. 23.

Crochettes, *sb. pl.* crockets, 1. 174. ' *Crockets,* projecting leaves, flowers, &c., used in Gothic architecture to decorate the angles of spires, canopies,' &c.; Glossary of Architecture. Du. *kroke,* a curl.

Crois, *sb.* cross, 1. 805. F. *croix,* Lat. acc. *crucem.*

Crombolle, *sb.* crumb-bowl; a large wooden bowl for broken scraps, 1. 437.

Croppis, *sb. pl.* tops, 13. 77. A. S. *crop,* a top; M. E. *crop,* top of a tree or plant.

Crosbowes, *sb. pl.* crossbows; *but put for* crossbowmen, archers, 15 *b.* 16.

Croukeþ, *pr. pl.* bend, bend down, 1. 751. E. *crook,* W. *crwg.*

Crounis, *sp. pl.* crowns; clyppit crounis = shaven heads, 22. 4568.

Crowd, *v.* to coo as a dove, 13. 299. From the sound *croo.*

Crowdis, *pr. s.* coos, 13. 237.

Crownell, *sb.* corolla, small crown, 13. 113.

Crucheþ, *pr. pl.* crouch, 1. 751. A mere variation of Croukeþ, q. v.

Cummerit, *pt. s.* F. encumbered, 6. 229. See Combren.

Curace, *sb.* F. cuirass, 19 *a.* 666. F. *cuirasse,* from *cuir,* leather, Lat. *corium.*

Curall, *adj.* coral, 4. 153.

Curious, *adj.* dainty, 1. 765.

Currours, *sb. pl.* F. runners, light-armed troops, 15 *b*. 93.

Curry, *pr. pl.* rub down, stroke, 1. 365. F. *corroyer*, to curry; O. F. *conroi*, preparation, from O. F. *roi*, order; from O. H. G. *reiti*, ready, cognate with A. S. *ræd*, E. *ready*.

Curteis, *adj.* F. courteous, 10. 153. Lat. *cohors*.

Cusyng. *sb.* F. cousin; *here put for* nephew, 6. 445.

Cutted, *pp.* cut short, 1. 434. Cf. '*cutty* sark' in Burns's Tam o' Shanter. W. *cwta*, short, bob-tailed.

Cutworks, *sb. pl.* intricately cut patterns, in lace and other materials, 26. 777.

Cylenius, a name of Mercury, 13. 5.

D.

Damme, *v.* F. condemn, 16. 210.

Dang, *pt. s.* threw, 22. 4600; *pt. pl.* Dange, beat, hit hard, 6. 411. Sc. *ding*, to drive, Sw. *dänga*, to thump, Dan. *dænge*, to bang.

Darklyng, *adv.* in the dark, 23. iii. 3. 58. Cf. 'we were left *darkling*;' King Lear, i. 4. 237.

Darnel, *sb.* a weed growing amongst corn, 21. 327.

Daungere, *sb.* demur, 2. 603. O. F. *dangier*, which has many meanings, the first being *feudal authority*; Low Lat. *damnum*, a fine.

Dauntyng, *pres. part.* taming, 18. xvii. 176. O. F. *danter*, Lat. *domitare*, from *domare*, to tame.

Dawes, *sb. pl.* daws, jackdaws, 14. 312, 23. iii. 3. 36. A jackdaw was considered a foolish, chattering bird. See Nares' Glossary.

Dawing, *sb.* S. dawning, dawn, 11 *b*. 1. A. S. *dægian*, to dawn.

Day, *sb.* 26. 1094. To *give day* is to fix a future time of payment, to give trust.

Days, *sb. pl.* does, 13. 181. A.S. *dá*.

De, *v.* to die, 7. 36; 22. 4713. Icel. *deyja*, Dan. *döe*.

Debate, *sb.* F. strife, 12. 13; discord, 24. 58; to set debate = to cause discord, 26. 1033. F. *battre*, Lat. *batuere*, to beat.

Debonayr, *adj.* F. well-mannered, 6. 294. F. *de bon air*, of a good mien.

Deburs, *v.* F. disburse, pay, 20 *c*. 60.

Dede, *pt. pl.* died, 3 *b*. 1181. See De.

Dede, *sb.* death, 6. 226. Dan. *död*.

Dedeyne, *pr. s. subj.* F. deign, 4. 168. Lat. *dignus*, worthy.

Defade, *v.* to cause to fade, 4. 170.

Defaste, *pp.* F. defaced, 22. 2.

Defautis, *sb. pl.* F. faults, sins, 5 *a*. 86. Lat. *fallere*.

Defundand, *pres. part.* pouring down, 13. 41. Lat. *defundere*.

Degoutit, *pp.* spotted (alluding to the ermine-tails), 4. 161. Lat. *gutta*, a drop.

Deir, *v.* to injure, harm, 22. 5575. A. S. *derian*, to injure.

Deit, *pt. s.* died, 6. 236. See De.

Del, *sb.* S. deal, part, 3 *b*. 1331; neuere a del, i.e. in no part, not at all, 3 *b*. 1332.

Delitable, *adj.* delightful, 4. 154.

Delyt, *sb.* F. delight, 11 *a*. 1. Lat. *delectare*.

Demaunded, *pp. prob. corrupted from* Demened, i.e. demeaned yourself, behaved, 12. 22.

Demen, *v.* to judge, 1. 814; Deme, to give an opinion, 20 *b*. 94. A.S. *déman*, to judge.

Demenyng, *pres. part.* expressing, 9. 169. O. F. *demener*, to lead, conduct, shew, manifest; *mener*, to guide. Low Lat. *minare*, to conduct; Lat. *minari*, to threaten.

Demyng, *sb.* S. supposition, guess, 8. v. 9. See **Demen.**

Dene, *sb.* a title of honour, answering (not to modern *dean*, but) to M.E. *Dan, don,* Lat. *dominus*, master.

Dent-de-lyon, *sb.* dandelion, 13. 119. Named from the resemblance of the edges of the leaves to *lion's teeth.*

Departen, *v.* to part; *wiþ vs to departen,* to share her goods amongst us, 1. 416; Departe, 10. 33, 18. xviii. 53; *pp.* Depart, separated, 13. 111.

Depaynt, *pp.* F. painted, 11 *a*. 3; Depaynted, depicted, 24. 58; *pt. pl.* Depeynt, reddened, 3 *b.*1259. Lat. *pingere.*

Depayntar, *sb.* painter, 13. 261.

Depured, *pp.* cleared, purified, 12. 1.

Der, *sb.* S. harm, damage, 6. 206, 359. A.S. *daro* or *daru,* harm.

Derbies, *in phr.* father Derbies bands, i.e. handcuffs, 26. 787.

Derked, *pp.* S. darkened, 10. 32.

Derring-doe, *sb.* (*prob. for* daring-do), deeds of arms, courage, feats, 28 *b.* 43.

Dert, *s.* dirt, 4. 170.

Descryue, *v.* F. to describe, 24. 10.

Desese, *sb.* F. dis-ease, discomfort, wretchedness, 3 *b.* 1302.

Desperate, *adj.* outrageous, 25.122.

Deuise, *sb.* F. device, *but here used for* report, 23. iii. 3. 1.

Devoir, *v.* F. to devour, 11 *a*. 18. Lat. *uorare.*

Deuoyr, *sb.* F. knightly duty, 8. iv. 32. Lat. *debere.*

Dewill, *sb.* S. the devil (used as an expletive oath), 6. 216.

Dewite, *sb.* F. duty, 22. 4732.

Dewle, *sb.* sorrow, 24. 14. See **Dule.**

Dey, *v.* to die, 10. 26. See **De.**

Diffame, *sb.* dishonour, 22. 4512.

Dight, *pp.* disposed, set in order, 20 *a*. 10; framed, 24. 55. A.S. *dihtan,* to dispose.

Digne, *adj.* dignified, haughty, 1. 355; disdainful, and hence repulsive, 1. 375. 'She was as *deyne* as water in a dich;' Chaucer, Reves Tale, 44. O.F. *dain,* Lat. *dignus.*

Dirige-money, *sb.* money paid for saying a *dirige,* or dirge, 16. 150.

Disclosed, *pt. s.* unclosed, 19 *a*. 314.

Disconfort, *v.* F. discompose (himself), 3 *b.* 1305.

Discrepant, *adj.* different, 18. xvii. 199.

Discryve, *v.* F. describe, 11 *a*. 6.

Discumfyst, *pp.* F. discomfited, 6. 429.

Discure, *v.* F. discover, reveal, 3 *b.* 1314.

Disguised, *pp.* made in an ill guise, odd-shaped, 25. 121.

Dispence, *sb.* F. expenditure, 2. 600; *pl.* Dispenses, 2. 624.

Dispende, *pr. s. subj.* spend, 2. 623; *pp.* Dispent, 2. 623.

Dispers, *adj.* dispersed about, 13. 90. Lat. *spargere.*

Dispitous, *adj.* F. contemptuous, full of despite, 3 *b.* 1084. O.F. *despit,* from Lat. *despicere,* to look down.

Disport, *sb.* F. sport, pleasure, 3 *b.* 1309. Lat. *dis,* apart, *portare,* to carry.

Dispoyled, *pp.* F. stripped, 19 *f*. 13. Lat. *spolium.*

Distraught, *pp.* distracted, 24. 28.

Distrayne, *v.* F. to vex, disquiet, 10. 37; *pp.* Distreyned, vexed, 24. 14. O.F. *destraindre,* to vex, Lat. *stringere.*

Do, *pp.* done, caused, 2. 624; Done, *v.* to do, 2. 624.

Doale, *sb.* S. a dole, a portion given away to the poor, 23. iii. 3. 65.

A.S. *dál, dǽl,* a *dole, deal,* part, G. *theil.*

Doing; *phr.* doing fleit = dripping, 11 *a.* 7; doing chace = chasing, 11 *a.* 8; doing spring, springing, 11 *a.* 22.

Domage, *sb.* F. damage, 18. xvii. 180. Lat. *damnum,* loss.

Dome, *adj.* S. dumb, i. e. mock, sham, false, 16. 147.

Donk, *adj.* dank, damp, 13. 45.

Doom, *sb.* S. judgment, 5 *b.* 13; Doome, 24. 13. A.S. *dóm;* whence *déman,* to deem, judge.

Dortour, *sb.* dormitory, 1. 211.

Doubted, *pp.* suspected, 28 *b.* 22.

Dout, *pr. pl.* F. fear, 15 *b.* 122. See Dowte.

Dow, *sb.* dove, 13. 297.

Downstilled, *pt. pl.* trickled down, 24. 75. Cf. E. *distil,* from L. *stilla,* a drop.

Dowte, *v.* F. to fear, 10. 62. The usual meaning in M.E.

Drawne (*for* Drawen), *v. refl.* to draw near, 3 *a.* 10.

Dre, *v.* S. to endure, hold out, 7. 98. Used by Burns. A.S. *dreógan,* to suffer.

Drecchep, *pr. pl.* vex, grieve, oppress, 1. 464. A.S. *dreccan.*

Dreeriment, *sb.* sadness, 28 *a.* 36.

Dreid, *sb.* dread, 13. 73; but dreid = without delay, 11 *b.* 15.

Drent, *pp.* drowned, 28 *a.* 37. A.S. *drencan,* to drown, *drench.*

Drere, *sb.* dreariness, woe, 24. 20.

Dresse, *v.* F. to direct one's course; Dresse hem = to turn their course, to go, 2. 608; Dresse him = direct himself, come, 4. 156; 1 *p. s. pr.* Dresse me, I address myself, 2.612; *pp.* Dressid, directed, 5 *b.* 54; Drest, treated; sore drest, ill treated, 4. 173. Lat. *dirigere,* to direct.

Droggis, *sb. pl.* drugs, 13. 144.

Drowe, *pt. s.* drew, 3 *b.* 1116.

Druggar-beste, *sb.* drudger-beast, drudging animal, 4. 155.

Dulce, *adj.* sweet, 11 *a.* 7; 13. 137. Lat. *dulcis.*

Dule, *sb.* mourning, 22. 5497. O. F. *duel,* Lat. *dolium* in comp. *cordolium,* heart-sorrow.

Dully, *adj.* dull, 11 *a.* 9. Sc. *dowie,* A.S. *dwollic,* erring, Mœso-Goth. *dwals,* foolish; G. *toll,* mad.

Dur, *sb.* S. door, 6. 238.

Durance, *sb.* endurance, duration, 28. *epil.* 2.

Dure, *v.* F. to endure, 24. 15; *pt. s.* Dured, 19 *a.* 595.

Duresse, *sb.* F. severity, harshness, 2. 298. Lat. *duritia.*

Dutchkin, *adj.* Dutch-like, i. e. German-like, 26. 1161.

Dyght, 1 *p. s. pt. refl.* prepared myself, 3 *a.* 16; *pp.* Dyght, disposed, set, 7. 84. A.S. *dihtan,* to array.

Dyke, *sb.* S. ditch, 15 *b.* 95.

Dynt, *sb.* S. a dint, dent, blow, 7. 94.

Dyonea, mother of Venus, 13. 1.

Dysconfited, *pp.* F. discomfited, 15 *b.* 43.

Dyttay, *sb.* indictment, legal charge, 6. 274. Lat. *dictatum.*

Dywlgat, *pp.* divulged, 13. 225. (The *w* = *uu* = *vu.*)

E.

E, *sb.* S. eye, 11 *a.* 13; 13. 4; *pl.* Ene, 11 *a.* 2; Eyn, 13. 39. A.S. *eágè,* pl. *eágan.*

Ear, *conj.* S. ere, 24. 5.

Earing, *sb.* ploughing, 26. 10. Mœso-Goth. *arjan,* A.S. *erian,* cognate with, not borrowed from Lat. *arare.*

Echeon, *for* Eche on, each one, 10. 179; Echon, 3 *b.* 1181.

Ee, *sb.* S. eye, 22. 5616. See E.

Effecte, *sb.* F. meaning, 12. 5.

Effeiris, *sb. pl.* qualities, 11 *a.* 19.

O. F. *afaire*, state, condition, *affair*; from Lat. *facere*.

Effray, *sb.* F. terror; do effray = cause terror, 11 *a.* 18. O. F. *effrei*, *effroi*, terror, *froior*, fear; from Lat. *frigus*, cold.

Eft, *adv.* again, 19 *a.* 314, 24. 18; Efte, 8. v. 41. A. S. *eft*, again.

Eftsithes, *an error for* Oftsithes, i. e. oftentimes, 19 *a.* 595. Virgil has *saepius*.

Eftir, *adv.* S. afterwards, 6. 196.

Egalle, *adj.* F. equal, 2. 301.

Egged, *pt. s.* urged, 1. 239. A. S. *eggian*, to excite, *egg* on.

Eik, *adv.* S. also, 11 *a.* 10; *also* Eke. A. S. *eác*, G. *auch*, Du. *ook*.

Eked, *pp.* eked out, 1. 244. Cf. A. S. *eácan*, to grow.

Elde, *sb.* S. old age, 24. 45. A. S. *yldo*, Mœso-Gothic *alds*, old age.

Eliche, *adj.* alike, 3. 624; Elyk, alike, equally, 11 *a.* 16. A. S. *gelíc*, like.

Ellis, *adv.* S. else, 10. 114.

Embassades, *sb. pl.* F. embassies, 14. 412. See **Ambassages**.

Embraue, *pr. pl.* decorate, deck, 28 *a.* 109. Cf. Sc. *braw*.

Eme, *sb.* S. uncle, 6. 269; Eyme, 6. 233. A. S. *eám*, G. *Oheim*.

Empaled, surrounded, enclosed, 24. 67.

Emportured, *pp.* pourtrayed, 14. 1154. Lat. *protrahere*, to draw out.

Emyspery, *sb.* hemisphere, 13. 28.

Enbrovd, *pp.* embroidered, 13. 65. F. *broder*, of Celtic origin; cf. W. *brodio*, to embroider, darn.

Enbroudin, *pp.* embroidered, i. e. decked, 4. 152.

Enches, *sb.* inches, 16. 276. A. S. *ynce*, an ounce, Lat. *uncia*, a twelfth part.

Ender, *in phr.* this ender daie = this day past, lately, 1. 239. Icel. *endr*, formerly; cf. Lat. *ante*. See **Hindir**.

Endlang, *prep.* along, 13. 100;

beside, 4. 152; all along, lengthways, *whence* endlang and ouerthwert, lengthways and across, both ways, 4. 167. See Chaucer, Kn. Ta. 1133. A. S. *andlang*.

Ene. See **E**.

Eneuch, *adv.* enough, 13. 224.

Engyne, *sb.* F. craft, subtility, wit, 3 *b.* 1197. Lat. *ingenium*.

Enhached, *pp.* marked, 14. 1078. F. *hacher*, to cut; cf. E. *hack*.

Enhastyng, *pres. part. refl.* hasting, hurrying himself, 3 *b.* 1075.

Enlumynyng, *pr. pt.* F. illumining, light-giving, 2. 282.

Ennewed, *pp.* renewed, 14. 1003.

Ensaumple, *sb.* F. ensample, 2. 627.

Ensaumplid, *pp.* F. exemplified, 5 *a.* 99.

Entayled, *pp.* sculptured, carved, 1. 167, 200. O. F. *entailler*, to cut; cf. Ital. *intaglio*.

Entendement, *sb.* F. understanding, intelligence, 2. 281.

Entent, *sb.* heed, attention, 3 *a.* 8, 16; intention, design, 4. 166. Lat. *in*, towards; *tendere*, to stretch.

Enteryd, *pt. s.* interred, 8. iii. 2. Lat. *in terra*, in the earth.

Environ, *adv.* around, 3 *b.* 1124; Envyroun, round about, 3 *b.* 1137. F. *environner*, to surround, from *virer*, to turn; cf. E. *whir*, *whirl*.

Eous, the morning-star, or the horse of the chariot of dawn, 13. 25. Gk. ἠώς, dawn.

Erberes, *sb. pl.* gardens for herbs, 1. 166. O. F. *herbier*, Lat. *herbarium*. (Quite distinct from E. *harbour*.)

Erd, *sb.* earth, 13. 78, 22. 5472. Du. *aarde*, G. *erde*, Sw. *jord*.

Ersche, *adj.* Erse, 6. 217.

Erst, *adv.* last, 28 *b.* 105. (Properly, it means *first*.) A. S. *ǽrest*, first, from *ǽr*, *ere*, formerly.

Escapes, *sb. pl.* wilful faults, 27. 82. F. *échapper*, Ital. *scappare*,

K k

to escape, lit. to get out of a cape
(*ex cappâ*).

Eschamyt, *pp.* ashamed, 13. 5, 285.

Eschew, *v.* F. to avoid, 12. 13.
O.F. *eschever*, G. *scheuen*, to shun,
shy at.

Eschue, *sb.* method of avoiding,
mode of escape, 20 *h.* 8.

Esement, *sb.* F. solace, 5 *a.* 78.

Esmayed, *pp.* dismayed, 9. 53.
O.F. *esmaier*, to lose courage ; a
hybrid word, from Lat. *ex*, out of,
and A.S. *magan*, G. *mögen*, to
have *might*. Similarly *dismay* is
from the Lat. *dis* and the root of
E. *may*, *might*.

Esperance, *sb.* F. hope, 9. 166;
Espirance, 22. 5633. Lat. *sperare*.

Euelles, *adj.* evilless, guiltless, 1.
242.

Even-forþ, *adv.* straightway, directly onwards, 1. 163.

Euer among, *adv.* continually, 28
b. 112.

Euer-eiþer, *adj.* each, 5 *b.* 102.

Euerilk, *adj.* every, 6. 209.

Evir, *adj.* ivory, 13. 14; Euour, 4.
155. Lat. *ebur*, ivory, Sanskrit
ibha, an elephant.

Euesed, *pp.* surrounded by clipped
borders, edged round, 1. 166.
A.S. *efesian*, to clip round; hence
E. *eaves*, which is a *singular* noun,
from A.S. *efese*, a border.

Euynsonge, *sb.* S. evensong, vespers, 15 *b.* 176.

Exerce, *imp. s.* exercise, exert, 11
a. 16.

Exhibition, *sb* F. a sum of money
to assist in defraying expenses of
education, 21. 63.

Expert, *v.* to experience, try, 28 *a.*
186. A coined word.

Expowned, *pp.* expounded, 17
c. 93. Lat. *ex*, and *ponere*, to
place.

Ewin, *adv.* evenly, 22. 5465.

Eye, *sb.* an egg; *gos eye*, goose's
egg. 1. 225. A.S. *æg*, G. *ei*.

Eyme, *sb.* S. uncle, 6. 233. See
Eme.

Eyn, *sb. pl.* eyes, 13. 39. See **E.**

Eyt, *pp.* eaten, 13. 94.

F.

Faccion, *sb.* F. fashion, 17 *c.* 69;
pl. Facions, 16. 330.

Fache, *v.* S. to fetch, 7. 117.

Faill, *sb.* greensward, 13. 88. Of
Celtic origin. Cf. Gael. *fal*, wall,
hedge, sod.

Fair, *v.* S. to fare, go, 6. 380.

Fall, *v.* to happen, befell; foule
mot ʒou fall = may evil happen to
you, 6. 430; *pr. s.* Falleth, hap-
pens, befalls, 15 *b.* 128.

Fallow, *v.* to mate oneself with,
match, be companion to, 11 *a.* 20.

Fallow, *sb.* fellow, 13. 211; *pl.*
Fallowis, associates, 22. 4684. See
Felow.

Fallyng, *pp.* fallen, 4. 164. This
form is only found in Old Scotch.

Falshede, *sb.* falsehood, 1. 419;
Falset, 11 *b.* 43.

Fand, *pt. s.* S. found, 6. 195, 232.

Fane, *sb.* a small banner, 12. 8.
25; *pl.* Fanys, streamers, 13. 47.
A.S. *fana*, E. *vane*, a flag, banner;
Mœso-Goth. *fana*, cloth ; Lat.
pannus, Gk. πῆνος.

Fantasy, *sb.* fancy, 14. 1135. F.
fantasie, notion, from Gk. φαντασία, a making visible, from φαίνειν,
to bring to light.

Far, *v.* to fare, go, 6. 338 ; Fair, 6.
380.

Farder, *adj. comp.* farther, 29. 70.

Farforth, *adv.* extremely (lit. far
forth), 24. 35 ; cf. st. 69.

Fassoun, *sb.* F. fashion, make,
shape, 11 *a.* 12. See **Faccion.**

Fauell, *sb.* F. flattery, cajolery,
deceit, 20 *b.* 67. Lat. *fabula*,
O.F. *favel*, talk, flattery.

Fawch-ʒallow, *adj.* fallow-yellow,

13. 108. A. S. *fealh*, G. *falb*, light yellow.

Fawely, *adv.* S. fewly, few in number, 6. 198.

Faym, *sb.* foam, 13. 197. A. S. *fǽm, fám.*

Fayn, *sb.* vane, 13. 71. See **Fane**.

Fayneden, *pt. pl.* F. feigned, 9. 138.

Fayntise, *sb.* feigning, pretence, 1. 251.

Fays, *sb. pl.* S. foes, 6. 280.

Faytoures, *sb. pl.* traitors, deceivers, 1. 758. O. F. *faiteor*, an agent, from Lat. *factor.*

Feale, *sb.* fail, 7. 24.

Feare, *v.* S. to frighten, 16. 4; *pp.* Feared, 16. 287. A. S. *fǽran*, to frighten, *fǽr*, fear; from *fǽr*, sudden, Du. *vaarlijk*, quickly.

Fechtaris, *sb. pl.* fighters, 6. 324. Cf. G. *fechter.*

Fede, *sb.* feud, enmity, 6. 354. A. S. *fǽhð*, feud, enmity, G. *fehde*; from A. S. *feón*, to hate. Cf. *foe, fiend.*

Fedramme, *sb.* plumage, 13. 163. A. S. *feðer-homa*, a feather-covering; Layamon has *feþerhame.* Cf. M. E. *likame* from A. S. *líc-hama.*

Feer, *sb.* S. companion, 24. 42; Feir, 11 *a.* 14. A. S. *geféra, féra,* one who *fares* with one, a travelling companion. See **Fere**.

Feild-going, *sb.* a walking out of doors, 22. 5534. See the note.

Feir, 11 *a.* 14. See **Feer, Fere**.

Feldes, *sb. pl.* S. fields, 16. 302.

Feldishe, *adj.* fieldish, belonging to the country, 20 *a.* 2.

Fele, *adj.* many; *fele wise*, many ways, 1. 484. A. S. *fela*, many.

Fell, *sb.* S. hide, skin, 26. 793. A. S. *fell*, Lat. *pellis.*

Fell, *adj.* S. fierce, 15 *b.* 35. 103.

Felle, *pl. adj.* many, 6. 323. See **Fele**.

Felle, *adj.* S. lit. cruel; probably here used to mean crafty, 2. 607.

Felloun, *adj.* F. cruel, harsh, 6.

205; Felloune, 6. 372. O.F. *felon*, cruel, perhaps from O. H. G. *fillan*, to torment, flay: from O. H. G. *vell*, A. S. *fell*, a hide. Cf. Du. *villen*, to flay.

Felonye, *sb.* F. wickedness, cruelty, 3 *b.* 1104, 4. 156.

Felow, *sb.* a fellow, mate, 10. 134. Icel. *félagi*, from *fé*, cattle (G. *vieh*, E. *fee*), and *lag*, law, society. It implies one who possesses property in partnership with others.

Fen, *sb.* mire, 1. 427. A. S. *fenn.*

Fend, *imp. s.* F. defend, 11 *a.* 19.

Fende, *sb.* S. a fiend, 12. 6. Mœso-Goth. *fijands*, hating, from *fijan*, to hate.

Fenystaris, *sb. pl.* windows, 13. 169. G. *fenster*, Lat. *fenestra.*

Ferde, *pp.* afraid, terrified, 20 *a.* 55.

Ferden, *pt. pl.* S. fared, 2. 603.

Fere, *sb.* S. companion, mate, 4. 155, 19 *f.* 46. See **Freer**.

Ferforth, *adv.* far forth, far, 3 *b.* 1320.

Ferleis, *pr. pl.* wonder, 13. 10.

Ferleis, *sb. pl.* S. marvels, 22. 5479. A. S. *fǽrlíc*, sudden, from *fǽr*, sudden, *fǽr*, fear, sudden, danger; cf. Du. *vaarlijk*, quickly, G. *gefährlich*, dangerous.

Fermans, *sb.* an enclosure, 13. 176. F. *fermer*, to shut, make *firm.*

Fermery, *sb.* an infirmary, 1. 212.

Fermes, *sb. pl.* farms, 26. 1154.

Ferrer, *adv.* further, 1. 207. A. S. *fyrre*, farther, comp. of *feor*, far.

Ferret-silke, *sb.* silk of an inferior quality, 26. 1095. Ital. *fioretto*, F. *fleuret*, floret-silk, flurt-silk, or ferret-silk; G. *florett*, the outer envelop of the silk-cord, ferret-silk. From Lat. *flos*, Ital. *fiore*, a flower.

Fery, *adj.* fiery, 4. 156.

Fesaunt, *sb.* a pheasant, 18. xviii. 73. Lat. *phasianus*, the Phasian bird, from Gk. φᾶσις, river in Colchis or Pontus.

Fest, *sb.* F. feast, festivity, 19 *a.* 316.

Fet, 1 *p. s. pt.* fetched, 24. 36 ; *pt. s.* Fet, 1. 808. A. S. *feccan*, to fetch, pt. t. *ic feahte*, whence M. E. *fette* and *fet*.

Feth, *sb.* F. faith ; i feth = in faith, 7. 68.

Fette, *v.* S. fetch, bring (back), 23. iii. 3. 92, 23. iii. 4. 141 ; made fetten = caused to be fetched, 3 *b.* 1348 ; *pr. s.* Fetteth, fetches, gets, 16. 149. See **Fet**.

Feuir3er, *sb.* February, 6. 363.

Fewnyng, *sb.* F. foining, thrusting, 8. iv. 27. See **Foyne**.

Fewte, *sb.* F. fealty, 11 *a.* 17. Lat. *fidelitas.*

Fickle, *adj.* fidgety, full of action, 23. iii. 5. 4. Cf. G. *fickfacken*, to fidget.

Figurie, *sb.* figured or embroidered work, 26. 776.

Fille, *pt. s.* fell, 3 *b.* 1135.

Fine, *sb.* F. end, 19 *a.* 728.

Firmentie, *sb.* furmity, made of hulled wheat, boiled in milk and seasoned, 26. 1077. See note.

Fit, *sb.* a song, a part of a ballad, being so much as is said without a break or stop, 23. iii. 3. 144 ; 7. 50. A. S. *fit*, a song.

Flat, *v.* to flatter, 13. 209.

Flaunt-a-flaunt, *adv.* flauntingly displayed, 26. 1163.

Flaw, *pt. s.* flew, 6. 405.

Fle, *sb.* fly, 13. 172.

Fleichit, *pp.* flattered, 11 *b.* 36. Du. *vleijen*, to flatter ; cf. G. *flehen*, to supplicate, Mœso-Goth. *thlaihan*, to caress.

Fleit, *v.* to flow, drip ; doing fleit = dripping, 11 *a.* 7. Sw. *flyta*, to flow, Dan. *flyde*, to flow, float.

Flemed, *pt. s.* S. banished, 8. vi. 6 ; *pp.* Flemit, driven away, dispelled, 11 *b.* 44. A. S. *flýman*, to banish, cause to *flee.*

Flete, *pr. pl.* float, 19 *c.* 8 ; *pres.*

part. Fletyng, 19 *a.* 259. See **Fleit**.

Fley, *v.* to frighten, 22. 5461. A.S. *flýgan*, to cause to flee, *fleógan* to fly, flee.

Fleyce, *sb.* covering (lit. fleece), 13. 80.

Fleyt, *v.* to flow, drip, 13. 137. See **Fleit**.

Flocke, *v.* to crowd round, 23. iii. 3. 33. Cf. 'Good fellows, trooping, *flock'd* me so ;' Nares, ed. Halliwell.

Flockes, *sb. pl.* S. flakes, tufts, lumps, 12. 2.

Flour-dammes, *sb. pl.* fleur-des-dames (ladies' flower), 13. 118. Cf. the terms *lady's-bedstraw, lady's-bower, lady's-comb, lady's-cushion, lady's-finger, lady's-hair, lady's-mantle, lady's-seal, lady's-slipper, lady's-smock, lady's-tresses,* all names of flowers.

Flour-de-lycis, *sb. pl.* fleurs-de-lys, 11 *a.* 14 ; Flour-de-lyss, *sing.* 13. 117. F. *lis*, lily ; Du. *lisch*, waterflag.

Fludis, *sb. pl.* floods, 13. 59.

Flurichep, *pr. s.* elaborates, varies capriciously, 1. 484. M. E. *floryschen*, to make flourishes in illuminating books ; Prompt. Parv.

Flyttyng, *sb.* the act of removing from one place to another, 6. 396 ; where *ga in our flyttyng* = go along with us.

Folde, *pp.* folded, 24. 11.

Foles, *sb. pl.* F. fools, 14. 312.

Foltred, *pp.* faltered, stumbled, 18. xvii. 78. Cp. Span. *faltar*, to fail ; see *Falter*, in Wedgwood.

Fond, *adj.* S. foolish, 25. 122. M.E *fonne*, a fool, which is used by Chaucer. Cf. Sw. *fåne*, a fool.

Fonde, *pt. pl.* found, 2. 622.

Fonded, *pp.* tried, made trial of, 1. 451. A. S. *fandian*, to try, test.

Fonden, *v.* to go, 1. 408. A. S. *fandian*, to try, O. Fries. *fandia*, to try, *also*, to visit the sick, visit, go.

Fongen, *v.* to receive, get, 1. 786. A. S. *fón,* G. *fangen.*

Foole, *adj.* F. foolish, 2. 598. O. F. *fol,* F. *fou.*

Foole-large, *adj.* F. foolishly lavish, 2. 623.

Foole-largely, *adv.* F. in a foolishly lavish manner, 2. 623.

Foon, *sb. pl.* S. foes, 3 *b.* 1149. A. S. *fáh,* pl. *fá;* but pl. *fán* is sometimes found.

For, *conj.* whether, 1. 350.

For-, *prefix,* corresponding to G. and Du. *ver.* It generally has an intensive force.

Forbathde, *pp.* deeply bathed, 24. 61.

Forbode, *sb.* 1. 415; *Godys forbode,* (it is) God's prohibition, God forbids it. A. S. *forboden,* forbidden.

Forboden, *pp.* forbidden, 17 *c.* 54.

Fordeden, *pt. pl.* did to death, slew, murdered, 1. 495; *pp.* Fordone, ' done for,' utterly spent, 24. 19. M. E. *fordo,* to destroy, do for.

Fordone. See above.

Fordynnand, *pres. part.* causing to resound loudly, filling with loud noise, 13. 240; Foredinning, 24. 72.

Fore-, *prefix,* beforehand; corresponding to G. *vor,* Du. *voor.*

Fore; to fore, *printed for* tofore, i. e. before, 9. 167.

Foredinning. See **Fordynnand.**

Forepast, *pp.* already past, that has happened beforehand, 24. 16.

Forespeking, *pres. part.* foretelling, 19 *a.* 314.

Forespent, *pp.* utterly spent, tired out, 24. 12. Should be spelt *forspent.*

Forfaynt, *pp.* rendered quite faint; *or else adj.* very faint, 24. 15.

Forgane, *prep.* opposite to, over against, 13. 60. Douglas also uses *foregainst.*

Forgit, *pp.* F. forged, constructed, made, 11 *a.* 3. Lat. *fabricare.*

Forgone, *pp.* gone quite away, 24. 49; *badly spelt* Foregone, 24. 47. The prefix is *for-;* the modern *forego* is misspelt.

Forhewed, *pp.* hewn about, hacked severely, deeply cut, 24. 57.

Forlore, *pp.* forlorn, utterly wasted, 24. 48; Forlorne, ruined, 22. 4720; bare, 24. 8. A. S. *forloren,* utterly lost, pp. of *forleósan,* to lose utterly.

Formfaderes, *sb. pl.* forefathers, 1. 808. A. S. *forma,* former, early; Mœso-Goth. *frums,* a beginning.

For-quhy, *conj.* because, 22. 4689. See **Forwhi.**

Forsonke, *pp.* deeply sunk, sunk down, 24. 20.

Fortill, *for* For to, 13. 76.

Fortune, *v.* F. to happen, 17 *c.* 193.

Forwaste, *pp.* utterly wasted, rendered wretched, 24. 11. The right form is *forwasted,* but the final *-ted* is contracted to *-t.*

For-werd, *pp.* worn out, 1. 429. A. S. *werod,* pp. of *werian,* to wear.

Forwhi, *conj.* S. because, 5 *a.* 20. A. S. *hwí,* Mœso-Goth. *hwe,* instrumental case of *hwas,* who; *for-whi* = on account of what.

Forwithered, *pp.* utterly withered, 24. 12.

Forwounded, *pp.* desperately wounded, 3 *b.* 1217, *rubric.* A. S. *forwundian,* to wound deeply.

Fostyr, *sb.* fosterer, nourisher, 13. 253.

Foull, *sb.* S. a bird; *used collectively for* birds, 11 *a.* 12. G. *vögel.*

Foundement, *sb.* foundation, 1. 250.

Fownys, *sb. pl.* fawns, 13. 181.

F. *faon*, O. F. *feön*, from Lat. *foetus*.

Foyne, *sb.* a foin, thrust, 8. iv. 69. Prov. F. *fouiner*, to push with an eel-spear; *fouine*, an eel-spear. (Mahn.)

Foynʒer (or Foynʒee; *the* MS. *is indistinct*), *sb.* the beech-martin, 4. 157. F. *fouine*; from Lat. *fagus*.

Fra, *conj.* from, from the time that, 6. 292. A. S. *fra, fram.*

Fraid, *pp.* scared, 25. 83. See **Frayd**.

Fraitur, *sb.* 1. 212. See **Fraytour**.

Fra-thine, *adv.* from thence, 6. 380. A. S. *fram*, from, *þanon*, thence.

Fraughted, *pp.* freighted, 24. 71. G. *fracht*, Sw. *frakt*, Du. *vragt.*

Frawart, *adj.* froward, malignant, 13. 7. A. S. *framweard*, fromward, perverse.

Fray, *sb.* fright, 22. 5612. F. *frayeur*, fright, from Lat. *frigus*, cold, horror.

Frayd, *pp.* frightened, 19 *a.* 637; Fraid, scared, 25. 83. See above.

Frayne, *v.* S. to pray, ask, 1. 153, 14. 397. A.S. *fregnan*, G. *fragen*, Lat. *precari*, whence E. *prayer.*

Fraytour, *sb.* a refectory, 1. 203.

Freate, *v.* to fret, feel vexed, 20 *a.* 112. G. *fressen*, to eat.

Freckys, *sb. pl.* men, 7. 66. See **Freyke**.

Freir, *sb.* F. friar, 11 *b.* 5. Lat. *frater.*

Freitour, *sb.* 1. 220. See **Fraytour**.

Freklys, *sb. pl.* spots, 13. 111. Cf. G. *fleck*, a spot, speck.

Fret, *pp.* adorned, 14. 1048. A.S. *frætwian*, to adorn.

Freyke, *sb.* a man, 7. 63. A. S. *freca*, a man.

Fricht, *pp.* frightened, 4. 162.

Frounced, *pp.* curled in a disorderly manner, frizzled, 25. 105. F.

froncer, to wrinkle, from Lat. *frons*, the forehead.

Fructuous, *adj.* F. fertile, fruitful, 2. 281. Lat. *fructus.*

Frustir; *in phr.* of frustir = in vain, 6. 313. Lat. *frustra.*

Fulʒeis, *sb. pl.* leaves, 13. 89. F. *feuille*, Lat. *folium*, a leaf.

Funding (*for* funden), *pp.* found, 22. 5517, 5599.

Fundit, *pp.* founded, 22. 4736.

Fur, *sb.* furrow, 13. 88. A. S. *furh.*

Fur-breid, *sb.* a furrow's breadth, 6. 405. See above.

Furder, *adj.* S. further, 11 *b.* 29.

Fureur, *sb.* F. fury, 9. 184.

Furth, *prep.* along, throughout, 4. 158; Furth of, forth from, 13. 99.

Fyall, *sb.* 13. 71. Perhaps meant for *fynall*, i. e. finial.

Fyn, *sb.* F. end, 3 *b.* 1190, *rubric.*

Fynd, *pp.* fined, i. e. refined, sifted, 28 *b.* 125.

Fynde, 1 *p. s. pr.* I end, 7. 50. A corruption of *fyne*, like *gownd* for *gown*. See **Fyn**.

Fyreflaucht, *sb.* lightning, 22. 5556. Lit. a *fireflake.*

Fyrth, *sb.* bay, estuary, frith, 13. 54. Dan. *fiord*, Sw. *fjärd.*

G.

Gage, *v.* to gauge, sound, 18. xvii. 132. O. F. *jale, jalon*, a bowl, (whence E. *gallon*); from whence *jauger*, to tell the number of bowls in a vessel.

Gaiff, *pt. s.* S. gave, 6. 244.

Gairding, *sb.* S. garden, 11 *a.* 7.

Gait, *sb.* S. way; *gang thar gait* = go their way, 6. 250. Sw. *gata*, G. *gasse*, a street; Mœso-Goth. *gatwo*, a way.

Gale, *sb.* gall, sore place, 21. 45. F. *gale*, scurf, itch; which Diez connects with G. *galle*, a stain, E. *gall*, in oak-gall.

Galys, *pr. s.* sings, 13. 241. A. S. *galan*, to sing; hence E. *nightingale*, a singer by night.

Galʒart, *adj.* sprightly, 13. 150. F. *gaillard*, a word of uncertain origin.

Gan, *pt. s.* did, 24. 4. Once very common.

Ganand, *pres. part. as adj.* suitable, meet, becoming, excellent, 6. 214, 382. Icel. *gegna*, to meet, suit, Sw. *gagna*, Dan. *gavne*, to avail, profit; cf. E. *ungainly*.

Gane, *v.* to yawn, 2. 625. A. S. *ganian*.

Gang, *v.* S. to go, 6. 298, 397.

Ganyde, *pt. pl.* availed, 7. 59. Dan. *gavne*, to benefit. It means 'their pride availed them not.' See **Ganand.**

Gaped, 1 *p. s. pt.* stared, 1. 156. Sw. *gapa*, from Sw. *gap*, mouth, G. *gaffen*.

Gar, *v.* to cause, 11 *a.* 12; *pt. s.* Gert, 6. 447; *pt. pl.* Garde, 7. 59. Sw. *göra*, Dan. *giöre*, Icel. *gjöra*.

Garites, *sb. pl.* garrets, 1. 214. The original sense is a watchtower, from O. F. *garer*, to be wary.

Garth, *sb.* garden, enclosure, 6. 257; 11 *a.* 7. Icel. *garðr*, a yard.

Gate, *sb.* gait, 28 *epil.* 8.

Gate, *sb. pl.* goats, 22. 5629.

Gate, *sb.* S. way, forward motion, 19 *a.* 269. See **Gait.**

Gaudying, *sb.* toying, 23. iii. 4. 1. M. E. *gaud*, a toy; Lat. *gaudium*.

Gaurish, *adj.* garish, staring, 25. 122. M. E. *gare*, to stare; cf. E. *gaze*.

Gaynage, *sb.* produce, 1. 197.

Gaynstand, *v.* withstand, stand against, 6. 268.

Gayte, *sb.* S. goat, 4. 156; *pl.* Gate, 22. 5629.

Geare, *sb.* S. business, 23. iii. 3. 14; matter, 23. iii. 146; material, 21. 105, where it seems to be applied to the *earth*, though it should rather refer to the plough. A. S. *gearwian*, to prepare.

Gemmyt, *pp.* covered with buds, 13. 101. Lat. *gemma*, a bud.

Generall, *adj.* universal, catholic, 1. 816.

Genowayes, *sb. pl.* Genoese, 15 *b.* 14.

Gent, *adj.* (lit. gentle), tall, fine, 13. 157; pretty, 11 *a.* 7.

Ger, *sb.* gear, 6. 435; clothing, 6. 220. A. S. *gearwa*, clothing, from *gearwian*, to prepare, *gearo*, ready, *yare*.

Gerraflouris, *sb. pl.* gillyflowers, stocks, 13. 121. *Gillyflower* is corrupted from M. E. *girofler*, and this again from F. *girofle*, a clove.

Gerss-pilis, *sb. pl.* blades of grass, 13. 92. Lat. *pilus*, a hair.

Gert, *pt. s.* caused; gert geyff = caused to be given, 6. 447. See **Gar.**

Gesserant, *sb.* a coat or cuirass of fine mail, 4. 153; Gesseron, 18. xvii. 122. O. F. *jaserant*, which Burguy connects with Span. *Jazarino*, Algerian, from the Arabic form of *Algiers*. (Jamieson's explanation is wrong.)

Gest, *sb.* story, poem, 1. 479. Lat. *gestum*.

Gestinge, *sb.* F. jesting; or, more literally, telling of *gesta* or stories, 16. 394. See above.

Geue, *conj.* if, 22. 4505.

Geyff, *v.* to give, 6. 447.

Geyn, *adj.* near, short, convenient, 3 *b.* 1102. Icel. *gegn*, Sw. *gen*, Dan. *gjen*, near, short (of a way).

Gife, *conj.* if, 11 *b.* 25. *Not* connected with *give*, as Horne Tooke says, but with Mœso-Gothic *iba*, if, Icel. *ef*, from Icel. *ef*, a doubt.

Gill, *sb.* a foolish woman, 23. iii. 4.

104. Short for *Gillian*, i.e. *Juliana*.

Gin, *sb.* contrivance, 19 *a.* 299. Lat. *ingenium*, F. *engin*.

Gise, *sb.* F. guise, way, 20 *a.* 57. F. *guise*, E. *wise*.

Glade, *v.* to gladden, 2. 603; Glaid, 13. 28.

Glaid, *adj.* glad, 13. 42.

Glaid, *pt. s.* glided, 6. 414.

Glave, *sb.* a sword glaive, 12. 16; 13. 6.

Glede, *sb.* a glowing coal, live ember, 7. 29. A. S. *gléd*, a hot coal; from *glówan*, to glow.

Glent, *pt. pl.* glided swiftly, glanced, past, 7. 13. See *glance* in Wedgwood. Cf. Dan. *glimt*, a gleam; *glimte*, to flash, *glindse*, to glisten, *glimre*, to glimmer; E. *glimpse*, *gleam, glim,* &c.

Glewis, *sb. pl.* destinies, lit. glees, 4. 160. Supplied from conjecture. *Glew* or *gle* in Scottish means (1) glee, game, (2) the destiny of battle.

Gleym, *sb.* bird-lime; hence, subtlety, craft, 1. 479; cf. 546. Cf. E. *clammy*.

Glore, *sb.* glory, 13. 51; 22. 5508. F. *gloire*.

Glose, *v.* to mislead, deceive, 1. 367; *pr. s.* Gloseþ, glosses, explains away by glosses, 1. 345. Gk. γλῶσσα, a tongue, gloss.

Glosis, *sb. pl.* glosses, commentaries on a text, 17 *a.* 11.

Glum, *v.* to look glum or gloomy, 12. 21. A. S. *glóm*, gloom.

Gnar, *v.* S. to snarl, 14. 297. Icel. *gnýr*, a clash.

Godspell, *sb.* gospel, 1. 345. A. S. *godspell*, the story of God, the life of Christ.

Goldbeten, *pp.* adorned with beaten gold, 1. 188.

Goldspynk, *sb.* goldfinch, 13. 240. Sc. *spink*, W. *pync*, E. *finch*.

Gon, *sb.* a gun, 25. 164.

Goo, *pp.* gone, 10. 90.

Good, *in phr.* a good, i.e. a good deal, plentifully, fully, 23. iii. 4. 148.

Goode, *sb.* goods, property, 2. 599.

Gos, *sb.* goose; *gos eye*, goose's egg, 1. 225.

Gosse, a profane oath, 23. iii. 4. 90. See the note.

Gostly, *adj.* spiritual, 21. 138.

Gostly, *adv.* spiritually, 21. 136. A. S. *gást*, the breath, a spirit. The E. *ghost* should be spelt *gost*; cf. G. *geist*, Du. *geest*.

Gothe (*better* Goth), *pr. s.* S. goes, 2. 602.

Gouernauncis, *sb. pl.* F. directions for conduct, rules; or else, modes of conduct, customs, 5 *a.* 98.

Gowland, *pres. part.* yelling, 22. 5487.

Gowlys, *adj.* red, 13. 107. E. *gules*, red (in heraldry), F. *gueules*, jaws, from Lat. *gula*, the *gullet*.

Graith, *adj.* readily, 1. 232. Icel. *greiðr*, ready; cf. G. *gerade*, direct.

Gramercies, *sb. pl.* great thanks (F. *grand merci*), 23. iii. 4. 117.

Granyt, *pp.* dyed in grain, dyed of a fast colour, 13. 15.

Grapers, *sb. pl.* grappling-irons, 15 *a.* 50. Allied to F. *grappin*, a grapnel, of G. origin.

Grathis, *pr. s.* attires, dresses, 6. 216. Icel. *greiða*, to furnish, equip; Mœso-Goth. *garaidjan*, to prepare.

Gravys, *sb. pl.* groves, 13. 190.

Gre, *sb.* F. good will; *in phr.* take in gre = agree to, put up with, 14. 444. From Lat. *gratus*.

Gre, *sb.* degree, quality, 13. 109. O. F. *grè*, Lat. *gradus*, a step.

Greahondes, *sb. pl.* grayhounds, 7. 13.

Greeing, *pres. part.* concordant, 19 *a.* 293. See Gre (good will).

Greete, *v.* to cry aloud, 3 *a.* 11. A.S. *grǽtan,* to cry.

Grehoundes, *sb. pl.* grayhounds, 18. xviii. 29.

Greit, *sb.* gravel, 13. 55. E. *grit,* G. *gries.*

Gresy, *adj.* grassy, 13. 103, 190.

Gretand, *pres. part.* weeping, wailing, 22. 5545. A.S. *grǽtan,* Mœso-Goth. *gretan,* to weep.

Grete, *adv.* greatly, 1. 501.

Grevis, *sb. pl.* S. groves, 7. 13; Gravys, 13. 190. A.S. *grœf,* a grave, cave; a *grove* is a space *cut out* in the woods. A.S. *grafan,* to grave, dig.

Grewance, *sb.* F. grievance, hurt, 6. 196.

Grey, *sb.* a gray, a badger, 4. 156.

Greyce, *adj.* gray, 13. 107. F. *gris.*

Greyn, *sb.* grain, i.e. dyeing *in grain,* 1. 230. See the note.

Grieslie, *adj.* horrid, 28 *b.* 69. A.S. *ágrísan,* to dread.

Grocched, *pt. s.* murmured, mumbled (lit. grudged), 3 *b.* 1249. O.F. *grocer, groucer,* to murmur.

Grotte, *sb.* a groat, 2. 607. Du. *groot,* great.

Grundyn, *sb.* ground, sharpened, 13. 6.

Gud, *sb.* goods, property, 6. 314.

Gudely, *adv.* in a good way, 6. 448.

Guerdone, *sb.* remuneration, 2. 627; Guerdon, 28 *a.* 45. O.F. *guerdon,* Ital. *guiderdone,* from Low Lat. *widerdonum,* corrupted from O. H. G. *widerlon,* recompense; from *wider,* again, back, and *lon,* a loan, gift.

Gukgo, *sb.* cuckoo, 13. 241.

Gyde, *sb.* a gown, dress, 6. 214. Chaucer has *gite,* a gown, which Tyrwhitt says is of French origin.

Gye, *v.* F. to guide, 3 *b.* 1118.

Gylt, *v.* to gild, 13. 40.

Gym, *adj.* trim, spruce, 13. 161. See **Gymp.**

Gymp, *adj.* jimp, slim, slender, 13. 121. W. *gwymp,* smart, trim.

Gynne, *v.* S. to begin, 3 *b.* 1394; *pr. s.* Gynnes, it begins, 28 *a.* 208. A.S. *ginnan.*

Gyrss, *sb.* grass, 13. 115.

Gyss, *sb.* guise, wise, manner, 13. 203. F. *guise,* G. *weise.*

Gysse, *sb. pl.* S. geese, 16. 384.

H.

Ha, *imp. s.* 3 *p.* let him have, 3 *b.* 1194.

Habilitie, *sb.* F. ability, 25. 157.

Hable, *adj.* able, 17 *c.* 108. Lat. *habilis.*

Haboundanle, *adv.* abundantly, 6. 376.

Haboundyt, *pt. s.* F. abounded, 6. 186.

Haiffeing, *pres. part.* having, 22. 4713.

Haile, *adv.* wholly, 6. 343; Haill, 22. 5564.

Hailsing, *pres. part.* saluting, greeting, 4. 166; *pt. s.* Halsit, 11 *a.* 2. Sw. *helsa,* to salute.

Hailsum, *adj.* wholesome, 13. 46.

Hairbis, *sb. gen. pl.* herbs', 11 *a.* 23.

Hairt, *sb.* S. heart, 11 *a.* 4.

Hait, *sb.* heat (?), 13. 137.

Halde, *imp. s.* S. hold, 4. 171.

Hale, *v.* to haul, to pull at, 4. 169; *pt. pl.* Haled, dragged, 19 *a.* 349. Du. *halen,* to fetch, pull; G. *holen,* to fetch.

Half, *sb.* S. side (often so used), 3 *b.* 1143.

Halflingis, *adv.* partly, half, 11 *a.* 27.

Halsit, *pt. s.* saluted, 11 *a.* 2. See **Hailsing.**

Halt, *pr. s.* holdeth, 1. 345. Contr. from *haldeth.*

Halwen, *pr. pl.* hallow, consecrate, 1. 356. A.S. *háligan, hálgian,* to hallow, from *hálig,* holy.

Halyde, *pt. s.* S. haled, hauled, drew, 7. 93. See **Hale.**

Han, *pr. pl.* have.

Hant, *v.* to practise, 13. 210; *pr. s.* Hantis, 13. 160. O. F. *hanter,* to frequent, practise; either from Icel. *hiemta,* Sw. *hämta,* to take home (Burguy), or from Breton *hent,* a path (Wedgwood).

Happis, *pr. s.* wraps, covers, 22. 4717.

Happy, *adj.* lucky, 6. 376. W. *hap,* luck.

Harborowe, *v.* S. to harbour, to lodge, 18. xviii. 16; Herberwe, 1. 215. A. S. *here,* an army, and *beorgan,* to hide.

Hard, 1 *p. s. pt.* heard, 22. 4737; *pt. s.* Hard say, heard it be said, 15 *b.* 137; *pp.* Hard, 11 *a.* 27.

Hardely, *adv.* S. boldly, 10. 123; 23. iii. 5. 110.

Haris, *sb. pl.* hairs, 13. 37.

Harlot, *adj.* base, scoundrelly, 6. 219.

Harneys, *sb.* F. armour, 3 *b.* 1176. F. *harnais,* G. *harnisch.*

Hartlesse, *adj.* not courageous, timid, 28 *b.* 28.

Haske, *sb.* a wicker basket for carrying fish in, 28 *a.* 16. Possibly connected with *hasel.*

Hastyfe, *adj.* F. hasty, 2. 229. O. F. *hastif,* hasty, from O. F. *haste,* Sw. *hast,* haste.

Hauld, *pr. pl.* hold, keep, 22. 4729.

Haunt, *v.* F. to practise, use, 5 *b.* 59; 25. 153; *pt. s.* Haunted, used, occupied, 2. 600. See **Hant.**

Haw, *adj.* azure, 13. 110. A. S. *hæwen,* azure-blue.

Hawbart, *sb.* halberd, 20 *a.* 78. M. H. G. *helmbarte* (the orig. form), an axe for cleaving helmets; from *helm,* a helmet, and *barte,* an axe.

Haye, *sb.* a springe, gin, or trap, 20 *a.* 88. Cf. E. *hedge, haw.*

Perhaps because set in a hedge. A. S. *hege,* a hedge.

Haylsede, 1 *p. s. pt.* saluted, 1. 231. Sw. *helsa.*

Haym, *sb. as adv.* home, homewards, 13. 198. Sw. *hem,* home, which agrees with the North E.

Haze, probably a corruption of *hae us,* or *ha' us,* i.e. have us, accept our terms, 23. iii. 5. 7.

He, *pron. pl.* they, 1. 471. A. S. *hi, hig.*

Heal, *sb.* S. hail, 7. 67.

Heale, *sb.* health, life, 23. iii. 3. 84. See **Hele.**

Heame, *put for* Home, 28 *a.* 98. See **Haym.**

Heare, *sb.* S. hair, 19 *a.* 725.

Hecht, *pt. s.* hight, was named, 6. 207; *pp.* Hecht, named, 6. 300. A. S. *hátan,* O. Fris. *heta,* G. *heissen,* to have for a name, be called.

Hecseities, *sb. pl.* 16. 318. A term in logic. Lat. *hic* (?).

Heer, *sb.* hair, 1. 423.

Hegh, *adj.* S. high, 3 *b.* 1251; *pl.* Heghe, 1254. A. S. *heáh, héh.*

Heir, *v.* S. to hear, 11 *a.* 1.

Heize, *adv.* high, on high, 1. 494, 551.

Hekkill, *sb.* heckle, cock's comb, 13. 156. A *heckle,* or *hackle* (derived from *hook*) is a toothed instrument for combing flax or hemp.

Hele, *sb.* health, salvation, 1. 264; health, 4. 169. A. S. *hælu,* health, from *hál,* whole.

Hely, *adj.* proud, haughty, 6. 211. A. S. *heáhlíc,* lit. high-like.

Hem, *pr. dat. pl.* to them, for them (mod. E. *'em*), 2. 603. A. S. *heom,* dat. pl. of *hí,* they.

Hendliche, *adv.* handily; hence, politely, 1. 231. Sw. *händig,* dexterous.

Henten, *v.* to seize, get, lay hands on, 1. 413; *pt. s.* Hent, took, 2.

602; *pp.* Hent, taken, 2. 618; rapt, caught, 28 *a.* 169. A.S. *hentan*, to catch.

Her, *poss. pr.* their, 2. 600. A.S. *hire*, of them, gen. pl. of *hé*.

Heraud, *sb.* herald, 1. 179. O.F. *herald*, from O. H. G. *haren*, to shout, proclaim; cf. Gk. *κῆρυξ*.

Herbere, *sb.* garden of herbs, 3 *b.* 1233; 13. 150. Lat. *herbarium*.

Herberwe, *v.* to harbour, lodge, 1. 215. See Harborowe.

Herce, *sb.* a hearse; hence a triangle, 15 *b.* 5. 'The origin (of *hearse*) is the F. *herce*, a harrow, an implement which in that country is made in a *triangular form*. Hence the name was given to a triangular framework of iron used for holding a number of candles at funerals,' &c. Wedgwood.

Herdeman, *sb.* a shepherd, pastor, 1. 231.

Here, *sb.* S. hair, 10. 110.

Herknere, *sb. used as adj.* listener, listening, 4. 156. (Obscure.)

Herield, *adj.* given as a heriot, or fine due to a superior, 22. 4734. See the note.

Herse, *sb.* rehearsal, burden of a song, 28 *a.* 60; cf. l. 170. This usage of the word, as an abbreviation of *rehearsal*, is incorrect, but Spenser has it again in The Fairie Queene, iii. 2. 48. He also uses *hersall* (F. Q. iii. 11. 18), which is equally unauthorized.

Hertely, *adv.* S. heartily, 10. 41.

Herteth, *pr. s.* S. gives heart to, encourages, 2. 282.

Herye, *v.* to praise, 28 *a.* 10. A.S. *herian*, to praise.

Hes, *pr. s.* has, 22. 4715.

Hestes, *sb. pl.* commandments, 1. 345. A.S. *hǽs*, a command.

Hestely, *adv.* F. hastily, 11 *a.* 7.

Hepen, *adv.* hence, 1. 408. Icel. *heðan*, hence.

Hew, *sb.* S. hue, 11 *a.* 3, 13. 38.

Hewed, *pp.* S. hued, coloured, 24. 59.

Hewynnis, *sb. gen. case*, heaven's, 6. 261.

Heynesse, *sb.* highness, haughtiness, 1. 265, 356; Hienes, majesty, 11 *a.* 11.

Hey3, *adj.* high, 1. 204.

High-copt, *pp.* high-topped, high-crowned, 26. 1163. W. *cop*, A.S. *copp*, a top; G. *kopf*, top.

Hight, 1 *p. s. pr.* I promise, 7. 70. A. S. *hátan*, pt. t. *ic héht*.

Hil, *sb.* prob. miswritten for *hool*, i. e. whole (though the Trinity MSS. also have *hille*), 3 *b.* 1328. The confusion is not surprising, as the word *hull* (shell of a pea) is spelt also *hool, hill*, and *hele*.

Hinde, *adj.* courteous, 7. 108. See Hendliche.

Hindir, *adj.* former, 11 *b.* 1. M.E. *ender*, former; cf. Germ. *ender*, former, and O. N. *endr*, formerly. (Stratmann.) See Ender.

Hird, *sb.* a shepherd, 22. 5629. Cf. G. *hirte*.

Hirnes, *sb. pl.* corners, 1. 182. A.S. *hirne*.

Hi3ede, 1 *p. s. pt.* hied, hastened, 1. 155. A.S. *higan*, to hasten.

Ho, *pron.* she, 1. 411. A.S. *heó*.

Hoball, *sb.* an idiot, 23. iii. 3. 18. Cf. *Hob* (short for Robert) a country clown, North E. *hobbil*, an idiot, *hob-hald*, a foolish clown, *hobbety-hoy*, &c. in Halliwell's Dict.

Hobies, *sb. pl.* hobbies, small-sized falcons, 18. xviii. 59. F. *hobereau*.

Hod, *sb.* hood, 1. 423.

Hoeues, *sb. pl.* hoofs, 18. xvii. 200. Du. *hoef*, Dan. *hov*.

Hoighdagh, *interj.* heyday! 23. iii. 3. 130. Cf. G. *heida*.

Hoip, *sb.* hope, 13. 206.

Hokshynes, *sb. pl.* gaiters, 1. 426, Ayrshire *hoskins, hoeshins, huskions*.

Ross *hoggers*, gaiters made of stockings without feet. *Hoskin* is a dimin. of *hose*. For the change of *sk* to *ks* compare E. *axe* (*akse*) and *ask*.

Hollyche, *adv.* wholly, 1. 796; Holly, 1. 815; 15 *b.* 40.

Holsome, *adj.* wholesome, 16. 305. A. S. *hál*, whole.

Holtes, *sb. pl.* S. groves, wooded hills, 8. v. 88; woods, 19 *f.* 29. A. S. *holt*, G. *holz*.

Hondes, *sb. pl.* S. hands, 2. 599.

Hongen, *v.* to hang, bend over, 1. 421; *pt. s.* Hong, 4. 160; *pt. pl.* Honged, 1. 429.

Hony, *sb.* S. honey, 16. 304.

Hoole, *adj.* whole, 3 *b.* 1178; hool my = my whole, 3 *b.* 1317. A. S. *hál*.

Hore, *adj. pl.* hoary, gray, 8. v. 88.

Horsecorsers, *sb. pl.* horsedealers, 26. 1084. Probably *corser* is put for M. E. *coser*. "*Mango*, a cosyr;" Wright's Vocab. 684. 40. Thus *coser* became *corser*; and, still later, *scorser*.

Hortis, *sb. pl.* hurts, 4. 156.

Houch-senous, *sb. pl.* hock-sinews, 6. 322.

Houed, *pt. s.* hovered, floated about, 8. v. 66. See Hufing.

Houris, *sb. pl.* F. hours of prayer; hence, orisons, songs of praise, lays, 11 *a.* 1.

Howe, *adj.* hollow, 22. 5491.

Hoyse, 1 *p. s. pr.* hoist, lift up, 24. 71. Du. *hijschen*, Sw. *hissa*, Dan. *heise*, F. *hisser*, which is distinct from F. *hausser*. Cf. Acts xxvii. 40.

Huddypeke, *sb.* a simpleton, or perhaps a rogue, 14. 326. On the probable origin of this word, see the note.

Hufing, *pres. part.* hovering, moving about slowly whilst keeping nearly in one spot, 4. 159. W.

hofio, hofian is borrowed from M. E. *hove*, to hover about.

Hugie, *adj.* huge, 24. 58, 65.

Humyll, *adj.* humble, 22. 4523. Lat. *humilis*.

Husbandis, *sb. pl.* husbandmen, 13. 259. Icel. *hús-bóndi*, master of a house; *bóndi* (Dan. *bonde*, a peasant) is for *búandi*, from *búa*, to build, live in.

Hycht, *sb.* height, 13. 92.

Hye, *sb.* haste; in hye = in haste, (common phr. in Sc.), 4. 158.

Hyen, *v.* to hie, hasten, 1. 409; Hye, 3 *a.* 9; 4. 164; 1 *p. s. pr.* Hyȝe, 1. 412; 1 *p. s. pt.* Hyed me, hastened, 3 *a.* 12. A. S. *higan*, to hasten.

Hyer, *adj.* S. higher, 2. 299.

Hyeth, *pr. s.* S. hies, hastens, 8. v. 20. See Hyen.

Hyndyr, *adj.* last past, 13. 221. See Hindir.

Hyng, *v.* to hang, 13. 131. See Hongen.

Hynt, 1 *p. s. pt.* seized, 13. 305; *pt. s.* Hynt, 6. 406. See Henten.

Hyȝe, *adj.* high, 1. 208.

I, J.

J is written like I in the MSS. Thus *Iaggde* is for *Jaggde*, and so on.

I-, *prefix*, used *chiefly* before past participles. A. S. *ge-*, Mœso-Goth. *ga-*, allied to Gk. γέ, Skt. *gha, ha*.

I, *adv.* aye, ever, 12. 9 (l. 6). Common in old editions of the dramatists.

Iaggde, *pp.* jagged, notched at the edges, 26. 1161. W. *gag*, an opening, cleft.

Iangled, *pt. pl.* talked fast, prated, 2. 611. O. F. *jangler*, to jest, from a Teutonic root; cf. Du. *janken*, to howl.

Iape, *sb.* F. a jest, 20 *a.* 31. F. *jape*, connected with E. *gab.*

Ich, *pron.* I, 1. 155. A. S. *ic.*

Ich a, *adj.* each one, each, 1. 432. Cf. Sc. *ilka.* A. S. *ælc*, each.

Ichon, *for* each one, 1. 476.

Iclyped, *pp.* S. called, 12. 16. A. S. *cleopian*, to call.

I-coruen, *pp.* carved, cut, 1. 161.

Ielofer, *sb.* a gillyflower, 14. 1053. F. *girofle*, a clove; of which *gilly-flower* is a corruption.

Iemis, *sb. pl.* gems, 11 *a.* 22.

Iennet, *sb.* a small, well-proportioned Spanish horse, 27. 85. Span. *ginete*, a nag; also, a horse-soldier.

Ientman, *sb.* gentleman, 23. iii. 3. 21. M. E. *gent* is often used for *gentle.*

Ieoperdie, *sb.* jeopardy, danger, 18. xvii. 166. F. *jeu parti*, Lat. *iocus partitus*, an even game, even chance.

Ierkins, *sb. pl.* jackets, 26. 1161. Diminutive of Du. *jurk*, a frock.

Ietting, *pres. part.* strutting, 23. iii. 3. 121. Used by Shakespeare. F. *jeter*, to throw; Lat. *iactare.*

Ijs, *sb.* ice, 1. 436. A. S. *ís.*

Ilke, *adj.* same, 4. 154. A. S. *ylc*, same.

Illumynat, *pp.* illuminated, 13. 54.

Illumynit, *pt. s.* F. shone, 11 *a.* 3.

Illustare, *adj.* F. illustrious, 11 *a.* 22.

Imps, *sb. pl.* shoots, grafts, scions, 26. 455.

In, *sb.* S. inn, lodging, house, 6. 243. See **Ynne**.

Inclinable, *adj.* capable of being inclined, 17 *c.* 293.

Incontinent, *adv.* F. immediately, 22. 5553.

Infere, *adv.* S. together, 2. 615; at the same time, 10. 14. A. S. *geféra*, a companion, from *faran*, to fare, go.

Inforce, *pr. pl. refl.* strive, endeavour, 18. xvii. 10.

Influent, *pr. part.* possessing influence, 13. 42. Lat. *fluere*, to flow.

Inhibitioun, *sb.* F. restriction, 11 *a.* 10. Lat. *inhibere*, to hold in, from *habere.*

In-till, *prep.* in, 6. 187. Cf. In-to.

Invnctment, *sb.* ointment, 13. 146. Lat. *inungere*, to anoint.

Iouisaunce, *sb.* rejoicing, joy, mirth, 28 *a.* 2. F. *jouir*, Lat. *gaudere*, to rejoice.

Iourney, *sb.* F. day, day's work, affair, 15 *b.* 66; day of battle, 15 *b.* 131. From Lat. *diurnus*, daily, *dies*, a day.

Joyneaunt, adjoining, 3 *b.* 1228.

Irkyt, 1 *p. s. pt.* became tired of, 13. 302.

Ischit, *pt. s.* issued; *ischit of =* issued from, 13. 14. O. F. *issir*, from Lat. *exire.*

Iubilie, *sb.* jubilee, 21. 181. Due to the Heb. *yóbél*, the blast of a trumpet.

Juges, *sb. pl.* F. judges, 14. 311. F. *juge.*

Iugledest, 2 *p. s. pt.* didst juggle, didst play false, 16. 70; 2 *p. s. pr.* Iuglest, 16. 101. Lat. *ioculari*, to make mirth.

Iugulynge, *sb.* F. juggling, 16. 18.

Iustlest, 2 *p. s. pr.* jostlest, pushest, 23. iii. 3. 129. O. F. *joster*, to joust, commonly referred to Lat. *iuxta*; but Wedgwood thinks the the word for a joust (combat) occurs in Dan. *dyst*, Sw. *dust.*

Iutte, *sb.* a piece of scornful behaviour, a slight, 23. iii. 3. 8. E. *jut*, another spelling of M. E. *jet.* See **Ietting**.

Ive, *sb.* ivy, 13. 97. A. S. *ífig.*

I-wisse, *adv.* certainly, 25. 17. O. Fries. *wis*, Icel. *viss*, certain, Du. *gewis*, adj. and adv. certain, certainly.

Iyen, *sb. pl.* S. eyes, 24. 11. See Eı.

Iȝe, *sb.* S. eye, 5 *b.* 28; *pl.* Iȝen, 122.

Iȝe-siȝt, *sb.* S. eyesight, 5 *b.* 14.

K.

Karmes, *sb. pl.* Carmelite friars, 2. 618.

Ken, *v.* to know, 28 *b.* 82; *2 p. pl. pr.* ye know, 22. 4574; *pt. pl.* Kend, 6. 204; *pp.* Kend, 22. 4588. Icel. *kenna,* G. *kennen,* to know.

Kep, *sb.* S. keep, heed, care, 3 *b.* 1359; Kepe, 24. 41.

Kepit, *pp.* kept, guarded, 11 *a.* 19.

Kerued, *pp.* S. carved, 18. xvii. 201. A. S. *ceorfan,* to cut.

Kest, *pt. s.* cast, threw (by re-flection), 13. 62.

Keuer, *v.* F. 10. 100.

Keysar, *sb.* Caesar, czar, emperor, 27. 227.

Kirtel, *sb.* a kind of petticoat, 1. 229; 10. 110. A. S. *cyrtel,* Sw. *kjortel.* See note to 1. 229.

Knackes, *sb. pl.* tricks, 26. 799. The original meaning is a crack or snap; Dan. *knag,* a crack, crash, E. *knock.*

Knap, *imp. s.* toll, strike (the bell), 23. iii. 3. 80. M. E. *knap,* to strike, break; cf. *knack, snap.* Du. *knappen,* to crack.

Knawen, *pp.* gnawn, gnawed, 24. 51. A. S. *gnagan,* to gnaw.

Knawin, *pp.* known, 22. 4563.

Knopped, *pp.* full of knobs or bunches, 1. 424. See below.

Knoppys, *sb. pl.* knops, buds, 13. 123. A. S. *cnæp,* a knop, button; E. *knab, knop, knob, nob.*

Knottes, *sb. pl.* knots, 1. 161. ' *Knot,* a boss, round bunch of leaves; also, the foliage on the capitals of pillars;' Glossary of Architecture.

Knyp, *pp.* nipped, nibbled, 13. 94.

Ko, *colloquial form of* quoth, 23 iii. 3. 21. See next word.

Koth, *pt. s.* S. quoth, said, 2. 611. A. S. *cwæð,* pt. t. of *cweðan,* to say; cf. E. *be-queath.*

Kundites, *sb. pl.* conduits, 1. 195.

Kunne, *v.* S. be able; kunne seie = be able to say, 5 *a.* 35. A. S. *cunnan.*

Ky, *sb. pl.* cows, kine, 13. 185; 22. 4715. A. S. *cú,* a cow, pl. *cý.*

Kychens, *sb. pl.* kitchens, 1. 210.

Kydst, *pt. s.* 2 *p.* knewest, 28 *b.* 92. (Properly, it means *shewedst.*) A. S. *cýðan,* to make known, shew; pt. t. *ic cýðde.*

Kynd, *sb.* S. nature, natural pro-perty, 6. 217; Kynde, natural occupation, 1. 760. A. S. *cynd,* nature.

Kynde, *adj.* natural; *kynde ypo-crites,* hypocrites by nature, 1. 489.

Kyne, *sb. pl.* cows, 6. 190. See Ky.

Kynrede, *sb.* kindred, 1. 486. A. S. *cyn,* kin, and *ræden,* condition, state. The first *d* in *kindred* is of late insertion; cf. *hatred.*

Kyrkis, *sb. pl.* churches, 13. 70.

Kyrnellis, *sb. pl.* battlements, 13. 69. F. *créneau,* O. F. *crenel,* a battlement, from F. *cran,* Lat. *crena,* a notch, *cranny.*

Kyrtel. See Kirtel.

Kyth, *v.* to shew, display, 13. 124 A. S. *cýðan,* to make known.

Kytlys, *pr. s.* excites pleasurably, enlivens, 13. 229. A. S. *citelian,* to tickle.

L.

Ladde, *pt. s.* S. led, 3 *b.* 1337; *pp.* Lad, 5 *b.* 55.

Laif, *sb.* S. remnant, the rest, 11 *a.* 19; oure the laif = above the rest, 11 *a.* 22; Layff, 6. 240. A. S. *láf,* a remainder, *læfan,* to leave.

Laitis, *sb. pl.* manners, gestures, 11 *a.* 17. Icel. *læti,* voice, gesture.

Lake, *sb.* blame, scorn, 22. 4515. A. S. *leáhan,* O. Fris. *lakia,* Du. *laken,* to blame.

Langar, *adv.* longer, 13. 8.

Lap, *pt. s.* S. leapt, 4. 153.

Largesse, *sb.* F. prodigality, 2. 598; bounty, 3 *b.* 1372.

Laser, *sb.* F. leisure, 22. 5537. F. *loisir,* from Lat. *licere,* as *pldisir* from *placere;* Diez.

Lasse, *adj.* less, 5 *a.* 91.

Latun, *sb.* latoun or latten, a mixed metal much resembling brass, 1. 196.

Laudacion, *sb.* Lat. praise, 12. 23.

Launcep, *pr. pl.* launch out, fling abroad, 1. 551. F. *lancer,* to fling.

Lauoures, *sb. pl.* lavers, cisterns, 1. 196.

Lauȝwe, *v.* S. to laugh, 5 *a.* 63; *pt. s.* Lauȝed, 67. A. S. *hlihan,* Du. *lagchen.*

Law, *adj.* S. low, 13. 76, 22. 5466.

Law, *adv.* lowly, humbly, 11 *a.* 11.

Lay, *v.* to lay it down, premise, 17 *c.* 46.

Laye, *sb.* lea, pasture, 28 *a.* 15 (but see the note); *pl.* Layes, 28 *a.* 188. M. E. *lay, lea, ley,* fallow-land. See **Leys.**

Layff. See **Laif.**

Leames, *sb. pl.* gleams, lights, rays, 24. 9. A. S. *leóma,* a beam of light.

Leche, *sb.* physician, 3 *b.* 1404; *pl.* Leches, 3 *b.* 1349. A.S. *læce.*

Lede, *sb.* lead, 4. 153; Leed, 1.193.

Ledys, *pr. pl.* lead; *dansys ledys,* lead dances, 13. 193.

Leef, *adj.* lief, dear, 2. 599; 8. *v.* 38; Leefe, 19 *f.* 48. A. S. *leóf,* lief, beloved.

Leeful, *adj.* lawful, 5 *a.* 49. Better spelt *leefful* or *lefful;* from M. E. *lef, leue,* permission, A. S. *lýfan,* to allow. See **Leifsum.**

Leel, *adj.* leal, loyal, faithful, 1. 390; Lel, 1. 344.

Leese, *v.* S. to lose, 20 *c.* 46; 26. 831; 1 *p. pl. pr.* we lose, 27. 129. See **Lose.**

Leesinges, *sb. pl.* lies; *l. lyep,* they lie their lies, 1. 379. A. S. *leás-ung,* lying, from *leás,* false, *loose.*

Leeue, 1 *p. s. pr.* I believe, 2. 623; *imp. s.* Leeue, 1. 363; *pp.* Leeued, 19 *a.* 313. Mœso-Goth. *laubjan,* G. *glauben* (for *ge-lauben*).

Leeuen, *pr. pl.* live, 1. 359.

Lef, *adj.* dear, lief, 1. 372; Leue, 1. 390. A. S. *leóf,* dear.

Lefte, *pt. s.* remained, 1. 374; 2. 607; Left, 3 *b.* 1174. A. S. *lǽfan,* to leave; cf. G. *b-leiben,* to remain.

Lege, *sb.* liege, liege lord, 13. 247.

Leide, *v.* to lead, carry, 6. 371.

Leiffe, 1 *p. s. pr.* live, 6. 310. A. S. *lybban.*

Leifsum, *adj.* allowable, i. e. it is allowable, 22. 4579. E. *leave,* permission, A. S. *léf, leáf;* cf. **Leeful.**

Lelliche, *adv.* leally, faithfully, truly, 1. 235; Lelly, 1. 384.

Lemand, *pres. part.* gleaming, 13. 34. See below.

Lemys, *sb. pl.* S. gleams, rays of light, 11 *a.* 3. A. S. *leóma,* a ray.

Lene, *v.* to lend, grant, give, 1. 445. A. S. *lǽnan,* to lend, give.

Lenger, *adv.* longer, 5 *a.* 91.

Lent, *pp.* inclined (lit. leant), 13. 200.

Lere, *sb.* cheek, complexion, 14. 1034. A. S. *hleór,* the cheek.

Lere, *imp. s.* teach, direct, commend, 1. 343. See below.

Lere, *v.* S. to learn, 4. 171, 28 *b.* 4; *pt. s.* Leryt, 6. 249. A. S. *lǽran,* G. *lehren,* to teach; A. S. *leornian,* G. *lernen,* to learn; but Du. *leeren* has *both* meanings, and so has Prov. E. *learn.*

Lerne, *v.* to teach, 1. 402. See above.

Lese, *v.* to lose, 15 *b.* 69. A. S. *leósan.* See **Leese.**

Less, *sb. pl.* lies; *but less,* without lies, 6. 321.

Leste, *pr. s. impers.* it pleases, 2. 612. See **List.**

Lesty, *adj. either* lusty (see Listy in Halliwell) *or* cunning (from A. S. *list,* cunning), 4. 157.

Lestyt, *pp.* lasted, 6. 412.

Lesyng, *sb.* S. losing, loss, 3 *b.* 1095.

Let, *v.* to hinder, prevent, delay, stop, 7. 5; 12. 9; Lette, 3 *b.* 1127; 15 *b.* 45; Letten, 1. 346; *pr. s.* Lettes, 19 *a.* 360; *pt. s.* Letted, forbade, 17 *b.* 13. A. S. *lettan,* Du. *letten.*

Let make, i. e. caused to be made, 8. vii. 16; wedden lete = caused to be wedded. 2. 598. A. S. *lǽtan,* G. *lassen,* Du. *laten,* to let, cause.

Lette, *sb.* S. hindrance, 15 *b.* 98.

Leuand, *pres. part.* living, 22. 5502.

Leue, *v.* S. to remain, 10. 45.

Leue, *adj.* See **Lef.**

Leue, *pr. s. subj.* permit, 1. 366. M. E. *leuen,* to permit, allow a thing to be done, is often wrongly confused with M.E. *lenen,* to grant, lend, give.

Leue, *v.* to believe; 2 *p. s. pr.* Leuest, 1. 342; *pr. pl.* Leueþ, 1. 754; *pt. s.* believed, 235.

Leuer, *adj. comp.* liefer, dearer, 20 *d.* 8; *adv.* rather, 10. 65; 17 *c.* 188. A. S. *leóf,* dear, *lief,* beloved.

Leueyed, *pp.* F. levied, 9. 11. Lat. *leuare.*

Levis, *sb. pl.* S. leaves, 11 *a.* 4; Leyvis, 13. 102.

Levis, *pr. s.* lives, 13. 206.

Lewch, *pt. s.* laughed, 6. 430; 13. 223. See **Lauȝwe.**

Lewde, *adj.* unlearned, base, 14.

569; ignorant, 14. 327, 17 *c.* 85. A. S. *lǽwed man,* a lay-man, an illiterate person.

Lewdnes, *sb.* S. ignorance, 17 *c.* 32. See above.

Lewyt, *pp.* left, 6. 435.

Leyen, *pt. pl.* lay, 1. 187.

Leyff, *sb.* leave, 6. 338, 448.

Leyffyt, *pp.* lived, 6. 318.

Leyn, *v.* S. to lay, 3 *b.* 1108. A. S. *lecgan,* G. *legen,* Du. *leggen,* to lay, place, cause to lie.

Leyn, *pp.* lain, 3 *b.* 1167. A. S. *licgan* (pp. *legen*), G. and Du. *liegen,* to lie.

Leys, *sb. pl.* leas, 13. 183. A. S. *leág,* a pasture. See **Laye.**

Leyvis, *sb. pl.* leaves, 13. 102. See **Leuis.**

Libbeþ, *pr. pl.* live, 1. 475. A. S. *lybban.*

Liberdes, *sb. pl.* leopards, 18. xviii. 8. Gk. λέων, a lion, and πάρδος, a pard.

Liche, *adj.* S. like, 3 *b.* 1154.

Lief; lief or loth = pleased or displeased, 3 *b.* 1071. A. S. *leóf,* dear, *láð,* hateful.

Lieftenants, *sb. pl.* lieutenants, deputies, 26. 438. F. *lieu-tenant,* holding place.

Light, *pt. s.* S. alighted, 19 *a.* 610.

Like, *v.* to please, 26. 1174; *pr. s.* Liketh, 2. 614; Likis, 6. 308.

Lilburne, *sb.* a heavy stupid fellow, 23. iii. 3. 18.

List, 1 *p. s. pr.* please, desire, 25. 173; *pr. s.* List, pleases, 19 *b.* 19; chooses, is pleased, 28 *a.* 19; 2 *p. pl. pr.* please, 3 *b.* 1313; *pt. s.* chose, was pleased, 3 *b.* 1067. A.S. *lystan,* to please; E. *list, lust.*

Liste, *pt. s.* it pleased (with dat. hem), 1. 165.

Liuelod, *sb.* livelihood, sustenance, 20 *a.* 3. A.S. *lif-láde,* from *ládu,* a voyage, food for a voyage. The proper word is *livelode,* of which *livelihood* is a corruption.

Liuing, *sb.* S. means of livelihood, 25. 123.

Lobcocke, *sb.* a lubber (a term of contempt), 23. iii. 3. 18. Cotgrave's Fr. Dict. has '*Baligaut*, an unweldie lubber, great *lobcocke*.' M.E. *lob*, to droop; cf. *looby*, *lubber*.

Lode-star, *sb.* a lode-star, i. e. a *leading* or guiding star, 14. 1226.

Logged, *pt. s.* F. lodged, 2. 605.

Lokrand, *pres. part.* curling, 13. 127. Icel. *lokkr*, a lock of hair.

Lollede, *pt. s.* lolled about, wagged about, 1. 224.

Longeth, *v.* S. belongs (to), is suitable, 10. 115. Cf. G. *gelangen*.

Loowes, *pr. s.* lows, bellows, 19 *a.* 282. A. S. *hlowan*.

Lorde, *pr. pl.* idle about, waste time idly, 21. 112. M. E. *loord*, a lout, lazy fellow (Spenser, F.Q. iii. 7. 12); M.E. *lurdein*, a lout; F. *lourd*, heavy, dull, from Lat. *luridus*.

Lording, *pres. part.* lazy, idling, 21. 95; loitering, lying lazily, 28 *b.* 70. This is better than supposing it to mean *behaving like a lord*, though Spenser may have intended the latter. See **Lorde**, and the note.

Lording, *sb.* idling about, laziness, 21. 109. See **Lorde**.

Lore, *sb.* teaching; also lesson, a thing to be learnt, acquirement, 10. 67. A. S. *lár*, lore, learning.

Lorels, *sb. pl.* abandoned wretches, 1. 755. Cf. Losells.

Lorne, *pp.* S. lost, 24. 77. A. S. *loren*, lost, G. *verlieren*, to lose, pp. *verloren*.

Losanger, *sb.* sluggard, 13. 281. O. F. *losenge*, flattery, F. *louange*, praise, from Lat. *laus*, praise; O. Sc. *losingere*, a flatterer, deceiver, sluggard.

Losells, *sb. pl.* abandoned wretches, good-for-nothing fellows, 1. 750.

Louerd, *sb.* lord, 1. 795. A. S. *hláford*.

Lough, *pt. pl.* laughed, 2. 615. Cf. Lewch.

Loure, *v.* to lower, frown, 12. 21; Louren, to look displeased, 1. 556. Sw. *lura*, to lurk, spy; Du. *loeren*, to peer about; Sc. *glowre*.

Loute, *v.* to treat as a *lout*, to contemn, 23. iii. 3. 33. Cf. *lowted* as used in Shakespeare, 1 Hen. VI, iv. 3. 13.

Lovyng, *sb.* praising, praise, 11 *b.* 16; Louyng, 22. 5639. A. S. *lof*, praise; G. *loben*, to praise.

Lovys, *pr. pl.* praise, 13. 247. A.S. *lofian*, to praise.

Lowe, 1 *p. s. pr.* approve of, praise, 23. iii. 3. 143. F. *louer*, to praise. Lat. *laudare*.

Lowis, *sb. pl.* lochs, lakes, 13. 153.

Lowkyt, *pp.* tightly closed (lit. locked), 13. 101.

Lowne, *adj.* serene, calm, 13. 54. Sw. *lugn*, calm, quiet.

Luffaris, *sb. pl.* lovers, 13. 288.

Luging, *sb.* F. lodging, 22. 5535.

Lugit, *pp.* F. lodged, 6. 233.

Luke, *v.* to look, 4. 170.

Lust, 1 *p. s. pr.* I like, 23. iii. 3. 36; 2 *p. s. pr.* choosest, art pleased with, 28 *a.* 21.

Lust, *sb.* inclination, 10. 97; pleasure, happiness, 19 *f.* 2. A. S. *lust*, desire, pleasure, G. *lust*.

Lustinesse, *sb.* beauty, verdure, 19 *b.* 2.

Lusty, *adj.* pleasant, 3 *b.* 1362; 11 *a.* 6. See **Lust**.

Lybbeþ, *pr. pl.* live, 1. 477. See **Libbeþ**.

Lyohtlynes, *sb.* lightness, i. e. jesting, insult, 6. 349.

Lyohtyt, *pt. pl.* alighted (from horseback), set (upon), 6. 409.

Lyokpeny, i. e. that licks up the penny, money-swallower, an epithet of London, 3 *a.*

Lyfly, *adv.* S. in a lively manner, spiritedly, 2. 282.

Lyft, *sb.* air, 13. 240. A. S. *lyft*, G. *luft*.

Lyghte, *v.* alight, descend, 7. 61.

Lyknes, *sb.* a likeness, i. e. a parable, 1. 263.

Lyms, *sb. pl.* S. limbs, 24. 18. A. S. *lim*.

Lym-ȝerde, *sb.* a lime-yard or limed twig, such as birds are caught with, 1. 564.

Lyn, *v.* to cease, stop, 24. 63. A.S. *linnan*, to cease, M. E. *blin* (i. e. *be-lin*), to cease.

Lynage, *sb.* F. lineage, 10. 170.

Lyntquhite, *sb.* linnet, 13. 240.

Lyplabour, *sb.* labour with the lips, recitation of prayers, 26. 857.

Lyss, *v.* to soothe, comfort, 13. 202. A. S. *liss*, grace, comfort; cf. *bliss*.

Lyssouris, *sb. pl.* pastures, 13. 183. A. S. *lǽsu*, prov. E. *leasowe*, *leese*, a pasture.

Lyst, 1 *p. s. pr.* choose, am pleased, 3 *a.* 15. See **List**.

Lyte, *adj.* little, 13. 112. A. S. *lyt*, little.

M.

M, the first letter of *master* or *mastership*; hence used as short for 'mastership,' a title of respect, 23. iii. 3. 133. See the note.

Maat, *adj.* exhausted, tired, 3 *b.* 1209. O. F. *mat*, from the Persian *shâh mat* (check-mate), the king is dead.

Macull, *sb.* stain, 11 *a.* 22. Lat. *macula*.

Magger, *sb.* F. in the phr. *in the magger of* = in spite of, 7. 3. See **Maugre**.

Maistow, *for* mayest thou, 4. 170.

Maistry, *sb.* F. mastery, proof of skill, 17 *a.* 13.

Make, *sb.* mate, husband, 19 *a.* 597; *pl.* Makys, 7. 117. A. S. *maca*, a husband; E. *match*.

Male, *sb.* F. mail, armour, 7. 62. F. *maille*, It. *maglia*, a ring of mail or chain-armour, from Lat. *macula*, a spot, a mesh in a net.

Malengyne, *sb.* F. malice, evil disposition, 9. 10. Lat. *malum in genium*.

Mamelek, *sb.* a mamuluke, slave, 14. 476. Span. *mameluco*, from Arab. *mamlûk*, a slave, from *malaka*, to possess.

Maner, *sb.* F. manner. The word *of* is frequently *understood* after it; see 3 *b.* 1395.

Manquellers, *sb. pl.* mankillers, 17 *c.* 37. A. S. *cwellan*, to kill.

Mantled, *pp.* covered, cloaked, adorned with flowers, 28 *a.* 128.

Marc, *sb. pl.* S. marks, 9. 6. Cf. our use of *foot* for *feet* in measurement. A *mark* was a coin worth 13*s.* 4*d.*

March, *sb*; in phr. *march-parti* = border country, the *marches*, 7. 120; cf. l. 122. A. S. *mearc*, a mark, boundary.

Martrik, *sb.* a marten or martin, 4. 157. A. S. *meard*, F. *martre*, G. *marder*.

Massage, *sb.* F. message, 3 *b.* 1065.

Masse-peny, *sb.* a penny given for the singing of masses, 16. 149.

Mate, *v.* to be checkmated, 4. 168. Mate is a *sb.* meaning checkmate in st. 169. See **Maat**.

Maugre, *adv.* in spite of, 3 *b.* 1149. Fr. *mal gré*.

Mavyss, *sb.* F. the song-thrush, 11 *a.* 24. O. F. *malvis*, F. *mauvis*, apparently of Celtic origin.

May, *adj. pl.* S. more, 6. 281. A. S. *má*.

May, *sb.* maid, 28 *a.* 39. A. S. *mæg*, Mœso-Goth. *mawi*.

Mayn, *sb.* main, i.e. strength, 6. 320. A. S. *mægen,* strength.

Mayne, *sb.* moan, 6. 189. A. S. *mǽnan,* to bemoan.

Mayny, *sb.* F. a household; hence, a flock (of sheep), 14. 292. See **Meany.**

Mayr, *adv.* more, 6. 188.

Me (*for* Men), people, used with sing. vb., like the French *on,* 9. 100.

Meane, *sb.* F. way, method, 17 *d.* 50; 26. 753. F. *moyen,* from Lat. *medius,* middle.

Meany, *sb.* F. company, suite, 7. 6. Meyne, 2. 620; Mayny, 14. 292. O. F. *maisne,* a household; supposed to be from Low Lat. *maisnada* short for *mansionata,* a household, a company of *menials.* A *menial* (*mansionalis*), is a household servant.

Meed, *sb.* S. reward, 3 *a.* 4; there mede = their hire, 3 *a.* 12.

Meeþ, *sb.* S. mead, 5 *a.* 90. A. S. *medu,* W. *medd,* Gk. μέθυ, wine, cf. Sanskrit, *madhu,* honey.

Meint, *pp.* mingled, 28 *a.* 203; Meynt, 3 *b.* 1260; Ment, 13. 22. Contr. from *menged,* pp. of A. S. *mengian,* to mingle.

Meked, *pp.* made meek, 16. 287.

Mekill, *adj.* mickle, much, 6. 183. A. S. *mycel.*

Mell, *v.* F. to meddle, 14. 375; *pp.* Mellit, 4. 152. Contr. from O. F. *mesler,* from Low Lat. *misculare,* which from Lat. *miscere,* to mix.

Mene, *adj.* mean, common, 1. 786. A. S. *gemǽne,* Goth. *gamains,* common.

Ment, *pp.* mingled, mixed, 13. 22. See **Meint.**

Menys, *pr. s.* bemoans, laments, 6. 432. See **Mayne.**

Merels, *sb. pl.* merelles, or nine-men's morris, a game played with counters or pegs, 5 *a.* 71. O. F.

merel, a counter; cf. F. *mérelle,* hop-scotch.

Merimake, *sb.* merrymaking, 28 *a.* 9.

Merkes, *sb. pl.* marks, tokens, 1. 177.

Merle, *sb.* F. the blackbird, 11 *a.* 25. Lat. *merula.*

Mess, *sb.* mass, 13. 304.

Mete, *adj.* scanty, close fitting, 1. 428. Prov. E. *mete,* scanty, small. A. S. *mǽte,* small; lit. closely measured, from the vb. *to mete.*

Mete-yarde, *sb.* S. a measuring rod, 16. 201.

Meued, *pp.* F. moved, 2. 628.

Meyn, *sb.* intent, design, 13. 210. Cf. A. S. *myne,* mind, intent; E. *mean,* to intend.

Meyne, *sb.* F. household, company, 2. 620. See **Meany.**

Meynt, *pp.* mingled, 3 *b.* 1260. See **Meint.**

Minges, *pr. s.* mingles, 19 *c.* 11. A. S. *mengian,* to mingle, mix.

Minyons, *sb. pl.* favourites, 21. 128. F. *mignon,* from O. H. G. *minni,* love.

Minyshe, *v.* F. to diminish, 17 *c.* 21. Lat. *minus,* less.

Mizzle, *v.* to rain slightly, 28 *a.* 208. O. Du. *mieselen,* to mizzle, connected with Du. and E. *mist.*

Mo, *adj.* more, 2. 603. A. S. *má.*

Mobyll, *adj.* moveable, 14. 522. Lat. *mobilis.*

Moich, *adj.* moist, misty, 13. 46. Sc. *moch, moich,* misty, close; E. *muggy.* Cf. W. *mwg,* smoke, fume.

Moist, *pr. s.* must, 22. 4716. See **Mot.**

Molte, *pt. s.* melted, 24. 78. A. S. *meltan,* pt. t. *ic mealt,* pl. *we multon,* pp. *molten.*

Mon, 2 *p. s. pr.* must, 13. 218. Icel. *ek mun,* I must.

Mone, *sb.* S. moon; mone shyne =

shining of the moon, moonlight, 3 *b*. 1123. A. S. *móna*, gen. *mónan*.

Moneþ, *sb*. month, 1. 248. A. S. *mónað*, month, *móna*, moon.

Mong-corn, (made of) mixed or mingled corn, hence, inferior, 1. 786. From A. S. *mengan*, to mix.

Monkrye, *sb*. monkery, the race of monks, 22. 4669.

Monstruous, *adj*. monstrous, 18. xvii. 203.

Moo, *adj. comp*. more, 16. 409. See **Mo**.

Moode, *sb*. mud; pekked moode = pecked mud, ate dirt, were humiliated, 2. 621. Du. *modder*, Sw. *mudder*, mud, slush.

Morow, *sb*. morning, 13. 304. Here *ayr* is an adjective, signifying 'early.'

Morrow, *sb*. morning, 11 *a*. 27. M. E. *morwe*, *morwen*. A. S. *morgen*.

Morrice-bells, *sb. pl*. bells for a morris-dance, 26. 785. *Morris* is for *Moorish*, which is from Gk. ἀμαυρός, dark.

Mort, *sb*. F. the note sounded at the death (*mort*) of the deer, 7. 16.

Mortal, *adj*. F. deadly, 3 *b*. 1141; Mortall, 13. 7.

Mot, *pr. s*. must, 1. 557; 2 *p*. Mot, mayest, 11 *b*. 17; 3 *p*. Mote, 3. 301. A. S. *ic mót*, M. E. *I mote*, is the present tense; A. S. *ic móste*, M. E. *I moste*, is the past tense. The modern E. *must* has to do duty for both.

Mought, *pt. s*. might, 18. xvii. 24. See **Mowe**.

Mounchynge, *pres. part*. munching, eating, 21. 181. F. *manger*, Lat. *manducare*.

Mountenaunce, *sb*. F. amount, duration, 14. 358. Lat. acc. *montem*, mountain.

Mowe, *pr. pl*. may, 5 *b*. 65; *pt. s*.

Mought, might, 18. xvii. 24. A. S. *magan*, to be able, *ic mæg*, I may, *ic meahte*, I might.

Mowing, *sb*. grimacing, 25. 119. F. *moue*, pouting, a wry face. Probably connected with *mock*. See *Mock* in Wedgwood.

Mowle, *sb*. mole, 27. 140.

Moylynge, *pres. part*. labouring, toiling, 21. 182. *Moil* also means to wet, from F. *mouiller*; hence probably the secondary meaning of to work in mud, to drudge.

Muddir, *sb*. S. mother, 11 *a*. 1.

Mum, *sb*. the least sound made by closed lips, 3 *a*. 4.

Munte, 1 *p. s. pt*. I disposed myself to go, purposed to go, from A. S. *myntan*, to intend, M. E. *minten*, to aim, attempt, 1. 171. See *Myntyn*, in Prompt. Parv.

Myddis, *adj. as sb*. midst, 4. 159. A. S. *middes*, gen. case of *midd*, adj. mid.

Myghe, *sb*. midge, 13. 172. A. S. *mycg*, *myg*.

Myllan, i.e. Milan steel, 7. 65.

Mynde, *sb*. S. remembrance, memory, 5 *b*. 115. Cf. phr. to *call to mind*.

Myne-ye-ple, *sb. prob. a corruption of* manople, a gauntlet, 7. 62. O. F. *manople*, a gauntlet, armbrace; Lat. *manus*. See Roquefort's Glossaire; and note.

Mysreuled, *pp*. misruled, misgoverned, disorderly, 2. 626.

Mystyrit, *pp*. injured by loss (of blood), 6. 361. Dan. *miste*, to lose.

Myteynes, *sb. pl*. mittens, 1. 428.

N.

Namelich, *adv*. especially, 5 *a*. 58.

Nappy, *adj*. sleep-inducing, heady, 20 *c*. 16. A. S. *hnæppian*, to slumber.

Natheles, *adv.* S. nevertheless, 2. 282. A. S. *ná,* not.

Naughte, *adj.* naughty, bad, 17 *e.* 79.

Nay; use of *nay* and *no,* 17 *d.* 16.

Nay whan, *interj.* nay, when? i.e. not so, when will you do it right, 23. iii. 3. 117.

Ne, *adv.* not, nor. A. S. *ne,* F. *ne.*

Neare, *adv.* never, 28. iii. 3. 133. See the note.

Nedes, *adv.* S. of necessity, of need, 2. 301. A. S. *neádes,* gen. of *neád,* need.

Neipces, *sb. pl.* F. grand-daughters, 26. 773. Lat. *neptis.*

Nemne, I *p. s. pr.* name, call, 1. 472. A. S. *nemnan,* to name.

New-fanglenesse, *sb.* fondness for novelty, 17 *c.* 68. See *Fangle* in Wedgwood.

Nobles, *sb. pl.* nobles (coins so named), 2. 609. A gold noble was worth 6*s.* 8*d.*

Nocht, *adv.* naught, not.

Nolde, *pt. s.* (*for* ne wolde), would not, 1. 190. Cf. A. S. *nyllan,* Lat. *nolle,* to be unwilling.

Nones, *in phr.* for the nones, i.e. for the once, for the occasion, 1. 183. M. E. *for the nanes,* a corruption of *for then anes.* See Ormulum, ed. White, vol. ii. p. 642.

Nonys; phr. for the nonys (mod. E. *for the nonce*), 3 *b.* 1167. See above.

Noonesteede, *sb.* S. noon-stead, place of noon, meridian, 24. 7.

Nosell, *pr. pl.* nuzzle, noursle, nurse, rear up, 16. 309. Lat. *nutrix.*

Note, I *p. s. pr.* know not, 2. 598. Equivalent to *ne wot.*

Nowne, *sb.* noon, 6. 372.

Noyss-thyrlys, *sb. pl.* nostrils, 13. 29. E. *nostril = nose-thrill,* from A. S. *þirlan,* to thrill, drill.

Nuly, *adv.* newly, lately, 15 *a.* 115.

Nummer, *sb.* F. number, 22. 5625.

Nutshales, *sb. pl.* nutshells, i.e. of small value, 14. 440. *Shale, scale, shell* are all the same word.

Nyce, *adj.* F. foolish, silly, full of tricks, 4. 155. O. F. *nice,* lazy, simple, orig. ignorant; from Lat. acc. *nescium.*

Nycht-hyrd, *sb.* guardian of the night, 13. 1.

Nycthemyne, a name for the owl, 13. 11. See note.

Nyl, *pr. s.* will not, 1. 249. A. S. *nyllan,* to be unwilling.

Nynt, *adj.* ninth, 11 *a.* 27.

Nyss, *adj.* curious, 13. 238. E. *nice.* See **Nyce.**

O.

O, *adj.* one, one and the same, 1. 440. See **On.**

Oblyste, *pp.* F. obliged, 22. 4691. Lat. *ligare,* to tie.

Observaunce, *sb.* F. homage, 13. 249.

Obumbrat, *pp.* overshadowed, 13. 66. Lat. *obumbrare,* to shade, from *umbra.*

Occident, *sb.* F. west, 22. 5559. Lat. *cadere,* to fall, sink.

Occupyed, *pt. s.* made use of, employed, 14. 557. Lat. *occupare,* to use, from *capere.*

Of-newe, *adv.* anew, 3 *b.* 1295.

Oliphant, *sb.* elephant, 4. 156. Probably from the Hebrew *aleph,* a bull.

On, *num.* one, 1. 789; Oon, 3 *b.* 1150; Oo, 10. 93; Oo point = one bit, one jot, 1. 198; O, one and the same, 1. 440. A. S. *án,* Lat. *unus,* G. *ein.*

On, *prep.* upon, in, 1. 342. A. S. *on,* G. *an;* only another form of *in.*

Onbydrew, *pt. s.* withdrew, continued to draw aside, 13. 6.

Ones, *adv.* once, I. 491. A.S. *ánes.*

Onepe, *adv.* scarcely, I. 217. See Vnneth.

Onlappyt, *pt. s.* unfolded, unlapped, 13. 114. A.S. *læppa,* a lap, flap.

Onlesum, *adj.* not permissible, unlawful, 13. 210. M.E. *lefsum,* from A.S. *leáf,* leave, permission. See Leifsum.

Onon, *adv.* anon, immediately, 6. 422. A.S. *on án,* in one.

Onschet, *pt. s.* un-shut, i.e. opened, 13. 17; *pt. pl.* 13. 121.

Onvale, *v.* to unveil, become unveiled, 12. 20.

Oo, Oon. See On.

Oost, *sb.* F. host, army, 9. I. Lat. *hostis.*

Or, *conj.* ere, before, 2. 618, 6. 181; Or than = ere then, 22. 5456. A.S. *ǽr,* ere.

Orchezardes, *sb. pl.* orchards, or rather, gardens, i.e. wort-yards, I. 166. A.S. *wyrt-geard.*

Ordand, *pt. s.* F. ordained, II *a.* II; *pt. pl.* 6. 274. Lat. *ordinare,* from *ordo.*

Ordynatly, *adv.* F. in good order, orderly, 15 *b.* 83. Lat. *ordinatus,* pp. of *ordinare,* from *ordo.*

Orient, *sb.* east, 13. 21. Lat. *oriri,* to arise.

Orleger, *sb.* clock, 13. 278; *pl.* Orologis, 5 *a.* 13. F. *horloge,* Gk. ὡρολόγιον; from ὥρα, hour, λέγειν, to tell.

Oper, *conj.* or, I. 480.

Ouersene, *pp.* overlooked, not blamed, 22. 4586.

Our, *sb.* F. hour, 10. 153. Gk. ὥρα.

Our, *prep.* over, 6. 241; 13. 153; Oure, II *a.* 6. A.S. *ofer.*

Ourfret, *pt. s.* adorned, 13. 89. A.S. *frǽtwian,* to adorn.

Our-hailing, *pres. part.* overhauling, i.e. considering, 4. 158.

Ourheldand, *pres. part.* covering over, concealing, 13. 46. Sc.

heild, a corruption of M.E. *hele,* to cover, A.S. *helan,* Lat. *celare.*

Our-small, i.e. over-small, too little, 6. 389. Cf. *our-mekill,* over-much.

Ourspred, *pt. pl.* overspread, 13. 48, 97; *pres. part.* Ourspredand, 13. 102.

Our-straught, *pp.* stretched across, stretching across, 4. 164. A.S. *streccan,* to stretch, pt. t. *ic strehte,* whence M.E. *I straught.*

Ourthwort, *prep.* overthwart, across, 13. 56. A.S. *þweor,* slanting, diagonal, across, G. *zwerch.*

Outbrast, *pt. pl.* S. burst out, 24. 11; *pres. part.* Owtbrastyng, out-bursting, 13. 29. M.E. *breste, berste,* from A.S. *berstan,* to burst.

Outbrayed, *pp.* brayed out, uttered loudly, 24. 18. F. *braire.*

Outrance, *sb.* F. confusion, 3 *b.* 1172. F. *outrance,* excess, from *outre,* O.F. *oltre,* Lat. *ultra,* beyond.

Outrayed, *pt. s.* F. destroyed (lit. outraged), 3 *b.* 1128, *rubric.* F. *outrage,* injury, Low Lat. *ultragium,* excessive dealing, from Lat. *ultra,* beyond.

Oware, *sb.* F. hour, 7. 15. See Our.

Owen, *adj.* own, 2. 602. A.S. *ágen.*

Owtbrastyng, *pres. part.* out-bursting, 13. 29. See Outbrast.

Owtrage, *adj.* F. outrageous, 6. 207. See Outrayed.

Oynementis, *sb. pl.* ointments, 3 *b.* 1348. F. *oindre,* to anoint, from Lat. *ungere.*

P.

Pacokkis, *sb. pl.* peacocks, II *a.* 18. A.S. *pawa,* G. *pfau,* Du. *paauw,* Lat. *pauo.*

Palke, *sb.* a poke, pouch, I. 399. So in MS.; for *pakke.*

Palme-play, *sb.* a game at ball, played with the hand, 'fives,' 19 *f.* 13.

Palmestrie, *sb.* palmistry, divination by examining the lines of the palm of the hand, 25. 115. Lat. *palma,* the palm.

Pament, *sb.* F. pavement, 5 *b.* 96.

Pantere, *sb.* panther, 4. 155. Gk. πάνθηρ.

Pantit, *pp.* painted, 13. 161.

Papingais, *sb. pl.* parrots, 11 *a.* 18. It. *papagallo,* i.e. talking cock; Bav. *pappeln,* to chatter. The ending *gallo* (cock) was changed in French into *gay* or *geai,* a jay. See Wedgwood.

Paragon, *sb.* a model, 23. iii. 4. 47. Sp. *paragon,* a model, from the compound prep. *para con,* in comparison with. (Diez.)

Parclos, *sb.* F. partition, 2. 605. Lit. an enclosure. Roquefort derives it from Lat. *perclaudere.*

Parti, *sb.* F. side; *on a parti* = aside, 7. 40.

Partly, *adv.* briskly, boldly, 23. iii. 4. 5. Prov. E. *peart,* pert, brisk; Short for *apert* (Murray).

Partriche, *sb.* F. partridge, 18. xviii. 73. F. *perdrix,* Prov. *perdiz,* Lat. *perdix.*

Partynere, *sb.* F. partner, 10. 91.

Pasand, *pres. part.* surpassing, excelling, 13. 161.

Passyng, *pr. pari. as adv.* surpassing, i. e. very, 2. 622.

Passyngly, *adv.* in a surpassing degree, largely, 2. 599.

Pastance, *sb.* a corruption of F. *passetemps,* i.e. pastime, 14. 1096, 23. iii. 3. 149; Pastans, 13. 212.

Patter, *pr. pl.* say repeatedly, 16. 89. Here used as if from *paternoster.* We have in Piers the Ploughman's Crede, ' And *patred* in my *pater-noster*;' l. 6.

Peare, *sb.* F. peer, equal, 26. 1117; *pl.* Pieres, 24. 10. Lat. *par.*

Pearst, *pp.* F. pierced, 24. 1.

Peas, *sb.* F. peace, 9. 5.

Peaste, *pt. s.* became peaceable, was quieted, 24. 72.

Peekgoos, 25. 131. See note on p. 469.

Peise, *sb.* F. weight, 5 *a.* 16. F. *poids,* Lat. *pensum.* See **Poys.**

Penny-breid, *sb.* penny's breadth, very small space, 22. 4533.

Penounes, *sb. pl.* pennons, small banners, 1. 562. F. *pennon,* from Lat. *penna,* a wing.

Pens, *sb. pl.* pence, 26. 1102.

Pepe, *interj.* peep! probably an imitation of the shrill cry of a mouse, as *cheep* is of a sparrow's, 20 *a.* 42. Cf. Du. *piepen,* to pipe, squeak.

Perchmentiers, *sb. pl.* parchment-makers, or parchment-sellers, 26. 1095. Or perhaps put for O. F. *parmentier,* a tailor (Cotgrave).

Perde, F., an oath adapted from F. *par dieu,* 10. 94; Perdee, 10. 128.

Perrochioun, *sb.* a parishioner, 22. 4692. F. *paroissien,* from *paroisse,* parish; from Gk. πάροικος.

Persand, *pres. part.* piercing, 13. 23.

Perseuer, 1 *p. pl. pr.* persevere, continue to do the same, 19 *a.* 310. Pronounced *perséver.*

Persone, *sb.* F. parson, 6. 311; Person, 16. 141.

Perss, *adj.* deep blue, dark rich blue, 13. 106. O. F. *pers,* Low Lat. *persus,* dark blue.

Pescodes, *sb. pl.* pea-pods, 3 *a.* 9. A. S. *pise,* Lat. *pisum;* and A. S. *codd,* a small bag.

Pewled, *pt. pl.* puled, whined, 24. 74. M. E. *pule,* F. *piauler,* to peep or cheep as a young bird, from *piau,* a bird's cry.

Peyce, *sb.* piece of ground, field, 13. 79.

Peynt, *pp.* painted; *peinttyl,* painted tiles, 1., 194.

Phantasie, *sb.* fancy, 25. 68. Gk. φαντασία, from φαίνειν, to shew.

Pheton, Phaëthon, 13. 30.

Philautia, *sb.* explained 'philosophy,' 16. 225. Gk. φιλαυτία, self-love.

Picke-purse, *sb.* thief, 21. 311. See note to Sect. iii. *a.* p. 373.

Pieres, *sb. pl.* F. peers, nobles, 24. 10. See **Peare.**

Pight, *pp.* pitched, fixed, 28 *b.* 134. M. E. *picche,* pt. t. *pihte* or *pighte;* cf. W. *picio,* to dart, *picell,* a dart, javelin.

Pigsnye, *sb.* a term of endearment, 23. iii. 4. 32. From *pigges nye,* put for *pigges ye,* pig's eye; the pig's eye being small. The use of *nye* for *eye* is sufficiently common. See Dyce's Skelton, ii. 97; and see the note to the line.

Pilche, *sb.* a fur garment, or skin garment with the hair on, 1. 243. A. S. *pylce,* from Low Lat. *pellicea* (= E. *pelisse*); from Lat. *pellis, fell,* skin.

Pilde, *pp.* peeled, bare, 24. 48; stripped of fur, 24. 77. M. E. *peel, pill,* to deprive of hair, from Lat. *pellis,* skin. See *Pill,* in Wedgwood.

Pilling, *sb.* robbery, 26. 445. O. F. *piler,* to *peel,* to rob; cf. E. *pillage.*

Pirries, *sb. pl.* storms of wind, hurricanes, 18. xvii. 74. See note. Sc. *pirr,* is a gentle breeze; but M. E. *bere* is violence, rush. Icel. *byrr,* wind; E. *birr, buzz,* a noise.

Piscence, *sb.* F. puissance, might, 11 *a.* 16. A Scottish spelling; it occurs again in Dunbar's Lament for the Makars; pr. in Shorter Eng. Poems, ed. Morley, p. 111. note 6. O. F. *poissant,* powerful, from Lat. *posse.*

Pistle, *sb.* epistle, letter, 17 *c.* 287.

Place; common place = court of common *pleas,* 3 *a.* 4; 14. 316.

Plane, *pr. s. subj.;* awey plane = plane away, remove, 2. 625. Lat. *planus,* smooth.

Plane, *v.* to complain of, lament, 11 *a.* 5. See **Playn.**

Planys, *sb. pl.* plains, 13. 82.

Platly, *adv.* F. flatly, fully, 3 *b.* 1133. Of Teutonic origin; cf. G. *platt,* Du. *plat,* flat.

Playn, *v.* F. to plain, lament, 19 *b.* 33; Plane, 11 *a.* 5; Pleyn, 13. 202. F. *plaindre,* Lat. *plangere.*

Playnyng, *sb.* complaint, 24. 22.

Plein, *adj.* F. plain, even, 5 *b.* 96. Lat. *planus.*

Plenyst, *pp.* replenished, filled, 13. 83. Lat. *plenus,* full.

Plesand, *pres. part. as adv.* pleasingly, pleasantly, 13. 83.

Plete, *v.* F. to plead, 14. 321.

Plettand, *pres. part.* plaiting, 13. 192. O. F. *pleit, plet,* a fold; Lat. *plicatum.*

Pletynge, *sb.* F. pleading, 14. 315. F. *plaid,* Prov. *plait,* a plea; from Lat. *placitum,* a decree, from *placere.*

Plewys, *sb. pl.* ploughs, 13. 259.

Pleyn, *v.* to complain of, lament, 13. 202. See **Playn.**

Plied, *pt. pl.* bent their way, 19 *a.* 260. Lat. *plicare,* W. *plygu,* to fold, bend.

Plomys, *sb. pl.* plumes, 13. 161.

Pluch-ox, *sb.* plough-ox, 11 *a.* 16.

Plyȝt, *pp.* plighted, 1. 240. A. S. *plihtan,* to plight.

Polleth, *pr. s.* exacts contributions from every person, exacts so much per *poll* or head, 16. 148.

Polling, *sb.* robbery, plunder, 26. 445. Lit. taking so much per *poll;* but *pill* and *poll* were often confused, and often joined together. Cf. 'Which *pols* and *pils* the poor in piteous wize.' Spenser, F. Q. v. 2. 6.

Pome, *sb.* pomade, 13. 144. F.

pomme, because pomade was formerly made of *apples* and lemons; Lat. *pomum*.

Pomels, *sb. pl.* pommels, 1. 562. ' *Pomel*, a knob, knot, or boss; used in reference to a finial, &c.;' Glossary of Architecture. O. F. *pomel*, a pommel, from *pomme*, an apple.

Popetrie, *sb.* popery, 21. 299.

Popyngay, *sb.* a parrot, 16. 83; *pl.* Popyngayes, 12. 2. O. F. *papegai*. The parts of it are from Bavarian *pappeln*, to chatter, *der papple*, a parrot; and F. *geai*, a jay. See **Papingais**.

Portis, *sb. pl.* ports, gates, 13. 19.

Portred, *pp.* pourtrayed, adorned, 1. 192. See **Purtreied**.

Porturat, *pp.* pourtrayed (the verb *ben = are* being understood), 13. 67.

Potent, *adj.* mighty, 13. 141. Lat. *potens*.

Pot-parlament, *sb.* a talk over one's cups, 17 *c.* 201.

Potshordes, *sb. pl.* S. potsherdes, 14. 478. A *sherd*, *shord*, or *shard* is the same as a *shred*; from A. S. *sceran*, to *share*, *shear*.

Potstick, *sb.* a pole; the ' precious potstick' is probably the rod on which the sponge was lifted up, a common symbol of the Passion; 23. iii. 3. 126. See **Poutstaff**.

Pouert, *sb.* F. poverty, 2. 623. F. *pauvre*, Lat. *pauper*, poor.

Poulderit, *pp.* powdered, i. e. oversprinkled, 22. 4550.

Povn, *sb.* peacock, 13. 161. F. *paon*, from Lat. acc. *pauonem*.

Poutstaff, *sb.* a pole used in fishing, for poking about in holes, 6. 402. Suio-Goth. *potta*, to poke about.

Poyntemente, *sb.* F. appointment, agreement, 8. iv. 14.

Poys, *sb.* F. weight, 9. 6; Peise, 5 *a.* 16. See **Peise**.

Prankie, *adj.* well adorned, fine, gorgeous, 23. iii. 3, 117. O. E. *prank*, to adorn, deck; Du. *pronk*, show, finery.

Pranys, *sb. pl.* prawns, 14. 1243. Prob. O. F.; cf. Lat. *perna*, a seamussel.

Preace, *sb.* F. press, throng, 15 *b.* 52; Prease, 20 *b.* 3. See **Prese**.

Prechoures, *sb. pl.* Preachers, i. e. Dominican friars, 2. 618.

Predicamentes, *sb. pl.* categories, 16. 317. A predicament or category constitutes one of the most general classes into which things can be distributed.

Prent, *sb.* F. print, 22. 5579.

Prese, *v.* to press forward, 1. 749. F. *presser*, from Lat. *premere*.

Prest, *adj.* ready, 2. 620; 24. 6; as *adv.* 24. 5. O. F. *prest*, F. *prêt*, from Lat. *præsto*, at hand. Observe W. *prest*, quick, *presu*, to hasten.

Preued, *pp.* proved, 2. 628.

Prevy, *adj.* privy, secret, 13. 218. Lat. *priuus*, single.

Pricket, *sb.* a buck in his second year, 28 *b.* 27. No doubt from his sharp, *pricking* horns; cf. Port. *prego*, a nail; also, the horn of a young deer.

Prief, *sb.* F. proof, 3 *b.* 1282.

Prijs, *adj.* chief, choice ones, 1. 256. F. *priser*, to value, *prize*; Lat. *pretium*.

Prime, *sb.* the time of the first of the seven 'hours' of service; or sometimes, the first hour of the day; but here, the first quarter of the day, 4. 171.

Primordyall, *sb.* first beginning, origin, 14. 486. Lat. *primus*, first, and *ordiri*, to begin.

Process, *sb.* story, talk, 11 *b.* 29. Cf. F. *procès*, procedure.

Prochinge, *pres. part.* approaching, 24. 1. F. *prochain*, near; Lat. *proximus*.

Promyt, *v.* F. promise, 11 *a.* 6.

Proue, *sb.* F. proof, 10. 157.

Proue, *imp. s.* test; *proue and asaye* = test and try it, 1. 247; *pr. s.* Prouyth, 10. 178. Lat. *probare.*

Proynd, *pp.* pruned, 26. 458. Less probably from A.S. *preon,* Dan. *preen,* Sc. *preen,* a bodkin, pin, whence *to preen,* to trim, than from F. *provigner,* to propagate vines.

Pryapus, Priapus, the presiding deity of gardens, 13. 81.

Pryklyng, *pres. part.* urging, inciting, 13. 299. Doubtless miswritten for *prykkyng.*

Pucell, *sb.* F. virgin, 12.9. Cf. Lat. *pullicenus,* dimin. of *pullus,* little; It. *pulcella,* a virgin.

Puissant, *adj.* F. mighty, 18. xvii. 86. Lat. *posse.*

Pulched, *pp.* polished, 1. 160. M.E. *pulche,* from F. *polir.*

Pulder, *sb.* powder, 13. 173. F. *poudre,* O.F. *puldre,* from Lat. *puluerem (puluis).*

Pulderit, *pp.* powdered, 13. 133. See above.

Pultery, *sb.* Poultry, the name of a street in London, 26. 791.

Pultrie, *sb.* F. poultry, 18. xviii. 72. From F. *poulet,* Lat. *pullus,* young.

Pure, *adj.* F. poor, 22. 4712.

Pure, *adv.* merely; *pure litel,* very little, 1. 170; *a pure myte,* a mere mite, 1. 267. Lat. *purus.*

Purlyche, *adv.* purely, completely, 1. 381. See above.

Purpour, *adj.* purple, 11 *a.* 8; 13. 107. Lat. *purpureus.*

Purpurat, *adj.* of a purple colour, 13. 16.

Purtenancis, *sb. pl.* F. appurtenances, suitable accompaniments, 5 *b.* 10. F. *appartenance,* Lat. *pertinere,* from *tenere,* to hold.

Purtreied, *pp.* F. pourtrayed, 5 *b.*

11. F. *portraire,* to pourtray, Lat. *protrahere,* to draw forth.

Purueid, *pp.* F. purveyed, provided, 10.146. F. *pourvoir,* Lat. *providere.*

Puysaunce, *sb.* F. power, might, 12. 16. Lat. *potentia.*

Pye, *sb.* magpie, 16. 83. Lat. *pica.*

Pykis, *sb. pl.* thorns, prickles (lit. *pikes*), 13. 98. Cf. E. *spike, peak, pick, peck, beak;* A.S. *pican,* to pick.

Pykland, *pres. part.* picking, 13. 158. (Doubtless miswritten for *Pykkand.*)

Pylle, *v.* F. to rob, plunder, strip, 8. iv. 88; Pyll, 14. 450; *pt. pl.* Pylled, pillaged, 9. 161. Cf. W. *pilio,* to peel; Dan. *pille,* to pick. See **Pilde, Pilling.**

Pyllars, *sb. pl.* robbers, 8. iv. 87.

Pyne, *sb.* S. pain, 4. 155, 175; trouble, 22. 4689. A.S. *pin,* pine, pain.

Pyrkis, *pr. s.* trims herself, 13. 237. W. *perc,* trim; cf. W. *pert,* spruce, *pert;* prov. E. *perky,* pert.

Q.

Quaile, *v.* to wither, 28 *a.* 21. Du. *kwelen,* to languish.

Quatriuials, *sb. pl.* the quadrivials, 4. 511. The *quadrivium* comprised the four lesser arts, arithmetic, music, geometry, and astronomy. Lat. *quatuor,* four, *via,* a way.

Queir, *sb.* choir, 22. 4677. Lat. *chorus.*

Quenche, *v.* to become quenched, go out, 9. 60; Quenchid, *pt. s. neut.* went out, 9. 46. A.S. *cwencan,* to quench, *cwincan,* to become quenched, to go out.

Queynte, *adj.* knowing, cunning, 1.482; curious, 552. O.F. *cointe,* from Lat. *cognitus;* often confused with O. F. *cointe*, from Lat. *comptus*. (Burguy).

Queynteli, *adv.* curiously, 1. 161. See **Queynte**.

Queyntyse, *sb.* cunning, sleight, 1. 388. O. F. *cointise*, from O. F. *cointe*, Lat. *cognitus*.

Quh-, often equivalent (in Scottish) to E. *wh*, A.S. *hw*; hence *quhyp* = whip, A.S. *hweop*, &c.

Quhair, *sb.* F. quire, book, 4. F. *cahier*, O. F. *quaier*, probably from Lat. *quaternum*. (Read *quair*.)

Quhairto, *adv.* wherefore, 11 a. 5.

Quhais, whose, 23. 38. A.S. *hwás*.

Quhalis, *sb. pl.* whales, 22. 5468. A.S. *hwæl*.

Quhare, *adv.* where, 4. 152. A.S. *hwær*.

Quhat, *used for* why, 6. 313. A.S. *hwæt*.

Quheill-rym, *sb.* wheel-rim, 13. 162.

Quhele, *sb.* wheel, 4. 159. A.S. *hweol*.

Quhens, Quham, &c.; *for* whence, whom, &c. Scottish.

Quhidder, *conj.* whether, 22. 5605.

Quhilk, *pron.* which, 11 a. 12. A.S. *hwylc*, Mœso-Goth. *hwa-leiks* (lit. who-like), Lat. *qualis*.

Quhill, *conj.* till, 6. 271; 11 a. 3; 13. 33.

Quhilum, *sb. dat. pl.* at times, 4. 160. A.S. *hwilum*, dat. pl. of *hwil*, a while, time.

Quhite, *adj.* white, 13. 111; Quhyt, 11 a. 1. A.S. *hwít*.

Quho, *pl.* whoever, 22. 5502. A.S. *hwá*.

Quhois, *gen. c.* of Quho, whose, 11 a. 1; 13. 67. A.S. *hwás*.

Quhyle, *sb.* S. while, season, 11 a. 6. A.S. *hwil*.

Quhyp, *sb.* whip, 13. 30. A.S. *hweop*.

Quhyrlys, *pr. s.* causes to whirl along, drives, 13. 30. A.S. *hweorfan*, to turn.

Quhyt. See **Quhite**.

Quidities, *sb. pl.* 16. 18. A quiddity relates to the essence of a thing, having reference to the question *quid est*, what is it?

Quyk, *adj.* living; *quyk myre*, a moving mire, quagmire, 1. 226; cf. E. *quicksand*; Quycke, alive, 14. 356. A.S. *cwic*, alive, whence *couch*-grass, *quitch*-grass, *quick*-set; cf. Latin *uiuus*.

Quyknar, *sb.* quickener, giver of life, 13. 253. A.S. *cwician*, to quicken, make alive.

Quyrry, *sb.* the quarry, a name given to the dead game, 7. 17. O. F. *curee*, *cuiree*, intestines wrapped in a hide, given to hounds; from Lat. *corium*.

Quyten, *v.* to requite with, pay, 1. 351. F. *quitte*, adj. quit, from Lat. *quietus*, quiet, at rest.

Quytteris, *pr. s.* twitters, 13. 241. Du. *kwetteren*, to warble.

R.

Racke, *v.* to stretch, value at the full amount, 26. 1039. A *rack-rent* is a rent estimated at the *full* value of the tenement. A.S. *ræcan*, to reach, extend, rack.

Rad, *pp.* S. read, 5 b. 36; Red, 5 b. 47.

Radious, *adj.* radiant, shining, 22. 5581; Radyous, 11 a. 15; Radius, 11 a. 19. Lat. *radiosus*.

Rageman, *sb.* a catalogue, list, 1. 180. Sc. *ragman-roll*, a roll with many seals to it; whence E. *rig-marole*, a long story.

Rair, *v.* to roar, 22. 5468.

Rakis, *pr. pl.* wander, roam, 13. 177. Icel. *reika*, to roam.

Ran, *sb.* S. rain, 7. 67; Reane, 7. 139.

Randes, *sb. pl.* strips, slices, 1. 763. 'Cut me into *randes* and sirloins;' Beaumont and Fletcher, Wild-goose Chase, A. v. sc. 2. '*Giste de bœuf*, a *rand* of beef, a longe and fleshy peece, cut out from between the flanke and buttock;' Cotgrave.

Rank, *adj.* thickly grown, luxuriant, 13. 167. A. S. *ranc*, proud; Sw. *rank*, tall.

Raparyt, *pt. pl.* F. repaired, 6. 350. F. *repaire*, a den, haunt; O. F. *repairer*, to return home; Lat. *repatriare*, from *patria*.

Rascalles, *sb. pl.* villains, low fellows, common sort of men, 15 b. 23, 53. The meaning of *rascal* is the scrapings and refuse of anything. Low Lat. **rasicare*, to scrape; from *radere*.

Rathe, *adv.* soon, 28 b. 98. A. S. *hraðe*, quickly, from *hræð*, quick.

Raught, *pt. s.* reached, caught hold of, 19 a. 625; *pt. pl.* 19 a. 273. A. S. *ræcan*, pt. t. *ic ræhte*.

Ravin, *adj.* ravenous, 4. 157. See next word.

Ravyne, *sb.* F. rapine, 11 a. 18. F. *ravin*, from *ravir*, to ravish, snatch, Lat. *rapere*.

Raw, *sb.* a row, 13. 177; *on raw* = in a row; Rawe, 4. 154. A. S. *ráwe*, G. *reihe*, Du. *rij*.

Raye, *sb.* a kind, of striped cloth, 3 a. 6. F. *raie*, Lat. *radius*.

Raylle, *v.* to flow, 3 b. 1156. Used by Spenser.

Rays, *sb. pl.* roes, 13. 182. A. S. *rá*.

Reall, *adj.* a *real* (philosopher), 16. 316. See the note.

Reane. See Ran.

Reas, *v.* to raise, 7. 10. Icel. *reisa*, Sw. *resa*, but in A. S. we find *ræran*, to rear, *rísan*, to rise.

Receits, *sb. pl.* receipts, 26. 1153.

Rechlesse, *adv.* recklessly, 20 b. 72. A. S. *recc*, care.

Recluse, *sb.* hermitage, 2. 620. O. F. *reclus*; see Burguy. Lat. *claudere*, to shut.

Recognisance, *sb.* F. an obliga-

tion binding one over to do some particular act, 26. 789.

Record, *sb.* F. witness, 3 b. 1202. Lat. *recordari*, to remember, get by heart, from *cor*, heart.

Recule, *v.* to recoil, 15 a. 39. F. *reculer*, from Lat. *re* and *culus*.

Reculyng, *sb.* recoiling, drawing back, 15 a. 60.

Recure, *sb.* F. recovery, 24. 49. See next word.

Recured, *pp.* F. recovered, made whole, 3 b. 1407. F. *recouvrer*, Lat. *recuperare*, to get again, from *capere*.

Recuyell, *sb.* F. collection, compilation, 9, *title*. O. F. *recueil*, from Lat. *colligere*.

Red, *pp.* read, 17 a. 5.

Rede, *sb.* S. advice, 10. 29.

Rede, *v.* to advise, 10. 49. A. S. *rædan*, to advise, from A. S. *ræd*, Dan. *raad*, G. *rath*, advice.

Redles, *sb. pl.* S. riddles, 16. 12. A. S. *rædels*, a riddle, from *rædan*, to interpret, *read*.

Reduced, *pt. s.* F. brought back, 24. 9; *pr. s.* Reduceth, brings back, 19 b. 14. Lat. *ducere*, to lead.

Redymyte, *adj.* crowned, adorned, 13. 128. Lat. *redimitus*, surrounded.

Reid, *adj.* S. red, 11 a. 1.

Reiosyng, *pres. part.* rejoicing, 13. 82. Lat. *gaudere*.

Rekkeles, *adj.* careless, inattentive to knightly duty, 3 b. 1296. See Rechlesse.

Rele, *v.* to roll, 4. 165.

Releschand, *pres. part.* relaxing (their notes), i. e. letting their notes die away as they continually rise higher, 13. 246. F. *relâcher*, O. F. *relascher*, to *relax*.

Relieue, *imp. s.* take up again, 28 a. 23. F. *relever*, to lift again.

Reliuen, *pr. pl.* live again, revive, 28 a. 89.

Relyue, *v.* to lift oneself up, rise, 15 *b.* 51 ; *pt. s.* Relyued, raised up again, 15 *b.* 100. See **Relieue.**

Remede, *sb.* F. remedy, 6. 225 ; 22. 4728. Lat. *mederi,* to cure.

Remenant, *sb.* F. remnant, rest, 17 *c.* 299. Lat. *manere.*

Remeue, *v.* F. to remove, change, 1b. 152 ; Remwe, to remove oneself, depart, 3 *b.* 1094.

Rendryng, *pres. part.* restoring, 13. 92. F. *rendre,* Lat. *reddere,* from *dare.*

Renne, *v.* S. to run, 2. 299 ; 10. 62. A. S. *rennan,* G. *rennen.*

Rennyng, *sb.* S. running, 5·*a.* 69. 18. xvii. 18.

Renome, *sb.* F. renown, 19 *a.* 736. Lat. *nomen,* a name.

Repeir, *sb.* F. return, home-journey, 3 *b.* 1381, See **Raparyt.**

Rerdit, *pt. pl.* sounded, echoed, 13. 240. A. S. *reord,* speech.

Rescous, *sb.* F. rescue, help, 10. 75. O. F. *rescosse,* from *escorre* ; hence it is compounded of Lat. *re,* and *excutere,* from *quatere.*

Respondes, *sb. pl.* responds, 1. 377. A *respond,* was a short anthem, sung after a few verses of a lesson from Scripture had been read, after which the lesson proceeded.

Ressaue, *v.* to receive, 13. 76.

Reste, *imp. s.* 3 *p.* give rest to, 2. 301.

Retcheles, *adj.* S. reckless, 24. 46. See **Rechlesse.**

Retourne, *v. act.* to turn back, 3 *b.* 1078.

Reve, *v.* to bereave of, take away from, 2. 299. A. S. *redf,* spoil, *reáfian,* to plunder ; cf. Lat. *rapere,* E. *rive, rip, rob.*

Reuer, *sb.* S. bereaver, taker away, 24. 42.

Reuert, *v.* to return, repair, 28 *a.* 191. Lat. *uertere.*

Revestyng, *pres. part.* re-clothing, 13. 78. Lat. *uestis,* a garment.

Rewe, *v.* S. to have pity, 3 *b.* 1293 ; to bewail, 24. 2 ; *pres. part.* Rewing, sorrowing, 24. 22. A.S. *hreów,* grief, *hreówan,* to rue, G. *reue,* repentance.

Rewis, *sb. pl.* rows, 5 *b.* 103. See **Raw.**

Rewle, *sb.* rule (of an order), 1. 377. A.S. *regol,* borrowed from Lat. *regula;* from *regere.*

Rewlyngis, *sb. pl.* shoes of undressed hide, with the hair on, 6. 219. Cf. A.S. *rifling,* a kind of shoe, *ryft,* a garment.

Riall, *adj.* F. royal, 4. 157. Lat. *rex.*

Ribaut, *sb.* ribald, worthless fellow, 3. 376. O. F. *ribault,* M. H. G. *ribalt,* prob. from M. H. G. *ribe,* O. H. G. *hrípa,* a prostitute; hence, perhaps, E. *rip.*

Richesse, *sb. sing.* F. riches, 2. 298. Now wrongly used as a plural noun. Mœso-Goth. *reiks,* rich.

Rieue, *v.* to reave, take away, 24. 16. A. S. *redfian,* to seize; E. *bereave.* See **Reve.**

Rin, *v.* S. to run, 25. 121. See **Renne.**

Ring, *v.* F. to reign, 11 *a.* 5. Lat. *regnare.*

Rishe, *sb.* a rush, a thing of small value, 25. 114 ; *pl.* Ryshes, 3 *a.* 11. A. S. *risce,* a rush.

Riueld, *pp.* wrinkled, 20 *c.* 61. A.S. *gerifled, gerifod,* wrinkled; cf. E. *ruffle.*

Roche, *sb.* F. a rock, 3 *b.* 1223; *pl.* Roches, 22. 5499; Rochis, 13. 68.

Rocks, *sb. pl.* distaffs, 26. 760. Icel. *rokkr,* Dan. *rok,* G. *rocken,* a distaff.

Rode, *sb.* S. rood, cross, 20 *a.* 45.

Rode, *in phr.* at rode = riding at

anchor, 18. xvii. 30. A.S. *rád,* a riding, also, a road.

Rois, Ross, *sb.* F. rose, 11 *a.*

Rok, *sb.* a distaff, 6. 244. See Rocks.

Rome, *sb.* S. room, place, office, 26. 438; *pl.* Rowmes, cells, 28 *b.* 68. A.S. *rúm,* space.

Roploch, *sb.* coarse woollen cloth, homespun, and not dyed, 22. 4722. Also spelt *raplach, reploch.*

Rost, *sb.* roast, *in phr.* rules the roast, 26. 429. *To rule the roast* is to take the lead, to domineer. See Nares.

Rotheren, *sb. pl.* rothers, heifers, 1. 431. A.S. *hryðer.*

Rouch, *adj.* rough, 6. 219. A.S. *rúh.*

Roue, *sb.* roof, 10. 88. A.S. *hróf.*

Roussat, *adj.* F. russet, 6. 239. Lat. *russus,* red.

Route, *sb.* rout, company, 3 *b.* 1178.

Routh, *sb.* S. ruth, pity, 3 *b.* 1301. See Rewe.

Rowle, *v.* to roll, 19 *a.* 618.

Rowmes, *sb. pl.* rooms, cells, 28 *b.* 68. See Rome.

Rownys, *pr. s.* whispers, 13. 211. A.S. *rúnian,* to whisper, speak mysteriously, from *rún,* a magical character, a *rune.*

Rowte, *v.* S. to snort, or make a noise, 14. 338, 22. 5468. A.S. *hrútan,* to snore, snort.

Royle, *sb.* a stumbling horse, 18. xvii. 76. M.E. *roile,* to roll about, Sw. *rulla,* to roll.

Royn, *sb.* scurfy, 13. 121. O.F. *roigne,* F. *rogne,* scurf, from Lat. acc. *robiginem,* rust, blight.

Roysters, *sb. pl.* rakes, rioters, swaggerers, 26. 789, 1113. O.F. *rustre,* a rioter, rake; O.F. *ruste,* rustic; Lat. *rusticus.* Now corrupted into *roisterer. Roister-doister* is a reduplicated form.

Rubicund, *adj.* reddish, 13. 68. Lat. *rubicundus,* from *ruber,* red.

Ruddes, *sb. pl.* blooms on the face, rednesses on the cheeks, 4. 1034. A.S. *rudu,* ruddiness.

Ruffelynge, *pres. part.* swaggering about (in clothes bought with the rents they receive), 21. 178. See below.

Ruffle, *pr. pl.* swagger, bully in a turbulent manner, riot, 26. 1113. M.E. *ruffle,* to make rough, hence to bully; Du. *ruifelen,* to rumple. Cf. E. *ruffian.*

Rummeis, *v.* to roar, bellow, 22. 5468. A.S. *hrýman,* to cry out, *hreám,* a cry, shout.

Ruthe, *sb.* S. pity, 10. 160; Ruth, 24. 11. A.S. *hreówe,* grief, repentance; G. *reue.* See Rewe.

Rutis, *sb. pl.* roots, 13. 142.

Ryall, *adj.* royal, 13. 18; Ryell, 11 *a.* 22.

Rybaudry, *sb.* F. ribaldry, 16. 389. See Ribaut.

Ryfe, *adj.* abundant, 2. 611.

Ryme, 1 *p. s. pr.* I make verses, 20 *b.* 101. The old spelling is more correct than *rhyme;* as it is the A.S. *rím,* G. *reim,* Du. *rijm,* Icel. *ríma,* F. *rime,* originally signifying *number.*

Ryngis, *sb. pl.* F. reigns, years of authority, 22. 4683.

Ryngis, *pr. pl.* reign, 22. 4499.

Ryng-sangis, *sb. pl.* songs adapted for ring-dances, or circular dances, 13. 193.

Rynne, *v.* S. to run, 14. 291; *pr. pl.* Rynnys, 13. 185. See Renne.

Ryse, *sb.* a branch, twig, 3 *a.* 9; in the ryse = on the branch; Ryss, 13. 237. G. *reis,* D. *rijs,* a twig.

Ryshes, *sb. pl.* rushes, 3 *a.* 11. See Rishe.

Rysp, *sb.* coarse grass, 13. 152. Sw. *rispa,* to scratch.

Ryss. See Ryse.

Ryȝt-lokede, *pp.* righteous, just, 1. 372. Cf. A.S. *rihtlíc,* righteous.

S.

Sad, *adj.* demure, discreet, firm, 6. 201 ; Sadde, *adj. as adv.* seriously, earnestly, determinedly, 2. 606. A. S. *sæd,* sated, full.

Sadly, *adv.* seriously, discreetly, 14. 1250.

Sadnes, *sb.* discreetness, 17 *c.* 275.

Safforne, *sb.* saffron, 3 *a.* 9. Arabic *za'farân.*

Saland, *pres. part.* sailing, 22. 5533.

Sale, *sb.* basket of willow-twigs for catching eels, &c. 28 *b.* 81. A. S. *sealh,* a willow, *sallow.*

Salfgard, *sb.* F. safe keeping, 13. 96.

Samplar, *sb.* a sampler, pattern of work, 20 *i.* 4. Lat. *exemplar.*

Samyn, *adj.* same, 22. 5523.

Sanctytude, *sb.* Holiness, 22. 4596.

Sang, *sb.* song, 13. 224. A.S. *sang.*

Sangwane, *adj.* sanguine (in heraldry), blood-colour, 13. 107 ; Sangwine, blood-red, 13. 16. Lat. *sanguineus,* bloody.

Sank, *sb.* F. blood, 4. 490. F. *sang.*

Sar, *adj.* sore, 6. 337. A. S. *sár.*

Sark, *sb.* shirt, 13. 269 ; Serk, 11 *a.* 7. A. S. *syrce.*

Sattell, *v.* to settle, 22. 5466. From A. S. *settan,* to *set,* place.

Sauacioun, *sb.* F. salvation, 2. 626.

Saugh, *pt. s.* saw, 3 *b.* 1123.

Saulfe, *adj.* safe; *hence,* saulfe garde = safeguard, safe keeping, 18. xvii. 163. Lat. *saluus,* F. *sauf.*

Saulfe, *prep.* save, except, 18. xvii. 185.

Saull, *sb.* soul, 22. 5593. A. S. *sáwel.*

Sax, *num.* six, 22. 4509.

Say, I *p. s. pt.* saw, I. 158 ; *pt. s.* Say, 7. 91. Cf. Saugh.

Sayntuaryes, *sb. pl.* holy things, lit. relics of saints, 9. 93.

Schakaris, *sb. pl.* drops of dew hanging down, 13. 131. A.S. *scacan,* to shake, tremble.

Schane, *pt. pl.* shone, 13. 60. A.S. *scínan,* pt. t. *ic sceán.*

Schapand, *pres. part.* forming, 13. 164.

Schaw, *v.* to shew, 13. 214. A.S. *sceáwian.*

Schawis, *sb. pl.* shaws, thickets, coverts, groves, 11 *a.* 15. A. S. *scaga,* Icel. *skógr.*

Schenden, *v.* to disgrace, I. 481 ; *pr. pl.* Schendeþ, ruin, I. 488. A. S. *scendan,* G. *schänden,* to bring to shame.

Schene, *adj.* shining, bright, 11 *a.* 9 ; clear, well-marked, 13. 68. A.S. *scíne,* bright, *scíne,* brightness, *sheen;* cf. Lat. *scintilla.*

Scherald, *adj. prob.* turfy, or covered with turf. Jamieson gives *scherald, sb.* a cut turf.

Scherand, *pres. part.* shearing, trenchant, 6. 414. A. S. *sceran,* to *shear, share.*

Scherpit, *pt. s.* sharpened, 11 *a.* 18. A. S. *scyrpan,* to sharpen.

Schew, *pr. pl.* shew, i.e. appear, 13. 68.

Scheyn, *adj.* shining, 13. 163. See **Schene.**

Schill, *adj.* shrill, 13. 194. M. E. *shill, shull,* shrill; Du. *schel.*

Scho, *pron.* she, 6. 261.

Schon, *sb. pl.* shoes, I. 424. A. S. *sceó,* a shoe; pl. *sceós, scós, gescý, scún,* or *sceón*; M. E. pl. *shoon.*

Schrowdis, *pr. s.* enshrouds, clothes, 13. 88 ; Schrowdith, clotheth, enshrouds, 13. 32 ; cf. ' Who coverest thyself with light *as with a garment;*' Ps. civ. 2. A. S. *scrûd,* a shroud, *scrýdan,* to clothe.

Scope, *sb.* mark (for shooting at), 28 *a.* 155. Gk. σκόπος.

Scriptour, *sb.* a pencase, 13. 305. Lat. *scriptorius,* belonging to writing.

Scripture, *sb.* F. writing, 2. 622; Scrypture, 12. 3.

Se, *sb.* a seat, 1. 558; See, 3 b. 1085. O. F. *se*, also *sed*, Lat. *sedes*.

Seales, *sb. pl.* sails, 15 a. 36. So spelt in both editions.

Seand, *pres. part. as conj.* seeing, since that, 13. 230.

Seare, *adj.* sere, withered, 28 a. 147. A. S. *séarian*, to dry up.

Sectour, *sb.* executor, 23. iii. 3. 62. O. F. *esseketeur*, Lat. *executor*, from *sequi*, to follow.

See, *sb.* F. seat, 3 b. 1085. See **Se.**

Seely, *adj.* simple, silly, 26. 1133. See **Sely.**

Seen, to seen (*gerund*), to sight, 24. 2.

Sege, *sb.* seat, 13. 41. F. *siége*, from Lat. acc. *sedem*.

Segge, 1 *p. s. pr.* say, 1. 793. A. S. *secgan.*

Seie, *v.* to say, 5 a. 1.

Seilye, *adj.* simple, humble, 22. 4663. See **Sely.**

Seir, *adj.* separate, several (applied to things numerous and separated), 13. 119. Dan. *sær*, singular.

Seirsand, *pres. part.* searching out, 13. 154. F. *chercher*, It. *cercare*, lit. to go round, from Lat. *circus.*

Seiȝ, 1 *p. s. pt.* I saw, 1. 208. A. S. *seón*, pt. t. *ic seáh.*

Seke; *in phr.* to seke = at a loss, like one who has to search for things, 14. 314.

Selcouth, *adj.* strange, wonderful, 13. 65. A. S. *sel-cuð* (for *seld-cúð*) strange, from *seld*, seldom, and *cúð*, known.

Self, *adj.* same, 4. 161.

Selvage, *sb.* selvage, edge, 13. 16. The *selvage* is the *self-edge*, that which makes an edge for itself without hemming. Cf. Du. *zelfkant*, self-border, selvage.

Selure, *sb.* a decorated ceiling, 1.

201. Perhaps from Lat. *cælatura.*

Sely, *adj.* poor, simple, 1. 442; 2. 601; silly, hapless, 20 a. 64; innocent, 20 b. 27; Seely, 26. 1133; Seilye, humble, 22. 4663; Selye, simple, 22. 4712. A. S. *sélig*, happy, G. *selig*, blessed; it came to mean innocent, then poor, simple, and even helpless.

Semblable, *adj.* F. like, 18. xvii. 190. Lat. *simulare*, from *similis.*

Semblably, *adv.* F. similarly, 18. xvii. 28.

Semblyde, *pt. pl.* assembled, 7. 16; *pt. s.* Semblyt, 6. 224. F. *assembler*, to gather together, from Lat. *simul*; *simul* is the A. S. *sam*, together, whence G. *sammeln.*

Sen, *conj.* since, 11 a. 20.

Send, *pt. s.* S. sent, 11 a. 12.

Sene, *in phr.* well sene, i. e. experienced, versed, 16. 227.

Sens, *sb.* incense, 13. 44. Lat. *incensus*, burnt, from *candere*, to glow.

Sens, *adv. as prep.* since, 18. xviii. 43. Shortened from M. E. *sithens.*

Sensing, *sb.* use of incense, 21. 307. See **Sens.**

Sepulture, *sb.* F. sepulchre, 9. 58, 19 a. 712; Sepultures, *pl.* burials, 1. 469. Lat. *sepelire*, to bury.

Serk, *sb.* S. shirt, 11 a. 7. See **Sark.**

Seroppes, *sb. pl.* syrups, 13. 145. F. *sirop*, Arabic *shurb*, a drink; cf. *sherbet.*

Serwis, 2 *p. s. pr.* deservest, 6. 399; *pt. s.* Serwit, served, 6. 283. M. E. *serue* means both to *deserve* and to *serve.*

Set, 1 *p. s. pr.* become fixed upon (the shore), 24. 71; *pt. s.* Sette, set, i. e. considered, heeded, 3 b. 1128.

Settys, *sb. pl.* young plants, shoots, 13. 133.

Sewane, *sb.* 13. 145. (The meaning is probably the herb savine; see Pliny, bk. 24, c. 11.

Sewintine, *num.* seventeen, 22. 4693.

Sey, *sb.* sea, 13. 26. A. S. *sǽ.*

Seych, *sb.* sigh, 22. 5493. A. S. *sícan*, M. E. *sike.*

Shear, *adj. evidently miswritten for* seir = several, separate, 7. 12, 16. North. *seir, sere*, several; which often thus follows its noun, as in 'resons sere,' Hampole's Pricke of Conscience, ed. Morris, l. 5966. See **Seir.**

Sheeuering, *pres. part.* shivering, 27. 270.

Shene, *adj.* S. shining, bright, 3 *b.* 1257; Sheene, fair, 28 *a.* 38. See **Schene.**

Sherch, *v.* to search, 16. 91; *pt. pl.* Sherched, 16. 96. F. *chercher.*

Shipwracke, *sb.* shipwreck, 26. 1054.

Shope, *pt. s.* shaped, contrived, 2. 601; intended, plotted, 2. 608; *impers.* it befel, 2. 615; *pt. pl.* Shope (them), shaped themselves, endeavoured, 19 *a.* 584.

Showell, *sb.* S. a shovel, 14. 557. Prov. E. *showl*, as in—' I, said the owl, With my spade and *showl.*' A. S. *scúfan*, to *shove*, remove.

Shrew, *sb.* a wicked or malicious person, 6. 211. A *screw* is a vicious horse. Cf. Du. *schreeuwer*, a bawler, from *schreeuwen*, to bawl, G. *schreien.*

Shriues, *sb. pl.* sheriffs, 26. 1103. Contr. from *shire-reves.*

Shryched, *pt. pl.* shrieked, 8. v. 85; *pt. s.* Shryght, 24. 18. Sw. *skrika*, to shriek, screech.

Shyttel-cocke, *sb.* shuttle-cock, 4. 351. Corrupted from *shuttle-cork*, a cork stuck with feathers, which is *shot* backwards and forwards like a weaver's *shuttle.*

Sicht, *pt. s.* sighed, 6. 311.

Sicophants, *sb. pl.* flatterers, 26.

1111. Gk. συκοφάντης, an informer about figs.

Side, *adj.* long, trailing, 26. 1157. A. S. *sid*, ample, vast, long.

Sidir, *sb.* F. cider, 5 *a.* 90. Lat. *sicera*, Gk. σίκερα.

Sike, *adj.* such, 28 *a.* 18.

Sikerer, *adv.* more securely, more certainly, 5 *b.* 108. D. *zeker*, G. *sicher*, sure; cf. Lat. *securus.*

Sikerly, *adv.* assuredly, 2. 604.

Singulare, *adj.* F. individual, 21. 143; Singuler, relating to one person only, 2. 282.

Sirculit, *pp.* F. encircled, surrounded, 11 *a.* 14.

Sith, *conj.* S. since, 10. 179. See below.

Siþen, *conj.* since, 5 *a.* 51. A. S. *siðð an*, afterwards, since; *sið*, adv. late; *sið*, *sb.* a turn, time. Cf. G. *seit, seitdem*, since.

Siþis, *sb.* S. times, 5 *b.* 35. A. S. *sið*, a turn, time.

Siþþe, *adv.* since, 1. 158; Siþe, 1. 353. A. S. *siðð an.*

Sits, *pr. s. impers.* it befits, 28 *a.* 26. Cf. the phr. 'that suit *sits* well;' and see **Syttis.**

Siȝede, *pt. s.* sighed, 1. 442.

Skaith, *sb.* S. scath, harm, 11 *a.* 16. G. and Du. *schaden*, to injure.

Skarrit, 1 *p. s. pt.* was scared, took fright (followed by *with* = at), 11 *b.* 6.

Slak, *sb.* a hollow, depression, gap or pass between two hills, 13. 46. E. *slack*, loose, depressed; Sw. *slak*, loose.

Slawe, *adj.* slow, 4. 155. A. S. *sláw.*

Slawe, *pp.* slain, 3 *b.* 1112. A. S. *sleán*, to slay, pp. *slagen.*

Sle, *adj.* sly, i. e. skilful, 6. 375. [Wallace was *not skilful*, but *lucky* on this occasion.]

Sle, *v.* to slay, 2. 281; Slee, 2. 282; *pr. s.* Sleth, 3 *b.* 1140; *pt. s.* Slow, 2. 299; Slough, 3 *b.* 1150; *pt. pl.*

Sloughe, 7. 53; *pp.* Slean, 7. 91. A. S. *sleán*, pt. t. *ic sloh*, pp. *slagen*, to smite.

Slep, *pt. s.* S. slept, 3 *b.* 1360. A.S. *slǽpan*, pt. *s. slép*, now corrupted into *slept.*

Slioke, *pr. pl.* anoint, smoothe with unguents, 26. 1144. Sw. *slicka*, to lick.

Slipper, *adj.* slippery, 19 *a.* 618; 28 *a.* 153. A. S. *slipor.*

Slokin, *v.* to quench, 4. 168. Cf. E. *slake*; and cf. st. 161. l. 4.

Slomering, *sb.* slumbering, slumber, 11 *a.* 2. A S. *slumerian*, to slumber, *sluma*, slumber.

Slong, *pp.* slung, thrown or cast away, 19 *a.* 617.

Sloppar, *adj.* slippery, 4. 163. See Slipper.

Slough, Slow. See Sle.

Sluggardy, *sb.* sloth, 13. 266. From the same root as E. *slack.*

Slungin, *pp.* slung, hurled, 4. 165.

Smaill, *adj.* small, 13. 119.

Smerted, *pt. s.* caused (me) to smart, 2. 624.

Smette, *pt. s.* S. smote, 3 *b.* 1134.

Snell, *adj.* S. sharp, 11 *a.* 10. A. S. *snel*, quick.

Sooht, *pt. pl.* S. sought, i. e. went, 6. 282; 13. 184; *pt. pl.* sought, 6. 245.

Sodeynly, *adv.* F. suddenly, 3 *b.* 1166. Lat. *subitaneus*, from *subire.*

Sollein, *adj.* F. solemn, sad, 28 *a.* 17. Lat. *solennis.*

Some, *sb.* F. sum, 9. 11; Somme, 2. 602.

Song, *pt. s.* S. sang, 3 *b.* 1250; *pt. pl.* Song, 11 *a.* 9; Songe, 3 *a.* 12.

Soote, *adj.* sweet, 3 *b.* 1234; 19 *c.* 1; Soot, 24. 2. Du. *zoet*, G. *süss.*

Soothe, *sb.* soothsaying, divination; *soothe of byrds*, augury, 28 *b.* 87. See Sothe.

Soppis, *sb. pl.* juices, moisture, 13. 45.

Sothe, *sb.* S. sooth, truth, 2. 614; Soþe, 1. 364. A. S. *sóð.*

Sothe, *adj.* south, 7. 46. A. S. *súð.*

Soþfast, *adj.* true, very, 1. 822. A. S. *sóð-fæst*, truth-holding, true.

Sothroun, *sb. pl.* Southerners, 6. 245; Suthroun, 6. 273.

Soudiours, *sb. pl.* F. soldiers, 18. xvii. 52. From Lat. *solidus*, O. F. *sol*, F. *sou*, a piece of money.

Soudly, *adj.* soiled, dirty, 6. 241. Sc. *suddle*, to sully, soil, Sw. *sudda*, to stain, soil; cf. E. *suds.*

Souenaunce, *sb.* remembrance, 28 *a.* 5. F. *souvenir*, to remember, Lat. *sub-venire*, to come up.

Souerte, *sb.* surety, 22. 4731.

Soun, *sb.* F. sound, 2. 608, 4. 152. Lat. *sonus.* The E. *sound* is a corruption of M. E. *soun.*

Sound, *sb.* S. swoon, 23. iii. 3. 94. A. S. *swindan*, to languish.

Soune, *adv.* soon, 12. 4.

Sowkand, *pres. part.* sucking. 13. 180.

Soutere, *sb.* cobbler, 1. 744. Lat. *sutor.*

Sowne, *sb.* a swoon, 8 v. 7. See Sound.

Sowped, *pt. pl.* F. supped, 9. 145. O. H. G. *súfan*, to sip.

Sowse, *v.* to drench, 20 *a.* 6. Another form of *sauce*, which is from Lat. *salsus*, salted.

Soyr, *adj.* sorrel-coloured, 13. 27. F. *saure*, sorrel-coloured; E. *sorrel*, from A. S. *súr*, sour.

Spangs, *sb. pl.* spangles, 26. 1162. Du. *spang.*

Sparres, *sb. pl.* spars, 19 *a.* 586. *Spar* is another form of *bar.*

Spede, *v.* S. to thrive, speed, succeed, prosper, 3 *a.* 1, 3 *b.* 1200; *pp.* Sped, 3 *a.* 11.

Spedfullest, *adj.* most full of good *speed*, most helpful, 1. 264.

Speir, *sb.* F. sphere, 11 *a.* 24; orbit, 13. 7.

Spendyd, *pt. s.* lit. spanned; hence, got ready, placed in rest, 7. 84. Dan. *spände,* to stretch, buckle; *at spände en Bue,* to bend a bow; G. *spannen.*

Sperd, *pt. s.* enquired, asked, 6. 282, 329. A.S. *spirian,* to track, investigate, *spór,* a track, *spoor.*

Spill, *v.* to destroy, harm, 23. iii. 4. 28; to kill, 24. 15. A.S. *spillan,* to destroy.

Spiritualty, *sb.* F. spirituality, i.e. spiritual advisers, 16. 253.

Splene, *sb.* the whim of a moment; on the splene = suddenly, 10. 165; fro the splene = with sudden fervour, rapidly, 11 *a.* 2. Cf. Shakesp. M. N. D. i. 1. 146. The *spleen* was supposed to be the seat of anger or caprice.

Sprange, *pt. pl.* S. (*active*), made to spring, roused, 18. xviii. 50.

Sprangis, *sb. pl.* stripes of a tinted colour, variegated rays, 13. 22. O. H. G. *sprengen,* to sprinkle; also, to mix of various colours; cf. E. to *sprinkle.*

Spray, *sb.* sprig, spray of a tree, 13. 90.

Sprayngis, *sb. pl.* drops of dew sprinkled about, 13. 132. A.S. *springan,* to *sprinkle.*

Spreit, *sb.* spirit, 22. 4527.

Sprent, 1 *p. s. pt.* leapt, sprang, 13. 269; *pt. s.* arose, was dispersed, 13. 142; Sprente, spirted, 7. 67; *pp.* Sprongen, sprung, 17 *c.* 63. A.S. *sprengan,* to *spring,* to *sprinkle.*

Sprutlyt, *pp.* speckled, 13. 180. Cf. Du. *sproettelig,* freckled, *sproet,* a freckle.

Sprynkland, *pres. part.* dispersing, darting in various directions, 13. 56. E. *sprinkle,* to scatter.

Spurn, *sb.* S. a kick, 7. 134. See the note.

Stable, *v.* to establish, confirm, 14. 533; *pp.* Stablit, made quiet,

made steady, 13, 52. Lat. *stare,* to stand.

Stale, *sb.* stale-mate, 4. 169. Jamieson explains it to mean 'prison;' but see the note.

Stall, *pt. s.* stole, withdrew, 13. 9.

Stallit, *pp.* placed, set, 4. 170. A.S. *gestalian,* G. *stellen,* to put.

Stalworthy, *adj.* S. stalwart, brave, 14. 345. A. S. *stælwirðe,* serviceable, excellent.

Stannyris, *sb. pl.* the small stones and gravel at the side of a river with sloping banks, 13. 60. A. S. *stán,* a stone.

Stant, *pr. s.* (contr. form) standeth, 4. 167.

Starep, *pr. pl.* shine, gleam, 1. 553. Cf. E. *star.*

Stark, *adj.* strong, 6. 191. A. S. *stearc,* strong, rigid; Gk. στερέος.

Starnys, *sb. pl.* stars, 13. 2. Cf. G. *stern,* Sw. *stjerna.*

Starven, *pp.* starved, 24. 51.

Statute-staple, *sb.* a jocose name for the staple to which a prisoner is by law attached, 26. 788.

Steok, *v.* S. to stick, stab, 6. 197; *pt. s.* Stekyt, 6. 226.

Sted, *sb.* S. a stead, place, 6. 353; Stede, 19 *a.* 611. A. S. *stede.*

Steiȝ, *pt. s.* ascended, 1. 810. A.S. *stígan,* to mount; prov. E. *stee,* a ladder; cf. E. *stirrup,* i. e. *sti-rop,* a rope to mount by, *stair,* a mounter, ladder, and *stile.*

Steir, *v.* to stir, move about, 13. 155.

Stemyng, *pres. part.* shining, gleaming, 20 *a.* 53. M. E. *stem,* a gleam, occurs in Havelok the Dane, and *stepe,* bright, in Chaucer. See **Stepe.**

Stent, *v.* S. to cease, 29. 32. See **Stint.**

Stent, *sb.* S. stopping-place, 24. 6. See **Stint.**

Stepe, *adj.* shining, glittering, 14. 1014. Cf. Chaucer's Prol. l. 201. See **Stemyng.**

Stered, *pp.* steered, directed, 2. 628.

Sterres, *sb. pl.* S. stars, 19 *a.* 603.

Sterue, 1 *p. s. pr.* I die, 20 *f.* 15; *pr. pl.* Sterue, die, 21. 125. A. S. *steorfan,* G. *sterben,* E. *starve.*

Stevynnys, *sb. pl.* notes, voices, 13. 238. A. S. *stefen,* a voice.

Stike, *sb.* a 'stich,' a verse, a line, 24. 21. Gk. στίχος, a row, line; cf. E. *hemistich.*

Stint, *imp. s.* cease, 24. 15; 26. 632. A. S. *stintan,* to be blunt or *stunted,* to faint.

Stiroppe, *sb.* stirrup, 18. xvii. 218. A. S. *stí-ráp,* mounting-rope, from *stigan,* to mount, G. *steigen.*

Stocke, *sb.* S. a post, 21. 58.

Ston, *sb.* rock, 1. 806.

Storour, *sb.* restorer, 13. 263.

Stounde, *sb.* S. time, portion of time, 2. 618; time, 23. iii. 4. 7; 28 *b.* 140. A. S. and G. *stund.*

Stoundmele, *adv.* at times, 3 *b.* 1258. A. S. *stund-mælum,* by little times, occasionally.

Stouth, *sb.* stealth, 13. 212. Cf. Sc. *stown,* stolen.

Stovys, *sb. pl.* vapours, 13. 46. Sc. *stew,* vapour, Sw. *stoft,* G. *staub,* fine dust.

Stowrand, *pres. part.* stirring quickly about, 13. 58. Sc. *stour,* to move rapidly about, A. S. *styrian,* to stir.

Stowre, *sb.* distress, conflict (of mind), 28 *b.* 66. O. F. *estour,* conflict, Icel. *styrr,* a battle.

Stoynde, *pp.* stunned, astonished, frightened, 24. 34. See **Astoynde.**

Straight, *adj.* (*put for* Strait), close-fitting, tight, pinching, 27. 21. Lat. *strictus,* from *stringere.*

Strain, *pr. pl.* distrain, 26. 1104.

Strake, *pt. s.* struck, reached, 19 *a.* 636.

Strandis, *s. pl.* streams, 13. 60. There are other examples of the word.

Streatly, *adv.* straitly, closely, strictly, 14. 438.

Streite, *adj.* F. strait, narrow, confined, 3 *b.* 1109. Lat. *strictus.*

Strekyng, *pres. part.* stretching, 13. 86.

Strenges, *sb. pl.* strings, 2. 625.

Strenthis, *sb. pl.* forts (lit. strengths), 6. 343.

Strocke, *pt. pl.* struck, 7. 62. The line seems to mean—'many stern (men) they struck down straight,' or, many stern (blows), &c.

Stroyed, *pp.* F. destroyed, 20 *a.* 14. Lat. *struere.*

Stude, *pt. pl.* stood, 13. 71.

Style, *sb.* prob. pen, writing-pen, 3 *b.* 1078. Lat. *stylus.*

Stynted, *pt. pl.* stopped; 8. iv. 33; *pt. s.* Stynttede, 7. 86. See **Stint.**

Sueþ, *pr. pl.* follow, 1. 454. Lat. *sequi.*

Suffragane, *sb.* assistant, helper, 11 *a.* 25. Lat. *suffragari,* to support with a vote, *suffragium,* a vote.

Sulʒart, *adj.* bright, shining(?), 13. 64. Cf. Gael. *soilleir,* bright; O. Irish *sollus,* bright.

Sulʒe, *sb.* soil, earth, 13. 74. O. F. *soille,* from Lat. *solum.*

Sumdeale, *adv.* (lit. some deal), somewhat, partially, 24. 37; Sumdeill, somewhat, 13. 27.

Supernale, *adj.* belonging to the upper regions, celestial, 13. 50. Lat. *supernus,* uppermost.

Supping, *pres. part.* supping up, swallowing, 24. 79.

Suposs, *conj.* although, 6. 374.

Sured, *pp.* securely bound by promise, 3 *b.* 1188.

Sutaille, *adj.* F. subtle, 6. 273.

Swage, *v.* F. assuage, i. e. diminish, 2. 601; to assuage, 24. 61. O. F. *assouager,* Prov. *assuaviar,* to make sweet, from Lat. *suavis.*

Swapte, *pt. pl.* struck, slashed, 7.

65. A. S. *swápan*, to sweep; *swipe*, a whip.

Swardit, *pp.* swarded, grass-covered, 13. 65. A. S. *sweard*, grass.

Swarve, *v.* to swerve, 24. 70; . *pres. part.* Suaruing, 19 *a.* 284; *pp.* Swarued, 19 *a.* 721. Du. *zwerven*; cf. *werpen*, to throw, A. S. *hweorpan*, E. *warp*.

Swat, *pt. pl.* S. sweated, 7. 65.

Swe, *v.* F. to follow, 3 *b.* 1093. See **Suep**.

Swelth, *sb.* mud, filth, lit. swillings, offscourings, 24. 31, 69. A. S. *swilian*, to swill, rinse.

Swincke, *pr. pl.* toil, 28 *a.* 154. A. S. *swincan*, to toil.

Swing, *sb.* S. free course of behaviour, license, 25. 95.

Swinge, *sb.* sovereignty, 24. 26.

Swirk, *v.* to dart swiftly away, 11 *a.* 12. Icel. *swirra*, to *swirl*; cf. *whirl*, *whir*.

Swogh, *sb.* a swoon, 3 *v.* 1287. See **Adawed**. It is a corrupted form of *swowne*. See **Sound**.

Swouchis, *pr. pl.* make a rustling sound, 13. 152. Sc. *souch*, a rushing or whistling sound, A. S. *swégan*, to sound.

Sye, 1 *p. s. pt.* saw, 4. 159; *pt. pl.* Sye, 2. 604. See **Seiȝ**.

Sygge, 1 *p. s. pr.* say, 1. 390. See **Segge**.

Syker, *adj.* secure, safe, 1. 350; *adv.* truly, 1. 237. See **Sikerer**.

Syn, *adv.* next, afterwards, 6. 244; Syne, 11 *a.* 18; 22. 4600. See **Siþen**.

Syng, *sb.* sign, 13. 311. Cf. Sc. *ryng* for *reign*. See **Ring**.

Synnamome, *sb.* cinnamon, 13. 145.

Synopar, *sb.* cinnabar, 13. 57. A pigment made from red sulphuret of mercury, of various shades of vermilion and brown. (A word of Eastern origin.)

Syon, *sb.* scion, shoot, 13. 135.

F. *scion* (for *secion*), a cutting, section; Lat. *secare*, to cut.

Syth, *conj.* S. since, 10. 45.

Syþen, *conj.* since, 1. 241; *adv.* afterwards, 1. 806. A. S. *siððan*.

Syttis, *pr. pl.* sit, suit; *syttis me sor* = sit heavily upon me, grieve me, 6. 439. See **Sits**.

T.

Ta, *v.* to take, 6. 222.

Tabernacles, *sb. pl.* cells for reconnoitring, 1. 168.

Takand, *pres. part.* taking, taking to, i. e. scouring across, taking his way over, 6. 421.

Taken, *pp.* given, 17 *c.* 198; *imp. pl.* Taketh, take ye, 2. 619. M. E. *take* often means to *give*.

Tallage, *sb.* a tang, bad savour, 17 *c.* 241.

Tancrete, *adj.* transcribed, copied out, 14. 417. ' *Tancrit*, transcrit, copié;' Roquefort. It seems a mere corruption of *transcript*.

Tane, *pp.* taken, 20 *h.* 6.

Tapese (*for* to apese), to appease, 3 *b.* 1352.

Tapite, *sb.* F. a piece of carpet, a cloth, 2. 607; *pl.* Tapets, tapestries, hanging cloths for ornament; metaphorically applied to the foliage of trees, 24. 1. Lat. *tapes*, Gk. τάπης, a carpet, rug.

Tappease, *for* to appease, 19 *a.* 295.

Tarieth, *imp. pl.* delay ye, 2. 618.

Tast, *sb.* taste, 17 *c.* 242. O. F. *taster*, as if from *taxitare*, frequent. of Lat. *taxare*, from *tangere*.

Taswage (*for* to aswage), to assuage, 3 *b.* 1352.

Tatered, *pp.* jagged, 1. 753. Cf. Icel. *tæta*, to card wool, to pluck in pieces (Egilsson).

Taucht, *pp.* S. taught, 6. 294.

Tawed, *pp.* hardened with labour,

24. 39. A.S. *tawian*, to dress leather.

Tayt, *adj.* brisk, 13. 184. Icel. *teitr*, joyful, brisk.

Tear, *sb.* S. a tear, rent, 7. 134.

Teind, *sb.* tithe (lit. tenth), 22. 4690.

Telde (*put for* Tolde *for the rhyme*), told, 24. 23.

Tellers, *sb. gen. sing.* counter's, of one who counts, 26. 1107. A. S. *tellan*, G. *zählen*, to count, tell.

Tencombre (*for* to encombre), to encumber, overwhelm, 3 *b.* 1098.

Tendure, *for* to endure, 3 *b.* 1201.

Tene, *sb.* S. vexation, extreme anger, 3 *b.* 1141; sorrow, 19 *b.* 51; vexation, 28 *a.* 41. A.S. *teóna*, vexation.

Tenforme, *for* to inform, 3 *b.* 1207.

Tennes, *sb.* tennis, a game with bat and ball, 25. 167.

Tenrage, *v. for* to enrage, 28 *b.* 89.

Tergate, *sb.* a small shield, 18. xvii. 123. O. F. *targe*, It. *targa*, Low Lat. *targa*, O. H. G. *targe*.

Testie, *adj.* testy, heady, head-strong, 23. iii. 5. 106. F. *tête*, O. F. *teste*, It. *testa*, the head.

Thaffirmatiue, *put for* the affirmative, 17 *d.* 33.

Thair-fra, *adv.* S. therefrom, 11 *b.* 10.

Thar, *pron.* their, 13. 66.

The, *bad spelling for* Thei, they, 7. 7, 24.

Thee, *v.* to thrive; *so mote I thee*, so may I prosper, 2. 620. A. S. *þeón*, to thrive, G. *gedeihen*.

Theffusion, *for* the effusion, 9. 55.

Thembatel, *for* the embatel, i. e. the battlement, 19 *a.* 581.

Thende, *for* the ende, 9. 191.

Thentent, *put for* the entent, i.e. the intent, 18. xviii. 9.

Thentrie, *for* the entrie, 19 *a.* 307.

Ther, *adv.* where, 3 *b.* 1256; There, where, when, 9. 15; Þere-as, where that, 1. 471. A.S. *þær*, where, there.

Therle, *put for* the erle, the earl, 15 *a.* 1.

Thewde, *pp.* conditioned, mannered, 14. 329. A. S. *þeáw*, a thew, a custom, manner, quality.

Thewtill, *sb.* S. a whittle, knife, 6. 218. A. S. *þweótan*, *þwítan*, to cut, cut off.

Thicke, *sb.* thicket, wood, 24. 27.

Þies, *pron. pl.* these, 1. 392.

Thir, *pron. pl.* those, these, 6. 267. Common in Scottish. Icel. *þeir*, they (masc.), *þær*, they (fem.); from *sá*, *sú*, *þat*, demonst. pronoun. In 13. 60 it may be an error for *thar*, their.

Tho, *conj.* then, 3 *b.* 1412. A. S. *þá*.

Thocht, *conj.* though, 6. 348.

Thold, *for* the old, 19 *a.* 665.

Þolede, *pt. s.* suffered, 1. 823. A.S. *þólian*, Du. *dulden*, Lat. *tolerare*, to suffer; Gk. τλῆναι.

Thoo, *dem. pron. pl.* those, 10. 59. A. S. *þá*, pl. of the article *se*, *seó*, *þæt*.

Þoruȝ, *prep.* through, throughout, 5 *a.* 60.

Thother, *for* the other, 20 *a.* 38.

Thoucht, *conj.* S. though, 22. 4693. A.S. *þeáh*.

Thouerwandred, *for* the over-wandered, 19 *a.* 380.

Thowis, 2 *p. pr. s.* sayest 'thou' to, addressest as 'thou,' 6. 399. The MS. has *dowis*, by a mere slip.

Thrall, *adv.* in bondage, slavishly, 20 *b.* 4. A. S. *þræl*, a slave.

Thre-sound, *adj.* three-voiced, giving three sounds at once, 24. 71.

Thrid, *adj.* third, 22. 4725. A. S. *þridda*.

Thrissil, *sb.* a thistle, 11 *a.* 19. A. S. *þistel;* but *thrissle* occurs in Burns, Globe ed. p. 10.

Throw, *adv.* eagerly, nimbly, 13. 182. Icel. *þrár,* eager, pertinacious.

Thuroh-hurt, *pp.* throughly hurt, much injured, viz. in the veins of the head, 6. 361. Cf. *thurgh-girt,* pierced through, in Chaucer, Knightes Ta. 152.

Thylke, *adj.* the same, 3 *b.* 1112. Scot. *that ilk;* A. S. *ylc,* same.

Tid, *sb.* S. time; *as this tid,* as at this time, now, 6. 313.

Tildep, 2 *p. pl. pr.* set up, 1. 494. See **Tyld.**

Till, *prep.* to, 11 *a.* 17, 11 *b.* 16. Sw. *till,* Dan. *til.*

Tinot, *pp.* tinged, dyed, 28 *a.* 107.

Tinsel, *adj.* showy, gaudy, 26. 776. F. *étincelle,* O. F. *estincelle,* Lat. *scintilla,* a spark.

Titmose, *sb.* titmouse, 28 *a.* 26. M. E. *tit,* small (which appears in *titlark,* and *tittle,* Du. *tittel*), and A. S. *máse,* a titmouse, G. *meise,* a small bird.

To, *conj.* until, 3 *b.* 1250.

To-dasht, *pt. s.* dashed (herself) in pieces, 24. 18. The prefix *to* is A. S. *tó-,* G. *zer-,* Lat. *dis-,* with the sense of *in twain,* asunder.

Toddis, *sb. pl.* foxes, 22. 4531. Probably named from the vile smell; cf. Icel. *tað, manure.

Tofore, *prep.* or *conj.* before, 4. 172, 9. 34.

To-forn, *adv.* before, beforehand, 1. 485; *toforn ar* = before that, 3 *b.* 1094.

To-forrow, *adv.* previously, already, 11 *a.* 27. See **Toforn.**

Tolde, *pt. s.* 1 *p.* S. counted, 2. 616. Cf. G. *zahl,* a number, *tale.*

Tolter, *adv.* unsteadily, totteringly, 4. 164. Cf. Sw. *tulta,* to waddle, totter.

Ton, *adj.* one; *the ton* = *that one* = the one; 7. 36, 10. 27. Similarly, *the tother* = *that other.*

Tong, *sb.* S. tongue, 17 *c.* 12.

Tonne, *sb.* a tun, 1. 221. A. S. *tunne.*

Topace, *sb.* topaz, 13. 37. Gk. τόπαζος.

Tote, *v.* to peep, spy, look, 14. 1146; Toten, to spy about, 1. 168; 1 *p. s. pt.* Totede, peeped, 1. 339; *pt. pl.* Toteden, peeped (out), 1. 425. Cf. M. E. *totehille,* a look-out hill; whence *Tothill.* Sw. *titta,* to peep.

Towe, *adj.* two, 7. 90.

Townish, *adj.* belonging to the town, 20 *a.* 4.

Traced, 1 *p. s. pt.* traced our way, went on, 24. 27. Lat. *trahere,* to draw.

Trade, *sb.* a trodden path, wellworn way, 19 *a.* 593. A. S. *trod,* a path.

Tradioion, *sb.* F. yielding up, 9. 65. Lat. *tradere.*

Trasyng, *pres. part.* tracing, marking, 13. 293.

Traytyse. See **Treatyce.**

Tre, *a misprint for* thre, i. e. three, 22. 4715. See l. 4723.

Treatise, *sb.* F. a passage (lit. a treatise), 17 *c.* 88.

Treatyce, *sb.* F. treaty, truce, 8. iii. 53; Traytyse, 8. iii. 67.

Trechurly, *adv.* treacherously, 1. 475.

Treddede, *pt. s.* trod, walked upon, 1. 425. The A. S. has both *tredan* (pt. t. *ic træd*), to tread upon, and *treddian* (pt. t. *ic treddode*), to go; the former form (*trod*), not the latter, should have been used here.

Treen, *sb. pl.* S. trees, 24. 1.

Treilȝis, *sb.* trellis, 13. 100. F. *treillis,* from *treille,* a vine-arbour; Lat. *trichila,* an arbour.

Trentall, *sb.* money paid for say-

ing masses for *thirty* days, 16. 149.
Fr. *trente*, thirty.

Tresour, *sb.* F. treasure, 2. 298.
It. *tesoro*, Gk. θησαυρός, from
τίθημι, I place, lay up.

Trey-ace, *sb.* a throw at dice, viz.
trois, three, and *ace*, one; hence,
a quick exclamation, 23. iii. 3.
142.

Trilleth, *pr. s.* trickles, 20 *h.* 2.
Sw. *trilla*, to roll.

Trimlyng, *sb.* trembling, 22. 5500.
Lat. *tremulus*, from *tremere*.

Tristes, *sb.* F. sadness, 9. 129.
Lat. *tristitia*.

Triuials, *sb. pl.* the trivials, 14. 512.
The three arts of grammar, logic,
and rhetoric. Lat. *tres*, three, and
uia, a way.

Trofle, *sb.* a trifle, 1. 352. O. F.
trufle, a trifle, from *trufler*, to
mock, cheat.

Trone, *sb.* throne, 13. 47.

Trosten, *v.* to truss, 1. 237; *on to
trosten*, to trust in, 1. 350.

Troweth, *pr. s.* S. believes, holds
to be true, 12. 13. A. S. *treów*,
trust, *treówan*, to believe.

Tryakill, *sb.* remedy (lit. *treacle*,
formerly a sovereign remedy), 13.
144. Lat. *theriacum*, Gk. θηριακὰ
φάρμακα, antidotes against bites
of animals, from θήρ, a wild
beast.

Tryg, *adj.* secure, safe, 13. 184. Sw.
trygg, Dan. *tryg*, secure, safe.

Trymlyt, *pt. pl.* trembled, 12.
243.

Tryst, *adj.* F. sad, sorrowful, sorry,
3 *b.* 1299. Lat. *tristis*.

Tuk, *pt. s.* took, i. e. hit, 6. 403.

Tutand, *pres. part.* poking, push-
ing out, 13. 123. M. E. *tote*, to
pry about. See **Tote**.

Twestis, *sb. pl.* twists, twigs, 13.
165; Twystis, 13. 100.

Twey, *num.* two, 1. 428. A. S.
twegen, masc., *twá*, fem. and
neuter; G. *zwei*, Du. *twee*.

Twyne, *v.* to separate, become
separated, 6. 421. Lit. 'to
divide in two;' see below.

Twynnen, *v.* to count as twins, to
compare, 1. 496; *pt. pl.* Twynned, departed, 2. 621. Icel.
tvinnr, two and two.

Twystis, *sb.* twigs, twining shoots,
13. 100.

Tyld, *pp.* set up like a tent, set up,
raised, 1. 181. A. S. *teldian*, to
spread a *tilt*, or tent.

Tyndis, *sb. pl.* tines, prongs of a
deer's horn, 13. 179. A. S. *tindas*,
(pl.) *tines*, teeth of a harrow.

V.

Vaine, *sb.* vein, order, 28 *a.* 8;
Vayn, vein, 13. 255.

Vale, *v.* to descend, 4. 172. F. *à
val*, to the valley, downwards;
whence *avalanche*.

Variand, *pres. part.* F. varying,
variable, 11 *a.* 1; Variant, 13. 62.

Vauntynge, *sb.* vaulting, 18. xvii.
217. O. F. *volter*, to leap; Lat.
uolutare, from *uoluere*, to roll.

Vaut, *v.* F. to vault, 25. 164. F.
volter, to vault, bound. The use
of *vaunt* (q. v.) makes it possible
that *vant* may be no misprint;
but *vaut* is more usual.

Vayleth, *pr. s.* avails, 20 *h.* 7. Lat.
ualere.

Vayn. See **Vaine**.

Voe, *sb.* F. use, 5 *a.* 106.

Veilys, *sb. pl.* calves, 13. 185. E.
veal, O. F. *veel*, Lat. *uitellus*, dim.
of *uitulus*.

Vengeable, *adj.* F. full of vengeance, 2. 298. Lat. *uindicare*,
from *uindex*.

Venust, *adj.* beautiful, 13. 87.
Lat. *uenustus*, from *Uenus*.

Verament, *adv.* F. verily, 7. 19.

Verlet, *sb.* F. varlet, servant, squire,
12. 22. E. and F. *valet*, Low
Lat. *uarletus*, dim. of *uassus*, from

W. *gwas*, a youth, servant. Cf. *vassal*, from W. *gwasol*, serving.

Vermel, *adj.* vermilion, 13. 124. F. *vermeil*, It. *vermiglio*, from Lat. *uermiculus*, a little worm, viz. the worm of the gall-nut used for the dye.

Viage, *sb.* F. voyage, 3 *b.* 1311. It. *viaggio*, Prov. *viatge*, from Lat. *uiaticum*, journey-money; Diez.

Violid, *pp.* F. violated, 9. 57.

Virelayes, *sb. pl.* roundels, 28 *a.* 21. F. *virer*, to turn. ' The *virelai* admitted only two rhymes, and, after employing one for some time, the poet was *virer*, or *to turn* to the other.' Nares.

Vitayle, *sb.* victuals, 10. 104. O.F. *vitaille*, from Lat. *uiuere*.

Vmaist, *adj. superl.* upmost, outermost, 22. 4711. A.S. *ufemest*, upmost, *ufa*, above.

Vmbrage, *sb.* shadow, 13. 72. Lat. *umbra*, shade.

Vncofred, *pp.* taken out of a coffer or box, 2. 607.

Vnderfong, *v.* to undertake, or perhaps, to receive, 28 *a.* 22. (It admits of both meanings.) A.S. *under-fón*, to undertake, from *fón*, contr. from *fangan*, to seize.

Vndermynde, *v.* to undermine, 14. 434.

Vndoubtabili, *adv.* without doubt, 5 *b.* 58.

Vneth, *adv.* scarcely, 18. xvii. 77; 23. iii. 5. 4. A.S. *uneáð*, uneasily, from *eáð*, easy.

Vniversales, *sb. pl.* 16. 318. A universal proposition is one in which the subject is taken in its widest extent.

Vnkempt, *pp.* uncombed; hence, rough, rugged, 28 *a.* 51. A.S. *cæmban*, to comb.

Unneth, *adv.* scarcely, 12. 19; 14. 1124. See Vneth.

Vnneth, *adv. as conj.* unless (but

probably misused; it should rather be *vnneth but* or *but vnneth*), 18. xviii. 70. A.S. *uneáð*, uneasy, from *eáð*, easy.

Vnpind, *pt. pl.* unpinned, unfastened, 19 *a.* 329.

Vnrest, *sb.* restlessness, 24. 26.

Vnshette, *pp.* unshut, 2. 607.

Vnsoote, *adj.* unsweet, bitter, 3 *b.* 1145, 28 *b.* 118. See Soote.

Vnsouerable, *adj.* F. insufferable, 6. 267.

Vnsounded, *pp.* not made sound, unhealed, 3 *b.* 1392.

Vnwarly, *adv.* unwarily, i. e. at unawares, 3 *b.* 1098.

Vnweldy, *adj.* unwieldy, 19 *a.* 715. A. S. *wealdan*, to rule, *wield.*

Voidis, *pr. s.* makes void, destroys (the effect of), does away with, 4. 155.

Voucheth, *pr. s.* avouches; hym voucheth = establishes his assertions, 2. 623. Lat. *uocare*, from *uox.*

Voyde, *imp. pl.* make room, make way, 23. iii. 3. 128.

Voys, *sb.* F. voice, report, 9. 29.

Vp, *prep.* upon, 3 *b.* 1095.

Upraiss, *pt. s.* S. uprose, 11 *a.* 26.

Vprist, *sb.* uprising, 3 *b.* 1257. Used by Chaucer, Kn. Ta. 193.

Vp-soo-doune, *adv.* upside down, 8. iii. 26.

Vpstowris, *pr. s.* is stirred up, rises, 13. 173. See Stowrand.

Vpwarpis, *pr. s.* throws up, lifts up, throws open, 13. 20. A. S. *weorpan*, to warp, throw; G. *werfen.*

Vse, *pr. pl.* are accustomed, 17 *b.* 7; *pt. s.* Vsyt, used; hence, used to go, 6. 209.

Vttring, *sb.* uttering, i. e. selling as complete, 26. 1068.

W.

Wach, *sb.* watch, one who keeps a look out, 13. 1; *pl.* Wachis, watches, sentinels, 6. 259. A. S. *wæccan*, to watch.

Waiker, *adj. comp.* weaker, 18. xvii. 15.

Wait, *pr. s.* S. wot, knows, 22. 4678. A.S. *wát*, knows, from *witan*, to *wit*, to know.

Waite, *imp. s.* look, watch, 1. 361. O.F. *gaiter*, to watch; E. *wait*, *watch*, *wake*.

Waith, *sb.* whatever is taken in hunting, or fishing, prey, catch, 6. 386. Icel. *veiðr*, the same, from *veiða*, to take, catch.

Waithyng, *sb.* a 'take,' 6. 387. See **Waith**.

Wak, *adj.* moist, 13. 45. Du. *wak*, moist, damp.

Walk, *v.* to wake, watch, 22. 5551; *pres. part.* Walking, waking, 4. 173. A.S. *wæccan*, to watch. The insertion of *l* is due to putting *l* for *k* in the form *wakke*; the symbol for *kk* looks like *lk*.

Wally, *adj.* wavy, surging, 13. 110. G. *welle*, a wave, E. to *well*, Sc. *wiel*, a whirlpool.

Walter, *sb.* water, 25. 4572, 5467. The converse, *Water* for *Walter*, occurs in Pierce the Ploughmans Crede.

Waltring, *pres. part.* lapping, rolling about, lolling, 19 *a.* 267. A.S. *wealtian*, to roll, reel.

Walxis, *pr. pl.* grow, become (lit. wax), 13. 151; *pt. s.* Wolx, became, 13. 136; *pt. pl.* Wolx, 13. 188. Here *Walxis = wauxis*, for *waxis*; and *wolx = woux = wox*. See **Wolx**.

Wambe, *sb.* belly, 22. 4515. A.S. *wamb*, womb.

Wane, *sb.* quantity, number, 7. 74. Sc. *wane*, a number of people; M.E. *wone*, a quantity. From A.S. *hwón*, a little, Sc. *quhoyn*, a few, afterwards extended to the notion of an indefinite number, a quantity.

Wanne, *v.* S. to ebb, *wane*, retreat (said of waves retreating after breaking), 8. v. 45. A.S. *wanian*, to wane, *wana*, want.

Wantonnes, *sb.* want of discretion, 17 *c.* 276. M.E. *wantowen*, ill educated, from *wan-*, prefix, signifying *want*, lack, and A.S. *togen*, educated, pp. of *teón.*

Wappe, *v.* S. to beat, lap (said of water 'lapping on a crag,' as Tennyson expresses it), 8. v. 45. E. *whop*, *whip*.

Wapynnys, *sb. pl.* S. weapons, 6. 193. A.S. *wǽpen*, a weapon.

Ward; to Pallas temple ward = towards the temple of Pallas, 19 *a.* 304. A.S. *weard*, a suffix signifying *towards*; Lat. *uersus.*

Warke, *sb.* work, 28 *a.* 64.

Wary, *v.* to curse, 22. 5473. A.S. *werigan*, to curse, *werig*, wicked.

Waseled, *pt. s.* bemired himself, 1. 430. A.S. *wós*, Prov. E. *wose*, E. ooze, mud.

Wat, 1 *p. s. pr.* wot, know, 7. 47. See **Witt, Wote**.

Wawes, *sb. pl.* S. waves, 8. v. 35, 45.

Waykely, *adv.* S. carefully, 8. iv. 79. A.S. *wacol*, watchful, *wacollíce*, watchfully.

Wayndyt, *pt. s.* blenched, became afraid, 6. 198. A.S. *wandian*, to fear, blench.

Wayntyt, *pt. pl.* were missing, were wanting, 6. 199. Icel. *vanta*, to be wanting.

Waynys, *sb. pl.* F. veins; *of waynys* = in the veins (of the head, as it appears), 6. 361.

Wayte; a wayte *printed for* awayte, *sb.* ambush, 9. 152. O.F. *agait*, ambush; from the Teutonic root of *wake* and *watch*.

Weal, *v.* (?) to clench so as to leave marks, to mark with *wales* by clenching, 7. 123. A.S. *walan*, wales. But see the note.

Wealked, *pp.* withered, 24. 12. G. *welken*, to fade. See **Welked**.

Wear, *put for* Were, 7. 7, 24.

Wedde, *sb.* S. pledge, 3 *b.* 1186. A. S. *wed*, Lat. *uas*, gen. *uadis*.

Wedis. See **Weid**.

Wedous, *sb. pl.* S. widows, 7. 118.

Weene, 1 *p. s. pr.* opine, suppose, imagine, 28 *a.* 40. See **Wene**.

Weid, *sb.* S. robe, garment, 11 *a.* 3, 11 *b.* 24; Weyd, 6. 240; *pl.* Wedis, clothes, 13. 303. A. S. *wǽd*, a garment; still preserved in the phrase ' widow's *weeds*.'

Weide, *v.* to go *wood*, i. e. to go mad, 9. 438. A. S. *wédan*, to be mad, *wód*, mad.

Weill, *adv.* well, i. e. about, nearly, 22. 4560.

Weir, *sb.* fear, doubt, 11 *b.* 50. Sc. *were*, *weir*, probably same as E. *war*. See **Wer**.

Weird, *sb.* fate, destiny, 22. 5473; Werd, 24. 63. A. S. *wyrd*, fate.

Weiris, *sb. pl.* S. wars, 11 *a.* 19.

Weld, *v.* to wield, 19 *a.* 680. A. S. *wealdan*, to rule.

Wele, *sb.* wealth, money, 1. 403; weal, prosperity, 4. 169. A. S. *wela*, weal; cf. E. *well*.

Weleaway, *interj.* wellaway, 20 *a.* 15. A. S. *wá lá wá*, woe, lo ! woe.

Welked, *pp.* shortened, 28 *a.* 13. Incorrectly used; to *welke* is an intransitive verb, meaning *to wither*. See **Wealked**.

Well, *sb.* well, spring of water, fount, 4. 168.

Weltering, *sb.* turning over, turning round owing to sudden overbalancing, 4. 163. M. E. *walter*, to roll, Sw. *vältra*, to roll.

Wende, 1 *p. s. pt.* weened, expected, 1. 452. See below.

Wene, 2 *p. pl. pr.* S. suppose, ween, 8. vi. 20; 1 *p. s. pt.* expected, 1. 452; *pp.* Wente, weened, thought, 8. v. 47. A. S. *wénan*, to suppose.

Wenges, *sb. pl.* wings, 2. 625.

Went, *v.* to wend, go, 6. 330. A. S. *wendan*, to turn, go.

Wente, *pp.* S. weened, 8. v. 47. See **Wene**.

Wente hym, *pt. s.* went (lit. turned him), 9. 2. A. S. *wendan*, to turn, go. See **Went**.

Wer, *sb.* S. war, 6. 205 ; distress, 6. 331 ; Weir, fear, doubt, 11 *b.* 50.

Wer, *v.* S. to wear, 6. 217.

Werche, *v.* to work, 1. 260.

Werches, *pr. s.* aches, 8. v. 1. Cf. A. S. *heáfod-wære*, a head-ache, lit. a head-*work*.

Werd, *sb.* S. fate, destiny, 24. 63. See **Weird**.

Weirdis, *sb.* (*gen. case*), of the world; werdis wele = worldly prosperity; 4. 169. *Werd* for *world* is North E.; Sc. *ward*. See below.

Werdliche, *adj.* worldly, 1. 371. O. Sc. *ward*, M. E. *werd*, often written for *world*.

Werely, *adj.* warlike, i. e. bristly, 4. 155.

Werwolues, *sb. pl.* werwolves, man-wolves, 1. 459. A. S. *wer*, a man.

Westermar, *adv.* more westward, more to the west, 6. 307.

Wethering, *sb.* seasoning (from exposure to *weather*), 21. 104.

Wex, *pt. s.* S. waxed, 3 *b.* 1157. A. S. *weaxan*, G. *wachsen*, to grow.

Weyd, *sb.* S. garment, 6. 240. See **Weid**.

What, *used for* why, 3 *b.* 1380.

Wher-as, *adv.* where that, 3 *b.* 1162.

Whette, *v.* S. to whet, i. e. use repeatedly as a means of advice, 16. 27, 37. A. S. *hwæt*, sharp.

Whilome, *adv.* once upon a time, 28 *b.* 19. A. S. *hwilum*, at times, dat. pl. of *hwíl*, a *while*, a time.

Whipling, *sb.* a murmuring, ·14. 347. Apparently the same word as the Lowl. Sc. *fippil*, to whimper.

Whit, *sb.* wight, man, 1. 430; Wijʒt, I. 233; *pl.* Whiʒtes, 1. 812. A. S. *wiht, wuht*, a wight, a creature, a *whit*.

Whome, *sb. as adv.* home, homewards, 16. 305.

Whough, *interj.* whew! 23. iii. 387.

Whouʒ, *adv.* how, I. 192; Whou, I. 234. A. S. *hwú, hú*, how.

Whyleere, *adv.* while-ere, formerly, 17 *c.* 235. A. S. *whíl*, a time, and *ér*, formerly.

Whypt, *pt. s.* fled swiftly, 24. 5. Cf. W. *chwif*, a whirl, turn, *chwipio*, to move briskly, *chwiff*, a *whiff*.

Wicht, *adj.* nimble, active, vigorous, 6. 184; Wycht, strong, 11 *a.* 18. Sw. *vig*, active.

Wiel, *adv.* well, 3 *b.* 1100.

Wijʒt, *sb.* a wight, I. 233. See **Whit.**

Wil, *adv.* while, 1. 416.

Wilfull, *adj.* full of wishing, desirous, 13. 270. A. S. *will*, will, wish.

Wilne, *pr. pl.* (*miswritten for* Willen), will, 1. 216. A. S. *willan*, to will.

Wilneþ, *pr. pl.* desire to have, covet, 1. 361. A. S. *wilnian*, to desire.

Wisse, *v.* S. to instruct, shew the way, 3 *b.* 1118; Wissen, to teach, 1. 233. A. S. *wissian*, to teach, make to *wit*.

Wist, *pt. s.* knew, 2. 599; 2 *p. s. pt. subj.* didst know, 20 *c.* 28; *pp.* known, 1. 452, 2. 628. See **Witt.**

Wiþinneforþ, *adv.* inwardly, 5 *b.* 46.

Wiþouteforþ, *adv.* outwardly, 5 *b.* 50.

Withoutyn, *prep.* without, 6. 195. A. S. *wið-útan.*

Witt, *v.* S. to know, 6. 312; *dide him to witt*, caused him to know, informed him, 6. 303; 1 *p. s.*

pr. Wat, I wot, know, 7. 47. A S. *witan*, to know, pr. t. *ic wát*, pt. t. *ic wiste*; Lat. *uidere*, to see.

Wobbys, *sb. pl.* webs, 13. 171. Sc. *wab*, A. S. *wæbb.*

Wode, *adj.* S. mad; *starke wode =* stark-mad, 14. 575. A. S. *stearc*, strong, *wód*, mad.

Wode-wrothe, *adj.* madly angry, 8. iv. 37. A. S. *wód*, mad.

Wolward, *adj.* 1. 788. ' *Wolwarde,* without any lynnen next ones body, *sans chemyse:*' Palsgrave. To go *woolward* (with the *wool* next one's skin) was a way of doing penance.

Wolx, *pt. s.* became (lit. waxed), 13. 136; grew, were found, 13. 188. Sc. *wolx, woux*, pt. t. of *wex*, to wax, grow. So also Sc. *walken, wauken*, to awake. See **Walxis.**

Womanhed, *sb.* womanhood, 10. 80.

Wombe, *sb.* belly, I. 762. A. S. *wamb*, womb, belly.

Wondir, *adv.* wondrously, 13. 84.

Wone, *sb.* dwelling-place, I. 164; Woon, a building, I. 172; Wun, 24. 23. A. S. *wunian*, M. E. *wonne*, to dwell.

Woned, *pp.* wont, accustomed, 5 *b.* 59. A. S. *wunian*, to dwell in.

Wont, *pp.* wont, accustomed (*used for* was wont), 28 *b.* 115. See above, and see **Woonted.**

Wood, *adj.* S. mad, very angry, 3 *b.* 1080; Woode, mad, 3 *b.* 1328, 28 *a.* 135. See **Wode.**

Wood-ward; to wood ward = toward the wood, 10. 112.

Woonted, *adj.* (*formed like a pp.*) accustomed, wont, 26. 442. A. S. *wunian*, M. E. *wonne*, to dwell; whence *wonned, wont*, and (the wrongly-formed) *wonted.*

Worne, *pp.* worn away, past, 19 *c.* 12.

Wortes, *sb. pl.* vegetables; *wortes flechles wroughte*, vegetables cooked without meat, 1. 787;

Wortis, plants (such as *hare*-mint, *hare*-wort), 4.156; herbs, 13.157. A.S. *wyrt*, a wort, a root, G. *wurzel*.

Worth. *pr. pl.* are, become, 13.186; *pt. s.* Worthed, became; *worthed vp* = got up, mounted, 3 *b.* 1213; *worthit to weide* = went mad, 6. 438. A.S. *weorðan*, G. *werden*, to become. See Worþen.

Worþ to, *v.* become, 1. 746. See Worþen.

Worþen, *v.* to become, be, 1. 748; wo mote ʒou worþen = may woe happen to you, evil be to you, 1. 493; *pp.* Worþen, 1. 431. A.S. *weorðian*, G. *werden*; cf. woe *worth* the day.

Worþely, *adv.* worthy, 1. 233. A.S. *wurðlic.*

Wote, 1 *p. s. pr.* S. know, wot, 2. 614; God wote, God knows, 24. 38. A.S. *ic wát*, I know, from *witan*, to *wit*. See Witt.

Wouche, *sb.* damage, 7. 55. A.S. *wóh*, an error, a wrong; *wóg*, crooked.

Wough, *interj.* woe! alas! 23. iii. 4. 86.

Wounnand, *pres. part.* dwelling, lodging, 6. 290. A.S. *wunian*, to dwell.

Wouʒ, *adv.* how, 1. 356.

Wow, *v.* to woo, 13. 298. A.S. *wógan*, to woo, lit. to bend; cf. A.S. *wóg*, a bending.

Wower, *sb.* wooer, 23. iii. 3. 2; Wowar, *sb. as adj.* one who wooes, wooing, 13. 300.

Wowyn, *pp.* S. woven, 6. 242.

Wrablis, *sb. pl.* warble, 13. 245. O. F. *werbler*, to warble, make turns with the voice, from G. *wirbeln*, to make a turn; cf. E. *whirl, whirr, swirl.*

Wrak, *sb.* wreck, ruin, 3 *b.* 1169. Du. *wrak*, adj. broken, *sb.* a wreck.

Wreaked, 1 *p. s. pt.* recked, cared, 28 *b.* 29. (Misspelt.)

Wrenche, *sb.* S. a severe twist; such a wrenche = so severely, 14. 318.

Wright, *v.* to write, 28 *b.* 136. (Misspelt.)

Wrinching, *sb.* S. wrenching, shrugging, 25. 119.

Wrink, *sb.* deceit, 11 *b.* 42. A.S. *wrence*, deceit, deception.

Wrocht, *pp.* S. wrought, 6. 295; Wroughte, cooked, 1. 787. A.S. *wyrcan*, to work, pt. t. *ic worhte*, I wrought.

Wrong, *pt. s.* S. wrung, 24. 11. A. S. *wringan*, pt. t. *ic wrang.*

Wrye, *v.* to turn, turn aside, 4. 164. Cf. *writhe* and *wry.*

Wsyt, *pp.* lit. used; hence, well-known, 6. 345.

Wtrage, *adj.* outrageous, cruel, 6. 340. O. F. *oltrage*, violence, excess, from Lat. *ultra*, beyond.

Wun, *sb.* S. dwelling, abode, 24. 23. See Wone.

Wy, *sb.* S. man, 11 *b.* 50. A.S. *wiga*, a warrior, *wig*, war.

Wycht, *adj.* powerful, strong, 11 *a.* 18. Sw. *vig*, active. See Wicht.

Wydder, *v.* to wither, 22. 5472. A.S. *wyderu*, withering, dryness; cf. *weder*, weather.

Wyld, *adj. pl. as sb.* wild (*the sb.* animals *being understood*), 7. 12.

Wyn, *v.* S. *lit.* to win; hence (like E. *get*) to go, make one's way; *win owt*, to make one's way out, get away, 6. 234.

Wynwe-schete, *sb.* a sheet used in winnowing corn, 1. 435. A.S. *windwian*, to expose to *wind*, to *winnow.*

Wyrry, *v.* to worry, 14. 296. Du. *worgen*, to strangle.

Wyst, 1 *p. s. pt.* knew, 3 *a.* 3; *pt. s.* 6. 225. See Wist.

Y.

Y-, as a prefix, generally before past participles, is the A.S. *ge-*, Mœso-Goth. *ga-.*

Yafe, *pt. s.* gave, 2. 599.

Yate, *sb.* S. gate, 2. 604. A. S. *geat*, Prov. E. *yett*.

Ybared, *pp.* bared, made bare, 24. 1.

Y-beld, *pp.* built, 1. 172; Y-buld, 157.

Y-benched, *pp.* furnished with benches, 1. 205.

Y-bent, *pp.* bent, prone, 28 *b.* 40.

Y-blessed, *pp.* blessed, 1. 520.

Ybound, *pp.* bound, 24. 38; Ybounde, 2. 618.

Yburied, *pp.* buried, 19 *a.* 338.

Y-clense, *v.* to cleanse, 1. 760. A. S. *geclǽnsian*.

Y-cnowen, *pp.* known, 1. 252.

Y-corven, *pp.* carved, 1. 173. A.S. *ceorfan*, pp. *corfen*.

Y-crouned, *pp.* crowned, 1. 805.

Y-diȝte, *pp.* fitted up, 1. 211; Y-dyȝt, prepared, made, 1. 228. A.S. *dihtan*, to prepare, pp. *gediht*.

Ye-bent, *pp.* bent, 7. 52. Here *ye-* represents A. S. *ge-*.

Yede, *pt. pl.* went, 2. 621; 8. iv. 86; *pt. s.* ȝeid, 6. 221. A. S. *ic eode*, pt. t. of *gán*, to go.

Yeding, *pres. part.* going, 24. 30. (Wrongly formed; for *yede* is a past tense, not an infinitive.)

Ye-feth, *put for* i feth, i. e. in faith, 7. 124.

Ye-noughe, *adv.* enough, 7. 52. A. S. *genóh*.

Yer, *conj.* S. ere, before, 16. 221. A. S. *ǽr*.

Yerle, *sb.* S. earl, 7. 39. A. S. *eorl*.

Yerly, *adv.* early, 7. 14. A. S. *ǽrlíce*.

Yerthe, *sb.* earth, 15 *b.* 124. A. S. *eorðe*.

Yfere, *adv.* S. together, 24. 74. A. S. *geféra*, a travelling companion, *faran*, to *fare*, travel.

Y-founde, *pp.* founded, 1. 242.

Y-gadered, *pp.* gathered, 1. 189.

Y-greiþed, *pp.* prepared, fitted, 1. 196. See Graþis.

Yhorsed, *pp.* provided with horses, 3 *b.* 1100.

Yhurt, *pp.* hurt, 3 *b.* 1175.

Y-hyled, *pp.* covered, 1. 193. A. S. *helan*, Lat. *celare*, to hide.

Ying, *adj.* S. young, 11 *a.* 22; ȝing, 6. 201. A. S. *geóng*.

Ylayne, *pp.* laid, 24. 46.

Y-leid, *pp.* laid, 1. 263. A. S. *lecgan*, to lay, pp. *geled*.

Yle, *sb.* F. isle, island, 3. 301.

Ylike, *adj.* like, 28 *b.* 36. A. S. *gelíc*.

Ymay, *pr. pl.* may, 24. 52.

Y-medled, *pp.* mixed, placed alternately (between the shields), 1. 177. O. F. *medler*, *mesler*, Low Lat. *misculare*, from Lat. *miscere*, to mix; cf. Ital. *mescolare*, to mix.

Ynewch, *adj.* enough, 6. 446. A. S. *genóh*. See Ynow.

Ynne, *sb.* inn, i. e. lodging, 28 *a.* 16, 28 *b.* 72. A. S. *inn*.

Y-noumbred, *pp.* numbered, 1. 178.

Ynow, *adv.* S. enough, 1. 230. A. S. *genóh*.

Yode, I *p. s. pt.* went, 3 *a.* 13. See Yede.

Yond, *pron.* yonder, 28 *a.* 42. A. S. *geond*, prep. beyond.

Yore, *adv.* formerly, long ago, 2. 602. A. S. *geára*.

Yornyng, *sb.* clamour, 18. xviii. 17. We find also *youl*, *yowle*, *yout*, *yowp*, *yelp*, and *gowle*, with the sense of *yell*; but the M. E. *yerne* is to be eager, and *yernyng* is eagerness, hence clamour.

Youngth, *sb.* youth, 28 *a.* 20. A. S. *geóguð*.

Youngthly, *adj.* youthful, 28 *b.* 75.

Your, *poss. pron.* yours, 10. 152. A. S. *eówer*, of you, pl. of *þú*, thou. The form is etymologically correct.

Y-paued, *pp.* paved, 1. 194.

Y-peynt, *pp.* painted, 1. 160.

Y-rayled, *pp.* bedecked, covered,

3 *b.* 1340. A. S. *hrægl,* a garment; M. E. *rail,* a kerchief.

Yrk, *adj.* weary, tired, 6. 331. A. S. *earg,* sluggish; cf. G. *arg,* bad, E. *irksome.*

Y-rosted, *pp.* roasted, 1. 764.

Y-sacred, *pp.* consecrated, sanctified, 1. 186.

Y-schrowdyt, *pp.* shrouded, clothed, 13. 163.

Y-sene, *pp.* seen, 20 *a.* 56.

Y-set, *pp.* set, 1. 201.

Y-sewed, *pp.* sewn, 1. 229.

Y-stabled, *pp.* put into a stable (or perhaps, merely) confined, 28 *a.* 15.

Y-stongen, *pp.* pierced, pricked through (lit. stung), 1. 553.

Y-suled, *pp.* soiled, sullied, 1. 753. F. *souiller,* or Dan. *söle,* to soil.

Yth, *put for* in the, 7. 25. Cf. the proper name *Strongitharm.*

Ythrungin, *pp.* crowded together, pushed together (upwards), 4. 165. A. S. *þringan,* to press, *throng.*

Y-tiȝt, *pp.* firmly built, solidly made, 1. 168. Cf. Du. *digt,* solid, *digten,* to make close; also 'Thyhtyn, or make thyht, *Integro, consolido, solido,*' and 'Thyht, *solidus,*' in Prompt. Parv.

Y-toted, *pp.* inspected, 1. 219. See **Tote.**

Y-wis, *adv.* certainly, 1. 555. Du. *gewis,* adj. certain, adv. certainly.

Ywounded, *pp.* wounded, 3 *b.* 1175.

ȝ.

ȝald, *pt. s.* yielded (up the ghost),

22. 4553. A. S. *gildan,* to pay, yield; pt. t. *ic geald.*

ȝard, *sb.* garden, 13. 95. A. S. *geard,* a garden, a *yard.*

ȝarrow, *sb.* S. the herb yarrow, milfoil, 11 *a.* 12. A. S. *gearwe,* G. *garbe,* yarrow. (Nature sends the *yarrow* on a message to the *flowers.*)

ȝeer, *sb.* S. year, 5 *b.* 86. A. S. *gear.* See **ȝer.**

ȝeerli, *adv.* yearly, 5 *b.* 108.

ȝeid, *pt. s.* went, 6. 221. See **Yede.**

ȝeir, *sb. pl.* years, 22. 4693. See **ȝer.**

ȝemede, 1 *p. s. pt.* regarded closely, 1. 159. A. S. *gýman,* to pay heed to.

ȝer, *sb. pl.* years, 6. 192. A. S. *geár.* The pl. *ȝer* is employed instead of *ȝeres* when used with numbers or collectively. See **ȝeir.**

ȝerne, *adv.* diligently, 1. 159. A. S. *georn,* diligent, *georne,* diligently.

ȝett, *sb.* S. gate, door, 6. 246. A. S. *geat,* Prov. E. *yett.*

ȝeue, *v.* S. to give, 5 *b.* 121.

ȝhit, *adv.* yet, 6: 191. A. S. *gyt.*

ȝing, *adj.* S. young, 6. 201. See **Ying.**

ȝisterevin, *sb.* yesterday evening, 13. 212. Sc. *yestreen,* A. S. *gyrsta,* G. *gestern,* yesterday.

ȝond, *adv.* beyond, far off, 13. 9. A. S. *geond.*

ȝong, *adj.* young, 13. 181; ȝyng, 13. 99. See **Ying.**

ADDENDA TO THE GLOSSARIAL INDEX.

Awayt, *sb.* guard, 3 *b.* 1248.

Byllets, *sb. pl.* pieces of firewood, 26. 785. See Murray's Dict.

Byrne, *v.* burn, 6. 254.

Chiefe, *sb. prob.* a crest, 28 *a.* 115; cf. the heraldic term *achievement*, for which see Murray.

Corage, *sb.* fury (lit. courage), 9. 190.

Er, *adv.* before; p. 364, last line.

Fer, *sb.* fear, 3 *b.* 1274.

Fey, *sb.* faith, 23. iii. 4. 93.

Flechles, *adj.* fleshless, i.e. without meat, 1. 787. (See note.)

Forbure, *pt. s.* avoided, 6. 259.

Force; no force, i. e. no matter, 20 *b.* 87.

Forswat, *pp.* covered with sweat; p. 364, st. 2.

Forswonke, *pp.* exhausted with toil; p. 364, st. 2.

Fully, *adv.* foully, shamefully; p. 364, st. 3.

Harnys, *sb.* harness, 13. 25. But Mr. Small gives the reading *hamis*, i.e. hames, pieces of wood on a horse-collar to which the traces are fixed. (Perhaps better.)

Hine, *sb.* peasant, hind; p. 364, st. 4.

Hors, *sb. pl.* horses, 6. 417.

Houe, *v.* lounge about, lit. hover, 19 *f.* 6. See Hufing (p. 508).

Iugulars, *sb. pl.* jugglers, 16. 340 (*margin*).

Leas, *sb. pl.* leas, pastures, 20 *b.* 84.

Leude, p. 365, l. 4; see Lewde.

Lige, *v.* lie; p. 364, st. 1.

Likle, *adj.* likely, promising, 6. 213.

Lout, *v.* bow down; p. 364, st. 3.

Mot, *sb.* a blast on a horn, 7. 16 (*footnote*).

Part; On part, partly, 6. 310.

Pennis, *sb. pl.* feathers, 11 *a.* 18.

Plat, *adv.* flatly; hence, forthwith; p. 364, st. 2.

Queint, *pp.* quenched, extinguished (as was done in excommunication), p. 365, l. 12.

Rowme, *sb.* official situation, high place, rule (lit. room), 6. 340.

Royn, *adj.* 13. 121. Perhaps it may mean 'roan,' or sorrel-coloured; and *levys* are petals.

Senged, *pp.* singed, i. e. sun-burnt; p. 364, st. 3.

Shent, *pp.* treated with contumely; p. 364, st. 3.

Spercled, *pp.* scattered, flung a-broad, 24. 67.

Swinke, *v.* toil; p. 365, l. 6.

Tabarde, *sb.* labourer's frock (properly a herald's coat); p. 364, st. 2.

Twichand, *pres. pt.* touching, regarding, 13. 271.

Vpholde, *pp.* held up, 3 *b.* 1206.

Wangtoth, *sb.* molar tooth (lit. cheek-tooth); p. 364, st. 2.

Weders, *sb. pl.* storms, 1. 435.

Weren, *v.* to protect, 1. 435.

Whiʒt, *adj.* white, 1. 552.

Wight, *sb.* creature, 24. 11. See Whit.

Wone, *adj.* one, 7. 97.

Wyne-grapis, *sb. pl.* vine-grapes, 13. 99.

ADDITIONAL NOTES.

Sect. VII. l. 1. The form *avowe* is further authenticated by *his avowe* in l. 130. There is no need to discuss here what has been called 'the redundant *and* in ballads'; cf. Shakespeare's Twelfth Night, v. 398. Norwegian poems sometimes begin with *aa*, meaning *and*; see Dr. Murray's letter in *The Academy*, April 25, 1874; but that is another matter.

Sect. XVIII. See the excellent notes in the edition of Elyot's Governour by H. H. S. Croft; 2 vols. 1883 (vol. i. p. 173).
12. Croft quotes Galen, *De San. tuend.* lib. ii. fol. 31.
20. See also Corn. Nepos, *Epaminondas*, cap. ii.
45. See Livy, lib. ix. c. 16.
47. See Plutarch, *Marius*, 34.
63. See Vegetius, *De Re militari*, i. 10.
80. See also Plutarch, *Poplicola*, 16.
158. See Valerius Maximus, lib. iii. c. 2. § 10.

Sect. XX (B), l. 100. Cf. Spenser, Shep. Kal., Sept. 153. See note in Pegge's Kenticisms, ed. Skeat (Eng. Dial. Soc.), pp. 61, 62.
. . . . . (H), l. 8. Imitated from Chaucer, Parl. of Foules, 140.

Sect. XXIV, st. 19. *Castell*, his castle, viz. health. Sir T. Elyot wrote a book called *The Castel of Helth*, first printed in 1533.
. . . . . st. 72, l. 4. Accent *horrible* on the *i*.

Sect. XXVI, 756. *Cast at heel*, out at heels, very destitute. Cf. '*cast* clothes.'
. . . . . 1083. This trick is still done. See *Blow*, § 22, in Murray's Dict.

Sect. XXVIII (B), 60. *Seate*, mansion; Leo, in astrology, is the 'mansion' of Venus.
. . . . . 136. Wrinkles beside the eyes are called *a crowfoot*.

INDEX TO THE PRINCIPAL SUBJECTS EXPLAINED IN THE NOTES.

The following Index refers to the principal matters discussed in the Notes. The references to the *words* explained can easily be found by means of the Glossarial Index; but a few words on which there are special notes are included in the present Index also. These are distinguished by being printed in *italics*. The references are to the pages of the volume.

More, Sir T., his juvenile poetry, 376; his statement about English bibles, 434.

Nay, No, use of, 436.
Nominalists, 433.
Northumberland, earl of, 420.
Nyctimene, 416.

Obsolescent words misused, 465, 478.
Otterburn, battle of, 402.
Ovid quoted, 466, 480; referred to, 443.

Palladium, 406.
Palmerius, 452, 453.
Panthers, 382, 475.
Peekgoos, 469.
Penthesilea, 406.
Persius imitated, 447, 448.
Philip Sparrow, 425.
Philomela, 420.
Pictures in churches, 389.
Piers Plowman, copied by Lydgate, 374, 375; by Gascoigne, 473; alluded to, 425, 480.
Pigsny, 460, 461.
Placebo, 458.
Plato, 477.
Pliny quoted, 439.
Ploughman's Complaint (or Tale), 362, 364, 367, 368, 369; Prologue to, quoted in full, 364.
Popes, pride of the, 452, 453.
Posterns in priories, 359.
Pot Parliament, 435.
Predicaments, 433.
Prime, 386; *high prime,* 366 (l. 443), 375.
Proverbs and Proverbial phrases: —a rolling stone, 449; an *M* at your girdle, 460; hunger pierces stone walls, 466; miller's golden thumb, 474; mouse's nest in a cat's ear, 425; Inglese Italianato, 475; the cat loves fish, 363; to bear in hand, 423; to have pepper in the nose, 423;

to make one's beard, 372; to rule the roast, 470; when bale is hext, 402.
Pythagoras, sayings of, 474, 475.

Quair, note on, 382.

r, strongly trilled, 384, 385.
Ragman rolls, 360.
Realists, 433.
Requiem, 459.
Riccartoun, 393.
Rock-day (Jan. 7), 471.
Roister Doister, plot of, 457.

Saints' emblems, 389.
Saturn inauspicious, 416.
Scapulars, 368.
Schoolmen, 432, 433.
Scotland, arms of, 411.
Scripture, things mentioned in; as *cloak, oven,* &c., 387, 388.
Sertorius, 438.
Seven deadly sins, 424.
Seven sciences, 424.
Shires, three, in Northumberland, 396.
Signs of the Judgment, 454.
Sir, title of, 453.
Sleeping naked, 420.
Sleeve on a helmet, 445.
Southampton burnt, 428.
Spenser's Faerie Queene, 414, 415.
Spenser to Sackville, 462.
Sphinx, 379, 466.
Spleen, 409.
Statius, 376; quoted, 378, 379, 380, 381, 480.
Statute-staple, 472.
Stemyng, 447.
Stepe, 425.
Swords, names of, 404.

Tenedos, 406, 441.
Terza rima, 446.
Thebaid, 377, 480.
Thistle of Scotland, 411.
Thopas, Sir, 449.
Thou, a term of contempt, 393.

THE END.

𝔚orks by

THE REV. W. W. SKEAT, Litt.D., LL.D.,

*Elrington and Bosworth Professor of Anglo-Saxon in
the University of Cambridge.*

—◆◆—

An Etymological Dictionary of the English Language.
4to. *Second Edition.* 2*l*. 4*s*.

**A Concise Etymological Dictionary of the English
Language.** *Third Edition.* Crown 8vo. 5*s*. 6*d*.

A List of English Words, the Etymology of which
is illustrated by a comparison with Icelandic. 4to. *stitched*.
2*s*.

Principles of English Etymology. First Series. The
Native Element. Crown 8vo. 9*s*.

Specimens of Early English. By R. Morris, LL.D.,
and W. W. Skeat, Litt.D. New and Revised Edition.

    Part I. **From Old English Homilies to King Horn** (A.D.
        1150–1300). Extra fcap. 8vo. 9*s*.

    Part II. **From Robert of Gloucester to Gower** (A.D. 1298–
        1393). 7*s*. 6*d*.

**Specimens of English Literature, from the 'Plough-
man's Crede'** to the 'Shepheardes Calender' (A.D. 1394–1579).
Second Edition. Extra fcap. 8vo. 7*s*. 6*d*.

LANGLAND. The Vision of William concerning
Piers the Plowman, etc. In three Parallel Texts. Together
with Richard the Redeless. 2 vols. Demy 8vo. 1*l*. 11*s*. 6*d*.

[P. T. O.

October, 1887.

𝔗𝔥𝔢 𝔆𝔩𝔞𝔯𝔢𝔫𝔡𝔬𝔫 ℜ𝔯𝔢𝔰𝔰, 𝔒𝔵𝔣𝔬𝔯𝔡,

LIST OF SCHOOL BOOKS,

PUBLISHED FOR THE UNIVERSITY BY

HENRY FROWDE,

AT THE OXFORD UNIVERSITY PRESS WAREHOUSE,
AMEN CORNER, LONDON.

* *All Books are bound in Cloth, unless otherwise described.*

LATIN.

Allen. *An Elementary Latin Grammar.* By J. BARROW ALLEN, M.A. *Fifty-seventh Thousand* . . . . . Extra fcap. 8vo. 2s. 6d.

Allen. *Rudimenta Latina.* By the same Author. Extra fcap. 8vo. 2s.

Allen. *A First Latin Exercise Book.* By the same Author. *Fourth Edition.* . . . . Extra fcap. 8vo. 2s. 6d.

Allen. *A Second Latin Exercise Book.* By the same Author. Extra fcap. 8vo. 3s. 6d.
A Key to First and Second Latin Exercise Books in preparation.]

Jerram. *Anglice Reddenda; or, Easy Extracts, Latin and Greek, for Unseen Translation.* By C. S. JERRAM, M.A. *Fourth Edition.* Extra fcap. 8vo. 2s. 6d.

Jerram. *Anglice Reddenda.* SECOND SERIES. By C. S. JERRAM, M.A. Extra fcap. 8vo. 3s.

Jerram. *Reddenda Minora; or, Easy Passages, Latin and Greek, for Unseen Translation.* For the use of Lower Forms. Composed and selected by C. S. JERRAM, M.A. . . . . . Extra fcap. 8vo. 1s. 6d.

Lee-Warner. *Hints and Helps for Latin Elegiacs.* Extra fcap. 8vo. 3s. 6d.
[*A Key is provided : for Teachers only.*]

Lewis and Short. *A Latin Dictionary*, founded on Andrews' Edition of Freund's Latin Dictionary. By CHARLTON T. LEWIS, Ph.D., and CHARLES SHORT, LL.D. . . . . 4to. 25s.

Nunns. *First Latin Reader.* By T. J. NUNNS, M.A. *Third Edition.* Extra fcap. 8vo. 2s.

Papillon. *A Manual of Comparative Philology* as applied to the Illustration of Greek and Latin Inflections. By T. L. PAPILLON, M.A. *Third Edition.* Crown 8vo. 6s.

Ramsay. *Exercises in Latin Prose Composition.* With Introduction, Notes, and Passages of graduated difficulty for Translation into Latin. By G. G. RAMSAY, M.A., Professor of Humanity, Glasgow. *Second Edition.* Extra fcap. 8vo. 4s. 6d.

Sargent. *Passages for Translation into Latin.* By J. Y. SARGENT, M.A. *Seventh Edition.* . . . . . Extra fcap. 8vo. 2s. 6d.
[*A key to this Edition is provided : for Teachers only.*]

[L]

Caesar. *The Commentaries* (for Schools). With Notes and Maps. By CHARLES E. MOBERLY, M.A.
>   Part I. *The Gallic War. Second Edition.* . . Extra fcap. 8vo. 4*s.* 6*d.*
>   Part II. *The Civil War.* . . . . Extra fcap. 8vo. 3*s.* 6*d.*
>   *The Civil War.* Book I. *Second Edition.* . . Extra fcap. 8vo. 2*s.*

Catulli Veronensis *Carmina Selecta,* secundum recognitionem ROBINSON ELLIS, A.M. . . . . . Extra fcap 8vo. 3*s.* 6*d.*

Cicero. *Selection of interesting and descriptive passages.* With Notes. By HENRY WALFORD, M.A. In three Parts. *Third Edition.*
>   Extra fcap. 8vo. 4*s.* 6*d.*
>   Part I. *Anecdotes from Grecian and Roman History.* . *limp,* 1*s.* 6*d.*
>   Part II. *Omens and Dreams ; Beauties of Nature.* . . *limp,* 1*s.* 6*d.*
>   Part III. *Rome's Rule of her Provinces.* . . . . *limp,* 1*s.* 6*d.*

Cicero. *De Senectute.* With Introduction and Notes. By LEONARD HUXLEY, B.A. *In one or two Parts* . . . '. Extra fcap. 8vo. 2*s.*

Cicero. *Pro Cluentio.* With Introduction and Notes. By W. RAMSAY, M.A. Edited by G. G. RAMSAY, M.A. *Second Edition.* Extra fcap. 8vo. 3*s.* 6*d.*

Cicero. *Selected Letters* (for Schools). With Notes. By the late C. E. PRICHARD, M.A., and E. R. BERNARD, M.A. *Second Edition.*
>   Extra fcap. 8vo. 3*s.*

Cicero. *Select Orations* (for Schools). *First Action against Verres ; Oration concerning the command of Gnaeus Pompeius ; Oration on behalf of Archias ; Ninth Philippic Oration.* With Introduction and Notes. By J. R. KING, M.A. *Second Edition.* . . . Extra fcap. 8vo. 2*s.* 6*d.*

Cicero. *In Q. Caecilium Divinatio* and *In C. Verrem Actio Prima.* With Introduction and Notes. By J. R. KING, M.A.
>   Extra fcap. 8vo. *limp,* 1*s.* 6*d.*

Cicero. *Speeches against Catilina.* With Introduction and Notes. By E. A. UPCOTT, M.A. *In one or two Parts.* . . Extra fcap. 8vo. 2*s.* 6*d.*

Cicero. *Philippic Orations.* With Notes, &c. by J. R. KING, M.A. *Second Edition.* . . . . 8vo. 10*s.* 6*d.*

Cicero. *Select Letters.* With English Introductions, Notes, and Appendices. By ALBERT WATSON, M.A. *Third Edition.* . . 8vo. 18*s.*

Cicero. *Select Letters.* Text. By the same Editor. *Second Edition.*
>   Extra fcap. 8vo. 4*s.*

Cornelius Nepos. With Notes. By OSCAR BROWNING, M.A. *Second Edition.* . . . . . . Extra fcap. 8vo. 2*s.* 6*d.*

Horace. With a Commentary. Volume I. *The Odes, Carmen Seculare,* and *Epodes.* By EDWARD C. WICKHAM, M.A., Head Master of Wellington College. *New Edition. In one or two Parts.* Extra fcap. 8vo 6*s.*

Horace. *Selected Odes.* With Notes for the use of a Fifth Form. By E. C. WICKHAM, M.A. *In one or two Parts.* . . Extra fcap. 8vo. 2*s.*

Juvenal. *XIII Satires.* Edited, with Introduction, Notes, etc., by C. H. PEARSON, M.A., and H. A. STRONG, M.A. . . Crown 8vo. 6*s.*
>   *Or separately, Text and Introduction,* 3*s.* ; *Notes,* 3*s.* 6*d.*

Livy. *Selections* (for Schools). With Notes and Maps. By H. LEE-WARNER, M.A. . . . . Extra fcap. 8vo.
>   Part I. *The Caudine Disaster.* . . . . . . *limp,* 1*s.* 6*d.*
>   Part II. *Hannibal's Campaign in Italy.* . . . . *limp,* 1*s.* 6*d.*
>   Part III. *The Macedonian War.* . . . . . *limp,* 1*s.* 6*d.*

Livy. *Book I.* With Introduction, Historical Examination, and Notes. By J. R. SEELEY, M.A. *Second Edition.* . . . . . 8vo. 6s.

Livy. *Books V—VII.* With Introduction and Notes. By A. R. CLUER, B.A. *Second Edition.* Revised by P. E. MATHESON, M.A. *In one or two parts.* . . . . Extra fcap. 8vo. 5s.

Livy. *Books XXI—XXIII.* With Introduction and Notes. By M. T. TATHAM, M.A. . . . . . Extra fcap. 8vo. 4s. 6d.

Ovid. *Selections* (for the use of Schools). With Introductions and Notes, and an Appendix on the Roman Calendar. By W. RAMSAY, M.A. Edited by G. G. RAMSAY, M.A. *Third Edition.* . Extra fcap. 8vo. 5s. 6d.

Ovid. *Tristia,* Book I. Edited by S. G. OWEN, B.A. Extra fcap. 8vo. 3s. 6d.

Persius. *The Satires.* With Translation and Commentary by J. CONINGTON, M.A., edited by H. NETTLESHIP, M.A. *Second Edition.* 8vo. 7s. 6d.

Plautus. *Captivi.* With Introduction and Notes. By W. M. LINDSAY, M.A. *In one or two Parts.* . . . . . Extra fcap. 8vo. 2s. 6d.

Plautus. *Trinummus.* With Notes and Introductions. By C. E. FREEMAN, M.A. and A. SLOMAN, M.A. . . . . Extra fcap. 8vo. 3s.

Pliny. *Selected Letters* (for Schools). With Notes. By the late C. E. PRICHARD, M.A., and E. R. BERNARD, M.A. *New Edition. In one or two Parts.* . . . . Extra fcap. 8vo. 3s.

Sallust. *Bellum Catilinarium* and *Jugurthinum.* With Introduction and Notes, by W. W. CAPES, M.A. . . . Extra fcap. 8vo. 4s. 6d.

Tacitus. *The Annals.* Books I—IV. Edited, with Introduction and Notes for the use of Schools and Junior Students, by H. FURNEAUX, M.A. Extra fcap. 8vo. 5s.

Tacitus. *The Annals.* Book I. By the same Editor. Extra fcap. 8vo. *limp,* 2s.

Terence. *Adelphi.* With Notes and Introductions. By A. SLOMAN, M.A. . . . . Extra fcap. 8vo. 3s.

Terence. *Andria.* With Notes and Introductions. By C. E. FREEMAN, M.A., and A. SLOMAN, M.A. . . . . . Extra fcap. 8vo. 3s.

Terence. *Phormio.* With Notes and Introductions. By A. SLOMAN, M.A. . . . . Extra fcap. 8vo. 3s.

Tibullus and **Propertius.** Edited, with Introduction and Notes, by G. G. RAMSAY, M.A. *In one or two Parts.* . . . Extra fcap. 8vo. 6s.

Virgil. With Introduction and Notes, by T. L. PAPILLON, M.A. In Two Volumes. . . . Crown 8vo. 10s. 6d.; Text separately, 4s. 6d.

Virgil. *Bucolics.* With Introduction and Notes, by C. S. JERRAM, M.A. *In one or two Parts.* Extra fcap. 8vo. 2s. 6d.

Virgil. *Aeneid I.* With Introduction and Notes, by C. S. JERRAM, M.A. Extra fcap. 8vo. *limp,* 1s. 6d.

Virgil. *Aeneid IX.* Edited with Introduction and Notes, by A. E. HAIGH, M.A. . . . Extra fcap 8vo. *limp* 1s. 6d. *In two Parts.* 2s.

GREEK.

Chandler. *The Elements of Greek Accentuation* (for Schools). By H. W. CHANDLER, M.A. *Second Edition.* . Extra fcap. 8vo. 2s. 6d.

Liddell and Scott. *A Greek-English Lexicon*, by HENRY GEORGE LIDDELL, D.D., and ROBERT SCOTT, D.D. *Seventh Edition.* . 4to. 36s.

Liddell and Scott. *A Greek-English Lexicon*, abridged from LIDDELL and SCOTT's 4to. edition, chiefly for the use of Schools. *Twenty-first Edition.* Square 12mo. 7s. 6d.

Veitch. *Greek Verbs, Irregular and Defective :* their forms, meaning, and quantity ; embracing all the Tenses used by Greek writers, with references to the passages in which they are found. By W. VEITCH, LL.D. *Fourth Edition.* Crown 8vo. 10s. 6d.

Wordsworth. *Graecae Grammaticae Rudimenta in usum Scholarum.* Auctore CAROLO WORDSWORTH, D.C.L. *Nineteenth Edition.* . 12mo. 4s.

Wordsworth. *A Greek Primer, for the use of beginners in that Language.* By the Right Rev. CHARLES WORDSWORTH, D.C.L., Bishop of St. Andrew's. *Seventh Edition.* . . . . Extra fcap. 8vo. 1s. 6d.

Wright. *The Golden Treasury of Ancient Greek Poetry ;* being a Collection of the finest passages in the Greek Classic Poets, with Introductory Notices and Notes. By R. S. WRIGHT, M.A. . *New edition in the Press.*

Wright and Shadwell. *A Golden Treasury of Greek Prose ;* being a Collection of the finest passages in the principal Greek Prose Writers, with Introductory Notices and Notes. By R. S. WRIGHT, M.A., and J. E. L. SHADWELL, M.A. . . . . Extra fcap. 8vo. 4s. 6d.

A SERIES OF GRADUATED READERS.—

Easy Greek Reader. By EVELYN ABBOTT, M.A. *In one or two Parts.* . . . . Extra fcap. 8vo. 3s.

First Greek Reader. By W. G. RUSHBROOKE, M.L., Second Classical Master at the City of London School. *Second Edition.* Extra fcap. 8vo. 2s. 6d.

Second Greek Reader. By A. M. BELL, M.A. Extra fcap. 8vo. 3s. 6d.

Fourth Greek Reader ; being Specimens of Greek Dialects. With Introductions and Notes. By W. W. MERRY, D.D., Rector of Lincoln College. . . . . Extra fcap. 8vo. 4s. 6d.

Fifth Greek Reader. Selections from Greek Epic and Dramatic Poetry, with Introductions and Notes. By EVELYN ABBOTT, M.A. Extra fcap. 8vo. 4s. 6d.

THE GREEK TESTAMENT.—

Evangelia Sacra Graece. . . . Fcap. 8vo. *limp,* 1s. 6d.

The Greek Testament, with the Readings adopted by the Revisers of the Authorised Version. Fcap. 8vo. 4s. 6d. ; or on writing paper, with wide margin, 15s.

Novum Testamentum Graece juxta Exemplar Millianum. 18mo. 2s. 6d. ; or on writing paper, with large margin, 9s.

Novum Testamentum Graece. Accedunt parallela S. Scripturae loca, necnon vetus capitulorum notatio et canones Eusebii. Edidit CAROLUS LLOYD, S.T.P.R., necnon Episcopus Oxoniensis.

18mo. 3s.; or on writing paper, with large margin, 10s. 6d.

The New Testament in Greek and English. Edited by E. CARDWELL, D.D. . . . . 2 vols. crown 8vo. 6s.

Outlines of Textual Criticism applied to the New Testament. By C. E. HAMMOND, M.A. *Fourth Edition.* . . Extra fcap. 8vo. 3s. 6d.

Aeschylus. *Agamemnon.* With Introduction and Notes, by ARTHUR SIDGWICK, M.A. *Second Edition.* . . . . . Extra fcap. 8vo. 3s.

Aeschylus. *Choephoroi.* With Introduction and Notes, by the same Editor. . . . . Extra fcap. 8vo. 3s.

Aeschylus. *Eumenides.* With Introduction and Notes, by the same Editor. *In one or two Parts.* . . . . . Extra fcap. 8vo. 3s.

Aeschylus. *Prometheus Bound.* With Introduction and Notes, by A. O. PRICKARD, M.A. *Second Edition.* . . . Extra fcap. 8vo. 2s.

Aristophanes. *The Clouds.* With Introduction and Notes, by W. W. MERRY, D.D. *Second Edition.* . . . . Extra fcap. 8vo. 2s.

Aristophanes. *The Acharnians.* By the same Editor. *Third Edition. In one or two Parts.* . . . . Extra fcap. 8vo. 3s.

Aristophanes. *The Frogs.* By the same Editor. *New Edition. In one or two Parts.* . . . . Extra fcap. 8vo. 3s.

Aristophanes. *The Knights.* By the same Editor. *In one or two Parts.* . . . . Extra fcap. 8vo. 3s.

Cebes. *Tabula.* With Introduction and Notes, by C. S. JERRAM, M.A. Extra fcap. 8vo. 2s. 6d.

Demosthenes. *Orations against Philip.* With Introduction and Notes. By EVELYN ABBOTT, M.A., and P. E. MATHESON, M.A., Vol. I. *Philippic I* and *Olynthiacs I—III. In one or two Parts.* . . . Extra fcap. 8vo. 3s.

Euripides. *Alcestis.* By C. S. JERRAM, M.A. Extra fcap. 8vo. 2s. 6d.

Euripides. *Helena.* By the same Editor. . Extra fcap. 8vo. 3s.

Euripides. *Iphigenia in Tauris.* With Introduction and Notes. By the same Editor. . . . . Extra fcap. 8vo. 3s.

Euripides. *Medea.* With Introduction, Notes and Appendices. By C. B. HEBERDEN, M.A. *In one or two Parts.* . . Extra fcap. 8vo. 2s.

Herodotus. Book IX. Edited with Notes, by EVELYN ABBOTT, M.A. *In one or two Parts.* . . . . . Extra fcap. 8vo. 3s.

Herodotus. *Selections.* Edited, with Introduction, Notes, and a Map, by W. W. MERRY, D.D. . . . . . Extra fcap. 8vo. 2s. 6d.

Homer. *Iliad,* Books I–XII. With an Introduction, a brief Homeric Grammar, and Notes. By D. B. MONRO, M.A. Extra fcap. 8vo. 6s.

Homer. *Iliad,* Book I. By the same Editor. *Third Edition.* Extra fcap. 8vo. 2s.

Homer. *Iliad,* Books VI and XXI. With Notes, &c. By HERBERT HAILSTONE, M.A. . . . . . Extra fcap. 8vo. 1s. 6d. each.

Homer. *Odyssey*, Books I–XII. By W. W. MERRY, D.D. *Fortieth Thousand.* . . . . Extra fcap. 8vo. 4s. 6d.

Homer. *Odyssey*, Books XIII–XXIV. By the same Editor. *Second Edition.* . . . . Extra fcap. 8vo. 5s.

Homer. *Odyssey*, Books I and II. By the same Editor.
Extra fcap. 8vo. each 1s. 6d.

Lucian. *Vera Historia.* By C. S. JERRAM, M.A. *Second Edition.*
Extra fcap. 8vo. 1s. 6d.

Plato. *The Apology.* With a revised Text and English Notes, and a Digest of Platonic Idioms, by JAMES RIDDELL, M.A. . . 8vo. 8s. 6d.

Plato. *The Apology.* With Introduction and Notes. By ST. GEORGE STOCK, M.A. *In one or two Parts.* . . . . Extra fcap. 8vo. 2s. 6d.

Plato. *Meno.* With Introduction and Notes. By ST. GEORGE STOCK, M.A. *In one or two Parts.* . . . . . Extra fcap. 8vo. 2s. 6d.

Sophocles. (For the use of Schools.) Edited with Introductions and English Notes by LEWIS CAMPBELL, M.A., and EVELYN ABBOTT, M.A. New and Revised Edition. 2 Vols. . . . . Extra fcap. 8vo. 10s. 6d.
Sold separately, Vol. I. Text, 4s. 6d. Vol. II. Notes, 6s.

Also in single Plays. Extra fcap. 8vo. limp,
Oedipus Tyrannus, Philoctetes. New and Revised Edition, 2s. each.
Oedipus Coloneus, Antigone. 1s. 9d. each.
Ajax, Electra, Trachiniae. 2s. each.

Sophocles. *Oedipus Rex:* Dindorf's Text, with Notes by W. BASIL JONES, D.D., Lord Bishop of S. David's. . Extra fcap. 8vo. *limp*, 1s. 6d.

Theocritus. Edited, with Notes, by H. KYNASTON, D.D. (late SNOW), Head Master of Cheltenham College. *Fourth Edition.*
Extra fcap. 8vo. 4s. 6d.

Xenophon. *Easy Selections* (for Junior Classes). With a Vocabulary, Notes, and Map. By J. S. PHILLPOTTS, B.C.L., Head Master of Bedford School, and C. S. JERRAM, M.A. *Third Edition.* . Extra fcap. 8vo. 3s. 6d.

Xenophon. *Selections* (for Schools). With Notes and Maps. By J. S. PHILLPOTTS, B.C.L. *Fourth Edition.* . . Extra fcap. 8vo. 3s. 6d.

Xenophon. *Anabasis*, Book I. With Notes and Map. By J. MARSHALL, M.A., Rector of the High School, Edinburgh. . . Extra fcap. 8vo. 2s. 6d.

Xenophon. *Anabasis*, Book II. With Notes and Map. By C. S. JERRAM, M.A. . . . . Extra fcap. 8vo. 2s.

Xenophon. *Cyropaedia*, Books IV, V. With Introduction and Notes, by C. BIGG, D.D. . . . . Extra fcap. 8vo. 2s. 6d.

ENGLISH.

Reading Books.

—— *A First Reading Book.* By MARIE EICHENS of Berlin; edited by ANNE J. CLOUGH. . . . . . Extra fcap. 8vo. *stiff covers*, 4d.

—— *Oxford Reading Book*, Part I. For Little Children.
Extra fcap. 8vo. *stiff covers*, 6d.

—— *Oxford Reading Book*, Part II. For Junior Classes.
Extra fcap. 8vo. *stiff covers*, 6d.

Skeat. *A Concise Etymological Dictionary of the English Language.* By W. W. SKEAT, Litt. D. *Second Edition.* . . . Crown 8vo. 5s. 6d.

Tancock. *An Elementary English Grammar and Exercise Book.* By O. W. TANCOCK, M.A., Head Master of King Edward VI's School, Norwich. *Second Edition.* . . . . . . Extra fcap. 8vo. 1s. 6d.

Tancock. *An English Grammar and Reading Book*, for Lower Forms in Classical Schools. By O. W. TANCOCK, M.A. *Fourth Edition.* Extra fcap. 8vo. 3s. 6d.

Skeat. *The Principles of English Etymology. First Series.* By W. W. SKEAT, Litt. D. . . . . Crown 8vo. 9s.

Earle. *The Philology of the English Tongue.* By J. EARLE, M.A., Professor of Anglo-Saxon. *Fourth Edition.* . . Extra fcap. 8vo. 7s. 6d.

Earle. *A Book for the Beginner in Anglo-Saxon.* By the same Author. *Third Edition.* . . . . . . Extra fcap. 8vo. 2s. 6d;

Sweet. *An Anglo-Saxon Primer, with Grammar, Notes, and Glossary.* By HENRY SWEET, M.A. *Third Edition.* . . Extra fcap. 8vo. 2s. 6d.

Sweet. *An Anglo-Saxon Reader.* In Prose and Verse. With Grammatical Introduction, Notes, and Glossary. By the same Author. *Fourth Edition, Revised and Enlarged.* . . . Extra fcap. 8vo. 8s. 6d.

Sweet. *A Second Anglo-Saxon Reader.* By the same Author. Nearly ready.

Sweet. *Anglo-Saxon Reading Primers.*
    I. *Selected Homilies of Ælfric.*   Extra fcap. 8vo. *stiff covers*, 1s. 6d.
    II. *Extracts from Alfred's Orosius.*   Extra fcap. 8vo. *stiff covers*, 1s. 6d.

Sweet. *First Middle English Primer, with Grammar and Glossary.* By the same Author. . . . . . . Extra fcap. 8vo. 2s.

Sweet. *Second Middle English Primer.* Extracts from Chaucer, with Grammar and Glossary. By the same Author. . . Extra fcap. 8vo 2s

Morris and Skeat. *Specimens of Early English.* A New and Revised Edition. With Introduction, Notes, and Glossarial Index. By R. MORRIS, LL.D., and W. W. SKEAT, Litt. D.
    Part I. From Old English Homilies to King Horn (A.D. 1150 to A.D. 1300). *Second Edition.* . . . . . . Extra fcap. 8vo. 9s.
    Part II. From Robert of Gloucester to Gower (A.D. 1298 to A.D. 1393). *Second Edition.* . . . . Extra fcap. 8vo. 7s. 6d.

Skeat. *Specimens of English Literature*, from the 'Ploughmans Crede' to the 'Shepheardes Calender' (A.D. 1394 to A.D. 1579). With Introduction, Notes, and Glossarial Index. By W. W. SKEAT, Litt. D.
    Extra fcap. 8vo. 7s. 6d.

Typical Selections from the best English Writers, with Introductory Notices. *Second Edition.* In Two Volumes. Vol. I. Latimer to Berkeley. Vol. II. Pope to Macaulay. . . Extra fcap. 8vo. 3s. 6d. each.

A SERIES OF ENGLISH CLASSICS.—

Langland. *The Vision of William concerning Piers the Plowman*, by WILLIAM LANGLAND. Edited by W. W. SKEAT, Litt. D. *Fourth Edition.* Extra fcap. 8vo. 4s. 6d.

Chaucer. I. *The Prologue to the Canterbury Tales; The Knightes Tale; The Nonne Prestes Tale.* Edited by R. MORRIS, LL.D. *Fifty-first Thousand.* . . . . Extra fcap. 8vo. 2s. 6d.

Chaucer. II. *The Prioresses Tale ; Sir Thopas ; The Monkes Tale ; The Clerkes Tale ; The Squieres Tale, &c.* Edited by W. W. SKEAT, Litt. D. *Third Edition.* . . . . Extra fcap. 8vo. 4s. 6d.

Chaucer. III. *The Tale of the Man of Lawe ; The Pardoneres Tale ; The Second Nonnes Tale ; The Chanouns Yemannes Tale.* By the same Editor. *New Edition, Revised.* . . . Extra fcap. 8vo. 4s. 6d.

Gamelyn, The Tale of. Edited by W. W. SKEAT, Litt. D.
Extra fcap. 8vo. *stiff covers,* 1s. 6d.

Minot. *The Poems of Laurence Minot.* Edited, with Introduction and Notes, by JOSEPH HALL, M.A. . . . Extra fcap. 8vo. 4s. 6d.

Wycliffe. *The New Testament in English,* according to the Version by JOHN WYCLIFFE, about A.D. 1380, and Revised by JOHN PURVEY, about A.D. 1388. With Introduction and Glossary by W. W. SKEAT, Litt. D.
Extra fcap. 8vo. 6s.

Wycliffe. *The Books of Job, Psalms, Proverbs, Ecclesiastes, and the Song of Solomon :* according to the Wycliffite Version made by NICHOLAS DE HEREFORD, about A.D. 1381, and Revised by JOHN PURVEY, about A.D. 1388. With Introduction and Glossary by W. W. SKEAT, Litt. D. Extra fcap. 8vo. 3s. 6d.

Spenser. *The Faery Queene.* Books I and II. Edited by G. W. KITCHIN, D.D.

    Book I. *Tenth Edition.* . . . . . Extra fcap. 8vo. 2s. 6d.
    Book II. *Sixth Edition.* . . . . . Extra fcap. 8vo. 2s. 6d.

Hooker. *Ecclesiastical Polity,* Book I. Edited by R. W. CHURCH, M.A., Dean of St. Paul's. *Second Edition.* . . . Extra fcap. 8vo. 2s.

Marlowe and Greene.—MARLOWE'S *Tragical History of Dr. Faustus,* and GREENE'S *Honourable History of Friar Bacon and Friar Bungay.* Edited by A. W. WARD, M.A. *Second Edition.* . . . Extra fcap. 8vo. 6s. 6d.

Marlowe. *Edward II.* Edited by O. W. TANCOCK, M.A. *Second Edition.* . . . . . Extra fcap. 8vo. *Paper covers,* 2s. *cloth,* 3s.

Shakespeare. Select Plays. Edited by W. G. CLARK, M.A., and W. ALDIS WRIGHT, M.A. . . . . . Extra fcap. 8vo. *stiff covers.*

    The Merchant of Venice. 1s.   *Macbeth.* 1s. 6d.
    Richard the Second. 1s. 6d.   *Hamlet.* 2s.

Edited by W. ALDIS WRIGHT, M.A.

    The Tempest. 1s. 6d.   *Coriolanus.* 2s. 6d.
    As You Like It. 1s. 6d.   *Richard the Third.* 2s. 6d.
    A Midsummer Night's Dream. 1s. 6d.   *Henry the Fifth.* 2s.
    Twelfth Night. 1s 6d.   *King John.* 1s. 6d.
    Julius Cæsar. 2s.   *King Lear.* 1s. 6d.
    Henry the Eighth (in the Press).

Shakespeare as a Dramatic Artist ; *a popular Illustration of the Principles of Scientific Criticism.* By RICHARD G. MOULTON, M.A.
· Crown 8vo. 5s.

Bacon. I. *Advancement of Learning.* Edited by W. ALDIS WRIGHT, M.A. *Second Edition.* . . . . . . Extra fcap. 8vo. 4s. 6d.

Bacon. II. *The Essays.* With Introduction and Notes. *In Preparation.*

Milton. I. *Areopagitica.* With Introduction and Notes. By JOHN W. HALES, M.A. *Third Edition.* . . . . Extra fcap. 8vo. 3*s.*

Milton. II. *Poems.* Edited by R. C. BROWNE, M.A. 2 vols. *Fifth Edition.* . Extra fcap. 8vo. 6*s.* 6*d.* Sold separately, Vol. I. 4*s.*, Vol. II. 3*s.*
In paper covers :—
Lycidas, 3*d.* *L'Allegro,* 3*d.* *Il Penseroso,* 4*d.* *Comus,* 6*d.*
Samson Agonistes, 6*d.*

Milton. III. *Paradise Lost.* Book I. Edited with Notes, by H. C. BEECHING, M.A. . . . . Extra fcap. 8vo.

Milton. IV. *Samson Agonistes.* Edited with Introduction and Notes by JOHN CHURTON COLLINS. . . . Extra fcap. 8vo. *stiff covers,* 1*s.*

Clarendon. *History of the Rebellion.* Book VI. Edited with Introduction and Notes by T. ARNOLD, M.A. . . Extra fcap. 8vo. 4*s.* 6*d.*

Bunyan. I. *The Pilgrim's Progress, Grace Abounding, Relation of the Imprisonment of Mr. John Bunyan.* Edited, with Biographical Introduction and Notes, by E. VENABLES, M.A.
Extra fcap. 8vo. 5*s.* *In white Parchment,* 6*s.*

Bunyan. II. *Holy War, &c.* By the same Editor. *In the Press.*

Dryden. *Select Poems.—Stanzas on the Death of Oliver Cromwell; Astræa Redux; Annus Mirabilis; Absalom and Achitophel; Religio Laici; The Hind and the Panther.* Edited by W. D. CHRISTIE, M.A.
Extra fcap. 8vo. 3*s.* 6*d.*

Locke's *Conduct of the Understanding.* Edited, with Introduction, Notes, &c. by T. FOWLER, D.D. *Second Edition.* . . Extra fcap. 8vo. 2*s.*

Addison. *Selections from Papers in the 'Spectator.'* With Notes. By T. ARNOLD, M.A. . Extra fcap. 8vo. 4*s.* 6*d.* *In white Parchment,* 6*s.*

Steele. *Selected Essays from the Tatler, Spectator, and Guardian.* By AUSTIN DOBSON. . . Extra fcap. 8vo. 5*s.* *In white Parchment,* 7*s.* 6*d.*

Berkeley. *Select Works of Bishop Berkeley,* with an Introduction and Notes, by A. C. FRASER, LL.D. *Third Edition.* . . Crown 8vo. 7*s.* 6*d.*

Pope. I. *Essay on Man.* Edited by MARK PATTISON, B.D. *Sixth Edition.* . . . . Extra fcap. 8vo. 1*s.* 6*d.*

Pope. II. *Satires and Epistles.* By the same Editor. *Second Edition.*
Extra fcap. 8vo. 2*s.*

Parnell. *The Hermit.* . . . . . *Paper covers,* 2*d.*

Johnson. I. *Rasselas; Lives of Dryden and Pope.* Edited by ALFRED MILNES, M.A. . . . . . Extra fcap. 8vo. 4*s.* 6*d.*
Lives of Pope and Dryden. . . . . *Stiff covers,* 2*s.* 6*d.*

Johnson. II. *Rasselas.* Edited, with Introduction and Notes, by G. BIRKBECK HILL, D.C.L. Extra fcap. 8vo. *limp,* 2*s. In white Parchment,* *s.* 6*d.*

Johnson. III. *Vanity of Human Wishes.* With Notes, by E. J. PAYNE, M.A. . . . . *Paper covers,* 4d.

Gray. *Selected Poems.* Edited by EDMUND GOSSE.
Extra fcap. 8vo. *Stiff covers,* 1s. 6d. *In white Parchment,* 3s.

Gray. *Elegy, and Ode on Eton College.* . . *Paper covers,* 2d.

Goldsmith. *Selected Poems.* Edited, with Introduction and Notes, by
AUSTIN DOBSON. . . . . Extra fcap. 8vo. 3s. 6d.
In white Parchment, 4s. 6d.

The Deserted Village. . . . . *Paper covers,* 2d.

Cowper. I. *The Didactic Poems of* 1782, with Selections from the
Minor Pieces, A.D. 1779-1783. Edited by H. T. GRIFFITH, B.A.
Extra fcap. 8vo. 3s.

Cowper. II. *The Task, with Tirocinium,* and Selections from the
Minor Poems, A.D. 1784-1799. By the same Editor. *Second Edition.*
Extra fcap. 8vo. 3s.

Burke. I. *Thoughts on the Present Discontents; the two Speeches
on America.* Edited by E. J. PAYNE, M.A. *Second Edition.*
Extra fcap. 8vo. 4s. 6d.

Burke. II. *Reflections on the French Revolution* By the same
Editor. *Second Edition.* . . . . . Extra fcap. 8vo. 5s.

Burke. III. *Four Letters on the Proposals for Peace with the
Regicide Directory of France.* By the same Editor. *Second Edition.*
Extra fcap. 8vo. 5s.

Keats. *Hyperion,* Book I. With Notes, by W. T. ARNOLD, B.A.
Paper covers, 4d.

Byron. *Childe Harold.* With Introduction and Notes, by H. F. TOZER,
M.A. . . . Extra fcap. 8vo. 3s. 6d. *In white Parchment,* 5s.

Scott. *Lay of the Last Minstrel.* Edited with Preface and Notes by
W. MINTO, M.A. With Map.
Extra fcap. 8vo. *stiff covers,* 2s. *In Ornamental Parchment,* 3s. 6d.

Scott. *Lay of the Last Minstrel.* Introduction and Canto I, with
Preface and Notes by W. MINTO, M.A. . . . . *Paper covers,* 6d.

FRENCH AND ITALIAN.

Brachet. *Etymological Dictionary of the French Language,* with
a Preface on the Principles of French Etymology. Translated into English by
G. W. KITCHIN, D.D., Dean of Winchester. *Third Edition.*
Crown 8vo. 7s. 6d.

Brachet. *Historical Grammar of the French Language.* Translated
into English by G. W. KITCHIN, D.D. *Fourth Edition.*
Extra fcap. 8vo. 3s. 6d.

Saintsbury. *Primer of French Literature.* By GEORGE SAINTS-
BURY, M.A. *Second Edition.* . . . . . Extra fcap. 8vo. 2s.

Saintsbury. *Short History of French Literature.* By the same Author. . . . . Crown 8vo. 10s. 6d.

Saintsbury. *Specimens of French Literature.* . . Crown 8vo. 9s.

Beaumarchais. *Le Barbier de Séville.* With Introduction and Notes by AUSTIN DOBSON. . . . . . . Extra fcap. 8vo. 2s. 6d.

Blouët. *L'Éloquence de la Chaire et de la Tribune Françaises.* Edited by PAUL BLOUËT, B.A. (Univ. Gallic.). Vol. I. *French Sacred Oratory.* Extra fcap. 8vo. 2s. 6d.

Corneille. *Horace.* With Introduction and Notes by GEORGE SAINTSBURY, M.A. . . . . . . Extra fcap. 8vo. 2s. 6d.

Corneille. *Cinna.* With Notes, Glossary, etc. By GUSTAVE MASSON, B.A. . . . . . Extra fcap. 8vo. *stiff covers,* 1s. 6d. *cloth,* 2s.

Gautier (Théophile). *Scenes of Travel.* Selected and Edited by G. SAINTSBURY, M.A. . . . . . . Extra fcap. 8vo. 2s.

Masson. *Louis XIV and his Contemporaries;* as described in Extracts from the best Memoirs of the Seventeenth Century. With English Notes, Genealogical Tables, &c. By GUSTAVE MASSON, B.A. Extra fcap. 8vo. 2s. 6d.

Molière. *Les Précieuses Ridicules.* With Introduction and Notes by ANDREW LANG, M.A. . . . . . Extra fcap. 8vo. 1s. 6d.

Molière. *Les Femmes Savantes.* With Notes, Glossary, etc. By GUSTAVE MASSON, B.A. . Extra fcap. 8vo. *stiff covers,* 1s. 6d. *cloth,* 2s.

Molière. *Les Fourberies de Scapin.* ⎱ With Voltaire's Life of Molière. By
Racine. *Athalie.* ⎰ GUSTAVE MASSON, B.A. Extra fcap. 8vo. 2s. 6d.

Molière. *Les Fourberies de Scapin.* With Voltaire's Life of Molière. By GUSTAVE MASSON, B.A. . . Extra fcap. 8vo. *stiff covers,* 1s. 6d.

Musset. *On ne badine pas avec l'Amour,* and *Fantasio.* With Introduction, Notes, etc., by WALTER HERRIES POLLOCK. Extra fcap. 8vo. 2s.

NOVELETTES :—

Xavier de Maistre. *Voyage autour de ma Chambre.*	
Madame de Duras. *Ourika.*	By GUSTAVE MASSON, B.A
Erckmann-Chatrian. *Le Vieux Tailleur.*	3rd Edition.
Alfred de Vigny. *La Veillée de Vincennes.*	Ext. fcap. 8vo.
Edmond About. *Les Jumeaux de l'Hôtel Corneille.*	2s. 6d.
Rodolphe Töpffer. *Mésaventures d'un Écolier.*	

Voyage autour de ma Chambre, separately, limp, 1s. 6d.

Quinet. *Lettres à sa Mère.* Edited by G. SAINTSBURY, M.A. Extra fcap. 8vo. 2s.

Racine. *Esther.* Edited by G. SAINTSBURY, M.A. Extra fcap. 8vo. 2s.

Racine. *Andromaque.* ⎱ With Louis Racine's Life of his Father. By
Corneille. *Le Menteur.* ⎰ GUSTAVE MASSON, B.A. Extra fcap. 8vo. 2s. 6d.

Regnard. . . . *Le Joueur.* ⎫ By GUSTAVE MASSON, B.A.
Brueys and Palaprat. *Le Grondeur.* ⎭   Extra fcap. 8vo. 2s. 6d.

Sainte-Beuve. *Selections from the Causeries du Lundi.* Edited by
G. SAINTSBURY, M.A. . . . . . .   Extra fcap. 8vo. 2s.

Sévigné. *Selections from the Correspondence of* **Madame de Sévigné**
and her chief Contemporaries. Intended more especially for Girls' Schools. By
GUSTAVE MASSON, B.A. . . . . .   Extra fcap. 8vo. 3s.

Voltaire. *Mérope.* Edited by G. SAINTSBURY, M.A. Extra fcap. 8vo. 2s.

Dante. *Selections from the 'Inferno.'* With Introduction and Notes,
by H. B. COTTERILL, B.A. . . . . .   Extra fcap. 8vo. 4s. 6d.

Tasso. *La Gerusalemme Liberata.* Cantos i, ii. With Introduction
and Notes, by the same Editor. . . . .   Extra fcap. 8vo. 2s. 6d.

GERMAN, &c.

Buchheim. *Modern German Reader.* A Graduated Collection of
Extracts in Prose and Poetry from Modern German writers. Edited by C. A.
BUCHHEIM. Phil. Doc.
    Part I. With English Notes, a Grammatical Appendix, and a complete
    Vocabulary. *Fourth Edition.* . . .   Extra fcap. 8vo. 2s. 6d.
    Part II. With English Notes and an Index. Extra fcap. 8vo. 2s. 6d.
    Part III. In preparation.

Lange. *The Germans at Home*; a Practical Introduction to German
Conversation, with an Appendix containing the Essentials of German Grammar.
By HERMANN LANGE. *Third Edition.* . . . .   8vo. 2s. 6d.

Lange. *The German Manual*; a German Grammar, a Reading
Book, and a Handbook of German Conversation. By the same Author.
                                                            8vo. 7s. 6d.

Lange. *A Grammar of the German Language,* being a reprint of the
Grammar contained in *The German Manual.* By the same Author. 8vo. 3s. 6d.

Lange. *German Composition*; a Theoretical and Practical Guide to
the Art of Translating English Prose into German. By the same Author.
Second Edition . . . .   8vo. 4s. 6d.
                [A Key in Preparation.]

Lange. *German Spelling*: A Synopsis of the Changes which it has
undergone through the Government Regulations of 1880 . *Paper cover, 6d.*

Goethe. *Egmont.* With a Life of Goethe, etc. Edited by C. A.
BUCHHEIM, Phil. Doc. *Third Edition.* . . .   Extra fcap. 8vo. 3s.

Goethe. *Iphigenie auf Tauris.* A Drama. With a Critical Introduction and Notes. Edited by C. A. BUCHHEIM, Phil. Doc. *Second Edition.*
                                                            Extra fcap. 8vo. 3s.

Heine's *Harzreise.* With a Life of Heine, etc. Edited by C. A.
BUCHHEIM, Phil. Doc.   Extra fcap. 8vo. *stiff covers,* 1s. 6d. *cloth,* 2s. 6d.

Heine's *Prosa*, being Selections from his Prose Works. Edited with English Notes, etc., by C. A. BUCHHEIM, Phil. Doc. Extra fcap. 8vo. 4*s*. 6*d*.

Lessing. *Laokoon*. With Introduction, Notes, etc. By A. HAMANN, Phil. Doc., M.A. . . . . . . Extra fcap. 8vo. 4*s*. 6*d*.

Lessing. *Minna von Barnhelm*. A Comedy. With a Life of Lessing, Critical Analysis, Complete Commentary, etc. Edited by C. A. BUCHHEIM, Phil. Doc. *Fifth Edition.* . . . Extra fcap. 8vo. 3*s*. 6*d*.

Lessing. *Nathan der Weise*. With English Notes, etc. Edited by C. A. BUCHHEIM, Phil. Doc. . . . . Extra fcap. 8vo. 4*s*. 6*d*.

Niebuhr's *Griechische Heroen-Geschichten*. Tales of Greek Heroes. Edited with English Notes and a Vocabulary, by EMMA S. BUCHHEIM. *Second Edition.* . . . . . Extra fcap. 8vo. *stiff covers*, 1*s*. 6*d*. *cloth*, 2*s*.

Schiller's *Historische Skizzen*:—*Egmonts Leben und Tod*, and *Belagerung von Antwerpen*. Edited by C. A. BUCHHEIM, Phil. Doc. *Third Edition, Revised and Enlarged, with a Map*. . Extra fcap. 8vo. 2*s*. 6*d*.

Schiller. *Wilhelm Tell*. With a Life of Schiller; an Historical and Critical Introduction, Arguments, a Complete Commentary, and Map. Edited by C. A. BUCHHEIM, Phil. Doc. *Sixth Edition*. . Extra fcap. 8vo. 3*s*. 6*d*.

Schiller. *Wilhelm Tell*. Edited by C. A. BUCHHEIM, Phil. Doc. *School Edition*. With Map. . . . . . Extra fcap. 8vo. 2*s*.

Schiller. *Wilhelm Tell*. Translated into English Verse by E. MASSIE, M.A. . . . . Extra fcap. 8vo. 5*s*.

Schiller. *Die Jungfrau von Orleans*. Edited by C. A. BUCHHEIM, Phil. Doc. [*In preparation.*]

Scherer. *A History of German Literature*. By W. SCHERER. Translated from the Third German Edition by Mrs. F. CONYBEARE. Edited by F. MAX MÜLLER. 2 vols. . . . . . . 8vo. 21*s*.

Max Müller. *The German Classics from the Fourth to the Nineteenth Century*. With Biographical Notices, Translations into Modern German, and Notes, by F. MAX MÜLLER, M.A. A New edition, revised, enlarged, and adapted to WILHELM SCHERER's *History of German Literature*, by F. LICHTENSTEIN. 2 vols. . . . . Crown 8vo. 21*s*.

GOTHIC AND ICELANDIC.

Skeat. *The Gospel of St. Mark in Gothic*. Edited by W. W. SKEAT, Litt. D. . . . . Extra fcap. 8vo. 4*s*.

Sweet. An Icelandic Primer, with Grammar, Notes, and Glossary. By HENRY SWEET, M.A. . . . . . Extra fcap. 8vo. 3*s*. 6*d*.

Vigfusson and Powell. *An Icelandic Prose Reader*, with Notes, Grammar, and Glossary. By GUDBRAND VIGFUSSON, M.A., and F. YORK POWELL, M.A. . . . . . . Extra fcap. 8vo. 10*s*. 6*d*.

MATHEMATICS AND PHYSICAL SCIENCE.

Aldis. *A Text Book of Algebra (with Answers to the Examples).* By W. Steadman Aldis, M.A. . . . . . . Crown 8vo. 7s. 6d.

Hamilton and Ball. *Book-keeping.* By Sir R. G. C. Hamilton, K.C.B., and John Ball (of the firm of Quilter, Ball, & Co.). *New and Enlarged Edition* . . . . Extra fcap. 8vo. 2s.

⁎⁎⁎ Ruled Exercise Books adapted to the above. (Fcap. folio, 2s.)

Hensley. *Figures made Easy: a first Arithmetic Book.* By Lewis Hensley, M.A. . . . . Crown 8vo. 6d.

Hensley. *Answers to the Examples in Figures made Easy,* together with 2000 additional Examples formed from the Tables in the same, with Answers. By the same Author. . . . . . Crown 8vo. 1s.

Hensley. *The Scholar's Arithmetic.* By the same Author.
Crown 8vo. 2s. 6d.

Hensley. *Answers to the Examples in the Scholar's Arithmetic.* By the same Author. . . . . . . Crown 8vo. 1s. 6d.

Hensley. *The Scholar's Algebra.* An Introductory work on Algebra. By the same Author. . . . . . . Crown 8vo. 2s. 6d.

Baynes. *Lessons on Thermodynamics.* By R. E. Baynes, M.A., Lee's Reader in Physics. . . . . . . Crown 8vo. 7s. 6d.

Donkin. *Acoustics.* By W. F. Donkin, M.A., F.R.S. *Second Edition.*
Crown 8vo. 7s. 6d.

Euclid Revised. Containing the essentials of the Elements of Plane Geometry as given by Euclid in his First Six Books. Edited by R. C. J. Nixon, M.A. . . . . Crown 8vo. 7s. 6d.

May likewise be had in parts as follows :—

Book I, 1s.   Books I, II, 1s. 6d.   Books I–IV, 3s. 6d.   Books V–IV, 3s.

Harcourt and Madan. *Exercises in Practical Chemistry.* Vol. I. *Elementary Exercises.* By A. G. Vernon Harcourt, M.A.: and H. G. Madan, M.A. *Fourth Edition.* Revised by H. G. Madan, M.A.
Crown 8vo. 10s. 6d.

Madan. *Tables of Qualitative Analysis.* Arranged by H. G. Madan, M.A. . . . . Large 4to. 4s. 6d.

Maxwell. *An Elementary Treatise on Electricity.* By J. Clerk Maxwell, M.A., F.R.S. Edited by W. Garnett, M.A. Demy 8vo. 7s. 6d.

Stewart. *A Treatise on Heat,* with numerous Woodcuts and Diagrams. By Balfour Stewart, LL.D., F.R.S., Professor of Natural Philosophy in Owens College, Manchester. *Fourth Edition.* . Extra fcap. 8vo. 7s. 6d.

Williamson. *Chemistry for Students.* By A. W. WILLIAMSON, Phil. Doc., F.R.S., Professor of Chemistry, University College London. *A new Edition with Solutions.* . . . . . . Extra fcap. 8vo. 8s. 6d.

Combination Chemical Labels. In two Parts, gummed ready for use. Part I, Basic Radicles and Names of Elements. Part II, Acid Radicles. Price 3s. 6d.

HISTORY, POLITICAL ECONOMY, GEOGRAPHY, &c.

Danson. The Wealth of Households. By J. T. DANSON. Cr. 8vo. 5s.

Freeman. *A Short History of the Norman Conquest of England.* By E. A. FREEMAN, M.A. *Second Edition.* . Extra fcap. 8vo. 2s. 6d.

George. *Genealogical Tables illustrative of Modern History.* By H. B. GEORGE, M.A. *Third Edition, Revised and Enlarged.* Small 4to. 12s.

Hughes. *Geography for Schools.* Part I, *Practical Geography.* Extra fcap. 8vo. [*Nearly ready.*]

Kitchin. *A History of France.* With Numerous Maps, Plans, and Tables. By G. W. KITCHIN, D.D., Dean of Winchester. *Second Edition.* Vol. 1. To 1453. Vol. 2. 1453–1624. Vol. 3. 1624–1793. each 10s. 6d.

Lucas. *Introduction to a Historical Geography of the British Colonies.* By C. P. LUCAS, B.A. . . . . Crown 8vo., with 8 maps, 4s. 6d.

Rawlinson. *A Manual of Ancient History.* By G. RAWLINSON, M.A., Camden Professor of Ancient History. *Second Edition.* Demy 8vo. 14s.

Rogers. *A Manual of Political Economy,* for the use of Schools. By J. E. THOROLD ROGERS, M.A. *Third Edition.* Extra fcap. 8vo. 4s. 6d.

Stubbs. *The Constitutional History of England, in its Origin and Development.* By WILLIAM STUBBS, D.D., Lord Bishop of Chester. Three vols. . . . . Crown 8vo. each 12s.

Stubbs. *Select Charters and other Illustrations of English Constitutional History,* from the Earliest Times to the Reign of Edward I. Arranged and edited by W. STUBBS, D.D. *Fourth Edition.* Crown 8vo. 8s. 6d.

Stubbs. *Magna Carta*: a careful reprint. . . . 4to. *stitched,* 1s.

ART.

Hullah. *The Cultivation of the Speaking Voice.* By JOHN HULLAH. Extra fcap. 8vo. 2s. 6d.

Maclaren. *A System of Physical Education: Theoretical and Practical.* With 346 Illustrations drawn by A. MACDONALD, of the Oxford School of Art. By ARCHIBALD MACLAREN, the Gymnasium, Oxford. *Second Edition.* Extra fcap. 8vo. 7s. 6d.

Troutbeck and Dale. *A Music Primer for Schools.* By J. TROUT-
BECK, D.D., formerly Music Master in Westminster School, and R. F. DALE,
M.A., B. Mus., late Assistant Master in Westminster School. Crown 8vo. *1s. 6d.*

Tyrwhitt. *A Handbook of Pictorial Art.* By R. St. J. TYRWHITT,
M.A. With coloured Illustrations, Photographs, and a chapter on Perspective,
by A. MACDONALD. *Second Edition.* . . . 8vo. *half morocco, 18s.*

Upcott. *An Introduction to Greek Sculpture.* By L. E. UPCOTT,
M.A. . . . . Crown 8vo. *4s. 6d.*

Student's Handbook to the University and Colleges of Oxford.
Eighth Edition. . . . . Extra fcap. 8vo. *2s. 6d.*

Helps to the Study of the Bible, taken from the *Oxford Bible for
Teachers,* comprising Summaries of the several Books, with copious Explanatory
Notes and Tables illustrative of Scripture History and the Characteristics of
Bible Lands ; with a complete Index of Subjects, a Concordance, a Dictionary
of Proper Names, and a series of Maps. . . . Crown 8vo. *3s. 6d.*

*** A READING ROOM *has been opened at the* CLARENDON PRESS
WAREHOUSE, AMEN CORNER, *where visitors will find every facility
for examining old and new works issued from the Press, and for
consulting all official publications.*

☞ *All communications relating to Books included in this List, and
offers of new Books and new Editions, should be addressed to*

THE SECRETARY TO THE DELEGATES,
CLARENDON PRESS,
OXFORD.

𝕷onoon : HENRY FROWDE,
OXFORD UNIVERSITY PRESS WAREHOUSE, AMEN CORNER.
𝕰oinburgꝫ : 6 QUEEN STREET.
⊕xforo : CLARENDON PRESS DEPOSITORY,
116 HIGH STREET.